Giles Milton was born in Buckinghamshire in 1966 and studied at the University of Bristol. A writer and journalist, in 1995 he wrote the acclaimed *The Riddle and the Knight: In Search of Sir John Mandeville.* He has contributed articles for most of the British national newspapers as well as many foreign publications and specialises in the history of travel and exploration.

In the course of his researches, he has travelled extensively in Europe and the Middle East.

Giles Milton lives in London with his wife and two daughters.

Nathaniel's Nutmeg

*How One Man's Courage
Changed the Course of History*

Giles Milton

SCEPTRE

For Madeleine and Héloïse

British Library C.I.P.
A CIP catalogue record for this title is available
from the British Library

ISBN 0 340 69676 1

Printed and bound in Great Britain by
Clays Ltd, St Ives plc

Hodder and Stoughton
A division of Hodder Headline
338 Euston Road
London NW1 3BH

ACKNOWLEDGEMENTS

The hand-written journals of the gentlemen adventurers who form the *dramatis personae* of this book are almost unreadable to the untrained eye. I owe a debt of gratitude to the handful of Victorian scholars – long deceased – who transcribed these voluminous writings. George Birdwood, Sir William Foster and Henry Stevens made this book possible, as did W. Noel Sainsbury and his indefatigable daughter Ethel who together edited and indexed more than five thousand pages of Jacobean script – all done without the aid of computers.

Thank you to Des Alwi on Neira Island for his hospitality, enthusiasm and the use of his twin-engined power boat; to Monsignor Andreas Sol of St Francis Xavier Cathedral in Ambon (Amboyna) for allowing me free access to his extensive library; and to James Lapian at the BBC's Indonesian Service.

In London, I am grateful to Marjolein van der Valk for rendering obscure Dutch chronicles into fluent English; to the staff of the London Library and the British Library's Oriental and India Office Collections; and to Frank Barrett, Wendy Driver, Maggie Noach and Roland Philipps.

I am particularly indebted to Paul Whyles and Simon Heptinstall, both of whom read numerous versions of the manuscript and suggested much-needed changes.

Finally, I wish to thank my wife Alexandra whose patience, encouragement and cheerfulness will always prove an inspiration.

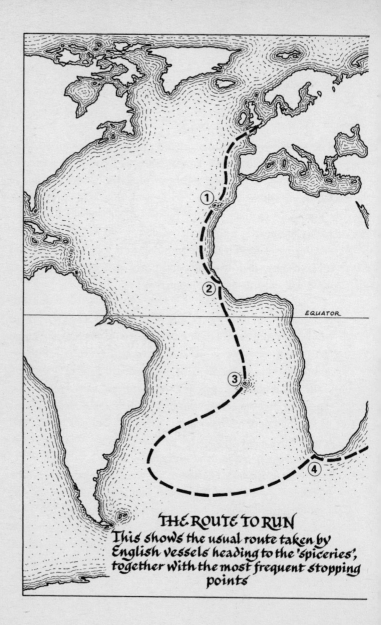

THE ROUTE TO RUN
This shows the usual route taken by
English vessels heading to the 'spiceries',
together with the most frequent stopping
points

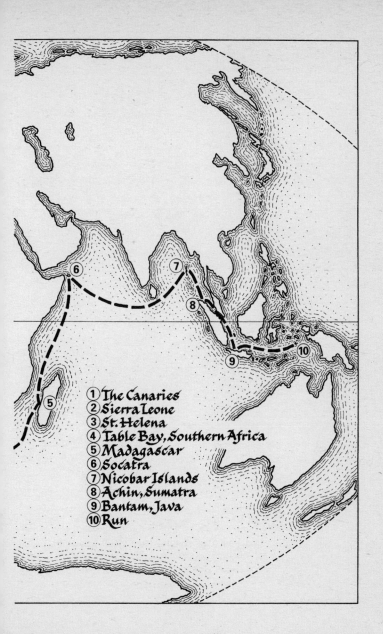

1. The Canaries
2. Sierra Leone
3. St. Helena
4. Table Bay, Southern Africa
5. Madagascar
6. Socatra
7. Nicobar Islands
8. Achin, Sumatra
9. Bantam, Java
10. Run

CONTENTS

LIST OF ILLUSTRATIONS

List of Illustrations

LIST OF MAPS

PROLOGUE

THE ISLAND CAN BE SMELLED before it can be seen. From more than ten miles out to sea a fragrance hangs in the air, and long before the bowler-hat mountain hoves into view you know you are nearing land.

So it was on 23 December 1616. The *Swan's* captain, Nathaniel Courthope, needed neither compass nor astrolabe to know that they had arrived. Reaching for his journal he made a note of the date and alongside scribbled the position of his vessel. He had at last reached Run, one of the smallest and richest of all the islands in the East Indies.

Courthope summoned his crew on deck for a briefing. The stalwart English mariners had been kept in the dark about their destination for it was a mission of the utmost secrecy. They were unaware that King James I himself had ordered this operation, one of such extraordinary importance that failure would bring dire and irrevocable consequences. Nor did they know of the notorious dangers of landing at Run, a volcanic atoll whose harbour was ringed by a sunken reef. Many a vessel had been dashed to splinters on the razor-sharp coral and the shoreline was littered with rusting cannon and broken timbers.

Courthope cared little for such dangers. He was far more worried about the reception he would receive from the native islanders, head-hunters and cannibals, who were feared and mistrusted throughout the East Indies. 'At your arrival at Run,' he had been told, 'show yourself courteous and affable, for they are a peevish, perverse, diffident and perfidious people and apt to take disgust upon small occasions.'

As his men rowed towards land, Courthope descended into his cabin and brushed down his finest doublet, little imagining the momentous events that were to follow. For his discussions with Run's native chieftains – conducted in sign language and broken English – would change the course of history on the other side of the globe.

The forgotten island of Run lies in the backwaters of the East Indies, a remote and fractured speck of rock that is separated from its nearest land mass, Australia, by more than six hundred miles of ocean. It is these days a place of such insignificance that it fails even to make it onto the map: *The Times Atlas of the World* neglects to record its existence and the cartographers of Macmillan's *Atlas of South East Asia* have reduced it to a mere footnote. For all they cared, Run could have slumped beneath the tropical waters of the Indies.

It was not always thus. Turn to the copper-plate maps of the seventeenth century and Run is writ large across the page, its size out of all proportion to its geography. In those days, Run was the most talked about island in the world, a place of such fabulous wealth that Eldorado's gilded riches seemed tawdry by comparison. But Run's bounty was not derived from gold – nature had bestowed a gift far more precious upon her cliffs. A forest of willowy trees fringed the island's mountainous backbone; trees of exquisite fragrance. Tall and foliaged like a laurel, they were adorned with bell-shaped flowers and bore a fleshy, lemon-yellow fruit. To the botanist, they were called *Myristica fragrans*. To the plain-speaking merchants of England they were known simply as nutmeg.

Nutmeg, the seed of the tree, was the most coveted luxury in seventeenth-century Europe, a spice held to have such powerful medicinal properties that men would risk their lives to acquire it. Always costly, it rocketed in price when the physicians of Elizabethan London began claiming that their nutmeg pomanders were the only certain cure for the plague, that 'pestiferous pestilance' that started with a sneeze and ended in death. Overnight, this withered little nut – until now used to cure flatulence and the common cold – became as sought after as gold.

There was one drawback to the sudden and urgent demand: no one could be sure from exactly where the elusive nutmeg originated. London's merchants had traditionally bought their spices in Venice, and Venice's merchants had in turn bought them in Constantinople. But nutmeg came from much further east, from the fabled Indies which lay far beyond Europe's myopic horizons. Ships had never before plied the tropical waters of the Indian Ocean and maps of the far side of the globe remained a blank. The East, as far as the spice dealers were concerned, could have been the moon.

Had they known in advance of the difficulties of reaching the source of nutmeg they might never have set sail. Even in the East Indies where spices grew like weeds, nutmeg was a rarity; a tree so fussy about climate and soil that it would grow only on a tiny cluster of islands, the Banda archipelago, which were of such impossible remoteness that no one in Europe could be sure if they existed at all. The spice merchants of Constantinople had scant information about these islands and what they did know was scarcely encouraging. There were rumours of a

The Banda Islands at the turn of the sixteenth century were the goal of every Elizabethan adventurer. 'There is not a tree but the nutmeg,' wrote one early English visitor, 'so that the whole countrey seemes a contrived orchard.' Run Island, marked Pulorin, is on the extreme left.

monster that preyed on passing ships, a creature of 'devillish possession' that lurked in hidden reefs. There were stories of cannibals and head-hunters – bloodthirsty savages who lived in palm-tree shacks decorated with rotting human heads. There were crocodiles that lay concealed in rivers, hidden shoals to catch captains unawares, and 'such mightie stormes and extreme gusts of winde' that even the sturdiest of ships were placed in grave risk.

None of these dangers deterred Europe's profit-hungry merchants who would chance everything in their desperation to be the first to find nutmeg's source. Soon the shipyards of Portugal, Spain and England were alive to the clatter of shipbuilding, a flurry of activity that sparked what would later become known as the spice race, a desperate and protracted struggle for control of one of the smallest groups of islands in the world.

In 1511, the Portuguese became the first Europeans to set foot in the Banda Islands, a group of six lumps of rock boasting rich volcanic soil and a strange micro-climate. Distracted by hostilities elsewhere in the East Indies, they did not return until 1529 when a Portuguese trader named Captain Garcia landed troops on the Bandas. He was surprised to discover that the islands which had caused such commotion in Europe had a combined area that was not much larger than Lisbon. Five of the Bandas were within gunshot of each other, and it was immediately apparent to Garcia that by building a castle on the principal island, Neira, he would have virtual control over the entire archipelago.

But one island, Run, was different. It lay more than ten miles to the west of Neira and was surrounded by dangerous and hidden reefs. It was also buffeted by the twice-yearly monsoon, putting it beyond the reach of Garcia's carracks for much of the year. This was galling to the Portuguese, for Run was thickly forested in nutmeg and its annual yield was enough to fill a large flotilla of ships. But Captain Garcia soon found himself troubled less by the inaccessibility of this outlying island than by the hostility of the native Bandanese whose warlike antics proved both tiresome and costly. Scarcely had his sailors set to work on a massive castle than a flurry of arrows and the threat of head-hunting sent them scurrying back to their ship. Henceforth, the Portuguese rarely visited the islands, preferring instead to buy their nutmeg from the native traders who were frequent visitors at their fortress in Malacca.

The misfortunes suffered by the Portuguese did not

discourage England's merchants from launching themselves
into the spice race and nor did it deter the captains chosen
to lead these expeditions; bold and fearless men who
steered their ships through such 'greevous stormes' that one
in three was lost. The weather was not the only threat:
scurvy, dysentery and the 'blody flux' killed hundreds of
men, and countless vessels had to be scuppered when there
was no longer a crew to sail them. When the ships finally
limped back from the East the surviving crews found the
wharves of London packed with people anxious to catch a
glimpse of these heroic men. The crowds were fuelled by
stories that the sailors on board were returning with untold
wealth; that they wore doublets of silk, that their main sail
was made of damask and their top sails trimmed with cloth
of gold. Although the humble sailors had been strictly
forbidden from indulging in 'private trade', the temptations
proved too great for many. After all, nutmeg commanded
fabulous prices in Courthope's day and brought spectacular
profits to all who traded in it. In the Banda Islands, ten
pounds of nutmeg cost less than one English penny. In
London, that same spice sold for more than £2.10s. – a
mark-up of a staggering 60,000 per cent. A small sackful
was enough to set a man up for life, buying him a gabled
dwelling in Holborn and a servant to attend to his needs.
London's merchants were so concerned about the illegal
trade in nutmeg when their first fleet arrived back in
London that they ordered the dockyard workers to wear
'suits of canvas without pockets'. This did little to deter the
sea-hardened mariners from filching their masters' spice
and although punishments grew ever more severe over the
decades, many still managed to amass private fortunes. As
late as 1665, Samuel Pepys records a clandestine meeting
with some sailors 'at a blind alehouse at the further end of

town' where he exchanged a sackful of gold for a small quantity of nutmeg and cloves.

The men that survived the expeditions to the Spice Islands returned with such fabulous tales and scrapes, true Boy's Own adventures, that their audiences were left spellbound. David Middleton had a dramatic escape from the cannibals of Ceram; the dilettantish William Keeling performed Shakespeare in the mangrove swamps of West Africa, whilst William Hawkins paid a visit to the Indian Great Moghul and spent the next two years watching gladiator battles of a scale and brutality not seen since the days of imperial Rome. There was Sir Henry Middleton, David's brother, who dropped anchor off the coast of Arabia and distinguished himself by becoming the first Englishman to visit the interior of the country, albeit as a prisoner with 'a great paire of fetters clapt upon my legges'. And there was James Lancaster, commander of the pioneering first expedition to be organised by the East India Company, who spent a delightful evening listening to a scantily clad gamelan orchestra that belonged to the lusty Sultan of Achin.

After all the disasters and false starts it was appropriate that England's first contact with the nutmeg islands should be with Run, the smallest and least accessible of them all. It was also fitting that they should arrive in such an undignified fashion, washed up as shipwrecks after a ferocious tropical storm in 1603. But what was all the more remarkable was that these English mariners, unlike the Portuguese, struck up an instant and lasting friendship with the native chieftains. Long before the sea-salt had stiffened their hair they were toasting each other with the local palm toddy.

England had scarcely launched herself into the spice race when she learned there was a new power to contend with.

In 1595, the Dutch despatched their first fleet eastwards with a crew more menacing and warlike than had ever before been encountered in the tropics. Faced with competition from both the English and Portuguese, they changed their goal from trade to conquest – the conquest of the Banda Islands – and they pursued this with a brutality that shocked even their own countrymen. But on the island of Run they were to meet their match. What happened on that remote atoll, just two miles long and half a mile wide, was to have consequences that no one could ever have imagined.

The extraordinary story of Nathaniel's nutmeg has been largely forgotten for more than three centuries. It is not always a pleasant tale, for although the captains and leaders of expeditions liked to refer to themselves as 'men of qualitye', that did not stop them from indulging in torture, brutality and gratuitous warfare. Such were the grim realities of life in the East, a harsh and bloody existence that was lightened by the occasional flash of humanity and courage – true feats of heroism that were epitomised by the bravery of Nathaniel Courthope.

But more than a century of expeditions and mis-adventures were to pass before Courthope set sail in the *Swan*. His story begins not in the sultry climes of the nutmeg islands, but in a land of icebergs and snow.

CHAPTER ONE

ARCTIC
WHIRLWINDS

IT WAS THE LOOK-OUT who saw them first. Two crippled vessels, rotting and abandoned, lay at anchor close to the shoreline. Their hulls were splintered and twisted, their sails in tatters and their crew apparently long since dead. But it was not a tropical reef that had wrecked the ships and nor was it malaria that had killed the crew. England's maiden expedition to the Spice Islands had come to grief in the ice-bound waters of the Arctic.

The historic 1553 voyage was the brainchild of a newly founded organisation known as the Mystery, Company and Fellowship of Merchant Adventurers for the Discovery of Unknown Lands. So impatient were these merchants to enter the spice race – yet so unprepared for the risks and dangers – that they allowed enthusiasm to overrule practicalities and long before the ships had left port a catalogue of errors threatened to jeopardise their mission. The choice of expedition leader, or 'pilot-general', was sensible enough. Richard Chancellor was 'a man of great estimation' who had gained some experience of seafaring in his formative years. His adoptive father, Henry Sidney, so eulogised his young charge when presented to the Company that the merchant adventurers thought they had a new Magellan in their midst. Sidney explained that it was Chancellor's 'good parts of wit' that made him so invaluable and, never shy to blow his own trumpet, added, 'I rejoice in myself that I have nourished and maintained that wit.'

When a doubting merchant tackled Sidney on his enthusiasm for being separated from Chancellor the old man had a ready answer. 'I do now part with Chancellor not because I make little reckoning of the man, or because his maintenance is burdenous and chargeable unto me. You know the man by report, I by experience; you by words, I by deeds; you by speech and company, but I by the daily trial of his life.'

Sidney's rhetoric won the day and Chancellor was promptly given command of the *Edward Bonaventure*, the largest of the expedition's three ships. The governors then turned to choosing a captain for the expedition's other large ship, the *Bona Esperanza*. For reasons that remain obscure they plumped for Sir Hugh Willoughby, a 'goodly personage' according to the records, but one who had absolutely no knowledge of navigation. Such a man would have been a risk for the short hop across the English Channel; to despatch him to the uttermost ends of the earth was to court disaster.

When it came to deciding the passage to the Spice Islands the merchant adventurers were most insistent. Although they had watched the Spanish and Portuguese successfully sail both east and west to the East Indies, they plumped for an altogether more eccentric option. Their ships, it was decided, would head due north; a route that would shave more than two thousand miles off the long voyage to the Spice Islands. It would have the added benefit of avoiding conflict with the Portuguese who had been sailing the eastern route for almost a century and had established fortified bastions in every port. There was also the question of illness and climate to consider. English mariners had seen the Portuguese ships return home with their crews decimated by dysentery and typhoid, often contracted in the tropical climes of the Indian Ocean. At least one man in five could expect death on the long voyage to the East but that number was frequently much higher and often entire ships had to be abandoned due to a shortage of crew. Since the Portuguese were acclimatised by birth to a hot climate men questioned how English sailors, brought up on the frosty fringes of northern Europe, could hope to return in rude health.

The expedition ran into trouble before it even set sail. During delays at Harwich, it was discovered that a large part of the provisions was already rotten, while the wine casks had been so badly assembled that the wine was leaking freely though the joints in the wood. But with the wind in their favour the captains decided there was no time to restock the ships and the expedition set sail on 23 June 1553.

So long as the vessels stuck together under the capable direction of Richard Chancellor they were unlikely to run into trouble. But as they rounded the rocky shores of northern Norway, 'there came such flows of winde and terrible whirlewinds' that Willoughby's ship was blown off course. Chancellor had planned for such an eventuality, suggesting that the ships regroup at Vardohuus, a small island in the Barents Sea. He waited for seven days but, hearing nothing of either the *Bona Esperanza* or the *Confidentia*, the third ship of the fleet, he pushed on eastwards towards the White Sea.

The other two vessels had also survived the storm. After riding out the gale, Sir Hugh re-established contact with

*Disaster strikes Dutch explorer William Barents, who believed there
was a quick route to the 'spiceries' via the North Pole. The engravings
(shown here and on pp. 17, 167 and 169) illustrate how his ship was
wrecked on 'a great store of ice' and how his men survived the winter.*

the *Confidentia* and both headed towards the coastline. Here
Willoughby's inexperience began to tell. He sounded the
sea floor, pored over charts and scratched his head before
concluding that 'the land lay not as the globe made
mention.' Failing to locate Vardohuus's or Chancellor's
vessel, he decided to press on with the expedition without
the flagship.

On 14 August 1553, he 'descried land', apparently uninhabited, at 72 degrees latitude but failed to reach it due
to the quantity of ice in the water. If this reading is correct,
his ship must have reached the barren islands of Novaya
Zemlya which lie, remote and isolated, in the Barents Sea.
From here he appears to have sailed south-east, then north–

west, then south-west, then north-east. The ignorance of Willoughby and his men is staggering, for their course, more than three hundred miles inside the Arctic Circle, must have taken them in a giant arc through a dangerous sea littered with melting pack-ice. On 14 September, they again sighted land and shortly afterwards 'sailed into a faire bay' somewhere close to the present border between Finland and Russia. Willoughby's men were cheered by the sight of 'very many seal fishes, and other great fishes; and upon the main we saw beares, great deere, foxes with divers strange beasts'. They planned at first to spend a week here but 'seeing the yeare far spent, and also very evill weather, as frost, snow, and haile', they decided to winter in the bay.

The expedition's directors in London must by now have hoped that their ships had found the North-East Passage, broken through it, and be well on their way to the Spice Islands. But instead of balmy evenings and gently swaying palm trees, Willoughby and his men had met with freezing fog, impenetrable ice, and the realisation that London's merchants had made a terrible mistake when they chose the route over the North Pole. Those merchants had voc-iferously defended their decision, presenting logical and compelling arguments to support their theories. As far back as the year 1527, Robert Thorne, an English trader living in Seville, had written to King Henry VIII with the exciting (and highly secret) news that the Spice Islands could be reached by way of the North Pole: 'I know it is my bounden duty to manifest this secret unto your Grace,' he wrote, 'which hitherto, as I suppose, hath beene hid.' The King was left in no doubt that 'by sailing northward and passing the Pole, descending to the Equinoctial line, we shall hit these islands [the Spice Islands], and it should be a much shorter way than either the Spaniards or Portingals have.'

The more the experts researched the north-eastern route to the Spice Islands the more plausible it proved to be. In an age when men still looked for perfect symmetry on their maps, the northern cape of Norway showed an exact topographical correspondence to the southern cape of Africa. Geographers agreed that this was indeed good news; the chilly northern land mass must surely be a second Cape of Good Hope. The writings of the ancients also lent credence to the idea of reaching the East Indies by a northerly route. Pliny the Elder had written of a circular sea at the top of the globe and a land called Tabis penetrating into the far north. To the east of Tabis there was said to be an opening which connected the Polar Sea to the warm waters of the Indian Ocean.

Such arguments were cold comfort to Willoughby and his men, stuck fast in an expanse of ice. The bay in which they had chosen to winter soon transformed itself into a desolate wilderness; fishing proved impossible due to the thickness of the ice and the wildlife disappeared with the first snows. Even the birds, aware of the onslaught of winter, migrated to warmer climes. Soon the ice floes had trapped, then crushed, the ships and there was no escape. With his crew growing hungrier by the day, Willoughby sent out search parties to look for food, for people, for help. 'We sent out three men south-south-west to search if they could find people,' wrote Sir Hugh, 'but [they] could find none.' Next he sent a party westwards, 'which also returned without finding any people'. A final team confirmed what Willoughby had feared – that they were imprisoned in an uninhabited wilderness.

More than five years was to pass before a search ship from England finally discovered what had happened to the *Bona Esperanza* and *Confidentia*. Sailing into the bay where

Willoughby had chosen to winter, the would-be rescuers stumbled across the ghostly and rotting hulks of the two ships – ships which had ended their days as charnel houses. The crew's final grim months remain a mystery, for Willoughby, racked by hunger, stopped recording daily entries in his ship's log. All that is certain is that he and his crew survived much of the winter, for the rescue party found wills dated January 1554, a full four months after the vessels had entered the bay.

The final, macabre twist in the tale was recorded by Giovanni Michiel, the Venetian ambassador to Moscow. The search party, he wrote, 'has returned safe, bringing with them the two vessels of the first voyage, having found them on the Muscovite coast with the men on board all frozen. And they [the rescuers] narrate strange things about the mode in which they were frozen, pen still in hand, and the paper before them, others at tables, platter in hand and spoon in mouth; others opening a locker, and others in various postures, like statues, as if they had been adjusted and placed in those attitudes.'

While Willoughby and his men froze to death, Richard Chancellor had fared rather better. Relying on the wit that had so enamoured him to his adoptive father, he quickly foresaw the danger of Arctic pack-ice. Dropping anchor in the White Sea close to present-day Archangel, he abandoned ship and trudged his way overland to Moscow. At first he was disappointed in what he found. The city, he thought, was 'very rude' and the houses 'all of timber'. Even the imperial palace was disappointing – 'rather low' and with 'small windows' it was 'much like the old buildings of England'. But Chancellor soon changed his tune when confronted with the barbaric splendour of Ivan the Terrible's court. Ivan greeted him in 'a long garment of beaten golde, with an imperial crowne upon his head and staffe of cristall and golde in his right hand'. The emperor's conduct was as majestic as it was awe-inspiring: at a courtly banquet he 'sent to every man a great sliver of bread, and the bearer called the party so sent to by his name aloud, and said, Ivan Vasilivich, Emperor of Russia and great Duke of Moscova doth reward thee with bread.' Even the wine goblets caught Chancellor's eye – weighing the golden beakers in his hand he declared they were 'very massie' and better than anything he had seen in England.

The time spent in Moscow was one of endless pleasure for Chancellor's crew. Many had expected their journey to end in disaster or death but instead they were living it up in the bejewelled pavilion of the Emperor of Russia. Chancellor was no less impressed: 'I have seen the King's majesties of England and the French King's pavilion,' he wrote, 'but none are like this.'

After lengthy negotiations, Ivan sent the English commander back to England with a letter conferring trading privileges upon a group of merchants in London. In doing so he had unwittingly laid the foundations of the Muscovy Company, a precursor to the East India Company.

Of the three ships that set sail for the Spice Islands not one achieved its goal of locating the elusive North-East Passage. The men who sailed north to escape the tropical diseases of the Indian Ocean little thought they would perish in the sub-zero waters of the Arctic. It would take another four hundred years, and a nuclear-powered submarine, before the northern route to the Pacific would finally be conquered.

While London's merchants anxiously awaited news of their historic first voyage to the Spice Islands, many people in

Barents' sailors faced continual danger from polar bears. 'We presently leaped forth to defend ourselves as well we could.'

the country were left wondering what all the fuss was about. Nutmeg, after all, made for an unpromising luxury. Dry, wrinkled and not much bigger than a garden pea it scarcely had the same appeal as a golden ducat or finely hewn sapphire.

The doubters were soon to learn that it was of potentially far greater value. London's leading doctors of physic made increasingly extravagant claims as to the efficacy of nutmeg, holding it to cure everything from the plague to the 'blody flux', both of which were regular visitors to the capital, sweeping through its insanitary back streets with devastating effect. One leading authority pronounced that his sweet-smelling pomander, which contained a large quantity of the spice, could even stave off the dreaded 'sweating syckness' that accompanied the 'pestiferous time of the pestilence'. Since this sickness – the plague – was said to kill in just two hours the pomander had to be made with all possible haste. After all, the old patter ran: 'mery at dinner, dead at supper.'

It was not just life-threatening illnesses that nutmeg was said to cure. A growing interest in the medicinal value of plants had led to an explosion in the number of dietary books and herbals, all of which claimed that nutmeg and other spices were beneficial in combating a host of minor ailments. For chesty coughs, doctors recommended mulled wine suffused with nutmeg. Cloves were said to cure earache, pepper stifled colds, while those embarrassed by trapped wind were recommended to take an extraordinary pot-pourri of fifteen spices including cardamom, cinnamon and nutmeg – a recipe that would have been out of reach of all but the flatulent rich. Spices were even held to revive those who had shuffled off this mortal coil. Ten grams of saffron taken with sweet wine was enough (it was claimed) to bring back the dead. There were not known to be any side-effects.

One of the more popular books was Andrew Borde's *Dyetary of Helth*, a guide to good living which earned the author even more fame than his seminal *Treatyse upon Beardes*. 'Nutmeges,' he wrote in his *Dyetary,* 'be good for them which have cold in their head and doth comforte the syght and the brain.' His home-produced nutmeg cocktail was said to be extremely efficacious; not only did it cleanse 'the mouthe of the stomacke and the spleen', it was also 'good against the blody flux', a virulent and dangerous strain of dysentery.

Borde's *Dyetary* is a curious mixture of herbal and lore. To any gentleman wishing to live a long life he suggests wearing a red petticoat and avoiding 'snaily rooms', while those able to 'rise with mirth' every morning were assured of good health. His suggestion that nutmeg dampens sexual desire had signally failed to work on him, for this celibate former monk died in disgrace. 'Under the colour of virginitie and of wearing a shirt of hair [he kept] three whores at once in his chamber … to serve not only himself but also help the virgin priests about in the country.' Borde of all people should have kept taking the nutmeg but as he wearily admitted, 'it is hard to get out of the flesh what is bred in the bone.'

Other authorities, turning Borde's misfortune to good effect, began to claim that far from dampening sexual desire, nutmeg was actually a powerful aphrodisiac. The licentious Charles Sackville, sixth Earl of Dorset, jested that Julius Caesar's libido was so low that even if Cleopatra had used 'nutmeg, mace and ginger' upon her 'Roman swinger' she would have failed to stir his loins. Such ingredients could scarcely have failed to work on his lordship, for he knew to his cost that a spoonful of nutmeg before bedtime could cause no end of sweet but troublesome dreams:

> Dreaming last night on Mrs Farley,
> My p – – – k was up this morning early,
> And I was fain without my gown
> To rise in th'cold to get him down
> Hard shift, alas, but yet a sure,
> Although it be no pleasing cure.

Sackville's love of nutmeg was to prove his downfall. His neighbour, Samuel Pepys, recorded how he was imprisoned for indecent exposure 'after running up and down all night almost naked through the street'.

Beneath all the quackery about nutmeg there lurked a grain of truth, particularly in the claims that it was a powerful preservative. Perishables had traditionally been conserved by salting, drying or smoking, none of which suppressed the foul taste of rank meat. A sprinkling of nutmeg over the viands not only disguised the stench, it also helped stay the natural process of rotting by dramatically slowing the rate of oxidation.

The use of spices as preservatives and flavourings was, in fact, nothing new. The ancient Egyptians had imported cumin, cinnamon and cassia to embalm the bodies of their pharaohs whilst the apothecaries of the Old Testament crushed spices into holy unguents for their temples. The Romans were more practical in their use of such luxuries, using nutmeg and aniseed to preserve meat and flavour wine, adding cumin to their pastries and using fennel as a flavouring for the city's famed vinegar sauces.

In Chaucer's day such spices had been a rare luxury. In the *Canterbury Tales* the doughty Sir Topaz speaks longingly of gingerbread, licorice and 'notemuge'-flavoured ale. By the time Shakespeare was writing, less than twenty years before Nathaniel Courthope arrived at Run, such luxuries were fast becoming commonplace. In *The Winter's Tale*, the clown has a lengthy list of ingredients needed for his dish of spiced pears, all of which were readily available in London: 'I must have saffron to colour the warden pies [pears]. Mace, dates, none; that's out of my note; nutmegs, seven, a race or two of ginger, but that I may beg; four pound of prunes, and as many raisins o'the sun.'

Throughout the Middle Ages, Venice had controlled the spice trade with an iron fist. Nutmeg, cloves, pepper and cinnamon all travelled across Asia to the great trading emporium of Constantinople where they were snapped up by Venetian merchants and shipped westward across the Mediterranean. From here they were sold, at vastly inflated prices, to traders from northern Europe. By the time Marco Polo made his 1271 voyage to China, Venice's monopoly on spices was complete, yet no one from the West had ever visited the countries from which these spices originated. Polo was the first European to describe the clove tree, 'a little tree with leaves like laurel', but his claim to have seen one in mainland China owes more to his imagination than to reality for, unbeknown to the Venetian, the tree could only be found on a handful of islands in the Indonesian archipelago.

In the two centuries that followed Polo's return, spices had become so popular that demand had long since outstripped supply. Venice's merchants were sufficiently adept at the art of money-making to know that a shortage of supply meant that prices could be kept high. So long as they controlled the trade routes and kept a monopoly over the souks of the Middle East they could retain their stranglehold on trade. But in the closing days of 1511 a startling and wholly unwelcome piece of news reached the Venetian merchants. A small flotilla of Portuguese ships, they learned, had just arrived in the Spice Islands and acquired a full lading of spices. After more than four centuries the Venetian monopoly had been broken.

The spice race could now begin.

The Portuguese had made spectacular progress in their quest to find a sea route to the East. Just forty years after their first tentative crossing of the equator in 1471, they had successfully sailed to the Spice Islands of the East Indies and returned with their ships crammed with pepper, nutmeg and cloves. These islands, known as the 'spiceries' or Moluccas, were scattered over an area of ocean more than half the size of Europe. Although these days they form

a single province of Indonesia, called Maluku, the hundred or so islands in fact fall into three distinct groups. To the north lie the volcanic islands of Tidore and Ternate, powerful sultanates which spent much of the sixteenth century fighting a desperate battle to retain their independence. Some four hundred miles to the south of here are the islands of Amboyna and Ceram, rugged places whose sweet-smelling cloves would eventually spark a terrible and infamous massacre. The southernmost group, the Banda Islands, were the richest and least accessible of them all, requiring bravado and a deft hand to steer a vessel safely through the archipelago's treacherous waters.

The Portuguese touched at all of these islands and, before long, were consolidating their position by force of arms. The important spice port of Malacca fell under their control in 1511 and, just months later, the remote Banda Islands were first visited by a Portuguese carrack. Next, they seized the spice ports on India's west coast, wresting control from the Muslim middlemen, before returning to the outlying and far-flung 'spiceries'. Here they built a series of heavily guarded forts and bastions and, within a few years, the islands of Ternate and Tidore, Amboyna and Ceram, had all fallen into their grasp.

The other countries of Europe had got off to a faltering start in the spice race. Columbus had sailed westwards across the Atlantic in 1492 convinced that he could detect the whiff of spice in the air. Although he went to great lengths to persuade the King and Queen of Spain that he had found the East Indies, he had of course discovered America. The Venetian explorer John Cabot also believed that the quickest way to the East Indies was to sail west and he visited Arabia at a very early age in order to quiz the local merchants about 'whither spices are brought by caravans from distant countries'. These merchants were understandably reticent to part with such priceless information and spoke vaguely of spices coming from the easternmost reaches of the world. It was exactly what Cabot had hoped to hear and he concluded that 'presupposing the rotundity of the earth' – not a foregone conclusion even in those days – the merchants must have bought the spices 'at the north towards the west'.

Cabot was unable to interest any Venetian sponsors in a westerly voyage across the Atlantic so he travelled to England and persuaded King Henry VII to commission his search for the 'spiceries'. Setting sail across the Atlantic in 1497 he landed at Cape Breton Island which he confidently declared to be an uninhabited part of China. Although spices were distinctly thin on the ground Cabot returned to an England fascinated by his supposed discovery. 'Great honour is paid him,' wrote a Venetian merchant living in London, 'and he dresses in silk; and these English run after him like mad people.' So, indeed, did the King who promptly provided the finances for a second expedition.

On this new voyage Cabot decided to follow the coast of 'China' until he reached Japan where 'all the spices of the world originate'. Certain he would return with his ships filled with nutmeg, his confidence only faltered when the mercury slumped below zero and the icebergs grew ever more threatening.

Despite his failure to bring home a single nutmeg, Cabot's voyages aroused considerable interest in the ports of Spain and Portugal. One man in particular was keen to know more about his discoveries: Ferdinand Magellan, a 'gentleman of great spirit', had long believed there was a far quicker route to the Spice Islands than the lengthy voyage around the Cape of Good Hope and was sure that Cabot had been right to sail westwards across the Atlantic.

Magellan had sailed to the East Indies in his youth and would certainly have returned had circumstances allowed. But after taking part in a military campaign in Morocco, he was accused of treachery and informed by the Portuguese king that his services were no longer required. King Manuel had made a grave error in dismissing Magellan for he was an expert navigator who had read widely the geographical theories of his day. He argued that the only reason that Columbus and Cabot had failed to find the Spice Islands was that they had not found a passage through the American continent.

Magellan travelled to the court of King Charles V of Spain in 1518 and 'acquainted the Emperour that the islands of Banda and of the Molucca's [were] the only one store-house of nature for nutmegs and mace'. The King immediately realised that Magellan offered him the best chance of challenging the seemingly indomitable position of the Portuguese, and placed him in charge of a fleet of ships which were to sail southwards down the coast of Brazil, find a passage through to the Pacific Ocean, then sail west until they reached the 'islands of Banda'. It is fortunate that Magellan took with him a scholar by the name of Antonio Pigafetta, for Pigafetta faithfully recorded everything that happened on that historic first Spanish voyage to the Spice Islands. His journal, in turn, found its way into the hands of the learned English vicar Samuel Purchas whose monumental anthology of exploration, *Purchas His Pilgrimes*, was to inspire London's merchant adventurers.

Magellan's voyage began well: he revictualled in the Canary Islands, crossed the equator, and reached the South

American coastline three months later. Here, simmering resentment between the Spanish crew and their Portuguese captain exploded into mutiny and Magellan was forced to hang the troublemakers from a hastily constructed gibbet. At that point the mutiny died down.

The remaining mutineers soon found their attentions diverted by the extraordinary behaviour of the natives; not least the giant-like menfolk of Patagonia who, noted Pigafetta, 'when they are sicke at the stomache they put an arrow half a yard downe the throat which makes them vomit greene choler and blood.' Their cure for headaches was no less dramatic; they gashed their heads open and purged the blood. And as soon as they detected the first chill of winter, 'they would truss up themselves so the genitall member is hidden in the body'.

A year after leaving Tenerife, Magellan's ship nudged through the straits that now bear his name and entered the warm waters of the Pacific. 'He was so glad thereof,' records his diarist, 'that for joy the teares fell from his eyes.' Magellan had been right all along: it was now simply a question of following the spice-filled breezes all the way to the East Indies.

Unfortunately it was not so simple. Magellan, like most explorers of his day, had no idea of the massive distances involved and after more than three months at sea with no sight of land his men began to starve. 'Having consumed all their biskits and other victuals, they fell into such necessitie that they were enforced to eate the powder that remained thereof, being now full of wormes and stinking like pisse by reason of the salt water. Their fresh water was also putrified and became yellow.' Soon even the worm-ridden powder ran out, forcing them 'to eate pieces of leather which were folded about certain great ropes of the shippes;

but these skinnes being very hard, by reason of the sunne, raine and winde, they hung them by a cord in the sea for the space of four or five days to mollifie them'. It was no diet for sick men and it soon took its toll: 'By reason of this famine, and unclean feeding, some of their gummes grew so over their teeth that they died miserably for hunger.'

Despite the terrible hardship, the ships limped on until they reached the Philippines where the men learned that they were nearing their goal. But Magellan was destined not to see the Spice Islands for he made the mistake of involving himself in a local power struggle and, during the fighting, was struck down and killed. It was a devastating blow to all those left alive and Pigafetta, shocked by the news, struggled to express their loss. 'There perished our guide, our light, and our support.'

So many men had died that a decision was taken to abandon one of the ships. The remaining vessels then sailed for the most northerly of the Spice Islands, sighting the clove-covered cone of Tidore's volcano in the first week of November 1521. Suddenly, the lurid descriptions that characterise Pigafetta's journal acquire a more practical tone. Magellan's men had sailed half-way around the world to make money and, for the next few pages, Pigafetta records every conceivable weight and measure in use on the island.

Laden with twenty-six tons of cloves, a cargo of nutmeg, and sackloads of cinnamon and mace, the expedition's remaining two ships finally left the Spice Islands in the winter of 1521. The *Trinidad* got no farther than the harbour: rotten, leaking and hopelessly overloaded, she needed extensive repairs before making the return journey. With a tearful farewell, the crew of the *Victoria* set sail alone. The men faced an appalling homeward journey and more than half of them died of dysentery. Pigafetta, diligent as ever, noted every sickness and death and even found significance in the way the corpses floated. 'The corpses of the Christians floated with the face towards heaven,' he wrote, 'but those of the Indians with the face downwards.'

Nine months after leaving the Spice Islands the *Victoria* at last reached Seville and, anchoring off the mole, 'discharged all her ordinance for joy'. Although her crew were half dead and Magellan was long-since buried, King Charles V was overjoyed and one of his first actions was to honour the captain, Sebastian del Cano, with a coat of arms. Its design included three nutmegs, two sticks of cinnamon and twelve cloves.

Portugal's merchants were livid at losing their short-lived monopoly and protested in the strongest terms to King Charles. They argued that the Spice Islands belonged to Portugal, not Spain, citing the infamous Treaty of Tordesillas. But their case was not as straightforward as they claimed. The Treaty of Tordesillas, signed some two decades previously, was based on a papal bull which had divided the world into two parts. Pope Alexander VI had drawn a line down the middle of the Atlantic which stretched 'from Pole Artike to the Pole Antartike' some hundred leagues west of the Cape Verde Islands. Any land discovered west of this line, declared the Pope, belonged to Spain. Everything east of the line belonged to Portugal. By the time the treaty had been signed, the Portuguese had successfully managed to shift the line westwards by several hundred miles allowing them to argue that Brazil, whose coastline was cut by the line, rightly belonged to them.

The treaty was easy enough to uphold with discoveries close to home but it was more complicated when dealing with distant and little-known islands. When continued on the far side of the world the Pontiff's line placed the Spice Islands unquestionably within the Portuguese sphere, but sixteenth-century maps were extremely inaccurate and the Spanish argued that these islands fell into their half of the globe and that their riches belonged to the king of Spain.

Unfortunately, no one could be sure who was right. In 1524, representatives from both sides submitted themselves to a board of inquiry but although they examined countless maps and charts no agreement was reached. It took a further five years of squabbling before King Charles of Spain sold his claims to the Spice Islands for the massive sum of 350,000 gold ducats.

This deal would have solved the problem had it been only the Spanish and Portuguese who were interested in the Spice Islands. But other powers were beginning to turn their attentions to the East: England, in particular, was developing an attachment to the sweet smell of spice. It could only be a matter of time before an English adventurer would once again attempt the journey.

Although the failure of Sir Hugh Willoughby's Arctic expedition brought to an abrupt end England's search for a North-East Passage, it did little to dampen the enthusiasm for sailing to the Spice Islands. Yet more than two decades were to pass before London's merchants contemplated financing a new expedition, and it was not until 1577 – some twenty-four years after Willoughby's voyage – that a flotilla of ships finally set sail under the command of Sir Francis Drake.

Drake's expedition was backed by Queen Elizabeth I and its ostensible object was to conclude trade treaties with the people of the South Pacific and to explore an unknown continent rumoured to exist in the southern hemisphere. But the Queen also gave Drake full licence to plunder Spanish ships and ports and to carry off as much treasure as his vessel could hold for, she told him, 'I would gladly be revenged on the King of Spain for divers injuries that I have received.' Since it was imperative that none of this information should fall into Spanish hands, the expedition was shrouded in secrecy from the very outset and the crew had no idea of their destination until the English coastline had receded into the distance.

The five ships under Drake's command, none of which exceeded the length of two London buses, used Magellan's route as their blueprint and revictualled in many of the same bays and harbours. These stops did not always go according to plan: dropping anchor in Patagonia the crew had fully expected to be entertained by giants vomiting 'green choler' and trussing up their genitals. Instead, they walked straight into an ambush and were only saved by swift intervention from Drake who picked up a musket, fired at a native, and, 'tore out his bellie and guts with greate torment, as it seemed by his crye, which was so hideous and horrible a roare, as if ten bulls had joined together in roaring'.

A few days later it was time to turn his fire on a fellow Englishman. One of Drake's subordinates, a 'gentelman' by the name of Thomas Doughty, was rumoured to be threatening mutiny. These rumours eventually reached the captain who promptly confronted Doughty with the allegations. What happened next is difficult to determine for Doughty had many enemies and each account tells a different story. But all follow a similar line: that Doughty admitted his guilt to an astonished Drake and was given three choices – to be executed, set on land, or return to

England to answer the charges before a full council. Doughty showed not a moment's hesitation: 'He professed that with all his heart he did embrace the first branch of the general's proffer … and without any dallying or delaying the time he came forth and kneeled downe, preparing at once his necke for the axe and his spirit for heaven.'

With this unpleasant episode over the ships continued on their way, successfully crossing from the Atlantic into the Pacific through the notoriously tempestuous straits. Drake's smaller vessels had already been abandoned. Now, sailing into a storm, he lost sight of the second ship in his fleet (it had, in fact, headed back towards England) leaving his flagship alone and in a perilous state. Tossed about 'like a ball in a racket' Drake raced up the South American coastline plundering wherever he could before steering his vessel westwards in the direction of the Spice Islands, a desolate journey for there was 'nothing in our view but aire and sea [for] the space of full sixty-eight dayes together'. At last – more than a generation after the Portuguese had first sailed to the East Indies – the English vessel sighted the luxuriant shores of the Spice Islands.

Drake had intended to drop anchor at the volcanic island of Tidore but as he edged his ship through the treacherous shallows a canoe drew alongside carrying a viceroy from the neighbouring island of Ternate. Arguing that Tidore was all but controlled by the hated Portuguese, he begged the English commander to change his course. Drake consented and, selecting a fine velvet cloak from his cabin, asked that it might be presented to the King with the message that he had come to buy spices. The messenger promptly returned with the news that the King 'would sequester the commodities and traffique of his whole island [and] reserve it to the intercourse of our nation'.

Drake and his men were treated to a fabulous display of Oriental politesse when the King at last visited their ship. His courtiers, all in white linen, rowed round and round the vessel and 'as they passed by us, did us a kind of homage with great solemnity, the greatest personages beginning first, with reverend countenance and behaviour, to bow their bodies right to the ground'. The King was not far behind. 'He also with six grave and ancient fathers in his canoe approaching, did at once, together with them, yield us a reverend kind of obeisance, in far more humble manner than was to be expected.' Drake found him 'of tall stature, very corpulent and well set together, of a very princely and gracious countenance; his respect amongst his own was such that neither his viceroy nor any other counsellors dared speak to him unless they were upon their knees'.

The English were at first unsure how to react to the affected manners of the East but they eventually commemorated the occasion in time-honoured fashion. They primed their cannon and listened with delight as 'our ordinance thundered, which we mixed with great store of small shot, among which sounding our trumpets and other instruments of music.' The King was dazzled by the fireworks and 'so much delighted that, requesting our music to come unto the boat, he joyned his canoe to the same, and was towed at least a whole hour together, with the boat at the stern of our ship'.

After a further blitz of cannon fire the King made his excuses and left, but not before he had sanctioned the English to buy whatever spices they needed from his island. By the time Drake was ready to leave Ternate his ship was so weighed down with goods – and so low in the water – that she was 'laid up fast upon a desperate shoal'. To lighten her, eight of the cannon were cast into the water, followed by much of the meal and pulse, and finally three tons of the precious cloves that he had bought. As the tide turned the ship was slowly lifted off the shoal and started on the long voyage back to England.

Drake arrived to a hero's welcome. Not only was his vessel, renamed the *Golden Hind*, laden with fragrant spices, she was also 'very richly fraught with gold, silver, pearls and precious stones', most of which had been pillaged from Spanish and Portuguese vessels. Men and women turned out in force to watch the arrival of the ship in Plymouth, and Queen Elizabeth herself came aboard the vessel at Deptford and conferred a knighthood on her gallant commander. Within days of his return, songs, sonnets, odes and poems were being composed in honour of his historic voyage.

Drake's astonishing feat of seamanship fired the imagination of Elizabethan England and fuelled the belief that the East was a land of fabulous potentates. But Drake had sailed as a freebooter, not a trader, and although he had successfully bought large quantities of spices in Ternate, their value was nothing compared to the gold and silver he had stolen from Spanish galleons. Worse still, he brought back little practical information about the market-places of the East. The records of his voyage include no details of prices, no mention of weights and measures, no clues as to the goods most sought after for barter. Yet his triumphant return caused great excitement among the merchants of London and they began to cast around for a suitable candidate to open trading links with the East Indies. Drake himself was the obvious choice but he had set his sights on some old-fashioned piracy and the merchants were forced to look elsewhere for a commander. Showing the singular lack of foresight that they had manifested when choosing Sir Hugh Willoughby for their Arctic adventure, they now entrusted command to a Nottinghamshire landowner called Edward Fenton, a headstrong man with little experience of seamanship.

Fenton came from a prosperous family and, had he so desired, could have lived a life of ignominious ease. Instead he chose a different path: eschewing the comforts of his stately home he sold his patrimony and embarked on a swashbuckling career as a soldier of fortune, allowing himself to be carried to wherever there was the chance for adventure. His first major expedition saw him travelling in the company of Martin Frobisher in search of the fabled North-West Passage and it was while on this expedition that Fenton first learned that orders given in London could be safely ignored once at sea. Landing on Baffin Island and finding what appeared to be large deposits of gold ore, Fenton abandoned his search for the North-West Passage and set up an impromptu mining venture with the aim of getting rich quick.

Fenton was a strange choice to lead a voyage to the East Indies: an incurable romantic, he had only a slim understanding of the responsibilities that befell a commander. His eccentricities had raised many an eyebrow before he even left England and there was considerable opposition to his appointment, but as the Earl of Leicester's preferred man he was duly entrusted with the post. When the merchants came to choose Fenton's second-in-command they plumped for a solidly dependable captain named William Hawkins, a relative of his more famous namesake, who had served in Drake's voyage to the South Seas. But they continued to harbour doubts about the whimsical Fenton and set down in great detail their plans for the voyage, including the exact route that he was to follow. 'You shall go on your course by the Cape of Good Hope,' they wrote, 'not passing the Strait of Magellan either going or returning … you shall not pass to the north-eastward of the 40 degree of latitude at the most, but shall take your right course to the Isles of Moluccas.'

Such instructions fell on deaf ears for hardly had Fenton set sail than he cooled on the idea of sailing to the East Indies, a hazardous and tiresome voyage that would profit the merchants far more than him. As his ship plied its way southwards down the Atlantic, the 'gentelman' commander spent the long hours at the helm indulging his dream of a nobler and more glorious profession. It is unfortunate that the records of the expedition fall silent just at the point when it slides into farce. The most interesting account of the voyage – the journal belonging to William Hawkins – was partially destroyed by fire in the last century. But its disintegrating pages are sufficiently legible to allow for a reconstruction of the tumultuous events on board the *Bear*. Fenton, it seems, had long realised that the quickest way to riches was to plunder and ransack the Portuguese carracks that made their way up and down the African coastline. But as his ship drifted listlessly in the mid-Atlantic he was struck by an altogether more fantastic idea. On 25 September 1582, he summoned his lieutenants to a meeting in his cabin and told them of his plan to seize the island of St Helena 'and theire to be proclaimed kyng'.

They could scarcely believe their ears. They were only too aware of Fenton's propensity for disregarding orders but this was an entirely unforeseen turn of events. Attempting to talk him out of this lunatic scheme only fuelled his desire and when the practical Hawkins became too vociferous in his arguments against the plan Fenton promised him 10,000 pounds of silver if he would change his mind, as well as great riches to 'all the well willers.' When news reached the on-board preacher he was horrified and 'fell down upon his knees and besought [Hawkins] that for God's sake he would not give his consent to this determination'. The crew had a similar reaction; they had no wish to spend the rest of their lives on the remote Atlantic islet that, two centuries later, would prove such an effective prison for Napoleon. Several pointed out the impracticalities of Fenton's plan, arguing that it would be almost impossible for them to defend the island against foreign vessels. Without mastery of the sea, King Edward of St Helena would be deposed before the year was out.

Hawkins agreed and, deciding to 'tell [Fenton] my mind', stormed back to the commander's cabin. Unfortunately the next few lines of his journal are illegible but he must have eloquently argued his case for Fenton abandoned his mad scheme with as much haste as it had originally been conceived. Perhaps he realised that without Hawkins's help, he would not even have been able to locate the island. His romantic dream in tatters, Fenton locked himself in his cabin in a mood of black despair. 'He saide then he would go back agayne to the islands of Cape de Verde to fetch some wine,' which, noted Hawkins, 'was only a desire to pick and steale'.

As his ship headed back towards England, Fenton awoke to the fact that he had done little to endear himself to London's merchants. He tried to silence Hawkins by clapping him in irons and threatening to kill him if he breathed a word about the more ludicrous episodes of the voyage. In the event, Hawkins survived but this final act completed Fenton's fall from grace and his name was conspicuously absent from any future expedition to the East. The detailed plans and orders laid down by the expedition's financiers proved to be entirely in vain: the 1582 expedition to the Spice Islands never even left the Atlantic.

The merchants of London now realised that the best way forward was for one of their own – a sober and hard-nosed businessman – to travel east to investigate the practicalities of trade. The man they chose to conduct this research was Ralph Fitch, a practically minded merchant of the Levant Company who left London in 1583 accompanied by four partners. The journal he compiled while travelling was filled with facts and figures about the ports and cities of the Indies and although it is not the most exciting of reads, its importance lies in the fact that it marked England's entry as a serious player in the spice race.

Fitch tells how he set off with four companions-in-trade – Messrs Newberry, Eldred, Leedes and Story – in the winter of 1583. After travelling by ship to Tripolis in Syria the small party teamed up with a caravan as far as Aleppo, then continued to the Euphrates on camel-back. Here they pooled their resources, bought a boat, and floated downstream to the Persian Gulf. Newberry had travelled this way once before and returned with stories about huge-breasted ladies with 'great rings in their noses and about their legs, arms and necks iron hoops'. Suffering from the stinking heat of midday, he had watched in amazement as they unblushingly 'threw their dugs over their shoulders'. Such a colourful tale would never have found its way into Fitch's journal; as Newberry eyed up the local ladies, his colleague was busy noting how their boat was constructed, the exact cost of the journey, and the weights and measures in use.

No sooner had the party of Englishmen arrived in Hormuz than the town's Portuguese authorities grew suspicious. Arrested and clapped in jail, they were eventually shipped to Goa to be dealt with by the Portuguese viceroy. Here, the men had a stroke of luck. One of the Jesuit fathers in the town was an Oxfordshire man named Thomas Steven who had arrived in Goa four years previously, earning himself the distinction of being the first Englishman ever to visit India. Hearing that a group of his compatriots were incarcerated in the town's 'fair stronge prison', Steven immediately provided sureties for them and the men were allowed to go free.

Once out of prison they went their separate ways. Story promptly locked himself up in a monastery to pursue his new-found vocation as a monk. Newberry found Goa to his liking and settled in the town, Eldred discussed trade with the local merchants, while Leedes entered the service of the Emperor Akbar and was never heard of again. But Fitch was not to be swayed from his original plans. In transporting him to Goa the Portuguese had unwittingly aided his project by dropping him behind enemy lines. Before they had the chance to rearrest him he fled the town in disguise and, after years on the road, eventually arrived in Malacca. Fitch shows no triumphalism in having finally reached his goal; he records his arrival with the same methodical detachment that marks the rest of his journey, compiling a dossier of information about commodities and prices.

After no less than eight years of painstaking research into the spice trade, Fitch decided it was time to return home. When he finally reached London, he was surprised to discover that he had become something of a celebrity and that his journal was eagerly sought after by the bards and playwrights of London. One who was particularly interested in his story was a young writer called William Shakespeare who adapted the opening sentence of Fitch's account for his new play *Macbeth*. Fitch had written: 'I did ship myself in a ship of London, called the Tiger, wherein we went for Tripolis in Syria, and from thence we took the way for Aleppo.' In *Macbeth* this is echoed in the words: 'Her husband's to Aleppo gone, master o'th' *Tiger*.'

While Fitch laid the groundwork for the first serious trading venture Sir Francis Drake was taking more practical measures to ensure its success. As King Philip of Spain's massive Armada sailed up the English Channel, Drake attacked the fleet, wreaking chaos on the would-be invaders. Each day he picked off straggling ships until, at the end of July 1588, 'the winds of God blew.' Surveying the destruction he had caused, Drake declared that none of the Spanish commanders 'will greatly rejoice of this day's service'.

The psychological effects of victory were to change England forever. For decades the high seas had been the exclusive preserve of Spain and Portugal but now there was a new power to be reckoned with. Within months, news of England's naval prowess had reached the kings and princes of the East Indies, rulers who had never before heard of England. In a region where military strength counted for everything, the local potentates of Java and Sumatra awaited their first glimpse of this newly victorious power, and when the first English mariners finally pitched up at the court of Sultan Ala-uddin of Achin – the most powerful ruler in Sumatra – they found that the Sultan knew every detail of the historic victory. So anxious was he to make an impression on this new naval power, and so keen to strike up a trading alliance, that he sent a train of elephants magnificently decked with streamers to meet them.

In the congratulatory letter that he sent to Queen Elizabeth I he was most effusive in his greetings. Imagining her as victorious ruler of vast swathes of Europe, he addressed his letter to the Sultana of England, France, Ireland, Holland and Friseland. Even good Queen Bess must have blushed at that.

CHAPTER TWO

WONDERFULLY
UNWHOLESOME
CLIMES

TWO MONTHS AFTER Sir Francis Drake's spectacular success against the Armada, London merchants heard rumours that an English vessel was sailing up the Channel after an adventurous voyage to the East Indies. The captain of this ship was Thomas Cavendish, the second Englishman to circumnavigate the globe, who was returning from his expedition laden with rich merchandise. On his home-bound journey he had attacked the huge Spanish galleon, *Great St Anne*, along with a staggering nineteen other vessels, and he arrived back in England to a rapturous welcome, a welcome that was heightened by reports that his sailors wore silken doublets and that his top sails were trimmed with gold.

Scarcely had Cavendish set foot on land than he was writing to his old friend, the Lord Chamberlain, urging him to promote an English expedition to the Spice Islands without delay. 'I sailed along the islands of the Moluccas,' he wrote, 'where our countrymen may have trade as freely as the Portugals if they themselves will.'

There was by now a pressing need to send a successful trading mission to the East Indies for, ever since King Philip II had acceded to the throne of Portugal in 1580, the markets of Lisbon had been closed to English shipping. Not only had this dramatically reduced the quantity of spice arriving in England, it had also closed an important export market for English broadcloths and woollens. The old argument against an English expedition to the Spice Islands – that the Portuguese had exclusive rights over the eastern sea routes – was no longer valid. The papal bull that had divided the world between the Catholic powers of Spain and Portugal was openly scorned in England and Queen Elizabeth I personally challenged its legality, famously arguing that 'it is as lawful for my subjects to sail [around the Cape] as the Spanish, since the sea and air are common to all men.' The voyages of Drake and Cavendish had demonstrated to the sceptics that English ships, though small, could indeed go anywhere they chose and when Drake captured a massive carrack in the eastern Atlantic it proved once and for all that such ships 'were no such bugs that they might be taken'. This particular bug was a rich prize indeed: its hold was filled with more than £100,000 of treasure.

In 1591, after years of vacillating, the merchants of London acted upon Cavendish's advice. They petitioned Queen Elizabeth for a licence to trade in the East Indies and, on gaining her consent, began searching for a suitable commander. This time they paid heed to their mistakes of the past and plumped for James Lancaster, an experienced merchant seaman who had fought bravely against the Spanish Armada.

Little is known of Lancaster's early life. His will relates that he was born in Basingstoke in 1554 or 1555 and died when he was well into his sixties. Known to be 'by birth of gentillity' he was despatched to Portugal at a tender age in order to learn the language and business of trade. Lancaster himself recorded only the briefest outlines of his years in

*James Lancaster survived two long journeys to the East Indies braving
scurvy, storms and Portuguese carracks. One of his letters, written
during a hurricane, entered the legends of the East India Company.
'I cannot tell where you should look for me,' he wrote,
'because I live at the devotion of the
winds and seas.'*

the country. 'I have been brought up among these people,' he later wrote, 'and have lived among them as a gentleman, served with them as a soldier, and lived among them as a merchant.' What else he did in Portugal remains uncertain, but it seems likely that he, like many other English living there, espoused the cause of Don Antonio in the struggle for the Portuguese throne and fought on his behalf. With the victory of Spain his days were numbered and he fled back to England as a virtual refugee, losing all his property and money in the process. But his knowledge of Portuguese was to stand him in good stead for by 1587, the year before the Armada, he was once again trading, this time from London.

An oil painting of James Lancaster has survived to show the manner of the man. Magnificently attired in buttoned doublet and flamboyant ruff he looks the typical Elizabethan, stiff and rigid with one hand resting on sword and the other fingering a globe. His journals and writings add flesh to what remains an archetypal Elizabethan portrait, revealing that Lancaster was a mixture of gruff sea dog and stern moraliser. A strict disciplinarian, he was a keen advocate of daily prayers on board ship and forbade any sort of gaming. He particularly abhorred bad language and instituted severe penalties 'against the blaspheming of the name of God and all idle and filthy communication'. Yet his disciplinarian nature was always tempered by compassion. When his vessel was in danger of sinking, he was at first furious that the accompanying ship ignored his orders to leave them to their fate. 'These men regard no commission,' he growled darkly; yet no one was punished when he later learned that they had remained alongside because of their love for him. The respect he showed for his crew was also a new departure: Lancaster did everything in his power to save the weak and, unlike many other captains, was genuinely horrified to watch helplessly as dozens of his crew succumbed to illness and death.

The vessel that Lancaster had captained against the Armada, the *Edward Bonaventure*, was not a warship; rather, she was one of the many London merchant vessels that sailed down the English Channel to aid in the defence of the realm. She was also destined to become, under Lancaster's skilful command, one of three ships to set off on the long 1591 voyage to the East Indies.

The merchants who financed this expedition viewed it as a reconnaissance mission rather than a trading venture and little cargo was loaded on board the ships. Instead, all available space was converted into living space for the large number of men on board, a necessary feature of long voyages into the unknown. Many would die on the outward trip and for those that survived there was a cornucopia of tropical diseases awaiting them on their arrival in the East.

Decked with streamers and bunting, the *Edward Bonaventure*, *Penelope* and *Merchant Royal* sailed from Plymouth on a warm spring day in 1591. A large crowd had assembled to bid the ships farewell and many families wept openly as they pulled away from the shore. Lancaster himself took the helm of the flagship, leading the other vessels into the choppy waters of the English Channel. His bullish optimism was not mirrored by the crowd gathered to see him off. The chances of them seeing their loved ones again were slim, and many were already questioning the wisdom of putting to sea so late in the season.

At first all went well; the ships arrived safely at the Canary Islands before setting off with the wind in their sails for Cape Verde and the equator. Here, they had the good fortune to capture a Portuguese caravel laden with sixty tons of wine, a thousand jars of oil and numerous barrels of capers. Despite this unexpected revictualling men began to die. Two expired on the *Edward Bonaventure* before she had even crossed the equator whilst others soon 'tooke their sicknesse in those hote climates, for they be so wonderful unwholesome'. Worse, the weather was on the turn. No sooner had the ships entered the southern hemisphere than 'we had nothing but tornadoes, with such thunder, lightening and raine that we could not keep our men drie three houres together which was an occasion of the infection among them.' With provisions running low, the ships followed the trade winds to Brazil before turning in the direction of the Cape of Good Hope.

The crew had by now been at sea for more than three months without eating any fresh fruit. Stuck in the doldrums and with nothing but 'salt victuals' and biscuits on board, they began to fall sick. Failure of strength and persistent breathlessness were the first signs that the body was beginning to weaken and many could no longer climb the rigging. Next, their skin turned sallow, their gums tender and their breath rank and offensive. 'The disease that hath consumed our men hath bene the skurvie,' wrote Edmund Barker, one of the on-board chroniclers of the expedition. 'Our soldiers, which have not been used to the sea, have best held out, but our mariners dropt away; which (in my judgement) proceedeth of their evil way of living at home.'

Most of Lancaster's men were soon suffering from these early signs of the sickness and it was not long before the scurvy took on a more dramatic form. Their teeth dropped out and purple blotches sprouted all over their bodies. Eating salted meat did nothing to assuage their condition;

indeed, it only seemed to make matters worse. As their muscles swelled and their joints stiffened, thin streams of blood began to trickle from their eyes and noses. By the time the ships staggered towards the Cape of Good Hope many were also suffering from acute diarrhoea, as well as from lung and kidney troubles.

The usual port of call for ships rounding the Cape was Table Bay, a sheltered watering place first discovered by the Portuguese in 1503. Here the English ships dropped anchor and sent an advance party ashore where they were met by 'certaine blacke savages, very brutish, which would not stay'. This first meeting between Lancaster's Elizabethan hosed and doubleted seamen and the natives of southern Africa must have made for a strange sight. Never had the English crew seen such a primitive and barbarous people and they watched the savages with a mixture of awe and disgust. 'They wear only a short cloake of sheepe or seale skinnes to their middle, the hairie side inward, and a kind of rat's skinne about their privities.' So wrote Patrick Copland, the priest on a later voyage who was unamused by the titillating behaviour of their womenfolk. 'They would lift up their rat skinnes and shew their privities.' Mealtimes were an occasion for even greater disgust. One Englishman watched in horror as a band of natives ravenously munched through a pile of stinking fish entrails that had lain for more than two weeks in the tropical heat. As the 'savages' smacked their lips and sucked their fingers he concluded that 'the world doth not yield a more heathenish people and more beastly', adding that their meals smelt so foul 'that no Christian could abide to come within a myle of it'. The jewellery worn by the women was equally offensive: 'Their neckes were adorned with greasie tripes which sometimes they would pull off and eat raw.

When we threw away their beasts' entrails, they would eat them half raw, the blood lothsomely slavering.'

For three weeks Lancaster's crew were disappointed in their search for fresh fruit. They managed to shoot geese and cranes with their muskets, and gathered mussels on the foreshore, but found it difficult to acquire food in sufficient quantities to feed all their company. But eventually they had some luck. After capturing a native and explaining in sign language their need for meat and fruit, he set off up country and returned eight days later with forty bullocks and oxen, as well as several dozen sheep. The men could not believe how cheap these animals were. One knife bought a bullock, two secured an ox, and a broken blade was all that was needed to buy a sheep. While the crew bartered on the foreshore, a small party set off around the bay in a small pinnace and returned with a huge number of seals and penguins. Lancaster even managed to shoot an antelope.

Despite all the fresh meat many of the men remained desperately sick. A health check revealed that less than two hundred men were 'sound and whole' and fifty were too ill to work. A decision was taken: the *Penelope* and *Edward Bonaventure* would continue eastwards while the *Merchant Royal* 'was sent home for England with diverse weake men'. The expedition was now down to two ships, both of which were dangerously undermanned.

It was only a matter of days before the expedition met with disaster. No sooner had the two remaining vessels rounded the Cape of Good Hope than a tremendous storm sank the *Penelope* with the loss of all hands:

We encountered with a mighty storme and extreme gusts of wind, wherein we lost our General's companie [the *Penelope*] and could never heare of him

nor his ship any more, though we did our best
endeavour to seeke him … Foure dayes after this
uncomfortable separation, in the morning, toward ten
of the clocke, we had a terrible clap of thunder, which
slew foure of our men outright, their necks being
wrung in sonder without speaking any word, and of
94 men there was not one untouched; whereof some
were striken blind, others were bruised in their legs
and arms, and others in their brests, so that they
voided blood two dayes after; others were drawne out
at length, as though they had been racked. But (God
be thanked) they all recovered, saving only the foure
which were slaine outright. Also with the same
thunder our main mast was torn very greviously from
the head to the deck, and some of the spikes, that
were ten inches into the timber, were melted with the
extreme heate thereof.

Lancaster's vessel, the *Edward Bonaventure*, was now alone, a
dangerous situation for a ship about to enter uncharted
waters. Worse still the ship's master, William Mace, was
killed by natives while making a sortie for water on the
shores of Mozambique. Luckily help was at hand. When a
Portuguese merchant-ship sent a message to Lancaster by
way of a negro in a canoe, 'we took the negro along with
us, because we understood he had been in the East Indies
and knew somewhat of the countrie.' This became a regular
practice among the English captains and the only sure way
of finding the remote and isolated Spice Islands.
Unfortunately, this particular 'negro' proved a disaster.
Allowing the ship to be blown hopelessly off course, he
missed the Laccadive Islands in the Arabian Sea where
Lancaster had intended to revictual and decided to head to

the Nicobar Islands instead. 'But in our course we were very much deceived by the currents,' and these islands also eluded the ship so that by the time she reached Penang off the coast of Malaysia the crew were once again in a desperate condition. Only thirty-three men were left alive, and eleven of these were so sick that they were unable to man the ship. After cruising the coastline for a few days, Lancaster spotted a large Portuguese ship sailing from Goa. To attack her was a great gamble but Lancaster was prepared to take the risk. Ordering the men to prime their cannon, he 'shot at her many shot, and at last shooting her maine-yard through, she came to anker and yielded'. The captain and crew escaped in little rowing boats leaving the English to ransack the vessel. She was loaded with a hotchpotch of cargo, including sixteen brass cannon, three hundred butts of Canary wine and a good supply of raisin wine 'which is verie strong', as well as red caps, worsted stockings and sweetmeats. As soon as these had been transferred onto the *Edward Bonaventure* Lancaster set sail in order to escape the danger of reprisals.

Sailing north-west towards Ceylon – and lost in the vastness of the Indian Ocean – the crew now decided that they had had more than enough adventure. With their captain languishing in his cabin, 'very sick, more like to die than to live', they refused to obey his orders and decided to head for England. Lancaster was reluctantly forced to agree.

Short of food and plagued with cockroaches, they safely rounded the Cape of Good Hope and, with the wind in their favour, headed straight to the island of St Helena where a group of men rowed ashore. Ever since the failure of Edward Fenton's mad scheme to proclaim himself king the island had been deserted. Ships occasionally stopped at the island to stock up on the 'excellent good greene figs, oranges, and lemons very faire', and the crew of one passing vessel had seen fit to construct a makeshift chapel on the island; but for the greater part of the year the island was uninhabited. It was with considerable surprise, therefore, and not a little fear, that Lancaster's men heard a ghostly chant emerging from the chapel. Kicking open the door, 'we found an Englishman, a tailor, who had been there 14 months.' His name was John Segar and he had been cast ashore the previous year by the captain of the *Merchant Royal* who, realising he was at death's door, reasoned that he stood a greater chance of survival on land than aboard the ship. But although the months on the island had cured his body, the loneliness, boredom and heat had begun to addle his mind. 'We found him to be as fresh in colour and in as good plight of body to our seeming as he might be,' wrote one witness, 'but crazed in mind and half out of his wits, as afterwards we perceived; for whether he were put in fright of us, not knowing at first what we were, whether friends or foe, or of sudden joy when he understood we were his olde consorts and countrymen, he became idle-headed, and for eight days space neither night nor day took any naturall rest, and so at length died for lacke of sleep.'

The journey home should have been almost over but as the crew set sail for home the wind dropped once again and they spent six weeks drifting helplessly in the mid-Atlantic. At last the breeze stiffened and Lancaster, who had by now recovered, suggested they let the winds carry them to the West Indies where they could obtain much-needed provisions. A chance encounter with a French ship enabled them to replenish their supplies of wine and bread but it was to be their last stroke of good fortune. A sudden storm arose which grew so fierce that 'it carried not only our sailes away, but also made much water in our shippe, so that wee had six foote water in holde'. The ship limped towards the outpost island of Mona and, relieved to have reached land, all but five of the crew rowed ashore. It was the last they would ever see of the *Edward Bonaventure*: at around midnight the ship's carpenter cut the moorings and, with a skeleton crew and a good measure of self-confidence, sailed off into the night leaving Lancaster and his men stranded.

Almost a month passed before a French ship was spotted on the horizon. Hastily lighting a bonfire to attract her attention the crew were eventually picked up and offered the passage home. By the time Lancaster and the pitiful remnants of his crew arrived back in England they had been away for three years, six weeks, and two days.

The voyage had proved a human and financial disaster. Of the 198 men who rounded the Cape, only 25 returned alive. Worse still, two of the three ships had been lost and the one that did manage to limp into port was carrying not spices but scurvy. Lancaster had proved – if proof was needed – that the spice trade involved risks that London's merchants could ill afford. It was not until they learned that the Dutch had entered the spice race, and achieved a remarkable success, that they would consider financing a new expedition to the islands of the East Indies.

The Dutch expedition had been planned in the utmost secrecy. For more than three years the inhabitants of Amsterdam's Warmoestraat, a genteel neighbourhood close to the city's main square, had watched an unusual amount of activity at the house of Reynier Pauw. This merchant, just twenty-eight years of age, had already made his fortune as head of an international lumber business. Now, it seemed, he had set his sights on a new and more ambitious project, for two of the regular visitors at his home, Jan Carel and Hendrik Hudde, were among the city's wealthiest merchants. There was a third man who joined them at their meetings – a bearded hunchback whose tight-fitting skull-cap emphasised his bulbous forehead. His name was Petrus Plancius, a gifted though dogmatic theologian who had studied in England before travelling to Amsterdam to preach his fanatical branch of Calvinism. But it was not

Cross staff was used to measure height of sun at noon and thereby determine latitude.

Expeditions set off to the Spice Islands with primitive instruments. Most navigational equipment was only useful in bright sunshine, and a common practice was to hire (or capture) a local 'pilot'. 'We took a negro along with us,' wrote James Lancaster, 'because we understood he had been in the East Indies.'

Cross staff in use, 1563. In bright sunshine it could damage the user's eye.

theology that brought him to Pauw's house: Plancius had come to show his maps of the Indies – maps that were said to be the most accurate in existence.

Men of religion do not, as a rule, make great men of science. Plancius was the exception and even when he preached from the pulpit his mind would frequently wander away from thoughts of God towards his fascination with geography. 'I have been told,' wrote one critic, 'that

The back staff did not require the user to look directly at the sun.

The astrolabe, also used to measure the height of the sun, was less accurate than the cross staff.

you frequently climb into the pulpit without having properly prepared your sermon. You switch then to subjects which have nothing to do with religion. You talk as a geographer about the Indies and the New World, or you discuss the stars.' This interest in geography strayed increasingly into his religious work. Commissioned to draw a map of Biblical sites for a new edition of the Bible, Plancius deftly crafted a map not of the Holy Land but of the entire world, including the Spice Islands. Soon he was concentrating more and more time on map-drawing until, in 1592, he published his important world map grandly entitled, 'A geographical and hydrographical map of the whole world, showing all countries, towns, places and seas under their respective degrees of longitude and latitude; capes, promontories, headlands, ports, shoals, sand banks and cliffs are drawn in the most accurate manner.'

Plancius drew on the work of two Dutch cartographers when he came to produce his maps. These men, Abraham Ortelius and Gerardus Mercator, had in turn derived their inspiration from the Roman geographer Claudius Ptolemy who had gone to immense lengths to determine the precise position of all known places. Ortelius's fascination with the science of cartography resulted in his magnificent *Theatrum Orbis Terrarum,* whilst Gerardus Mercator had been struggling throughout the 1560s to draw his pioneering world map on the projection that now bears his name. The finished work was similar in detail to that of Ortelius but differed in its novel projection, for although he drew all the lines meeting at right angles he pulled the parallels of latitude farther apart as they reached the poles. This, of course, distorted the distances to a huge degree, to the point that Greenland became the size of North America, but it also meant that the position of places relative to one another remained correct. His discovery gave Dutch cartographers a virtual monopoly on map-making for more than a century and enabled them to furnish their explorers with practical and up-to-date information when they set sail on their voyages to the East Indies.

Even with access to these maps, the Dutch merchants planning their first expedition remained cautious. They were aware that it took a huge sum of money to equip a fleet which, given the record of the English, was almost certain to suffer substantial losses on the long route to and from the East. But in the winter of 1592, Plancius arrived at Pauw's house with a new and unknown face whose weather-beaten features suggested that he had been abroad for some considerable time. The name of this stranger was Jan Huyghen van Linschoten and he had indeed been on a long voyage – nine years in the Indies – and had returned with reams of information about the spice ports of the East.

Linschoten was the antithesis of Fitch and, had the two men met in the souks of Malacca, they would have found little in common. The Dutchman's tales are a colourful mix of fact and fantasy and his book is filled with 'luxurious and unchaste women', rampaging elephants and giant rats 'as big as young pigges'. Most extraordinary of all is his tale of the monstrous fish of Goa which are 'in bigness as great as a middle sized dog, with a snout like a hog, small eyes, no eares, but two holes where his eares should bee'. As he tried to sketch this extraordinary creature, 'it ranne along the hall upon the floore and in every place snorting like a hog.'

Unlike Fitch, Linschoten was not travelling in order to research the cost and availability of spices; rather, his aim was to collect weird and wonderful fables from the East and he would quiz every merchant and mariner he met and transcribe their marvels into his bulging diary.

It was not until he returned to Holland and began to tell people of his travels that their true worth was realised. Unwittingly, Linschoten had compiled an immense encyclopaedia of knowledge about the islands of the East Indies. He knew exactly what the native merchants wished to exchange for their spices, had discovered that pieces-of-eight were the coins most sought after by traders, and had inadvertently researched all the most suitable ports for revictualling on the long journey to the East. The resulting book, the *Itinerario*, stretched to five weighty volumes, one of which included descriptions of the produce of every island in the Indies as well as a list of languages of most use to foreign traders. There were lengthy accounts of the nutmeg and clove trees along with a section on the healing and curative properties of these spices: 'nutmegs fortify the brain and sharpen the memory,' he wrote. 'They warm the stomach and expel winds. They give a clean breath, force the urine, stop diarrhoea, and cure upset stomachs.'

Linschoten's account and Plancius's maps convinced the three merchants that the time was now right to send an expedition to the East. Yet still they hesitated, deciding to await the return of a spy they had sent to Lisbon, a headstrong man named Cornelis Houtman whose unstable temperament was to cause so much trouble in the future. Exactly what Houtman discovered in Lisbon is not known, but it convinced the merchants that there was no time to be lost in entering the spice race and, 'after many discussions, it was finally resolved that, in the Name of God, a beginning should be made with the navigation and other affairs.' Six more merchants were summoned to help finance the project, four ships were built, and cannon were

borrowed from various towns. Embarrassingly, not enough
firearms could be found and an agent had to be despatched
to England to buy some extra weaponry.

In stark contrast to the English expeditions, the Dutch
voyage was meticulously planned. The ships were equipped
with spare masts, anchors and cables and the begrudging
pilots were compelled to have lessons in navigation from
Petrus Plancius: 'five days a week, from Monday till Friday,
from nine in the morning until five in the evening'. But in
common with all the English voyages prior to that of James
Lancaster, save that of Sir Francis Drake, the Dutch
merchants made one critical mistake: they put unsuitable
and inadequate men in command.

One of these was Cornelis Houtman, the very man
whose clandestine activities in Lisbon had helped get the
project off the ground. As a spy he was in his element; as a
leader of men he was a disaster. Houtman was given the
important post of chief merchant on the *Mauritius* which,
had it been his only job, would have limited his potential
to cause mischief. Unfortunately, he was also given a place
on the ships' council with a special status that allowed him
to speak first on any issue.

Setting sail in the spring of 1595, the expedition's four
vessels headed first for the Cape Verde Islands in the mid-
Atlantic and then set sail towards the equator. Here they
entered the doldrums, drifting across the ocean for almost
a month before the coastline of Brazil was sighted. From
here, the ships changed course with the trade winds and let
themselves be carried back towards southern Africa.

Many of the men were by now desperately sick and, as
the ships rounded the Cape, good hope proved elusive for
the seventy-one sailors who succumbed to scurvy. Worse
still, discipline broke down completely as simmering

discontent exploded into outright warfare. In normal circumstances, such unruly behaviour would have been treated with the utmost severity. According to a Dutch code of discipline, any fight that drew blood would result in the antagonist having one hand strapped behind his back and the other nailed to the mast. There he would remain until he tore himself lose. If the fight ended in death, the man was bound to his victim and tossed into the sea. Even pulling a knife in jest was a serious misdemeanour – the offender would suffer three lengthy dunkings from the yardarm. Refusing to obey the captain commanded the death penalty; desertion was rewarded with flogging, and the most serious offences were dealt with by keel-hauling – a terrible punishment which involved being hauled underneath the keel while the ship was moving. In the majority of cases, the victim's head was ripped off.

None of these deterred the crew of this pioneering Dutch expedition from indulging in the most violent and brutal behaviour. The troubles began when the skipper of the *Amsterdam* died of scurvy and the ship's chief merchant, a hothead named Gerrit van Beuningen, assumed control. The ships' council was furious and accused Beuningen of a series of crimes, including an attempt on the life of Cornelis Houtman, and demanded he be hanged from the ship's mast without further ado. Others supported Beuningen and vowed to defend him with force. Calmer counsel eventually prevailed and the merchant was clapped in irons instead. History has failed to record whether or not he regretted his action, but he was certainly given time to repent. When the *Amsterdam* finally arrived back in Holland two years later, Beuningen was still in irons.

Discipline now broke down completely and it was only when the ships reached Sumatra that the men called a temporary truce and patched up their quarrels. As they sailed through the shallow coastal waters, the natives rowed out in dug-out canoes and exchanged rice, water-melons and sugar-canes for glass beads and trinkets. Fresh food and water helped to heal the rifts but it was not long before new quarrels began. On arriving at the wealthy port of Bantam in Java, Houtman had hoped to buy spices for a song and was incensed when he discovered the prices to be sky-high. Worse still, all native authority in the town had disappeared as rival traders bickered and courtiers fought for possession of the throne.

Such an explosive situation was doomed to end in disaster. Angered by the escalating price of spices, Houtman lost his temper. 'And thus,' wrote one of the crew in a terrifyingly matter-of-fact entry in his journal, 'it was decided to do all possible harm to the town.' What followed was an orgy of destruction that was to set the pattern for the Dutch presence in the East Indies. The town was bombarded with cannon fire and prisoners were sentenced to death. A brief pause in the fighting allowed the Dutch commanders to debate the different means of disposing of prisoners (the choice was to stab them, shoot them with arrows, or blow them from cannons – unfortunately, no one recorded which method they settled for) and once this thorny question was resolved the battering continued. At one point the king's palace was hit; at another, a group of newly captured prisoners were tortured. 'And after we had revenged ourselves to the approval of our ship's officers,' wrote the same crew member, 'we prepared to set sail.' The ships proceeded to the nearby port of Sidayu where they were surprised by a group of Javanese natives who boarded the *Amsterdam* and hacked twelve men to death, including the skipper, before finding themselves under attack. The

Dutch 'then chased the natives back to the shore in our own rowing boats and executed the Javanese who had killed our colleagues'. Few paused to question why everyone was acting with such brutality. The voice of conscience is never loud in the journals of sixteenth-century mariners but one crew member did wonder why his fellow tradesmen had suddenly become such bloodthirsty cut-throats. 'There was nothing missing and everything was perfect except what was wrong with ourselves,' he wrote.

Events were to prove that the killing had scarcely begun. As the Dutch ships passed Madura, a low-lying island off the Javanese coast, the local prince (not yet privy to the events in Bantam) decided to put on a display of friendship, welcoming the Hollanders with a little flotilla of native prahus. The oarsmen rowed slowly and ceremoniously towards the Dutch vessels and at the centre of their display was a magnificent barge decorated with an elevated bridge on which stood the local prince, smiling broadly.

The Dutch grew agitated as more and more natives rowed out to the ships. Some whispered that it was an ambush; others were convinced there was treachery afoot and argued for a pre-emptive strike. Houtman agreed and, relying on the time-honoured principal that the best defence is attack, his ship 'opened fire and killed all on the big boat'. It was the signal for a general massacre. Within minutes, dozens of cannon were being fired into the flotilla, sinking boats and slaughtering the welcome party. No sooner had the floating parade been blasted out of the water than the Dutchmen lowered their rowing boats and concluded the day's business with hand-to-hand fighting. By the end of the battle, all but twenty natives were dead, among them the prince whose body was relieved of its jewels before being returned to a watery grave. 'I watched the attack not without pleasure,' admitted one Dutch sailor, 'but also with shame.'

The ships and crew were by now in a pitiful condition. Rival factions were at each other's throats while the various commanders – of whom Houtman was in the ascendant – were scarcely on speaking terms. Hundreds of men had died and those who were still alive were suffering from tropical diseases picked up at Bantam. Worse still, the ships themselves were in a sorry state of disrepair. Bearded with marine growth and encrusted with barnacles, they looked as if they had been raised from the depths of the ocean. Many were honeycombed with teredos (shipworms) which bored through the Dutch oak and allowed water to filter through the holes. On deck the tropical sun had so dried the timbers that the gaps between the planks were more than half an inch wide.

Then there was the question of spices. Despite many months at sea, Houtman had so far failed to buy any spices apart from the tiny quantity acquired when his ships first arrived in Sumatra. Having rejected trade with the merchants of Bantam, the Dutch were fast running out of suitable marketplaces.

A plan of action had to be made and a decision taken. Houtman argued that they should sail east to the Banda Islands where they were assured of a cargo of nutmeg at a reasonable price. But the captain of the *Mauritius*, Jan Meulenaer, disagreed. He said that the ships were virtually unseaworthy and that to make such a long voyage would be risking almost certain death. In the event, death came to Meulenaer rather sooner than he expected. Just hours after a particularly ferocious argument with Houtman he collapsed on deck and expired. There could be no doubt that there had been foul play. Two of the ships' on-board barbers proclaimed in front of the council that Meulenaer 'was completely blue and purple; poisoned blood came not only from his mouth but from his neck as well; and even his hair fell out at the slightest touch. A child,' they concluded, 'could tell he had been poisoned.'

A murder. A motive. And a body. It did not take long to find the suspect. The crew of the *Mauritius* accused Houtman of murder and promptly clapped him in irons. They then summoned the ships' council to convene for a second time and asked it to condemn him to death. But in this last demand they were to be disappointed for the council reasoned that there was insufficient evidence to execute Houtman and he was released.

The ships' crews now decided to abandon their quest for spices and sail for home. The *Amsterdam* was so rotten that she was emptied of supplies and set on fire. Then, making a final stop at Bali in order to take advantage of the amorous charms of local girls – and leaving behind two men who found those charms irresistible – the Dutch set sail for home.

When they finally reached Amsterdam more than two years had passed and two out of every three men on board had died. For the merchants who had financed the voyage the lack of spices was far more galling than the lack of men. They watched the ships' return to port fully expecting them to be laden with nutmeg, cloves and pepper. As it was, the cargo unloaded on that August day was silver reals – the same reals that they had watched being loaded two years previously. Incredibly, the price of spices had become so inflated while the ships had been in the East Indies that the tiny quantity Houtman carried home was enough to make the venture a profitable one. Had he been a more responsible commander he could have netted them a fortune.

The troubles that had plagued Holland's inaugural voyage to the East did little to deter Amsterdam's merchants from risking yet more of their money in the spice race. They argued that they had met with far greater success than the English who had not only lost two ships on their first expedition, one more than theirs, but had failed so far to reach the spice port of Bantam.

Less than seven months after Houtman's return, the merchants placed this unruly commander in charge of a second Dutch expedition to the East Indies, signalling that they had learned nothing from the mistakes of the previous voyage. But if Houtman was not up to the job, the chief pilot was more than qualified. His name was John Davis and he was an Englishman from Devon. A brilliant navigator, whose pioneering Arctic explorations had already carried him to the frozen shores of Greenland, he not only guided the ships to the East Indies and back, but also kept detailed notes on every coastline, port and harbour. Within weeks of completing the long voyage, Davis was hired for a second trip. But this time he was sailing on an English vessel under the command of the veteran James Lancaster. And this time, the two men were sailing as servants of the newly founded East India Company.

CHAPTER THREE

Music
and
Dancing Damsels

O N THE EVENING OF 24 September 1599, a loud
cheer was heard coming from the half-timbered
Founders Hall in London's Lothbury Street. For
much of the day the city's merchant adventurers had been
deep in discussion about sending a new fleet of ships to the
East Indies. Now they had at last reached a decision. With
a unanimous show of hands and a roar of excitement it was
decided to apply to Queen Elizabeth I for her assent to a
project that was 'intended for the honour of our native
country and for the advancement of trade of merchandise
within this realm of England'.

No painting survives to record the scene behind the
mullioned windows of Founders Hall on that September
evening but with the Company scribe recording every last
detail for posterity it is not hard to assemble a picture of the
historic events unfolding. Some fourscore men had
gathered to discuss the practicalities of the intended voyage.
These were not aristocrats nor landowners, nor were they
members of the courtly circle; most were merchants and
burghers, men who made their living by speculating on
trading ventures.

Some of the leading lights in this new enterprise had

considerable experience of international trade. Richard Staper and Thomas Smythe, for example, had been principal founders of the Levant Company and had helped to build a successful business in the eastern Mediterranean. Others, like Sir John Hart and Richard Cockayne were well-known faces in the City of London. Three of the men had held office as Lord Mayor of London and the chairman of the meeting, splendidly dressed in wig and robes, was Sir Stephen Soane, the present occupant of the Lord Mayorship.

Not all were merchants: among the aldermen and freemen of the London guilds were sailors and soldiers, bearded and weather-beaten sea dogs who wore gold rings in their ears and good-luck amulets about their necks. James Lancaster and John Davis could be seen among the crowds and so, too, could Francis Pretty, close friend of Thomas Cavendish. A few of Drake's crew pitched up for the meeting, as did some who had sailed with Fenton and Hawkins. Arctic explorer William Baffin put in an appearance as did the three Middleton brothers – John, Henry and David – who would all meet with disasters on the long voyage to and from the Spice Islands.

Such men were crucial to the success or failure of this, the Company's first venture. They were familiar with the sight of Portuguese carracks laden with costly spices and knew the best ports to obtain fresh water and new provisions. They also knew that although the Spanish and Portuguese had a vigorous commerce with the East, only a dozen or so ports were under their direct control. These were scattered over a huge area from Madagascar to Japan, and even Goa, the jewel in the crown of Portugal's eastern outposts, only housed a small settlement of traders and merchants. It scarcely deserved its suffix – dorado. In the 'riche and innumerable islands of the Mollucos and the

Spiceries', where nutmeg and cloves could be had for a song, the Portuguese influence was spread even more thinly. They had just two small forts on the islands of Tidore and Amboyna, leaving dozens of other atolls and skerries to be claimed, remote places like the nutmeg-producing Banda Islands.

Since it had become an axiom in international law that European nations could only claim such places as they had fortified or in which they had erected some visible symbol of possession, there were many who argued that it would make sense to head for these lonely outposts of the Spice Islands. If the flag could be raised in the Banda Islands, for instance, then England would have a toehold in the richest of all the islands in the East Indies.

When everyone had had the chance to speak Sir Stephen Soane called the meeting to order. There were important matters to be settled, not least of which was to prevent the large sum of money which had been subscribed just two days earlier from being contributed in any form other than cash. It was also decided to entrust the day-to-day running of the Company to fifteen directors who would organise and regulate the forthcoming voyage.

It was late by the time the meeting finally broke up. The sailors and adventurers trudged their way back to their homes in Shoreditch and Wapping, the merchants to their gabled dwellings in Charing Cross and Lincoln's Inn Fields. All must have felt that at long last they were on the brink of partaking in a successful trading enterprise to the East Indies.

To those subscribers who had gambled their money on the voyage there were huge riches to be had if it ended in success. Elizabethan London was home to an affluent aristocracy who clamoured for every luxury. Queen

Elizabeth herself determined the fashion of the age with her famous wardrobe of three thousand dresses, and the ladies of the court followed suit, cloaking themselves in brocades and satins trimmed with costly laces, sables and embroideries. The Queen loved the pomp, ceremony and luxuries that her state afforded her. In her palaces at St James, Greenwich, Windsor and Hampton Court she was surrounded by baubles, trinkets and precious objets d'art, as well as a magnificent library of Greek and Latin poets, richly bound in velvet.

Some of her more puritanical ministers reacted against the wanton extravagance of her court. At the wedding of one member of the aristocracy the celebrant priest, dismayed by the sight of so much finery, decided to speak his mind. Aware, perhaps, of the moves afoot for a great expedition to the East, he clambered into the pulpit and delivered a damning but topical sermon about the fripperies of Elizabethan fashion. 'Of all qualities,' he said, 'a woman must not have one quality, and that is too much rigging. What a wonder to see a ship under full sail, with her tackling and her masts, and her tops and top-gallants, with her upper deck and her nether decks, and so be-dekt with her streamers, flags, and ensigns ...' Pausing to survey the assembled ladies he continued: 'what a world of wonders it is to see a woman, created in God's image, so miscreate oft times with her French, her Spanish, and her foolish fashions, that He ... shall hardly know her with her plumes, her faunes, and a silken vizard, with a ruffle like a saile.'

The sermon fell on deaf ears. Elizabeth's courtiers were not about to abandon their new-found pleasures for this was an age that demanded excess. They needed to be richly clad for the pageants, masques and tournaments they attended and their frivolous needs were reflected in the trite ballads, odes and sonnets of the day. They loved curios and oddities, the unusual and the exotic, and it was to satisfy this vogue that had settled the merchants of London on their latest venture.

Queen Elizabeth herself was keen for the expedition to set sail at the earliest opportunity, especially when she learned that the Portuguese and Dutch had unexpectedly raised the price of pepper from three to eight shillings a pound. Pepper had become a basic commodity and with the price now beyond the means of all but the wealthy few it was imperative that a well-organised expedition be sent to seek it at its source. A handful of attempts had been made in the wake of James Lancaster's voyage but all had ended in disaster. The most recent, which had sailed under the captainship of Benjamin Wood, had disappeared without trace. It was, recorded Samuel Purchas, 'a double disaster; first in the miserable perishing of the fleet, and next in the losse of the historie and relation of that tragedie'. Rumours slowly filtered back to London reporting that the crew had been ravaged by disease and, one by one, perished at sea. 'Some broken plankes, as after a shipwracke, have yet beene encountered from the West Indies, which give us some notice of this East Indian disadventure.' Just four survivors managed to swim to a small island on the horizon and three of these were promptly despatched by a cut-throat Spaniard leaving just one man alive. Even he was not fated to live for long; fleeing the island aboard a passing ship, he soon succumbed to a dose of poison.

On 16 October 1599, less than a month after their first meeting, the London merchants received the Queen's official blessing. She instructed them to obtain from the Privy Council a warrant allowing them to proceed with the voyage, as well as a permit enabling them to carry overseas the five thousand pounds of bullion which the merchants needed for their proposed trade. The merchants were overjoyed at the Queen's enthusiasm, but the Privy Council, though outwardly enthusiastic, was determined to stop this voyage in its tracks. Delicate negotiations were just beginning with Spain and if this expedition were to set sail with the Queen's blessing – and against the wishes of the Pope – then Philip of Spain would be well within his rights to withdraw from the discussions. The merchants were warned in no uncertain terms that any voyage would have to be accommodated to the state of public affairs. Suddenly the expedition had been blocked at the highest level.

The merchants were furious to see their enterprise undermined by a handful of haughty lords in Elizabeth's court. They begged the Queen to intervene but although they had her full sympathy there was little she could do. The merchants now stiffened their resolve. Blithely ignoring the lords they 'did enter into the preparation of a voyage the next yeare following', poring over every map, chart and book of travels about the region they intended to visit. All this new-found information was then compiled into a document under the title: 'Certayne reasons why the English Merchants may trade into the East Indies, especially to such rich kingdoms and dominions as are not subjecte to the Kinge of Spayne and Portugal; together with the true limits of the Portugals conquest and jurisdiction in these oriental parts.'

Their reasoning as to why the voyage should go ahead was nothing less than a stoutly argued refutation of the Treaty of Tordesillas. 'Let the Spaniards,' they wrote, 'shewe any juste and lawful reasons ... why they should barre her Majestie and all other Christian princes and states, of the use of the vaste, wyde and infinitely open ocean sea, and of access to the territories and dominions of so many free princes, kings and potentates in the East.' These dominions, they argued, should be free to all merchants, 'for [the Spaniards] have noe more soveriegn comaund or authoritie, than wee, or any Christians whatsoever'.

The Queen read the document with great interest, then handed it to the learned Fulke Greville, Treasurer of the Navy, who concurred with every word and proceeded to strengthen its central argument by adding references to the spice trade from books in his impressive private library, 'espetially owt of the voyages of John Huighen [Lindschoten],' the man who had made possible the first Dutch voyage. Greville also provided a list of all the eastern kings already trading with Spain, leaving the inescapable conclusion that any potentates yet to sign a trading alliance were free to be exploited by whichever country reached them first.

When the London merchants held another meeting, on 23 September 1600, exactly a year had passed since their first gathering, yet they were no closer to setting sail for the East Indies. Increasingly impatient, they now resolved to 'goe forwards with the voiage' whether or not they had permission from the lords. Just two days after the meeting they bought their first ship, the *Susan*, for the princely sum of £1,600 and, on the following day, purchased the *Hector* and *Ascension* as well.

The obsequious courtiers, who had done so much to throw obstacles in the path of the merchants, now realised they had been wrong-footed. Instead of continuing their policy of refusing consent for the voyage they decided, instead, to wrest control from the merchants by placing one of their own in overall command. There was an obvious candidate: for months one of the chief players at court, the gentleman adventurer Sir Edward Michelborne, had been petitioning for an exclusive patent for trade to the Indies. Now, the Lord High Treasurer recommended Michelborne to the London merchants, politely instructing them to give him the position of 'principal commander'.

The merchants, mindful of Edward Fenton's disastrous expedition to St Helena, refused to be dictated to, even by so grand a luminary as the Lord Treasurer. They declined to take up his offer, explaining with considerable relish that they had resolved 'not to employ any *gentleman* in any place of charge', and added that they preferred to 'sorte their business with men of their own qualitye, lest the suspicion of the employment of gentlemen being taken hold of by the generalitie, do drive a great number of the Adventurers to withdraw their contributions'.

Michelborne was livid at this snub and refused to pay the subscription for which he had signed up. His name, in consequence, was removed from the Company's roll and, fuming and humiliated, he dropped from the scene to nurse his grievances. It was to be four years before he made his first independent foray into the eastern trade; when he did so, it had a devastating effect.

The merchants now settled on equipping a voyage to set sail in the spring of 1601 but the ships they had already bought were tiny, even by the standards of the time. Realising they would need a larger flagship if they were to have any hope of seeing off any war-mongering Portuguese carracks, they began to scout around for a more impressive vessel. The Earl of Cumberland had just the ship they needed: called the *Malice Scourge*, of 600 tons, she was offered for sale at the high price of £4,000. A deal was struck, she was bought for £3,700, and renamed the *Red Dragon*. She was a sturdily built and seaworthy vessel and although her construction was better placed for the chill waters of the north than for the tropics, she made an impressive sight on the Thames, her towering stern and carved poop betraying the large and comfortable living quarters for the captain and his lieutenants. Her low waist caused her to sit deep in the water, and she had a jutting prow adorned with an elaborate figurehead. She subsequently had a glorious career in the East Indies and was not sunk by the Dutch until a 'cruel, bloody fight' in October 1619.

After numerous arguments and deliberations the merchants settled on a mixed cargo of lead, iron (both wrought and unwrought), Devonshire cotton kerseys, broadcloth and Norwich woollens, as well as several boxes of trinkets and playthings suitable for presenting to the various potentates who would be encountered on the voyage. These included girdles, a case of pistols, ostrich plumes, looking glasses, spoons, glass toys, spectacles, and ewers wrought from silver.

The provisions were a subject of even more careful thought with every last pea and carrot calculated in individual portions. Food was not supplied for the time when the ships were in port: it would be up to the captains to barter from the natives enough to feed their crew. Even so, the detail that went into provisioning the ships is proof enough that the merchants were determined this voyage should succeed.

Bread for 16 months of 30 days p month

	c	lb		ll	s	d
at 24lb p man	1714	1 4	tons 150	1028	08	0

Meal for 4 months at 30 li p man p month

	535	2 24	tons 30	267	17	4

Beer for 4 months at a pottle p man p day
the hoggeshead accoumpted clear of leakage 80 gallons

		ll	s	d
g 30000	tons 170	510	00	00

Cider for 8 months at a quart p day at the former rate

g 30000	tons 170	680	00	00

Wine for 8 months at a pint p day at the former allowaunce

g 15000	tons 80	960	00	00

Beef for 4 months at 1 li p man p day

c	q	li				
538	2	14	tons 30	428	10	00

Porke for 10 months at 1/2li p man p day

c	q	li				
669	2	16	tons 40	669	12	6.

And so the list continues. There were peas and beans to go with the pork, three months' supply of salted fish, oatmeal, wheat, 'olde holland cheese', butter, oil, vinegar, honey, sugar, and rice. The crew were even allowed a couple of pounds of nutmeg, cloves and pepper to help disguise the taste of rank meat, as well as fourteen hogshead of aqua vitae.

The merchants, though busy preparing the victualling of the ships, had not overlooked the appointment of the various captains and commanders. After electing Sir Thomas Smythe, a man of ripe experience, as the first governor of the Company, they next turned to the day-to-day running of the expedition itself. It came as no surprise that James Lancaster was named as 'General' or Admiral of the Fleet, nor that John Davis – only recently returned from the Dutch voyage – was appointed as pilot-major in charge of navigation. John Middleton, William Brund and John Heyward, all of whom had previously covered the route in various ships, were given command of the other three vessels.

There were also the on-board merchants, known as factors, to be chosen. These men were professional traders upon whose shoulders the financial success of the voyage would hinge. Selected with considerable care, they numbered 36 and would, all being well, settle in the East Indies and establish trading bases for future voyages. Those with foreign languages were particularly favoured, especially those who could speak Portuguese, Spanish or Arabic, the languages of trade in many of the larger ports in the East. Along with the crew the total tally came to 480 men, most of whom were experienced mariners.

Soon the wharves of London were alive with the clatter of ships being loaded with ropes, anchors, pennants, kegs of powder, and muskets. The cargo was loaded, the holds were filled and finally the heavy kegs of ale and cider were lashed to the decks.

There was one final business to attend to before the ships could set sail: the Queen's signature was still needed on the charter of what had now become known as the Governor and Company of Merchants trading to the East Indies. In this document, drawn up by the merchants themselves, they were to be granted a total monopoly of trade over 'traffic and merchandise to the East Indies, the countries and ports of Asia and Africa, and to and from all the islands, ports, towns, and places of Asia, Africa, and America, or any of them beyond the Cape of Bona Esperanza [Good Hope] and the Straits of Magellan'.

On 31 December 1600, it was at last signed by the

Queen. Valid for fifteen years, it conferred massive powers upon a small group of men – 218 in total. The merchant adventurers were given the exclusive right to trade with the East Indies – a vague geographical term which included the entirety of South-East Asia – without any interference from the Crown. They could take as much bullion out of the country as was necessary, found trading posts wherever they wished, and govern as they saw fit. In return for these sweeping powers they were to furnish a fleet of six ships annually.

The few regulations imposed upon this first trading expedition were drawn up by the merchants rather than the Crown. Lancaster was warned to be on his guard against any sailors who attempted to dabble in private trade and told that 'due inquisition shall be made into all and every ship, by search of all chests, boxes, packs, packets, writing, and other means whereby discovery may be made of this breach of present ordenance'. Unfortunately, this stricture proved impossible to enforce. Individual sailors were paid next to nothing for the long and hazardous voyage and many set sail with the full intention of smuggling home a sackful or two of nutmeg.

The Queen coined new money specifically for the Company. Minted at the Tower of London and bearing her arms on one side and a portcullis on the other, it soon became known as portcullis money. She also granted the merchants a new flag which, with its blue field and background of thirteen red and white stripes, prefigured the one adopted by the Thirteen Colonies of America some 175 years later.

On a cold February day in 1601, Lancaster's five ships slipped slowly down the Thames. They made a colourful sight as they passed the wharves at Woolwich. Bedecked

with streamers, pennants and colourful bunting, they flew
from their main mast the blood-red cross of St George.
The banks of the river were lined with merchants, relatives
and well-wishers, a crowd and a send-off not repeated
until 1610 when Nathaniel Courthope would leave
London on the greatest sailing ship ever built by the East
India Company.

Scarcely had Lancaster's vessels reached the Thames
Estuary than the wind dropped and for almost two months
the sails hung loose. It was not until Easter that his
fleet finally reached Dartmouth. Delayed again at Torbay,
Lancaster sent instructions to each of the ships listing ports
and harbours where they should rendezvous in the event of
becoming separated. And then, with the wind once more
filling their sails, the ships set off down the English Channel
and had an uneventful passage all the way to Gran Canaria.

Here, the wind again died and for more than a month
the fleet floated idly at sea, inching slowly towards the
equator. Just two degrees short of the line Lancaster
had a stroke of good fortune. A lone Portuguese ship,
accidentally separated from her accompanying carracks,
was spied on the horizon. The five English vessels circled
her then closed for the kill. She was boarded, her crew
disarmed and a team of men sent down into the hold. She
proved to be a very rich prize: she was laden with 146
butts of wine and 176 jars of oil and her captured cargo
was shared out among the English ships according to the
number of men on board. And then, without further ado,
they set sail once again.

As with Lancaster's first voyage men began to fall sick as
soon as they crossed into the southern hemisphere and it
was not long before 'the weakness of men was so great that
in some of the ships the merchants took their turn at the

helm and went into the top to take in the topsails.' But while men grew weaker on the smaller vessels, the diarist on board Lancaster's *Red Dragon* could not help noticing that her crew were completely immune to the illness. 'And the reason why the general's men stood in better health than the men of other ships was this; he [Lancaster] brought to sea with him certain bottles of the juice of lemons, which he gave to each one, as long as it would last, three spoonfuls every morning, fasting; not suffering them to eat anything after it till noon ... by this means the general cured many of his men and preserved the rest.' How Lancaster stumbled upon the cure for scurvy remains a mystery; it may be that he noticed the spectacular recovery that men made as soon as they were able to add fresh fruit and vegetables to their diet of salted food. On his first voyage the on-board chronicler Henry May had observed that one particularly ill crew member had made a full recovery after eating the oranges and lemons found on St Helena. Tragically Lancaster's cure was soon forgotten and more than 170 years were to pass before Captain Cook rediscovered the beneficial effects of citrus fruit in combating scurvy.

Although scurvy and sickness were a constant concern, life on board had its lighter moments. Journals and diaries make frequent mention of the play-acting, singing and clowning around that enlivened the tedium of the voyage. Music was extremely popular and on one vessel 'a virginal was brought for two to play upon at once.' This proved a great success for no sooner had the music commenced than 'the jacks skip up and down in such a manner as they will.' A later expedition even boasted a cornet player who used to regularly play for his colleagues. So accomplished was he at the instrument, and so wide was his repertoire, that on arriving in India he found himself blowing his brass for the Great Moghul himself.

The merry-making was helped along by the huge quantities of alcohol consumed by the crew. Although attempts were made to regulate the drinking, it was universally ignored until men began to drop dead of liver disorders caused by the 'inordinate drinking of a wine called tastie [toddy] distilled from the palmetto tree'.

After merry-making their way across the southern Atlantic, Lancaster's expedition finally slipped into South Africa's Table Bay on 9 September 1601, where the commander knew he could barter for fresh meat and provisions. As had happened on his first voyage the crew viewed the natives as wild barbarians who were laughably easy to exploit. Neither side was able to communicate with each other for, 'their speech is wholly uttered through the throat, and they cluck with their tongues in such sort that, in seven weeks which we remained here in this place, the sharpest wit among us could not learn one word of their language.'

Instead, the English sailors 'spake to them in the cattle's language'. When they wanted to buy oxen they would say 'moo'. When they wanted sheep, they would say 'baa'. The animals cost next to nothing: the natives did not demand silver or gold but seemed content with a couple of old iron hoops. After twelve days, the ship's company had bought more than a thousand sheep and several dozen oxen.

When his ships finally set sail Lancaster must have been pleased that his time in Table Bay had passed without incident. Aware that this was an essential revictualling point for ships heading east he did everything possible to ensure that negotiations with the natives progressed smoothly. Such a policy was in stark contrast to that of

A man and woman att the Cape of good Hope

The Table

Souldanja bay

Elizabethan sailors were fascinated by the primitive natives of
southern Africa. 'The world doth not yield a more heathenish people,'
wrote one Englishman. 'Their neckes were adorned with greasie tripes
which sometimes they would pull off and eat raw. When we threw
away their beasts' entrails, they would eat them half raw, the blood
lothsomely slavering.'

Cornelis Houtman who had treated the natives of
southern Africa with brutality and paid for it with the loss
of thirteen crew.

Although every inch of space on the vessels was taken
up with fresh supplies, the hot southern climate was still
taking its toll on the crew and it was decided to land at the

island of Cirne – now known as Mauritius – where lemons were said to be plentiful. Unfortunately, the wind unexpectedly changed direction and the little fleet was blown towards Madagascar instead. Arriving on Christmas Day in the bay of Atongill a reconnaissance party discovered a series of carvings on a rock close to the water. It had long been the practice to carve upon rocks the dates of arrival and departure of ships so that straggling vessels might know the fate of the rest of their fleet. From these carvings, Lancaster discovered to his dismay that five Dutch ships had called here just two months earlier. They had lost more than two hundred men to dysentery while they lay at anchor.

History soon began to repeat itself on the English ships. First the *Red Dragon*'s master's mate died, then the preacher, the surgeon, and ten crew members. Others suffered more violent deaths: as the master's mate was lowered into the ground, the captain of the *Ascension* rowed ashore to attend the funeral. While doing so, he had the misfortune to enter the line of musket-shot that was frequently fired on such occasions and both he and the boatswain's mate were killed, 'so that they that went to see the buriall of another,' records the ship's diarist, 'and were both buried there themselves'.

It was a most unfortunate accident; Captain William Brund was popular among the sea dogs he commanded and was sorely missed. His death reinforced the growing feeling that Madagascar was not a place to linger, so as soon as the *Red Dragon*'s little pinnace had been assembled (it was brought out from England in kit form) the fleet once more set sail.

The expanse of the Indian Ocean presented Lancaster with fewer problems than the Atlantic. A near-catastrophe was avoided when the pinnace detected the reefs and shoals surrounding the Chagos Archipelago and by the second week of May the ships had caught sight of the remote Nicobar Islands – missed on Lancaster's first voyage – where they resolved to revictual. To their surprise they discovered that the fantastical writings of medieval travellers, which spoke of men with horns and green faces, appeared to be correct. According to the ship's journal, the island priest 'had upon his head a pair of horns turning backward', while others had 'their faces painted green, black, and yellow, and their horns also painted with the same colour; and behind them, upon their buttocks, a tail hanging down, very much like the manner as in some painted clothes we paint the devil in our country'.

It is ironic that just as sceptics in England were beginning to question the veracity of accounts by medieval 'explorers' like Sir John Mandeville, genuine travellers were reporting sights that bore witness to their more outlandish tales. Sir Walter Ralegh was one of those sceptics who changed his opinion of Mandeville after hearing the reports filtering back from the mysterious East. 'Mandeville's reports were holden for fables many yeeres,' he wrote, 'and yet since the East Indies were discovered, we find his relations true of such things as heretofore were held incredible.'

On 5 June 1602, more than sixteen months after leaving Woolwich, Lancaster's fleet finally arrived at the Sumatran port of Achin. A rich, powerful and cosmopolitan city, its sea power enabled it to exert influence over the western approaches to the East Indies and the Malay Peninsula. Although its shipping proved unable to compete with the Portuguese fleet anchored off Malacca on the far side of the Straits, Achin was nevertheless a vibrant commercial centre.

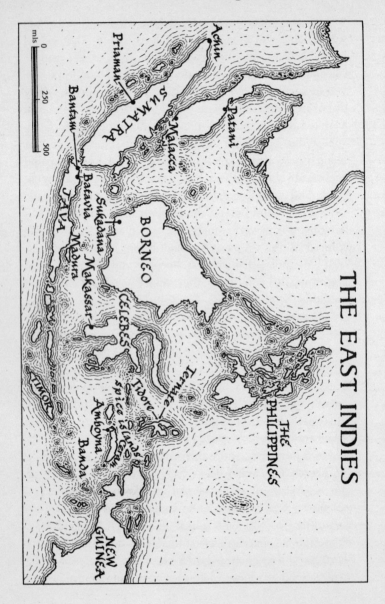

When Lancaster arrived here he counted no fewer than sixteen ships at anchor, including vessels from Gujarat, Bengal, Calicut and the Malay Peninsula.

Lancaster's chief pilot, John Davis, had visited Achin on his voyage with Cornelis Houtman and vividly recorded his meeting with the city's powerful ruler Ala-uddin Shah. The Sultan, he had discovered, was a keen Anglophile and had chatted enthusiastically to Houtman about England's seafaring victories – an enthusiasm not reciprocated by the Dutchman. When Ala-uddin learned that Houtman had a genuine Englishman on board he demanded to meet him immediately. 'He inquired much of England,' wrote Davis in his diary, 'of the Queen, of her Pashas, and how she could hold wars with so great a King as the Spaniard (for he thinks that Europe is all Spanish.) In these his demands he was fully satisfied, as it seemed to his great good liking.'

While in audience with the Sultan, Davis was gathering important information about Ala-uddin's personality and tastes; information which proved invaluable when he arrived back in England. Not only was the Company able to draft a suitable letter to the Sultan written in Queen Elizabeth's own hand, they were also able to buy him presents that were likely to find favour. He was a man of extravagant tastes; 'a lusty man, but exceeding gross and fat' – according to Davis – who was more than one hundred years old, 'as they say'. According to local tradition, he had been brought up a humble fisherman but, courageous and daring in wartime, was given command of the army and married to a relative of the reigning monarch. Ala-uddin promptly murdered the king and assumed the purple, ruling the country with an iron fist. Born to fight, he had held Queen Elizabeth in the highest regard ever since news of the Spanish Armada's defeat had filtered across the

Indian Ocean. Now, with Lancaster's fleet anchored in the bay, he was keen to meet one of her most trusted servants.

John Middleton, captain of the *Hector*, was the first to step ashore; he told the Sultan he had been sent by Lancaster to inform His Majesty that their fleet bore a letter from the Queen of England. The Sultan was most pleased and, presenting Middleton with a turban wrought with gold, he invited Lancaster to come ashore after he had rested himself for a day.

Lancaster acquitted himself well and, if the accounts are accurate, handled the Sultan with aplomb. Stepping ashore, he was welcomed by Ala-uddin's messengers who immediately demanded the Queen's letter so they could take it to the King. Lancaster refused, saying that such a letter, from so powerful a monarch, might be delivered only by himself.

The Sultan, too, was anxious to impress upon Lancaster the magnificence of his court and lavished every available resource on the English entourage:

He presently sent six great elephants, with many trumpets, drums, and streamers, with many people, to accompany the generall [Lancaster] to the court, so that the presse was exceeding great. The biggest of these elephants was about thirteene or fourteene foot high; which had a small castle like a coach upon his back, covered with crimson velvet. In the middle thereof was a great basin of gold, and a peece of silke exceedingly richly wrought to cover it, under which Her Majestie's letter was put. The generall was mounted upon another of the elephants. Some of his attendants rode; others went on foote. But when he came to the court gate, there a nobleman stayed the general, till he had gone in to know the king's further pleasure … And when the general came to the king's presence, he made his obeysance after the manner of the country, declaring that hee was sent from the most mightie Queene of England to congratulate with High Highnesse, and treat with him concerning a peace and amitie with His Majestie, if it pleased him to entertaine the same.

First, Ala-uddin was presented with the gifts: a basin of solid silver with a fountain in the middle, a huge silver goblet, a rich looking glass, a case of fine pistols, a magnificent headpiece, and a finely wrought embroidered belt. The Sultan received all these graciously, but was particularly taken by the fan of feathers he was given. He called for one of his attendant mistresses and ordered that she fan him continually. This, the cheapest of all the gifts, was a runaway success: 'the thing that most pleased him'.

Now it was time to present the Queen's letter which, it was hoped, would make a favourable impression. Wrapped in silk, decorated with fabulous swirls of calligraphy and delivered to the Sultan in a gold ewer securely fastened to a huge bull elephant, it was given the most dramatic billing possible.

The letter's contents were, by turn, flattering, obsequious, anti-Portuguese and businesslike. Pandering to the Sultan's vanity, but at the same time imploring favourable trading privileges, it described Ala-uddin as 'our loving brother', recognising 'the honorable and truly royall fame which hath hither stretched'. After glorifying him for his 'humane and noble usage of strangers', it went on to attack the Portuguese and Spanish who 'pretend themselves to be monarchs and absolute lords of all these kingdomes and provinces'. Finally, after more than two pages of preamble, it arrived at the substance. Queen Elizabeth I, it said, would like to begin regular commerce with Ala-uddin, to settle merchants in his capital and open a warehouse for the stockpiling of provisions. 'Trade,' it grandiloquently informed His Highness, 'not only breeds intercourse and exchange of merchandise ... but also engenders love and friendship betwixt all men.'

Reading it in private Ala-uddin was captivated by the Queen's sentiments and found himself agreeing whole-heartedly. He told Lancaster that he was well pleased with what he had read and accepted all the Queen's requests. Once the deal had been signed it was time for the Sultan's banquet, a dizzying affair in which prodigious quantities of food and alcohol were followed into the banqueting room by a troupe of the Sultan's damsels and musicians. The food was served on beaten golden platters while the arak, a fiery and extremely alcoholic rice wine, was knocked back in copious quantities. Throughout the meal the Sultan, who sat aloft in a gallery, kept offering toasts to his new-found friend. Lancaster had to beg Ala-uddin that he might mix his arak with water, 'for a little will serve to bring one asleep'. The Sultan, gracious as ever, consented.

Next came the cabaret. Sultan Ala-uddin 'caused his damosels to come forth and dance, and his women to play musicke unto them; and these women were richly attired and adorned with bracelets and jewels'. This performance was a special treat, 'for these are not usually seene of any but such as the king will greatly honour.' But the entertainments did not end here; there were endless other activities to amuse the newcomers including a lengthy bout of cock-fighting, the Sultan's favourite sport. And although not recorded in the ships' journals, it is quite possible that some of the more daring crew members took part in the celebrated Achinese speciality, the sub-aqua drinking bouts in which guests perched on low stools in a river while court butlers served generous beakers of arak.

Although Lancaster was delighted by the Sultan's reception he soon grew concerned that he had yet to buy a single ounce of spice. Worse, he now learned that pepper – far from costing four pieces-of-eight for the hundredweight – was actually being sold for almost twenty. Realising that he could not hope to fill his ships in Achin, Lancaster returned to the Sultan and diplomatically asked for his permission to set sail for other ports. Ala-uddin agreed, but there was an important condition attached. 'Thou must bring me a fair Portugall maiden when thou returnest, and then I am pleased.' Lancaster smiled, the Sultan chuckled, and the English ships prepared to depart.

Lancaster sent the *Susan* to the port of Priaman on Sumatra's southern coast while he, together with the rest of the fleet, sailed into the Straits. Almost immediately he spied a huge Portuguese carrack heading for Malacca and opened fire with the *Red Dragon*'s great guns. Six cannonballs were all it took to disable her; her main yard was split in two and crashed onto the deck with a tremendous boom. Completely marooned, the *Santo Antonio* gave up the fight and surrendered to the English. When Lancaster saw what he had captured he rubbed his eyes in disbelief: she was laden with Indian calicoes and batiks which, though almost valueless in England, were worth a small fortune in the ports of South-East Asia. Here, at last, was something which could readily be exchanged for nutmeg, cloves and pepper.

It took a full six days to unload the *Santo Antonio* and, by the time all her goods were stowed aboard the English

James Lancaster attacks the Portuguese Santo Antonio *in the Straits of Malacca. He was astonished when he saw what he had captured: she was richly laden with calicoes and batiks worth a fortune in the Spice Islands.*

ships, Lancaster realised it was imperative that he found a supply depot, a base for future trading, where the cloth could be stored. Achin, he now knew, was useless for although an important centre for trade it was not the source of the spices he was seeking. He decided to head for the spice port of Bantam on the north-west coast of Java, but thought it diplomatic to first return to Ala-uddin to bid him farewell.

The Sultan congratulated Lancaster on his success against the Portuguese, 'and jestingly said he had forgotten the most important business that he requested at his hands, which was the fair Portugal maiden he desired him to bring with him at his return. To whom the general [Lancaster] answered that there was none so worthy that merited to be so presented. Therewithall the king smiled and said: if there be anything here in my kingdom may pleasure thee, I would be glad to gratify thy goodwill.'

The request for maidens was not an unusual one among the potentates of the East. To ensure their harems retained an international flavour, they liked to procure youthful damsels from as far afield as possible. Ala-uddin's successor took his harem very seriously indeed and put in a request to London for an English rose or two. This put the Company's puritanical merchants into something of a quandary: if they sent two girls they would be seen to be condoning bigamy and that was unthinkable. There was also the problem of religion. Achin was an Islamic country and there was a theological objection to uniting a good Christian girl in holy matrimony with a Mohammedan. Ironically, the directors' most difficult task – that of finding a suitable virgin – was easily overcome. A London gentleman 'of honourable parentage' offered his daughter without further ado. She was, he explained, 'of excellent parts for musicke, her needle, and good discourse, also very beautiful and personable'. He even wrote a lengthy tract justifying mixed marriages. What the girl in question thought about all this has unfortunately not been recorded but she probably heaved a sigh of relief when King James I declined to sanction the presentation of such an unorthodox gift.

Lancaster was on the brink of departing from Achin when the increasingly eccentric Ala-uddin had an even stranger request. He asked the English captain if he possessed a book of the Psalms of David and, as soon as a copy had been produced, begged Lancaster that he and his court might sing one as a duet. This done, the Sultan wished the English crew his best wishes for the rest of their voyage. His last act was to present Lancaster with a letter addressed to Queen Elizabeth I and written in fine Arabic calligraphy. So magnificent was this calligraphy, in fact, that its eventual translator, Reverend William Bedwell of St Ethelburga's in Bishopgate Street, could scarcely read it. He did eventually produce a draft in English. It was absurdly grandiose and full of hyperbole and Queen Elizabeth was given a string of honorific titles. By the time the letter arrived back in England, she was no longer alive to read it.

Lancaster's fleet sailed from Achin in November 1602. The *Ascension*, by now fully laden with pepper and spice, set course for England while the rest of the ships headed towards Java, meeting with the *Susan* on the way. She had fared well in the port of Priaman and her captain had bought a large stock of spices for an extremely competitive price: in Bantam, Lancaster was to find the prices lower still.

Bantam's king was a boy of ten or eleven years. After showing him all the usual courtesies and presenting the customary gifts, Lancaster turned to his Protector to settle the finer points of trade. The English merchants were cordially received and prices for pepper and spice were fixed. A 'factory' or warehouse was established so that the English could unload their wares, and commerce was begun with enthusiasm. A problem of local thieving threatened to sour the buying and selling, but after Lancaster had slaughtered six robbers – a right he had been granted by the Protector – the thieving halted completely.

For five weeks spices were bought and bartered until two hundred and thirty sackfuls had been loaded onto the ships and there was not an inch of space left on board. The local natives were particularly curious to know why the

English required such huge quantities of pepper and there was much scratching of heads until it was finally agreed that English houses were so cold that the walls were plastered with crushed pepper in order to produce heat.

One sad episode marred the stay in Bantam. The languid heat was taking its toll on the men who had gone ashore, while those who remained on their vessels, including Captain John Middleton, 'fell sicke aboord his ship in the road'. Middleton's fever grew steadily worse until Lancaster, himself not well, became alarmed. Paying a visit to his old friend, he watched Middleton pace slowly up and down the deck, growing weaker with every step. That night, the *Hector* lost its captain and Middleton was buried at Bantam. The crew, though used to the sight of death, wept openly.

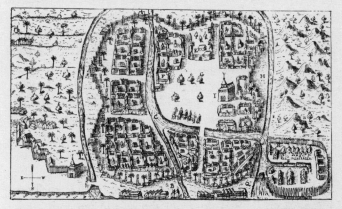

The Javanese port of Bantam was the headquarters of the English in the East Indies. Known as 'that stinking stew', the sailors had to brave the constant threat of head-hunting, as well as malaria and dysentery. 'Bantam is not a place to recover men that are sick,' wrote one, 'but to kill men that come thither in health.'

It was time to depart for England. Lancaster was aware that if trade between England and the East Indies was to succeed it was essential to establish a permanent base in the East. So, shortly before setting sail, he appointed eight men and three 'factors' or merchants to stay behind in Bantam, leaving in their charge all the goods he had so far been unable to sell.

He had also realised that the price of spices fell sharply the further east he sailed. The prices in Achin were astronomical while in Bantam they were much lower. He was certain that if he had been able to sail even further east, to the Banda Islands, the very source of nutmeg, those prices would dip still further. Before he left Bantam Lancaster therefore instructed the men staying behind to sail eastwards in the forty-ton pinnace left in their charge and buy as much nutmeg, mace and cloves as was possible.

In February 1603, the fleet set sail for England with a thunderous blast from their cannon. The first half of the return voyage proved remarkably uneventful and it was not until the ships reached Madagascar that they were buffeted by their first storm which so smashed their ships 'that they were leakie all the voyage after'. Two weeks later they were hit by a 'very sore storme which continued all the night, and the seas did so beate upon the ships quarter that it shooke all the iron-worke of her rudder'. Huge waves raged around the ships, lashing their weakened hulls and allowing water to seep into the holds. Early on the morning of the fourth the rudder of the *Red Dragon* 'brake cleane from the sterne of our shippe and presently sunke into the sea'. Unable to steer, 'our ship drove up and downe in the sea like a wrecke, which way soever the wind carried her.' Every attempt to make a new rudder failed and, as the rain turned to 'hayle and snow and sleetie cold weather', the men began to abandon all hope of surviving. 'It was a great miserie unto us,' wrote one, 'that pinched us exceeding sore, so that our case was miserable and very desperate.' Even Lancaster felt the end was near. Descending into his cabin, he penned a letter to the Company in London, a letter whose unfailing spirit would become legendary among the sailors of the East India Company. 'I cannot tell where you should looke for me,' he wrote, 'because I live at the devotion of the winds and seas.' And then, sending the letter over to the *Hector*, he bade her head for England leaving his own ship to her fate. The *Hector*'s captain refused and shadowed the *Red Dragon* until the storm finally abated. And so, side by side, the ships sailed first to St Helena and then into the English Channel.

On 11 September 1603, some two years and seven months after they had set sail from the Thames, the vessels finally anchored off the Downs, 'for which thanked be Almightie God, who hath delivered us from infinite perils and dangers in this long and tedious navigation'.

Compared to previous expeditions, this one had been an unqualified success. Wherever the Portuguese had been encountered in the Indian Ocean they had been of little threat – indeed the English were proving remarkably adept at disabling their unwieldy carracks. In the spice port of Bantam, Lancaster had found few difficulties in acquiring a full lading of spice and had even been allowed to build a small warehouse close to the harbour and leave behind a permanent staff. Even more impressive was the fact that all five of his ships had returned safely and more than a million pounds of spices had been successfully brought into the kingdom. But Lancaster had his misgivings. He had lost almost half his men, including his friends John Middleton and William Brund, and had failed to reach the islands far to the east of Bantam. As he kneeled before the King and received his knighthood, Sir James could only hope that the men he left behind – those eight crew and three merchants – would have the courage to sail to the Banda Islands in their tiny pinnace.

CHAPTER FOUR

IN THE PAWS
OF THE
LION

THE ENGLISH TRADERS left in Bantam watched the departure of Lancaster's fleet with deep misgivings. They had no idea when they might see their next English vessel but it was certain to be at least two years. In the meantime they were in a wholly unfamiliar environment, living in this fly-blown port on sufferance of the boy-king's Protector and terrified that they would soon succumb to the same sickness that had killed so many of their colleagues.

Lancaster had only reinforced their sense of vulnerability when he wrote down the hierachy of command to be adhered to if and when they died. William Starkey was put in overall charge with Thomas Morgan as his deputy, but 'if it please God to lay his hand upon you and take you out of this world' then Edmund Scott was to take control. In the event such caution proved all too necessary. Starkey died in June 1603, having already outlived Morgan by two months. Only Edmund Scott survived to see the arrival of the East India Company's second expedition and, to his evident relief, was allowed to join the fleet when it headed back to England.

Lancaster showed a similar concern for the moral well-being of his men. Bantam was infamous in the East for its loose women and lax morals and an air of profligacy hung over the town like the plague of typhoid that frequently descended on its inhabitants. He ordered Starkey that 'you meet together in the morninges and eveninges in prayer. God, whom ye serve, shall the better bless you in all your affairs.' He also begged them to 'agree together lovingly, like sober men [and] govern yourselves so that there be no brabbles among you for any cause'.

These men, who for so long had complained about the strict daily routine on board ship, now found themselves comforted by an ordered existence. The day began at dawn with William Starkey offering prayers of thanksgiving, and this was followed by a light breakfast. The main meal was at midday at which all the factors would sit together at a long table, seated in strict accordance with his position. The rice, mutton and tropical fruit which they ate, all of which was bartered in Bantam's souks, was washed down with locally distilled arak, a fiery spirit that was glugged in considerable quantity by these drink-hardened men. One captain who arrived in Bantam a few years later professed himself horrified at the drunken behaviour of the factors. 'If any be found by excessive drinking or otherwise like to prove a scandal to our nation,' he said, 'use first sharp reprehensions, and if that work not reformation then by the first ship send him home with a writing showing the reasons thereof.'

Once the English were familiar with life in Bantam they prepared to carry out Lancaster's instructions. Three of the factors were to remain in the city and buy pepper in preparation for the Company's second voyage. The rest of the men were to sail to the remote Banda Islands under the command of Master Keche and acquire as much spice as was available. Lancaster was most specific in his request

The native rulers of Bantam travelled in chariots pulled by white buffalo. Dissolute and quarrelsome, their irrational behaviour so terrified the English that 'our men in their sleepe would suddainely leape out of their beddes and ketch their weapons.'

for nutmeg: 'Have you a great care to receive such as be good,' he told them, 'for the smallest and rotten nutmegs be worth nothing at home.' Such a warning was born from experience. It had long been the custom of wily merchants to fill their sacks with old and rotten spices, as well as dust and twigs, in order to increase the weight and swell their profits.

The little pinnace hoisted its sails soon after the English fleet had departed from Bantam and gingerly headed east into uncharted waters. But no sooner had it come within sight of the 'spiceries' than contrary winds began to blow and the ship drifted off course. What happened next remains unclear for the report written by the men has been lost and only a couple of letters survive. Struck by 'contrarietie of wynde', the ship spent two months 'beating up and down in the seas' in a desperate attempt to reach the outlying Banda Islands. This proved wholly unsuccessful until a tremendous storm washed the boat up on Run's remote shores. The hardy English sailors were given a friendly welcome by the islanders who thought them too few to be of any threat. They were soon busily trading nutmeg with these storm-tossed sailors and even allowed them to construct a flimsy bamboo and thatch warehouse on the island's northern coastline.

Lancaster's fleet arrived back to a London steeped in gloom. The capital was in the grip of the plague and the streets and alleys around the Company's house in Philpot Lane were silent but for the rattle of tumbrels and barrows bearing corpses out of the city. The plague had not spared the Company directors: two had already succumbed to the disease while others had fled London for the safety of the countryside.

Hearing that the first of Lancaster's ships had arrived in Plymouth the Company directors bestirred themselves. Bestowing the princely sum of five pounds to the local courier 'for his pains in riding hither with the first report of the coming of the Ascension', they sent strict orders back to Plymouth that the ship's cargo was not to be touched until she was safely moored in the Thames. Even then they could not be too careful; the six porters charged with unloading the ship were instructed to wear pocketless

(Opposite) *James Lancaster returned to a London stricken with the plague. To the voyage-hardened crew, death was treated with a cavalier contempt. 'Walker died laughing,' reads one account. 'Woodes and I staked two pieces-of-eight on his body, and I won.'*

suits, just in case they should feel the urge to filch some spice.

The *Ascension* had made speedy progress back to England and arrived in advance of the other ships. Lancaster, together with the rest of the fleet, sailed up the Thames in September 1603, by which time almost 38,000 Londoners had fallen victim to the plague. There were none of the cheering crowds that had seen them off two-and-a-half years previously. The wharves lay silent and the dockyards were closed for Londoners were too scared to venture out of doors. The playwright Thomas Dekker summed up the sombre mood that hung over the city in his ironically titled *The Wonderfull Yeare*:

> No musick now is heard but bells,
> And all their tunes are sick mens knells;
> And every stroake the bell does toll,
> Up to heaven it windes a soule.

Even the physicians had fled for their lives, leaving only a handful of brave practitioners to sell their 'pomanders and what not' and reap enormous profits from their nutmeg potions: 'I confesse they are costly,' explained one doctor to his ailing client, 'but cheape medicines are as dear as death.'

To the voyage-hardened crew, death had become so commonplace that it was treated with a cavalier contempt. 'Walker died laughing,' reads one journal. 'Woodes and I staked two pieces-of-eight on his body, and after a long play, I won.' But one death caused many a sailor to shed tears: just a few months earlier Queen Elizabeth I, the last of the great Tudor monarchs, had passed away at her palace in Richmond. There was now a new ruler on the throne – Elizabeth's haughty Scottish cousin King James – who showed far less sympathy than his predecessor to the likes of the common burghers who formed the backbone of the East India Company.

Despite the general gloom, Lancaster was given an enthusiastic reception on his return and duly received his knighthood from the King. But the pressing problem facing the merchants was how, in the midst of the worst plague London could remember, to dispose of more than a million pounds in weight of pepper. Cash was desperately needed to pay off the sailors who had survived the voyage, the subscribers were anxiously clamouring for money, and preparations for the second voyage were unthinkable until the present stock had been sold.

Unfortunately, the financial institutions of the city had been paralysed by the plague for those dealers who were still alive had also fled to the country. Worse still, the King himself had recently acquired a huge quantity of pepper – probably the contents of a captured Portuguese carrack – and was keen to dispose of it as quickly as possible. Citing his kingly prerogative, and invoking a royal edict, he declared that the merchant adventurers could not sell a single peppercorn until he had first disposed of his own stock.

The Company was in dire straits and its future hung on a thread. It seemed ironic to many that it was so woefully short of funds as to threaten its survival at the very moment when the first voyage had ended in such triumph. A single event saved the day. When Queen Elizabeth had originally granted the merchants their charter she had specified that it was on the understanding that a trading expedition should be sent to the 'spiceries' annually. Now, sensing the merchants' vulnerability, the Privy Council threatened to hand over the Company's trading rights to another individual unless a second expedition set sail immediately.

No names were mentioned but it was clear whom they had in mind: Sir Edward Michelborne, whose name had been so humiliatingly deleted from the Company's lists, had nursed his grievances for long enough. He now wanted revenge.

The Company was shocked by the possibility of losing their privileges and acted with uncharacteristic decision, despatching a beadle to all the city merchants to collect subscriptions for a second voyage. The merchants were understandably reluctant to finance a new voyage before they had reaped the profits of the old and a mere £11,000 was subscribed. It was therefore decided that everyone who had invested £250 in the first voyage was obliged to subscribe a further £200 for the second. It was not a popular move but it saved the Company in its hour of need and within a few months preparations were under way for a second voyage.

Lancaster had no intention of commanding this new expedition: wealthy, knighted and understandably reluctant to tempt fate by sailing to the East Indies for a third time, he graciously accepted the desk-bound post of director. He was placed in charge of planning the new expedition and his influence is everywhere apparent: although the ships were to call at Bantam in order to rendezvous with the English factors, their mission was to sail east to the 'Molloccos', or Spice Islands, which Lancaster himself had failed to reach. Here, the ships were to buy the most valuable of the spices, nutmeg and cloves, and leave factors behind in anticipation of the Company's third voyage. Lancaster's instructions once again placed special emphasis on the crews' spiritual well-being and asked that concern be shown for the men he had left behind, particularly chief factor William Starkey who was to be 'provided for and well placed in such ship as he shall be shipped as a man that we hold in good regard and to be respected accordingly'. He did not know that Starkey was long since dead.

The man charged with leading this second expedition was Henry Middleton who had sailed under Lancaster's command on the first venture and proved himself to be both capable and trustworthy. Energetic and resolute, he was always respected by his subordinates and his leadership never came under fire, even when he guided his fleet through dangerous and uncharted seas. Although given to impetuosity and hot-headedness, he dealt with both the Dutch and Portuguese, as well as the native chieftains, with considerable diplomacy.

With no shortage of funds to finance the voyage it was decided to send four ships to the East – the *Hector*, *Ascension* and *Susan*, with the trusty *Red Dragon* once again serving as flagship. Following Lancaster's instructions to the letter, Middleton headed directly to Bantam where he found the few remaining Englishmen in a desperate plight after receiving much harsh treatment from the local traders. The arrival of his ships on 22 December 1604 was the best Christmas present these men could have asked for. 'Towards evening we descried our ships coming into the road, to all our extreaordinary great joy.' So wrote Edmund Scott, by now the most senior Englishman still alive in the city. 'But when we came aboard of our admiral, and saw their great weakness, also hearing the weakness of the other three ships, it grieved us much.'

Middleton went straight to business on his arrival at the port. Presenting the boy-king with a hotchpotch of presents – including two gilt cups, a spoon and six muskets – he struck a deal, loaded the *Hector* and *Susan* with pepper, and sent them directly back to England. His last task before bidding them farewell won him widespread popularity from his crew. Having listened to endless complaints about the tiresome habits of Master Surfflict, the preacher on the *Red Dragon*, Middleton decided to despatch him back to England. He had proved completely useless on the outward journey and few tears were shed when he dropped dead on the return.

More deaths were soon to follow. Middleton continued eastwards to the Spice Islands as instructed but no sooner had he left Bantam than his ship was afflicted by the 'blody flux' – a life-threatening strain of dysentery. With the list of casualties growing by the day, the ship's journal becomes little more than a roll-call for the dead: 'The seventeenth day died of the flux William Lewed, John Jenkens, and Samuel Porter ... the twentieth dyed Henry Stiles our master carpenter, and James Varnam, and John Iberson, all of the fluxe. The twenty-second day died of the fluxe James Hope; the twenty-fourth dyed John Leay and Robert Whitthers.' The atmosphere on board was sombre indeed and still the men kept dying. Three more succumbed on the following day, then another two, and by the time the ships sighted land another five men had died of the 'flux'. It was with considerable relief that the ships at last arrived at Amboyna, a clove-fringed island that lay at the very heart of the 'spiceries'.

Middleton stepped ashore to greet the local king and entreat him for a trading deal but was promptly informed that all trade was forbidden without prior permission of the Portuguese garrison stationed on the island. The English commander now showed his colours as an accomplished diplomat. Aware that the Portuguese were unlikely to part with their cloves, especially to their old adversaries the English, he sent a letter to their captain informing him that there was at last peace between the two nations and that he 'desired that the like might be between us, for that our comming was to seeke trade with them'. What he said was true: King James I and King Philip III had indeed signed a peace treaty but Middleton can hardly have been aware of this for it had been agreed more than five months after he left England.

The news had the desired effect and the Portuguese commander, safely ensconced in the stout bastion that guarded Amboyna's natural harbour, sent word of his agreement to a deal. But before the two men even had the chance to shake hands, they learned that there was trouble on the horizon. In the far distance, and fast disappearing into the twilight, a formidable fleet of vessels could be seen approaching the island. To Middleton's dismay, these were neither Portuguese nor English: this veritable armada was flying the Dutch colours from its flagship.

When the sun rose the following day there were no less than nine ships in the offing, together with an auxiliary fleet of pinnaces and sloops. These slowly sailed into the harbour and 'came to an anker within a musket shot of the fort'. The Portuguese commander immediately ingratiated himself with his Dutch counterpart, asking him 'wherefore they came thither' and stating that 'if they came in friendshippe they should be welcome'. But the Dutch had certainly not come in friendship and their general 'made answer that his comming thither was to have that castel from them; and willed them to deliver him the keyes [which,] if they refused to do, he willed them to provide for themselves to defend it, for he was minded to have it before he departed'.

Middleton now found himself in an unenviable position. It was clear that his fleet was no match for the

Dutch, but if he went ashore and joined forces with the Portuguese there was a slim chance that together they could successfully defend the island. If so, the dividends would be rich indeed for Amboyna's mountainous interior was thickly forested in clove trees. But before he had time to reach a decision he learned that the battle for Amboyna was over. Although the Portuguese bragged that 'they would never yeild up their fort, but fight it out to the last man', they capitulated after a short bombardment and the only death occurred when their commander mysteriously expired. His unhappily married wife later took credit for his death, explaining that she had poisoned him in order to save his honour and reputation.

With Amboyna lost to the Dutch, Middleton put to sea with not a single clove on board. He was growing increasingly concerned by the difficulties of trading in the 'spiceries' and wisely decided that his two vessels, the *Red Dragon* and the *Ascension*, should separate and sail for different islands. While the *Ascension* headed south to the unknown Banda Group, he directed his own ship to the most northerly of the Spice Islands, Ternate and Tidore, which had been loosely under the control of the Portuguese for some decades.

As the *Red Dragon* approached these islands, Middleton heard the crack of musket-shot split the air and saw two galleys 'making all the speed possible toward us'. The foremost vessel contained the King of Ternate while behind him, and hot on his heels, were dozens of pirates rowing furiously and firing with their guns. Realising that the king would be an invaluable ally should his life be saved, Middleton immediately ordered the *Red Dragon*'s sails to be hauled down and ropes to be thrown over the side. In the nick of time the king was pulled aboard the vessel, but not before his oarsmen had been captured by the pirates and 'put to the sword, saving three men which saved their lives by swimming'.

Middleton for once had the upper hand. Leading the King down to his private quarters, he handed him one of the letters of trade and friendship drafted by King James and, without even having time to affix the King of Ternate's name to the top, kindly requested him to sign it. Although quaking with fear, the king hesitated for he had only recently signed a secret agreement with the Dutch in which he promised to reserve all his spices for their merchants. But he soon realised that he was in no position to bargain and scrawled his signature on Middleton's treaty, even taking the trouble to write a personal missive to King James explaining how 'we have been informed that Englishmen were of bad disposition, and came not as peaceable merchants, but as thieves and robbers to depose us of our countries. But by the coming of Captain Henry Middleton we have found to the contrary, and we greatlie rejoice.'

Middleton's luck was not to last. Just a few hours after his triumph a small Dutch fleet stormed the island of Tidore, capturing its sturdy bastion from the Portuguese and threatening to repeat the exercise on neighbouring Ternate. They had been extremely fortunate in the ease of their conquest for 'the Portugals manfully defended their honour against the assailants, till an unfortunate fire (how or whence uncertaine) lighting in their powder blew up a great part of their castle with sixtie or seventie of their men.'

Middleton watched these events unfold with a growing sense of anger. 'If this frothy nation [the Dutch] may have the trade of the Indies to themselves,' he wrote, 'their pride and insolencie will be intollerable.' The victory of the Dutch gave them control of both the northern and central groups of the Spice Islands, leaving the Banda Islands as the only group of 'spiceries' that still offered the possibility of trade without competition.

It was to the Bandas that Captain Colthurst had steered the *Ascension*, ordered by Middleton to 'seeke a lading of nutmegs and mace'. Hoping to trade in peace, he watched in disbelief as a flotilla of Dutch ships followed in his wake. Unfortunately, there are few records of Colthurst's time here – save for a brief account which gives depth readings and soundings of various harbours in the archipelago – and it is necessary to turn to later accounts for a description of these verdant and grandiose islands.

Dominating them all was Gunung Api, a classically shaped volcanic island with steep sides and a hole at the top. At the beginning of the seventeenth century, it was entering one of the more energetic periods in its history, 'yeelding nothing but cinders, fire and smoake' and frequently erupting with such violence that 'it carried stones of three or four tunnes weight from the one iland into the other.' These boulders would rain down upon neighbouring Neira Island which, although not the largest in the group, had long been the centre for the nutmeg trade. It was to Neira that Captain Garcia had steered his Portuguese carrack in 1529 and, without consulting with the native chieftains, had attempted to construct a castle. Although Garcia was driven away by the local warriors, Neira remained popular with captains and traders on account of its fine natural harbour – once the volcano's caldera – which provided a safe anchorage for far larger vessels than the *Ascension*.

Less than half a mile from Neira was the kidney-shaped

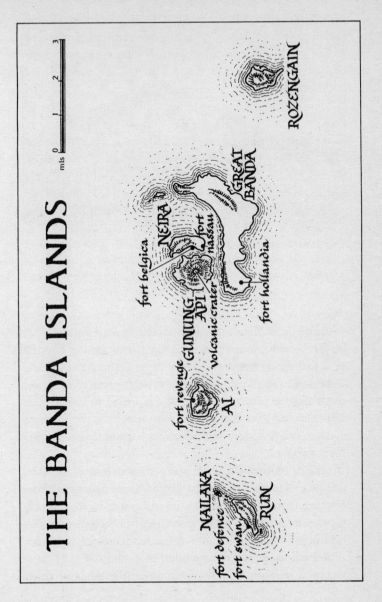

THE BANDA ISLANDS

mls 0 1 2 3

ROZENGAIN

fort belgica
NEIRA
fort nassau
GREAT BANDA
fort hollandia

fort revenge
GUNUNG API
volcanic crater
AI

NAILAKA
fort defence
fort swan
RUN

The Banda Islands' volcano, Gunung Api, had a habit of erupting every time a Dutch fleet arrived. 'The hill cast forth such hideous flames,' wrote one observer, 'such store of cinders and huge streames that it destroyed all the thicke woods.'

island of Great Banda, 'strong and almost inaccessible, as [if] it were a castle'. Great Banda's rocky backbone was covered in a mantle of greenery – almost all nutmeg trees – and there was 'scarce a tree on the iland but beareth fruit'. These fruits were jealously guarded by the native inhabitants, an aggressive and warlike people who had built an elaborate system of defensive fortifications around the island's shelving coast.

The other two islands, Ai and Rozengain, were less than an hour's sailing from Great Banda. Rozengain had little nutmeg and was therefore of no interest to Captain Colthurst, whilst Ai had an extremely treacherous shoreline which deterred all but the most foolhardy of mariners. Nevertheless, it was 'the paradice of all the rest [for] there is not a tree on that iland but the nutmeg, and other delicate fruits of superfluitie; and withall, full of pleasant walkes so that the whole countrey seemes a contrived orchard with varieties'.

The only other island of note was Run, a tiny and outlying atoll whose cliffs and mountain were so tangled with nutmeg trees that they yielded a massive third of a million pounds of the spice every year. But Run, more than two hours from Neira, was the most dangerous of all the Banda Islands for its small harbour was ringed by a sunken reef which had claimed the timbers of many a vessel attempting to put in to port. Such dangers appear to have deterred Colthurst from landing on the island and he returned to Neira where the Dutch commander generously invited the English captain to dinner. According to Dutch records, Colthurst arrived bearing a freshly baked chicken pie, not out of courtesy but because he disliked Dutch food.

He left the Bandas with a valuable cargo of spice, as well as a friendly letter from a local headman offering King James I a generous gift of nutmeg. It was several years before this headman received a reply, but when he did he was overjoyed. The King, courteous as ever, thanked him for his kind present which, he said, 'we accepted with all kindness.'

Middleton and Colthurst sailed together for England, following in the wake of the *Hector* and the *Susan*. The *Susan* was destined never to make it home. Caught in a ferocious storm off southern Africa, she sank with the loss of all hands. The *Hector* almost shared a similar fate; stricken by sickness she was spotted by the *Red Dragon* 'in lamentable distress' and drifting helplessly in the waters around Table Bay. With just fourteen men left alive, the captain was about to scupper her when Middleton arrived on the scene. He oversaw her repair, waited until her surviving crew had been nursed back to health, and eventually accompanied her back to England, arriving in the spring of 1606.

The joyous welcome that greeted Middleton and his surviving men on their arrival home was to prove short-lived. For no sooner had his ships' cargo of nutmeg, cloves and pepper been unloaded than a vessel arrived in London bearing news of appalling happenings in the harbour at Bantam: ships had been ransacked, cargoes stolen and men indiscriminately slaughtered. At first it was thought that only the Dutch or Portuguese could wreak such terror, but London's merchants were soon to learn otherwise. The perpetrator of these outrages was none other than the 'gentelman' adventurer Sir Edward Michelborne.

Sir Edward had made good his promise to have his revenge. Flattering King James with his patrician charm and bad-mouthing the East India Company in the same breath, he persuaded the King to grant him a royal licence for a voyage of discovery to the Far East, a licence that was valid 'notwithstanding any grant or charter to the contrary'.

The Company were incensed at this sudden loss of their monopoly but not unduly surprised. Unlike his predecessor, King James had failed to grasp the fact that trade with the East Indies could only succeed if it was carried out by a monopoly and with the full backing of the Crown. He was also blind to the problem of the occasional ship sailing into eastern waters, even when that ship was captained by a loose cannon like Sir Edward. It was with the King's sanction and blessing, therefore, that the *Tiger*, together with a pinnace christened the *Tiger's Whelp*, set sail from the Isle of Wight on 5 December 1604.

The *Tiger* was a minuscule ship of just two hundred and forty tons and the East India Company directors might reasonably have hoped that she would be lost in the first storm. But Michelborne had a trump up his sleeve. Catching them unawares he announced that his chief pilot was the hugely experienced John Davis, veteran of James Lancaster's expedition and survivor of two difficult voyages to the East Indies. The Company was most surprised to hear this and wondered how Michelborne had managed to seduce Davis on board. In fact, the intrepid navigator had not needed much persuading for he was still angry at having returned from Lancaster's expedition under a cloud. Lancaster himself had complained about Davis, informing the directors that he was 'not a little grieved' that his navigator had been wrong about both the ease with which pepper could be bought in Achin and also the price. Davis was unfairly made a scapegoat and, offered the chance by Sir Edward Michelborne to have his revenge, he promptly signed up to join the *Tiger.*

No sooner had they reached Bantam than the mayhem began. Spotting a fully laden vessel on the horizon Michelborne 'fell in fight with her' and she was captured. She was a poor prize, a rice-laden cargo boat, and a dismayed Michelborne recorded that she 'was not suffering the worth of a penny to bee taken from them'. Other ships were stopped and searched in the shallow coastal waters around Bantam until the natives of one vessel, indignant at this blatant act of piracy, set upon the Englishmen and inflicted terrible injuries before leaping overboard and 'swimming away like water spaniels'.

Undeterred, Sir Edward next waylaid an Indian vessel of eighty tons and ransacked her. Emboldened by his success he now sailed into Bantam harbour where five enormous vessels, all Dutch, were riding at anchor. Chuckling at his own audacity he sent a message to each captain informing them 'that hee would come and ride close to their sides, and bad the prowdest of them all that durst to put a piece of ordnance upon him'. There was a warning attached to his message: if any ship so much as loaded a musket 'hee would either sinke them or sink by their sides.'

The Dutch were most upset to find themselves at the receiving end of such threats and complained to the King of Bantam that all Englishmen were the same, 'being thieves and disordinate livers'. Yet they steadfastly refused to take up Michelborne's challenge, cowering below deck as Sir Edward tacked up and down the harbour and, 'whereas the Hollanders were wont to swagger and keep great stirre on shore all the time before our being there, they were so quiet that wee could scarcely see one of them.'

Sir Edward had so far been lucky; he had acted with daring and bravado and no one had called his bluff. But he was shortly to meet his match. As the ship drifted in calm waters off the Malay Peninsula, a cry was suddenly raised from the look-out. A mysterious ship was approaching, a huge junk, whose decks were lined with more than eighty men. They were strange-looking fellows: short, squat, and with an almost total lack of expression on their faces. Sir Edward despatched a heavily armed boat to discover if these people were friend or foe and, after a brief exchange in which the English learned that the vessel was 'a junke of the Japons', they were invited on board and shown around. When they enquired of the Japanese as to their line of business the men made no bones about their trade. The junk, like the *Tiger*, was a pirate ship and the men were proud of her devastating progress through the waters of South-East Asia. She had pillaged the coasts of China and

Cambodia, plundered half a dozen ships off Borneo, and was now heading back to Japan laden with spoils.

When the English party were safely back on the *Tiger*, Sir Edward weighed up his options. Trusting to his previous good fortune, he decided to ransack the junk and, to this end, sent a second band of Englishmen on board to stake her out. Although it was clear to the Japanese that Michelborne's buccaneering sailors were assessing the strengths and weaknesses of the vessel, they welcomed the English with open arms and allowed them free access to the ship's hold. They even pointed to the choicest items on board, astonishing the crew of the *Tiger* who had never met with such an odd race of men. 'They were most of them too gallant a habit for sailors,' wrote one, 'and such an equalitie of behaviour among them that they all seemed fellows.' When they asked to visit the English vessel all agreed that it would be impolite to refuse.

Here Michelborne's inexperience told for the first time. He was unaware that the Japanese had the reputation in the Indies for being a 'people so desperate and daring that they are feared in all places' and was ignorant of the fact that all eastern ports demanded that any Japanese sailor coming ashore must first be disarmed. Davis, too, was 'beguiled by their humble semblance'. Not only was he of the opinion that disarming them was unnecessary, he offered them the run of the ship and let them freely fraternise with the crew. As more and more Japanese clambered aboard, beakers were raised and the two crews joked and chatted among themselves.

In a flash everything changed: unbeknown to the English, the Japanese had, in the words of Michelborne, 'resolved with themselves either to gaine my shippe or to lose their lives'. The smiles vanished, the laughter died and the Japanese suddenly transformed themselves into brutal 'rogues' who stabbed and slashed at their English adversaries. The crew of the *Tiger* had never faced such hostility and scarcely had a chance to resist before the deck was swarming with Japanese wielding long swords and hacking men to pieces. Soon they reached the gun room where they found Davis desperately loading muskets. 'They pulled [him] into the cabbin and giving him sixe or seven mortall wounds, they thrust him out of the cabbin.' He stumbled on deck but the sword wounds had severed one of his arteries and he bled to death. Others, too, were in their final death throes and it seemed inevitable that the *Tiger* would shortly be lost.

It was Michelborne who saved the day. Thrusting pikes into the hands of his best fighters he launched a last-ditch attack on the Japanese soldiers 'and killed three or four of their leaders'. This disheartened the Japanese who slowly found themselves at a disadvantage. Armed with knives and swords, they were unable to compete with Michelborne's pikemen and found themselves driven down the deck until they stood en masse by the entrance to the cabin. Sensing their predicament, they let out a terrific scream and dashed headlong into the heart of the ship.

The English were at a loss as to know how to evict them. Not one man volunteered to follow them into the cabin for to do so would be to court certain death. It was equally hopeless to send a large group down. The passageway was low and narrow and the men would end up wounding themselves rather than the Japanese. Eventually, a bright spark on board had a simple but devastating solution. Two thirty-two-pound demi-culverins were loaded with 'crosse-barres, bullets, and case-shot' and fired at point-blank range into the most exposed side of the cabin. There was a deafening crash as the shrapnel tore through the woodwork and 'violently marred therewith boords and splinters'. A terrible shriek followed, a cry of agony, and then there was silence. When the smoke cleared and the dust settled, the cabin was entered and it was found that only one of the twenty-two Japanese had survived. 'Their legs, armes and bodies were so torne, as it was strange to see how the shot had massacred them.'

It was now time for Michelborne to have his revenge. Training every last cannon on the Japanese junk, he fired shot after shot into her sides until the men on board begged for mercy. When this was refused they vowed to go down fighting and the battle raged until all resistance was quelled and the junk fell silent. Only one Japanese attempted to surrender. Diving into the water he swam across to the *Tiger* and was hauled aboard. When quizzed by Sir Edward as to the motive for the attack he 'told us that they meant to take our shippe and to cut all our throates'. Having said this, and terrified by the crowd of hostile onlookers, he told Michelborne that his one desire was 'that hee might be cut in pieces'. Michelborne preferred a less bloody method of execution and ordered the man to be strung up at the yardarm. This sentence was duly carried out but the rope snapped and the man dropped into the sea. No one could be bothered to haul him in and as the coast was not far away it was presumed that he escaped with his life.

The English crew were by now weary of their piratical adventure and elected to return home, eventually sailing back into Portsmouth in the summer of 1606. Michelborne was totally discredited by his conduct and retired in disgrace, but far more serious than the damage to his own career was the damage he had done to the reputation of English shipping. The Dutch in particular seized on his acts of piracy and used them to blacken the name of England among the native princes òf the East. The English traders living in Bantam were in particular peril, for the King of Bantam was furious about what had happened. So damaging was Michelborne's voyage, in fact, that the Company sent a protest to the Lords of the Privy Council calling upon them to seize all the goods that Sir Edward had pillaged and reminding them that 'Sir Edward Michelborne has taken and spoiled some of our friends there, whereby not only the utter overthrow of the whole trade is much endangered, but also the safety of our men and goods.'

The spice race had by now been under way for more than ten years; time enough to judge who had gained the upper hand. Although London's merchant adventurers were flushed with success after Middleton's return, they had a nagging suspicion that they were steadily losing the race. They had so far despatched three fleets to the East (including the ships of Lancaster's maiden voyage) with a combined total of twelve vessels. Of these, one in three had either sunk or simply disappeared without trace. The loss in men was an even greater cause for concern. Of the approximately twelve hundred men who had sailed on these expeditions, some eight hundred had died either of scurvy, typhoid or the 'blody flux'. Two captains had been lost – one accidentally shot by his crew – and only one ship, the *Ascension*, had reached the distant Banda Islands. The profits, of course, had been enormous, even given the difficulties of disposing of Lancaster's cargo of pepper; and the Company warehouses were currently filled with sweet-smelling nutmeg and cloves. But the report that Middleton had submitted on his return suggested that it might be the last cargo they received. For the Dutch, latecomers to the spice race, were proving formidable rivals. Within a few years of Houtman's return they had managed to despatch a staggering fourteen fleets comprising sixty-five ships. Unlike the English commanders, who preferred 'a quiet trafficke', the Dutch had entered the race with cannons blazing. They had achieved a remarkable success against the Portuguese, ousting them from virtually all the 'spiceries' in which they had an interest. Now they were turning their attentions to the Banda Islands and seemed poised to capture these by force.

Faced with such a threat the Company took the view that they needed to expand their activities with all possible haste. They still had only one 'factory' or warehouse in the East, at Bantam in Java, and this was on a much smaller scale than those belonging to either the Dutch or Portuguese. If they were going to compete successfully against their rivals this factory needed to be expanded and new factories established right across the region.

There was a good case for expansion. One of England's most important exports, woollens, was understandably unpopular in the stifling climate of the Spice Islands. Instead of cloaks and blankets, the natives wanted cottons and calicoes which could be picked up cheaply in the ports along India's west coast. Already there was a brisk trade in these cottons and local ships regularly plied their trade between Gujarat and Bantam. Since India was believed to present a more favourable market for English woollens (as well as lead, iron and tin), the London merchants reasoned that if they could exchange these goods for cottons, then barter cottons for spices, they would have established a triangle of trade which would benefit everyone. Better still, they would be able to dramatically reduce the amount of gold being exported from England.

But there was a problem with trade with India. Much of the subcontinent was under the control of the mighty Moghul Emperor, Jehangir, the self-styled 'Conqueror of the World' who had already granted extensive and exclusive trading rights to the Portuguese – rights which they jealously guarded. Since a military assault on their fortified factories was out of the question, the only solution was to send an ambassador to Jehangir and beg his permission to build a factory on the western coast of India. If the Emperor agreed, the Portuguese would be powerless to intervene.

The governors began to search around for a suitable candidate to bear their petition to the Moghul Emperor. There were, they soon realised, few men qualified for the task and after several weeks of searching, their shortlist still contained only one name, William Hawkins, a sea captain whose background remains obscure but whose name links him to one of the most distinguished seafaring families of the Elizabethan age. He may have been the Hawkins who travelled across the Atlantic with Edward Fenton; he may also have put to sea in the *Griffin* against the Spanish Armada. But there were so many of the Hawkins family at sea during this period – including four named William – that it is not possible to untangle their exploits. Why the Company alighted on this particular Hawkins is easier to ascertain. Having spent some years trading in the Levant he was able to speak Turkish, an invaluable aid in any eastern country. He was also familiar with the customs and manners of the Orient and would be able to make an impression on the Moghul Emperor.

Hawkins set sail in the *Hector* in 1607 and arrived at

Surat on India's north-western coastline some sixteen months later. The journey was apparently uneventful for Hawkins makes scant mention of the storms, hunger and sickness that invariably afflicted the Company's voyages. Even the first sighting of the lush Gujarat coast, watered by the recent monsoons, failed to move him.

The town of Surat lay some twenty miles up the River Tapti and was reached by way of a muddy estuary which was only navigable by the smallest of vessels. The *Hector* therefore anchored off the sandy bar that blocked the estuary's mouth and Hawkins – accompanied by several of his crew – rowed upstream towards the town, watched by a crowd who had gathered to stare at these new and unfamiliar faces. The town's governor was too drunk to speak with Hawkins so he and his companions made his way to the Custom House where their personal possessions were 'searched and tumbled to our great dislike'.

While Hawkins explained that he wanted to establish a trading base his companion, Will Finch, set off to explore. The city, he discovered, was a pleasant one and home to a large number of merchants. Keeping a look-out for a suitable residence Finch noted that the finest houses were those fronting the river and those next to the castle where, to his surprise, he stumbled across 'a pleasant green, in the midst of which is a maypole'.

The customs' official spoke kindly to the English but was wary. He informed them that he was powerless to grant trading rights – that was the prerogative of the Moghul official in overall charge of the Gujarat ports – but assured Hawkins he would make their stay as comfortable as possible. Assigning them sleeping quarters in the porter's lodge of the Custom House, a room that Finch considered rather 'poore lodging', he then secured them an invitation to dinner at the home of one of the richer merchants in town.

Unfortunately what should have been a jovial meal proved to be painfully embarrassing. The merchant was none other than the owner of one of the ships that Sir Edward Michelborne had seized a couple of years earlier. Although he was gracious when he noticed their embarrassment and tactfully pointed out that 'there were thieves in all countries', Hawkins and Finch could not help but feel their mission had got off to a poor start.

It was soon to take a turn for the worse. While the two Englishmen awaited the return of the Moghul official whose permission they sought, the Portuguese took matters into their own hands. They were most upset when they heard of Hawkins' request to set up shop in the town and, seizing an English skiff packed with crew from the *Hector*, they arrested the men and threatened to pack them off to Goa to be dealt with by the Portuguese Viceroy.

Hawkins was annoyed but placed his trust in tact and diplomacy. He sent a polite but firm letter to the Portuguese commander reminding him that their two countries were at peace and asking that 'he release my men and goods, for that we were Englishmen.' The commander was in no mood to be lenient and sent Hawkins a return letter 'vilely abusing His Majesty [King James I] terming him King of Fishermen, and of an island of no import'. Worse still, he described Hawkins as 'a fart for his commission'. Hawkins exploded when he read that last insult. Labelling him a 'base villain and a traitor to his king', he immediately challenged 'the proud rascal' to a duel. The commander ignored the challenge and promptly despatched the English prisoners to Goa.

The *Hector* had by now sailed for Bantam leaving

Hawkins and Finch in a particularly vulnerable position, the more so when Finch fell 'extreme sick of the blody flux'. 'After the departure of my ship,' wrote Hawkins, 'I was so misused that it was insuferable. [I was] environed with so many enemies, who daily did nothing else but plot to murther me and cosen me of my goods.' The arrival of the Moghul official, Mukarrab Khan, did little to further his cause. Proud, arrogant and avaricious, Mukarrab had originally entered the emperor's service as court physician, only to be elevated to the governorship after curing the Emperor of a particularly nasty disorder. With the lucrative port of Surat now under his control, he proceeded to milk any arriving trader. Hawkins was not exempt from this policy – Mukarrab impounded the Company's wares, pocketed the choicest articles that had been brought ashore, and listened attentively to the lies and deceits told him by the Portuguese. 'He outwardly disembled and flattered with me almost three moneths,' wrote Hawkins, 'feeding me with faire promises and kindnesses. In the meantime he came to my house three times, sweeping me cleane of all things that were good so that when he saw that I had no more good things left, he likewise by little and little degraded me of his good looks.'

With enemies in every camp the two Englishmen were now in the gravest of dangers. 'I could not peep out of doors for fear of the Portugals,' records Hawkins, 'who in troops lay lurking in by-ways to give me assault to murder me.' Soon, they chose more direct action. Learning that the English captain had been invited to dinner with a friendly Moghul official they hatched a plot to murder him. While a company of Portuguese troops fanned out along the shoreline, three soldiers bristling with weapons stormed the marquee. Hawkins reacted quickly, grabbing his musket and stopping them in their tracks. The Moghul official then shouted to his followers and the Portuguese, suddenly outgunned, fled from the scene.

It was not long before they tried again. A band of forty men, egged on by Portuguese monks, tried to storm Hawkins' home, 'but I was always wary, having a strong house with good doores'. The man engineering the attacks was a Jesuit priest called Father Peneiro. Fanatically anti-English and a close friend of 'the dogge Mocreb [Mukarrab]' he did everything he could to whip up hatred against Hawkins and Finch throughout their stay in India.

By February 1609, Hawkins realised he would achieve nothing by staying in Surat and set out for Agra, the imperial capital, leaving behind a much-recovered Finch. To protect him during the ten-week journey he hired fifty Pathan horsemen, 'a people very much feared in these parts', though not so feared as to stop two more attempts on his life before he reached the capital. News of his arrival had preceded him, causing quite a stir at court. The Emperor wished to meet this curiosity immediately and 'presently charged both horsemen and footmen in many troupes, not to leave before I was found, commanding his knight marshall to accompany me with great state to the Court as an ambassador of a king ought to be'. So keen were they to bring Hawkins to his audience with the Emperor that he was scarcely given time to change into clean clothes. He was unprepared in another respect. It was well known that Jehangir expected anyone to whom he gave an audience to arrive with a large bag of presents. Paintings, toys and trinkets were his favourites, but he had a keen eye and did not take kindly to gifts of an inferior quality. Hawkins had arrived in India with half a cartload of presents but all had been stolen by 'the dogge' in Surat.

Rummaging through his baggage for a gift, the only item he could find was a small bundle of cloth; 'a slight present,' he admitted later, 'and not esteemed'.

Despite all the setbacks Hawkins found himself heartily welcomed by Jehangir and chatted to him for two hours in Turkish, informing him of all the problems he had faced in Surat. Despite their different stations in life, the two men struck up an instant friendship and the Emperor 'spake unto mee in the kindest manner that could be [and] with a most kind and smiling countenance'. Jehangir loved curiosities and an Englishman at his court was something truly exotic. Hawkins was given lodging and instructed to appear before the emperor every morning.

Each day Hawkins questioned him about the possibility of opening an English factory in Surat. Each day Jehangir stalled for time and urged him to be patient until, tiring of the constant petitions, he suggested that England would be best served if Hawkins stayed at his court on a semi-permanent basis. As an inducement he offered an annual pension of £3,200 a year, four hundred horses and the title of Inglis Khan: 'the title for a Duke'. It was a tempting offer and the captain-turned-duke weighed up the options. Eventually he agreed to stay for 'halfe a doozen yeeres', deciding it would be foolish to turn down this opportunity to 'feather my nest'.

He now became an intimate member of the Emperor's inner circle. Not only did he take part in the ceremonial duties that accompanied the daily durbar, where he sat in the little railed enclosure reserved for the highest nobility, but he also became a regular guest at the nightly wassails that filled the inner recesses of the palace with debauched laughter. It was at one of these drinking binges that Jehangir was struck by a brilliant idea. 'He was very earnest with me to take a white maiden out of his palace' – not as a mistress, but as a wife. For a free spirit like Hawkins the idea of settling down to a life of domesticity was far from appealing but he knew that he would have to be diplomatic when refusing the Emperor's kind offer. Quick-thinking as ever, he told Jehangir he was theologically opposed to marrying a Muslim, but jested that if the Emperor found him a good Christian girl, why, he would be up the aisle in a trice. 'At which speech,' says Hawkins, 'I little thought a Christian's daughter could be found.' Nor did he realise that he had thrown down the gauntlet. It became a matter of honour for the Emperor to find Hawkins a wife and after much searching he learned of an Armenian Christian who had recently lost her father and was all alone in the world. Hawkins found himself unable to refuse. 'Therefore I took her,' he writes, 'and for want of a Minister, before Christian witnesses, I married her.' He later discovered that such a marriage was unlawful, 'upon which news I was new married again'. Surprisingly, the couple fell head over heels in love and 'for ever after I lived content and without feare, she being willing to goe where I went and live as I lived.'

Throughout his time in Agra, Hawkins gives almost no description of the place, save to mention that it was 'one of the biggest cities in the world'. Although the Taj Mahal had yet to be built, the city was nonetheless adorned with outlandish public monuments, none of which was more beautiful than Jehangir's palace built inside the walls of Agra Fort. From here, richly caparisoned elephants would carry the imperial court up into the hills for numerous hunting expeditions. Here, too, a steady stream of courtiers, sycophants and imperial flatterers from all over India would arrive to pay homage to the Emperor. And as word got around of the influence of the Englishman at court – and as jealousies flared – the web of intrigue grew ever more complex.

'The Jesuits and Portugalls slept not,' recorded Hawkins with evident relish, 'but by all means sought my overthrow; and to say the truth, the principal Moslems near the king were exceeding envious that a Christian should be so close unto him.' Hawkins was shrewd enough to hold his own against men like Mukarrab Khan and the Portuguese Jesuits, and this latter group received a stern warning from the emperor that if Hawkins 'died by any extraordinary casualty, they should rue for it'.

He was fortunate to be invited to partake in the numerous daily drinking binges at court for they brought him ever closer to the Emperor. Jehangir liked to spend the greater part of every day completely drunk and was quite open about his love of alcohol, stating in his memoirs that he began to drink wine at the age of eighteen and increased his consumption day by day until it no longer intoxicated him. Then he moved on to spirits until, by the end of his life, his hand shook so much that he could no longer drink from his cup.

The imbibing would begin as soon as the day's official business was over. Jehangir would eat his main meal of the day, then retire to his private quarters with a few of his closest friends. These invariably included Hawkins, who describes how the Emperor would drink himself into a stupor. Then, after consuming a large quantity of opium to heighten his sense of well being, he 'layeth him down to sleep, every man departing to his own home'.

Hawkins knew that if he was ever to acquire the elusive trading privileges so desperately sought by the East India Company he needed to have a constant supply of novelties and trinkets to present to the Emperor. He wrote several letters to London urging them to send high-quality presents, a call that repeatedly fell on deaf ears. Several times the directors sent paintings of inferior quality and letters had to be despatched to London warning them 'to be very wary what they send'. In the end Jehangir took matters into his own hands, writing a list of his favourite presents which included 'any figures of beasts, birds, or other similes made of glass, or hard plaster, or silver, brass, wood, iron, stone or ivory'.

It was the expectation of more gifts that at long last led Jehangir to grant Hawkins his request for an English factory in Surat. Learning of the imminent arrival of the *Ascension*, he gave his approval for the establishment of an English trading base and allowed Hawkins to send a message to William Finch with the good news. Finch was most impressed with Hawkins' work and was duly deferential in his reply, addressing him as 'my Lord' and 'my Worship', rather than 'the captain'.

The Moghul officials and the Portuguese now redoubled their efforts to revoke the Emperor's licence. They proved successful for hardly had Jehangir's order reached Surat than it was inexplicably countermanded. There was more bad news in store for Hawkins and Finch. The *Ascension* 'was cast away' off Gujarat, presumably after striking a reef and, although many of the crew were saved, the 'disorder and riot committed by some of them' caused Finch untold trouble, especially when a certain Thomas Tucker butchered a cow in the street – 'a slaughter more than murder in India'.

Hawkins, meanwhile, was trying to mend his fences with the emperor, all the while making observations about Jehangir's unpredictable character. Most afternoons he accompanied him to lion and elephant fights which were of a scale and brutality akin to those of imperial Rome. Relishing the quantities of blood spilt, Jehangir took increasing delight in gladiatorial contests between man and beast, as Hawkins relates in a particularly gruesome anecdote.

A Pathan warrior from the frontier approached one of the Emperor's sons for a job but, when asked what pay he expected, said he would not work for less than 1,000 rupees a day. The prince was taken aback and asked how he could justify asking for such a huge salary. 'Make trial with me with all sorts of weapons,' he said, 'and if I do not perform as much as I speak, then let me die for it.'

Later that evening, the prince went to visit his drunken father and repeated this amusing story. The Emperor immediately commanded that the Pathan be brought before him and also asked for the strongest and most savage lion he possessed to be led into the palace. When asked by the emperor why the Pathan thought he was worth such a great salary, the man repeated his earlier challenge. Jehangir, bleary-eyed from drink and by now slurring his words said, 'That I will … go wrestle and buffet with this lion.'

The Pathan protested, saying that to fight a lion without a weapon was no test of strength. But Jehangir was in no mood to change his mind. 'The King,' writes Hawkins, 'not regarding his speech, commanded him to buckle with the lion, who did so, wrestling and buffeting … a pretty while: and then the lion being loose from his keepers, but not from his chaines, got the poore man within his clawes, and tore his body in many parts: and with his pawes tore the one halfe of his face, so that the valiant man was killed by this wilde beast.' The Emperor so enjoyed the spectacle that he called for ten of his horsemen to wrestle with the lion, three of whom lost their lives.

He was no less unpredictable with his ministers. One of Hawkins' friends at court, the Chief of the King's Wardrobe, had the misfortune to smash one of Jehangir's favourite Chinese dishes. Knowing the Emperor would be furious if he discovered the accident, he sent a servant to travel over the whole of China to find a replacement. The man searched in vain. Two years after the accident – and with still no sign of the servant – the Emperor asked the Chief of the King's Wardrobe for the dish and was told it was broken. 'Now when the king heard [this] he was in a great rage, commanding him to be brought before him and to be beaten by two men, with two great whips made of cords: and after he had received one hundred and twenty of these lashes, he commanded his porters, who he appointed for that purpose, to beate him with their small cudgels till a great many of them were broken. At least twenty men were beating him, till the poore man was thought to be dead, and then he was hauled out by the heels and commanded to prison.'

The following morning the Emperor demanded to know whether the man was still alive; when told that, yes, the man had survived the ordeal, he ordered that he spend the rest of his days in prison. At this point Jehangir's son intervened, secured the poor man's release and nursed him back to health. But still the Emperor was angry. Summoning the trembling fellow into his presence once again, he dismissed him from his court and told him 'never to come again before him until he had found such a like dish, and that he travel through China to seek it'. The man voyaged the length and breadth of the country for fourteen months but had no success in finding a copy. At length he discovered that a similar dish was owned by the King of Persia who sent it to him out of pity.

Hawkins eventually tired of the constant bloodshed and debauchery and grew fearful that the capricious Emperor would turn against him. One minute he was in favour, the next minute he was despised: 'Thus', he writes, 'was I tossed and tumbled in the kind of a rich merchant, venturing all he had in one bottom and, by casualtie of storms or pirates, lost it all at once.' When he was told his allowance had been annulled Hawkins knew it was time to pack his bags. He headed back to Surat with Mrs Hawkins and found himself in luck. A new English fleet under the command of the recently knighted Sir Henry Middleton had just arrived from Arabia and was presently at anchor off the bar at Surat.

Hawkins sailed home a disappointed man. He had been sent to India with high hopes of striking a deal with the emperor but, after almost three years of constant petitioning, he had left the court empty-handed. On a personal level, the mission had also failed. Jealous of Hawkins' influence over the Emperor, his fellow sailors did their utmost to undermine his reputation on their return. Purporting to be scandalised by his drunkenness, they told the East India Company directors that his debauchery at court had led to his disgrace. It was an unlikely charge but it stuck. In any case, Hawkins was in no position to defend himself for he fell sick on the long journey home and died shortly before arriving in England. The loyal Mrs Hawkins was distraught. Unable to live on her own she sold a very valuable diamond, married a factor called Gabriel Towerson, an experienced East India trader, and accompanied him back to the East.

CHAPTER FIVE

'ADMIRAL, WE ARE BETRAYED!'

To the handful of observers gathered on Dover's cliffs there had rarely been a more magnificent sight. A flotilla of ships was flying up the Channel, the wind filling their sails and their pennants streaming behind them. But these were not English vessels, nor were there any English sailors on board. The fleet was commanded by a Dutchman, Jacob van Neck, who was about to bring untold wealth to his mercantile masters in Amsterdam.

Rarely would expeditions pass as smoothly as Jacob van Neck's, which returned to Holland in the summer of 1599. He sailed to the East without any untoward incident and successfully bought an enormous quantity of spices in Bantam before heading for home. On later voyages he would find himself accused of sodomy, would lose his hand in a gun battle and eat a poisonous fruit which temporarily afflicted him with 'madnesse, seeing angels, devils, serpents, all things and nothing'. But on this occasion he was spared such troubles and his return was a cause for joyous celebration, for 'as long as Holland has been Holland there have never arrived ships as richly laden as these.' Indeed they were: nearly a million pounds in weight of pepper and cloves as well as half a ship-load of nutmeg, mace and cinnamon. The commander and his men were fêted as heroes: led by a band of trumpeters they were paraded in triumph through the streets of Amsterdam while the city's church bells rang out in celebration. The merchants presented van Neck with a glittering golden beaker (a generosity somewhat marred by the discovery that it was only gold-plated) and the crew were given as much wine as they could drink.

The success of the voyage was due to van Neck's skill in dealing with the natives in Bantam. Three years previously the choleric Cornelis Houtman had battered the town with his formidable firepower, slaughtered hundreds of the local population, and even had the audacity to train his largest cannon on the King's palace. Van Neck was a shrewd enough operator to realise that any redress for Houtman's behaviour would be welcomed. Not only did he agree to the King's prices, he boldly suggested that he pay over the odds for the goods in order to cement their new-found relationship. 'Some may think', he wrote in his journal, 'that we are a bit too liberal with the money of our masters. But if they will look at it soberly, they will have to agree that, at places where our nation previously left as an enemy, a certain amount of goodwill is not misplaced.' He was aided in his task of mending fences by Bantam's merchants who had recently captured three Portuguese vessels, stripped them of everything of value, and set fire to them. Aware that the Portuguese were sure to avenge this wanton act of piracy, the Bantamese were desperately in need of a powerful ally.

A brisk trade followed van Neck's arrival and within four weeks the three ships under his direct command were filled with spices. His only concern was what had happened to the second squadron of his fleet, not sighted since Madagascar. But as New Year's Eve approached and van Neck planned festivities for his crew, these other ships, commanded by the splendidly named Vice Admiral Wybrand van Warwyck and the Arctic explorer Jacob van Heemskerck, sailed into view. 'They were joyously received,' records the ship's journal, 'and made welcome.'

None was happier than Jacob van Heemskerck who, just two years earlier, had been stranded in the Arctic when his search for the fabled North-East Passage was brought to an icy halt. Now, basking in the tropical heat of Bantam, Heemskerck found himself in considerably more genial surroundings. Back among old friends, he threw himself into the festivities. His own voyage had been better than many; stumbling across a paradisal island in the middle of the Indian Ocean – which he named Mauritius – his men stuffed their bellies with the easy-to-catch wildlife and amused themselves by lounging on the beaches and riding four-abreast on giant tortoises. Realising that Mauritius could be a valuable port of call for Dutch ships Heemskerck put a rooster and some hens ashore and planted orange and lemon seeds, invoking 'the Almighty God's blessing that He may lend His power to make them multiply and grow for the benefit of those who will visit the island after us'.

Jacob van Neck's frantic buying had left the port of Bantam bereft of spices. Before sailing for home he suggested that the rest of the fleet sail east to the Spice Islands where it was certain they would be able to procure a full cargo of nutmeg and mace. This they duly did: Warwyck headed for the northernmost island of Ternate where he fired so many rounds of ammunition in celebration of his safe arrival that the very island was said to quake. Heemskerck, meanwhile, had sailed into even remoter seas. Fearless and daring, he had his eye on the Banda Islands – as yet unvisited by either the Dutch or English – and sailed eastwards with a bravado that was not always appreciated by his on-board merchants. When one of their number suggested that the captain should be more careful with his ships, Heemskerck exploded: 'When we risk our lives,' he said, 'the Lords of the Company may damn well risk their ships!'

He also had to risk a monster, a creature of 'devillish possession' which was said to live in the Banda Islands and prey on passing ships. Fortunately his Indian pilot knew just the method of dealing with such monsters: 'With a terrible ghastly countenance [he] thrust forward the boat-hook' as if to kill the devil. This did the trick, the monster remained out of sight and in mid-March, 1599, Heemskerck dropped anchor at Great Banda and petitioned the local chieftain for trade.

The Bandanese were less than happy to see this band of Dutchmen arrive at their shores. Almost ninety years of contact with the Portuguese had taught them to treat all foreigners with mistrust and the arrival of the Dutch seemed to portend some new and menacing threat. Scarcely had Heemskerck's vessels dropped anchor in the huge natural harbour at Neira than Gunung Api, a volcano which had lain dormant for centuries, suddenly burst into life and sent a spectacular display of fireworks into the tropical sky. 'The hill cast forth such hideous flames, such store of cinders, and huge streames that it destroyed, burnt, and broke downe all the thicke woods and mightie trees, overwhelming them as it were her owne vomiting so that a greene leafe could not be seene in all that part of the iland.' The locals were reminded of a prophecy, told them five years earlier by a Muslim holy man, that an army of white strangers would shortly arrive at the islands and take them by force. Since the Dutch ships were heavily armed, and Heemskerck appeared to take a keen interest in the local feuding, it was widely agreed that this was that white army.

After the presentation of lavish gifts, and repeated assurances from Heemskerck that he was a sworn enemy of the Portuguese, his men were allowed to land on Great Banda and barter their knives and mirrors for nutmeg and mace. The Dutchmen spent almost a month buying spices and were allowed to trade peacefully and undisturbed, though not without quarrels: 'A man needs seven eyes,' recorded Heemskerck, 'if he does not want to be cheated. These people are so crooked and brazen that it is almost unbelievable.' Nevertheless, the prices they paid for nutmeg were laughably low (less than one English penny for ten pounds of nutmeg) and their cargo would increase many thousand-fold in value by the time they arrived back in Holland.

A house was rented on Great Banda and soon local boats began arriving from the neighbouring island of Neira. Trading was temporarily halted when the Banda Islands were plunged into war as rival chieftains embarked on a series of ambitious head-hunting expeditions. The menfolk of Neira, together with their allies on nearby Ai Island, went on the rampage, killing their enemies and adorning their boats with the bloody trophies of battle. They even chopped off women's heads, contrary to tradition, although they had the good grace to 'burie these heads in cotton clothes'. On their return, 'with their swords yet bloody, [they] made glorious muster of themselves four or five days together.'

Such localised wars were a recurring feature in the

Banda Islands and the Dutch were soon to exploit them to devastating effect. But for the moment Heemskerck was happy to watch from the sidelines and gather intelligence for future expeditions. When he finally set sail on his homeward journey he left behind a party of twenty-two Dutchmen and instructed them to stockpile nutmeg in preparation for the next Dutch fleet. His parting conversation with the headman of Great Banda provoked an unusual request: drawing Heemskerck to one side the headman confessed to an abiding passion for horology and begged the Dutch commander to return to the island with a large grandfather clock, adding the proviso that any representation of man or beast must be removed since it would cause offence to his Muslim islanders. Heemskerck agreed, but as there is no further mention of the clock, the request seems to have been conveniently forgotten.

The Dutch captain finally arrived back in Amsterdam in the spring of 1600 and was accorded a welcome no less rapturous than had been given to van Neck. When his nutmeg was finally unloaded into the city's warehouses, 'the air of the whole neighbourhood was sweetened by their savoury smell.'

'But before the returne of any of these ships, in the yeere 1599, the Dutch set forth another fleet.' Much to the chagrin of Amsterdam's merchants, this new expedition had been despatched by their trading rivals in Rotterdam and Zeeland who had long been keen to involve themselves in the spice trade. Amsterdam responded by toughening its stance, informing its commanders to deal harshly with any competitors. 'You know as well as we do what losses it would cause us if the Zeeland ships were to arrive before ours are fully loaded. Therefore, buy. Buy everything you

Nutmeg-traders in the Banda Islands, 1599. Local merchants added
grit to their spices to increase the weight and swell their profits.
'Have you a great care to receive such nutmegs as be good,'
Lancaster warned his merchants, 'for the smallest nutmegs
be worth nothing at home.'

can lay your hands on, and load it as quickly as possible. Even if you have no room for it, keep on buying and bind it to yourselves for future delivery.'

Their advice came too late. With more and more ships heading for the 'spiceries', and with prices rising by the month, the merchants of Amsterdam petitioned their delegates in the States General, the body that represented all the provinces of the United Netherlands, for a total and exclusive monopoly on the spice trade. 'For many and varied reasons,' they wrote, 'it is advisable that this commerce be conducted by one administration.'

It was an outrageous demand and it was soon thrown out. Yet the man who led the opposition, Johan van Oldebarnvelt, who as Advocate or Attorney-General of Holland was the most powerful man in the land, realised that some sort of monopoly was essential if the spice trade was to flourish. He rejected Amsterdam's proposal, insisting instead that small-time investors from the entire country should be included 'so that these men can discuss ways and means whereby this aforementioned navigation and trade shall be secured for many years to come'. It was not a popular move and was bitterly opposed by the Amsterdam merchants, but on the evening of 20 March 1602, an agreement was struck and the Dutch East India Company officially came into being. Known as the VOC (Vereenigde Oost-Indische Compagnie), or more colloquially as the Seventeen after its seventeen-strong council, it was given a total monopoly over the spice trade for a period of twenty-one years. It was to prove a formidable rival to its English counterpart.

The Seventeen wasted no time in sending their first fleet to the East Indies. Just eleven days after putting their signatures to the charter, they despatched three ships under the robust command of Sebald de Weert whilst the rest of the fleet, under Wybrand van Warwyck, left the Texel some two months later. The men were ordered to establish trading links with scores of countries and princedoms including Java, Sumatra, Ceylon and the 'spiceries'. As if that was not enough, van Warwyck was also instructed to sail to China and open trading bases up and down the coast. Military action was both permitted and expected: 'attack the Spanish and Portuguese wherever you find them,' read the instructions, and it was not long before the Dutch ships found themselves embroiled in local hostilities. No sooner had Sebald de Weert arrived at Ceylon than the maharajah 'protested much his hatred to the Portugall and began to explore the possibilities of a joint assault on their castles'. De Weert struck up an instant rapport with this candid but jovial ruler who, he learned, had been brought

up by the Portuguese, converted to Christianity and taken
the name Dom Joao. Now, his friendship had turned sour
and he was planning his revenge, suggesting to de Weert
that if the Dutch vessels blockade the island's principal
port, he would attack the Portuguese castle with his land
forces. They could then repeat this exercise up and down
the coastline until the Portuguese had been decisively
trounced. In return, he promised to turn over the
Portuguese battlements to the Dutch and 'reserve his
merchandising for them'. This was too good an offer to
turn down and de Weert whole-heartedly embraced the
project.

The good humour was not to last. De Weert's crew
were exhausted after their long journey and although
there was plenty of fresh fruit on the island, the humid
climate made them jumpy and irritable. 'They were
disquieted with flies and gnats which would not suffer
them to sleepe.' Even more annoying were the natives
'who made fire and smoake all the night'. But what really
angered the Dutch crew was the fact that they were still
living off the by now putrid salt beef loaded onto the ships
in Holland. 'The king entertained them well,' records one
journal, 'but their religion prohibiting to eat beefs and
buffals – whereof they had great plenty – they would not
sell any to the Hollanders.' This was all the more galling
since the surrounding fields and meadows, and even the
streets, were crowded with plump cattle and buffalo. To the
Singhalese, these were holy animals who harboured the
souls of their deceased relatives. But the Dutch, sick of
gnawing rancid gristle, saw juicy steaks in every cow that
passed. De Weert listened politely as Dom Joao explained
why he could not sell any cattle but privately he scoffed at
the suggestion of sacred cows and allowed his 'unruely'

men to go on the rampage, butchering cows and roasting the meat over camp-fires.

The natives were horrified when they saw what was happening and none more so than Dom Joao. 'The Portugals had never offered such indignitie,' he stormed. De Weert's apologies did little to dampen the fury over the 'sacriligious murther of beefs', nor did his offer of payment for the butchered cows. 'From that time on,' wrote Dutchman Jacob Rycx, 'we were on a bad footing with the king and his subjects.'

The incident was temporarily forgotten when the military campaign against the Portuguese was resumed, but resentment towards the Dutch continued to simmer and when Dom Joao learned that his son had been allowed to fall into enemy hands he decided that it was time to act. With an outward show of friendship he invited de Weert and his staff to a fabulous banquet and there had his bloody revenge:

> While the Vice-Admiral and the King discussed various matters, there was quite a bit of drinking. Suddenly the King berated the Vice-Admiral for having allowed the Portuguese to escape. By then De Weert was pretty drunk. He denied the accusation heatedly and insisted that the King and his retinue pay him a courtesy visit on his ship, adding: 'The Dutch are not accustomed to bend their knee without receiving some respect in return.' This added fuel to the fire and the King apparently convinced himself that the Dutch were not to be trusted, and that the invitation was for the sole purpose of taking him prisoner. At a signal the King's followers drew their swords, slaughtering the Vice-Admiral and all

those who were with him. There were three hundred Singalese hidden in the woods near the beach, and when they learned what was happening in the palace they attacked those of us who were ashore. In all we lost forty-seven men and six wounded ... And so it was all enmity and we knowing what had caused this because we thought we were all friends.

Dom Joao soon tried to mend fences with the Dutch but there was an understandable lack of goodwill on the part of the survivors. 'We are sailing for other lands where we shall be treated less treacherously,' they informed the maharajah.

Long before news of the massacre reached Holland, yet more ships had been despatched eastwards under the command of Steven van der Hagan. These headed straight to the Banda Islands where the commander intended to build a fortified factory. He had expected to be greeted by the party of Dutch traders left behind by Heemskerck but as he stepped ashore and knocked on the factory gates he was most surprised to find himself answered by a cheery English voice. It was Christopher Colthurst, captain of the *Ascension*, who extended a gleeful welcome to van der Hagen. The Dutchman quizzed Colthurst about the fate of the Dutch settlers, only to learn that they had all been murdered by the natives after a fiery argument. The cause of their quarrel 'was a strangenesse', according to the records. Two of the Dutchmen were said to have renounced Christianity shortly after arriving in the Banda Islands and had adopted the Islamic beliefs of the natives. 'They were slaine by three Hollanders which, in revenge, were slaine by the natives.' This led to a blood feud which ended only when all the Dutchmen were dead.

Van der Hagen was outraged by what he heard and

made veiled threats to the Bandanese. 'Stormie weather followed,' writes Samuel Purchas in his colourful account of the event, '… wherein all the beasts of the forrest crept forth, the young lions roared after their prey; the ghastly ghosts walked abroad in the darke, and the rulers of the darknesse … domineered at pleasure.' Gathering the island's headmen together, the Dutch commander duped them into signing a document that granted him a total and permanent monopoly over their supply of nutmeg. To the native chieftains, such a document was scarcely worth the paper it was written on, but the Dutch treated it as a legally binding agreement and would later use it as the justification for their annexation of the Banda Islands.

By the time van der Hagen set sail for Holland the Dutch could boast three forts in the Spice Islands which gave them a virtual monopoly on the world's production of cloves – and had secured a written agreement with the Banda Islands, theoretically capturing the priceless nutmeg supply as well. But van der Hagen's mistake was to leave behind insufficient forces to guarantee this treaty he had concluded. Scarcely had he left the Banda Islands than a fleet equipped by the English East India Company sailed into port and experienced few difficulties in buying nutmeg from the local islanders.

News of Holland's success was a cause of grave concern to the directors of the English East India Company. Less than four years after launching themselves into the spice race they found that most of the 'spiceries' were already lost to the Dutch. This caused panic among the Company directors who resolved to challenge the Dutch authority by building factories on the clove-producing islands of Tidore and Ternate as well as on the nutmeg-producing Bandas.

They reasoned that having 'factors' or merchants permanently living on these islands was an essential requisite to trade in the Spice Islands; not only could these factors stockpile spices at the time of harvesting when prices were low, they would also be able to keep an eye on the movements of the Dutch and appraise newly arrived fleets of the current situation.

In 1607 they despatched their third expedition to the East, supplying it with £17,600 of gold bullion (but just £7,000 of home-produced merchandise). The captains were urged to stay one step ahead of the Dutch. 'Take your speedy course along the coast of Malabar,' read their orders, 'that you may come [to Bantam] before the Hollanders ... for they will do what they can to anticipate you at the Molluccas.' The directors also took the opportunity to remind all crew members that gambling and swearing was strictly prohibited, and this time an extra clause was added. With the thought, perhaps, that cleanliness is next to godliness, men were asked 'that there be a diligent care to keep the lowest decks and other places of the ships clean and sweet, which is a notable preservation of health'. This sudden concern for on-board hygiene owed less to a concern for the crew's health than to the fact that the Company had learned that 'the Dutchmen do far exceed us in cleanliness, to their great commendation, and to the great disgrace of our people.'

The directors had one other request – a trifling matter, really, but one they felt obliged to fulfil. 'Remember to do your best to bring for the Lord of Salisbury some parrots, monkeys, marmasetts, or other strange beasts and fowls that you esteeme rare and delightful.' The Lord of Salisbury was the celebrated Robert Cecil, Secretary of State, who had been pestering the Company for months for exotic animals to add to his collection. The leaders of the third expedition surpassed themselves when it came to meeting this request, for when the *Hector* at last docked at the Thames-side wharves onlookers were amazed to discover a 'blacke savage' gazing wistfully across the London landscape. His name was Coree, a native of Table Bay, who had made the mistake of clambering on board ship as she revictualled in southern Africa. Realising what a stir he would cause in London, the acting captain Gabriel Towerson took Coree captive and carried him back to England. He proved tiresome company, for 'the poore wretch' moaned throughout the long voyage, not through lack of creature comforts but – according to the ship's journal – 'merely out of extreme sullenness, for he was very well used'.

Sir Thomas Smythe strode down to the Thames to extend a personal welcome to Coree and to assure him that the East India Company would do everything in its power to make his stay as enjoyable and comfortable as possible. Despite these promises, the homesick Coree caused the London merchants much disquiet for he singularly failed to offer them any word of thanks. 'He had good diet, good cloaths, good lodging and all other fitting accommodations,' they said, 'yet all this contented him not.' Indeed the longer he stayed in London, the less he appeared to like the city and 'would daily lie upon the ground and cry very often thus in broken English, "Coree go home, Saldania go, home go." '

It was a surprise present of a suit of chain mail, including a brass helmet and breastplate, that gave Coree a change of heart. He was overjoyed with his gift and would don his 'beloved metal' every morning and clatter through the capital's markets proudly displaying his armour to astonished passers-by. When he was at last shipped back to southern Africa having escaped an undignified end as a stuffed accompaniment to Lord Salisbury's collection of hunting trophies, Coree was still wearing his suit of chain mail. However, the novelty of the armour soon wore off, 'for he had no sooner sett foot on his own shore but did presently throw away his cloaths, his linen and other covering and got his sheepskin upon his back and guts aboute his necke'.

It had long been intended that the Company's third expedition should consist of three ships under the overall command of William Keeling, but the irrepressibly energetic David Middleton, captain of the diminutive *Consent*, tired of the slow progress of the *Red Dragon* and *Hector* and decided to press on without them. It was a wise decision for by the time Captain Keeling reached the Spice Islands, Middleton had already returned to England and was planning his next expedition to the East Indies.

David Middleton was the youngest of the intrepid Middleton trio and the most impatient and businesslike of them all. Never one to dawdle in foreign ports, his overriding concern was to conduct his business in as short a time as possible. Travelling at breakneck pace across the Atlantic he arrived at Table Bay with the loss of just one man, 'Peter Lambert [who] fell off the top-most head, whereof he died.' He paused briefly to stock up on fresh food and was soon under way again, this time heading towards Madagascar. Here Middleton stopped to inspect the island but, after a cursory glance, decided 'there was nothing on it' and continued with his voyage, arriving in Bantam less than eight months after leaving Tilbury.

Almost every expedition that made it to Bantam did so in poor shape. Men on board would be sick and dying while the factors living in the town were generally found

to be in an advanced state of degeneracy. Not so on this
occasion. The ever-efficient David Middleton headed
straight ashore for a meeting with Gabriel Towerson, the
factor left behind by his brother Henry in 1604, and 'found
the merchants in very good health and all things in good
order'. Towerson expressed concern that the youngest
Middleton lacked in experience what he made up for in
enthusiasm and warned him that any dealings with the
Spanish or Portuguese would be viewed with hostility by
the Dutch. But Middleton needed no lectures on how to
conduct business: although sailing in a tiny vessel and
without an accompanying fleet he was full of bravado and
informed Towerson that he 'cared little for their threats and
brags'. Towerson recorded all this in a lengthy letter to his
superiors in London and although scrupulously impartial
when writing about this youngest Middleton, his verbatim
report of Middleton's behaviour does the captain few
favours. Towerson clearly felt that Middleton's headstrong
nature betrayed his youth. But Middleton was no fool and
played a clever game of cat and mouse when he reached
the spice-rich Moluccas. Having dashed across the Indian
Ocean to get here, he now spent more than two months
wining and dining the Spanish and Portuguese, apologising
for not participating in sorties against the Dutch but
explaining that it would run contrary to his orders. He
cared little that the Spanish steadfastly refused to sell him
spices for, in the words of Samuel Purchas, his men 'had
privy trade with the people by night, and were joviall and
frolicke by day with the Spaniards'.

Setting sail from Tidore, his next port of call was the
island of Celebes where he found himself royally
entertained by the King of Butung or, as the jovial crew
nicknamed him, the King of Button. This island was almost

unknown to the English but Middleton enjoyed his stay here and found the King a curious fellow who was only too keen to entertain his guests with banquets and sweetmeats. Some meals were novel affairs; the ship's purser found himself eating in a room whose interior decor consisted entirely of rotting human heads dangling from the ceiling.

Scarcely had the English made their final farewells to the King of Button than they had a stroke of good fortune. The captain of a passing junk sent a message to Middleton that he was laden with cloves which were for sale. Middleton jumped at this piece of news. He bought the lot and, not bothering to sail to the Banda Islands to buy nutmeg, immediately returned to England. One mishap marred their leaving: 'Our captain had bought some slaves from the king,' records the ship's journal, 'and as we were busy this night, one of them stole out of our captain's cabbin door and leaped into the sea, and swum ashore, and was never heard of.' The few captains who later followed Middleton's lead and bought slaves all met with similar problems. They either escaped when the ships reached port or died en route. Slaves apart, the *Consent* had a trouble-free return to England. Middleton had spent just £3,000 on cloves but when they were sold on the London market they reaped more than £36,000.

The rest of the fleet was making painfully slow progress towards the East Indies. Setting sail from England on April Fools' Day, 1607, it was beset by troubles from the very beginning. So numerous were the 'divers disasters', in fact, that its commander, William Keeling, tired of describing them and contented himself with a list: 'Gusts, calms, rains, sickness, and other marine inconveniences.' Keeling was the antithesis of the businesslike David Middleton. In the journal of his voyage he cuts a flamboyant figure whose erratic behaviour was to cause many problems for the Company directors. On a later trip he smuggled his beloved wife on board ship, contrary to Company rules, and kept her hidden in his cabin. She was discovered soon after the ship left England and a rowing boat was sent to bring her back to land, though not before Keeling had written dozens of letters to the exasperated directors in London informing them that he loved his wife dearly and thought their actions to be mean-spirited.

Keeling's other great passion was the plays of William Shakespeare and, as his ship drifted listlessly in the mid-Atlantic, he spent his leisure time planning a magnificent performance of one of the bard's plays. While the men on the *Hector* were busy mending ropes and caulking the decks, the crew of Keeling's vessel were learning speeches, sewing costumes and performing dress rehearsals. Finally, the big day arrived. Dropping anchor off the coast of Sierra Leone the dilettantish Keeling watched a final rehearsal and decided that his men were as good as they would ever be. A select audience was invited from the *Hector* and the play performed under the star-studded African sky. 'We gave,' wrote the proud captain, 'the tragedie of Hamlett.' If this is correct it must have been one of the earliest amateur performances of the play, staged not in the Globe Theatre but on the mangrove-tangled shores of equatorial Africa.

What Keeling's crew thought of these dramatics has passed unrecorded. More certain is that the spills and adventures of English mariners provided Shakespeare with an endless supply of material for his plays, and it was surely one of the East India Company's sailors, mimicking the strictures of his superiors, who put the words into the mouth of Shakespeare's Clown in *Twelfth Night*: 'I would have men of such constancy put to sea, that their business might be everything and their intent everywhere; for that's it that always make a good voyage of nothing.' Other plays echo the risks that investors took when they ploughed money into the spice trade and many merchants must, like Antonio's friend in *The Merchant of Venice*, have spent their waking hours thinking,

> of shallows and of flats;
> And see my wealthy Andrew dock'd in sand
> Vailing her high-top lower than her ribs
> To kiss her burial. Should I go to church
> And see the holy edifice of stone,
> And not bethink me straight of dangerous rocks,
> Which touching but my gentle vessel's side
> Would scatter all her spices on the stream,
> Enrobe the roaring waters with my silks;
> And, in a word, but even now worth this,
> And now worth nothing?

Drama was not the only diversion provided by Keeling. Realising the importance of keeping his men busy he organised a fishing expedition for his crew who, spurred on by his enthusiasm, managed to catch six thousand fish in a single hour. Never one for half measures, he then rowed ashore for a shopping trip and returned with three thousand lemons. He also carted back a massive elephant tusk as a wall-hanging for his cabin. It cost him eight pounds of iron and a couple of yards of cloth.

This last purchase set him thinking: if the natives could slaughter an elephant with their primitive spears, then he would certainly be able to kill one with his musket. And so, 'on the seventh of September in the afternoon, we went all

together ashore to see if we could shoot an elephant.'
Trekking through the African bush they spied an enormous
bull elephant and Keeling and his men immediately
opened fire with their muskets: 'We shot seven or eight
bullets into him, and made him bleed exceedingly as
appeared by his track, but being near night we were
constrained aboard without effecting our purposes on him.'

With his men restored to good health it was time to set
sail once more. No sooner was the *Red Dragon* clear of the
land than Keeling and his men were rehearsing
Shakespeare's *King Richard II*. By the end of September the
captain thought them sufficiently good to send a boat
across to the *Hector* and once again invite Captain Hawkins
aboard to watch the play. Keeling was in his element and
ordered an elaborate fish dinner to be cooked in honour of
the event. Mindful that such entertainments were
discouraged by the Company's directors, he justified his
actions by explaining that amateur dramatics 'keeps my
people from idleness and unlawfull games or sleep'.

After almost nine months at sea the *Red Dragon* and
Hector at last neared the Cape of Good Hope. They had still
received no word from Middleton, but putting into Table
Bay to revictual Keeling stumbled across a rock carved with
the words: '24 July, 1607: David Middleton in the Consent.'
Since then, half a year had passed yet still Keeling was in no
hurry. After allowing his crew a leisurely few weeks ashore,
he reluctantly put to sea, only to drop anchor again as soon
as they reached Madagascar. This time Keeling paused to
give his men a chance to wash their clothes, an attention to
cleanliness that cost one man dear. Stepping ashore, a
certain George Evans was 'sore hurt with a crocodile, or
alligator, which had siezed upon the man's leg [as] he had
been washing a shirt by the boat's side'. This unfortunate

man had been tugged into shallow water where he managed to kick the crocodile so hard that it momentarily released its jaws. Even so, Evans was 'sorely wounded, and recovered the boat, making no other account but that his foot was gone, till he saw that the hind part of the small of his leg was bitten clean asunder both flesh and sinews to the bone; and had the alligator got him into deep water, assuredly he had been carried clean away'.

Another stop, another Shakespeare play, and the ships made their stately progress towards Socotra, a parched island off the Horn of Africa. Even the unhurried Keeling could find little to detain him here and after buying a huge supply of aloes, noted for their efficacy against constipation, he again set sail, this time for Bantam.

Bantam held good news and bad. Keeling was less than happy to be greeted by six Dutch ships in the harbour but overjoyed when the king told him that he was desperate to 'have commerce with so great a king as his Majesty of England with whom, he understood, the King of Holland was not comparable'. True to his word, he allowed the *Red Dragon* to be loaded immediately and, two days before Christmas 1608, she set sail for England. Keeling was not on her: just a few days earlier, he transferred all his goods onto the *Hector* which he now intended to sail to the Banda Islands.

The first of these islands that came into sight was the tiny outpost of Run. Instead of stopping here Keeling sailed east for another ten miles until he reached the larger islands of Great Banda and Neira where there was 'a very fair and spacious harbour' and a safe anchorage was assured. Scarcely had he entered this huge natural harbour than a party of Dutchmen rowed out to his vessel, intrigued by the unexpected arrival of these Englishmen. At first they

*Bantam market, circa 1600. It was here that one Englishman, William
Clarke, was attacked by a Dutch gang who stripped him naked and
'cruelly cut his flesh, and then washed him with salt and vinegar.'*

were cordial in their greetings; they blasted their cannon in
Keeling's honour and even invited him to a feast. But their
friendship soon turned sour when they discovered that
Keeling had presented the local headman with a letter from
King James I, along with a gilded beaker, an ornamental
helmet and a first-class musket. Resorting to underhand

tactics, they sent a message over to the *Hector* informing
Keeling that there were plots against his life and that he
should set sail immediately.

The English captain was unmoved and, after paying some
four hundred pieces-of-eight to the headman of Great
Banda, his men began buying large quantities of nutmeg
from the local growers. He was unhurried in his trade for
he knew that the winds which had carried him to the
Banda Islands were on the brink of shifting direction and,
with the imminent arrival of the monsoon, was confident
that no more Dutch ships would be able to sail east from
Bantam. It was with considerable surprise, therefore, that he
opened the curtains of his cabin on the morning of 16
March 1609, and saw three Dutch vessels sail into view.

The crew of these new ships came to visit the *Hector* and
were outwardly friendly, but 'an Englishman [serving on one
of the ships] reporteth that they mean to surprise us ere a
month expire'. They were, in fact, already hampering
Keeling's business and within days of their arrival the price
of nutmeg had rocketed. Abandoning trade with Great
Banda, the English captain 'made a secret accord with the
chief of Ai Island' and prepared to send a factor there. But less
than a week had passed before there was further bad news.
Not only had the Dutch learned about this secret deal and
vowed to undermine it, they had also received reinforcements in the shape of six more vessels. This was an entirely
unexpected development and left Keeling with very few
options. 'Sixty-two men against a thousand or more
could not perform much,' he wrote. Outnumbered and
outgunned, he realised that friendship was his only option
and as the Dutch ships approached he lamely ordered his
men to welcome them with a burst of cannon fire. Keeling
also discovered that he was fast developing an allergy to

nutmeg and that far from curing sickness it was actually making him ill. 'I went aboard,' he writes irritably, 'to cure mine eyes which, by the heat of the nuts, were very sore.'

He was by now thoroughly dispirited. The Dutch were treating him 'most unkindlye, searching his boate disgracefullye ... and not suffering him to have any further trade, not to gather in his debts, but with a peremptory comaund, to be gone'. Keeling held a secret meeting with the ruler of Neira and tentatively suggested that he surrender his authority to King James I in return for trade and protection. He was pleased to learn that the headman was interested in the proposal but, 'doubted their inconstancies'. He continued to play his game of bluff with the Dutch, warning them that 'his majesty of England, our sovereign, would not permit his subjects to sustain any damage by their means without special and sound satisfaction.' The Dutch simply ignored him for they were getting a perverse enjoyment in goading Keeling. When they filched some sacks of rice from under his nose, the English commander lost his temper. Grabbing the Dutch admiral's messenger, 'I requested [him] to tell his admiral ... that if he were a gentleman, he would not permit his base people to abuse me as I walked among them.' The messenger sniggered when he heard this and replied that his admiral was not a gentleman but a weaver.

Keeling was in a hopeless position. Denied spices and spied upon day and night, he could have been forgiven for abandoning the Company's orders and setting sail for England. But no sooner had he considered such an option than the entire situation changed. Yet another Dutch fleet arrived in the Banda Islands, and it was carrying new and wholly unwelcome orders.

★

The commander of this latest fleet, Peter Verhoef, was a spirited fighter who had first acquitted himself at the Battle of Gibraltar two years previously when he masterminded the annihilation of the Spanish fleet. Now, he was despatched on a mission which, although ostensibly to buy spices, had an unambiguously military objective. 'We draw your special attention to the islands in which grow cloves and nutmeg,' wrote the Seventeen in their instructions, 'and we instruct you to strive to win them for the Company either by treaty or by force.'

Following their instructions to the letter, Verhoef sailed directly to the Banda Isles with his impressive fleet which carried at least a thousand Dutch fighting men, as well as a contingent of Japanese mercenaries. On his arrival at Great Banda he ceremoniously presented the headman with his credentials and summoned all the local chieftains to a meeting 'under a greate tree'. Reading from a prepared script, first in Portuguese and then in Malayan, he admonished them for breaking their promise 'to have trade only with them, who had now traded there sixe yeares ... and were often much abused'. He went on to explain that he intended to construct a castle on Neira Island 'to defend themselves and the whole countrey from Portugals'. This news was greeted with 'uprore' by the natives who, 'but for feare of their shipping would have slaine the Hollanders'.

Verhoef found it impossible to negotiate with the chieftains who seemed to lack any overall authority. Although numerous documents refer to a 'King of Banda' there was no such person. Instead, every island and every village had its own headman whose authority extended over a few hundred people at most. In informing more than two hundred headmen of his intentions, Verhoef had at a stroke made himself a common enemy.

Ignoring their threats, he promptly landed 750 soldiers on Neira and instructed them to start digging the foundations. The building, whose massive walls are still visible beneath a curtain of creepers, was constructed on the site of a Portuguese fort which had been abandoned almost a century previously. The headmen watched with alarm as the fort's outer walls grew in height and on 22 May 1609, they asked for a meeting with the Dutch commander. Verhoef immediately agreed, hoping that they would at last consent to his plans.

After the passing of almost four centuries it is hard to piece together exactly what happened next. The Dutch records suggest that William Keeling helped instigate the ensuing massacre, but this accusation contradicts his own diaries. Although he had certainly struck a number of secret deals with the natives, there is nothing to suggest he was actively inciting them to violence. Indeed, he was busy buying nutmeg at Ai Island, a day's sailing from Neira, when rumours of a plot began to circulate.

The first hint of trouble was conveyed to Keeling by the chief of the island. He was told that on no account should he set sail for Neira unless he wanted to be henceforth regarded as an enemy. Keeling was intrigued and took to his bed in order to puzzle over this cryptic message. The following night things became clearer. 'As I was going to bed, there came a command upon our lives that we should not stir out of doors. And presently I heard that the Dutch were upon their knees to the people.' Throwing on his clothes, 'I armed myself and went out among them, where I found the Dutch overcome with fear.' One of their colleagues had been shot in the leg while the others had been threatened with their lives.

If the situation on Ai was unsettled, on Neira it had

turned murderous. Verhoef had sailed to the island's eastern coastline in order to meet the native headmen, but when he stepped ashore he discovered that the headmen were nowhere to be found. This was strange. He had certainly got the right day and he knew for certain that this was the village where the two sides had agreed to meet. As he pondered what to do next, a lone native appeared from the woods and 'told the admiral that the orang-kayas, and other chiefs of the isles, were nearby in the woods but were so frightened by the soldiers that the admiral had with him that they feared to come unto him'. The native messenger asked Verhoef and his advisors if they would leave the soldiers and weapons on the beach and step into the woods for the meeting. Amazingly, Verhoef agreed and led the cream of the Dutch command into a deadly trap. 'And being entered among them he found the woods replenished with armed blackamoores, Bandanese, and orang-kayas who instantly encircled them and without much conference between them passed, were by them treacherously and villainously massacred.'

The last words Verhoef heard were those of his subordinate, Jan de Bruin, who cried in panic, 'Admiral, we are betrayed!' Defenceless and unarmed, there was nothing the men could do. All forty-two Dutchmen who entered the grove were butchered and their heads severed from their bodies. The Bandanese then attacked the soldiers on the beach before inciting a general uprising.

The Dutch now found themselves in a perilous position. An emergency council was summoned and elected a new leader, Simon Hoen, who hurried back to the half-built castle and urged his men to work even harder to complete the construction. Hoen did not waste any time in taking his revenge; the blood-flag was hoisted from his flagship and the Dutch made a formal declaration of war against Neira Island and began to 'execute and practise all revenge possible'. Villages were burned, vessels destroyed and natives butchered.

On 10 August 1609, a peace treaty was at last signed on board Hoen's flagship. This pact, agreed by only a handful of orang-kaya, stated that henceforth Neira Island was to be placed under Dutch dominion and 'to be kept by us forever' – the first territorial acquisition by the Dutch in the East Indies – while the rest of the islands were to suffer similar losses to their freedom. Furthermore, the headman was forced to 'sweare that they would thereafter have trade with none other nation whatsoever it were but sell all their nuts and mace to the Hollanders only'. Hoen sent a letter to Captain Keeling informing him of this fact and commanding him to sail from the Banda Isles within five days and never to return – the beginning of 'the warres betwixt the English and Dutch'.

Keeling, having suffered so many indignities at the hands of the Dutch, now felt he was in a position to act defiantly. He sent a reply stating that there was no question of him leaving the Banda Islands since he had just managed to procure a large batch of spices which would take a full twenty-five days to load on board. He also informed Hoen that he intended to leave a permanent English factory on Ai Island.

Keeling's bluff worked. He was well aware that 'oftentimes rash men threaten to kill which they durst not for life perform': so it was on this occasion. He loaded his spices in peace and, happy to bid farewell to the Banda Islands, set sail for England. At last, after months of hardship, he had time to perform some Shakespeare again.

CHAPTER SIX

A Rebel
at Sea

IN THE SUMMER OF 1558, almost five years after Sir Hugh
Willoughby's fateful expedition to the Arctic, a piece of
disconcerting news filtered into London. It was
rumoured that a resourceful young explorer from Brussels
called Oliver Brunel had travelled a considerable distance
along the northern shores of Russia and claimed he was on
the verge of discovering the North-East Passage. Confident
of success, he was now planning to board a Russian ship and
continue sailing until he reached the Spice Islands – a route
that would slash two thousand miles and more than a year's
sailing time off the long journey east.

This news was a cause of great anxiety to London's
merchants for Brunel's sympathies lay with the Dutch and
any discovery would be to their benefit. It was imperative
that Brunel's exploration should be stopped in its tracks
and, to this end, the merchants of the newly formed
Muscovy Company promptly denounced him to the
Russians as a spy and the unfortunate Brunel spent the next
twelve years in prison.

Lesser men might have found their enthusiasm for
foreign travel dampened by this experience. Not Brunel: no
sooner had he been released from jail than he set off
eastwards again, this time in the employ of the Strogonov
family. Exploring the ice-shattered coastline of Arctic

Russia, he compiled endless notes and charts and eventually returned to Holland to find a string of geographers waiting to meet him, including the distinguished Gerardus Mercator. Mercator was overjoyed to discover that Brunel brought the news he had been waiting so long to hear; for years a constant trickle of hearsay and rumour had reached both Amsterdam and London suggesting that there was indeed a navigable North-East Passage that led to the Spice Islands. Many of these stories were decades old, and even more were complete fiction, but each new finding saw geographers redrawing their charts of the Arctic, much of which remained a vast white blank known only as Terra Incognita.

What was particularly interesting about Brunel's findings was that he claimed to have reached the fabled River Ob which, it was believed, wound a golden route in the direction of the Indies. 'It is,' wrote one trader, 'a common received speech of the Russes that are great travellers, that beyond the Ob to the south-east there is a warm sea, which they express in these words in the Russe tongue: "Za Oby reca moria Templa;" that is to say, "beyond the River Ob is a warm sea." '

No one could be sure whether or not this was true and even Brunel had not managed to sail down the River Ob, but a persistent stream of rumours suggested that the Ob did indeed lead to the tropics. Certainly the dependable merchants of the newly formed Muscovy Company believed the stories and often added their own tales to the increasing dossier of evidence. Chief merchant Francis Cherry told his London bosses that he had eaten a sturgeon from the Ob; others, more tantalisingly, declared that they had seen 'great vessels, laden with rich and precious merchandise, brought down that great river by black or swart people'.

This caused great excitement among London's spice merchants; the more so when they learned that the people living on the shores of the Ob appeared to be of Chinese descent for 'whenever they make mention of the people named Carrah Colmak (this country is Cathay) they fetch deep sighs and, holding up their hands look to heaven signifying, as it were, and declaring the notable glory and magnificence of that nation.'

Despite all the evidence, the English were wary about furnishing a new expedition in search of the northern route to the 'spiceries'. A handful of bold adventurers continued to try their hand at sailing into the Arctic and an expedition despatched in 1580 managed to sail a considerable distance across the Kara Sea before finding its path blocked by pack-ice. But the mission was not a complete failure for the crew returned to England with a strange horn, some six feet long and decorated with a spiral twirl. Ignorant of the existence of the narwhal – that strange member of the whale family that has a single tusk protruding from its head – the rough English mariners confidently declared that this odd piece of flotsam had once belonged to a unicorn, a highly significant find, for 'knowing that unicorns are bred in the lands of Cathay, China and other Oriental Regions, [the sailors] fell into consideration that the same head was brought thither by the course of the sea, and that there must of necessity be a passage out of the said Oriental Ocean into our Septentrionall seas.'

The English were urged on in their Arctic endeavours by Samuel Purchas who called upon all intrepid and adventurous men to set sail in search of a passage, reminding them that their journey towards the 'spiceries' would shorten with every step they took towards the Pole, 'where that vast line at the Circumference itself becomes no line anymore, but a Point, but Nothing, but Vanitie'. Purchas's poetry failed to stir his English compatriots but his enthusiasm was echoed in Holland by the more practically minded Mercator who gave repeated assurances that Arctic exploration was not as dangerous as was commonly supposed. 'The voyage to Cathay by the east is doubtless very easy and short,' he wrote dismissively, 'and I have oftentimes marvelled that being so happily begun it hath been left off, and the course changed to the West, after more than half of the voyage was discovered.'

Advice of a more concrete sort came from Petrus Plancius, the man who would help to despatch the first Dutch expedition to the Indies in 1595 and who was as keen as ever on sending a fleet over the top of the North Pole. Arguing that fresh water froze more easily than salt, he maintained that the coastline of Russia was continually choked with ice because of all the water pouring into the sea from freshwater rivers such as the Ob. His advice to the Dutch explorers was to sail further north, away from the land, where they would find a sea completely free from ice.

In the wake of such demonstrable logic three fleets set sail in succession. The first, which left the Texel in 1594, was so confident of success that it carried letters in Arabic to be handed to the eastern potentates on arrival in the Spice Islands. Splitting into two groups, the first squadron was commanded by an accomplished mariner called William Barents who was destined to go down in history as one of the greatest of all polar explorers. But even his navigational skills were useless in the frozen wastes of the Arctic and it was not long before his ship reached a 'great store of ice, as much as they could descry out of the top, that lay like a plain field of ice'. He sailed more than fifteen hundred miles in search of a passage through this ice but was eventually forced to admit defeat.

Cornelis Nay, commander of the second group, was more fortunate. Sailing through the Strait of Vaygach to the south of Novaya Zemlya, he had a trouble-free passage into the Kara Sea and would have continued eastward if summer had not come to an abrupt end. He returned to Holland and boldly pronounced that he had discovered the North-East Passage, informing the Dutch merchants that it was 'ready-made and certaine'. Nay was fêted as a hero. Northern Russia was renamed New Holland, the Kara Sea became the New North Sea, and the Strait of Vaygach was rechristened Strait Nassau.

There was no time to lose for other nations, particularly the English, were certain to hear such momentous news. The following summer a second fleet was sent with the full expectation of it reaching the Spice Islands by Christmas. It was not to be. Strait Nassau was choked with ice and the New North Sea was frozen solid. Morale plummeted when two men, caught stealing pelts from natives, were disciplined in accordance with the rules of the ship. This involved being keel-hauled three times in a row – a brutal enough punishment in the warm waters of the Indies but even more dangerous when performed in the glacial Arctic. The first man had his head ripped off as he was pulled under the vessel. The second survived only to be cast ashore where he froze to death. A small mutiny followed, resulting in the hanging of five men, and by the time the expedition arrived back in Holland, the crew had lost their enthusiasm for their Arctic adventure.

The States of Holland and Zeeland decided to abandon the project, arguing that they had already spent a fortune on an increasingly futile venture. But the merchants of

The Dutchmen built a shelter and survived by eating bear-meat. One bear 'did us more hurt than her life, for after we ripped her belly we dressed her liver and ate it ... but it made us all sick.'

Amsterdam were undeterred by the repeated failures and promptly equipped a third fleet of two ships which set sail in the spring of 1596 under the overall command of William Barents, with Jacob van Heemskerck as captain. Trapped in ice somewhere to the north of Novaya Zemlya, the two men were convinced that their experience of Arctic climes would enable them to survive the winter. Building a temporary shelter out of logs and driftwood – a shelter so well constructed that it was still standing three centuries later when visited by Englishman Charles Gardiner – they hibernated for eight months. Good humour helped them win their battle for survival. In January they feasted on flour after crowning their ship's constable King of Novaya Zemlya whilst in February they shot a polar bear 'that gave us a hundred pounds of fat'. In June the ice at last began to thaw revealing that the ship had been crushed beyond repair. Two small craft were hastily built by the remaining survivors who were encouraged in their endeavours by the jocular Barents. Although desperately sick he kept everyone in good spirits: 'Our lives depend on it, boys,' he jested. 'If we cannot get the boats ready we shall have to die here as burghers of Novaya Zemlya.'

A few days later he expired, leaving Heemskerck to guide the little boats through the ice. Nearly two months passed before the survivors spied a Dutch ship close to the Kola Peninsula, which came to the rescue. When Heemskerck and his men eventually reached Holland and had an audience with their Amsterdam financiers they betrayed a considerable cynicism about any northern route to the Spice Islands. To reinforce the message that the North Pole was no place to go looking for spices, they pitched up at the meeting dressed in full Arctic clothing, including 'fur caps made of white foxes'.

With the failure of this third expedition, enthusiasm for the northern project waned. Although a prize of 25,000 guilders awaited anyone who did break through the ice, more than a decade was to pass before any ship, Dutch or English, ventured further east than the White Sea port of Archangel. The Reverend Purchas was distraught: 'That which I most grieve at,' he wrote, 'is the detention of further discovery of the Pole and beyond.' He believed that it was the duty of rich merchants to finance polar exploration, for 'they might get the world and give us the world better if Charitie were their Needle, Grace their Compasse, Heaven their Haven, and if they would take the height by observing the Sun of Righteousness in the

As the temperature plummeted, 'it froze so sore within the house that the walls and the roof thereof were frozen two fingers thick with ice.'

Scripture-astrolabe, and sounding their depth by a Leading Faith, and not by a leaden bottomless Covetousness.'

In 1608, word reached Purchas that an English explorer by the name of Henry Hudson had made two journeys northwards, setting sail with the intention of crossing the pole and continuing on to the 'islands of spicerie'. Although he had failed in both these aims he had covered considerable distances, touching land at Novaya Zemlya, Spitzbergen and even the eastern coastline of Greenland. But what really excited Purchas was that Hudson had travelled further north than any mariner before him; sailing, indeed, to within less than ten degrees of the Pole.

The London merchants expressed interest in Hudson's findings but were too preoccupied with bringing their ships home around the Cape of Good Hope to entertain the idea of equipping a new expedition to the north. Not so their Dutch counterparts; learning of Hudson's voyage and fearing that the North-East Passage might be discovered by their English rivals, they instructed their wise old consul in London, Emanuel van Meteren, to make contact with Hudson and bring him back to Holland.

Hudson arrived in Amsterdam in the winter of 1608 and was immediately granted an audience with the directors of the Dutch East India Company, to whom he presented his discoveries as the eighth wonder of the world. He told them of his conviction that there was an open sea at the North Pole, as Plancius had suggested, explaining that the further north he had sailed the warmer the climate became; and that instead of being confronted with ice and snow he had found land covered with grasses and wild flowers as well as many different species of animals living solely from the produce of the land.

The merchants were intrigued and asked Hudson why their own mariners had failed to find this temperate land. To this the English explorer had a ready explanation. In order to reach the mild climate of the North Pole, he said, it was necessary to push beyond 74 degrees latitude – the point at which the Dutch ships had always found their path blocked by ice – into the open sea where the great depth of the water and the swell of the waves prevented any ice from forming. Furthermore, he confidently asserted that if 83 degrees latitude was reached – somewhere to the north of Franz Josef Land – it would be possible to turn eastwards and break through to the warm seas of the East Indies.

Hudson's theory sounded plausible but the merchants had suffered so many failures in their Arctic exploits that they demanded further evidence. Summoning Petrus

Plancius to their meeting, they asked for his opinion of Hudson's findings. Not only did Plancius concur with every word, he actually reinforced the Englishman's claims with his own evidence. He argued that although the heat of the sun is extremely weak at the North Pole, the fact that it shines uninterrupted for almost five months of the year enables a permanent warmth to build up at the top of the world. To prove his point he reminded the directors that a small fire kept alight for a long time in the same place gives out considerably more heat than a large fire that is constantly extinguished.

The Amsterdam directors were impressed with this explanation but hesitated in equipping a fleet immediately, largely because Company rules dictated that an expedition to the Spice Islands could only set sail with the unanimous consent of the Council of Seventeen. Since that only met two or three times a year they would not be able to agree to any project until its next meeting which was scheduled for late spring 1609. Unfortunately this would be too late in the season to send an expedition across the Arctic, so Hudson would have to wait a further year before he could set sail.

This uncharacteristic hesitation nearly cost the directors dear. The charter of the Dutch East India Company gave them a monopoly on any trade passing by way of the Cape of Good Hope or the Magellan Straits, but there was no mention of any northern route to the Spice Islands, leaving the inescapable conclusion that if any dissident merchant were to go in search of the North-East Passage it would be beyond the power of the Seventeen to stop him. By the time Hudson visited Amsterdam just such a situation had arisen. Isaac Lemaire, one of the city's wealthiest merchants, had grown increasingly dissatisfied with what he considered to be Holland's overly cautious approach to trade and, in 1605, promptly withdrew his support. He was now their enemy, and a dangerous one at that, for he vowed to do everything in his power to undermine his former partners. When he heard that they had effectively turned down Hudson's proposal for an immediate voyage to the North he made contact with the English navigator and suggested the two men form a partnership. Lemaire had powerful backing: King Henry IV of France had watched with growing jealousy the Dutch ships sail up the Channel and was anxious to have his share of the riches of the East Indies. When he learned of Lemaire's rift with his erstwhile partners the King made contact with the Dutchman through his ambassador, Pierre Jeannin.

The ensuing negotiations had to be conducted in the utmost secrecy lest the Seventeen, who were 'fearful above all things of being forestalled in this design', should learn of the plan. A meeting was sought with Hudson, and the English explorer, irritated that the Seventeen were dragging their feet, placed his Arctic research at the disposal of the two men.

As soon as Jeannin had read these findings he wrote to the French King urging him to finance a Hudson-led expedition to the Arctic. He predicted that the return journey to the Spice Islands would take just six months, with the added advantage that not a single foreign carrack would be met en route. 'It is true,' wrote Jeannin, 'that the success of this undertaking cannot be promised with certainty, but Lemaire has long been making inquiries as to what results could be expected from this enterprise and he is regarded as a prudent and industrious man.' He added that 'it is the opinion of Plancius and other geographers that there are other lands which have not yet been discovered and which God may be reserving for the glory and advantage of other princes … Even if nothing should come of it, it will always be a laudable thing, and the regret will not be great since so little will be risked.'

The King acted promptly on receipt of this letter. Although sceptical about the project he was sufficiently enthused to send a draft for four thousand crowns. Unfortunately the money arrived too late. Learning of Lemaire's secret meetings with Hudson, the Seventeen urgently recalled the Englishman and this time acted swiftly. A contract was drawn up in which Hudson was named as captain of an expedition to discover the northern route to the Spice Islands and which included details of the route he was to take, the payment he would receive, and the obligations placed upon him. 'The above named Hudson shall about the first of April, sail, in order to search for a passage by the North, around by the North side of Nova Zembla, and shall continue thus along that parallel until he shall be able to sail Southward to the latitude of sixty degrees.' Throughout the voyage he was to 'obtain as much knowledge of the lands as can be done without any considerable loss of time and, if it is possible, return immediately in order to make a faithful report and relation of his voyage to the Directors, and to deliver over his journals, log-books and charts, together with an account of everything whatsoever which shall happen to him during the voyage without keeping anything back'. In return for his services, 'the Directors shall pay to the said Hudson … the sum of eight hundred guilders; and in case (which God prevent) he do not come back or arrive hereabouts within a year, the Directors shall further pay to his wife two hundred guilders in cash; and thereupon they shall not be further liable to him or his heirs.'

The contract throws light on the considerable risks that

explorers like Hudson were prepared to take. The vessel he was to sail in was tiny – sixty tons is scarcely bigger than a modern yacht – and poorly equipped for seas littered with icebergs. The financial reward, too, was paltry, whilst payment for any success was left entirely in the hands of his employers who 'will reward the before named Hudson for his dangers, trouble and knowledge in their discretion'. Nor was he offered any assurance of future employment; the contract was for a single exploratory voyage only. Even more surprising is that Hudson should agree to such a pitiful sum being paid to his wife in the event of him dying while at sea. Possibly he could not persuade the Seventeen to part with any more money, but more probably he had supreme confidence in his own abilities.

A curious set of additional instructions were handed to Hudson shortly before he set sail. These stated in even greater detail the route that he was to take and explicitly ordered him 'to think of discovering no other routes or passages, except the route around by the North and North-East above Nova Zembla'. Why the Seventeen added this last clause remains a mystery but perhaps, even now, they had an inkling that Hudson would ignore all their instructions once he had set sail. Certainly there was some disquiet about this headstrong Englishman for one of the Company letters, referring to a dispute over the crew's wages, states: 'If he begins to rebel here under our eyes what will he do if he is away from us?'

Subsequent events were to prove that they were right to be concerned about Hudson's behaviour and were fully justified in mistrusting his leadership. But what the Dutch merchants could never have imagined was that his 1609 voyage would have such a profound and lasting consequence on the spice race.

The *Half Moon* set sail in March of that year with a mixed crew of Dutch and English mariners. The vessel was built with a high forecastle and poop, and resembled in appearance the shallow-bottomed *vlie* boats used in the calm waters of the Zuider Zee. Few who watched its slow progress towards the North Sea, and fewer still among its crew, could have guessed that Hudson had no intention of sailing along the northern coastline of Russia; and that unbeknown to anyone he had set sail with his cabin piled high with charts and maps relating not to the North-East Passage, but to the North-West Passage, and it was this western waterway that he now wished to research.

Hudson's own account of the voyage has been lost but two contemporary journals have survived. One, written by Robert Juet, Hudson's mate, is a colourful and personal account of events on board; whilst the other, by Emanuel van Meteren, is drawn from conversations with Hudson's crew on their return. Juet provides little information about the early weeks of the voyage and records scant detail until the *Half Moon* had edged her way towards the Arctic pack-ice. He does mention a 'black fortnight' and refers to 'much trouble' although whether this is due to the crew or the 'close stormie weather, with much wind and snow', is not clear.

Emanuel van Meteren tells a more intriguing story. He relates that even in these early weeks there were bitter quarrels between the Dutch and English sailors and that some of the crew staged an abortive mutiny against their captain. The appalling weather only increased their discomfort for some of the Dutch crew were only recently returned from the Indies and were used to sailing in the languid heat of the tropics. Now they were heading into altogether colder climes where it was necessary to chip blocks of ice off the ropes before they could be hauled through the pulleys.

At exactly noon on 21 May 1609, the crew of the *Half Moon* were called on deck to watch something peculiar happening to the sun. 'We observed the sunne having a slake', says Juet, 'and found our height to be 70 degrees, 30 minutes.' The word 'slake' means 'an accumulation of mud or slime', suggesting that Juet was describing a sun spot. If so, this is the earliest recorded sighting, for the observation of astronomer Thomas Hariot – usually considered the first on record – was not until the winter of 1610.

Troubled by tempestuous winds and snow showers, as well as a rebellious crew, Hudson now decided to abandon his search for the North-East Passage and instead head westwards across the Atlantic. According to van Meteren, 'Master Hudson gave [the crew] their choice between two things': to head to the Spice Islands by way of the Davis Straits far to the north of Baffin Island, or to sail down the eastern seaboard of America until they reached the 40 degrees latitude at which point he hoped to force his passage through to the Pacific. This latter route, Hudson's preferred option, had been drawn to his attention by the English navigator George Weymouth who had explored America's eastern coastline in 1602 and 1605 and had, on at least one of these expeditions, reached the entrance to the Hudson River. Weymouth himself would have proceeded upstream had it not been for 'the imbecility of his crew' who forced him to return home.

How Weymouth's charts and maps came into Hudson's possession remains unclear. According to a Dutch account, 'the journals of George Weymouth, which fell into the hands of Domine P Plancius ... were of the greatest service to Hudson in his exploration of this famous strait, for in the year 1609, when he was negotiating with the Directors of the [Dutch East] India Company ... he begged these journals from D P Plancius.' This suggests that even as Hudson was signing up for an expedition to discover the North-East Passage, his real interest was in sailing westwards across the Atlantic.

A week after Hudson's crew had chosen the second option – an attempt on the supposed southerly passage – the *Half Moon* came in sight of the jagged silhouette of the Faroe Islands. Hudson had visited these islands before and knew they were a good place to revictual. Anchoring far from the shore for fear of the treacherous rocks and dangerous whirlpools, he sent a small party ashore to fill the ship's casks with fresh water. On 30 May 1609, the weather brightened and the crew caught a glimpse of the sun, prompting Hudson to lead all the men ashore for some exercise. Unfortunately Juet, keeper of the journal, stayed aboard so there is no record of what the sailors made of these primitive, cormorant-eating islanders who traded seal skins and still spoke a peculiar dialect of ancient Norse.

Setting sail once again they kept a sharp look-out for Busse Island, discovered thirty years previously by Martin Frobisher, but the rolling sea mists had grown too thick. Storms and gale-force winds plagued them for days on end and at one point grew so ferocious that the foremast cracked, splintered and was hurled into the sea. It was with considerable relief that the crew sighted through the mist the coast of Newfoundland – a vague geographical term in Hudson's day – at the beginning of July. They dropped anchor in Penobscot Bay, some one hundred miles west of Nova Scotia.

It was not long before the Indians on shore caught a glimpse of the vessel and, 'at ten of the clock, two boats came off to us, with six of the savages of the country, seeming glad of our coming. We gave them trifles, and they ate and drank with us; and told us that there were gold, silver and copper mines hard by us; and that the Frenchmen do trade with them; which is very likely, for one of them spoke some words of French.' The French, in fact, had been fishing these rich waters since the days of the Cabots and often ventured ashore to barter knives, hatchets and kettles for beaver skins and other furs. They must have treated the natives well for the *Half Moon* was given a warm welcome, a reception not reciprocated by Hudson's crew who headed ashore armed with muskets and stole one of the Indians' small boats. Realising that the Indians were powerless to defend themselves, they rowed ashore for a second time armed with 'two stone pieces or murderers', drove the 'savages' from their houses and 'took the spoil of them'.

Such barbarous and confrontational acts repeatedly stain the pages of Juet's journal. Throughout his account he views the native Indians – always described as 'savages' and usually treacherous ones at that – with a distrust approaching hatred and sees nothing untoward in firing at approaching canoes. What Hudson made of such behaviour can only be guessed at. His personality is shadowy in the extreme and much that is known of him is derived from the writings of others who usually bore a grudge against their captain. He was, perhaps, morose and suspicious, and quite possibly indulged his favourites at the expense of others, yet in the few surviving fragments of his own writings he always speaks kindly of the native Indians and appears to have held them in the highest respect. He and his crew seem to have disagreed entirely on how the Indians should be treated and while his personal acts of kindness to the natives were reciprocated with friendship, his crew's hostility was met with mistrust. Hudson's weakness was that he was unable to keep his subordinates under control, and it comes as no surprise that his eventual end, on his next voyage west, should be not at the hands of an irate Indian but of his own mutinous crew.

The *Half Moon* now headed south towards Cape Cod pausing briefly to allow a particularly jolly Indian to come on board, plying him with so much liquor that he 'leaped and danced and held up his hands'. As the ship passed the English colony of Virginia, the captain's cat mysteriously ran from one side of the ship to the other, wailing and mewling all night and causing considerable anxiety aboard.

Towards the end of August 1609, the *Half Moon* reached Cape Charles, the southernmost point of its voyage, and the men caught their first glimpse of Chesapeake Bay, 'a white sandy shore [which] sheweth full of bays and points'. From here they headed north once more and, two days later, reached Delaware Bay. They had now entered the region in which Hudson thought he might find the channel that would lead their ship to the Spice Islands and all the men were told to keep a watch for any inlet or estuary that looked promising. Juet climbed the mast several times to look for the elusive channel but each time he was disappointed. A forest fire broke the darkness on 2 September but the shoreline remained indistinct and even when the first rays of the sun rose above the horizon it was hard to chart the coastline for it was 'all like broken islands'. At last the light strengthened and Harbour Hill on Long Island hove into view followed, a few hours later, by the gleaming flats of Sandy Hook. When the *Half Moon* finally dropped anchor, Hudson found himself in 'a very good harbour, and four or five fathoms, two cables length from the shore'. According to American tradition, he had arrived at Coney Island at the mouth of the Hudson River.

★

Hudson was not the first explorer to discover the Hudson: that honour goes to Giovanni da Verrazano, a navigator in the service of the French King François I who had sailed into the natural harbour some eighty-five years earlier. Like Hudson, he was searching for a passage through to the Pacific and had also been struck by the natural beauty of the landscape. In a letter to the King he wrote that 'we found a very pleasant situation among some steep hills, through which a very large river, deep at its mouth, forced its way to the sea; from the sea to the estuary of the river, any ship heavily laden might pass, with the help of the tide, which rises eight feet.' Verrazano would have continued upstream had it not been for a 'violent contrary wind' which suddenly blew in from the sea and forced him to depart. 'I did not doubt that I should penetrate by some passage to the eastern ocean,' he recorded in his journal. It was this passage that Hudson now hoped to discover, a passage that would slash thousands of miles off the journey to the 'spiceries'.

After dropping anchor off Coney Island, Hudson sent a small party ashore on a reconnaissance mission. They returned with a band of curious natives who had watched with wide-eyed astonishment as the *Half Moon* had approached their island. Dressed in deer skins and proffering green tobacco, they expressed an interest in acquiring knives and glass beads. The following day the crew rowed ashore again though this time they headed towards either New Jersey or Staten Island. Here they were amazed by the 'very goodly oaks' that were 'of a height and thickness that one seldom beholds'. Indeed everywhere they landed they were astonished by the abundance of fruit that grew without cultivation: the blue plums, red and white vines, and whortleberries, not to mention the poplars, linden trees, 'and various other kinds of wood useful in ship building'.

So far the trigger-happy crew had been well received by the native Indians but they were soon to discover that their arrival was not everywhere greeted with the same enthusiasm. Hudson had sent Englishman John Coleman with a party of four others through the Narrows, and as the men chatted about the beauty of the landscape and savoured the 'very sweet smells' that came from the flowers on the foreshore, a hail of arrows descended without warning upon their boat, piercing Coleman's throat and killing him instantly. The others rowed desperately away from the shore but dusk descended before they could regain the *Half Moon* and they spent the rest of the night fighting the current with their grapnel and trying to stop their boat being dragged out to sea. It was not until ten o'clock in the morning when they finally rejoined the ship, and almost noon by the time they buried their colleague at Coleman's Point, close to Sandy Hook.

Incensed by the attack, and now fearful of stepping ashore, the crew weighed anchor and set sail up the Hudson River. On the way they bartered with the natives for provisions and even brought a small party of 'savages' aboard the *Half Moon*. This was not done in a spirit of friendliness: mindful of Sebastian Cabot's famous advice that 'if [a native] may be made drunk with your beer or wine you shall know the secrets of his heart', Hudson now plied his Indian guests with 'so much wine and aqua vitae that they were all merrie'. Unfortunately, they soon became so 'merrie' that they were unable to tell him anything about the supposed passage that led to the Indies and it was only with considerable difficulty that they managed to row back to the shore. But although Hudson learned nothing about the geography of the region from his impromptu drinks party, the gathering did help to restore relations between the crew and the natives and the next day saw the two groups once again bartering their goods. Continuing upstream the *Half Moon* soon arrived at 'that side of the river that is called Manna-hata'. Some six months after leaving Holland, and more than four thousand miles from where he was supposed to be, Hudson had arrived at the island of Manhattan.

Although most of Hudson's writings have been lost, a fragment of his journal was transcribed by a Dutch merchant called John de Laet. De Laet quotes Hudson's account of being paddled ashore by an elderly Indian, a passage that throws considerable light on the English captain's personality. There is none of the intolerance shown by Juet and his men. Instead, Hudson seems intrigued by the Indian customs and impressed by their kindness. 'I sailed to the shore in one of their canoes with an old man who was the chief of the tribe,' he writes, 'consisting of forty men and seventeen women; these I saw there in a house well constructed of oak bark, and circular in shape, so that it had the appearance of being well built, with an arched roof.' Hudson was surprised at the abundance of food, for the house 'contained a great quantity of maize or Indian corn, and beans of last year's growth, and there lay near the house for the purpose of drying, enough to load three ships, besides what was growing in the fields'. He was immediately made welcome by the Indians who, 'on our coming into the house, [spread] two mats ... and immediately some food was served in well made red wooden bowls'. It soon became apparent that Hudson was to partake in a lengthy feast:

Two men were also despatched at once with bows and arrows in quest of game, who soon after brought in a pair of pigeons which they had shot. They likewise killed a fat dog, and skinned it in great haste, with shells which they had got out of the water. They supposed that I would remain with them for the night, but I returned after a short time on board the ship.

The land is the finest for cultivation that I ever in my life set foot upon, and it also abounds in trees of every description. The natives are a very good people, for when they saw that I would not remain they supposed that I was afraid of their bows, and taking the arrows, they broke them in pieces and threw them into the fire.

The journals and letters written by men like Hudson and Juet, along with the accounts preserved by the English East India Company, form an invaluable record of the first European contact with native tribes. Much rarer are the records of what the natives thought of the unshaven English mariners who pitched up on their shores. Hudson's arrival at Manhattan is the exception, a result of the work undertaken by a diligent American missionary called Reverend John Heckewelder. In January 1801, almost two centuries after the *Half Moon* dropped anchor on Manhattan's western shoreline, Heckewelder wrote to a friend in Jerusalem explaining that he had spent several years working with native Indians and had struck up friendship with many of the chieftains. As he chatted about their early history he was surprised to learn that Hudson's arrival had long ago entered tribal lore. Learning that the story had been handed down from father to son, but was nowhere written down, Heckewelder reached for his notebook: 'A long time ago,' he wrote, 'when there was no such thing known to the Indians as people with a white skin, some Indians who had been out a-fishing … espied at a great distance something remarkably large swimming or floating on the water, and such as they had never seen before.' Immediately returning to their homes, the men gathered their bravest warriors and set out to discover what it might be. But the closer they got to this strange object, the more puzzled they became. 'Some concluded it either to be an uncommon large fish or other animal, while others were of opinion it must be some very large house. It was at length agreed among those who were spectators, that as this phenomenon moved towards the land, whether or not it was an animal, or anything that had life in it, it would be well to inform all the Indians on the inhabited islands of what they had seen and put them on their guard.'

The various chieftains duly arrived to discuss this strange object and there was a great deal of argument. At length they agreed that it was a giant canoe in which Mannitto, the Supreme Being, lived and that he was coming to pay them a visit. This sent the assembled crowds into a panic: men were sent to search for meat for a sacrifice, women were ordered to prepare fine victuals, idols were repaired and repainted and a grand dance was organised in order to please their god.

While preparations were under way, news arrived from the fleet of runners sent to monitor the floating object. Having observed it for some hours they confidently declared it to be a large house painted in different colours and filled with people. Not only were these of a different colour to them, but they wore peculiar garments around their bodies. The one dressed in red, they said, was Mannitto himself who was behaving in a most undignified manner, shouting and bawling to those on the shore and creating the most ungodly noise.

At length, Hudson came ashore with two colleagues and saluted the chieftains and wise men. The chieftains returned the salute, all the while studying this strange character and wondering what type of cloth would shimmer so brightly in the sunlight. (It was Hudson's lace ruff.) They watched in astonishment as Mannitto opened a bottle of pure alcohol, poured it into a glass beaker, and gulped down the lot. He then handed the bottle and glass to the nearest Indian chieftain and instructed him to drink.

'The chief receives the glass but only smells it, and passes it to the next chief who does the same. The glass thus passes through the circle without the contents being tasted by anyone; and is upon the point of being returned again to the red-clothed man when one of their number, a spirited man and great warrior, jumps up, harangues the assembly on the impropriety of returning the glass with the contents in it.' He argued that Mannitto had offered them the glass in the spirit of friendship and for the peace of their people, 'and that as no-one was willing to drink it he would, let the consequence be what it would. He then took the glass and bidding the assembly a farewell, drank it off. Every eye was fixed on their resolute companion to see what an effect this would have upon him, and he soon beginning to stagger about, and at last dropping to the ground, they bemoan him. He falls into a sleep, and they view him as expiring.'

But after a few minutes the man suddenly leaped to his feet and, to gasps of amazement from the crowd, declared that he had never felt so happy in all his life and demanded that he be given another glassful. 'His wish is granted, and the whole assembly soon join him, and become intoxicated.'

This last detail gives the story the ring of authenticity. Juet's journal frequently records how only a tiny quantity of alcohol was needed to get the Indians drunk, 'for they could not tell how to take it'; and tales of the drunkenness that greeted Hudson's arrival persisted among the native Indians until the last century. Indeed Heckewelder claims that the name Manhattan is derived from the drunkenness that took place there, since the Indian word *manahactanienk* means 'the island of general intoxication'.

When the Indians had sobered up Hudson stepped ashore once again to distribute beads, axes, hoes and stockings. The Indians were overjoyed with their presents although they had no idea of their use. It was a cause of much mirth when it was later discovered that they were wearing the axes and hoes as jewellery and using the stockings as tobacco pouches.

On 19 September 1609, the *Half Moon* continued its journey upstream in search of the passage that, it was hoped, would lead to the warm waters of the Pacific. Hudson anchored somewhere in the region of Albany and sent his Dutch mate and four others upstream in the ship's small boat. They returned at dusk bearing bad news. The channel narrowed and the water became shallow; it was clear to all on board that this mighty river did not lead to the spices of the East.

Their return journey was marred by a series of violent interludes. Dropping anchor 'down below the mountains', presumably the Highlands near Peekskill, Hudson's crew invited a band of natives on board and proudly showed off their weaponry. All was amicable until Juet spotted an Indian, who had been paddling his canoe around the stern of the ship, clamber onto the rudder and filch a pillow and two shirts from his cabin. The guns that had caused so much wonder were now demonstrated with deadly effect. Taking aim at the Indian, Juet blasted him in the chest, killing him instantly. His action caused a sudden panic and the Indians dived into the water, many of them still clutching items they hoped to buy, while the crew of the *Half Moon*, furious at losing their goods, jumped into their little boat and forcibly recovered their possessions, shooting several Indians in the process.

When all were back on ship, the *Half Moon* set sail down the Hudson with the ill-tempered Juet still fuming over the treachery of the natives. To assuage his anger he fired indiscriminately at Indians gathered on the banks of the river, noting in his diary whenever he had success. The gratuitous violence makes for distasteful reading: 'We discharged six muskets and killed two or three of them ... I shot a falcon at them, and killed two of them ... I shot at [a canoe], and shot it through, and killed one of them.'

The ship soon reached the mouth of the Hudson and, with clear weather and a blustery wind, 'we set our main sail, and sprit sail, and our top sails, and steered away.' Less than five weeks later they had recrossed the Atlantic and caught sight of the English coastline.

Had Hudson followed his instructions he should have continued up the Channel and not stopped until he reached Amsterdam. Instead, he dropped anchor in Dartmouth and sent notice to his Dutch employers informing them of his return. There was no mention of his travelling to Amsterdam; indeed his letter requested a further fifteen hundred florins to be forwarded to Dartmouth so that he could set sail once again, this time to explore the northern coastline of Newfoundland.

The Dutch directors were incensed by Hudson's behaviour and ordered him to return immediately. But the English government, hearing rumours that Hudson had actually discovered a passage through to the Spice Islands, issued an Order in Council accusing him of undertaking a voyage 'to the detriment of his own country', and forbidding him from leaving England. This proved too much for Emanuel van Meteren, the Dutch consul in London: 'Many persons thought it rather unfair that these sailors should have been prevented from laying their accounts and reports before their employers,' he wrote in his official report. In his private correspondence he was less diplomatic. 'The English,' he declared, 'are inconstant, rash, vainglorious, light and deceiving, and very suspicious, especially of foreigners whom they despise. They are full of courtly and affected manners and words, which they take for gentility, civility, and wisdom.'

Reports of Hudson's discovery of a 'groote noordt rivier' slowly filtered back to Holland where it was greeted with a mixed reception. Van Meteren himself was dismissive of the discovery, recording that the Englishman had merely stumbled across a river in Virginia; whilst others, though interested in Hudson's route down America's eastern seaboard, state that he 'achieved nothing memorable by this new way'. Nevertheless, wrote one, 'it was thought probable that the English themselves would send ships to Virginia to explore the aforesaid river.'

Although the Dutch East India Company showed little interest in Hudson's findings, a handful of individual merchants were intrigued to learn that 'the land is the finest for cultivation that I ever set foot upon', and extremely interested to read of the abundance of skins and furs. Less than a year after Hudson's return, 'some merchants again sent a ship thither, that is to say, to the second river discovered, which was called Manhattes.'

These merchants soon found that Hudson had not exaggerated the richness of the countryside around Manhattan. They informed the Indians that 'they would

Half a world away, Fort New Amsterdam on Manhattan Island was a carbon copy of Fort Belgica in the Banda Islands. Its capture by the English was a response to the 'inhuman proceedings' in the Spice Islands four decades previously.

visit them next year again' and would bring gifts and trinkets, but added that because 'they could not live without eating, that they should then want a little land of them to sow seeds in order to raise herbs to put in their broth.' Had the native Indians been able to foresee the future, they would not have been so obliging to these Dutch sailors. Within a few years the English and Dutch were squabbling over land rights and the Hollanders had built a couple of shacks on the island's southern tip. These would become a castle, then a town, and, within a decade, New Netherland. But little did anyone realise, least of all Hudson, that its future would be inextricably entwined with the nutmeg-producing Banda Islands.

CHAPTER SEVEN

THE CANNIBALS' COUNTRY

S CARCELY HAD WILLIAM KEELING sailed away from the Banda Islands in the autumn of 1609 than David Middleton arrived on his second voyage to the East. 'He passed us in the night,' noted Keeling with bitterness, 'else we should have surely seen him.' More than two years had passed since he had last spoken to his mercurial colleague and he must have been seriously wondering if he would ever hear from him again.

Middleton had made a brief stop at Bantam and learned from the English factors that the situation in the Banda Islands was not good. The Dutch were deadly serious about enforcing the treaty they had imposed on the islanders and were muttering dark threats about defending their monopoly at all costs. A governor had been left behind on Neira to monitor the coming and going of all shipping and a strong garrison posted in Fort Nassau to safeguard Dutch interests. Any vessel arriving at the Banda Islands was ordered to anchor close to the Dutch castle and submit to inspection, and no foreigner was allowed to settle without a Dutch permit. Even inter-island trade, upon which the survival of the outer islands depended, was forbidden unless authorised by the Dutch.

These laws and strictures sounded harsh but they proved

impossible to enforce and were soon being openly flouted by the Bandanese who realised that the Dutch were in a far weaker position than had first appeared. The fleet of ships commanded by Simon Hoen, Verhoef's replacement, had been plunged into chaos shortly after the imposition of the treaty and the morale of the crew had never been lower. Few showed any respect to their new master and when Hoen dropped dead, presumably from poison, his ship was left in the hands of an uncontrollable rabble. Life was little calmer on land where the garrison left to guard the Banda Islands found itself under a constant state of siege. There were numerous tales of 'the blacks killing divers Hollanders in a wood; of a kinde of siege of their castle; [of] bloody fight; the castle almost famished; all in the same yeere that this peace was concluded'.

News of the Dutch woes came as music to David Middleton's ears. Never short on confidence, he sped eastwards across the Java Sea and arrived at Neira displaying the 'flag and ensign, and at each yardarm a pendant, in as comely manner as we could devise'. To make his presence felt, he blasted every cannon and musket on board the *Expedition* and provocatively moored well within gunshot of the Dutch vessels riding at anchor.

The Dutch governor, Hendrik van Bergel, was infuriated by Middleton's effrontery and despatched a messenger to demand the reason for his coming. Ordered to surrender his commission from London, the English commander refused, consenting only to read the first paragraph to prove, as he put it, that he came as an authorised trader and not a pirate. When the messenger asked Middleton to clarify if he was a merchant or a man-of-war the English captain gave an equivocal answer, saying that 'I would pay for what I take' and 'defend my selfe' if attacked.

The Dutch retired to their castle to plan their response but Middleton had already won the war of words and the natives, who had watched the chicanery from the shore, rowed out to the *Expedition* to greet the English commander. Middleton was in his element and 'knowing well that in troubled waters it is good fishing', wasted no time in cultivating his friendship with the native merchants. Within a few days he had struck a profitable deal with a nutmeg trader from Ai Island who agreed to sell to the English all the spice he could gather.

Middleton could have saved himself any further argument with the Dutch by setting sail for this outlying island, but he was rather enjoying his new-found status as irritant and antagonist. Although warned by the Dutch governor not to remain anchored so close to their ships, he sent reply that 'I would ride there until I found the inconvenience [too great to bear] and then I would come into the best of the harbour.'

He then despatched a second letter informing van Bergel of the deal he had struck with the merchants of Ai and explaining that he was writing not out of courtesy but because he was keen to know whether the Dutch would be challenging him or not. After reminding the governor that both Ai and Run maintained their total independence from the Dutch (their headmen had steadfastly refused to sign the 1609 agreement), he insolently offered any assistance that the governor might require. 'If your worship stand in need of any thing that I have,' he wrote, 'I pray you make bold to demand it, and I will be as ready to perform it to my power.'

This last sentiment so angered van Bergel that he began to plot his revenge. The *Great Sunne*, a dilapidated Dutch vessel which was no longer seaworthy, was to be towed towards the *Expedition* under cover of darkness, chained to its hull, and 'there set her selfe a fire'. She was loaded with thirty kegs of gunpowder so it would not take long for the fire to spread to the English ship. As a precaution against failure, van Bergel suggested that the rest of his vessels spray the decks of the *Expedition* with musket shot.

Middleton's spies brought news of this plot and the English captain, never one to shy away from confrontation, 'thought it fit to goe and speake with the Governour my selfe, and before wee would try it with battaile, to see what hee would say to my selfe'. After all the bluffs and threats the two men met in Fort Nassau and were surprised to discover a mutual respect for each other. 'So there passed words between us, some sharpe and some sweet; but at the length they began to be more mild, and [the governor] called for a cup of wine, then the company rose all up, drank a cup of wine, and went to walke and to view the castle.' Having expected to be expelled after a fiery argument, Middleton ended the day examining suits of armour with van Bergel and discussing the varied merits of different types of musket.

With the hostilities postponed Middleton assured the governor that he did not wish to cause any trouble and, in return for the right to buy spices, offered a large sum of money 'which often maketh wise men blind'. The governor seemed genuinely sympathetic to Middleton's request but 'he told me plainly that he durst not give me leave to deal for any spice, under pain of losing his head.' When he heard this Middleton knew the time for talking was over. Although he left the castle in friendship and 'the governor caused all the ordnance to be shot off', he realised that buying spice would almost certainly lead to confrontation with the Dutch. This caused him not the slightest worry, but he was concerned that his men might not have the stomach for the fight. So, 'I called all my company to know their minds, and told them plainly that if they would stand by me, I meant to set up my rest, to make my voyage to those islands [Ai and Run], let the Hollander do what he could: and promised them that if any man were maimed, he should have maintenance during his life.' The men did not hesitate to place their trust in Middleton and shouted their assent to a man.

As they prepared to head for Ai, the wind suddenly changed direction and it proved impossible to sail west in the cumbersome *Expedition*. So Middleton sent his assistant, Augustus Spalding, in the ship's pinnace to establish a factory on the island while he and the rest of the crew set up base on the rugged island of Ceram, some one hundred miles to the north. From here they could run a shuttle of pinnaces to and from Ai, enabling Middleton to lade his ship with little danger of attack from the Dutch.

The strategy proved a great success. With Spalding successfully established on Ai, the little *Hopewell* plied its hazardous way to and from the island with its cargo of nutmeg and mace. It was wearisome work and Middleton cursed the Company directors who, although aware of the great difficulties of buying nutmeg, were as fussy as ever about what he spent their money on. 'Make choice of such nutmeg as be large and sound,' they had told him before he left London, 'and at the lading therof [do not] lime them too much, for that doth burn them.' They were no less concerned about his treatment of the mace. 'Lay [it] in cannisters in some fit place by itself so that it be not spoiled by the heat of the other spice, taking good heed to buy that which is bright, and not withered or red or dark brown.'

After making no fewer than nine exhausting trips in the

Hopewell Middleton needed a rest. Electing a new crew to man her – not an easy matter, for he was desperately short of men – he bid her God's speed as she sailed on her tenth journey. He fully expected her to be back within seven days, but a week passed, and then a fortnight, and still there was no news of the *Hopewell*. Each day Middleton scanned the horizon for the tiny craft until a third week had gone by and he decided to lead a search party, hoping to find her adrift in the treacherous currents that surround the Banda Islands. 'Having not a sound man with me that could stand on his legges, I hired three blacks and put to sea. Being out of sight of land, there arose a grievous storme that I was fain to spoone afore the sea, to save our lives.' Middleton was fortunate to be blown back towards Ceram, but with the velocity of the wind increasing by the hour he found it increasingly difficult to stop the boat being dragged onto the rocks. 'Night being at hand, we strove all we might to keepe her upon the sea till day, the storme increaseth, that no remedie but that we must hazzard all to put into the breach over a ledge of rockes. This we did, and no man durst forsake the boat for [fear of] being beaten to pieces against the rocks.'

All night Middleton and his 'blacks' fought to keep the skiff out of danger and when dawn broke they found they had been washed further along the coastline to a shallow bay where they could safely beach her. 'We laid hands on the boat and got her out of the suffe of the sea, and gave God thankes for preserving us from so apparant danger. Being extreme foule weather, with much raine, we could not tell what to doe.'

Middleton sent his men to reconnoitre the bay but they soon returned with grim news:

The Blacks told us that we must goe to sea presently
if we meant to save our lives. I asked one of them the
reason; who said, it was the canibals countrey, and if
they got sight of us they would kill us and eate us, and
nothing would ransome a man if they take him; and
all Christians that they get, they roast them alive for
the wrongs that the Portuguese have done them. And
therefore, if we would not goe to sea they would go
hide themselves; for the canibals would be at the
water side as soon as they can look about to descry if
they can discover any fishermen or passengers that by
stealth pass by in the night.

This news alarmed Middleton and he put to sea without
further ado. But his woes did not end with his escape from
the cannibals. An approaching rowing boat brought the
unwelcome news that the *Expedition* had broken its anchor
and was in danger of being washed onto the rocks. It was
imperative that Middleton return to the ship as soon as
possible in order to organise a rescue operation, but with
the wind blowing a gale the only way back was a twelve-
mile hike overland. The English captain and his guides were
almost half-way into their walk when they found their path
blocked by a great river. The guides made the unhappy
discovery that the river was full of alligators, but Middleton
was unconcerned by the danger, even when told 'that if I
saw any [alligator] I must fight with him or he would kill
me'. With this warning ringing in his ears he waded into
the water:

I being weary, not having slept in two nights, tooke
the water before the Indians, knowing they would
bee over before me. The river being broad and with a

swift current, which the great raine that had fallen had made, the Indians would have had me turn backe, but being the better halfe way, I was very unwilling.

[While] in the water, one of the Indians that carried my mandilion had got a great cane (which I knew not of) and strooke me on the side, who feeling the stroke, suspecting it had beene an alligata, dived under water where the current got such a hold on me that before I could come up I was in the sea; and there the sea threw me against the beach and bruised my backe and shoulder till the time that he came and gave me the end of the cane, whereof I got hold and he pulled me out, neere hand drowned, being tossed with the sea, that every suffe washed me into the sea againe.

Headhunters were greatly feared by the English mariners. 'They lay in the rivers on purpose to take off the heads of all they can overcome,' wrote one English factor of the dyak warriors.

Such dangers had a happy ending. Not only was the *Expedition* saved from the rocks but the *Hopewell*, which had now not been seen for a month, suddenly hove into view. She had, it transpired, been blown thirty leagues to the east of the Banda Islands in a terrible storm and it had taken more than a fortnight to bring her back to Ceram.

Middleton's success in buying spices had not escaped the notice of the Dutch. In his own words they were 'starke madde' from the moment he arrived in the Banda Islands, for the local traders had ferried all their available nutmeg over to Ai. This was all the more galling since two of their ships were only half laden with spice and required many more tons before they could sail for Holland.

The Bandanese had been encouraged by Middleton's presence and now rose up against the Dutch, massacring all who had the misfortune to be caught outside the walls of Fort Nassau. And, 'being fleshed with the slaughter of some of the straggling Hollanders which they had murdered, [they] took all the able men to give assault to the Hollander's castles; and determined to fire their ships.'

With the sound of musket fire ricocheting across the harbour, Middleton set sail for Bantam and home. His voyage had been a triumph, for against all the odds he had not only bought a massive quantity of nutmeg but also left the Dutch in an extremely vulnerable position. The Company directors were overjoyed and penned a letter to the Earl of Salisbury, Lord High Treasurer, drawing special attention to Middleton's guile and courage: 'Seeking trade at Banda . . . he was, with many reproachful and insolent speeches, forcibly put from all trading in those parts. What he got [was] with strong hand against their will, from other broken islands near adjoining, with extreme hazard and danger (they devising and oftentimes attempting to

The Dutch-built Fort Nassau on Neira Island. Built against the wishes of the native islanders, its construction led to a massacre of the entire Dutch high command. The Dutch, in return, began 'to execute and practise all revenge possible.'

surprise, consume by fire and cut off by any indirect means both ship, men and goods.)'

With a temporary power vacuum in the Banda Isles, the directors began once again to pore over their maps. It was the island of Run, some ten miles to the west of Great Banda, on which their eyes would eventually settle.

Although the return of Middleton's ship was a cause for great joy, the directors of the East India Company were concerned that their licence would be rescinded by King James I. Courtiers and rival merchants were constantly petitioning the King for their own trading licences arguing, like Edward Michelborne, that one company should not be allowed a total monopoly on trade. Queen Elizabeth I's licence had been for fifteen years and would soon expire. Sir Thomas Smythe, aware of the pressure that certain courtiers were placing on the King, decided that to exclude nobles from their enterprise was no longer advisable. Rallying King James's favourites to his cause, he now petitioned the King for a renewal of the Company's privileges, explaining the absolute necessity of retaining a monopoly on trade with the Indies. King James at length accepted their arguments, agreed to their demands and, instead of limiting his licence to a further fifteen years, he now granted them 'the whole, entire and only trade and traffic to the East Indies . . . forever'. There was just one proviso: if the trade 'should not prove profitable to the realm' the licence could be withdrawn, although even in this extreme situation the King would have to give the merchants three years notice.

Smythe and his directors were overjoyed at this extension of their privileges for it instilled a new-found confidence – and increased investment – in the spice trade. But the nobility, who had played such an important role in convincing the King to grant that extension, were not among those who would pour their money into future voyages. Reticent to sully their hands with trade, they preferred instead to be linked by association to this most fashionable of enterprises. It became de rigueur to be a freeman of the East India Company, a title which involved the participant swearing an absurd and solemn oath forbidding him from revealing 'the secrets and privities of the said Company, which shall be given you in charge by the Governor or his deputie to conceale'. It was a stroke of brilliance on the part of the directors, for aristocrats were soon queuing up to become members of what they excitedly saw as a semi-secret society. Acceptance went quite to the heads of some: the Earl of Southampton was so overjoyed when he heard he had been made a freeman that he sent a brace of bucks to the directors 'to make merry withal in regard to their kindness in accepting him of their Company'. The quick-thinking directors promptly formed a Venison Committee whose sole function was to provide the finest game for banquets at Sir Thomas Smythe's house.

With the King's signature safely on the charter the time was ripe for a new expedition. The Company beadle was sent around London to collect subscriptions and, on his return, it was found he had raised no less than £82,000. With such a vast sum at their disposal, the directors decided to build their own vessel rather than relying upon the inferior ships of previous voyages. At 1,100 tons this new ship was a veritable leviathan, more than double the size of the standard East Indiaman and not exceeded in tonnage until the era of steam. Such a ship could only be launched by the King and so, on 30 December 1609, James I, accompanied by the Queen and Prince Henry, travelled to Deptford for a right royal celebration. The ship was aptly named the *Trades Increase* and was to be accompanied by two smaller vessels – the *Peppercorn* and the *Darling*. The launch was followed by a triumphal banquet served on priceless China-ware and, as desserts were served, the King called Sir Thomas Smythe to his side and slipped 'a greate chaine of golde and a medal about his necke with his own hands'.

This marked the start of a constant flow of gifts between the King and the Company and when the sixth fleet finally set sail it was given instructions to 'carefully keep and reserve for his majesty and the lords all such rare fowles, beasts or other thing as are by you or any of your company brought from those parts'. Mindful, perhaps, of the problems caused by the morose Coree, all three captains studiously ignored these instructions.

The fleet was scheduled to depart London in the spring of 1610 and a rigid timetable was imposed on all involved to ensure it would leave on time. By November the Company was interviewing potential factors and crew, and it is in the list of these new recruits that the name of Nathaniel Courthope first appears. Nothing is known of Courthope's life prior to his joining the East India Company. It is quite possible that he had worked as a trader in London and, like so many of his fellow factors, was lured eastwards by the hope of making his fortune. He certainly made an impression on the sober-minded directors for on 13 November 1609, just five days after petitioning for employment, he was told that his application had been successful. Several of his fellow factors were hired on that same day: 'Benjamin Greene who speaks Spanish, French and Italian [and] Rowland Webb who speaks French and Spanish'. Of Courthope we are told only that the Company 'has an agreement with Nathaniel Courthope for seven years'; two years longer than the other men hired. These extra years were to prove highly significant and would, because of Courthope's bravery, mark a turning point in the history of the Spice Islands.

The fleet sailed in April 1610 under the command of the experienced Sir Henry Middleton with the equally skilful Nicholas Downton in charge of the *Darling*. The governors decided that the two men should head for the Banda Islands and cement the friendship with the native traders. Middleton was also instructed to exploit the anti-Dutch feeling by 'presenting such gifts to the Governor [of Banda] as in your discretion shall seem fitting; and there provide three hundred tons of nutmeg of the best and

soundest that may be gotten, freed from dust and rumps ...
also twenty tons of mace, the largest and brightest that may
be gotten, but none that is dark coloured red maces, which
are feminine maces and here little worth'. Having secured
his cargo, he was told to leave a large number of factors on
the islands – including Nathaniel Courthope – to prepare
for the arrival of future fleets.

Sir Henry was also requested to stop at numerous ports
en route, not to buy spices but to continue the search for
markets for England's 'wollen comodities' in order that 'we
may be able to drive a trade without the transportation of
money which is the cheefe scope of our desires.' It was this
desire that led Sir Henry, after a tiresome journey around
the Cape, to nudge his fleet towards the parched port of
Aden on the south-western tip of the Arabian Peninsula.

'Wednesday at sun-setting,' wrote Nicholas Downton in
his diary, 'on the sudden we descried Aden, which is
situated under the foot of an unfruitful mountain, a place I
should scarce have looked for a town, but it is set there for
strength, where it is very defencible, and not by any enemy
easily to be won.' The castle reminded him 'of the Tower of
London, which is not by enemies to be in haste ascended'.

Middleton, too, was impressed by Aden's fortifications
but was more concerned about the welcome he would
receive. This corner of Arabia was under the nominal rule
of the Ottoman Sultan, but most of the towns lay in the
hands of unscrupulous local governors, whilst the
mountainous interior had been carved into private
fiefdoms by warring Arab tribesmen. Stopping a local
craft, Middleton asked the Arabs on board whether the
local Pasha was a good man. Their reply was ominous
indeed. The last Pasha was 'very bad', the present was only
'a little better', and the Turks in general were 'stark

naught'. Middleton's mind was made up; instructing Downton to anchor the *Darling* off the coast of Aden, he decided to sail to the Red Sea port of Mocha and try his chances there.

It was a decision he would soon come to regret for as he edged the *Trades Increase* towards the town's harbour the enormous ship stuck fast on a sand bank and could not be moved. This put Middleton in a quandary; the only possibility of refloating her was to unload everything on board, but to land goods without an on-shore factory ran contrary to Company policy. Fortunately the local governor, a renegade Greek named Rejib Aga, was most obliging. When Middleton sent a message explaining that he was an English merchant in need of assistance he received answer that 'if we were Englishmen we were heartily welcome, and should not fail of that we look for.'

There was more good news to follow: Laurence Femell, the expedition's amply girthed chief factor, had struggled ashore in a rowing boat and managed to strike a beneficial trading deal with the governor. To celebrate this deal Rejib Aga invited Middleton to an extravagant banquet at which he heaped honour after honour upon the English commander, which an increasingly embarrassed Middleton felt obliged to accept. After being assured of 'good and peaceable trade', Sir Henry might have hoped that this exaggerated display of Oriental politesse was drawing to a close. In fact Rejib Aga had scarcely begun. After offering a waterfront house for the English to use as a base, 'he caused me to stand up, and one of his chiefe men put upon my backe a vest of crimson silke and silver, saying, I needed not to doubt of any evill; for that was the Grand Seignor's protection. After some few complements I took my leave: I was mounted upon a gallant horse with rich furniture, a great man leading my horse; and so in my new coate with the musicke of the towne, conveyed to the English house.'

The next few days passed most pleasantly. The Aga sent daily messages to Middleton 'willing me to be merry' and promising that as soon as Ramadan had come to an end the two men would ride together in his private pleasure gardens. Middleton's initial scepticism as to the Aga's sincerity evaporated with these sugar-coated pleasantries and – foolishly – he took the Aga's words at face value.

On 28 October 1610, he rowed ashore in order to stretch his legs and stroll around the town. It was a glorious evening; the sky had been cloudless all day and Middleton proceeded to the English house in order to watch the desert sun sink slowly into the Red Sea. 'The sunne being set I caused stooles to be set at the doore where my selfe, Master Femell and Master Pemberton sat to take the fresh aire, suspecting nothing of the present ensuing harm that did befalle us.' At eight o'clock a messenger arrived from the governor but because none of the Englishmen present spoke Arabic he was sent away. Soon after he returned with an interpreter who informed Middleton that Rejib Aga's message was simply that the English should make themselves merry. Taking the governor at his word Middleton uncorked a bottle of Madeira and handed it around to his friends, but they had scarcely had time to toast each other before there was a loud bang on the door: 'My man returnes in great feare telling us we were all betrayed: for that the Turkes and my people were by the eares at the backe of the house.' Middleton dashed inside to warn the crew of the danger and to urge them to fortify the house as quickly as possible:

But whiles I was thus speaking I was strooke upon the head downe to the ground by one which came

behind me. I remained as dead till such time as they
had bound my hands behind me, and so straite that
the extreame paine thereof brought me to my
memorie. As soone as they saw me stirre they lifted
me upon my feet, and led me betweene two of them
to the Aga, where I found divers of my companie in
like taking as I was my selfe. On the way the souldiers
pillaged me and tooke from me such money as I had
about me, and three gold rings, whereof one was my
seale, the other had seven diamonds which were of
good worth, and the third a gimmall ring.

This was only the beginning of his misfortune. When all the
Englishmen in the town had been captured, including
Nathaniel Courthope, they were herded together and
clapped in irons; 'my selfe with seven more were chained by
the neckes all together: others by their feete, others by their
hands.' When this was done, the soldiers left them in the
company of two heavily armed guards who 'had compassion
for us and eased us of our bands, for the most of us had our
hands so straite bound behind us that the blood was readie
to burst out at our fingers' end, with pain unsufferable'.

Middleton still had no idea why he had been attacked,
but he was soon to learn the scale of the Aga's treachery.
Not only had eight of his men been killed in the 'bloudie
massacre' and fourteen severely injured, he now heard that
a band of one hundred and fifty Turks had put to sea 'in
three great boats' with the intention of taking the *Darling* –
now anchored off Mocha – by force. The attack caught the
Darling's crew completely unawares. Knowing nothing of
the treachery ashore they first realised something was
amiss when dozens of Turks were seen boarding the ship,
their swords unsheathed. The situation quickly became

desperate; three Englishmen were killed outright while the rest of the company rushed below deck to gather their weapons. By the time they had armed themselves the ship was almost lost. 'The Turkes were standing very thicke in the waist [of the ship], hollowing and clanging their swords upon the decke.' It was a quick-thinking crew member who saved the day. Realising their plight was helpless he gathered his strength and rolled a huge barrel of gunpowder towards the Turkish attackers, then hurled a firebrand in the same direction. The effect was as dramatic as it was devastating. A large number of Turks were killed instantly while the rest retired to the half-deck in order to regroup. This hesitation cost them their lives for the English had by now loaded their weapons which they 'set off with musket shot, and entertayned [the Turks] with another trayne of powder which put them in such feare that they leaped into the sea, hanging by the ship's side, desiring mercy, which was not there to be found, for that our men killed all they could finde, and the rest were drowned, only one man was saved who hid himselfe till the furie was passed, who yielded and was received to mercie'.

The *Darling* had been saved but Middleton's situation was now even more precarious. Still chained by the neck he was led to the Aga to be told the reason for his arrest. 'He with a frowning (and not his wonted disembling) countenance, asked me how I durst be so bold as to come into this their port of Mocha, so near their holy citie of Mecca.' Middleton remonstrated most strongly, reminding the Aga that it was he who had invited the English to land and persistently invoked them to be merry. The Aga chose to ignore this last remark, telling him that the Pasha in Sana'a had been given orders from the Sultan in Constantinople to arrest all Christians who attempted to land at any of the Red Sea ports. He also told Sir Henry that the only way for him to gain his freedom was for him to send letters to the *Trades Increase* and *Darling* ordering them to capitulate. Middleton refused, and when the Aga told him he would starve the ships into submission the English commander gleefully informed Rejib that they had enough supplies to last two years. 'He urged me againe to write to will them to come all ashore and yeeld the ship or he would cut off my head. I bade him doe so; for therein he should doe me a great pleasure for I was weary of my life; but write to that effect I never would.'

This answer did not find favour with the Aga. 'I was taken out of my chaine and coller and a great paire of fetters clapt upon my legges, and manacles upon my hands, and so separated from the rest of my company: they stowed me all that day in a dirty dogges kennell under a paire of stairs . . . my lodging was upon the hard ground, and my pillow a stone, my companions to keepe me waking were griefe of heart and multitude of rats which, if I chanced to sleep, would awake me with running over me.'

Sir Henry would soon find himself longing for that 'dogges kennell'. The Aga instructed him to send a letter to the *Trades Increase* with the message that all the warm clothing on board should immediately be sent ashore. Middleton was perplexed and, asking the reason for such a strange request, was told that the Pasha in Sana'a wanted to interrogate the men and 'that we should find it very cold in the mountain country'. Middleton, sweltering in the heat of Mocha, scoffed at the Aga's talk of frost and snow and dismissed the request for woollen clothing. And so, on 'the two and twentieth of December, our irons were knockt off all our legges . . . and my selfe and foure and thirtie persons more of us were appointed to goe up for

Sana'a, the chief citie of the kingdome where the Pasha is resident.'

One of the men, William Pemberton, managed to give his guards the slip and it was many hours before his absence was noticed. He eventually reached the *Trades Increase* by trekking back to the coast, stealing a canoe and putting to sea. With no food and nothing to drink except his own urine he rowed for several days through choppy waters until a look-out on the flagship spied him in the far distance and sent a pinnace to the rescue. His arrival was invaluable to Downton for it provided him with information about the guards and sentries travelling with Middleton and enabled him to carry on a regular, though clandestine, correspondence with the commander using secret envoys and middlemen. Pemberton twice sent letters to Middleton urging him to plan an escape, suggesting that he could easily pass himself off as an Arab if he disguised himself in Oriental dress, cut the hair from his face, and took to 'besmutting' his skin. He added that he had fully intended to 'besmut' himself but decided that his 'pock-eated' face would have given him away.

The correspondence between Downton and Middleton at times betrays the great stress they were under. When Middleton refused permission for Downton to raid local craft on the grounds that his life would be placed in even graver danger, Downton wrote a strongly worded reply suggesting that he alone could judge what was best in the situation. Sir Henry was most upset at the petulance of his erstwhile friend and replied in what Downton described as 'a very carping and most distasteful letter'. But just as relations between the men seemed in danger of rupturing completely, Downton came to his senses and sent a note with the message that while he was hurt by the tone of

Middleton's letter he would write no more angry words for their mutual enemies to 'cant, construe and cavil at'. In reply, Sir Henry wrote a 'very kind letter' asking forgiveness for his 'melancholie letter' which, he explained, was written while suffering from acute depression.

That depression was soon to get worse as the weather grew ever colder during the enforced march to Sana'a. Middleton now realised his mistake in refusing the woollen gowns, recording that 'I would not beleeve at Mocha, when I was told of the cold we should have upwards, and that made me go but thinly clothed my selfe.' With the little money he still possessed he now bought his men fur gowns, without which they would all have perished. Few can have expected to see a white Christmas in the blistering Arabian Peninsula but as the English prisoners stumbled into the city of Taiz on Christmas Day 1610, the first few flakes of snow began to fall. William Pemberton's 'boy', who had failed to escape with his master, fell sick from cold and was lodged in the governor's house; the rest continued up into the mountains where 'every morning the ground was covered with horie frost, and . . . we had ice a finger thick.'

At last they came to Sana'a, 'a citie somewhat bigger than Bristol,' where their fur gowns were confiscated and they were forced to march barefoot through the city like common criminals. Middleton was in no mood for diplomacy. Dragged by 'two great men' to an audience with the Pasha he gave vent to his fury, accusing Rejib Aga of duplicity, falsehood and murder. The Pasha listened 'with frowning and angry countenance', blamed Sir Henry for causing him numerous problems, then led the Englishmen to a common prison where they were once again 'clapt in waightie irons'.

They had spent almost a month in jail when the Pasha suddenly called Sir Henry into his presence and told him that all the men would be released without delay and were free to return to Mocha. What induced the Pasha's sudden clemency is far from clear but it was rumoured that an influential merchant from Cairo, to whom the Pasha was indebted, had intervened on behalf of the Englishmen. Their release came just in time, for 'many of our people in the meane while fell sicke and weake through griefe, cold, naughtie aire, bad diet, evill lodging, and waightie irons.'

The chameleon-like Pasha now transformed himself into a kindly and avuncular figure, providing the men with a large mansion, suggesting a tour of the city's sights, and even presenting them with six cows on which to feast themselves. Middleton was singled out for special treatment, receiving a purse of 150 gold coins as recompense for his sufferings. In return he was obliged to listen to one of the Pasha's insufferable speeches in which he gave fulsome praise to his own wisdom, insight and mild temper. The English commander was bemused by the turn of events but not altogether surprised; he was fast learning of the inconstancies of these Turkish governors who could flick from friend to foe without even losing their smile.

In mid-February the men at last left Sana'a for the long march back to Mocha. Middleton still had niggling doubts as to the Pasha's sincerity but any fears about returning to Mocha were dispelled when he was told that 'if Rejib Aga wrong you I will pull his skinne over his eares and give you his head.' On their arrival at Taiz, the men hoped to recover Mr Pemberton's boy who had been lodged with the town's governor since collapsing through weakness. But herein lay a problem: 'the governor, Hamet Aga, had forced him to turne Turke, and would by no meanes part with him.' The poor boy had suffered a terrible ordeal during his weeks with the governor: when he refused to convert to Islam, 'some of the Aga's servants [carried] him to a hot-house where they had him naked circumcised perforce.' The governor steadfastly refused to give up his boy and the Englishmen had no option but to continue without him, but Middleton, to his great credit, never forgot the boy and refused to sail from Arabia until he had been released.

On his arrival in Mocha, Middleton was taken straight to the Aga who 'received me after his wonted dissembled shew of love and kindnesse, bidding me and the rest welcome, saying he was glad of our returne safe, and sorrie and ashamed of what was passed, and prayed me to pardon him'. But long before the Englishmen were able to return to their ship they found themselves marched to a 'great strong house' and once again placed under armed guard. Sir Henry's suspicions had proved all too correct and he now knew that escape was his only option. His plan was a simple one: under cover of darkness he sent a letter to the *Trades Increase* asking that a bottle of aqua vitae be smuggled into the prison. With this he planned to get his guards drunk, steal their keys and, aware that his face was well known throughout the town, hide himself in an empty barrel and get his men to roll him down to the beach.

The hour at last arrived. The aqua vitae was successfully smuggled into prison and a boat surreptitiously moored on the southern edge of town. When the guards saw they were being offered alcohol they were unable to refuse and 'fell to drinking hard'. By noon everything was ready: 'the boat being come, and keepers all drunk, and all things fitted ... I began to put my business in execution.' Unlocking the door to their 'strong house', Sir Henry popped into a barrel as planned and was rolled down to the beach where he

clambered into the waiting boat and rowed across to the
Darling which was riding at anchor.

Not everyone had been so lucky: the ships' armourer,
Thomas Eves, was so fearful of being recaptured that he
'took off his shoes and ran through the streets with all the
speed he could, whereupon all the towne rise after him'. It
was only a matter of minutes before Mocha was crowded
with soldiers who, one by one, picked up the sick and
wounded. Lawrence Femell soon found himself in
difficulty. Unable to run because of his 'unwieldy fatness' he
was hounded by a band of troops as he waddled down to
the waterfront. He 'discharged a pistoll in the face of one
of them that pursued him, and mortally wounded him' but
was eventually captured while up to his armpits in water.
He later blamed 'the foolish dealing of that idiot and white-
livered fellow the coxswain who, we being in the water . . .
fell to leeward of us'. The capture of Femell was a setback, but Middleton was safe and after offering his thanks
to God 'for his great mercy towards us' he joined the
celebrations on board the English vessels.

He was now in a strong position to gain the freedom of
Master Femell, Nathaniel Courthope and the other men,
including poor Mr Pemberton's boy who was still
incarcerated in Taiz. Sending a letter to Rejib Aga, he
bragged of his powerful cannon and threatened that unless
all the men were immediately released he would sink
every ship that entered the port 'and do my best to batter
the towne about his ears'. He also wrote a reassuring letter
to Femell repeating the threat and adding that 'if I shoot at
the town he saith he will requite me with the like, which
he cannot do as you well know for his ordnance is far
inferior to mine . . . Though I should fire the town and
beat it smooth about their ears, whether it be pleasing or

displeasing to the Grand Seignor I care not, [for] I am out
of reach of his long sword . . . let the Pasha and Regib Aga
likewise consider that the King of England will not take
well the betraying, robbing and murdering of his subjects.'

The Aga stalled for time but after his port had been
blockaded for a month he was forced to 'sing a new song'
and all the men were released. Master Femell did not, alas,
enjoy his freedom for long; three days after coming aboard
'at about two of the clock in the morning he ended his life,
as we thought, by poison.' He had bragged once too often
about the power of the English and the enraged Aga,
knowing that the chief factor never turned down a meal,
had dosed his food with delayed-action poison.

With the safe return of Mr Pemberton's boy everyone
still alive was back on board. The sixth fleet of the East
India Company could at long last continue on its voyage to
the Banda Islands.

It was now August 1611, and the fleet which had set sail
with such high expectations some sixteen months
previously had so far accomplished nothing. If the crew
were dispirited by their misfortunes the captains were even
more depressed. A rare insight into this depression has
survived in the form of a private memo that Downton
penned at the height of the troubles; a memo given added
poignancy by the fact that its tone so belies the brave
good-humour that Downton struggled to present to his
crew. In private he was 'environed with swarms of
perplexed thoughts' that now, 'after two years travel [we
find] our victuals spent, our ships, cables and furniture far
worn, men's wages for 24 months already passed, ourselves
deluded and abused in most places we have come . . ..
Whether we wish a languishing end, or a shameful return,

God only direct, for our counsel is weak and our case doubtful.'

Before sailing from Mocha the two captains took stock of the situation. Their overriding duty was to sail to the Banda Islands to buy nutmeg and mace, but their instructions from the Company allowed them to sail first to India to discover how William Hawkins was faring at the court of Jehangir. They chose this latter option and headed for Surat, but when Middleton learned that trade had been denied he once again put to sea, taking Hawkins with him. Fuming at Jehangir's intransigence, the commander decided

The Indian Great Moghul, Jehangir, struck up friendship with English sailor William Hawkins. A capricious alcoholic, he forced Hawkins to watch gruesome gladiator fights.

to sail back to the Red Sea and there compel the Indian dhows to sell their cottons to the English. The benefits would be threefold: the Aga in Mocha would be infuriated by the loss of trade, the Indians would be roundly punished and Middleton would acquire the calicoes he so desperately needed to exchange for nutmeg and mace.

It was unfortunate that just as Middleton's ships were setting up their blockade of the Bab-el-Mandeb, the entrance to the Red Sea, John Saris, commander of the East India Company's seventh fleet, was nudging his way towards Mocha. Saris brought with him a letter of recommendation from the Sultan in Constantinople and, ignoring Middleton's warnings about trade with the Arabs, he sailed gaily into the harbour at Mocha. Lavishly entertained by the new Aga – Rejib had since been dismissed – he struck a deal and sent a mission to Sana'a to pay its respects to the Pasha.

When the Aga learned that Middleton was 'rommaging' ships from India he was incensed and immediately annulled the trading deal he had granted to Saris. The English captain protested in the strongest terms and offered repeated assurances that he was not in league with Middleton, but the Aga refused to believe such a story. Saris now turned his fury on Middleton, boarding the *Trades Increase* and berating Sir Henry for his stupidity. He vowed to do everything in his power to break Middleton's blockade, 'wherat Sir Henry swore most deeply that if I did take that course he would sink me and set fire of all such ships as traded with me'. What followed was an explosive row in which the two commanders 'used very grosse speeches not fitting to men of their ranks, and were so crosse the one to the other as if they had been enemies.'

The two men did eventually strike a deal in which they

shared the spoils of the 'rommaging', but Saris's heart was not in the work and he soon set sail for Bantam without paying Middleton the usual compliment of a parting salute. Sir Henry was as angry as he was upset. Realising that his policy of harming the Aga was futile he sailed for Sumatra and Java, finally anchoring in the great harbour at Bantam. Here the East India Company's sixth fleet, which had set out with such high hopes, floundered in the malarial shallows. The *Trades Increase* was discovered to be riddled with teredos (shipworm) and no longer seaworthy, while the crew had fared little better: dozens succumbed to typhoid, dysentery and malaria and died on board their rotting flagship.

'I saluted them with three peeces,' wrote John Jourdain, a merchant on the next English ship to arrive in the Indies, 'but noe awnswere nor signe of English coulours, neither from the shipp nor from the towne.' Suspecting that the ship had been captured by locals, 'I shott annother peece ... with determination nott to go a land untill I had certaine notice from thence.' At length Jourdain 'perceived a prow cominge from the shore, wherein came Edward Langley, Christopher Luther, Nathaniel Courthope, and Thomas Harwood, all of them like ghostes or men fraighted. I demanded for the Generall and the rest of our freindes in particuler; [but] I could not name any man of noate but was dead to the number of 140 persons; and the rest which were remayneinge, as well aland and aboard the Trade, weare all sicke, these four persons beinge the strongest of them, whoe were scarce able to goe on their leggs.'

Most of the men were in the final stages of illness. Middleton himself was dead – some said of a broken heart over the loss of his ship – and the *Trades Increase* had miserably failed to live up to her name. Of her last days a merchant named Peter Floris wrote: 'She was lying on the ground without mast, with three and thirtie men, the greatest part sicke, the ship being sheathed on one side and not on the other. In her had deceased one hundred English and more Chinese which wrought for wages, and eight Dutch by some strange sicknesse.' Her final demise came all too soon; a renegade Spaniard set fire to her timbers and the once-great vessel, pride of the East India Company, was rapidly reduced to ash.

The *Darling* had not fared much better; on arrival at Patani on the Malay Peninsula she was inspected and considered to be in too poor a condition to sail back to England. She would end her days shuttling factors to and from the islands of the East Indies. Only the *Peppercorn* survived the long voyage home, but even she was unable to reach London and Downton suffered the ignominious fate of having to hire a Frenchman to tow her into Waterford in Ireland. There was no triumphal welcome and none of the crowds that had cheered her off three and a half years before. Instead, Downton stepped onto dry land in October 1613, only to find himself arrested and charged with piracy for his part in the Red Sea 'rommaging'. He was eventually released, but it did little to boost his morale and his diary ends in a mood of black despair. 'And so concluded,' he wrote, 'this tedious and out-tyring journey.'

CHAPTER EIGHT

THE BANNER
OF
SAINT GEORGE

FOUR MONTHS BEFORE THE *Trades Increase* had sailed from London, the governor of the East India Company, Sir Thomas Smythe, renewed his acquaintance with Henry Hudson. Smythe was in ebullient mood, for confidence in the spice trade had never been higher and with the successful return of William Keeling, large sums of money were pouring into the East India Company coffers.

He had long been considering financing a new voyage of exploration to the Arctic and, just a few months previously, had reminded his committee 'that three yeares since, this Companie did adventure £300 per annum for three yeares towards the discovery of the North-West Passage' – money that remained unspent. These were not the only funds at his disposal: Sir Thomas was also governor of the Muscovy Company whose merchants were growing increasingly enthusiastic about searching for a northern route to the Indies.

Two other men of importance attended the meeting between Smythe and Hudson. Sir Dudley Digges was a wealthy individual who would shortly write a book entitled *Of the Circumference of the Earth, or a Treatise of the North-West*

Sir Thomas Smythe, the first governor of the East India Company, was instrumental in ensuring the success of James Lancaster's pioneering expedition to the East.

Passage, a turgid piece of prose that led one critic to remark that 'many of his good friends say he had better have given four hundred pounds than have published such a pamphlet.' Nevertheless, Digges harboured a passion for discovery and was in possession of a large enough fortune to indulge that passion. The third man at the meeting was John Wolstenholme, Farmer of Customs, who also had a long record of promoting voyages to unknown lands.

All three had studied Hudson's reports of the area around Manhattan and accepted that the mighty river did not lead through to the Pacific Ocean. But there was one last region of North America that held the possibility of a North-West Passage to the Spice Islands – the mysterious 'furious overfall' described by John Davis. This treacherous passage of water, later known as Hudson Strait, had been attempted by many adventurers (George Weymouth was so confident of reaching China via this route that he carried a preacher equipped for converting the heathen spice traders) and although none had been successful in their quest, most had returned with tales of its certain existence.

With permission from King James sought and gained, Hudson set sail in April 1610 on a mission 'to search and find out a passage by the north-west of America to the sea of Sur, comonly called the South Sea [intending] to advance a trade' to the spice-producing islands of the East Indies. His voyage through the 'furious overfall' was one of the utmost difficulty for spring had yet to arrive and the water was choked with icebergs. Many of the less-experienced crew members began to fear for their lives while the sour-minded Robert Juet, who had accompanied Hudson on his previous voyage, jeered at his hope 'of seeing Bantam by Candlemasse'. The captain was determined to prove Juet wrong and, as he steered the ship into Hudson Bay, pronounced himself 'confidently proud that he had won the passage'. But as the first snows began to fall and the men were forced to winter in desolate James Bay, their enthusiasm plummeted and a handful of conspirators began to whisper of mutiny. 'It was darke,' wrote crew member Abacuk Prickett, 'and they in readinesse to put this deed of darknesse in execution ... Now every man would go to his rest, but wickednesse sleepeth not.'

Stepping out of his cabin, Hudson found himself seized by two men, pinioned with a rope, and cast into the ship's shallop along with seven of his closest supporters. The mutineers then cut the cable and put up the sails, leaving Hudson and his company 'without food, drink, fire, clothing or other necessaries'. As their little boat drifted off into the night, any lingering hopes of discovering a North-West Passage to the Spice Islands seemed to have died and Hudson, one of the great Arctic explorers, was never seen again.

He was destined not to be forgotten, for some seven years after being cast adrift a spirited captain by the name of Thomas Dermer began a detailed study of all the material relating to Hudson's earlier voyages. Dermer had been obsessed since childhood with discovering a quick route to the 'spiceries' and, after scouring the explorer's charts, plans and journals, he confidently declared that the elusive passage did indeed lie in the region around Manhattan. How he reached this decision remains uncertain, but he had sufficient evidence to persuade his financiers and, soon afterwards, he set off on the first of two voyages to the Hudson.

Sailing through Long Island Sound and its ever-narrowing inlet, Dermer passed into Upper Bay where he rowed ashore and got into conversation with a group of

Indians. To his immense satisfaction these men confirmed everything that Dermer had earlier argued. 'In this place,' he wrote excitedly, 'I talked with many savages who told me of two sundry passages to the great sea on the west [coast of America], offered me pilots, and one of them drew me a plot with chalke upon a chest.' The good news was tempered by bad: 'they report one [passage] scarce passable for shoalds, perillous currents; the other no question to be made of.'

Dermer was not prepared to allow their warning to dampen his enthusiasm and, excited about the imminent fulfilment of his life's dream, 'hastened to the place of greatest hope, where I purposed to make triall of God's goodnesse towards us, and use my best endeavour to bring the truth to light'. But no sooner had he reached the 'passage' than the wind whipped up a storm and forced him to turn and flee, 'hardly escaping with our lives'.

Despite this temporary setback, Dermer was thrilled with his discovery and dashed off a letter to Samuel Purchas informing him of the historic news. He even drew a map of the passage, 'yet dare not part with it for feare of danger. Let this [letter] therefore serve for confirmation of your hopes.' Purchas was sufficiently impressed to include the letter in his anthology of exploration, but Dermer's financiers in England were decidedly sceptical about the 'discoveries' of their quixotic adventurer and promptly recalled him to England. Dermer refused, 'resolutely resolving to pursue the ends he aymed at'.

As he sailed towards the mouth of the Hudson on his second attempt, Dermer was surprised to see 'divers ships of Amsterdam and Horna who yearly had there a great and rich trade'. He was even more perturbed to find 'some Hollanders that were settled in a place we call Hudson's River, in trade with the natives'. Curtly informing them that the land belonged to England, Dermer 'forbad them the place, as being by his Majestie appointed to us'. The Dutchmen apologised for their mistake and told him they sincerely hoped 'they had not offended'. Nevertheless, they made no effort to move themselves elsewhere, for the trade in beaver pelts was more profitable here than anywhere else on the coastline.

The news that the Dutch were settling the land around Manhattan aroused considerably more interest in England than had Dermer's supposed discovery of the North-West Passage. King James was already fuming at the belligerence of the Dutch in the 'spiceries' and was determined to prevent them from repeating their successes in America. As far as he was concerned, the American coastline belonged to him by virtue of the discoveries of John and Sebastian Cabot who had sailed in the service of King Henry VII more than a century previously. Although neither one of this intrepid duo had staked England's claim to the land, Queen Elizabeth I had later argued that merely setting foot in America implied sovereignty, a view championed by Richard Hakluyt, author of *The Principall Navigations*.

Despite this, England's merchants had been far too preoccupied with the spice race to show much interest in settling the American seaboard and it was not until 1606 that an ambitious merchant called Sir Ferdinando Gordes petitioned King James for a charter for two new companies, one based in London and one in Plymouth. These were given the right to plant colonies 'in that part of America commonly called Virginia', but were ordered to remain one hundred miles apart, a fatal decision, for it was into this gap – in the Hudson River region – that the Dutch had neatly staked their claim.

When the King learned of the Dutch settlements he

granted Sir Ferdinando a much larger swathe of land which made him the proprietor of a huge region that stretched from the Hudson to the St Lawrence. Although forbidden from seizing any land already belonging to any Christian prince, the charter noted that King James was of the opinion that no prince was in possession of this stretch of land 'by any authority from their sovereigns, lords, or princes'.

With Manhattan and the Hudson River now safely placed under English jurisdiction – on paper at least – King James wrote to his ambassador in Holland, Sir Dudley Carleton, asking him to investigate whether or not the Hollanders had indeed planted colonies and were in the process of sending vessels to supply them. Sir Dudley, who had spent years arguing with the Dutch over their claims to the Spice Islands, wrote back with the alarming news that the Amsterdam merchants did indeed have a regular trade with the land around Manhattan and 'kept factors there continually resident'. But he added that stories of a Dutch colony had been somewhat overblown and rejected claims that one had been 'either already planted or so much as intended'. The King nevertheless insisted that Sir Dudley register a formal complaint to the effect that, 'the King's government has lately been informed that the Hollanders have planted a colony in these regions, and renamed the ports and harbours, as is their fashion'.

The King was, in fact, wrong to draw a parallel between the traders in Manhattan and those in the 'spiceries', an ironic mistake given the future destiny of these islands. Although a handful of Dutchmen were indeed living in wooden shacks in the Hudson River area – they had arrived in 1611, soon after Hudson's report of a rich and fertile land reached their ears – they would hardly have labelled themselves colonists for they only remained on land for as long as it took to barter their trinkets for the beaver pelts that were in such plentiful supply. Like nutmeg and mace, these pelts fetched astronomical prices on the open market and had been eagerly sought after in northern Europe for centuries, particularly in Germany and Russia where 'they are used for mantle linings; [and] whoever has the costliest fur trimmings is esteemed the greatest.' They retained their value even when they had been worn for years by the Indians and were 'foul with sweat and grease'; indeed, worn skins were often the most highly prized of all for 'unless the beaver ... is greasy and dirty it will not felt properly.'

The spectacular success of the Dutch in the East Indies drove King James to be ever more vociferous in his claims to the land around Manhattan. But the hard work of his ambassador, Sir Dudley, proved to be of no avail for in June 1621, less than three years after Dermer had encountered Dutch vessels in the Hudson, the States General bestowed their charter upon the Dutch West India Company, an organisation modelled on its eastern counterpart. The Company was granted exclusive rights to trade with both the east and west coasts of America and was permitted to conclude treaties with native princes, build castles and settle provinces.

It was not long before the first settlers began to arrive in what was now known as New Netherland. In the spring of 1623, the appropriately named *New Netherland* slipped out of the Texel carrying a handful of families, 'all of the Reformed religion,' on the long journey across the Atlantic. Their departure did not go unnoticed by the crew of the *Bonnie Bess*, an English vessel which had only recently been commissioned by 'high authorities' to sail to Manhattan, conduct a search of the area and, 'if we there find any strangers, as Hollanders or others, we are to give them fight and spoil or sink them down into the sea.'

In the event the *Bonnie Bess* never got to execute these orders and the colonists on board the *New Netherland* arrived safely at their destination after a trouble-free voyage. Only one of the settlers' names is known, Caterina Trico, who wrote her memoirs some six decades after arriving in America. Although she muddles dates and names, she remembers 'that four women came along with her in the same ship … which four women were married at sea'. She is equally forgetful about the voyage itself and it is only from maritime records that we learn the *New Netherland* sailed first to the Canary Islands and the 'Wild Coast' (Guiana) before heading towards the mouth of the Hudson. Later settlers would not forget the trials of the long sea voyage quite so easily as Madame Trico. As with the ships that sailed to the East Indies, there were only a handful of cabins reserved for those who could afford the substantial fare of one guilder a day and everyone else was crammed into the stinking and claustrophobic confines between decks. For two months in summer, and many more in winter, scores of passengers lived, unwashed, in total squalor, sharing their floor space with the filth of pigs, sheep and chickens. Dysentery and fevers were rife and although most settlers carried their own medicine chests, the homespun pills and unguents they contained were useless against life-threatening disease. It is hardly surprising that many went into raptures when they at last spied the eastern coastline of America. 'There came the smell of the shore,' wrote one early traveller, 'like the smell of a garden.' It was as if they had arrived at the Spice Islands.

The natural beauty of Manhattan also made a deep impression after the long sea voyage. 'We were much gratified on arriving in this country,' reads one account.

'Here we found beautiful rivers, bubbling fountains flowing into the valleys, basins of running waters in the flatlands, agreeable fruits in the woods. There is considerable fish in the rivers, good tillage land; here is, especially, free coming and going, without fear of the naked natives of the country.'

The settlers spread themselves over a wide area of land. According to Caterina Trico, two families and eight men went to Delaware, six to the mouth of the Connecticut River and the rest – totalling eighteen – sailed up the Hudson to Fort Orange, close to the site of present-day Albany. Only eight, all men, were left behind on Manhattan 'to take possession' of their new home. Unlike their fellow colonists in Bantam and Banda who were generally drunkards and 'wholly unsuitable for the plantation of colonies', the settlers despatched to the Hudson were honest and hard-working. They were reliant upon their own labour for food and shelter, but their work paid handsome dividends and it was not long before they were 'bravely advanced' and the grain they had planted was 'nearly as high as a man'. They did have one complaint: 'Had we cows, hogs, and other cattle for food (which we daily expect by the first ships) we would not wish to return to Holland, for whatever we desire in the paradise of Holland is here to be found.' In fact, the cows, hogs and other cattle were on their way. In a meticulously planned operation, a relief expedition set sail carrying more than one hundred horses, cows and sheep on three vessels imaginatively named the *Horse*, the *Cow* and the *Sheep*.

It is not easy to picture the Manhattan of those first settlers. The terrain of the island in those days was hilly and rugged and at its southern end, close to the present-day site of the World Trade Center, were a series of low wooded hills dotted with freshwater ponds. It was here that work started on the much-needed Fort New Amsterdam. Engineer Cryn Fredericks and a number of builders had been sent out with 'special instructions' outlining the precise dimensions of the fort. A carbon copy of the impregnable Fort Belgica on Neira Island in the Bandas, it was shaped like a pentangle and stretched more than a thousand feet in circumference. For additional security, the entire structure was surrounded by a wide moat. The outlines of the fort can still be traced today. Beaver Street, Broad Street, Pearl Street and Whitehall Street in Lower Manhattan all follow engineer Fredericks's original ground plan, as do Broadway, Park Row and Fourth Avenue.

It was while work on the fort was in progress that Peter Minuit, the first governor-general of New Netherland, arrived on the island. One of his first acts was to purchase Manhattan from the native Indians, a transaction that the merchants in Amsterdam had been urging for some time. 'In case there should be any Indians living on the aforesaid island or claiming any title to it,' they wrote, '… they must not be expelled with violence or threats, but be persuaded with kind words (to let us settle there), or otherwise should be given something for it to placate them or be allowed to live amongst us, and a contract should be made of such an agreement to be signed by them in their manner'.

Minuit obliged by purchasing the island from the native Indians, paying them to the value of sixty guilders in trinkets. A copy of this transaction, was sent to The Hague and records that 'here arrived yesterday, the ship Arms of Amsterdam … they report that our people [on Manhattan] are of good cheer and live peaceably. Their wives have also borne children there. They have bought the island Manhattes from the savages for the value of sixty guilders. It is 11,000 morgens in extent. They had all their grain sown by the middle of May and harvested by the middle of August. They send small samples of summer grain, such as wheat, rye, barley, oats, buckwheat, canary seed, beans and flax'.

By the time this letter arrived in Holland, the fledgling settlement in Manhattan had survived its first difficult years. But although the population soon began to grow, New Amsterdam was never really considered to be a colony by the directors. As with the settlements in the Banda Islands, in Bantam and elsewhere in the East Indies, it was nurtured not for its own sake but for the sake of a profitable trading company. What Amsterdam's merchants could never have imagined is that in seizing Manhattan from the English they had gained themselves a bargaining chip of immense value.

Nathaniel Courthope was one of the sickly few who survived Sir Henry Middleton's disastrous 1610 expedition to the East Indies. His contract still had five years to run when the *Trades Increase* ran aground in Bantam harbour and he would soon find himself despatched in the near-rotten *Darling* to search for potential trading partners in the lesser-known Spice Islands. In the meantime he and his fellow survivors recuperated from their trials in the Javanese port of Bantam.

Bantam was the hub of English activity in the East Indies and the first port of call for most of the Company's vessels. Although the city was almost a thousand miles from the 'spiceries,' it was nevertheless from Bantam that ships sailed, factors were despatched and trade organised; and it would eventually be the men living in the port upon whom Courthope's fate was to rest. It had gained the unenviable reputation of being the least hygienic place in the East Indies – 'that stinking stew,' wrote Nicholas Downton, after watching most of his men die in the town. Few disagreed with such a conclusion: 'Bantam is not a place to recover men that are sick,' wrote one, 'but rather to kill men that come thither in health.'

The annals of the East India Company are filled with notices of plagues, sicknesses and deaths that occurred in Bantam but only one journal, written by Edmund Scott, charts the full horror of life in this rotting, disease-ridden port. For more than two years Scott held the post of chief factor to the dozen-strong English community: a period of unremitting hardship in which he witnessed his two superiors die in rapid succession and his men succumb to typhoid and cholera. Malaria, too, was rife, for the oozing mud flats and tidal swamplands that surrounded Bantam provided a fertile breeding ground for swarms of mosquitoes.

Scott's men lived in constant fear of attack and scarcely a day passed without one of their number being assaulted by thieves or bandits. For almost two years their flimsy wooden warehouse, surrounded by a palisade of sharpened stakes, was under a state of siege and 'these continuall alarames and greevous outcryes of men, women, and children grew so rife in oure eares,' wrote Scott, 'that our men in their sleepe would dreame that they were pursuing the Javans and suddainely would leape out of their beddes and ketch their weapons.'

The English looked in vain for any support from the native government for the King was but a child and real power lay in the hands of an unscrupulous Protector who was forever haranguing the foreign traders in the town. Business could only be transacted after proffering large bribes to native officials, yet the bustling commercial life of Bantam continued to attract rival traders from all over the region and within its fly-blown alleys lived a mêlée of residents whose mutual animosities created endless troubles. Chinese, Indians, Christians and Muslims all lived within a stone's throw of each other and were equally loathed by the quarrelsome Javanese who only tolerated these foreigners because they depended upon their trade. A more worrying threat to the English was the town's unscrupulous head-hunters who faced a constant shortage of heads. 'There were some Javan women that would cut off their husbands' heads in the night and sell them to these people,' records Scott. 'They did linger much about our house; and surely, if we had not kept good watch, they would have attempted the cutting of our throats, if not our heades.' Such was the shortage of heads in the town that 'many times they would digge up such as were new buried at Bantam and cut off their heads.'

There was an unrelenting rivalry between the English and Dutch in all matters pertaining to business. Fuelled by the heat and insufferable humidity, disagreements frequently boiled over into violence and it was only when faced with serious trouble from the natives that the two nations presented a united front. Indeed, it was Dutch support in times of strife that saved the small English factory from extinction. 'Though we were mortall enemies in oure trade,' penned Scott in one of his more conciliatory moments, 'yet in other matters we were friendes and would have lived and died for one another.' Even this occasional amicability vanished in later years. 'The Flemings thunder it most terribly in these parts,' wrote an English factor a decade later. 'Their untruths are daily more discovered, and they are rather feared than respected by their brutal carriage.'

An additional problem that faced the English in Bantam

was the frequent fires that threatened to ravage their warehouse. It was a favourite ploy of would-be thieves to light a fire to the windward of the English warehouse and, in the ensuing confusion, raid the premises and carry off the spices. 'Oh this worde fire!' writes Scott. 'Had it been spoken neere mee, either in English, Mallayes, Javanese or Chynese, although I had been sound asleepe, yet I should have leaped out of my bedde; the which I have done sometimes when our men in their watch have but whispered one to another of fire; insomuch that I was forced to warne them not to talk of fire at night.'

One night, the threat of fire became all too real. At around ten o'clock, as the second watch took over from the first, the men noticed the acrid smell of smoke filtering out from the warehouse. Summoning Scott, they made a thorough search of the premises yet were unable to locate its source. 'Then one of them remembered a hole which a rat had made behind a trunk, that went through the ceiling down into the cloth warehouse.' Heaving the trunk away from the wall, they saw that the smoke was indeed coming from this hole and that the little-used lower warehouse was on fire. There was no time to lose, for two huge jars of gunpowder were stored in the same room 'which caused us greatly to fear blowing up'.

The Englishmen tried again and again to extinguish the flames but the fire had by now taken hold and the smoke was so thick that they were continually forced back outside. The situation was desperate for there was more than a thousand pounds of gold stored in the upstairs room which would soon be lost. There was no alternative but to call for help from the 'damned Chinese' who lived next to the English warehouse and who agreed to empty the building in return for a large share of that gold.

'When the fire was all out,' wrote Scott, 'I stood musing alone by myselfe how this fire could come, being verie much grieved in minde.' What disquieted him was the fact that the fire appeared to have started underground and had only spread so rapidly because it had already taken hold in the joists beneath the floorboards. His suspicions of treachery were confirmed when he wrenched up a short length of the floor and discovered a tunnel leading in the direction of the house opposite. Vowing to have his revenge, Scott stormed around to this building, seized two men and marched them back to the warehouse where he had them clapped in irons.

He was keen that everyone involved in the plot should be punished and with the judicious application of a branding iron soon had a list of all the guilty men. One of these, handed over by the authorities, refused to admit his part in the affair even though he had openly bragged about his involvement around town. 'Wherefore,' wrote Scott in a matter-of-fact entry in his journal, 'I thought I would burne him a little (for we were now in the heate of our anger.)'

What follows is a clinical account of the torture, a barbarous affair which makes for painful reading even when one allows for the fact that the employment of torture to extract confessions was standard procedure in the English judicial system:

First, I caused him to be burned under the nayles of his thumbes, fingers, and toes with sharpe hotte iron, and the nayles to be torne off. And because he never blemished at that, we thought that his handes and legges had beene nummed with tying; wherefore we burned him in the arms, shoulders, and necke. But all was one with him. Then we burned him quite thorow the handes, and with rasps of iron tore out the flesh and sinewes. After that, I caused them to knocke the edges of his shinne bones with hotte searing irons. Then I caused colde screws of irone to be screwed into the bones of his armes and sodenly to be snatched out. After that all the bones of his fingers and toes to be broken with pincers. Yet for all this he never shed a teare; no, nor once turned his head aside, nor stirred hand or foot, but when we demaunded any question, he would put his tongue betweene his teeth and strike his chynne upon his knees to bite it off. When all the extremity we could use was but in vaine, I caused him to be put fast in irons againe; where the emmets [white ants] (which do greatly abound there) got into his wounds and tormented him worse than we had done, as we might well see by his gesture.

The King's officers desired me he might be shott to death ... wherefore, they being verie importunate, in the evening we led him into the fields and made him fast to a stake. The first shott caried away a peece of his arme bone, and all the next shot struck him thorough the breast, up neare to the shoulder. Then he, holding down his head, looked upon the wound. The third shott that was made, one of our men had cut a bullet in three partes, which strooke upon his breast in a tryangle; whereat he fell down as low as the stake would give him leave. But betweene our men and the Hollanders, they shot him almost to peeces before they left him.

Power was commensurate with brutality in Bantam but despite the horrific barbarity inflicted on the instigators of the fire, life got no easier for the English. The stresses of living cooped up in a confined space, coupled with the lack of sleep caused by round-the-clock watches, began to tell on the men. 'What with overwatching and with suddaine waking out of our sleepe (we beeing continually in feare of our lives) some of our men were distract of their witts; especially one, who sometimes in the night would fall into such a franticke rage that two or three of his fellowes could hardly keepe him in his bed.' On more than one occasion the men began fighting among themselves and could only be brought to their senses by being clapped in irons.

Scott soon realised that one of the main reasons why they faced the constant threat of violence was that the native Javanese were unable to distinguish between the English and Dutch. The Hollanders, who lived in Bantam in considerable numbers, paid scant regard to the sensitivities of the local population and thought nothing of staggering home through the streets of this staunchly Muslim town after a lengthy drinking bout. Their behaviour led to 'much falling out betweene the Hollanders and the countrey people, by means of the rude behaviour of some of their marriners; and many of them were stabbed in the eveninges'. The situation was made worse by the fact that some of the Dutch would pretend they were English if they thought it would be to their advantage when buying spices. It was Scott's subordinate, Gabriel Towerson, who dreamed up a clever way to draw a distinction between the two nations. Realising that the anniversary of Queen Elizabeth I's coronation was drawing near – 'for at that time we knew no other but that Queene Elizabeth was lyving' – he suggested they celebrate the event in the most extravagant manner possible. Then, when quizzed about the pageantry, they could explain to the natives that they, unlike the other rabble, were commemorating their monarch.

Scott listened to Towerson's plan but was initially sceptical. 'I stood in doubt many times whether I should put this in practise or not,' he wrote, 'for feare of being counted fantasticall when it should be knowne in England.' In the end he relented and ordered the small English community to dress themselves in white silk, don scarves of red and white taffeta, make 'a flagge with the redde crosse thorow the middle', and dust down their military drums.

'Our day beeing come, we set up our banner of Sainct George upon the top of our house, and with our drumme and shott we marched up and downe within our owne grounde; being but fourteene in number, wherefore we could march but single, one after the other, plying our shotte.' The performance had the desired effect. Hundreds of curious locals, including many of the most important personages of the town, flocked to the English factory to enquire the reason for the celebration. 'We told them that that day sixe and fortie yeares our Queene was crowned; wherefore all Englishmen, in what country soever they were, did triumph on that day. He [a local dignitary] greatly commended us for having our prince in reverence in so farre a countrey.'

Others were bewildered by the behaviour of the English and asked why the other Englishmen in the town were not celebrating the Queen's anniversary. It was exactly the question Scott had hoped they would ask and, with a distinct note of pride, 'told them they were no Englishmen, but Hollanders, and that they had no king, but their land was ruled by governours'. Some were sceptical when they heard this explanation and told him that these so-called

Hollanders had persistently called themselves English. 'But we told them againe that they were of another countrey, neere England, and spake another language; and that, if they did talke with them now, they should heare they were of another nation.'

The day ended in triumph. As a constant stream of shot was fired in celebration from the English factory a procession of children wound through the streets shouting ' "*Oran Enggrees bayck, orak Hollanda jahad*," which is: "the Englishmen are good, the Hollanders are naught." '

Scott was fast learning that when dealing with the native Javanese, style was every bit as important as substance. Now, with a feast day to celebrate the king's circumcision just weeks away, he prepared to lay on a gift that, while less costly than that of the Dutch, would be guaranteed to leave a deep impression. 'Amongst all others,' he wrote, 'we were to make a show, the best we could.' While the local chieftains, princes and Dutch merchants were buying gifts of gold and jewellery, the English 'bought a very faire pomegranate tree, being full of fruite growing on it ... which we set in a frame beeing made of rattan or carrack-rushes, somewhat like a bird's cage, but very wyde. At the roote of this tree we placed earth, and upon that greene turfe, so that it stood as if it had been still growing. Uppon these turfes we put three silver-headed conies [rabbits] which our Vice-Admirall had given me; and at the top, and round about upon the boughs, we with thread made fast a number of smalle birds which would ever be cherping. Soe that tree was ... full of faire fruite, and birdes merily singing on the top.'

The men spent some days on their handicraft and Scott was delighted with the end result. He would have liked to deliver it to the King accompanied by a troupe of English damsels but, 'we had no women; wherefore we borrowed thirty of the prettiest boys we could get.' Once again Gabriel Towerson proved his usefulness. 'Master Towerson had a very pretty boye,' writes Scott, 'a Chinese, [who] we attyred as gallant as the King, whom we sent to present these thinges and to make a speach to him.' The procession was led by a trumpeter and followed by ten musketeers, all dressed in the red and white colours of England. Next came the pikemen, all Chinese, and finally the 'pretty boye' who had a canopy held over him to screen the sun.

The King was overjoyed with the gift, the more so when he learned that the English entourage had filled their pockets with fireworks which they proceeded to light for his amusement. The day came to a climax with a tiger parade, a circus act and, unhappily for the King, his circumcision. Whether he made immediate use of his favourite present, a 'fair quilted bed with twelve bolsters and pillows of silk', is not recorded.

When Scott finally came to leave Bantam he expressed amazement that he had survived his ordeal: throughout his years in the city he had dug many a grave for his fellow countrymen and been a witness to (and participant in) unprecedented brutality. Yet the harsh treatment he received had done nothing to dent his pride in being English, and his dogged determination to defend his country's flag became the inspiration for the factors who followed – men like Nathaniel Courthope for whom patriotism and devotion to duty were more important even than trade.

'And here it is not fit I should omit one thing,' writes Scott in the final pages of his journal, 'and yet to make relation of it, some may thinke I do it of a vaineglorie to myselfe and those that were with me ... It was a common talke among all straungers and others how we stoode at defiance with those that hated us, [and] it will be a thing generallye talked of, in all parts of the worlde, what different carriage we have beene of, when it is likely there will be no English [left in Bantam].'

His prophetic words would in time be fulfilled, but the English presence in the East still had more than a decade to run. Although Sir Henry Middleton's second expedition had ended in disaster, the East India Company directors remained in buoyant mood and were considering expanding their trade in the East. By the time Courthope arrived in Bantam in 1611, they had factors dotted all over the region searching for markets for English goods, and the Company records are filled with letters from obscure backwaters reporting on the feasibility of trade. These missions often ended in disaster: in Macassar the factor was forced to flee for his life after 'a pitiful tragedy' caused by the Dutch who 'murdered the King's most dearly loved nephew more like cannibals than Christians'. In Johor it was the English who made a bad impression; so bad, indeed, that the King of Johor sent a letter to a neighbouring king warning him to steer clear of what he described as 'a vile people, drunkards and thieves'. Even China, which had once been viewed as a most promising market, was henceforth out of bounds. The King of Cochin attacked an English trading vessel and overturned it, and 'both English, Dutch and Japans, their followers, [were] cut to pieces and killed in the water with harping irons like fishes.'

The London merchants proved incredibly resilient to the continued bad news and resolved not only to search for trade 'at other places' but to appoint a far greater number of factors. Yet for all their enthusiasm, most English factories were never more than temporary bases which

lasted for only as long as the factor stayed in good health –
usually little more than a few months. For if life was
unremittingly hard in Bantam, it was often far worse on the
island outposts to which Courthope would find himself
posted. The steady trickle of letters from the Company's
factors contain a litany of complaints and grievances for,
notwithstanding the constant threat of sickness and disease,
most found themselves afflicted with homesickness and
extreme loneliness. For some the loneliness quite addled
their minds, as is revealed in an extraordinary letter written
by one William Nealson, factor in Firando. Full of riddles,
puns and strange allusions it begins: 'Morrow, bully;
morrow morrow. To recover my health, I forgot not,
fasting, a pot of blue burning ale with a fiery flaming toast
and after (for recreation's sake) provided a long staff with a
pike in the end of it to jump over joined stools with. Hem.'

Others retained their sanity only to complain bitterly at
the treatment they received from their employers. 'At
home men are famous for doing nothing;' wrote one
disgruntled factor, 'here they are infamous for their honest
endeavour. At home is respect and reward; abroad
disrespect and heartbreaking. At home is augmentation of
wages; abroad no more than the third of wages. At home
is content; abroad nothing so much as griefs, cares and
displeasure. At home is safety; abroad no security. At home
is liberty; abroad the best is bondage. And, in a word, at
home all things are as a man may wish, and here nothing
answerable to merit.'

The complaint that wages had gone unpaid is frequently
heard and one that grieved factors greatly since most had
only been lured eastwards by the prospect of making
money. More frightening was the ever-present spectre of
the grim reaper who demanded a high price from those

who settled in the East. The average life expectancy for factors was no more than three years and it is little wonder that many followed the example of William Hawkins in India who brazenly admitted to using his time to 'feather my nest'. Nathaniel Courthope was no exception: in a letter sent from Bantam to London in the winter of 1613 he, along with a number of other factors, was accused of 'purloining the Company's goods, deceiving private men, insolent behaviour, and vanity in wearing buckles of gold in their girdles'. Furthermore, the Company's attention is drawn to 'the great wealth they have gathered suddenly, being worth £500 or £600 each', and the fact that 'they are false and unjust to their masters.'

With the threat of his 'great wealth' being confiscated by the next vessel to arrive in the East – and doubtless concerned that he would be left penniless and without prospects in these distant lands – Courthope repented of his misdemeanours and wrote 'a voluntary confession' of his wrong-doings. It was a shrewd move for he soon found himself back in favour and, in the spring of 1614, was instructed to sail to Sukadana, a port on the south-west coast of Borneo where, it was rumoured, 'the best diamonds in the world [are] to be procured'.

Sukadana was already home to one of the Company's more flamboyant factors, a professional sailor called Sophony Cozucke. Known as 'Sophony the Russe', but more probably Sophonias the Kazak, he had established a base at the only place in the East where diamonds were indeed in plentiful supply. With the help of Courthope, 'of whom there is great hopes that he shall do your Worships good service,' the two men set about expanding this lucrative trade and investigating what goods were of greatest value for barter.

The hardships they faced in Sukadana were similar to those facing all factors in such remote spots. As they were totally dependent on English vessels for food and money, it only took one supply ship to be blown off course for a factory to be plunged from prosperity to near-starvation. When the *Darling* re-entered the harbour at Sukadana after a lengthy absence, its captain was alarmed to find the factory 'indebted to the Hollanders, and in a poor, beggarly state, because the junk that was despatched from Bantam first touched at Macassar'. Although in good health, Courthope and Sophony were 'altogether unfurnished with money [and] report that they had in consequence been obliged to refuse 1,000 carats of diamonds'.

Once Courthope had turned Sukadana into a going concern, buying gemstones on the cheap and exporting them to Bantam for re-sale, he was keen to expand his trade. Learning that Borneo was rich in gold, diamonds and bezoar stones, a concretion taken from the stomach of animals which was believed to be an antidote, he despatched Sophony to the island on a reconnaissance mission. His instructions, a copy of which he forwarded to Bantam, ordered 'the Russe' to 'proceed to Landak and confer with the governors of those parts upon what security the English may settle a factory there'. In addition he was 'to learn privately whether they stand in fear of the Sukadanians or not, for if so, I see not how our people can be safely with them'. With characteristic cynicism – a cynicism that would become more pronounced during his long years in the Banda Islands – he ended with a caution: 'Above all, be not flattered with fruitless hopes, but if possible, bring firmans [written confirmation] for what they say or promise.'

The mission was not a success, largely because of the

'savageness of the people … who lie in the rivers on purpose to take off the heads of all they can overcome'. Sophony and his two companions were attacked by a mob of a thousand men and 'escaped a miraculous danger', only surviving the onslaught when they discovered the natives were 'not used to powder and shot [and] were fain to run ashore'. A second, heavily armed expedition had more success, largely because of the English muskets. 'The force of the whole country,' wrote Sophony, 'was not able to withstand nine men.'

In the summer of 1616, Courthope relinquished his lonely job as chief factor in Sukadana and returned to Bantam. The energy he had put into his work had not passed unnoticed and it was with regret that the Company allowed him to leave. Within months of his departure the diamond trade was 'in hugger mugger', there was much 'stealing and griping' and Sukadana became a haven for 'heavy and unprofitable hangers-on that have meat, drink and money to do harm'. Those in responsibility called for Courthope's return, 'for it is fitting that it be a man that hath experience here'.

The request went unheeded for Courthope was needed for a mission of far greater importance. A new chief factor had arrived in Bantam, a man by the name of John Jourdain who had considerable experience of life in the East Indies and who brought with him an unbounded enthusiasm for the task ahead. He was determined to stake his country's claim to the Banda Islands and, in Nathaniel Courthope, he had just the man for the job.

CHAPTER NINE

CONFLICT BETWEEN GENTLEMEN

JOHN JOURDAIN TRAVELLED TO London in the winter of
1607 to seek employment as a chief factor with the
East India Company. It is unclear what drove him to
this decision for he was involved in a profitable shipping
concern in the Dorset port of Lyme Regis and, as son of
the town's mayor, was able to involve himself in many
overseas business ventures. Perhaps he was lured to the
East India Company by the hope of getting rich quick,
but a more compelling reason is that relations with his
wife were strained and he chose self-imposed exile in
preference to a life of domestic unhappiness. By the time
he came to write his will, the marital breakdown was
complete and he totally excluded her from the
management of his estate, leaving her a paltry sum of
money. The poor woman's final years were spent 'begging
from door to door' and writing endless letters to the East
India Company asking for 'some competent yearly means
proportionable to her birth and breeding'.

The directors responded by despatching the occasional
gift to Dorset – the least they could do for a widow whose
husband was to prove the greatest of all the Company
factors. Jourdain had long held that the future of the spice
trade lay in the Banda Islands and he did everything in his

power to promote English interests in the region. Returning home after a stint of more than five years in the East he penned a persuasive document in which he argued the importance of strengthening trading links with these remote islands. He sent this document directly to Sir Thomas Smythe who declared himself most impressed with what he read and called a special meeting in order to make public 'his [Jourdain's] opinion concerninge the contynueinge and prosecutinge of trade in the Indies'. After discussing its contents the committee summoned Jourdain to the Company headquarters and listened attentively as he set out the weaknesses of the English in the region and argued that it was essential to 'saufeguards their buysines at Bantam and attempt trade at Banda'. When a number of members protested that this would surely bring them into conflict with the Dutch, Jourdain assured them 'that the Flemings neither dare not or will not sett upon the English'. It was a disingenuous answer for Jourdain had already concluded that future trade in the Spice Islands would inevitably involve coming to blows with the Dutch, a conclusion that had been more than reinforced by his previous trip to the East. Sailing from Bantam in the winter of 1613 he had headed for Amboyna, a clove-rich island under the firm control of the Dutch. Jourdain was only too aware of their presence on Amboyna: graciously introducing himself to the Dutch captain at Hitu, a village on the north of the island, he suggested that instead of buying cloves from the natives, thereby driving up prices, he should buy them from the Dutch at a little over cost price. The captain expressed interest in this proposition but said he would have to clear the matter with his superiors, a response that irritated Jourdain who 'awnswered that this country did nott belonge to the Dutch'.

When he was at last handed the official reply to his

proposition, Jourdain was stunned by its strong language. In a 'skoffing' two page letter, the governor 'marvelled that we would presume to thrust ourselves into a countrye where they had made a contracte with the people for all the cloves growinge upon the iland', and strongly advised Jourdain 'nott to deale with the contrye people for any cloves; which if we did they would seek their uttermost to prevent us'. They proved all too willing to carry out this last threat, for no sooner had native chieftains started to offer the English small quantities of spice than the Dutch sent a warning that 'they would build a castle at Hitu and burn their town.' This was enough to panic the natives who were 'made soe fearfull that they durst not give us any enterteynement'.

When Jourdain finally met the Dutch governor he could scarcely contain his rage, accusing him of deceit, arrogance and lies. The helplessness of his situation was a cause of great amusement to the governor who goaded Jourdain about his failure to buy any spices and made a number of cruel jokes about the diminutive size of the *Darling*. These proved too much for Jourdain, who told the governor that the Dutch followed the English 'as the Jews did Christ' and added, in a threat that would pass into legend at the East India Company, that they would one day answer for their arrogance 'betwixt Dover and Calais'. Still smarting from the insults, he then put to sea and headed to the neighbouring island of Ceram where David Middleton had successfully set up his temporary base.

He stepped ashore only to find himself face to face with Jan Coen, the youthful captain of one of the Dutch vessels and a man destined to become the most ruthless of all of Holland's governor-generals in the East. The first meeting between these headstrong men developed, appropriately enough, into a scrap with both men accusing and abusing each other. Coen upbraided the English captain 'in a chollericke manner'; whilst Jourdain employed character-istically insulting language, the product of many years in the company of mariners. Asked to show his commission, 'I replyed that I wondred much that he should be soe well acquainted with my comission; but seeinge he knewe it so well, his long beard (for he had none att all) could not teach me to followe my comission.' This jest, he knew, would wound Coen's pride for the smooth-faced Dutchman was just twenty-six years old and acutely conscious of his youth. Indeed, he never forgave Jourdain the insult and would spend the next six years plotting his bloody revenge. Coen also took the trouble to send an account of his meeting with Jourdain to his superiors in Amsterdam; an account which praised his opponent in order to boost his own standing. 'Jourdain gave us much trouble,' he wrote, 'and I had many disputes with him; for he is a clever fellow and left no means untried which would in any way serve his designs ... We on our side did everything to frustrate his endeavours, for it would have been all up with us there had he succeeded.'

It was not long before Jourdain found his chance to humiliate the Dutchman for a second time: when Coen boasted that the natives hated the English, Jourdain summoned a great council of local chieftains and, cajoling Coen into attendance, asked them to publicly declare whom they preferred as trading partners. 'In awnswere of which they all with one accord stoode up, sayinge: Our onelie desire is to deale with the English, but we are daylie threatned by the Hollanders ... so we dare not almost to speake with you for fear of their forces which are neere.' The council gave Jourdain the moral victory and even provided him with a little spice, for the natives were emboldened by his presence and began to sell him cloves 'oute of sight of the Hollanders'. When continued Dutch threats caused them to abandon their trade, a disillusioned Jourdain set sail for Bantam.

Here the news could hardly have been worse. The last survivors of Sir Henry Middleton's expedition were on their deathbeds and trade had ground to a virtual standstill because of animosities between rival factors. As Jourdain stepped ashore and probed the trusty Nathaniel Courthope for news it became apparent that discipline had broken down completely. The two groups of merchants in the town, those of the sixth and eighth voyages, were engaged in bitter in-fighting and neither was happy at the arrival of Jourdain who had been named as chief factor by Middleton shortly before his death. Jourdain was aware that 'they did not greatly care for my coming aland, and that they were determined not to receive me as principal merchant' but he did not realise that his presence would create such hostility. 'Not knowing of any civil wars,' he made the mistake of visiting the factors who lived in the lower town before proceeding to those in the upper. The latter group treated this as a snub and greeted Jourdain with open hostility. A headstrong mariner called Robert Larkin, 'though not able hardly to stand on his legs,' proclaimed himself chief factor and consented to speak with Jourdain only if he returned later in the day. Jourdain duly obliged, only to find Larkin 'haveinge lost his paine and sicknes, came runninge forth like a madman, askinge for the bilboes, threatninge that if I would not begone out of his house (as he tearmed itt) he would sett me into them'.

Characteristically, Jourdain took the threats in his stride. 'I laughed to see the world soe much altered,' he noted in his diary, perhaps because he realised that in this total breakdown of authority lay his strongest chance of recovering his position. But when he returned the following morning to demand the keys and accounts, 'they, beeinge armed with guns, halberts and swordes, came out against me as in defiannce, sayinge that they knewe me not for cheife factour, neither should I have any thinge to doe in thatt buysines.' Thoroughly disheartened, Jourdain told them that 'I would not staie in Bantam to trouble them; and I, as much desirous to be rid of their companie, made as much haste as might be to fitt our shipp.' True to his word, the *Darling* was made ready and put to sea within a few days.

Six weeks later an unforeseen event brought Jourdain back to Bantam. As he sailed along the coast of Sumatra, he caught sight of two English vessels which, he discovered, were under the captainship of Thomas Best, commander of the East India Company's tenth fleet. Best was an 'ungratefull, covetous and prowde' man whose rumbustious personality was not always appreciated by his crew. When he learned that the *Darling* was laden with half a cargo of cloves he was struck by the brilliant idea of buying this cargo, thereby saving himself the trouble of sailing to either Amboyna or the Banda Islands. Jourdain was most unhappy about this and suggested a number of other solutions but 'all this could not satisfie the Generall [Best], the cloves smellinge so sweete that we must retourne for Bantam in his companie; and seeinge no remedy, I was content.' Best had, in fact, struck an agreement whereby he would use his authority to reinstate Jourdain as chief factor in return for the cloves on board the *Darling*.

No sooner had the men arrived in Bantam than Best put his plan into action. Summoning the English factors to a general meeting 'he propounded that he understoode of some disorders and controversie that there was betwixt the factors of the sixth and eighth voyages, as alsoe of other voyages formerlie.' To much nodding of heads, he now turned on the factors, haranguing them for 'the greate disgrace it was to our nation and the Honourable Companie, our employars, to have so many houses in one place, seperated both in qualitie and friendshippe, beeing all as it were for one Companie; which was a greate scandall to our nation'.

In speaking these words Best had got to the heart of the problem. Although the men in Bantam were all employed by the East India Company, each voyage sought its own profit and not the general profit of the Company. In forcing Jourdain to sell his cloves, Best was behaving no more honourably than the men he was chastising but he did at least have the foresight to realise that the English community in Bantam could only survive if there was some central authority which could override the claims of individual voyages. 'It was fittinge,' he concluded, 'there should be but one head in the countrye.'

Who that 'one head' might be was never in doubt. 'After perswations of the Generall and them all,' writes Jourdain modestly, 'I was content (though against my will) to take the place.' At last Bantam had a chief factor, and one who had a vision for the future of trade in the East Indies.

Jourdain was convinced that the English should now concentrate their activities on the Banda Islands and sent word to the native chieftains that his merchants would shortly be arriving in far greater numbers. But despite his title and influence Jourdain was powerless to decide the final destinations of vessels arriving at Bantam. It was up to expedition commanders to choose which islands they would visit, and Jourdain's authority only extended over a handful of pinnaces based in the Javanese port. It angered him that for more than a year he was unable to send a single ship to the Bandas and he scribbled a strongly worded letter to London complaining that '[because] there is not any ship gone this year they [the natives] will be out of hope; for that they did depend much upon the English this year, which now they will be frustrate of their hopes and hold the Hollanders' words to be true, who tells them that they shall never see any English ship there but once in four years, and then some small ship which can do them no good.'

A small English vessel did touch at Great Banda in the spring of 1614 and its captain, Richard Welden, wrote to Jourdain to inform him of his visit and urge him to send a ship – any ship – to the islands. 'For the Bandanese do much marvel that in so long a time there have come no English shipping there, protesting if they come they will live and die with the English, for now all the Bandanese hath open wars with the Hollanders and have slain many of them.' Welden added that trade in Banda was more profitable than in previous years and that he was resolved to sail there again 'at the first of the next monsoon'.

His letter arrived at a fortuitous time, for Jourdain had recently found himself with two small ships at his disposal. Fitting out the *Concord*, together with a pinnace called the *Speedwell*, he despatched two factors, George Ball and George Cokayne, to explore the possibilities of increased trade with Banda. Ball was instructed to 'confer with the country people concerning the estate of their business; and if you perceive them to be willing of trade … you may leave there Mr Sophony Cozucke and Richard Hunt, with one English more, and some black that is willing to serve them.' This was a significant development – the first time that someone of influence had proposed a permanent English presence in the Banda Islands.

The news from Banda was not good. Gerald Reynst, the

Dutch governor-general had recently arrived in the islands bringing with him a fleet of eleven ships, an army of a thousand soldiers, and orders to impose his unchallengeable control over the Banda Islands. As he sailed into Neira harbour the volcano, Gunung Api, erupted in spectacular fashion, convincing the superstitious islanders that something portentous was about to occur.

The two Georges, Ball and Cokayne, arrived soon after, sailing straight to Neira and anchoring before the Dutch castle. The Hollander vessels caused them a moment's anxiety but they saluted them with a couple of cannon shots and prepared to visit Reynst the following morning. They used the intervening hours wisely. Both men rowed over to Great Banda and made contact with the native chieftains, enquiring about the possibility of building a fortified English factory. The sight of the Englishmen caused the natives to pour out their feelings and one of the headmen, 'pointing to the Fleming castle, [said] that it makes old men to weep, and will the child that is unborn, saying as God hath given them a country to them and their, so He hath sent the Hollanders as a plague unto them, making wars upon them and by unjust proceedings seeking to take their country from them'.

So far the English vessels had been untroubled by the Dutch, but as the men returned to their ships a Dutch pinnace crowded with soldiers stopped them and ordered them to a meeting with the governor-general. After a brief stand-off the soldiers opened fire and Ball, realising the futility of resistance, sent Cokayne ashore as his messenger.

Reynst had been fuming ever since he watched the English ships sail into his harbour. Now, with the Englishman standing in front of him, he demanded to see Cokayne's East India Company papers. Cokayne's refusal sent Reynst into an apoplexy of rage. 'He then standing up, fluttering his papers at my face, saying we were rogues and rascals, not having anything but from Thomas Smythe of London, most vilely railing of our Honourable Company.' He added that King James I had recently declared that the Dutch 'had all the right that might be, and no others, to these places of Banda'. After a few further words of abuse Reynst finished by saying 'that we came to steal more voyages from them as others had done before, naming Keeling and Middleton'.

It was clear that the English were not going to have much luck trading at Neira or Great Banda and the following morning they hoisted their sails and headed for Ai, five miles to the west of the main islands. Reynst immediately ordered a squadron of Dutch ships to follow them but these were shaken off in a gale and Cokayne slipped ashore unhindered, the islanders 'much rejoicing of our coming'. Reynst's control over this small, nutmeg-rich island was almost non-existent but Ai's chieftains were nonetheless nervous about the thousand soldiers barracked on Neira and, fearing attack, provided the English with a warm welcome. They knew from the antics of Keeling and Middleton that the English were united in their hatred of the Dutch and, when they learned of their desire to settle a permanent factory on the island, consented immediately. An agreement was struck, a factory built, and Ball and Cokayne sailed away laden with nutmeg, leaving Sophony Cozucke and a few men to guard the island. One of these, a trader called John Skinner, felt so confident of their impregnable position that he wrote to a friend: 'Truly I durst lay all that I ever shall be worth whilst I live that the Hollanders never get the islands of Banda, for all the Bandanese will lose their lives before they will be under the Hollanders.' What gave him even greater satisfaction was that Gunung Api, the volcano, was now erupting with such force that huge boulders were raining down on the Dutch castle on Neira. Skinner claimed that the soldiers had 'begun to make way to leave the castle' and believed that were it not for the choleric Reynst they would have fled the islands altogether.

The Dutch governor-general soon knocked the waverers into shape, informing them not only that they were here to stay, but that they were about to launch a massive offensive against Ai. Many were only too keen to escape the dangers posed by the volcano, unaware that Ai's awkward geography made an invasion extremely hazardous. 'The sea shoare is so steepe that it seemeth nature meant to reserve this iland particularly to herselfe,' wrote one observer. 'There is but one place about the whole iland for a ship to anchor in; and that so dangerous that he that letteth fall his anchor seldome seeth the weighing of it againe; besides he incurreth the imminent dangers of his ship.' The invasion was scheduled for the morning of 14 May 1615, and Reynst – who dismissed the difficulties – declared himself confident that it would be in Dutch hands within a matter of hours. He was taking no chances; almost a thousand Dutch and Japanese soldiers were pitched against Ai's five-hundred-strong fighting force and the Hollanders were armed to the teeth with muskets and cannon. But from the moment they launched their attack the Dutch troops were surprised by the resistance they encountered. The native marksmanship was far more accurate than anything they had experienced on Neira or Great Banda and the island strongholds were particularly well designed. These fortifications snaked upwards from the shoreline to the hills so that even when the Dutch captured long sections of wall they found to their annoyance that they were open to attack from defenders higher up the hillside.

The English on Ai had spent time and effort preparing themselves for the invasion. Not only had they planned a detailed defence of the island, they had also trained the natives to use muskets and taught them how to hold their positions. Had they not been faced with such an overwhelmingly larger force, the men of Ai might well have saved the island from capture. But successive waves of Dutch attackers gradually disheartened the defenders and by nightfall their army had succeeded in overrunning most of the island, leaving only one remote fort still controlled by the Bandanese. As the sun went down the Dutch celebrated their victory, then went to sleep in the knowledge that tomorrow the whole island would be theirs.

It was a fatal mistake, for in the early hours the Bandanese crept out of their fort and launched a savage counter-attack. The Dutch soldiers, heavy with sleep and in unfamiliar surroundings, were sitting ducks. Twenty-seven were killed outright and dozens more wounded as they fought their way back to their ships. Two Dutchmen, convinced that all was lost, suddenly switched over to the enemy. One of them clambered into a tree and killed two of his erstwhile comrades with a single shot. The Dutch humiliation was complete. As the ships limped back to Neira, the scale of their defeat gradually became apparent. In one day's fighting they had lost thirty-six soldiers, with two hundred wounded and two defections. Reynst was devastated, never recovered from the humiliation and died a few months later.

The role of the English in this debacle did not pass unrecorded by Jan Coen who sent two letters to the Seventeen in Amsterdam. In the first he informed them that the English 'want to reap what we have sowed, and they brag that they are free to do so because their king has authority over the Netherlands nation.' In the second he

The crumbling entrance to Dutch-built Fort Revenge on Ai. Dozens of Englishmen were imprisoned in its dungeons and complained bitterly about their harsh treatment. 'They pissed and **** upon our heads,' wrote one, 'untill such time as we were broken out from top to toe like lepers.'

was more forthright. 'You can be assured,' he wrote, 'that if you do not send a large capital at the earliest opportunity ... the whole Indies trade is liable to come to nothing.'

The Seventeen, in fact, had every intention of continuing their war against the island of Ai and in the spring of 1616 they despatched Admiral Jan Dirkz Lam to the Banda Islands with one simple order: Ai was to be brought under Dutch control. The natives on Ai knew that the Dutch would return to punish them and were equally certain that they would be unable to withstand a second attack. They therefore asked Sophony Cozucke to sail one of their chieftains to Bantam so that he could personally deliver a letter to John Jourdain.

'We have all heard even from farr countryes of the greate love and peace that the Kinge of England has with all the world ...' it read, 'and hath done no hurt to any of our religion, or doth seeke to overthrowe our lawe, and doth not by force attempt to overcome any man's kingdome, but only peace and frindshipp doth seeke trade without violence.'

Therefore we all desire to come to an agrement with the Kinge of England, because that nowe the Hollanders do practize by all meanes possible to conquer our country and destroy our religion, by reason whereof all of us of the Islands of Banda do utterly hate the very sight of theis Hollanders, sonnes of Whores, because they exceede in lying and villainy and desire to overcome all men's country by trechery. These are the occasions whie we soe extreamely hate them. We have nowe therefore with one general consent, resolved never hereafter to trade with them, but allwayes to esteeme them our utter enimyes, wherefore we all thought good to send this lettre ... that if so be the kinge of England out of his love towards us will have a care of our cuntry and religion and will help us with artillary powder and shott and

help us to recover the castle of Neira, whereby we
may be able to make warrs with the Hollanders, by
God's helpe all the spice that all our island's shall
yeald, we will onely sell to the King of England, and
to no other nation in the world.

There was only one proviso attached to the agreement:
'that [if] in small matters the Bandanezers should give
occasion of discontent to the English, or the English doe
that which might be distastful to the Bandanezars, that then
with mutuall consent like frinds they would beare with
each others errors; onely we all desire that you doe not
seeke to overthrowe our religion, and that you do not
comitt offence with our weomen, because theis twoe onely
we are not able to endure'.

Such words were music to the ears of Jourdain who was
already dreaming of expanding the English factory in Ai.
Now was the time to act and, in December 1615, he
assembled a squadron of three ships, the *Thomas*, the *Concord*
and the *Speedwell*, and instructed them to sail for Banda
without further ado. But just as they were about to leave
Bantam Jourdain received a note from Jan Coen warning
him that henceforth all English shipping was banned from
the Banda Islands and that any vessel contravening this order
would be expelled by force and 'if any slaughter of men
happened ... they would not be culpable.'

The arrival of two new English ships under the
command of Samuel Castleton strengthened Jourdain's
resolve. Castleton had always intended to sail to the Banda
Islands and had no intention of being deflected from his
mission by an arrogant letter from Jan Coen. He suggested
that all the ships sail together in a mini-armada, and set off
in January 1616 on what was to prove one of the most

bizarre English expeditions ever to reach the Banda Islands. This was largely due to the eccentricities of its commander whose behaviour left the Dutch both puzzled and bemused. Castleton had already caused raised eyebrows among the Company directors in London after trumpeting his unorthodox methods for preserving the health of his sailors. These included the daily baking of fresh bread on board his ships, the manual grinding of corn which he considered 'an exercise fit to preserve men in health' and the distilling of fresh water from salt by means of an elaborate system of stills and furnaces. Had this worked, he intended that each of his vessels would have its own mobile desalination plant. Unfortunately it proved a complete failure, his crew still died, and Castleton concluded that it was their own fault since they were all confirmed alcoholics.

By the time his fleet arrived off Ai Island a new Dutch armada under the command of Admiral Lam had anchored in the shadow of Fort Nassau. Lam had come in even greater numbers than his predecessor: a fleet of twelve ships and more than a thousand soldiers who were shortly joined by a second fleet and military reinforcements. For a few days they watched the English ships lurking around Ai and Run Islands before Lam realised that both islands were being fortified and that on Run the English were building some sort of castle. He immediately ordered his men to prepare for a full-scale invasion of Ai, but scarcely had their squadron of ships set sail from Neira than they discovered they had a fight on their hands. Castleton had manoeuvred his five vessels into the deep channel separating the two islands, blocking access to Ai. A few shots were fired and the men were about to do battle when a curious incident brought the fighting to an abrupt halt. Castleton, it seems, had only just learned the name of the Dutch commander and, despatching a rowing boat over to Lam's ship, he offered his compliments to the commander and explained that he, an Englishman, was so deeply grateful for a service Lam had once rendered him that he was unable to bring himself to continue with the battle. To an astonished Lam he added that he was ordering his vessels to withdraw and apologised for any offence he might have caused.

Castleton did indeed have good cause to thank Lam. Some three years previously he had been watering at the Atlantic island of St Helena when he was surprised by two Portuguese carracks and forced to put to sea, leaving half his men on the island. Two Dutch vessels commanded by Lam had just left the island; vessels which Castleton chased after and begged for assistance. Lam agreed to attack the Portuguese, an action which saved the English sailors but cost him dear for he lost one of his ships in the fight.

Now, in very different circumstances, Castleton wished to repay Lam's former kindness. Invited over to the Dutch commander's ship, Castleton found himself heartily welcomed by Lam who was only too happy to strike a gentleman's agreement in which the Englishman would withdraw his fleet and provide intelligence about Ai's defences in return for freedom of trade with Ai once the Dutch had occupied the island. The two men shook hands and Castleton, perhaps a little ashamed at the way he had just abandoned the islanders of Ai, sailed to Ceram while Lam conquered the island. His last act was to instruct Richard Hunt, the resident English factor on Ai, to observe a strict neutrality throughout the forthcoming battle.

The island elders watched in despair as the English vessels sailed away. A council was convened at which they pinned their last hopes on Hunt, formerly surrendering Ai and Run to him and dutifully raising the flag of St George from the island's battlements. There was little else to do but await the Dutch onslaught.

Despite their overwhelming superiority the Dutch found their second battle for Ai no less challenging than the first. Once again a huge force of Dutch and Japanese soldiers were landed and they fought their way from stronghold to stronghold, surprised by the tenacity of their Bandanese foes. By nightfall they had taken most key positions but still the island was not under control. Fearful of a repeat of the previous year's catastrophe the men remained on their guard all night and in the morning a large band of reinforcements were landed. Violent rainstorms hindered the Dutch and it was a further two days before the island was finally brought under their control. By this time the Bandanese had run out of ammunition and most escaped to Run Island where they could continue their resistance to the Dutch.

Lam took no chances once he had conquered Ai. He built a sturdy fort close to the shoreline, provided it with a permanent garrison and gave it the appropriate name Fort Revenge. 'It is a regular pentagon, well fortified, and furnished with all manner of provisions and souldiers, and is held to bee the strongest castle the Dutch have in the Indies.' It stands to this day, its neglected ramparts overgrown with climbing ivy and its parade ground home to a family of goats. But the battlements are in a fine state of repair and a rusting cannon still points towards Run, the letters VOC – Vereenigde Oost-Indische Compagnie – embossed on the barrel.

Lam drew up a formal agreement with the conquered Bandanese and took the opportunity to confirm Dutch authority over most of the Banda Islands. Great Banda and Neira reluctantly signed up to the Dutch monopoly; tiny

Rozengain soon followed suit. Ai got the worst deal of all for Lam fixed the price of nutmeg at 20 per cent less than on the other islands. Of all the Bandas, Run now stood alone – the only island that remained unoccupied by Dutch troops and was party to no agreement with the Dutch East India Company.

It was to Run that Richard Hunt now fled 'in fear of his life, the Hollanders having sworne to hang him, and did offer great sums of money for his person'. He eventually arrived back in Bantam where news of his clandestine activities had spread far and wide and where he had the misfortune to become a walking symbol of the Dutch hatred for the English. In the words of John Jourdain, 'Richard Hunt, passinge in a very narrowe streete, mette with two of the Dutch marchannts, which came abrest towards him and would nott give him way to passe by. Soe Hunt put one of them aside to make waye, whereupon they fell to blowes. The Dutch beeinge neere their backe dore called for their slaves who presentlie came, to the number of 20 persons, and fell upon him and beate him very sore, and halled him through the durte by the haire of the head to their owne howse.' Vowing to make him suffer before they killed him they 'sett him in the boults at their gate in the hott sunne, without hatt'. All this was done very publicly in order to demonstrate to the townspeople that the Dutch were a force to be reckoned with. Jourdain realised this and decided to meet force with force, threatening to seize 'the best of their marchannts', clap them in irons, and put them on display outside the English gates. But Hunt was unexpectedly released before he had a chance to carry out his threat, and a new English fleet arrived in the bay of Bantam. Its commander, the experienced William Keeling, urged restraint and although annoyed by the treatment of Hunt, was 'was willing to wink at it, and so the matter rested'. Individuals continued to fight in the streets, and even to kill one another, but on an official level the two nations remained at peace.

Peace was something that the office-bound directors of both the English and Dutch East India Companies recognised as essential if the spice trade was to continue to be profitable. Yet the peace had always been an uneasy one and, in the remoter islands of the East Indies, had all too often spilled over into a virtual state of war. As early as 1611 the English directors had felt the need to complain about the warlike stance taken by some of the Dutch commanders. Enraged by persistent reports of violence shown to their employees, and 'having long and patiently endured sundry notorious wrongs and injurious courses at the hand of the Hollanders', they were 'enforced at last to break silence'. In a lengthy letter to the Lord High Treasurer of England they set out their woes and requested help in their desire to enter into dialogue with the States General. King James approved the idea and instructed his minister in The Hague to set the ball rolling. Although the Dutch disputed most of the English complaints they agreed to meet in 1613 'in order to promote friendly feeling and good neighbourly relations'.

The Dutch negotiating team was a distinguished one, led by the noted jurist Hugo Grotius who had published his celebrated *Mare Librum* in the previous year. Grotius, whose book had the significant subtitle, *A Discourse concerning the right which the Hollanders claim of trade to India*, argued, as had the Dutch in Manhattan, that as soon as a nation erected a building on a piece of land, the land automatically became the property of that nation. He added that the Dutch, unlike the English, had spent vast sums of money fighting the natives in the East Indies and, in view of that, it was totally unfair of the English to dispute their rights to trade with these islands. The English East India Company disagreed, maintaining its right to trade with the Spice Islands by virtue of the fact that it got there first. 'Before these regions were known to you,' announced the directors grandly, 'we stood legally approved by their leaders and peoples, in pacts and agreements, as we can easily prove.' The conference ended with no formal agreement, but it had achieved the useful result of bringing the two sides together and many felt that it would be foolish not to continue the dialogue. It was therefore agreed that the teams should meet again within two years.

This second conference, which took place against a backdrop of much bloodshed in the Banda Islands, was to prove one of the more extraordinary events in the saga of the two companies. The conference began in a similar manner to its predecessor with each side retreading the same old ground. But after a few days the English contingent were invited to a meeting with the Attorney-General of Holland who made the startling suggestion that the two companies unite to form one unbeatable organisation. Chief negotiator Sir Henry Wooten immediately wrote to the directors in London pointing out the benefits: 'If we joined with them to beat the Spaniards out of the East Indies we shall make them as profitable unto us as the West Indies should be unto them.'

Although the English directors remained extremely sceptical, a detailed proposal concerning the merger was prepared and plans were formulated for the finance of the giant company. The benefits were deemed to be enormous: each year more than £600,000 of spices could be shipped from the East, the maximum that western Europe could consume annually. Spain would quickly be forced out of the region, native chiefs would be compelled to reduce duties paid at Bantam and trade with China would be vigorously pursued. Even discipline among sailors would be improved since there would no longer be any rivalry between the two nations.

So keen were the Dutch to prove conciliatory that shortly before the suggestion was mooted the Seventeen wrote to the hot-headed Jan Coen ordering him to avoid any conflict or 'maltreatment' of the English. Coen was stung by this letter and immediately penned a sarcastic reply: 'If by night and day proud thieves broke into your house, who were not ashamed of any robbery or other offense, how would you defend your property against them without having recourse to "maltreatment?" This is what the English are doing against you in the Moluccas. Consequently, we are surprised to receive instructions not to do them bodily harm. If the English have this privilege above all other nations, it must be nice to be an Englishman.'

In the event the negotiations in The Hague broke down and the English, who had presented their own list of propositions, found they were rejected by the Dutch. After all the excitement and many months of discussions, both parties found themselves back at the drawing board. By late spring 1615 the English commissioners realised there was nothing left to discuss and they returned to London.

It was during the years in which these negotiations were taking place that Jan Pieterszoon Coen began his spectacular climb to the top. He had first sailed east in 1607, a most unfortunate introduction to the spice trade for it was while he was stationed in the Banda Islands that Verhoef and his lieutenants were massacred. Coen was in

Ten pounds of nutmeg cost one penny in the East Indies yet sold in London for fifty shillings. Apothecaries reaped vast profits from their pomanders, particularly during the plague. 'I confess they are costly,' wrote one, 'but cheape medicines are as dear as death.'

no doubt that the English had played a significant role in planning the ambush and much of his hatred seems to have stemmed from this belief.

In 1612 he sailed to the Spice Islands for a second time and it was on this occasion, while serving as chief merchant, that he engaged in his first scrap with John Jourdain. The men shared the similar aim of capturing the entire Bandanese spice trade but Coen was willing to employ far bloodier methods to pursue his goal. He wanted to conquer islands, subjugate the natives and plant Dutch colonies as a balance to the English presence in the region. Although the Seventeen had already sent out a handful of settlers they were hardly what Coen had in mind; a motley crew much given to 'drinking and whoring'. In later years Coen would persistently call for a better class of settler, particularly those with manual skills. 'Even if they come naked as a jaybird,' he wrote, 'we can still use them.'

A portrait of Coen hangs in the Rijksmuseum in Amsterdam. Painted in Bantam, it depicts a tall, upright figure with a long and narrow face and deep-set eyes. His lips are thin, his nose aquiline and his cheeks hollow and pale. It is by no means a flattering portrait but it does suggest that Coen was a man in total control of his destiny. The few contemporary descriptions of Coen are far from complimentary. One of his colleagues describes him as 'full of Italian tricks' whilst others refer to his bony hands and pointed fingers. His nickname was De Schraale, which means 'thin and lanky' but also refers to his grim character.

His numerous letters give a greater insight into his character. Coen was a reserved man who was preoccupied with what he considered to be his duty and who did not suffer fools gladly. He never hesitated to speak his mind, frequently admonishing his superiors for what he believed to be their stupidity and short-sightedness. He was a practical man, a great mathematician, who, as a strict Calvinist, was devoid of any frivolities. As for a sense of humour, he had none.

His rise through the ranks was rapid. A year after proving himself a successful chief merchant he was promoted to the important post of book-keeper general and, after a further twelve months, was made a member of the influential Council of the Indies. He might have hoped that when Gerald Reynst died shortly after his abortive attack on Ai he would be promoted to the position of governor-general. As it turned out, the Seventeen in Amsterdam elected Laurens Reael, an effete aristocrat who appears to have spent much of his time concerned with his dress. Coen, not surprisingly, could not stand the man and argued vehemently against his tactics in dealing with the English. Reael responded by countermanding Coen's instructions forbidding the English from sailing to the Banda Islands, ordering him that 'no harsh measures were to be used to disperse the English by force, fearing that this might not only lead to war in these quarters but might spread to Europe as well.'

Coen studiously ignored these instructions and continued his attacks on English shipping. 'If I did wrong,' he wrote in a letter to Amsterdam, '(which I do not believe) please tell me and I will act accordingly. The English threaten to hang me in effigy on the highest gallows in England and to pickle my heart ... Reael cannot decide to deal firmly with the English, demanding more pertinent orders. I hope that your latest orders will satisfy him and change his attitude.'

The Seventeen had initially expressed concern about their bellicose servant in the East, but as his detailed letters, documents and balance sheets poured into their headquarters in Amsterdam they were convinced that they were dealing with someone of remarkable talent. Despite the shortage of capital he continued to send back huge cargoes of spice, and the directors, hinting that he might one day be considered a suitable candidate for the top job, raised his salary and promised it would keep rising if Coen continued the good work. The directors got no thanks from their industrious servant. 'I thought my services were more valuable to you than what you offer,' he wrote in his characteristically sneering style, referring to the fact that others received far more than him 'and accomplish little'. This barbed comment was directed at Reael who was also deeply dissatisfied with his pay rise. Determined to force the directors into reconsidering their offer, Reael upped the stakes considerably by resigning from his position as governor-general. He then dropped heavy hints to the effect that he would be only too willing to resume his post when his pay rise had been satisfactorily sorted. 'It being human nature to change one's mind ...' he wrote, 'I might be induced to stay longer if the situation, and especially a good salary, would warrant it.' In resigning, Reael had seriously misjudged his employers. The Seventeen had long been considering removing him from his post and he had now presented them with the perfect opportunity. Writing a polite letter accepting his resignation, they promptly installed Jan Coen, just thirty-one years old, in his place.

The time for being conciliatory was over: in a letter to Coen they instructed him that 'something on a large scale must be done against the enemies; the inhabitants of Banda must be subjugated, their leaders must be killed or driven out of the land, and if necessary the country must be turned into a desert by uprooting the trees and shrubs.'

Coen was only too keen to carry out these wishes. Courthope was determined to stop him.

CHAPTER TEN

RAISING THE
BLOOD-FLAG

NATHANIEL COURTHOPE was appointed commander
of two ships, the *Swan* and the *Defence,* in October
1616. He was given the post by John Jourdain
who had long recognised Courthope's abilities and was
now sending his friend on a mission of the utmost
importance. Courthope was to sail his ships to Macassar in
order to buy rice and provisions, then proceed directly to
Run where it was hoped that the natives 'expected him and
would be ready to receive him.' It was critical that he
should be successful in taking control of the island for of
the six principal Bandas, only Run still lay outside the grasp
of the Dutch. If they seized this island, as they had seized
Ai, they would control the world's entire supply of nutmeg.
They would also have completed their stranglehold on the
Spice Islands, leaving the English without a single base
from which to launch future attacks.

Jourdain was only too aware of the consequences of
failure and provided Courthope with detailed instructions
about his mission. He was to gather together the chieftains
of Run and Ai and confirm whether or not they stood by
their former surrender to Richard Hunt, the factor on Ai
Island, to whom they had proclaimed their allegiance to
King James I. If they did, Courthope was to get this

confirmed in writing; if not he was to coerce them into submission. Jourdain added that if the Dutch 'offered violence, to the utmost of his power, even to the loss of lives and goods, to make the good the same'. Little could he have imagined how thoroughly Courthope would fulfil this last command.

The *Swan* and the *Defence* sailed on the last day of October and, helped by a freshening breeze, arrived before Run Island on 23 December 1616. The ever-cautious Jourdain had warned his friend to be wary of treachery on the part of the natives: 'At your arrival at Run,' he said, 'show yourself courteous and affable, for they are a peevish, perverse, diffident and perfidious people and apt to take disgust upon small occasions, and are, being moved, more cumbersome than wasps.' Fearing a hostile reception, Courthope anchored in the bay and 'sent my skiff ashore to understand the state of the islanders'. It became immediately apparent that far from planning treachery the natives were overjoyed at the sight of the English ships for they had been worn down by their constant struggles with the Dutch and many were in a pitiful state having fled to Run as refugees from Ai. Since then, the island had been under a virtual blockade and much of the population was on the verge of starvation.

Courthope records with great precision the formal surrender of the island; a wise precaution, for it was his documentation that was later used as incontrovertible proof of England's sovereignty over Run. Inviting the chief orang-kayas aboard the *Swan*, he asked them 'whether they had made any contract with the Hollanders, and given them any surrender; they all replied, they had not, nor never would; but held them as mortal enemies'. Indeed the island's headmen surpassed themselves in their protestations of loyalty to England, repeatedly assuring Courthope that their former submission still held.

When asked to record their surrender in writing, the orang-kayas obliged by producing an agreement which made over the island of Run to the English Crown 'forever'. 'And whereas King James by the grace of God is King of England, Scotland, France and Ireland, is also now by the mercy of God King of Pooloway [Ai] and Poolaroone [Run].' It was a title that King James would come to cherish, and with good reason. On reading these lines one of Courthope's men wryly remarked that these two islands would prove a great deal more profitable than Scotland ever had.

The document continued: 'Moreover, we doe all of us make an agreement that the commodities in the two foresaid ilands, namely mace and nutmegs, we cannot nor will sell to any other nation, but only to the King of England his subjects … And whereas all the orankayas of the foresaid ilands have made this agreement, let it be credited that it was not made in madnesse or loosely as the breathing of the wind, but because it was concluded upon in their hearts, they cannot revolt from or swerve from the same againe.'

There was one condition attached to the treaty: 'that we doe desire of his Majestie that such things as are not fitting in our religion, as unreverent usage of women, mayntayning of swine in our countrey, forceable taking away of men's goods, misse-using of our men, or any such like… that they be not put in practice, being out of our use and custome.' The document was duly signed by eleven of the islands' headmen and the two sides shook hands. There was one last ceremonial which was to prove, above all else, that the chieftains stood by their pledge. A nutmeg seedling wrapped in the unique soil of the country was handed to

Courthope as a gesture of loyalty, an act that was more than mere symbolism for it demonstrated that they placed all their trust in his leadership. The colourful little ceremony that followed, which threw a carnival-like atmosphere over the proceedings, was undertaken with great sincerity on the part of both the orang-kayas and Nathaniel Courthope. As the English fired all their cannon in celebration of the island's 'capture', the village elders reciprocated by raising the flag of St George and the next two days were spent in friendly festivities.

It is unfortunate that there is no record of what the local headmen made of this strangely attired Englishman – nor has any portrait of Courthope survived – but letters in the East India Company archives testify to his impressive stature and

In Elizabethan times, the nutmeg tree only grew in the Banda Islands. Its fruit was believed to cure the 'sweating sickness' – the plague – that accompanied the 'pestiferous time of the pestilence'.

he appears to have engendered an instant respect both from his fellow men and from the native Bandanese. He was honest, straight-talking and scrupulously fair, and his sense of justice and strict morals were in striking contrast to those of the Dutch commanders so despised by Run's islanders.

The festivities presided over by 'the captain' were brought to an abrupt halt on Christmas Day when a Dutch ship was spied approaching from the west. A hastily convened council agreed that the island should be urgently fortified and, to this end, three of the largest cannon were landed and heaved up to a makeshift platform atop Run's highest cliff. This proved to be a wise precaution for three days later the vessel sent its pinnace into the bay 'within shot of our fort'. A tense stand-off followed before the Dutch ship raised the blood-flag to signify the start of hostilities, then hastily sailed for Neira. This gesture ended Courthope's fading hope that his stay on Run would be a short one. It was clear that the Dutch had no intention of allowing the English to remain on the island and were prepared to use force in order to evict them.

Yet Courthope was not unduly worried by threats of Dutch aggression for he knew that Run's natural defences would make it extremely hard for any enemy to capture the island. Its southern coastline consists of a long bank of precipitous cliffs which are virtually impossible to scale without ropes. The sea here is a boiling fury for the strong current hurls the waves against the black rock with tremendous force. Any vessel attempting to land would almost certainly be dashed to pieces on the rocks or wrecked on the reef that lies just below the surface. The island's northern shore, where the *Swan* and *Defence* lay at anchor, presented Courthope with more of a problem. Its small harbour was accessible to ships arriving from either east or west and, once anchored in the bay, they would have few difficulties in targeting Run's only settlement. But here, too, Courthope had geography on his side. The western end of the harbour is overlooked by a high cliff that commands a splendid view of the bay: by fortifying this bluff of rock the English could effectively bar enemy ships sailing from Java from coming within shot of the village.

The harbour's eastern entrance was the most difficult part of the island to defend – a long coral reef linking Run with the tiny islet of Nailaka, a low-lying atoll of powdery beaches and palm-trees. This islet was of great importance to the islanders because its surrounding shallow waters provided rich pickings for fishermen. It was essential that in times of siege Nailaka remained in their hands. As Courthope made a study of the little island he realised that if he set cannon pointing eastwards he could attack any ship sailing from Neira long before it got within shot of Run harbour. By placing a second battery facing west he would have virtual command over all shipping sailing from Bantam.

His men began work on the fortifications shortly after Christmas. One bastion was christened Fort Defence, the other Fort Swan, and each was armed with three stout cannon. Scarcely were these guns in place than a small fleet of Dutch ships took advantage of the stiff easterly wind and sailed over from Neira, catching the English unawares. Before Courthope had even primed his cannon, the ships had sailed into Run harbour and moored alongside the *Swan* and the *Defence*, cutting off any assistance from the shore.

Courthope's immediate task was to inform the Dutch that Run had surrendered to England. He therefore sent a

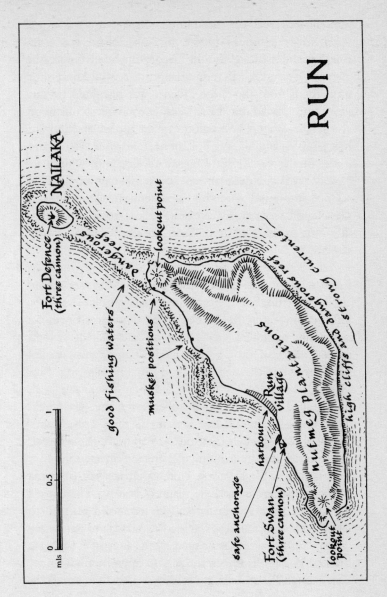

messenger across to the Dutch flagship to warn the commander, Cornelis Dedel, that the island was now English, and that he should 'depart the road before six glasses were run, for that the islanders ... would have shot unto them from the shore'. Dedel was intrigued by this news and played for time, asking to meet Courthope aboard the *Swan*. The English captain agreed 'and shewed him the surrender of Polaroone, and our right and possession there for his Majesty of England, which we would hold and maintain to our utmost power'. Dedel seemed impressed with the document and, according to the English account of the event, took it in his hands and, 'perusing it, he said with these words: "This is a true surrender."'

Yet he refused to leave the harbour. Although 'the glass was running in the Great Cabin' he wished to learn more about the English commander and probed him for information about the forces at his disposal. Courthope repeatedly reminded Dedel that he had hidden cannon trained on the Dutch vessels and that the natives would open fire when the sixth glass had run. Having gauged his man, Dedel at last took this threat at face value and, outmatched and outgunned, sullenly retreated to Neira. The English later learned that he had come with instructions to attack the island but had not reckoned with the batteries that Courthope had erected on the shore.

Less than a week later a Dutch pinnace was observed taking soundings around the island of Nailaka. This caused Courthope serious concern and he instructed his men to let fly with their muskets, forcing the pinnace to put hastily to sea. This event was later used by the Dutch as evidence that the English had been the first to open hostilities.

Although Run's defences made a Dutch assault unlikely,

The narrow channel separating the central group of Banda Islands provided safe anchorage for English and Dutch vessels. Although the English were banned from mooring here, most captains treated Dutch threats to their shipping with derision.

at least in the short term, Courthope realised that the island was extremely vulnerable to a sea blockade, a situation aggravated by the fact that he had landed on Run with scarcely any provisions. His two ships had been loaded with only a few chickens and a small quantity of rice and arak, most of which had been consumed on the journey to Run. Unable to restock en route, the Englishmen arrived to find that the island offered little in the way of food. Although nutmeg grew in abundance, there was not enough fresh fruit or vegetables to feed the native islanders and the only other plant that thrived was the sago palm whose pithy trunk could be boiled down into a glutinous, porridge-like starch. The inhabitants of Run had always depended on their neighbouring islands for their supplies, but all of these were now firmly under Dutch control. Their only hope of replenishing stocks lay in the occasional junk or trading craft that happened to put into the island's natural harbour.

More serious was the shortage of water. Run had no water reserves and the islanders had traditionally survived by collecting the monsoon rains in 'jarres and cisternes' and using the water sparingly during the dry season. But Courthope's men brought an increased demand and water soon began to run low. A group of them offered to sail across to Neira or Great Banda to replenish supplies but Courthope considered such a move far too dangerous and ordered them to survive on reduced rations. But his authority over one group of rebellious spirits, never strong, was now weakened by dissension between the ships' companies. Many of the professional sailors were horrified at the prospect of spending many months on this remote island and, led by John Davis, the master of the *Swan*, they announced their intention of sailing to Ceram to fill the water casks. Unrelated to his more famous namesake, Davis was nevertheless a sailor of ripe experience who had taken part in no fewer than five voyages to and from the East Indies. But his abilities as a leader of men were not so obvious. His quarrelsome disposition upset many of his own crew while his deep attachment to the bottle frequently clouded his judgement.

Courthope, 'very sick,' pleaded with him to rethink but Davis had already tired of Run and refused to stay on land, 'obstinately contrarying my command'. He was about to set sail when a native pinnace arrived from Great Banda with some surprising news. The elders of one of the villages on that island, hearing of events on Run, had held a meeting at which it was decided to surrender themselves 'unto his Majestie'. The island of Rozengain, four miles farther to the east, had followed suit and also asked for English protection.

Since Davis was adamant about putting to sea, Courthope ordered him to call first at Great Banda and then at Rozengain in order to receive the islanders' formal submission. He also suggested that Sophony Cozucke and three other merchants should hoist the flag of St George on the latter island and establish a factory there. Davis carried out these instructions but was unable to persuade Cozucke to step ashore at Rozengain. As soon as the village elders had surrendered their islands to the English king, the men set sail for a watering hole on the coast of Ceram.

The casks were soon filled and Davis shaped his course for Run, but scarcely had he put to sea than the *Swan* found itself in difficulty. The wily Dutch commander, Cornelis Dedel, had been spying on the English from his ship the *Morgensterre* and now decided to attack. The *Swan* was of a similar size to the Dutch vessel and at one time a 'very warlike ship,' but its crew were sick and hungry and most its guns were ashore on Run. Sensing his vulnerability, Davis tried to outsail the *Morgensterre* but 'they did shoote at me twice before I began, although I was in the sea eight leagues off when they chased me.' Aided by the wind, Dedel managed to manoeuvre his ship alongside the *Swan*, enabling his men to hurl grappling irons onto the decks of the English vessel. The Dutch then boarded the ship and, swords drawn, began a bloody hand-to-hand battle. 'We fought almost boord and boord for the space of one houre and a halfe,' recalled Davis, 'untill they had killed five men, maymed three and hurt eight. And when we began we had not thirtie men able to doe anything, nor no wind to worke withall.' Those who hid inside the ship were flushed out with musket fire; those on deck were cut down with swords. One of the dead was the adventurous Sophony Cozuke, 'torne in pieces with a great shot,' while those who were 'maimed' were unlikely to live, 'having lost legs and arms, and almost all hope of life, if not dead already'.

After the *Swan* had been ransacked, her cabins smashed to pieces and all the trunks thrown into the sea, she was towed in triumph to Neira, the Hollanders 'much glorying in their victory, and showing the Bandanese their exploit, in the great disgrace of the English ... saying that the King of England might not compare with their great King of Holland, and that one Holland ship would take ten of the English ships, and that Saint George is now turned child'. It was three weeks before Courthope learned for certain of the *Swan*'s capture – the news being brought to him by a local merchant who described how she was lying crippled and rifled under the guns of Neira Castle. One of Courthope's most trusted men, Robert Hayes, was despatched to Neira under a flag of truce to demand the restitution of both the ship and her crew. Not surprisingly the Dutch refused, boasting that it would only be a matter of weeks before they had captured the *Defence* as well. They also warned Courthope that unless he submitted without a fight, 'there will be much slaughter about it.'

The loss of the *Swan* was a terrible blow for the Englishmen left on Run for they were totally reliant on their ships, both for supplies and for escaping in an emergency. Although the *Defence* was still seaworthy, Courthope desperately needed her cannon to make his island fortress secure. Since disarming her would render the ship unserviceable, his only option was to draw her up onto the beach where she would be protected by the on-shore gun batteries. This would maroon him on Run, a precariously exposed position which left him unable to replenish his supplies.

He was soon struck by further misfortune: long before he had a chance to land the *Defence*'s weaponry, the ship mysteriously drifted from her anchorage and floated out to sea. Courthope initially thought this had happened through carelessness but it soon became apparent that the cable had been deliberately cut by 'a plot of knaves' whose long months on Run had proved more than they could endure. The ship was sailed to Neira where her crew surrendered to the Dutch and proceeded to hand over detailed plans of all the defences on Run and Nailaka. They were, remarked one of Courthope's more loyal companions, 'a company of treacherous villains who have deserved hanging better than wages'.

It was shortly after this unfortunate event that the Dutch governor-general, Laurens Reael, arrived in the Banda Islands to take over the handling of the crisis. Informed of the hopelessness of Courthope's position, Reael decided to bring to an end the English stand on Run by negotiation rather than force, inviting Courthope to Neira for discussions. But although the Dutch governor-general held the upper hand, his position was an awkward one for he could scarcely ignore Courthope's treaty, nor could he claim any authority over Run. Instead, he took the line that the islanders had pledged to sell their spices to the Dutch after the 1609 murder of Verhoef – which was not true – and argued that this pledge still held.

Courthope agreed to meet with Reael as long as suitable hostages were sent to Run as a sign of good faith. These duly arrived bearing a letter from John Davis who languished in Neira prison. 'If I lose any more men by your arrogance,' he warned Courthope, 'as I have here lost by sicknesse already, their lives and blouds shall rest upon your heads … and this I will write with dying hand.' Courthope ignored the note and rowed across to the Dutch castle on Neira to discuss the future of the Banda Islands. Reael was the first to lay his bargaining chips on the table, offering to return the captured ships and men, pay compensation for everything that had been rifled and assist the English in leaving Run with a full cargo of nutmeg. In return he demanded that England sign away forever her rights to the island. Courthope flatly refused to countenance such an offer, answering that 'I could not, unless I should turne traitor unto my King and Countrey, in giving up that right which I am able to hold; and also betray the countrey people, who had surrendered up their land to our King's Majestie.'

It was the sort of answer he might have expected from the Englishman, but Reael had naively assumed his offer would be accepted and, infuriated by such defiance, 'threw his hat on the ground and pulled his beard for anger'. Courthope now placed his chips on the table, informing Reael that he would leave Run immediately if the Dutchman would agree to the question of sovereignty being settled in Bantam or Europe. This time it was Reael's turn to refuse and the two men parted with the island's fate unresolved. It was clear that the issue could only be settled by war, and the Dutch governor-general curtly informed Courthope that within three days he 'would bring all his forces and take us perforce'.

These forces were not inconsiderable. In addition to his bases on Neira, Great Banda and Ai, Reael had more than a dozen ships at his disposal as well as a thousand soldiers. He had a total mastery of the sea, leaving Courthope with no option but to sit tight, knowing that Reael could stop any supply ships from reaching the island of Run.

Courthope had taken an enormous risk in declining Reael's offer but he remained confident that the Dutch would find it almost impossible to mount a frontal assault on Run, even with their overwhelmingly superior forces. The battery on Nailaka was virtually impregnable and Courthope had a brave and highly competent network of spies at his disposal – local men – who rowed backwards and forwards between Run and the other islands keeping him informed of every development.

In the spring of 1617 he took a gamble, despatching six men to Bantam in a hired vessel, a small native pinnace, in order to urgently request reinforcements and aid. The man in charge of this perilous journey was Thomas Spurway, one of Courthope's most trusty lieutenants who, after numerous mishaps, pitched up in Bantam to plead Courthope's case. To his dismay, he discovered that John Jourdain had left for England some months earlier and instead found himself dealing with George Ball who had visited Run the previous year and must have understood the precariousness of Courthope's position. But Ball's promotion had quite gone to his head and he spent much of his time tending to his extensive and lucrative private ventures. A man of inordinate pride and vanity he maintained a personal guard of fifty negro slaves and was preoccupied with continual quarrels with other factors, caring little for the Company's concerns. Indeed, for an entire year not a single ship was laden for England, even though there were six vessels in Bantam harbour and plenty of money in the coffers. Despite continued pleas from Spurway, Ball refused to send a ship to relieve Courthope.

Reael, too, had returned to Bantam, determined to bring to a satisfactory conclusion the tiresome business in the Banda Islands. He wrote to Ball ordering the immediate evacuation of Run and declaring that any ships found in the Banda Islands, or anywhere else in the Moluccas, would be sunk. 'If you refuse,' he fulminated, 'we shall have to help ourselves with all means time and opportunity will give us, believing ourselves to be guiltless before God and the world.' Ball scoffed at this threat and stood defiant, so infuriating Jan Coen that he posted a declaration of war on the gates of the Dutch compound, 'threatening to put them [the English] to the edge of the sword'. Hostilities between the English and Dutch now became so serious that even the local ruler became alarmed. When he asked to see a copy of the Dutch declaration of war, the English ran back to the Dutch compound 'and when they were unable to detach the paper, they tore down the gate and brought it to him (document and all)'.

Ball now decided it was time to act. In a letter to Reael he wrote: 'for your threats, I respect them not, having God and a just cause for my comfort, and you a foul and horrid and shameful matter … Hitherto I have shed no blood willingly; and if blood must be shed, it shall not be my fault, it being lawful in defence of myself.'

That Ball had shed no blood was hotly disputed by the Dutch. Fifteen of their compatriots had recently been massacred in Macassar, an atrocity they ascribed to the machinations of the English factor. Worse still, a number of Spanish and Portuguese prisoners had escaped from a Dutch ship in Bantam harbour and the English had promptly given them asylum. This last event tipped the balance from hatred into warfare and every day there were skirmishes on the streets of Bantam as rival sailors attacked each other with knives and cutlasses. The East India Company archives are littered with accusations of Dutch brutality; a steward named

William Clarke, for example, claims to have been wandering through the marketplace when set upon by a gang of Dutch sailors, stripped naked, and whipped across his bare back. They 'cruelly cut his flesh, and then washed him with salt and vinegar, and laid him again in irons'.

The seas around Bantam had become equally dangerous. In November 1617, the English pinnace *Speedwell* was met by three Dutch vessels carrying a Dutch dignitary from Bantam to Jakarta. She was ordered to lower her flag and submit to a search by Dutch troops but before she had a chance to comply (according to the English report) she was 'shot through and through, and lastly entered and taken, having one man wounded and one killed'. Her crew were manacled and the vessel towed towards Bantam in triumph, 'and it was verily thought they [the English and Dutch] would have fought together in the Road, for the General of the Hollanders had brought thither fourteen great ships ready to fight, where the English had nine, which they fitted for defence; but they fought not, for the Governor of Bantam forbade them to fight in his Road, and threatened them that if they did fight, contrary to his command, he would cut the throats of all their men that he should find upon the land.'

The English, still fuming over the seizure of the *Swan* and the *Defence*, now had the *Speedwell* to add to their list of grievances. They sought all possible means to recover the ships, as Coen recounted in a gleeful letter to Amsterdam. 'It caused a great to-do,' he wrote. 'One day they threaten to sail to Banda in force and take revenge, and the next they say they will attack our ships at sea. They expect to get even by reprisals in the Channel at home and they are going to break our heads. Daily they come up with new threats which clearly shows that they are quite confused.'

All the time that these arguments were raging in Bantam, Courthope had been maintaining his dogged stand on Run. Although he and his men were plagued by a constant lack of supplies, the occasional junk broke through the Dutch blockade and landed rice and arak on the island, to everyone's great relief. Many were suffering from malnutrition and dysentery – a result of their bland diet and the putrid and infected water. But after more than fifteen months of hardship, 'the captain' learned from a passing trader that help was on its way. In the spring of 1618, three English ships were despatched to Run with orders to relieve Courthope and develop trade with the rest of the islands. The crew were bullish and ready to fight, believing their force sufficient to scatter any Dutch ships sent to intercept them.

As one of the ships, the *Solomon*, neared the Banda Islands a cheer went up from the little force of besieged Englishmen on Run. It was a moment of great excitement and they scrambled up Run's cliffs for a better view of the vessel. She was 'some five leagues from Polaroon [Run],' wrote Courthope in his journal, 'comming from the westwards with the very last of the westerly windes'. She was a large ship and was heavily laden with hundreds of tons of rice, fish and 'six hundred jarres of arack'. With the wind blowing a stiff westerly they confidently predicted that she would make the harbour in less than an hour.

Four Dutch vessels had been despatched from Neira to monitor the *Solomon*'s progress but these were unable to reach Run due to the wind, a cause of much mirth to Courthope's men. But their jeering was brought to an abrupt halt when the wind suddenly changed direction and the sails of the Dutch ships 'were taken with an easterly'. The Hollanders were now able to give chase and the

Englishmen watched in horror as the unequal forces prepared to do battle.

'The fight was in sight of Polaroon [Run],' recorded a nervous Courthope, 'some three leagues off.' Stuck on his island prison, he could only hope that the *Solomon* would score an early success and send the Dutch ships scurrying back to Neira. But almost from the beginning the English found themselves at a massive disadvantage for the *Solomon* was so deeply laden with supplies that she was unable to use her lower tier of ordnance, dramatically reducing her ability to fight. The crew put up a valiant resistance, answering 'shot for shot all that afternoone, but our powder was naught, and could not carrie the shot home'. The Dutch, meanwhile, 'plyed their great ordnance upon us, killing three men and hurt thirteene or fourteene others'.

For almost seven hours the ships did battle, peppering each other with shot until they were 'almost board and board' and the rival soldiers were engaged in hand-to-hand combat. The English captain, Cassarian David, soon found himself within shouting distance of the Dutch commander who ordered him to take in his colours, strike his sails, and come aboard to negotiate. Perceiving his situation to be hopeless the Englishman agreed, descending into the commander's cabin for discussions. When several hours had passed and Cassarian did not return the crew assumed that he had been taken prisoner.

It was during this lull in the fighting that a party of warlike Bandanese had rowed out to the *Solomon*. To them, surrender was both shameful and unthinkable and the English feared that if these fighters learned that their captain was negotiating a truce they would go on the rampage, killing everyone irrespective of nationality. Muttering vaguely about a cease-fire they disarmed the

Bandanese of their weapons, taking special care to relieve them of their deadly *kris* daggers. It was a wise precaution for when the Dutch finally came to take possession of the ship, eight Bandanese who had managed to conceal their daggers hurled themselves at the invaders. 'They played their parts excellently,' wrote one of the crew, 'for they drove the Flemings overboord, by fortie at once; some up into the foure shrouds, some one way, and some another, that they had scoured the deckes of them all. I thinke that if the Bandanese had had them upon plaine ground, they would have put the Flemmings to the sword, every man of them.' After wreaking havoc on the Dutch, the Bandanese were overpowered and all but seven were killed.

Courthope was exasperated as he watched these events from the cliffs of Run. In a letter to the directors in London he informed their worships that rather than yielding in the disgraceful way that the *Solomon*'s captain had done he 'would have sunke downe right in the sea first'. It was a characteristically defiant attitude and doubtless Courthope meant every word. He was bitterly disappointed by his continued misfortune and speaks of 'the hard fortune fallen to our ships bound thither this year.' He placed much of the blame on the authorities in Bantam who sent the ships so close to the monsoon that they invariably did not even get within sight of Run.

I much marvel you sent this year with so weak forces, you seeing they use all the means possible they can to bar us of all trade in these parts ... Therefore, if you mean the Company to have any trade with these islands, or the Moluccas, it must not be deferred any longer, but to send such forces the next westerly monsoon to maintain that we have, or

Run seen from neighbouring Nailaka. Nathaniel Courthope built a bastion on this low-lying atoll which was to prove critical to Run's defence. When ordered by the Dutch commander to surrender his stronghold, he vowed to fight to the last man. 'And if they win it,' he wrote, 'by God's help I make no doubt but they shall pay full dearly for it with effusion of much blood.'

else all is gone, and not to be expected hereafter any more trade this way.

This year I have withheld it from them with much difficulty, without any relief or aid ... not so much as one letter from you to advise me what course you intend to take in this business, I having but 38 men to withstand their force and tyranny, which is a very weak strength to withstand their unruly odds of forces. Our wants are extreme; neither have we any victuals or drink, but only rice and water, which had not God sent in four or five junks to have relieved us with rice I must have been fain to have given up our

King's and Company's right for want of relief, which relief is weak. Therefore I pray you consider well of these affairs, and suffer us not to be forced to yield ourselves into such tyrants hands ... I am determined to hold it out until the next westerly monsoon, in despite of them, or else we are determined all to die in defence of it. At present they have eight ships here, and two gallies, and to my knowledge all fitted and ready to come against us; so I look daily and hourly, and if they win it, by God's help I make no doubt but they shall pay full dearly for it with effusion of much blood.

Courthope's position had never been weaker. His small force had been decimated by sickness and his supplies were almost non-existent. With just a couple of sacks of rice left in their storehouse, his beleaguered garrison was now forced to subsist on the revolting sago porridge, supplementing their diet with the occasional fish caught in the waters surrounding Nailaka. 'Had not foure of five Java[nese] junkes come in,' he wrote in his diary, 'for want of victuals we must have given up; and still [we] live on rice only, with a little fish, which in foule weather is not to be found.' Worse still, they were 'daily expecting an assault from the Hollanders' and had to keep a constant watch from the battlements. Such threatened attacks rarely materialised, but the fear of assault wearied the men who were already suffering the effects of prolonged hardship and starvation. Yet Courthope continued to exert a powerful influence over both his own men and the local islanders and when the Dutch attempted a landing on Run some weeks after the *Solomon*'s capture, the invading force was crushed by a group of Bandanese warriors.

Courthope managed to stay in close contact with the English prisoners; both those from the *Swan* and the *Defence*, and also the survivors from the *Solomon*. Under the cover of darkness, his Bandanese troops repeatedly put to sea and smuggled letters to and from the English held on Ai Island and Neira. One of the first replies he received was from Cassarian David whose decision to surrender the *Solomon* had earned him good treatment at the hands of the Dutch. Ignorant of Courthope's anger about the manner in which he submitted, he wrote to the English commander gleefully explaining that 'my selfe with one English boy to attend me remayne on Pooloway, where the Generall and his Councill doe abide, at whose hands I doe daily find much favour and kind usage.'

The same could not be said of the other English prisoners. Most had been incarcerated in Fort Revenge on Ai Island from whose dungeons there was no hope of escape. Chained together by the neck and with nowhere to relieve themselves, conditions soon became intolerable. The Dutch made life even less bearable by their routine humiliation of their captives. 'They pissed and ★★★★ upon our heads,' wrote Bartholomew Churchman, 'and in this manner we lay, untill such time as we were broken out from top to toe like lepers, having nothing to eat but durtie rice, and stinking rainewater.' That they were still alive at all, he writes, is thanks to a Dutch woman 'named Mistris Cane, and some poore blackes, that brought us a little fruit'.

Others had similar complaints. 'We were very hardly and inhumanely used,' wrote one, 'being fettered and shackelled in the day time, and close locked up at nights.' 'They keep many of us fast bound and fettered in irons,' recorded another, 'in most loathsome and darke stinking dungeons, and give us no sustenance, but a little durtie rice to eat ... many have dyed, who were fetcht out of the dungeons and so basely buried, more like dogges than Christians.' Those that dared to complain were given an even harsher regime. Churchman found himself 'clapt in irons and [placed] in the raine and the cold stormes of the night, and in the day time where the hot sunne shone upon him, and scorched him, without any shelter at all'. All this was because he berated a Dutchman for insulting King James I's wife. Others would be set in the sun until they were blistered with sunburn, then chained below the sewers 'where their ordures and pisse fell upon them in the night'.

Courthope was even more horrified to learn that the English prisoners were being used as pawns in a nasty game of propaganda played out by the Dutch governor-general. 'Lawrence Reael ... caused grates and cages to be made in their ship, and did put us therein, and carried us in them bound in irons from port to port amongst the Indians, and thus in scornfull and deriding manner and sort spake unto the Indians as followeth: "Behold and see, heere is the people of that Nation, whose King you care so much for." '

After many months of such treatment the English prisoners could endure no more and wrote to the Dutch governor-general pleading for mercy. But to their dismay they found that Reael had been replaced by an even less compromising individual, a man they knew as John Peter Sacone but whose real name was Jan Pieterzoon Coen. They begged him to 'consider of our extreame wants and miseries, and help us to some better sustenance'. Unfortunately they could not have picked a worse man to ask for clemency for Coen 'most wickedly replied with base speeches, and bade us be gone, and trouble him no more; for if we did, he would cause us all to be hanged speedily'. Courthope wrote frequent letters to the prisoners urging them to bear their trials with fortitude: 'For make no question but this year to be all set free ... [and] what extremity the Dutch useth unto you,' he told them, 'they shall have their measure full and abounding either in gentleness or rigour; and whereas they have heretofore protested fire and sword, fire and sword they shall have repaid unto their bosoms.' The English prisoners never forgot their grievances, reserving particular hatred for Coen, and long after the Run saga had drawn to a conclusion the survivors continued to complain of their hardships and demand compensation from the Dutch government.

Courthope's had ceased to count the passing weeks and months. Each new day brought boredom and fear, punctuated by lengthy watch duties from the battlements and an endless battle against hunger. The little pinnace that Courthope had managed to acquire from a passing junk proved to be of little use. After a single journey to the island of Ceram, from which she returned laden with yet more sago, she was 'so full of leakes ... that we haled her on shoare and found her so rotten that we saved what we could and set fire on the rest'. When the rains failed to materialise in the autumn of 1618, the island's water reserves became precariously low and were soon so teeming with tropical parasites and worms that the men had to drink through clenched teeth to sieve out the fauna. At one point a group of them could stand their hardships no longer and threatened Courthope with mutiny. For a while the situation looked desperate but Courthope's 'mild carriage and earnest protestations' won them back and the men eventually repented.

It was not until January 1619, more than two years after they had arrived on Run, that the English had an inkling of good news. A local junk which managed to sail undetected into the harbour brought a letter arrived from Bantam, a letter written by Sir Thomas Dale who had sailed from England with a huge armada. 'Master Courthope,' began Sir Thomas's letter, 'as unknown I remember my love, which I will always be ready to express in respect of your worthy service for the honour of our country and the benefit of our honourable employers.' His mission was to expel the Dutch from Java and when that had been accomplished he intended to race eastwards to relieve Courthope's brave band of men. Attached to his letter was a note from John Jourdain who had returned to the Indies with Dale's fleet to take up his new position as 'President of the English' living in the East. Jourdain promised that as soon as the Dutch had been defeated, 'we determine to proceed for Banda … hoping in God that we shall be able to lay some part of their insolent pride.'

Courthope was most pleased to learn that the English fleet was under the command of Sir Thomas Dale. Dale was a man of great experience, a 'heroike lion', who had excelled in a number of different capacities. Previous to his employment with the East India Company he had been selected by the Virginia Company in London to serve as governor of their fledgling colony in America, 'the hardest task he ever undertook,' but one he carried out with such aplomb that he left the colony 'in great prosperity and peace'. When he arrived back in England in 1616, he did so in style, bringing with him the celebrated Indian princess Pocahontas. Soon after his return, Dale was called to a meeting with the East India Company and was offered the job of chief commander of a critical expedition to the

East. He accepted and was given the command of five ships and an annual salary of £480.

The outward journey was not without its incidents. At the Cape both Dale and Jourdain almost drowned when a little skiff capsized, whilst a few weeks later the aged and corpulent Captain Parker, vice admiral of the fleet, dropped dead. Far more serious was an accident at Java when Dale's magnificent flagship, the *Sun*, was wrecked on the island of Engano. The heavy loss of life troubled Dale less than the fact that he had lost his possessions and he bemoaned in a letter to London that 'the *Sun* was cast away, wherein I lost all that I had in that ship to my shirt.' He later returned to the site of the wreck to see if he could recover his goods but was disappointed to find nothing of value. Although a number of his crew had managed to swim ashore, not a single one was left alive and the only trace of their existence was a pile of eighteen skulls lying on the beach. As revenge for this apparent act of cannibalism Dale shot two natives, burned their houses and cut down all their trees. Such a response was typical of this pugnacious commander who was ruthless in his revenge. Punctilious in official matters and slow to give praise, he was feared rather than loved by his men. 'It was always "I will and require" ', wrote one of his juniors, ' "this must be done," and "this shall be done," and yet in the end we must signe what he says.' All too often he allowed his temper to overrule his judgement, a fault which would prove dangerous when pitched against the calm detachment of Jan Coen.

The loss of the *Sun* sharpened Dale's resolve and he determined to revenge himself on the Dutch. As he sailed towards the Javanese coast he spied a richly laden Dutch ship called the *Black Lion* sailing through the straits. He promptly set upon her and the ship was soon captured.

Continuing towards Bantam he was delighted to see a large number of other English vessels at anchor, bringing his total fleet to no less than fifteen ships – 'the bay was not large enough to harbour them all.'

The Dutch were now seriously alarmed and Coen immediately sent a letter of protest to Dale demanding the release of the *Black Lion*. When Dale was handed this letter he 'only scolded, stamped on the ground, swore, cursed [and asked] why the letter was written in Dutch and not in French, Spanish or any other language'. He finally sent the messenger on his way, 'swearing and cursing that he would take all he could get.'

Dale was driven by revenge, as he admitted in his letter to Courthope: 'My stay [in Bantam] is to revenge the abuses received from them [the Dutch], having now an opportunity by a difference between them and the King of Jakarta.' Jakarta, a small port that lay fifty miles to the east of Bantam, had become increasingly important to the Dutch: Coen found life in Bantam intolerable and petitioned the King of Jakarta for permission to build a fort in his town, intending to make it the future centre of Dutch activities. A few weeks later he learned that the English were also in the process of erecting a fortified factory, presumably to stop the Dutch from gaining the upper hand. In the ensuing game of cat and mouse the Dutch retaliated for the capture of the *Black Lion* by burning this factory to the ground.

Dale toyed with the idea of destroying the Dutch factory in Bantam but was soon struck by an altogether more destructive plan. With a large fleet at his disposal and the Hollanders in the middle of moving to Jakarta, he made a pact with the native ruler and vowed to wipe them out altogether. Coen panicked: 'I am sitting here in a cage,' he wrote, 'surrounded by various bulwarks and batteries, the river closed with piles, and a very strong battery at the place of the English.' Realising that an attack was imminent and defeat a certainty, he convened an emergency council and, after much deliberation, it was decided to withdraw most of the men to the ships and contest the issue at sea.

On the morning of 30 December 1618, the English fleet gathered within sight of Jakarta. Dale had eleven ships at his disposal, with four more left to protect Bantam, while Coen had just seven ships, many of them in a deplorable state. He was outnumbered and outgunned and had a total fighting force of just seventy men. Yet Dale seemed in no hurry to press the attack and spent the day sailing to and fro, hoping that the sight of his vastly superior fleet would weaken the Dutch resolve. In the afternoon he sent a messenger to Coen demanding that his entire fleet surrender. Coen refused, only to be informed that the English admiral intended to sink each and every ship. When Coen shrugged off this threat a battle became a certainty and the two sides spent that night, New Year's Eve, in a state of nervous excitement. Yet it was not until 2 January, after another day's stand-off, that the battle finally began. The two fleets fought all day, 'a cruel bloody fight,' according to Sir Thomas, 'with 3,000 great shot between both the fleets, many men maimed and slain on both sides, but they had (as we are given to understand) four times as many men slain and maimed as we'. The English should have trounced the Dutch; as it was, they appeared hesitant and defensive, the unfortunate consequence of Dale's armada consisting of three separate ventures, each with its own commander who refused to risk his own ships for the common good. As night closed the battle still hung in the balance.

Coen called a council of war to decide what to do. The

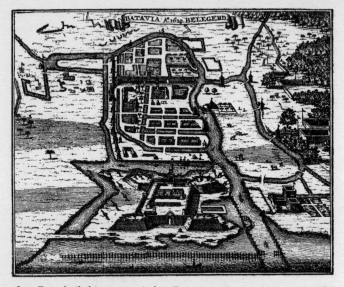

Jan Coen built his new capital at Batavia in Java (now Jacarta). After 'a cruel bloody fight,' the English came close to capturing the city in 1619, but snatched defeat from the jaws of victory.

Dutch were now in a perilous position for their ammunition had run low, they had numerous wounded and their vessels were scarcely seaworthy. Some argued in favour of retreat, others wanted to continue the fight, but 'all glumly looked at each other, not being able to come up with the answer.'

It was the English who made up their minds. As dawn broke, Dale's fleet was joined by another three ships (those from Bantam) and he prepared to renew the battle. Coen immediately ordered his men to hoist the sails and head for the Banda Islands. The indomitable Dutch were in retreat.

It was now that Dale made his greatest mistake. He should have chased after Coen with his overwhelmingly superior force and pressed the battle to its inevitable conclusion. Instead, he chose to remain where he was, arguing that Coen's flight would enable him to capture their Dutch headquarters. Yet a letter to London reveals that he was doubtful about his strategy and wondered if he had made the wrong decision: 'Their fleet [sailed] away eastward for Banda,' he wrote, '... and so by this means we lost them which troubled me very much.'

Coen also wrote home, castigating the Seventeen for their lack of support and for not listening to his warnings. 'And now see what has happened,' he said, informing them that the Company is faced with 'a thousand perils ... even if the Almighty wills us his best'. He ended the letter with a stark warning: 'If your Lordships have no intention to send me yearly large numbers of ships, people, and other necessities, I pray once more that you release me at the soonest, because without such means I cannot execute your wishes.'

In the event, the Dutch were saved by Dale's hesitancy. Had he defeated Coen at sea he would have been able to return to Jakarta, seize their headquarters, then sail to the Banda Islands and relieve Courthope and his men. Instead, he allowed the Dutch fleet to escape intact and even bungled the storming of their fort, snatching defeat from the jaws of victory. Dale now lost heart completely. Rankled by the feeling that he failed where he should have been victorious, he ordered his fleet to sail for India's Coromandel Coast. The voyage was a tiresome one for his officers were close to mutiny and more than eighty of his crew died at sea. Soon after arriving at Masulipatam, Dale became grievously ill and, for the next twenty days, he fought his illness, talking contemptuously of death and testifying to his good Christianity. On 19 July 1619, he 'departed this life in peace' and his body was 'enclosed and housed in form of a tomb, which is almost finished'.

Coen was overjoyed when he heard of Dale's death but was soon to learn of even better news. His old adversary, John Jourdain, had taken charge of two ships and, concerned about his friend Nathaniel Courthope, set sail for the East. But no sooner had he reached a sheltered harbour on the Malay Peninsula than he realised he was being tailed by three Dutch vessels. These blocked the harbour's entrance and attacked the English while they were at anchor. Jourdain fought fiercely but when almost fifty men had been killed he raised the flag of truce and prepared to negotiate. 'He showed himself aboard the Sampson before the main mast ... where the Flemings espying him, most treacherously shot at him with a musket, and shot him into the body near the heart, of which wound he died within half an hour after.' His death caused a scandal, particularly when everyone questioned confirmed that he was in the midst of negotiating a surrender. 'Our noble minded President was slain in parley with Henrie Johnson [the Dutch commander],' wrote one crew member. 'The President had sounded a parley and in talking with Hendrike Johnson received his death wound with a musket,' recorded another. Others claimed that Coen himself had ordered Jourdain's death. 'General John Peter Sacone [Coen] gave Hendrike Jansen a gold chain worth 1,400 guilders, putting it himself about his neck. He also gave 100 reals to the man who actually shot the President.'

The directors of the Dutch East India Company were embarrassed by the incident and took the unusual step of issuing an official statement of what had happened:

Your President and our Commander came above the

hatches and began to confer (while the two ships were alongside). Our other ships could not be advertised of the aforesaid parley by reason of shortness of time. The Morning Star coming up fired in ignorance of what before had passed between the chiefs of both fleets. A musket shot hit your President in the belly, without any special aim, but the mishap might as well have befallen our own Commander because a cannon ball (from the Morning Star) went through his own ship.

Whether true or not, Coen's position was considerably strengthened by the deaths of Dale and Jourdain. He now had just one thorn in his side, Nathaniel Courthope, who was as resolute as ever about the defence of his island fortress.

The dreadful news about Sir Thomas Dale's fleet took time to reach Run. On 13 February 1619, more than a month after the sea battle, Courthope spied three Dutch ships heading for Neira, 'one whereof had her beak-head shot off, and shot through in forty places'. His spies informed him that Coen was at Amboyna, busily assembling a huge fleet with which to launch a massive attack against Jakarta. Soon after, Courthope learned to his dismay that the bulk of Dale's fleet had sailed for India. 'This was cold comfort to me,' he wrote in his journal, 'which had neither direction nor stocks.' The news soon got worse. Courthope was informed of Jourdain's death in a letter from his old friend George Muschamp, himself on the verge of death. 'I [am] in miserable torture with the losse of my right legge (shot off with a canon) for want of medicines to apply to it … I doe not much value my life, and have every day lesse comfort and courage to remain in these parts.' His letter ends with the news that Courthope's defiance has spread far and wide: 'and I make no question [that] our honourable Masters will truly value your deserts'. Indeed they did: with glowing reports of Courthope's defiance filtering back to London the directors voted that he be awarded a gift of £100 a year for services to King and Company.

When Courthope learned that he and his men had been abandoned to their fate his most sensible course would have been to surrender to the Dutch. His heroic stand had been way beyond the call of duty and he could have retired with honour intact. But to submit now, after more than three years of hardship, was not in Courthope's nature. He was to choose a far more glorious path, vowing to fight to the bitter end in defence of his island stronghold. He no longer had any money and was reduced to bartering his men's remaining possessions for essential supplies, but there was never enough food for everyone and the sick began to die, often from dysentery contracted from the foul water. 'We have rubbed off the skinne alreadie,' he writes, referring to their destitution, 'and if we rub any longer, shall rub to the bone.' Each day Courthope would rally his malnourished men, urging them to stand resolute in the face of Dutch brutality. And each day his men would vow to stand by 'the captain', greeting his words with noisy acclaim. They manned their defences, primed their cannon, and awaited the imminent Dutch onslaught.

On 18 October 1620, Courthope was heartened by some good news. The men of Great Banda had risen up against the Dutch and plunged the island into turmoil. It was rumoured that they now wished to join Courthope's men in a full-scale attack on the hated Hollanders. For Courthope, this news came not a moment too soon and he immediately decided to visit Great Banda and instil in the natives the same sense of resolution that he had brought to his band of Englishmen. But these men, reliant for so long on their captain, were most unhappy about him sailing to Great Banda — even under the cover of darkness — and petitioned him to think again. 'I prayed him to stay,' wrote Robert Hayes, his number two, 'but hee refused.'

'Thus went he over that night with his Boy William, wel fitted with muskets and weapons; promising to returne in five dayes.' But unbeknown to anyone there had been a traitor lurking on Run. A lone Hollander, who had passed himself off as a deserter, had sent message of Courthope's movements to the Dutch governor-general in Neira. The governor-general could scarcely believe his good fortune and acted immediately, equipping a heavily armed pinnace and despatching it to sea with one simple order: kill the troublesome Englishman. Nothing was left to chance; the assassins planned precisely where they would attack Courthope, in a treacherous channel of water where the current and tides would leave him no manoeuvrability.

The Dutch soldiers put to sea as night fell and lay in wait some two miles off Ai's coastline. For hours they saw nothing but the dim outline of the island, but at 'about two or three a clocke in the morning' a lantern came into view — Courthope's boat. In the pitch darkness they waited until he was almost upon them, trapped and surrounded, before suddenly opening fire with their muskets. In a flash Courthope was firing back, his weapon ready loaded in preparation for just such an attack. But right from the outset it was an uneven battle. Although Courthope momentarily silenced the Dutch guns, he noticed a second boat approaching, armed with 'some fortie small shot'. Undeterred, he returned shot for shot until his 'piece being choked', he could fire no more. Hurling his gun into the water, he was now a sitting duck – an unarmed and defenceless target for more than fifty Dutch soldiers. His final end was not long in coming. 'Receiving a shot on the brest [he] sate downe ... then leapt over-board in his clothes.' It was the last time he was seen alive.

News that Courthope had been 'slain by Hollanders' filtered slowly across the Banda Islands and it was not until 27 October 1620, more than a week after his death, that the Englishmen on Run learned of the treachery that had killed their captain. They were devastated by what they were told. For four years they had been led by the inspired Courthope and had suffered the greatest of hardships in withstanding a force hundreds of times stronger than their own. Now, 'the captain' was dead and their future as bleak as it was uncertain. After allowing the men to recover from the initial shock, Courthope's second-in-command, Robert Hayes, summoned a council and asked them if they would accept him as their leader. There was not a moment's hesitation. With a tremendous cry, 'they all promised that as they had been ruled by the captaine, so now they would be ruled by Robert Hayes.'

It was a brave show but with Courthope's death the men had lost their defiance and their heroic stand on Run was nearing its tragic end. With the loss of more men to sickness, the long nightly watches broke the spirit of these half-starved survivors, particularly as there was no longer 'the captain' to rouse them. Their last day came soon enough. The Dutch governor-general sent twenty-five ships and a huge army to Run with the intention of leading a massive frontal assault on the island, 'whereupon the blacks came to Mr Hayes and asked him whether he would defend them, and told him if he would then they would fight it out to the last man. But Mr Hayes answered that he was not able, nor could not.'

So the Dutch 'landed unopposed' and harangued the 'poor miserable people of the island'. Knowing that the tiny band of Englishmen were finished, the Dutch reserved all their anger for the natives. 'They forced the country people to dismount the ordnance from the two English forts on the great island, and threw them down on the rocks; four were broken, the rest remained on the sands altogether unservicable.' Next they ordered the natives to demolish the island's defences 'with their own hands ... so that before night there was not one stone left upon another; and ranging the whole island, caused all the walls, little and great, to be made even with the ground, not so much as sparing the monuments of the dead'. Once this was complete they took all the chieftains prisoner, publicly humiliating them by compelling each and every one to submit to the Dutch 'by presenting them with a nutmeg tree in a basin, as is the custom of these parts'. Their last act before sailing away was to rip down the flag of St George that was still flying in the village. It was replaced by the Dutch colours, signifying the end of a siege that had lasted 1,540 days.

The English were no less humiliated. Forced to watch their island fortress being dismantled, they were then summoned to the Dutch commander who contemptuously informed them that they could keep Nailaka, the sandy atoll adjoining Run. With no nutmeg trees it was useless to the Dutch; with cannon trained upon it from Run, it was equally useless to the English. Hayes and his men stayed on the island only long enough to catch a passing boat and escape to Amboyna.

'Thus was Pooloroon lost,' wrote Captain Sir Humphrey

Fitzherbert, the newly arrived captain of an English fleet, 'which in Mr Courthope's time by his good resolution with a few men maintained itself to their [the Dutch] disgrace, and now by the fearfulness of Mr Hayes and his irresolution is fearfully lost'. Such words are unfair on Hayes and do not sit easily with Captain Fitzherbert's own actions. When he arrived in the area in charge of a heavily armed vessel, the only shots he fired were a brief salvo nervously to celebrate the Dutch victory.

Courthope's defiance would ultimately pay handsome dividends, but his cruel death passed quietly into English history and we look in vain for any tomb or epitaph commemorating this very English hero. Even his final resting place remains a mystery: 'And what became of him I know not,' wrote Hayes at the time, 'but the blacks said surely he there sunke, by reason of his wounds and his clothes all about him.'

Yet he later received information, brought by a Dutchman, that suggested the English captain had been buried with full honours and given a tomb befitting to his heroism. 'The Captaine Nathaniel is killed in the prow,' said this Dutchman, 'for which God knoweth I was heartily sorie. We have buried him so stately and honestly as ever we could fitting for such a man.'

CHAPTER ELEVEN

TRIAL BY
FIRE AND WATER

NATHANIEL COURTHOPE'S MURDER left Coen in a seemingly invincible position. For almost four years this stubborn Englishman had been a thorn in his side, thwarting his ambitions of total dominance in the Spice Islands. Now he was dead, leaving the Dutchman with unchallenged control of the Banda Islands.

During the long years of siege, Coen had concentrated his efforts in other parts of the East Indies. He had wasted no time in regrouping his forces after his flight from Sir Thomas Dale. Heading for Amboyna, he had trained his men for battle, then led them back to Jakarta where he vowed to flatten every building in the town. He attacked within two days of arriving, leading his thousand-strong force from the front. Although the local population outnumbered the Dutch by more than three to one, they soon lost heart and their defences crumbled. True to his word, Coen had the towers and fortifications destroyed and the rest of the town burned to the ground. By the end of the day Jakarta had ceased to exist. When it rose again from the ashes it was built to Coen's specifications as befitted the 'capital' of the Dutch East Indies. It was given the new name Batavia in honour of the first tribes who had settled in the Netherlands.

*Jan Pieterszoon Coen, circa 1626, when Governor-General of the
Dutch East Indies. Ruthless in crushing opposition, he sold most of
the Bandanese population into slavery. 'They are indolent people,' he
wrote, 'of whom little good can be expected.*

Coen immediately informed Amsterdam of his triumph: 'It is certain that this victory and the fleeing of the English will create quite a furore throughout the Indies,' he wrote. 'This will enhance the honour and the reputation of the Dutch nation. Now everyone will want to be our friend.'

Within a week of his arrival in Java, Coen had reversed the balance of power. His next plan was nothing less than the total annihilation of the English fleet whose ships were scattered over a wide area of ocean. But scarcely had he given the order to sink every vessel east of Arabia than a messenger arrived at Batavia bearing wholly unexpected news. To Coen's astonishment he was informed that in July 1619, the Dutch East India Company, together with its English counterpart, had signed an agreement whereby all fighting between the two companies must cease at once. The document, known as the Treaty of Defence, was the fruit of the third Anglo-Dutch conference which had been summoned to discuss the deteriorating situation in the East. After much argument the two sides decided that all grievances should be 'forgiven and forgotten'. Captured ships were to be returned, prisoners released and employers, 'both high and low, should henceforth live and converse as trusted friends'. The most important clause of the treaty stated that the English were to be granted one third of all trade in the Spice Islands. In return, the English agreed to take active steps to defend the region from the Spanish and Portuguese.

Coen was stunned when he read the terms of the treaty. 'The English owe you a debt of gratitude,' he wrote to his employers, 'because after they have worked themselves out of the Indies, your Lordships put them right back again ... it is incomprehensible that the English should be allowed one third of the cloves, nutmegs and mace [since] they cannot lay claim to a single grain of sand in the Moluccas,

Amboyna, or Banda.' With the stroke of a pen all his hard work had come undone.

Had the Dutch directors known the true picture in the East Indies it is doubtful that they would have signed the treaty. But with their signatures duly attached Coen was left with just two options: to abide by its terms or to wreck it. Given his hatred of the English it is scarcely surprising that he chose the latter option, playing his hand with characteristic skill.

The treaty had called for the establishment of a joint Fleet of Defence in which the English would supply one third of the men, money and ships and the Dutch would supply the rest. This fleet was to complete the expulsion of the Spanish and Portuguese from the East Indies, destroying their remaining bases in the Malay Peninsula, China, and the Philippines, and to act as a naval patrol force to guard the monopoly on spices. Coen was well aware that the English had few ships at their disposal and with this in mind proposed long and time-consuming expeditions across huge expanses of ocean. Within months the English were struggling to meet their side of the deal.

Coen now saw his chance. He had always vowed to crush the Banda Islands but had hesitated in recent months because any military expedition would have to include English ships. Knowing that these were all currently at sea, Coen now proposed a massive expedition and when the English argued that they lacked resources he accused them of reneging on the deal and haughtily informed them that he would proceed without them.

His fleet arrived at Neira Island in the spring of 1621, anchoring under the guns of Fort Nassau. Here he gathered his forces, assembling a fleet of 13 large ships, 36 barges and 3 messenger boats, as well as an army of 1,600 men and 80

Japanese mercenaries, most of them experts in the art of execution. It was the largest force ever seen in the Bandas and it was augmented by a band of freed slaves, Dutch townspeople and the 250-strong garrison of Fort Nassau.

Despite the humiliating capitulation of Run, a handful of English were still living on the Banda Islands. Great Banda was home to an English merchant, two helpers and eight Chinese guards, while a couple of men continued to stage a token resistance to the Dutch on the tiny atoll of Nailaka. To these hardy survivors Coen now sent a message inviting them to take part in the forthcoming invasion of Great Banda. All declined his offer – a response that came as no surprise to Coen who had been informed that there were many other English secretly training Bandanese soldiers.

The forthcoming invasion placed the English merchant, Robert Randall, in something of a quandary. Many of the village elders stood by their former submission to the English king and, claiming that Great Banda was technically English soil, reminded Randall that any attack on the island would effectively be an attack on His Majesty. Desperate to delay the invasion, Randall wrote a strongly worded letter to Coen advising him 'not to attempt any violence'. Needless to say Coen was most displeased to receive such a letter and 'threw [it] from him in a great rage, scarce vouchsafing to reade it over, and caused the messenger to be thrust out of doores'. As the poor man picked himself up from the dirt, Coen warned him to escape while he could, 'for whomsoever he should find [on Great Banda] he would take them as his utter enemies, and they should fare no better than the inhabitants'.

Prior to his attack Coen sent his yacht, the *Hert*, to circle its coastline. The boat came under sustained and extremely accurate musket fire which cost the lives of two crew members and injured ten others. The *Hert's* commander reported that he had identified no less than a dozen forts close to the shore. Furthermore, all the island's ridges were heavily fortified, and he had sighted numerous English gunners.

Great Banda had long been a magnet for thousands of disaffected Bandanese who had taken refuge in its wild and inaccessible mountain range. It was, according to one English visitor, 'the greatest and richest iland of all the iles of Banda; strong and almost inaccessible, as it were a castle'. The village of Lonthor on the island's northern coastline was an almost impregnable stronghold 'situate on the brow of a sharpe hill, the ascent as difficult as by a ladder'. It had three lines of fortifications and each of these was lined with cannons and muskets which could be trained on passing ships with devastating effect. Coen's men knew the risks of attacking the island and lost heart before the fight had even begun. To rally his troops the Dutch governor-general made an impassioned speech about glory and destiny, urging his men to fight with honour and courage. Then, hoping to confuse the enemy, he landed them at a number of different points on Great Banda. The Dutch fought with considerable daring, scaling the sea cliffs and crawling along ledges and promontories in order to capture key positions. It was an uneven struggle and the invaders were repulsed on numerous occasions because 'one man above was worth twenty below', but by the end of the first day they had most of the lowlands under their control. In this they were helped by the treachery of the Bandanese. At the strategic position of Lakoy, a native guided the attackers through a hidden rear entrance in return for two hundred and fifty pieces-of-eight, while at Orantatta small purses of gold were awarded to any Bandanese who would betray his fellow fighters. With the use of bribes, treachery and daring Great Banda was eventually brought under control and the great defences of Lonthor fell into Dutch hands after a tough struggle on the evening of the second day. The Dutch lost just six men in the attack with a further twenty-seven injured.

The leading orang-kayas now visited Coen aboard his vessel, bringing with them gifts of gold and copper and offering to sue for peace. Coen's terms were harsh; they were to destroy all fortifications, hand in all weapons, vow never again to resist the Dutch, and present their sons as hostages. They were also ordered to sell exclusively to the Dutch East India Company and recognise Dutch sovereignty. This last clause was significant for any future uprising would not be considered as an act of war but an act of treason, and treason in Holland was punishable by death. The chieftains duly signed the agreement – they had little alternative – but Coen was in no doubt that they would renege on it. When they did he vowed to crush them completely.

Robert Randall had wisely kept a low profile throughout the invasion. He and his colleagues had locked themselves into the English warehouse and 'kept themselves within doores' until the island had fallen. His neutrality did little to endear him to the Dutch soldiers who 'sacked our house, tooke away all our goods, murthered three of our Chinese servants, bound the rest (as well English as Chinezes) hand and foote, and threatned them to cut their throats'. The Japanese mercenaries took particular delight in tormenting their prisoners: having decapitated the Chinese, they rolled the severed heads around the feet of the English captives, laughing at the panic they were causing. Then, 'with their weapons readie drawne out, [they] did put a halter on our principall factor's necke, drawing up his head, and stretching out his necke, readie to put him to death'. But they stopped short of executing Randall. Instead, 'as they were bound hand and foot (as foresaid) [they] tumbled them downe over the rocks like dogges, and like to have broken their neckes, and thus bound, carried them aboord their shippes, and kept them prisoners in irons.' Randall was convinced that the Dutch had ordered his execution but that the Japanese had failed to understand the command.

Coen was correct in his belief that the Bandanese had no intention of honouring his treaty. The weapons they handed in were rusty and quite useless whilst the fortifications they demolished were soon replaced by new battlements. Worse still, most of the native population had fled into Great Banda's mountainous hinterland where they staged irregular attacks on stray Dutch troops. On one occasion they ambushed a large group of soldiers, killing nine and leaving twenty-five others with serious injuries.

Coen still had forty-five orang-kayas aboard his ship and these were now interrogated. After a judicious application of burning irons they confessed that the Bandanese never had any intention of abiding by the terms of the surrender and that they planned to launch a counter-offensive against the Dutch within a few weeks. On hearing this the Dutch council condemned the hostages to death – an execution that left at least one Dutch eyewitness horrified and disgusted:

> The forty-four prisoners [one had committed suicide] were brought within the castle, the eight foremost orang-kaya – those, who it was said had 'belled the cat' – being kept apart, the others being herded together like sheep. A round enclosure was built of bamboo just outside the castle, and into it were brought the prisoners, well bound with cords

and surrounded by guards. Their sentence was read out to them for having conspired against the life of the Heer Generael and having broken the terms of the peace. Before the reading of the sentence it was forbidden on pain of death for anyone else to enter the enclosure except only fathers and mothers.

The condemned victims being brought within the enclosure, six Japanese soliders were also ordered inside, and with their sharp swords they beheaded and quartered the eight chief orang-kaya and then beheaded and quartered the thirty-six others. This execution was awful to see. The orang-kaya died silently without uttering any sound except that one of them, speaking in the Dutch tongue, said, 'Sirs, have you then no mercy' but indeed nothing availed.

All that happened was so dreadful as to leave us stunned. The heads and quarters of those who had been executed were impaled upon bamboos and so displayed. Thus did it happen: God knows who is right.

All of us, as professing Christians, were filled with dismay at the way this affair was brought to a conclusion, and we took no pleasure in such dealings.

Coen's conscience was untroubled by the deaths of so many Bandanese: 'They are indolent people,' he wrote, 'of whom little good can be expected.' But the directors in Amsterdam found his brutality distasteful and wrote: 'We had wished that it could have been accomplished by more moderate means.' Coen could rightly feel indignant at such criticism since it was the directors themselves who had originally recommended that 'the Bandanese should be overpowered, the chiefs exterminated and chased away, and the land repopulated.'

Repopulation had long been on Coen's mind and he now prepared the way by rounding up whole communities of Bandanese and shipping them to Batavia to be sold as slaves. The total number transported from the islands remains unknown, but one ship alone was registered as carrying nearly nine hundred people of whom a quarter died en route.

The conquest of the Banda Islands was almost complete. The natives who remained were totally at Coen's mercy for their leaders were dead and their defences in ruins. The English, too, were no longer a threat. All who had survived the siege of Run were now either imprisoned on Ai or in chains on board one or other of the Dutch ships. With little possibility of further trouble, Coen now set sail for Batavia and Holland. On the way he took the opportunity to stop at Amboyna and warn the governor, Herman van Speult, to be on the look-out for any suspicious activities. He was convinced that the English would try to strike back at the Dutch, either in Amboyna or in the Banda Islands and told van Speult to nip any conspiracy in the bud. 'We hope to direct things according to your orders,' replied van Speult, 'and if we hear of any conspiracies … we shall with your sanction do justice to them without delay.'

Carrying out Coen's command to the letter, van Speult employed a large network of agents to inform him of any suspicious activity in town. The events that followed, which would become known across Europe as the Massacre of Amboyna, destroyed any hope that England might have had of recovering ground in the Spice Islands. They also brought England and Holland to the brink of war.

The island of Amboyna was of great importance to the Dutch, both strategically and in terms of the spices it produced. Not only was it the principal port for ships setting sail for the Banda Islands, it was also rich in cloves with much of its 280 square miles given over to clove plantations. 'Amboyna sitteth as Queene between the Iles of Banda and the Molucas,' wrote Captain Humphrey Fitzherbert in his *Pithy Description of the Chiefe Ilands of Banda and Moluccas*. 'Shee is beautfied with the fruits of severall factories and clearly beloved of the Dutch.' Coen had chosen the town of Amboyna as his principal headquarters in the Spice Islands and ordered the building of a 'very stronge castle' from which he could keep an eye on all shipping heading towards the Banda Islands.

One side of Amboyna Castle was washed by the sea while the rest of the building was divided from the town by a moat five fathoms wide which was filled with sea water. The walls and ramparts were strongly fortified with each corner boasting a tower upon which were mounted 'six great pieces of ordnance'. The garrison comprised two hundred Dutch soldiers and a company of free burghers. In addition there were four hundred *mardikers*, or free natives, who could be summoned to defend the castle at a moment's notice. In the harbour eight Dutch vessels lay at anchor as a further line of defence.

That the English could have launched any sustained campaign against the Dutch is most unlikely. By the time Coen sailed for Amsterdam the small band of Englishmen still living in the East Indies were struggling to make ends meet. They received little support from London and the factories they guarded were for the most part broken and half derelict. All were on the brink of insolvency and had virtually abandoned the trade in spices. Indeed the question of closing down these factories had been discussed in the winter of 1622 and the final decision postponed only when it was agreed that advice was needed from London.

The small English factory on Amboyna was in the principal town, also called Amboyna. Here there were a dozen or so men. On the same island, at the villages of Hitu and Larica, resided a handful of other factors bringing the total number of Englishmen to eighteen – a motley band of merchants, sailors, a tailor and a barber who doubled as a surgeon. Between them, these men could muster a total arsenal of three swords and two muskets. Their chief factor was Gabriel Towerson, a veteran merchant who had married William Hawkins' widow, the regal Armenian lady, and chosen to settle in the East. He was a formidable survivor who had outlived all of his contemporaries by many years, and his letters reveal that he was quick to adapt to unfamiliar surroundings and had a shrewd understanding of eastern customs. He was indolent yet reliable, fond of pomp yet intensely practical. When he pitched up at Ahmedabad in India, the new English ambassador Sir Thomas Roe complained that Towerson 'is here arrived with many servants, a trumpet, and more show than I use' – a clear sign that Towerson knew how to win influence at the Moghul court. He held the Dutch in deep distrust, of that there can be no doubt, but he bore no malice against the Dutch governor of Amboyna, Herman van Speult, who had helped him to secure lodgings for the English factors. Indeed even as Van Speult was worrying himself about conspiracies, the Englishman was writing to his superiors in Bantam asking that they send a letter of thanks to the Dutch governor 'together with some beer or a case of strong waters, which will be acceptable to him'. Towerson and his men were frequent guests at the castle and had been given virtually free access to the place, coming and going as they pleased. Towerson himself often dined with the Dutch governor and always came away charmed by his 'courtesies' and 'love'.

Fort Victoria, Amboyna – scene of the torture and execution of the entire English population of the island. Dutch claims that the English wished to seize the castle were unsubstantiated.

He would soon learn how hollow those courtesies were to prove. On the night of 10 February 1623, a Dutch sentinel patrolling the walls of the castle stumbled across one of the Japanese mercenaries regularly employed by the castle authorities. There were about thirty Japanese serving the castle but they were looked upon with suspicion by the regular garrison and, for this reason, they were lodged in a house in the town. The sentinel grew suspicious of the line of questioning pursued by the Japanese and at the end of his watch declared to his colleagues that there was a spy staking out the castle. This news soon reached the ears of the governor who arrested the Japanese and questioned him more closely. The man admitted that he had asked questions concerning the strength of the castle but said they were prompted by mere curiosity and 'without any malicious intentions'. It was a common practice among soldiers, he said, to learn the strength of a watch 'so that they might know how many hours they might stand'.

Such a reply would have satisfied most men, but van Speult confessed himself to be totally unconvinced by this answer and ordered the man to be tortured. He 'endured pretty long', according to the official Dutch report, but eventually the torture had the desired effect and the poor man 'confessed' that the Japanese had organised a plot to seize the castle by force. That such a plot existed was unbelievable, preposterous even, but the Dutch were so terrified by what they heard that the rest of the Japanese were arrested and similarly tortured. All this time 'the English men went to and from the castle upon their businesse, saw the prisoners, heard of their tortures and of the crime laid to their charge.' After fifty-six hours the Dutch interrogators got the answer they had been looking for all along. The Japanese, mangled and burned, confessed that they were conspiring together with the English and that it was Towerson and his men who had instigated the plot to storm the castle.

There was at this time an English surgeon called Abel Price in solitary confinement in the castle dungeon. Price was a drunkard who had got himself into trouble by threatening to set a Dutchman's house on fire after a particularly debauched evening. It was now decided to bring Price to the torture chamber to see what he knew about the conspiracy. It was dawn when he was brought to face the fiscal, the Dutch legal official, and his head was still swimming with drink. Told of the Japanese confessions and shown their wounds, the Dutch inquisitors scarcely had to heat the torture irons before Price confessed 'whatever they asked him'. In fact, they asked him very little; all they required was for him to agree to their version of events. Price duly obliged, confessing, according to the Dutch records, that 'on New Yeares Day, Captain Towerson had called them together, viz. the English merchants and the other officers, and first had had them take their oathe of secrecy and faithfulness on their Bible. After this he pointed out to them that their nation was greatly troubled by us and treated unjustly, and was very little respected; for which he thought to revenge himself. If they would helpe him and assist him faithfully, he knew how to render himself master of the castle, to which some of them had objections, saying their power was too small. On which the said Captain Towerson replied that he had already persuaded the Japanese and others and they were willing to assist him. He would not (he said) have want of people for all of them were willing.'

Price went on to give details of the attack. The Japanese, he said, were to be the first into the castle and it was their job to murder the guard and governor. Once this was accomplished the rest of the men would storm the gates and murder all the Dutchmen who refused to capitulate. The money and merchandise would then be divided among the victors.

'I was extremely surprised when I heard of this conspiracy,' said van Speult when told of the confession, and well he might have been for the English were in no position to capture a heavily fortified castle. Even if they had incited a rebellion throughout Amboyna, with just three swords and two muskets such a plan would certainly have failed, while to attempt such an attack without an escape ship waiting off-shore would have been little short of suicide. But Coen had warned van Speult that this was exactly the sort of conspiracy to expect and the governor decided it was his duty to investigate the matter more closely.

On the pretext of wishing to discuss some important business matters he sent word to the English house asking that they come to the castle immediately. All answered the summons save one who was left to guard the house. No sooner had they been brought to van Speult than they were accused of conspiracy and told they would be held as prisoners 'until further notice'. Towerson was locked inside the English factory with a guard of Dutch soldiers while Emanuel Thomson was kept in the castle. The rest of the men, John Beomont, Edward Collings, William Webber, Ephraim Ramsey, Timothy Johnson, John Fardo and Robert Brown, were manacled together and cast into confinement aboard a Dutch vessel at anchor. Afterwards Samuel Coulson, John Clarke and George Sharrocks who lived at Hitu, and William Griggs and John Sadler, who were at Larica, were brought to Amboyna. Lastly, John Powle, John Wetherall and Thomas Ladbrook, who were based at Cambello, were arrested and imprisoned. The English house was then ransacked and all the merchandise seized, along with chests, boxes, books and letters.

The men were still oblivious to the charges laid against them and faced their imprisonment with little anxiety. They had always maintained good relations with van Speult and felt sure that the misunderstanding would soon be clarified and they would be set free. In this they were mistaken, for even before the last prisoners had arrived from Cambello the first tortures were under way.

An account of the proceedings was published in a 1624 pamphlet entitled *A True Relation of the Unjust, Cruel and Barbarous Proceedings against the English at Amboyna*. With no detail of the tortures left to the imagination, this grisly

account became a bestseller in England and ran into dozens
of editions, with reprints still being made forty years after
the event. Such was its effect on the English public that
many clamoured for war against the Dutch. Even in
Holland the account caused a stir and the States General
professed itself horrified by its details.

John Beomont and Timothy Johnson were the first to be
called before the fiscal. While Johnson was led into the
torture chamber, the trembling Beomont was left standing
outside, guarded by soldiers. This refinement of cruelty
allowed him to hear his friend being tortured before being
cast into the chamber himself. He did not have to wait long
before the fiscal set to work upon Johnson. Beomont heard
him 'cry out very pitifully, then to bee quiet for a little
while, and then loud again'. After a 'taste of the torture,'
Johnson was released for a moment while Abel Price was
wheeled in and forced to accuse him. 'But Johnson not yet
confessing anything,' runs the report, 'Price was quickly
carried out and Johnson brought again to the torture
where Beomont heard him sometime cry aloud, then quiet
again, then roare afresh. At last, after he had been an houre
in this second examination, hee was brought forth wailing
and lamenting, all wet, and cruelly burnt in diverse parts of
his body.' He was thrown into a corner 'with a soldier to
watch him that he should speak with nobody'.

Next into the chamber was Emanuel Thomson. At fifty-
one years old he was an old man but his age did nothing to
save him from the hideous interrogation. For more than
one and a half hours he endured the torture, although he
was heard 'to roare most lamentably and many times'.

At last the fiscal called for the trembling Beomont who
had been outside the torture chamber all this time. He was
repeatedly questioned and accused, 'all of which hee denied

with deep oaths and protestations'. His denials were to no
avail for he was strung up against the wall with a cloth
bound tightly around his neck, and the bloody instruments
of torture displayed to him. But before they could be used
the Governor suddenly halted Beomont's torture and
declared that 'hee would spare him a day or two because he
was an old man'.

The following day was a Sunday. After a longer than
usual service at the castle chapel attended by van Speult and
his gang of interrogators the tortures continued. First into
the chamber was Robert Brown, a tailor, who broke down
and confessed before the fiscal had a chance to torture him.
Collins, the next in line, caused them more of a problem.
Informed of the accusations laid against him, he denied
everything 'with great oathes and execrations'. This angered
the fiscal who ordered his henchmen to 'make his hands
and feete fast to the rocke [and] bound a cloth about his
throate'. When Collins saw what he would have to endure
he begged to be taken down, promising to confess
everything. But no sooner had he been released than he
once again denied any knowledge of the plot, stating that
since they were determined to use torture, 'to make him
confesse any thing, though never so false, they should do
him a great favour, to tell him what they would have him
say, and hee would speake it to avoid the torture'.

'The fiscal hereupon said: "What? Do you mocke us" and
bade, "Up with him again," and so gave him the torment of
water which he not being able to endure prayed to be let
down again to his confession. Then he devised a little with
himself and told them that about two months and a half
before himself, Thomson, Johnson, Brown and Fardo had
plotted with the help of the Japans to surprise the castle.'

'Here he was interrupted by the fiscal and asked whether

Towerson were not of the conspiracy. He answered, "No."

' "You lie," said the fiscal. "Did he not call you to him and tell you that those daily abuses of the Dutch had caused him to think of a plot and that he wanted nothing but your consent and service?"

' "Yes," interjected a Dutch merchant – one John Joost – that sat by: "Did you not swear upon the Bible to be secret to him?"

'Collins answered with great oaths that he knew nothing of any such matter. Then they made him fast again. Whereupon he then said all was true that they had spoken. Then the fiscal asked him whether the English in the rest of the factories were not consenting to this plot. He answered "No." The fiscal then asked him whether the president of the English at Jakarta or M Welden in Banda were not plotters or privie to the business. Againe he answered "No." '

The fiscal now asked Collins how the Japanese planned to carry out their attack, at which poor Collins 'staggering and devising of some probable fiction', at length turned to the fiscal and silently shook his head. The fiscal was only too willing to help, supplying him with the story that was wanted: 'Should not the Japaners have gone to each point of the castle, and two to the Governors chamber doore; and when the hurly-burly had been without, and the Governor coming to see what was the matter, the Japaners to have killed him?'

Even the torturers were shocked when they heard the fiscal put such leading words into Collins' mouth and 'one that stood by said to the fiscal, "Do not tell him what he should say but let him speak for himself." ' After further torments, Collins agreed to everything that was asked of him and was sent away in chains, 'very glad to come clear of his torture though with certain belief that he should die for his confession'.

Next in line was Samuel Coulson, factor at Hitu, who was so distraught when he saw Collins, 'his eyes almost blowne out of his head,' that he chose to confess everything, 'and so was dismissed, comming out weeping, lamenting, and protesting his innocency'.

John Clarke, also from Hitu, proved the most resilient of all, refusing to confess to a single crime. 'They tortured him with water and fire' for two hours but still he protested his innocence. Like the others he was subjected to the horrific 'torment of water' which left the person grotesquely deformed. 'First they hoisted him up by the hands with a cord on a large dore, where they made him fast upon two staples of iron, fixd on both sides at the top of the doreposts, haling his hands one from the other as wide as they could stretch. Being thus made fast, his feete hung some two foot from the ground, which also they stretched asunder as far as they would reach and made them fast.' This being done they bound a thick piece of canvas about his neck and face leaving an opening at the top. Then, 'they poured the water softly upon his head untill the cloth was full, up to the mouth and nostrils, and somewhat higher, so that he could not draw breath but he must suck in all the water.'

This was continued for hours until water 'came out of his nose, eares and eyes; and often as it were stifling and choking him, at length took away his breath and brought him to a swoune or fainting'. At this point the torturers had to act quickly. Releasing the cloth from his face and neck 'they made him vomit up the water' and as soon as he was breathing again 'they triced him up.'

Clarke endured this terrible torment four times in succession, 'till his body was swollen twice or thrice as bigge as before, his cheekes like great bladders, and his eyes staring and strutting out beyond his forhead'. Still he refused to confess, at which point the fiscal and torturers grew worried, 'saying that he was a Devill, and no man, or surely was a witch; at least had some charme about him, or was enchanted, that he could bear so much. Whereupon they cut off his haire very short, as supposing he had some witchcraft hidden therein.'

There was a brief discussion as to whether they should continue the torture. All agreed that it was necessary, whereupon 'they hoisted him up againe as before, and then burnt him with lighted candles in the bottome of his feete, untill the fat dropt out the candles; yet then applyed they fresh lights unto him. They burnt him also under the elbowes, and in the palmes of the hands, likewise under the arme-pits, until his inwards might evidently be seene.'

At last he was taken down and, 'being thus wearied and overcome by the torment, he answered yea to whatsoever they asked.' With the confession down on paper and, 'having martyred this poor man, they sent him out by foure blacks who carried him between them to a dungeon, where he lay five or six daies without any surgeon to dress him until (his flesh being putrified) great maggots dropped and crept from him in a most loathsome and noisesome manner.' With the torturers now exhausted after their ordeal, 'they thus finished their Sabbath day's work.'

Over the next week the rest of the English were individually brought into the torture chamber. All endured various degrees of disfiguration before being thrown back into the castle dungeon burned and bleeding, their sores and wounds infected and putrefied. Griggs confessed early on, saving himself from being burned, Fardo endured the water torture before breaking, and then Beomont, the aged invalid, was carried in for the second time. Several of his tortured colleagues were brought in to denounce him but Beomont denied all the charges 'with great earnestness and deep oaths'. The fiscal soon tired of waiting for a confession and the stubborn prisoner was 'triced up and drenched with water till his innards were ready to crack'. After an hour or so of endurance, 'he answered affirmatively to all the fiscal's interrogatories' and 'had a great iron bolt and two shackles riveted to his legs and then was carried back to prison.'

Desperate to avoid torture George Sharrocks was the most inventive in his story. Seated before a water butt and surrounded by candles he was told that unless he confess he would be tortured to death then 'drawne by the heels to the gallows and there hanged up'. This was too much for the poor man and he began a rambling tale of conspiracies against the Dutch. Since the prisoners were forbidden from talking to each other, his story bore little resemblance to the others that the fiscal had been told. Sharrocks continually denied that Towerson had ever spoken to him on the subject and said that he had not seen his fellow countrymen for four months – long before the so-called conspiracy was hatched – since he lived on the north of the island. Despite these protests his confession was prepared and read out and Sharrocks was asked if it was true. ' "No," said Sharrocks. "Why then," said the fiscal, "did you confess it?" "For fear of torment," replied Sharrocks.' At this, 'the fiscal and the rest in a great rage told him he lied; his mouth had spoken it, and it was true, and therefore he should subscribe it.'

At long last Gabriel Towerson was brought to the examination chamber 'deeply protesting his innocence'. The fiscal told him that all the others had accused him of conspiracy, then ordered three of them into the room to reaffirm in Towerson's presence the crimes they had accused him of perpetrating. Coulson was the first brought in: pale and trembling he stood silent, his head hung in shame. At length he was told he would be tortured again if he did not speak, at which point Coulson 'coldly re-affirmed' his confession. Next Griggs and Fardo were led in and stood before Towerson. A dramatic scene then followed, for Towerson 'seriously charged them, that as they would answer it at the dreadful day of judgement, they should speak nothing but the truth. Both of them instantly fell down upon their knees before him, praying him for God's sake to forgive them, and saying further openly before them all, that whatsoever they had formerly confesed was most false and spoken only to avoid torment.' On hearing this the fiscal exploded and threatened them with more torture, 'which they would not endure, but then affirmed their former confessions to be true'.

Towerson bowed his head silently, realising now that his situation was hopeless. Neither Griggs nor Fardo could stand further torture and both assented to sign a declaration of guilt. When Griggs signed his confession he asked the fiscal 'upon whose head he thought the sinne would lie; whether upon his that was constrained to confesse what was false, or upon the constrainers?' At this the fiscal left the room to confer with van Speult before returning and ordering Coulson to sign. ' "Well," quoth he, "you make me to accuse myself and others of that which is as false as God is true: for God is my witness, I am as innocent as the child new borne." '

What happened to Towerson after the signing of these confessions remains uncertain. There is no doubt that the most brutal treatment was reserved for him yet he withstood the torture to the very end. The two survivors later recorded that van Speult's henchmen used even more brutal methods, such as 'the splitting of the toes and lancing of the breast and putting in gunpowder, and the firing the same, whereby the body is not left entire, either for innocency or execution'. The stench of burned flesh was said to be so pungent in the castle dungeon 'that no one was able to endure the smell'.

There was a two day respite from the torture before the prisoners were assembled in the great hall of the castle to learn their fate. A handful, believing their sufferings would entitle them to compassion, were certain that they would be banished rather than murdered. But van Speult was not a man noted for his clemency. Seated at a massive table and flanked by his officers he gravely 'stated his suit and drew his conclusions'. All the men had confessed their guilt – all except Towerson whose continued protestations of innocence had so incensed the fiscal. As the men waited to hear the judgement read out, Towerson was once again 'brought up into the place of examination, and two great jarrs of water carried after him'. What he suffered during the hours he was interrogated will never be known for he was next seen at the scaffold, his features blenched and drawn.

Before the fiscal read the sentence, 'prayers were said to the Lord that He might govern their [the Council's] hearts in this gloomy consultation and that He might inspire them only with equity and justice.' With this done the fiscal called the room to order. Towerson was condemned to be decapitated and quartered and his head to be suspended from a post as a warning to others. The rest of the men were to be spared the quartering; they would simply be decapitated, along with their Japanese conspirators. As the men listened in horror a whisper arose among the Dutch officers. It was realised that by executing all of the men they would leave themselves with the burden of having to administer the affairs of the English factory. It was therefore decided to reprieve two of the men to look after the Company's interests. Beomont was one of the men spared; he was fortunate enough to have a Dutch merchant friend who argued for his release. To choose the second man it was decided that Coulson, Thomson and Collins should draw lots. They knelt on the cold flagstones and joined hands in communal prayer, and this being done they each delved their hands into the lottery box. Collins drew the right paper and was duly set free. The others resigned themselves to their deaths.

They were led back to their prison cells for their last night before execution. The men were visited by Dutch ministers who 'telling them how short a time they had to live, admonished and exhorted them to make their true confessions; for it was a dangerous and desperate thing to dissemble at such a time'. The English continued to protest their innocence, 'and prayed the Ministers that they might all receive the sacrament as a seale of the forgivenesse of their sinnes and withall thereby to confirme their last profession of the innocencie'. This was too much for the ministers and 'would by no means be granted'.

Coulson now begged the minister that he might ask a question. '"You manifest unto us the danger of dissimulation in this case," he said, "but tell us, if we suffer guiltlesse, being otherwise also true believers in Jesus Christ, what shall be our reward?"'

To this the minister had a ready answer: '"By how much the cleerer you are, soe much the more glorious shall be your resurrection."' The narrative continues:

With that word Coulson started up, embraced the preacher and gave him his purse with such money as

*The Massacre of Amboyna deeply shocked the English nation.
The East India Company merchants were tortured with fire
and water before having their limbs blown off with gunpowder.
After enduring a week of brutality, they were executed by the
Dutch commander.*

hee had in it, saying, 'Domine, God bless you. Tell the Governor I freely forgive him; and I entreat you to exhort him to repent of this bloody tragedy wrought upon us poor innocent souls.'

Here all the rest of the Englishmen signified their assent to this speech.

Then spake John Fardo to the rest in the presence of the ministers as followeth; 'My countrymen and brethren that are heere with mee condemned to dye, I charge you all as you will answer it at God's Judgement Seat if any of you bee guilty of this matter, whereof we are condemned, discharge your consciences and confesse the truth for satisfaction of the world.' Hereupon Samuel Coulson spake with a loud voyce, saying: 'According to my innocency in this treason so, Lord, pardon all my sinnes and if I be guiltie thereof, more or lesse, let me never be partaker of Thy heavenly joys.' At which words every one of the rest cryed out, 'Amen for me, amen for me, good Lord!' This done, each of them knowing whom he had accused, went one to another begging forgiveness for their false accusation, being rung from them by the pains or feare of torture. And they all freely forgave one another: for none had bene so falsely accused but he himself had accused another as falsely.

The Dutch ministers found themselves deeply moved by the spectacle of these condemned men professing their innocence and one of them offered to bring them a barrel of wine in order that they might 'drive away their sorrow'. But the men steadfastly declined the offer, not wishing to spend their final hours in a state of drunkenness. Instead they asked the ministers for ink and sat quietly writing their final protestations of innocence. One of these, bearing Samuel Coulson's signature, is inscribed into his copy of the Psalms of David which eventually found its way back to Europe. Written on 5 March 1623, 'aboard the Rotterdam lying in irons', it begins:

> Understand that I, Samuel Coulson, late factor of Hitto, was apprehended for suspicion of conspiracy; and for anything I know must die for it: wherefore having no meanes to make my innocency knowne, have writ in this book, hoping some good Englishman will see it. I do here sweare upon my salvation, as I do hope by His death and passion to have redemption for my sinnes, that I am cleere of all such conspiracy: neither do I know any Englishman guilty thereof, nor other creature in the world. As this is true, God bless me – Samuel Coulson.

William Griggs also managed to scribble a few lines on that final night: 'We, through torment, were constrained to speake that which we never meant, nor once imagined; the which we take upon our deaths and salvation, that tortured as with that extreme torment of fire and water, that flesh and blood could not endure ... And so farewell; written in the dark.'

How Towerson passed his final night is unknown for he was still held in isolation and unable to communicate with his compatriots. Everything he wrote was confiscated and destroyed except for a couple of lines which he scrawled onto a bill of debt against the Company. This passed undetected until it fell into the hands of an English agent in the Banda Islands: 'Firmed by the firme of me, Gabriel Towerson, now appointed to die, guiltless of anything that can be justly laid to my charge. God forgive them their guilt and receive me to His mercy. Amen.'

That his suffering was at least as great as the rest of the men is clear from an account by Beomont, one of the released, who visited him on the morning of his execution and 'found him sitting in a chamber all alone in a most miserable condition, the wounds of his torture bound up'. He clutched Beomont's hand weakly and prayed him that if he ever reached England he should seek out his brother Billingsley and certify him of his innocence 'which,' he said, 'you yourself know well enough'.

As day broke the men were reminded of their impending execution by the beat of drums and tramp of soldiers echoing through the town. This was to summon spectators wishing to view the bloodshed about to take place. Executions in Amboyna were colourful events; flags and bunting were strung out, bands played, and large crowds 'flocked together to behold this triumph of the Dutch over the English'. The prisoners, meanwhile, were assembled in the great hall for the last time. At the door stood 'the quit and pardoned', those lucky two who had been released on the orders of the governor. To these men the condemned now made their last farewells and solemnly charged them 'to bear witnesse to their friends in England ... that they died not traitors, but so many innocents merely murdered by the Hollanders, whome they prayed God to forgive their blood-thirstinesse and to have mercy upon their own soules'.

As they spent their last minutes in the hall the Japanese prisoners were ushered in and lined up against the opposite wall. This spectacle angered both parties for each believed the other group to be the cause of their present plight. ' "Oh you Englishmen," said one of the Japanese in a voice of despair, "where did wee ever in our lives eat with you, talk with you, or (to our remembrance) see you?" The Englishmen replied: "Why then have you accused us?" ' It was only at this point that all realised the scale of the Dutch deception and 'the poore men, perceiving they were made believe each had accused others before they had so done, indeed, showed them their tortured bodies and said, "If a stone were thus burnt, would it not change his nature? How much more we that are flesh and blood?" '

The men then embraced each other before being ushered into a courtyard where their sentence was read out by an official standing in a gallery. Here they were reunited with Towerson whose wounds and sores had become so festered that he could scarcely walk. Then, accompanied by five companies of soldiers, they were led in procession to their place of execution, a long and melancholy cortège that wound through crowds of cheering onlookers before arriving at the execution ground.

As they stood facing their executioner Samuel Coulson drew from his pocket a short prayer which ended in a defiant declaration of his innocence. This being done, he threw the paper into the wind and watched as it fluttered high into the air before being caught by a soldier and taken straight to the governor.

One by one the men stepped forward to the block. Before the executioner proceeded with his bloody work, each man affirmed in a clear voice that he was innocent of all the crimes of which he was accused. 'And so, one by one, with great cheerfulness, they suffered the fatal stroke.'

Only Towerson was singled out for special treatment. As the leader of the little English contingent he was accorded the special honour of having a small piece of black velvet tied to the block prior to his being beheaded. In a bill of charges later received by the English East India Company, the cost of this cloth was added to the list on the grounds that it was so bloodstained as to be unusable.

If van Speult had any qualms about his rough justice, he was about to receive an admonishment from on high. 'At the instant of the execution there arose a great darknesse with a sudden and violent gust of winde and tempest; whereby two of the Dutch shippes riding in the harbour were driven from their anchors.' Worse was to come; within two weeks of the execution 'there happened a great sickness on the island such as was there never seen or heard of, so that the people cried out that it was a plague upon them for the innocent blood of the English.' When the sickness finally subsided, more than a quarter of the island's population had lost their lives. The surviving Englishmen took comfort in these events, remembering Emanuel Thomson's dying words that 'he did not doubt but God would show some sign of their innocencie.'

The small English community in Batavia knew nothing of these events until they met with two pallid Englishmen disembarking from a vessel in the harbour. When asked to explain their miserable state these men poured out the story of the Amboyna massacre. The English were shocked by what they heard and sent an immediate protest to the new Dutch Governor-General, Pieter de Carpentier, remonstrating against van Speult's 'presumptuous proceedings' in 'imprisoning, torturing and bloodily executing his majesty's subjects' and 'confiscating their goods in direct violation of the Treaty, whereby the King was disgraced and dishonoured and the English nation scandalized'.

Carpentier treated the protests with cool detachment, but the letters he sent back to Holland reveal that he realised the matter was of the utmost gravity. Although believing that Towerson and his fellow men had indeed been engaged in conspiracy, he condemned in the strongest words the methods used by the fiscal. 'He called himself a lawyer and had been taken into the Company's service as such,' he wrote, but he 'should have shown better judgement in the affair'. He continued: 'We think the rigour of justice should have been mitigated somewhat with Dutch clemency (with consideration to a nation who is our neighbour), especially if such could be done without prejudice to the state and the dignity of justice, as we think could have been done here.'

When news of the massacre reached London there was uproar. King James at first refused to believe it, claiming it was too foul. But when he heard the story from the mouths of the survivors he was deeply shocked and although not accustomed to show emotion was said to have shed tears over the fate of Towerson and his companions. The Lords of the Privy Council also wept when they were told of the tortures, while the merchants of the East India Company were stunned to silence. Stranger was the reaction of the English public who indulged in what was little short of a national outpouring of grief. Up and down the country pamphlets and broadsheets were published with graphic details of the tortures and in towns and villages men eagerly discussed the gruesome business. A mob gathered around the Dutch Chapel in Lothbury and jeered at the congregation as they entered the church. 'Hypocrites, murderers,' they shouted, 'Amboyna will cost you paradise.' More than fifty years later the poet John Dryden used the massacre to whip up anti-Dutch feeling, publishing his tragedy *Amboyna, or The Cruelties of the Dutch to the English Merchants*.

All through the winter indignation grew, and the directors of the East India Company did not fight shy of stoking the public outrage. They commissioned artist

Richard Greenbury to produce a huge oil painting depicting the agonies of Towerson and companions, with van Speult and the fiscal gloating over their bloody victory. Greenbury apparently excelled himself, painting a gruesome picture in which he 'lively, largely and artificially' depicted the tortures. The work was to be exhibited in the Company headquarters 'as a perpetual memorial of Dutch cruelty and treachery' and the public were invited to come to view it. So effective was the painting in inciting hatred against the Dutch that the directors were ordered by the government not to display it until after the Shrove Tuesday holiday for fear of a general uprising against the large population of Hollanders living in London.

Greenbury himself was delighted with the reaction and demanded £100 from the directors. In this he was to be disappointed for they told him that 'one proffered to cut it out in brass for £30, which was a great deal more labour and workmanship than to draw it on cloth.' In the end Greenbury settled for £40.

With anti-Dutch protests growing in London there was a feeling that something had to be done. 'For my part,' wrote one notable to Sir Dudley Carleton, the English ambassador at The Hague, 'if there were no wiser than I, we should stay or arrest the first Indian ship that comes in our way and hang up upon Dover cliffs as many as we should find faulty or actors in this business and then dispute the matter afterwards: for there is no other course to be had with such manner of men, as neither regard law nor justice, nor any other respect or equity or humanity, but only make gain their God.'

The States General were extremely concerned at the aftermath of the Amboyna Massacre and unsatisfied with an official report compiled by the directors of the Dutch East India Company. Far from denying that van Speult used torture it actually justified his methods, arguing that 'the torture of the water is much more civill and less dangerous than other tortures for the paine of water doth but cause and produce an oppression and anxiety of breath and respiration.' The report was riddled with inconsistencies and offered no real evidence against the English. After deliberating over its contents the States General recalled van Speult to Holland to answer for his brutality, but he died before he reached Amsterdam. Others made it back to Holland but the special court that convened to investigate their conduct deliberated for months before declaring it could find no reason to punish them for something they did in the belief that they were acting in the best interests of their country.

The directors of the English East India Company protested, informing the King that they would be forced to abandon trade with the Spice Islands unless 'the Dutch make real restitution for damages, execute justice upon those who had in so great fury and tyranny tortured and slain the English, and give security for the future'. The King acted upon their advice, appointing a committee comprising the country's most distinguished servants to examine all the evidence that had arrived in England. This committee concluded that the massacre had less to do with any conspiracy than with a Dutch plan to permanently evict the English from the Spice Islands. They recommended to the Lord High Admiral that a fleet should be sent to patrol the entrance to the English Channel, lay hold of any outward or homebound Dutch East India ships and keep them in England until suitable compensation was forthcoming. What form that compensation should take was never in doubt. There was only one possible way for the Dutch to atone for the Amboyna Massacre, and that was to hand back the tiny island of Run.

CHAPTER TWELVE

STRIKING
A DEAL

SOME FIFTEEN YEARS AFTER the Massacre of Amboyna, a renegade Dutchman arrived in London bearing some disquieting news. He informed the directors of the East India Company that he had recently visited Run and was surprised to discover that every nutmeg tree on the island had been chopped down. Where once there had been a verdant forest covering Run's mountainous backbone, there was now nothing but exposed soil.

The news was yet another blow to England's increasingly forlorn hopes of recovering a foothold in the region. It required only a cursory glance at an atlas for London's merchants to see the tragic story writ large. The Banda Islands were now totally under Dutch control: studded with castles and defended by permanent garrisons, they were probably lost forever. Amboyna, too, was indisputably in Dutch hands. They had chosen it as their regional centre of operations and its jagged coastline was protected by a string of imposing forts. It was much the same story in the northerly islands of Ternate and Tidore which had slowly but surely fallen under the Dutch sphere of influence.

To the dwindling band of Englishmen who lingered in Coen's new capital, Batavia, there were more tangible reasons for pessimism. Every month saw the arrival of more factors from abandoned outposts; haggard, destitute men who had struggled to keep trading until insolvency or the machinations of the Dutch forced them to flee. Even such far-flung settlements as Siam, Patani on the Malay Peninsula, and Firando in Japan – of which there had been such high hopes – had come to nothing. One by one their traders had been forced to abandon them, leaving decaying warehouses and tarnished reputations. The only places that managed to continue a trade of sorts were those scattered along the coastline of India, but even these would soon be brought to their knees by a devastating and wholly unexpected famine.

The horrific news of events in Amboyna sent a wave of panic through the small English community still living in Batavia. Despised by both the Dutch and the natives, they lived in the town on sufferance of Pieter de Carpentier, the new governor-general, who showed little concern or interest in their welfare. He dismissed their protestations about the massacre at Amboyna, unsettling the English who felt themselves to be in the most vulnerable of positions, surrounded by enemies and with no obvious means of escape. If Carpentier chose to emulate the butchers of Amboyna, they would be unable to resist.

A meeting of the factors ended in decision: scouts were to put to sea at once in order to search for a suitable island upon which the English could build a new headquarters, and the Company's president was to write to London to beg the directors to 'liberate us from the intolerable yoke of the Dutch nation'. Although his letter evoked no response, the scouts soon returned with good news. After sailing around the southern coastline of Sumatra they chanced upon the low-lying island of Lagundi which, they confidently declared, was perfectly suited to their needs.

Why they alighted on this blighted spot remains unclear for it had an extremely unhealthy climate and no source of fresh water. But in October 1624, the remaining Englishmen in Batavia heaved a heavy sigh of relief and fled 'this perfidious people', sailing directly to Lagundi. The flag was raised, the supplies landed, and Lagundi was renamed Prince Charles Island.

Hardly had they made the island their home than their luck once again deserted them. Many of the men succumbed to tropical fevers and dysentery and the wretched remnants spent as much time digging graves as they did on constructing their warehouse. After only a few months a meeting was convened and the survivors elected to return to Batavia, a decision that was fraught with difficulty. Too few to man a ship, the men were forced to beg a Dutch captain to carry them back to the port. They were welcomed with rude cheers and 'a merciless whipping in the public market place'.

The news from London during this troubled period gave few grounds for optimism. Although King James was determined to have his revenge for the heinous crimes perpetrated at Amboyna, more than three years were to pass before a fleet of India-bound Dutch vessels was seized in the English Channel and towed into Portsmouth. By then, King James was dead and it was left to his successor, King Charles I, to pursue the claim for reparations. The directors at last saw a real chance of obtaining redress, but no sooner had they compiled a report of their grievances than they learned that the King had inexplicably released the vessels. He justified his extraordinary behaviour by explaining that the Dutch had promised to send a negotiating team to England, but few believed such an explanation and rumours of backhanders to the King only fuelled the belief that a secret deal had been struck. One report claimed the King had been handed £30,000 by the Dutch captain; another said he had been given three tons of gold. The Dutch themselves stoked the fire by bragging they had bought the King's jewels back from his pawnbroker.

The Company was about to enter its darkest hour. The number of ships sailing to the East dropped by almost two thirds and, with trade at a virtual standstill, its stock slumped by more than 20 per cent. In the good years subscribers had freely stumped up more than £200,000 per annum; now the Company beadle was lucky to collect a quarter of that figure. More worrying was the news that the debts were spiralling out of control: when the auditors checked their accounts in the spring of 1629 they were horrified to learn that they were more than £300,000 in the red.

A series of meetings was called to discuss the parlous state of the Company's finances and it was reluctantly decided that the overheads and expenses should be slashed. The eighteen London employees were the first to feel the squeeze. A list was prepared of their salaries and expenses, together with suggestions of how money could be saved. A few were to be fired, ineffectual workers were to have their pay docked, and others would be retained on much-reduced salaries. First on the list was Mr Tyne, the book-keeper, whose salary was cut from £100 to his 'former proportion' of £80. The apologetic directors explained that with so few ships returning from the Indies he no longer had much book-keeping to do. Mr Handson, the auditor, was the next victim but when he learned that the axe was about to fall he chose to depart with honour, graciously standing down from his position and thereby saving the Company £100 a year. Mr Ducy, a timber measurer, was no less fortunate: his annual £50 salary was cancelled and he was, in future, to be paid by the day. Others found they were surplus to requirements: Richard Mountney was informed that his salary had been 'recalled' as his services were no longer required.

Such petty measures were cosmetic and useless in halting the Company's decline. Further cuts in salaries were followed by the abandonment of shipbuilding activities and, in 1643, the forced sale of the Deptford shipyard. 'We could wish,' wrote the directors to their long-suffering factors, 'that we could vindicate the reputation of our nation in these partes [the East], and do ourselves right … [but] of all these wee must brave the burden and with patience sitt still, until wee may find these frowning times more auspicious to us and our affayres.'

Throughout these 'frowning times' the directors clung to the hope that Run would one day be restored. In both 1632 and 1633 they sent letters to their Bantam merchants ordering them to reoccupy the island and, in the following year, they actually despatched a vessel to the Banda Islands but the untimely arrival of the monsoon forced it to return to Bantam. In 1636 a spirited English merchant sailed single-handedly to Neira to demand the return of Run. He was welcomed by the gleeful Dutch commander who told him that if he rowed across to survey the island he would be a little less hasty in demanding its return. The Dutch, increasingly concerned by the continued English interest in the island, had taken 'all courses to make the iland little or nothing worth'. One onlooker watched with astonishment the Hollanders 'demolish and deface the buildings [and] transplant the nutmeg trees, plucking them up by the roots and carrying them into their owne ilands of Neira and of Poloway [Ai] … and at last finde a meanes to dispeople the iland and to leave it so as the English might make no use of it'.

The Dutchman who brought this news to England had been dismissed from the Dutch Company and was determined to have his revenge. He offered to pursue the King's claim for damages in return for a small fee and, to this end, was despatched to Holland to work in tandem with England's ambassador. The men were armed with reams of evidence about Dutch brutality, including a lengthy report investigating 'the barbarous behaviour of the Governor of Banda in burning and torturing the inhabitants, robbing them of gold, silver, jewels, and goods and destroying the nutmeg trees and other spices'. They also had documents listing the 150 Englishmen who had been murdered over the past two decades and a further list of 800 who had been sold into slavery.

The ensuing negotiations fill page after page of East India Company records – a litany of complaints, grievances and hard bargaining. The English team were given considerable flexibility when it came to discussing reparations but the bottom line was that Run should be replanted with nutmeg trees and restored to England. In addition, the directors demanded a one-off payment of £200,000 for losses suffered, both human and financial. This sum dropped steadily over the months that followed but still the Dutch refused to pay a single guilder.

By unhappy coincidence it was during these long years of negotiations that the Banda Islands entered their most productive period, producing hitherto undreamed of quantities of nutmeg and mace. In the five years between 1633 and 1638, for which records are still extant, the combined weight of nutmeg and mace exported to Holland exceeded four million pounds. That, of course, was only the official quantity. Many Dutch settlers on the islands were amassing private fortunes by clandestinely selling nutmeg to native merchants and traders. Although this practice was strictly prohibited by the Dutch authorities, the ragged coastline of the Banda Islands proved impossible to police and the settlers had few difficulties in finding buyers for their spice.

The success of the nutmeg plantations was due, in no small part, to Coen's strategy of ridding the islands of their native inhabitants and replacing them with Dutchmen. Before leaving the East Indies, he had announced that the Dutch Company was inviting applications for grants of land in the Banda archipelago. In return for defence against foreign attack and slaves to work the plantations, applicants had to agree to settle permanently and produce spices only for the company. Many 'free burghers' living in Batavia – men who had completed their contracts but remained in the East – proved only too willing to take up Coen's offer and applications were soon flooding in. The Banda Islands were parcelled into small estates, sixty-eight men were chosen to farm them, and the surviving Bandanese were compelled to teach them how to cultivate the nutmeg tree.

Success and riches went to the heads of most settlers who, having procured the necessary slaves to work their land, sank into a life of dissolute drunkenness. Coen himself complained that most of the settlers were 'wholly unsuitable for the planting of colonies [and] some are worse than animals'. In this he was correct: they were generally lazy and unruly and needed harsh measures to keep them in check. A journal kept by one Company employee records that in the space of one five-year period he witnessed the following punishments: two persons burned alive, one broken on the wheel, nine hanged, nine decapitated, three garrotted, and one 'arquebussed' – a punishment which entailed being shot to pieces by the matchlock arquebus gun favoured by the Dutch.

The Dutch grasp over the Banda archipelago was now so complete that the English directors began to despair of ever recovering Run, especially when the outbreak of the English Civil War put paid to any immediate hopes of despatching a fleet to the East. 'Wee are fearfull how far wee shall be able to performe in this troublesome tymes,' they wrote, 'when all trade and commerce in this kingdome is fallen to the ground through our owne unhappie divisions at home.' Intermittent fighting, a breakdown of communications, heavy taxation and increased risks at sea caused a complete loss of trade and the directors bemoaned that 'as the badnesse of trade and scarsity of monyes are here, so is all Europe in little better condition, but in a turmoyle.'

By the winter of 1656 the East India Company was on its knees. For more than four decades its merchants had struggled to compete with the Dutch, despatching increasingly decrepit ships to the Spice Islands and clinging to the last threads of their trade. Now, even that had come to nothing: the grand fleets that had once sailed majestically down the Thames were little more than a distant memory. The Deptford shipyard had been sold, the warehouses lay empty and the employees were on the breadline, only drawing money on the rare occasions when a ship limped back from the Indies.

Overseas the Company's remaining assets were of little worth. The factors still living in Bantam had almost ceased trading and their sole success during this grim period – the acquisition of a modest cargo of pepper – was immediately scuppered when the Dutch captured the ship and gleefully towed her to Batavia. On India's north-west coastline the trading post at Surat had, for a while, reaped considerable profits for the Company. But it had been hit hard by pirates and its fortunes were dealt an even harsher blow when the great famine of 1630 wiped out the town's population. 'The land was allmost voyde of inhabitants,' wrote one of the factors living in Surat, 'the most part fledd, the rest dedd.' His vivid account of the crisis left the London directors in no doubt that it would be many years before their Surat trade would recover. 'Noe less lamentable was it to see the poor people scrapeing the dunghills for food, yea in the very excrement of beastes … our noses were never free of the stinck of corpses [for] they dragg them out by the heels stark naked of all ages and sexes, till they are out of the gates, and there they are left so that the way is half barred up.' Surat had become a ghost town and when the factors at last strayed out of their compound 'we hardly could see any living persons where heretofore was thousands … women were seen to roast their children [and] men travelling in the waie were laid hold of to be eaten.'

The other factories in India had also been brought to their knees by famine. For a brief moment the Company's fledgling settlement in Madras had offered a ray of hope: no sooner had the battlements of Fort St George risen above the shoreline than native artisans flocked here in their hundreds, lured by the promise of calico weaving and chintz painting. After fourteen years of relative prosperity the famine virtually eliminated the local population and decimated the small English garrison. Just ten soldiers and two factors were left alive, and even these proved too expensive for the Company to maintain. The directors publicly declared that three ships would shortly be sent to the East in order to wind up their affairs.

The crunch came on 14 January 1657. The governor of the East India Company, William Cockayne, summoned a general court of all the adventurers who still had money invested in the Company. To a grim-faced audience he explained that the coffers were empty and that there was no hope of a revival in fortunes. Every avenue had been explored, every hope extinguished. The Lord Protector, Oliver Cromwell, had been petitioned for help but had repeatedly refused to come to the Company's aid, pleading too many 'great affaires'. As Cockayne spelled out the enormity of the crisis it slowly dawned on the merchants that this really was the end. The Company was no longer viable, the balance sheet did not add up. As the sun set on that chill winter's evening the adventurers threw in the towel and declared for liquidation.

'It is resolved to appoint a sale of the island [Run], customs, houses and other rights in the Indies.' So read the minutes of that historic final meeting. The suggested value was a mere £14,000 – the low price explained by the fact that most of these were paper assets – for which the buyer would receive the titles to Run, the factories in Bantam, Surat and Madras, and a remote customs post in Persia. Their business at an end, the merchants ordered a beadle to post bills in the Exchange advertising the forthcoming sale.

As the door closed on that sombre evening there was a deep sense of shock among the merchant adventurers. This, then, was the end; the dying hours of a Company that had blazed such a glorious path to the East. In the early years there had been so much hope. The pioneering expeditions of Sir James Lancaster; the indomitable Middleton trio; the doughty William Hawkins – all had risked their lives in sailing to the Indies and some had returned with undreamed of quantities of spice. Once, the Thamesside wharves had been filled with the scent of nutmeg and the estuary cluttered with ships from the Indies. The King himself had sent expeditions on their way and cheering crowds had welcomed them home.

Now, more than half a century later, it was time to count the price of failure. Numerous ships had been sunk in the great spice race and hundreds, possibly thousands, of men had lost their lives. For nothing had the victims of Amboyna met their gruesome ends; in vain had Nathaniel Courthope laid down his life in the heroic defence of Run. That very island, lost after such a struggle, was now up for sale with an asking price lower than the cost of a small ship. It was an end of which no one could be proud.

This should have been the conclusion to the story; the final death throes of a Company and a dream. But unbeknown to the merchant adventurers of London, no one would be given the opportunity to make an offer for their few remaining assets in the East. For scarcely had news of the sale been announced than they found themselves summoned to a meeting with Cromwell's Council of State – a meeting to discuss the future of the East India Company.

Oliver Cromwell and his Council of State were genuinely alarmed by the news from the Exchange. For too long they had refused to listen to the arguments put forth by the Company – that trade with the East Indies was doomed to fail unless organised as a regulated, joint-stock system, a system that allowed no room for privateers to spoil the trade. Now, learning of the Company's plight, the Council of State invited the merchants to put their side of the argument, then withdrew to consider their verdict.

The Council reconvened the following morning and,

without hesitation, pronounced itself swayed by the arguments. Twelve days later Cromwell agreed, thereby snatching the Company from the jaws of death. A new charter was drawn up, sanctioned by Parliament, and passed the Great Seal on 19 October 1657. With the stroke of a pen, the East India Company found itself reborn as a modern, permanent and united joint-stock corporation. The very same day a meeting was called by the jubilant directors and a new subscription posted in the Exchange. London's merchants responded with unbounded enthusiasm and within a matter of months a staggering £786,000 had been raised. Trade with the East could begin once again.

But it was not to the Spice Islands that the merchants despatched their ships. Throughout the lean and desperate years it was the Indian subcontinent that had kept the East India Company afloat, surviving off a modest trade between Surat and Persia and a much smaller trade between India and London. Although the Company continued to import 'long pepper, white pepper, white powdered sugar, preserved nutmegs and ginger myrabolums [a plum-like fruit], bezoar stones [and] drugs of all sorts', spices had ceased to be its mainstay. They had been replaced by silks and saltpetre, the latter an essential ingredient in gunpowder which was freely available in India.

As the factories in the Spice Islands fell into decay, new ones sprang up on the Indian coastline and when Surat officially replaced Bantam as the eastern headquarters of the East India Company it was clear to all that its horizons had changed forever. 'Behold then,' wrote Sir Thomas Mun in 1667, 'the true form and worth of foreign trade, which is the great revenue of the King, the honour of the

Kingdom; the noble profession of the merchant; the school of our arts; the supply of our wants; the employment of our poor; the improvement of our lands; the nursery of our mariners; the walls of our Kingdom; the means of our treasure; the sinews of our wars; the terror of our enemies.'

His triumphalism was a far cry from the laments of old and it would grow ever louder as the Company's fortunes grew. Under King Charles II's benevolent rule the directors were granted even more extensive rights: to acquire territory, declare war, command troops, and exercise civil and criminal jurisdiction. When the directors passed a 1689 resolution about local government in India, it was clear that the Company was irrevocably changing. Arguing that good government would lead to increased profits they concluded, ''tis that must make us a nation in India.' With these words the story of the East India Company had, in effect, become the story of British India.

The Company's turn-around in fortunes was an astonishing and wholly unexpected event, yet there was to be an even more extraordinary twist in the tale. In the yellowing archives of the East India Company are a handful of documents that lie unnoticed and unread; documents which reveal that Run – defended with such courage by Nathaniel Courthope – was to yield a far greater dividend than anyone could ever have imagined.

London merchants had never abandoned their dream of recovering Run, their 'ancient and rightfull inheritance'. and held regular meetings to discuss how this could be achieved. But it was not until the affairs of the Company were in the process of being wound down that they saw a glimmer of hope on the horizon.

In April 1654, the Anglo-Dutch war was terminated by a peace treaty, the Treaty of Westminster, in which it was decreed that all claims for damages – claims that stretched back decades – should at long last be settled. Each side was given three months to prepare its case. The English not surprisingly called for the immediate restoration of Run, but upped the stakes considerably by also demanding the island of Great Banda. In addition, they filed a staggering £2,695,990 claim for lost revenue as well as decades of accumulated interest. If they thought this would place them in a strong bargaining position they were in for a rude shock. The Dutch argued that their trade had been seriously damaged by the English and responded with a counter-claim of almost three million pounds.

The commissioners charged with dealing with the claims wisely chose to ignore them and instead spent their time sifting through the evidence. Their findings were straightforward and favoured the English: Run was to be immediately restored and £85,000 was to be paid in damages, plus a further £4,000 to the families of the victims of Amboyna. To the surprise of everyone both sides agreed the deal and the Treaty of Westminster was duly signed. Almost fifty years of hatred, bloodshed and mutual animosity were, on paper at least, 'obliterated and bury'd in oblivion.'

In London, news of the treaty was greeted with weary enthusiasm by the cash-strapped directors of the East India Company. The parlous state of their finances, together with continuing legal wrangles with the Dutch, delayed any hope of immediate action and it was not until Cromwell had unexpectedly rescued the Company – more than three years after the treaty was signed – that London's merchants were able to consider sending an expedition to Run.

The receipt of a letter from Jeremy Sambrooke, a servant of the Company, gave them cause for optimism. Sambrooke had recently sailed to Run and assured his superiors that once the English were 'setled upon Pollaroone they will find the Indians [and] inhabitants of the adjacent islands ready to come and inhabite, plant and trade with them'. He added that the natives were 'soe well affected to this nation that assuredly they will deal for the clothing etc. and returne spices untill this island shal be reestablished to its former condition, as in former times of peace'. Sambrooke also reported that the island's nutmeg groves were once again flourishing and that the Company could look forward to an annual yield of more than a third of a million pounds in weight of the spice. When they learned this, the directors immediately established a special Committee for Pulo Run which, at its inaugural meeting, 'resolved to send sixty men of several conditions to remain on the said island, they to be either English, Scotch, or Irish'. These men were to include 'seven house carpenters, seven bricklayers and masons, six gardeners, four smiths and armourers, four coopers, and two plumbers', as well as 'twenty youths from fourteen years upwards, and ten young husbandmen'. Run was to be England's glorious colony in the East. In the winter of 1658, Captain John Dutton was selected to be the first governor of Run, a job which was to earn him a generous £200 a year salary, a further £100 in expenses, and the right to travel with his beloved wife. His orders were to take possession of the island and 'with drum and trumpett proclaime the same,' and he was asked, en route, to stop at the Atlantic island of St Helena and claim it for the Company as well. Unfortunately it took so long to select the settlers for Run that by the time Dutton put to sea, England and Holland were once again on the brink of war. Concerned for the safety of his ship he decided to remain on St Helena until he received further orders. And so, in May 1659, this strategically placed island received its first inhabitants and a small settlement, Jamestown, was built on its northern coastline.

A whole year was to pass before the East India Company considered it safe enough to despatch another fleet to Run. This time they prepared four supply ships under the command of John Hunter and selected a further thirteen colonists for the island, all of whom were to be paid a salary of £12 a year except for the appropriately named George Smallwood who, 'by reason of smallnesse of stature,' was to receive only £10.

The aim of the voyage was clear: 'The King [has] given authority, under the great seal of England, to the Governor and Company or to such as they may appoint, to receive, possess, plant, and fortify the Island of Roone.' The island was to be permanently settled and it was the duty of the colonists 'to keep possession of the said island'.

The ships sailed first to St Helena where they picked up an impatient Captain and Mrs Dutton, then headed directly for Batavia where the couple requested an audience with the Dutch governor-general. The governor-general was initially most welcoming, volunteering the information that his superiors in Amsterdam 'doe order, command and advise' him to hand over the island in accordance with the Treaty of Westminster. But there was a small matter of bureaucracy to be settled before he could sanction their voyage. He required a letter from 'His majestie of Great Britain', written in the King's fair hand, stating that Dutton was a bona fide employee of the East India Company. This request caught the captain by surprise: he was not in possession of such a letter and when he explained this to the governor-general he was met with an icy stare. The governor-general began to rail at the

Englishman, saying he was most displeased to hear that the King was once again creating troubles for the Dutch and 'doth renew and ripp open severall ould sores and debates formerly enacted which have bine long buried'. In short, he intended to refuse the English the necessary permission to sail to Run.

Dutton was astonished by this change of heart and vowed to sail to the Banda Islands without further ado. He hoped to be able to induce the local governor to let him settle the island and, if not, entertained the possibility of taking the place by force. But in this too he was to be disappointed. His arrival at Neira was greeted with anger by the Dutch governor who gave an 'obstinate denial to surrender the island' and added that any attempt on Run would be met with gunshot and cannon fire.

Dutton was not surprised; he had long suspected that the English were being duped and that the Dutch Company 'never really intended to deliver the island which, after many years' detention by them, has been the most profitable blood in the veins of their trade'. His two options were to return to Batavia to plead with the Dutch authorities or to storm the island. Although the records of his mission have been lost, he appears to have chosen the latter option until discovering that his subordinate, John Hunter, adamantly refused to take part in such a plan. Having lost the confidence of his crew there was little Dutton could do but write to the directors in London informing them of the sorry state of affairs. His letter elicited from the directors a stern reprimand for Hunter, finding that his cowardly behaviour compared unfavourably with Courthope's heroic defence of the island some forty years previously. 'Wee cannot but conclude,' they wrote, 'that if our Agent [Hunter] had byn

posessed with the head and heart of a man, hee would ...
have done something worthie the name of an Englishman,
and not have retorned back soe dishonourably, to our
greate losse in perticulaer and to the generall shame of the
nation.' Despairing of ever recovering their beloved island,
the directors once again resorted to adding up their losses
that stemmed from the debacle which they now computed
to be 'above four millions'.

After all the fuss and bluster it is ironic that when Run
did at long last slip back into English hands, it passed
unnoticed in both London and Amsterdam. On 23 March
1665, two English vessels pulled into the island's little
harbour, made contact with the handful of Dutch traders,
and demanded Run's surrender. An agreement was struck,
the Dutch packed up their belongings, and after an interval
of two days they sailed to Neira and left the English to
unload their supplies. 'Concerning all this,' records a memo,
'the Company have no certain knowledge because their
letters were lost in the Royal Oak.'

Run's liberation was to prove short-lived. No sooner
had word of a new outbreak of hostilities between England
and Holland reached the East Indies than the Dutch
promptly despatched a vessel to Run and recaptured the
island. To dissuade the English from ever again attempting
a landing, 'great waste and spoilation [was] committed on
the island'. The nutmeg groves were once again chopped
down and the vegetation burned to its roots. Run had
become a barren and inhospitable rock.

Although the high-handed tactics of the Dutch failed to
stir the temperate King Charles II, they incensed his
brother, the impetuous James, Duke of York. He was stung
into action by the news trickling back from the East Indies
and, as head of the powerful Royal African Company, was

determined to avenge the wrongs. 'The trade of the world is too little for us two,' he declared imperiously, 'therefore one must lie down.' Already in 1663, James had commissioned four vessels to sail down the African coastline and seize the Dutch trading post of Cape Corso on the Gold Coast. Flushed with success, he now ordered his vessels to cross the Atlantic and seize the Dutch-held territory of New Netherland. This brazen act of aggression was justified as being in response to the 'inhuman proceedings' at Amboyna four decades previously. ''Tis high time to put them out of a capacitie of doeing the same mischeife here,' declared the royal commission.

In choosing to attack Manhattan, James had picked an easy target. The island's principal defence, Fort Amsterdam, was a decrepit bulwark whose walls were in an advanced state of decay. The barracks and church were built of wood and vulnerable to fire while the outer walls were lined with wooden houses. The town's governor, Peter Stuyvesant, was also hampered by a lack of weapons. The fort's twenty-four guns were rusting and useless and the available powder was old and damp. 'If I begin [to shoot] in the forenoon,' said the chief gunner, ''twill all be consumed by the afternoon.'

The English had the added advantage of their fleet looking considerably more impressive than it was. As Stuyvesant surveyed the Hudson from Fort Amsterdam he could see four ships carrying a total of a hundred guns. But only one, the *Guinea*, was a ship of war. The others were rotting trading vessels that had been hastily converted before sailing from Portsmouth. The number of men on board had also been grossly exaggerated. Stuyvesant had been told that the ships were carrying a crew of eight hundred. In fact, there were less than half that number.

The governor was nevertheless undeterred and vowed to

go down fighting. But the confidence of his men had been drained by stories of the war-like English soldiers and none in New Amsterdam had a stomach for the fight. When the English offered an honourable surrender, Stuyvesant was reluctantly forced to agree. On Monday, 8 September 1664, he signed away the Dutch rights to Manhattan and, two hours later, his small band of troops left their fort 'with their arms, drums beating, and colours flying'.

When he heard the news of the town's capitulation, King Charles II was delighted. 'You will have heard of our taking New Amsterdam,' he wrote to his sister in France. ''Tis a place of great importance … we have got the better of it and 'tis now called New York.' The Dutch did not share the king's enthusiasm and protested in the strongest terms, arguing that the English had seized the island without 'even a shadow of right in the world.' King Charles shrugged off the protests; after all, the Dutch had behaved with equal aggression when they had seized Run, an island to which they had even less claim than Manhattan.

With no resolution in sight, the two countries once again tumbled into war, fighting it out on the high seas for more than two years with neither side gaining the upper hand. The English had small consolation when they captured two richly laden East India ships – lucrative prizes which were filled with nutmeg, mace and other precious commodities. So valuable was their cargo that Samuel Pepys made a special journey down the Thames Estuary to view the prize. 'The greatest wealth lie in confusion that a man can see in the world,' he wrote. 'Pepper scattered through every chink, you trod upon it; and in cloves and nutmegs I walked above the knees; whole rooms full. And silk in bales, and boxes of copper plate, one of which I saw opened … as noble a sight as ever I saw in my life.'

With the war dragging on inconclusively it was agreed, in March 1667, that both sides should meet at Breda to discuss their grievances. The English demands were predictable: compensation for Dutch outrages and the immediate return of Run. The Dutch grievances were equally well rehearsed: compensation for English piracy and the return of New Amsterdam. Although the English negotiating team were given considerable flexibility in their handling of the talks, on the question of Run they were allowed no leeway. They were to 'represent to the ambassadors that the detaining of Pulo Run is one of the greatest foundations of the vast profits and strength of the Dutch in the Indies, but extremely prejudicial to the English nation.' To this they were met with a familiar cry: 'New Netherland must be restored'. As the talks faltered and broke down, the peace commissioners stepped in and proposed the only remaining solution: that in return for the Dutch keeping Run, the English should be allowed to retain Manhattan.

Still the English hesitated, fearful of signing away their richest asset. They deliberated for days but were unable to reach a decision and wrote to London asking for advice. On the morning of 18 April 1667 there arrived a letter with one simple instruction: 'we acquiesce.' A deal had at last been struck.

The resultant treaty, the Treaty of Breda, was a work of exquisite diplomacy, tactfully naming neither of the islands that had caused so much bloodshed. But the exchange, which included the whole of the New Netherlands, was there for all to see, enshrined in article three. 'Both parties shall keep and possess hereafter, with plenary right of sovereignty, propriety, and possession, all such lands, islands, cities, forts, places, and colonies ... [as] they have by force of arms, or any other way whatsoever, gotten and detained from the other party.'

As the ink dried on the treaty, few can have realised that they were signing one of the most significant documents in history. In exchanging a tiny island in the East Indies for a much larger one on America's eastern seaboard, England and Holland had sealed the destiny of New York. Until 1667, Manhattan had been a small trading centre with a population of less than one thousand. Now, the island was set to enter a new and ever more prosperous period in its history – a period that would see it rise and rise until the name New York was fabled around the globe. By the time of the War of Independence, the city had become the largest city in North America and was the natural choice to be the country's new capital.

That a deal should have been struck between England and Holland was due, in no small part, to the courage of a simple trader, Nathaniel Courthope, whose defiance and heroism forty-seven years earlier had sparked an unstoppable train of events. His bravado in defending Run, his stand against an army hundreds of times more powerful than his own, and his devotion to his country's flag became the rallying cry for the East India Company. Yet Courthope's motivation was simple: patriotism, duty, and an unswerving belief that what he was doing was right. He always knew that he would die for his ideals; indeed he looked 'daily and hourly' for his final end. When given a final opportunity to surrender the sovereignty of Run he had countered with an emphatic refusal: 'I could not,' he replied, 'unlesse I should turne traitor unto my King and Countrey.' For Courthope, a trader, there were some things too precious to be bought and sold.

Almost four centuries after his death, Courthope finds

himself on the margins of history, forgotten by English and Americans alike. No statue of him graces the streets of Manhattan; no plaque commemorates his achievements in Westminster Abbey. Yet the stand he made on Run was to reshape history on the other side of the world, and although his death robbed England of her nutmeg, it gave her the biggest of apples.

EPILOGUE

AT AROUND MIDNIGHT ON 9 August 1810, a small party of Englishmen could be seen loading weapons into a tiny boat moored off Great Banda. They carried no torches or lanterns and were working in total silence for their mission was one of great secrecy. Led by an irrepressibly energetic commander by the name of Captain Cole, their task was to storm the Dutch castle on Neira and force the governor to surrender. They were then to take control of the rest of the archipelago.

The Dutch knew nothing of the English presence in the Banda Islands for Captain Cole had kept his men out of sight until long after dark. Suspecting neither treachery nor attack, the garrison of Fort Belgica were all asleep and even the night watches, bored with pacing the battlements, had retired inside. Undetected by anyone, Cole and his men drew up their boat on Neira's rocky foreshore, seized the battery and redoubt without a fight, and began scaling the stone-lined walls of Fort Belgica. By the time the Dutch alarm had been sounded, the English were in virtual control of the fort and there was only the briefest of skirmishes before the Dutch troops surrendered. Cole then directed the bastion's formidable firepower onto Fort Nassau, the island's other castle, and blasted shot after shot at its battlements until they crumbled to dust. Here, too, the Dutch capitulated and

*Nutmegs being harvested in traditional manner. The English sounded
the death-knell for the Bandanese economy in the 19th century when
they uprooted hundreds of nutmeg seedlings and transported them to
Ceylon, Pinang and Singapore.*

without the loss of a single man, Cole found himself in effective control of the Banda Islands.

The English commander justified his action on the grounds that Napoleon might use the 'spiceries' as the base for a campaign against India. Such a threat was always remote, but Cole's forces remained in the Bandas until 1817 when they abruptly pulled out, explaining to a bewildered population that a Holland deprived of the Indies would make for a very weak ally in Europe.

Although Cole's action serves as little more than a footnote in the history of the Bandas, it did have one significant and devastating effect on their future. Before they left, the English uprooted hundreds of nutmeg seedlings along with several tons of the unique soil and transplanted them to Ceylon, Pinang, Bencoolen and Singapore. Within a few decades, these thriving new plantations were far outstripping the production on the Bandas.

The decline of the archipelago had, in fact, set in many years earlier. Although the islands had for a time reaped fabulous dividends, the Dutch settlers proved hopelessly indolent and corrupt and allowed their poorly managed estates to go to ruin. Even more damaging was the volcano, Gunung Api, which was entering one of the most violent and unpredictable phases in its history with no fewer than five major eruptions during the seventeenth century, all followed by devastating earthquakes and tidal waves. In 1629, Neira town was virtually swept out to sea; whilst the winter of 1691 ushered in five years of misery as the volcano belched sulphur and lava in the direction of the governor's residence. Nature was scarcely less destructive in the eighteenth century. In 1778, the twin forces of an eruption and earthquake, followed by a hurricane and an immense tidal wave, all but wrecked the Banda Islands' nutmeg groves. One out of every two trees was felled and production of nutmeg plummeted to a fraction of its former levels.

Although descendants of the early Dutch settlers doggedly clung to their land, the overseas English plantations had sounded the death knell for the Banda Islands. As demand for nutmeg in Europe steadily fell, even the great Dutch East India Company found itself lurching from one financial crisis to another and when auditors examined the accounts in the 1790s they found the Company to be a staggering twelve million guilders in the red. Soon afterwards, the monopoly was lost and the Company slipped quietly into the history books.

Despite the decline, few of the older residents were inclined to return to Holland – a country that most had never even visited – preferring instead to enjoy the substantial inherited fortunes that many still possessed. The end of the nineteenth century saw the islands enter a twilight golden age as vast sums of money were squandered on grandiose waterfront mansions, all of them filled with the choicest antiques and crystals, marble and glass. Each evening the burghers of Banda would dress in their finery and stroll up and down the promenade to the rousing music of a military brass band, and when the Dutch governor-general arrived in the winter of 1860 he was welcomed with such extravagance and excess that he could almost have been fooled into believing that the islands were as rich as they had ever been. His triumphant procession through Neira town was led by a troupe of musicians, dancers and players, all dressed in costume, and the main (and only) street was gaily decked with flags, flowers and bunting.

No less diverting than His Excellency's official visit was the regular arrival of one or another of the local steam packets, bringing naturalists and wealthy Europeans in search of the exotic and unusual. All were delighted with what they found in this tropical archipelago, as testified in their numerous journals and diaries. 'A sail of two nights and a day [from Amboyna],' wrote the naturalist Henry Forbes, 'brought us to Banda. Coming on deck, before breakfast, we found ourselves slowly steaming in through a narrow winding entrance between thickly foliaged cliffs … it was the most lovely spot we had yet visited. Fronting us as the steamer warped itself to the jetty lay the town as a cluster of white houses … [and] from an elevated plateau, a battlement fort overlooked us, the scarlet of its Dutch ensign floating in the wind.'

Although the frivolity and heady excess of fin-de-siècle Banda provided the illusion of prosperity, many of the younger generation soon tired of the stagnant social life and lack of prospects and bought themselves one-way tickets to Holland, leaving the islands to their fate. With Dutch expenditure on the Bandas far outweighing revenue, they became an increasingly costly drain on resources and it was not long before the governor himself was withdrawn and the archipelago returned to an obscure provincial backwater seldom visited by Dutch officials. There were a few brief moments that reminded the world of the existence of these islands. In the 1930s, two prominent anti-colonialists, Mohammed Hatti, later vice-president of Indonesia, and Sutan Sjahrir, who served as prime minister, spent six years in exile on Neira Island; whilst in 1944 the Japanese bombed and then occupied the archipelago. Although they found the islands of little interest except as a rendezvous for shipping, their

The Banda Islands entered a twilight golden age in the 1890s as residents squandered inherited fortunes. But younger inhabitants tired of the stagnant social life and lack of prospects and bought one-way tickets to Holland.

occupation did have one malign consequence: with few supplies reaching the islands, the locals were forced to cut down many of their remaining nutmeg trees and turn the land over to vegetable cultivation.

The end of the war brought tragedy to the Bandas. An American bomber raiding Japanese bases in the region appeared in the skies above Neira in the spring of 1945 intent on destroying the shipping anchored in the harbour. But one stray bomb scored a direct hit on the town of Neira, exploding directly above a wedding party and killing more than a hundred guests.

Today, the Banda Islands have once again retreated into obscurity – an archipelago so small and insignificant that it rarely features on a map of the region. Scarcely more accessible than in the days of Nathaniel Courthope, it requires patience and a good deal of luck to reach the islands. In the summer of 1997, the antiquated fourteen-seat Cessna plane that used to fly between Amboyna and Neira was flipped over by the monsoon winds and dashed to pieces on the airstrip. Now, the only way to reach the Bandas is on the KM *Rinjani* ferry, an eight-hour journey through the choppy waters which separate Neira from Amboyna.

Neira remains the 'capital' of the Banda Islands, home to a couple of stores, a fish market, two streets and two cars. A wander through the town reveals a Dutch church (the hands of its clock stuck at 5.03, the exact time of the Japanese invasion), a handful of crumbling villas and the former Dutch governor's residence which today lies empty and abandoned, its baroque chandeliers slowly shedding their crystal-glass finery. The only other 'sight' is the pentangle-shaped Fort Belgica which occupies a commanding position on a bluff of rock above the port – impregnable to all but volcanic boulders and Captain Cole's intrepid troops. The castle has recently received a much-needed face-lift but the restorers have been over-zealous in their work, rendering walls and installing doors. The ghosts that were until recently said to trudge its ramparts have been forced to flee to other castles in the archipelago – rambling, ivy-clad places where one can still scoop musket-shot from the sand-filled dungeons.

Unlike the central group of Bandas – connected to each other by prahus or native canoes – the outlying island of Run can only be reached by twin-engined powerboat. Even so, the journey is a treacherous one, especially when the monsoon whips up a storm and sends mountainous waves roaring through the ten-mile channel that separates Neira and Run. As our boat smashes its way through these waters in defiance of nature, we slowly catch a fragrance in the wind – the sweet, odoriferous scent of nutmeg blossom.

We land on the island's northern shoreline – the point at which Nathaniel Courthope landed 381 years previously – which is sheltered from the monsoon by the island's precipitous cliffs. A couple of fishermen glance at this newly arrived stranger while their womenfolk wander off to fetch us some coconut milk, but otherwise nothing stirs. The island's small wooden settlement is a soporific place; a village of swept alleys, tidy gardens and shaded verandas lined with flowerpots.

No one here knows anything of the extraordinary history of their island, even though they are forever turning up coins and musket-shot in their vegetable plots. Nor are they aware that their home – just two miles long and half a mile wide – was once considered a fair exchange for a very different island – Manhattan – on the far side of the globe.

Yet they are unmoved when told of the cruel blow that fortune has dealt them, happy to see out their days on this unknown and unspoiled atoll. For although their flickering televisions allow them a glimpse of America through reruns of *Cagney and Lacey* and *Starsky and Hutch*, they will tell you that the view from their windows is infinitely more magnificent than Manhattan's glittering skyline.

For there on the cliffs, high above the translucent sea, the willowy nutmeg tree is once again setting its roots, bursting into flower each spring and filling the air with a heady, languorous scent.

BIBLIOGRAPHY

Nathaniel's Nutmeg has been drawn largely from original journals, diaries and letters. A brief glance at this bibliography will reveal the author's indebtedness to Samuel Purchas who collected the writings of East India Company adventurers and transcribed them into his monumental *Purchas His Pilgrimes*. The 1625 edition is now extremely rare and even the twenty-volume 1905 reprint is only to be found in specialist libraries.

The Hakluyt Society is the other source for original writings but most of these volumes are also long out of print. They can be found in the British Library's Oriental and India Office Collections, along with many original manuscripts.

Those wishing to delve further into the letters written by overseas factors, or to read the official Company documents, will need to turn to the East India Company archives and Colonial State Papers – a task not for the lighthearted since they run to forty-five volumes. The relevant editions are listed below.

The two standard works on the Dutch East India Company are K. J. Johan de Jonge's thirteen-volume *De Opkomst*, a collection of journals written in old Dutch; and François Valentijn's *Oud en Nieuw Oost-Indien*. Full details are to be found below.

Contemporary journals and diaries

Borough, Stephen, in Hakluyt's *The Principall Navigations*, 1599.

Chancellor, Richard, in Hakluyt's *The Principall Navigations*, 1599.

Courthope, Nathaniel, in *Purchas His Pilgrimes* (vol. 1).

Davis, J., *Voyages and Works of,* Hakluyt Society, 1880.

Dermer, Thomas, in *Purchas His Pilgrimes*; see also I. N. Phelps Stokes, *The Iconography of Manhattan Island*, 1922.

Downton, Nicholas, *Voyage to the East Indies*, ed. Sir William Foster, Hakluyt Society, 1939; see also *Purchas His Pilgrimes* (vol. 1).

Drake, Sir Francis, *The World Encompassed by Drake*, Hakluyt Society, 1854; see also *New Light on Drake*, ed. Z. Nuttall, Hakluyt Society, 1914.

Finch, William, in *Purchas His Pilgrimes* (vol. 1).

Fitch, Ralph, in *Purchas His Pilgrimes* (vol. 2).

Fitz-Herbert, Sir Humphrey, in *Purchas His Pilgrimes* (vol. 1).

Floris, P.W., *His Voyage to the East Indies in the Globe*, ed. W. H. Moreland, Hakluyt Society, 1934; see also *Purchas His Pilgrimes* (vol. 1).

Hakluyt, R., *The Principall Navigations*, 1599.

Hawkins, William, in *The Hawkins Voyages During the Reigns of Henry VIII, Queen Elizabeth, and James I*, ed. C. Markham, Hakluyt Society, 1878. (This is the journal kept by the William Hawkins who sailed with Edward Fenton.)

Hawkins, William, in *Purchas His Pilgrimes* (vol. 1). (This is the William Hawkins who lived in India.)

Hayes, Robert, in *Purchas His Pilgrimes* (vol. 1).

Hudson, Henry, *Henry Hudson the Navigator*, Hakluyt Society, 1860. See also *Purchas His Pilgrimes* (vol. 3).

Jourdain, John, *The Journal of*, ed. W. Foster, Hakluyt Society, 1905.

Keeling, William, in *Purchas His Pilgrimes* (vol. 1).

Lancaster, Sir James, *Voyages of Lancaster to the East Indies*, Hakluyt Society, 1877.

Michelborne, Sir Edward, in *Purchas His Pilgrimes* (vol. 1).

Middleton, David, In *Purchas His Pilgrimes*, (vol. 1).

Middleton, Sir Henry, *Voyage to Bantam and the Maluco Islands*, Hakluyt Society, 1855; *Voyage to the Moluccas, 1604–6*, ed. Sir William Foster, Hakluyt Society, 1943.

Roe, Sir Thomas, *Embassy to the Great Moghul* (2 vols), Hakluyt Society, 1899.

Saris, John, *Voyage to Japan, 1613*, Hakluyt Society, 1900; see also *Purchas His Pilgrimes* (vol. 1).

Willoughby, Sir Hugh, in Hakluyt's *The Principall Navigations*, 1599.

Bibliography

Letters and state papers

Calendar of State Papers: Colonial (vols 1–9), ed. W. Noel Sainsbury, 1860–93.

Chalmers, George, *A Collection of Treaties between Great Britain and Other Powers*, 1770.

Collections of the New York Historical Society (vol. 1), 1841.

East India Company, *Calendar of the Court Minutes of, 1640–79* (11 vols), ed. Ethel B. Sainsbury, 1907–38.

East India Company, *The Dawn of British Trade to the East Indies ...*, *1599–1603*, ed. Henry Stevens and George Birdwood, 1886.

East India Company, *The English Factories in India, 1618–1669* (13 vols), ed. William Foster, 1906–27.

East India Company, *Letters Received from its Servants in the East* (6 vols), ed. F. C. Danvers and William Foster, 1896–1902.

East India Company, *Register of Letters etc. of the Governor and Company of Merchants of London trading into the East Indies, 1600–1619*, ed. George Birdwood and William Foster, 1892.

East India Company, *Selected Seventeenth Century Works*, 1968.

East India Company, *A True Relation of the Unjust, Cruel and Barbarous Proceedings against the English at Amboyna, 1624. The Answer unto the Dutch Pamphlet made in Defence of the Unjust and Barbarous Proceeding against the English at Amboyna, 1624. A Remonstrance of the Directors of the Netherlands and the Reply of the English East India Company, 1624.*

A General Collection of Treatys, etc. (4 vols), 1732.

Reference works

Borde, A., *Fyrst Boke of Introduction to Knowledge.* Early English Texts Society edition of 1870 (ed. F. J. Furnivall) contains Borde's *Dyetary of Helth.*

Chaudhuri, K. N., *The English East India Company 1600–40*, 1965.

Crawfurd, John, *A Descriptive Dictionary of the Indian Islands and Adjacent Countries*, 1856.

Danvers, F., *Dutch Activities in the East*, 1945.

Dodwell, H. H. (ed.), *Cambridge History of India*, vol. 4, 1929.

Elyot, Sir Thomas, *The Castel of Helth*, 1541.

Flick, Alexander (ed.), *History of the State of New York* (10 vols), 1933.

Foster, W., *England's Quest of Eastern Trade*, 1933.

Foster, W., *John Company*, 1926.

Gerard, J., *Gerard's Herbal*, 1636.

Hanna, Willard A., *Indonesian Banda*, 1978.

Hart, Henry, *Sea Road to the Indies*, 1950.

Jonge, Johan K. J. de., *De Opkomst van het Nederlandsch Gezag in Oost Indie* (13 vols), 1862–88.

Keay, J., *The Honourable Company*, 1991.

Khan, Shafaat Ahmad, *The East India Trade in the Seventeenth Century*, 1923.

Loon, Hendrik van, *Dutch Navigators*, 1916.

Masselman, George, *The Cradle of Colonialism*, 1963.

Murphy, Henry C., *Henry Hudson in Holland*, 1909.

Parry, J. W., *The Story of Spices and Spices Described*, 1969.

Penrose, Boies, *Travel and Discovery in the Renaissance*, 1952.

Phelps Stokes, I. N., *The Iconography of Manhattan Island*, 1922.

Pinkerton, J., *A General Collection of the Best and Most Interesting Voyages*, 1812.

Powys, Llewelyn, *Henry Hudson*, 1927.

Rink, Oliver, *Holland on the Hudson: An Economic and Social History*, 1986.

Rosengarten, F., *The Book of Spices*, 1969.

St John, Horace, *The Indian Archipelago* (2 vols), 1853.

Valentijn, François, *Oud en Nieuw Oost-Indien* (5 vols in 8 bindings), 1724–6.

Van der Zee, Henri and Barbara, *A Sweet and Alien Land: The Story of Dutch New York*, 1978.

Van Rensselaer, Schuyler, *History of the City of New York in the Seventeenth Century*, 1909.

Venner, Tobias, *Via Recta ad Vitam Longam*, 1637.

Vlekke, Bernard, *The Story of the Dutch East Indies*, 1946.

Willson, Beckles, *Ledger and Sword*, 1903.

Wilson, F. P., *The Plague in Shakespeare's London*, 1927.

Wright, Arnold, *Early English Adventurers in the East*, 1917.

INDEX

Index

Index

Raymond Khoury is the *Sunday Times* and international bestselling author of *The Last Templar* and *The Sanctuary*. An acclaimed screenwriter and producer for both film and television whose credits include *Spooks* and *Waking the Dead*, he lives in London with his wife and two children. Visit his website at www.raymondkhoury.com.

By *Raymond Khoury*

THE LAST TEMPLAR
THE SANCTUARY
THE SIGN

THE SIGN

RAYMOND KHOURY

An Orion paperback

First published in Great Britain in 2009
by Orion
This paperback edition published in 2009
by Orion Books Ltd,
Orion House, 5 Upper St Martin's Lane,
London WC2H 9EA

An Hachette UK company

1 3 5 7 9 10 8 6 4 2

A CIP catalogue record for this book
is available from the British Library.

ISBN 978-1-4091-0213-7

Printed and bound in Great Britain by
CPI Mackays, Chatham, ME5 8TD

The Orion Publishing Group's policy is to use papers that
are natural, renewable and recyclable products and
made from wood grown in sustainable forests. The logging
and manufacturing processes are expected to conform to
the environmental regulations of the country of origin.

www.orionbooks.co.uk

This one's for Suellen

The idea that religion and politics don't mix was invented by the Devil to keep Christians from running their own country.

—Jerry Falwell

My kingdom is not of this world.

—Jesus Christ (John 18:36)

PROLOGUE

I.

Skeleton Coast, Namibia – Two years ago

As the bottom of the ravine rushed up to meet him, the dry, rocky landscape hurtling past Danny Sherwood miraculously slowed right down to a crawl. Not that the extra time was welcome. All it did was allow the realization to play itself out, over and over, in his harrowed mind. The gut-wrenching, agonizing realization that, without a shadow of a doubt, he would be dead in a matter of seconds.

And yet the day had started off with so much promise.

After almost three years, his work – his and the rest of the team's – was finally done. And, he thought with an inward grin, the rewards would soon be his to enjoy.

It had been a hard slog. The project itself had been daunting enough, from a scientific point of view. The work conditions – the tight deadline, the even tighter security, the virtual exile from family and friends for all those intense and lonely months – were even more of a challenge. But today, as he had looked up at the pure blue sky and breathed in the dry, dusty air of this godforsaken corner of the planet, it all seemed worthwhile.

There would be no IPO, that much had been made clear from the start. Neither Microsoft nor Google would be paying big bucks to acquire the technology. The project, he'd been told, was being developed for the military. Still, a significant on-success bonus had been promised to every member of the team. In his case, it would be enough to provide financial security for him, his parents back home, and for any not-too-overly profligate wife he might end up with along with as many kids as he could possibly envisage having – if he ever got around to it. Which he conceivably would, years from now, after he'd had his fun and enjoyed the spoils of his work. For the moment, though, it wasn't on his radar. He was only twenty-nine years old.

Yes, the cushy future that was materializing before him was a far cry from the more austere days of his childhood in Worcester, Massachusetts. As he made his way across the parched desert soil, past the mess tent and the landing pad where the chopper was being loaded for their departure, and over to the project director's tent, he thought back on the experience – from the lab work to the various field tests, culminating with this one, out here in this lost netherworld.

Danny wished he'd be allowed to share the excitement of it all with a few people outside the project. His parents, firstly. He could just imagine how stunned, and proud, they would be. Danny was making good on all the promise, all the lofty expectations they'd heaped on him since, well, birth. His thoughts migrated to his older brother, Matt. He'd get a huge kick out of this. Probably try and get Danny to back him in some dodgy, harebrained, borderline-legal scheme, but what the hell, there'd be plenty to go around. There were also a few big-headed jerks in the business that he would have loved to gloat to about all this, given the chance. But he knew that any disclosure outside the team was strictly – *strictly* – not allowed. That much had also been made clear from the start. The project was covert. The nation's defense was at stake. The word *treason* was mentioned. And so he'd kept his mouth shut, which wasn't too hard. He was used to it. The highly competitive industry he was in had a deeply ingrained subterranean culture. Hundreds of millions of dollars were often at stake. And when it came down to it, the choice between an eight-figure bank account and a dingy cell in a supermax federal penitentiary was a no-brainer.

He was about to knock on the door of the tent – it was a

huge, air-conditioned, semi-rigid-wall tent, with a solid door and glass windows – when something made him pull his hand back.

Raised voices. Not just raised, but angry.

Seriously angry.

He leaned closer to the door.

'You should have told me. It's my project, goddammit,' a man's voice erupted. 'You should have told me right from the start.'

Danny knew that voice well: Dominic Reece, his mentor, and the project's lead scientist – its PI, short for principal investigator. A professor of electrical engineering and computer science at MIT, Reece occupied hallowed ground in Danny's world. He'd taught Danny in several of his formative classes and had kept a close eye on Danny's work throughout his PhD before inviting him to join his team for the project all those months ago. It was an opportunity – and an honor – Danny couldn't possibly pass up. And while Danny knew that the professor had a habit of expressing his opinions more forcefully and vociferously than most, he detected something else in his voice now. There was a hurt, an indignation that he hadn't heard before.

'What would your reaction have been?' The second man's voice, which wasn't familiar to Danny, was equally inflamed.

'The same,' Reece replied emphatically.

'Come on, just think about it for a second. Think about what we can do together. What we can achieve.'

Reece's fury was unabated. 'I can't help you do this. I can't be a party to it.'

'Dom, please—'

'No.'

'Think about what we can—'

'No,' Reece interrupted. 'Forget it. There's no way.' The words had an unmistakable finality to them.

A leaden quiet skulked behind the door for a few tense

moments, then Danny heard the second man say, 'I wish you hadn't said that.'

'What the hell does that mean?' Reece shot back.

There was no reply.

Then Reece's voice came back, tinged with a sudden unease. 'What about the others? You haven't told any of them, have you?' An assertion, not a question.

'No.'

'When were you planning on letting them in on your revised mission statement?'

'I wasn't sure. I had to get your answer first. I was hoping you'd help me win them over. Convince them to be part of this.'

'Well that's not going to happen,' Reece retorted angrily. 'As a matter of fact, I'd like to get them all the hell away from here as soon as possible.'

'I can't let you do that, Dom.'

The words seemed to freeze Reece in his tracks. 'What do you mean, you can't let me do that?' he said defiantly.

A pregnant silence greeted his question. Danny could just visualize Reece processing it.

'So what are you saying? You're not going to . . .' Reece's voice trailed off for a beat, then came back, with the added urgency of a sudden, horrible realization. 'Jesus. Have you completely lost your mind?'

The outrage in the old man's tone froze Danny's spine.

He heard Reece say, 'You son of a bitch,' heard thudding footfalls striding toward him, toward the door, heard the second man call out to Reece, 'Dom, don't,' then heard a third voice say, 'Don't do that, Reece,' a voice Danny knew, a harsh voice, the voice of a man who'd creeped Danny out from the moment he'd first met him: Maddox, the project's shaven-headed, stone-faced head of security, the one with the missing ear and the star-shaped burn around it, the man he knew was nicknamed 'The Bullet' by his equally creepy men. Then he heard Reece say, 'Go to hell,' and the door swung open, and Reece was suddenly there, standing before Danny, a surprised look in his eyes. Danny heard a distinctive, metallic double-click, a sound he'd heard in a hundred movies but never in real life, the all-too-familiar sound of a gun slide, and the second man, the man who'd been arguing with Reece all along and who Danny now recognized, turned to the Bullet and yelled, 'No – '

 – just as a muffled, high-pitched cough echoed from behind Reece, then another, before the scientist jerked forward, his face crunched with pain, his legs giving way as he tumbled onto Danny.

Danny faltered back, the suddenness of it all overwhelming his senses as he struggled to keep Reece from falling to the ground. A warm, sticky feeling seeped down his hands as he struggled to support the stricken man, a thick, dark red liquid gushing out of Reece and soaking Danny's arms and clothes.

He couldn't hold him. Reece thudded heavily onto the ground, exposing the inside of the tent, the second man standing there, horrified, frozen in shock, next to the Bullet, who had a gun in his hand. Its muzzle was now leveled straight at Danny.

Danny dived to one side as a couple of shots cleaved through the air he'd been occupying, then he just tore off, running away from the tent and the fallen professor as fast as he could.

He was a dozen yards or so away when he dared glance back and saw Maddox emerging from the tent, radio in one hand, the gun in the other, his eyes locking onto the receding Danny like lasers as he bolted after him. With his heart in his throat, Danny sprinted through the temporary campsite – there were a few smaller tents, for the handful of other scientists who, like him, had been recruited for the project. He almost slammed into two of them, top minds from the country's best universities, who were emerging from one of the tents just as he was nearing it.

'They killed Reece,' he yelled to them, pausing momentarily and waving frantically back toward the main tent. 'They killed him.' He looked back and saw Maddox closing in inexorably, seemingly carried forward on winged feet, and took off again, glancing back to see his friends turn to the onrushing man with confused looks, crimson sprouts erupting from their chests as Maddox gunned them down without even slowing.

Danny had ducked sideways, behind the mess tent, out of breath, his leg muscles burning, his mind churning desperately for escape options, when the project's two ageing Jeeps appeared before him, parked under their makeshift shelter. He flung the first car's door open, spurred the engine to life, threw the car into gear, and floored the accelerator, storming off in a spray of sand and dust just as Maddox rounded the tent.

Danny kept an eye on the rearview mirror as his Jeep charged across the harsh gravel plain. He clenched the steering wheel through bloodless knuckles, confused thoughts assaulting his senses from all directions, his heart feeling like it was jackhammering its way out of his chest, and did the only thing he could think of, which was to keep the car aimed straight ahead, across the deserted terrain, away from the camp, away from that crazed, insane maniac who'd killed his mentor and his friends, all while fighting for a way around the horrifying truth of his predicament, which was that there was nowhere to run. They were in the middle of nowhere, with no villages or habitations anywhere near, not for hundreds of miles.

That was the whole point of being there.

That fear didn't have much time to torment him as a loud, throaty buzz soon burst through his frazzled thoughts. He looked back and saw the camp's chopper coming straight at him, reeling him in effortlessly. He pegged the gas pedal to the floor, hard, sending the Jeep bounding over the small rocks and undulations of the outback, slamming his head against the inside of the car's canvas roof with each jarring leap, avoiding the occasional boulder and the lonely bunches of dried up quiver trees that dotted the deathly landscape.

The chopper was now on his tail, its engine noise deafening, its rotor wash drowning the Jeep in a swirling sandstorm. Danny strained to see ahead through the tornado of dust, not that it made much difference since there was no road to follow, as the chopper dropped down heavily on the car's roof, crushing the thin struts holding up the roof and almost tearing Danny's head off.

He veered left, then right, fishtailing the car as he fought to avoid the flying predator's claws, sweat seeping down his face, the car careening wildly over rocks and cactus bushes. The chopper was never more than mere feet from the Jeep, connecting with it in thunderous blows, slapping it from side to side like it was toying with a hockey puck. The thought of stopping didn't occur to Danny: He was running on pure adrenalin, his survival instincts choking him in their grasp, an irrational hope of escape propelling him forward. And just then, in that maelstrom of panic and fear, something shifted, something changed, and he sensed the chopper pulling up slightly, felt a spike of hope that maybe, just maybe, he might make it out of that nightmare alive, and the twisting cloud of sand around his Jeep lifted –

– and that's when he saw the canyon, cutting across the terrain dead ahead of him with sadistic inevitability, a vast limestone trench snaking across the landscape like something from the Wild West, the one he'd seen in countless cowboy films and had hoped to visit someday but hadn't yet, the one he now knew, with a savage certainty, that he'd never get a chance to see, as the Jeep flew off the canyon's edge and into the dry desert air.

II.

Wadi Natrun, Egypt

Sitting cross-legged in his usual spot high up on the mountain, with the barren valley and the endless desert spread out below him, the old priest felt a rising unease. During his last few visits to that desolate place, he'd sensed a more ominous ring to the words that were reverberating inside his head. And today, there was something distinctly portentous about them.

And then it came. A question that sent a straightening spasm shooting up his spine.

'Are you ready to serve?'

His eyes fluttered open, blinking against the soft dawn light. He glanced around instinctively, as he'd done many times before, but it was pointless, as it had been each time before. He was alone up there. There was no one around. Not a soul, human or animal. Nothing at all, as far as the eye could see.

Despite the early morning chill, sweat droplets sprouted across his bald pate. He swallowed hard, and concentrated again.

And then it came, again.

The voice, the whisper, coming from inside his own head.

'The time of our Lord will soon be upon you. Are you prepared to serve?'

Hesitantly, with a tremor in his voice, Father Jerome opened his mouth and stammered, 'Yes, of course. Whatever you ask of me. I am your servant.'

There was no reply at first. The old priest could feel the individual droplets of sweat sliding down the rugged skin on his forehead, one after the other, skating across the ridge of his brow before dropping onto his cheek. He could almost hear them trickling down, a slow, tortuous progress across his tightened, weather-beaten face.

Then the voice inside his head came back.

'Are you ready to lead your people to salvation? Are you prepared to fight for them? To show them the errors of their ways, even though they may not want to listen?'

'Yes,' Father Jerome cried out, his voice cracking with equal doses of passion and fear. 'Yes, of course. But how? When?'

A suffocating silence gripped the mountain, then the voice returned, and simply told him, 'Soon.'

CHAPTER 1

The static that hissed through the tiny, noise-isolating earpiece disappeared, replaced by the authoritative-yet-soothing voice of the show's anchorman.

'Talk us through why this is happening, Grace?'

Just then, another wall of ice crumbled behind her and collapsed on itself, crackling like distant thunder. Grace Logan – Gracie, to her friends – turned away from the camera and watched as the entire cliff plummeted into the gray-blue water and disappeared in an angry eruption of spray.

Perfect timing, she thought with a glimmer of satisfaction, a brief respite from the solemnity she'd been feeling since she'd arrived on the ship the day before.

Under normal circumstances, this could well have been a pleasant, sunny, late-December day, December being the height of summer in the Southern Hemisphere.

Today was different.

Today, nature was in turmoil.

It felt as if the very fabric of the earth was being ripped apart. Which it was. The slab of ice that was tearing itself off the rest of the continent was the size of Texas.

Not exactly the kind of Christmas present the planet needed.

The breakup of the ice shelf was now in its third day, and it was only getting started. The cataclysm had kicked up a ghostly mist that thinned out the sun's warming rays, and the cold was starting to get to Gracie, even with the adrenalin coursing through her. She could see that the rest of her team – Dalton Kwan, the young, breezy Hawaiian cameraman she'd worked with regularly over the past three years, and Howard 'Finch' Fincher, their older, über-fastidious and annoyingly stoic veteran producer – were also far from comfortable, but the footage they were airing was well worth it, especially since, as far as she could tell, they were the only news crew around.

She'd been out there for over an hour, standing on the starboard observation deck of the RRS *James Clark Ross*, and despite the thermals and the gloves, her fingers and toes were shivering. The royal research ship, a beefy three-hundred-foot floating oceanographic and geophysical laboratory operated by the British Antarctic Survey project, was currently less than half a mile off the coast of Western Antarctica, its distinctive deep-red hull the only blip of color in an otherwise bleak palette of whites, blues, and grays. Gracie, Dalton, and Finch had been on the continent for a couple of weeks, shooting footage in the Terra Firma Islands for her big global warming documentary. They had been ready to pack up and head home for Christmas, which was only days away, when the call from the news desk back in D.C. had come in, informing them that the shelf's breakup had started. The news hadn't been widely circulated at that point; a contact of the network inside the NSIDC – the National Snow and Ice Data Center, whose scientists used satellite data to track changes in the spread and thickness of the polar ice caps – had given them the heads-up on the sly. With the competition snoozing and the *James Clark Ross* a day's sail away from the action and already heading toward it, Gracie and her crew had jumped on the opportunity for an exclusive scoop. The BAS had graciously agreed to have them on board to cover the event, going so far as to arrange for a Royal Navy chopper to ferry them in from the island.

Several of the ship's onboard scientists were also on deck, watching the walls of ice disintegrate. A couple of them were filming, using handheld video cameras. Most of the crew were also out there, staring in resigned and awed silence.

Gracie turned back to face the camera and pulled her microphone closer. In between the irregular, thunderous collapses of the cliff face, the air reverberated with the distant, muffled retorts of the ice's tortured movement farther inland.

'This breakup was probably caused by a number of factors, Jack, but the main suspect in this very complicated investigation is just plain old meltwater.'

She heard more hissing as the signal bounced off a couple of satellites and traveled ten thousand miles to the network's climate-controlled newsroom in D.C. and back, then Roxberry's voice returned, slightly confused. 'Meltwater?'

'That's right, Jack,' she explained. 'Pools of water that build up on the surface of the ice as it melts. This meltwater is heavier than the ice it's sitting on, so – basic law of gravity – it finds its way down into cracks, and as more and more water pushes through, it acts like a wedge and these cracks grow into rifts that grow into canyons, and if there's enough meltwater to keep pushing through, the ice shelf eventually just snaps off.'

The physics of it were simple. The highest, coldest, and windiest continent on the planet, an area one and a half times as big as the United States, was almost entirely covered by a dome of ice over two miles thick at its center. Heavy snowfalls blanket it in winter, then spread downward by gravity, flowing like ice-cold lava to the coast. And when this ice floe runs out of land, it keeps going, beyond the edge of land, but it doesn't sink: It floats, cantilevering over the sea in what we refer to as ice shelves. They can be over a mile thick at the point where they start floating, tapering to a no-less-staggering quarter mile at the water's edge, where they end in cliffs of a hundred feet or more above the waterline.

There had been a handful of major breakups in the last decade, but none this big. Also, they were rarely captured live on camera. They were usually only detected long after the event, after scrutinizing and comparing satellite images. And even though what Gracie was witnessing was only a localized portion of the overall upheaval – the collapse of towering cliffs of ice at the shelf's seaward edge – it was still an astounding and deeply troubling sight. In twelve years in television news, a career she'd dived into straight after getting her BA in political science from Cornell, Gracie had witnessed a lot of tragedies, and this one ranked right up there with the worst of them.

She was watching the planet fall apart – literally. 'So the big question then is,' Roxberry asked, 'why is it happening now? I mean, as I understand it, this ice shelf has been around since the end of the last ice age, and that was, what, twelve thousand years ago?'

'It's happening because of us, Jack. Because of the greenhouse gases we're generating. We're seeing it at both poles, here, up in the Arctic, in Greenland. And it isn't just part of a natural cycle. Almost every expert I've talked to is now convinced that the melting is accelerating and telling me we're close to some kind of tipping point, a point of no return – because of man-made global warming.'

Another block of ice disintegrated and crashed into the sea.

'And the concern here is that this ice shelf breaking off and melting will contribute to rising sea levels?' Roxberry asked.

'Well, not directly. Most of this ice shelf is already floating on water, so it doesn't affect sea levels in itself. Think of it as an ice cube floating in a glass of water. When it melts, it doesn't raise the level of water in the glass.'

'Doesn't it?'

'I guess I'm not the only one who's forgotten their sixth-grade physics,' she grinned.

'But you said there's an indirect effect on global sea levels.' Roxberry's voice exuded expertise, as if he were generously allowing her a chance to display her knowledge.

'Well, this area, the West Antarctic ice sheet, is the one place on the planet that scientists have been worried about most, in terms of ice melts. More specifically, they're worried about the massive glaciers sitting on land, behind this ice shelf. They're not floating.'

'So if they melted,' Roxberry added, 'sea levels would rise.'

'Exactly. Up until now, ice shelves like this one have been keeping back the glaciers, sort of like a cork that's holding in the contents of a bottle. Once the ice shelf breaks off, the cork's gone, there's nothing left to stop the glaciers from sliding into the sea – and if they do, the global sea levels rise. And this melting is happening much faster than forecasts had predicted. Even the data we have from last year is now considered too optimistic. In terms of disaster scenarios due to climate change, Antarctica was considered a sleeping giant. Well, the giant's now awake. And, by the looks of it, he's really grumpy.'

Roxberry quipped, 'I'm trying real hard to avoid saying this could just be the tip of the iceberg—'

'A wise choice, Jack,' she interjected. She could just picture the smug, self-satisfied grin lighting up his perma-tanned face and groaned inwardly at the thought. 'A grateful audience salutes you.'

'But that's what we're talking about here, isn't it?'

'Absolutely. Once these glaciers slide into the sea, it'll be too late to do anything about it, and . . .'

Her voice suddenly trailed off and dried up, as something distracted her: a ripple of sudden commotion, shrieks and gasps of shock and outstretched arms pointing out at the ice shelf. The words still caught in her throat as she saw Dalton's head rise from behind the viewfinder of the camera and look beyond her. Gracie spun around, facing away from the camera. And that's when she saw it.

In the sky. A couple of hundred feet above the collapsing ice shelf.

A bright, shimmering sphere of light.

It just appeared there, and wasn't moving.

Gracie concentrated her gaze on it and inched over to the

railing. She didn't understand what she was looking at, but whatever it was, she couldn't take her eyes off it.

The object – no, she wasn't even sure it was an object. It had a spherical shape, but somehow, it didn't seem . . . *physical*. It had an ethereal lightness to it, as if the air itself was glowing. And its brightness wasn't uniform. It was more subtle, graded, intense at its core then gradually thinning out, as in a close-up of an eye. It had an unstable, fragile quality to it. Like melting ice, or, rather, just water, suspended in midair and lit up, if that were possible, only Gracie knew it wasn't.

She darted a look at Dalton, who was angling the camera toward the sighting. 'Are you getting this?' she blurted.

'Yeah, but,' he shot back, looking over at her, his face scrunched up in sheer confusion, 'what the hell is it?'

CHAPTER 2

Gracie's eyes were locked onto it. It was just there, suspended in the pallid sky over the edge of the ice shelf. Mesmerizing in an otherworldly, surreal way.

'What *is* that?' Finch asked. His hands went up to his glasses, fidgeting slightly with their position, as if it would help clarify things.

'I don't know.' A surge of adrenalin spiked through her as she struggled to process what she was seeing. A quick, almost instinctive trawl through the possibilities of what it could be didn't get any hits.

This was unlike anything she was even vaguely familiar with.

She glanced across at the knot of scientists crowding the railings. They were talking and gesticulating excitedly, trying to make sense of it too.

'Gracie? What is that behind you?' Roxberry's voice came booming back through her earpiece.

For a second, she'd forgotten this was going out live. 'You're seeing this?'

A couple of seconds for her question and his reply to bounce off a satellite or two, then he came back. 'It's not perfectly clear, but yeah, we're getting it – what is it?'

She composed herself and faced the camera squarely, trying to keep any quiver out of her voice. 'I don't know, Jack. It just suddenly appeared. It seems to be some kind of corona, a halo of some sort . . . Hang on.'

She looked around, scanning the sky, checking to see if anything else was around, noting the sun's veiled position, unconsciously logging her surroundings. Nothing had changed. Nothing else was out there apart from their ship and the . . . *what was it?* She couldn't even think of an appropriate name for it. It was still shimmering brightly, half-transparent, its texture reminding her of a gargantuan, deep-sea jellyfish, floating in midair. And it seemed to be rotating, ever so slowly, giving it a real sense of depth.

And, oddly, she thought, a sense of being somehow . . . *alive.*

She stared at it, resisting all kinds of competing, outlandish thoughts, and focused her mind on getting a handle on its size. As big as a large hot air balloon, she first thought, then adjusted her thinking upward. Bigger. Maybe as big as a fireball in a fireworks display. It was huge. It was hard to judge without a point of reference for scale. She ran a visual comparison to the height of the cliff face below, which she knew to be roughly a hundred and fifty feet tall. It seemed to be around the same size, maybe a hundred and fifty feet in diameter, maybe more.

Dalton looked up from behind the camera and asked, 'You think it's some freaky aurora borealis thing?'

She'd been thinking the same thing, wondering if it was a trick of the light, an illusion caused by a reflection off the ice. In Antarctica, the sun never set during the austral summer. It just circled around at the horizon, a little higher during the 'day,' a little lower – almost a sunset – during the 'night.' It had taken some getting used to and it played tricks on you, but somehow Gracie didn't think it explained what she was seeing. The sighting seemed more substantial than that.

'Maybe,' she replied, almost to herself, lost in her thoughts, 'but I don't think it's the time of year for them . . . and I'm pretty sure they only appear when it's dark.'

'Gracie?' Roxberry again, waiting for an answer. Reminding her that she was going out live.

To a world audience.

Christ almighty.

She tried to relax and put on a genial smile for the camera, despite the tiny alarms buzzing through her. 'This is just . . . It's pretty amazing, Jack. I've never seen anything like it.

Maybe someone else on this ship knows what it is, we've got quite a few experts on board.'

Dalton lifted his tripod and tracked along with Gracie as she edged over to the scientists and crew members on deck with her, keeping the apparition in frame.

The others were discussing it in excited, heated tones, but something about their body language worried Gracie. If it was a rare, but natural, phenomenon, they'd be reacting differently. Somehow, she got the impression that they weren't comfortable with what they were seeing. Not just uncomfortable, but . . . rattled.

They don't know what it is.

One of them, who'd been watching it through binoculars, turned and met her gaze. He was an older man, a paleoclimatologist she'd met on arrival named Jeb Simmons. She read the same confusion, the same unease, on his face that had to be radiating from hers. It only confirmed her feeling.

She was about to speak up when another wave of gasps broke out across the deck. She turned in time to see the shimmering shape suddenly pulse, brightening up to a blazing radiance for a heartbeat before dimming back to its original pearlescent glare.

Gracie glanced at Simmons as Roxberry's excited voice crackled back. 'Did it just flare up?'

She knew the image on the screen he was looking at would be grainy, maybe even a bit jumpy. The live video uplink back to the studio was always compromised, nowhere near as clear as the original, high-definition footage on Dalton's cameras.

'Jack, I don't know how clearly it's coming through to you, but from out here, I can tell you, it's not like anything I've seen before.' She tried hard to hang onto her unflustered expression, but her heart was racing now. This didn't feel right.

She suddenly remembered something, and turned to Finch and Dalton. 'How quickly can you get the bird up?'

Finch nodded and turned to Dalton. 'Let's do it.'

'We're sending the skycam up for a closer look,' Gracie confirmed into her mike, then turned to Simmons, breathless, and clicked her mike off. 'Tell me you know what this is,' she said with a tense smile.

Simmons shook his head. 'I wish I could. I've never seen anything like it.'

'You've been here before, right?'

'Oh yes. This is my fourth winter out here.'

'And your specialty's paleoclimatology, right?'

'I'm flattered,' he smiled, 'yes.'

'And yet . . .'

He shook his head again. 'I'm stumped.'

Gracie frowned, her mind spinning, and pointed at his binoculars. 'May I?'

'Sure.' He handed them over.

She looked through them. It didn't add anything to what she'd already observed. The shimmer was more pronounced. It appeared hazy, slightly more mirage-like . . . but it was definitely there. It was real.

She gave the binoculars back to Simmons as a few of the others congregated around them. They seemed as bewildered as he was. She darted a look behind them. Finch had the skycam's arms clicked into place while Dalton was double-checking the second camera's harness and settings, both of them keeping an eye on the sighting. She noticed the captain coming out on deck. Two crew members hurried to join him. Gracie turned to the others. 'None of you have any idea what we're looking at here?'

'I first thought it might be a flare,' one of the other crew members said, 'but it's too big and too bright, and it's just there, you know? I mean, it's not moving, is it?'

The sleek noise of air being whipped around startled them just momentarily. It was a sound they'd heard earlier that day, when Gracie and Dalton had used the small, unmanned remote-controlled helicopter to get some panoramic establishing shots of the ice shelf.

Dalton shouted, 'We've got liftoff,' over the whirr of the skycam's rotor blades.

They turned to watch it rise. The Draganflyer X6 was an odd-looking but brilliant piece of engineering. It didn't look anything like a normal helicopter. It was more like a matte-black alien insect, something you'd expect to see in a Terminator movie. It consisted of a small central pod that was the size of a large mango and housed the electronics, gyroscopes, and battery. Three small collapsible arms extended out from it horizontally, at twelve, four, and eight o'clock positions. At the end of each arm was a whisper-quiet, brushless motor, each one driving two parallel sets of molded rotor blades, one above it and another underneath. Any type of camera could be fitted to the rig under its belly. It was all powered by rechargeable lithium batteries, and the whole thing was made of black carbon fiber that was incredibly strong and yet superlight – the Draganflyer weighed less than five pounds, high-definition video camera with a helicopter-to-ground link included. It gave great aerial shots with minimal fuss, and Dalton never traveled anywhere without it.

Gracie was watching the black contraption rise above the deck and glide away slowly, heading toward the ice shelf, when a female voice yelled out, 'Oh my God,' and Gracie saw it too.

The sighting was changing again.

It flared up again, then dimmed down from its outward rim inward, shrinking until it was barely a tenth of its original size. It held there for a couple of tantalizing seconds, then slowly flared back to the way it was. And then its surface seemed to ripple, as if it were morphing into something else.

At first, Gracie wasn't sure what it was doing, but the

second it started changing, something deep within her knotted. The sighting had clearly come alive. It was shapeshifting, twisting into itself, but always within the confines of its original envelope. It was taking on different compositions with alarming speed, all while keeping up its barely noticeable rotation, and they were all perfectly symmetrical, almost as if it were a kaleidoscope, but less angular, more rounded and organic. The patterns it took on melted from one to another continuously at an increasing, dazzling rate, and Gracie wasn't sure of what they were, but they reminded her of cellular structures. And in that very moment, she felt a deeply unsettling sensation, as if she were staring at the very fabric of life itself.

The small gathering froze, equally dumbstruck. Gracie glanced over at them. A whole range of emotion was etched across their faces, from awe and wonder to confusion – and fear. None of them was debating what it could be, not anymore. They just stood there, rooted to the deck, eyes fixated on it, their only words brief expressions of their amazement. Two of them – an older man and woman – crossed themselves.

Gracie saw Dalton check on the fixed camera, making sure it was still capturing the event. He held the skycam's remote control unit, which was suspended from a neck strap, at waist level, his fingers expertly controlling both joysticks.

She caught his gaze and moved her mike down. 'This is . . . Jesus, Dalton. What's going on?'

He looked up at the sighting. 'I don't know, but . . . Either Prince has a new concert tour coming up, or someone's spiked our coffee with some serious shit.' Dalton could usually see the humor in anything, but right now, he sounded different to Gracie. His tone was drained of all light.

She heard a few gasps, and someone said, 'It's slowing down.' All eyes strained in nervous unison as the sighting moved to take on a final shape.

For a second, it felt to Gracie as if her heart had stopped beating. Every pore of her body was crackling with fearful tension as she stared dead ahead at it. Without daring to take her eyes off it, she said, almost to herself, 'Jesus.'

The brighter zones of the sphere were being consumed by a spreading darkness, and it kept going until the sphere's entire surface looked blackened and coarse, as if it had been carved from a lump of coal.

CHAPTER 3

A ripple of terror spread among the crowd. The apparition had lost all of its splendor. In the blink of an eye, it had gone from being strangely wonderful to sinister and lifeless.

Finch moved close to Gracie, both of them riveted by the ominous sight.

'This isn't good,' he said.

Gracie didn't reply. She glanced down at the skycam's control box. The image on its small, five-inch LCD monitor was very clear, despite the light mist. Dalton had guided it in a wide, slight arc, in order for it not to come between them and the sighting. With the Draganflyer now more than halfway to the shelf, Gracie was able to get more of a sense of scale. The apparition dwarfed the approaching flying camera, like an elephant looming over an ant. It held the dark, lifeless skin it had assumed for a minute or so, bearing down on them with what seemed like a malevolent intent, then it flared up again, burning brightly, only this time, it took on a more distinct shape, defined by the light which was radiating with different strengths. It now looked unquestionably like a three-dimensional sphere, and at its core was a bright ball of light. Around it were four equal rings, running along the sphere's outer face, evenly spaced. As they weren't facing the ship head-on but were at a slight angle, they appeared like elongated ovals. The outer shell itself was brightly illuminated too, and rays of light were projecting outward from the core, between the rings, petering out slightly beyond the edge of the sphere. The whole display was hypnotic, especially as it blazed away against the dull, gray backdrop.

The sight was beyond breathtaking. It electrified the crowd and brought some of them to tears. The couple who had crossed themselves were holding each other close. Gracie could see their lips trembling in silent prayer. Her own body stiffened, and her legs went numb. She felt a confusing surge of euphoria and fear, which seemed echoed in the faces around her.

'Whoa.' Dalton recoiled.

Finch was also motionless, gaping at it. 'Tell me I'm not really seeing this,' Finch said. 'Tell me it's not really there.'

'It is,' Gracie confirmed as she just stood there, enthralled. 'It absolutely is.'

She held the mike up and struggled for words as everything around her faded to oblivion, a complete sensorial disconnect from her surroundings, her every thought consumed by the apparition. It was beyond understanding, beyond definition. After a moment, she emerged momentarily from her trance, and faced the camera again.

'I hope you're still getting this, Jack, 'cause everyone here is just stunned by this . . . I can't even begin to describe the sensation out here right now.' Her eyes dropped away for a passing glance at Dalton's monitor. He was using the joysticks to zoom in on the apparition, which filled the screen with its radiance before he pulled back out.

She looked out at it again. The skycam was closing in on it. 'How far from it do you think it is?' she asked Dalton.

'A hundred yards. Maybe less.' His voice had a slight quiver in it as his eyes darted from the monitor to the apparition and back.

Gracie couldn't take her eyes off of it. 'It's just magnificent, isn't it?'

'It's a sign,' someone said. It was the woman Gracie had noticed crossing herself. Gracie looked over, and Dalton panned over to her.

'A sign? Of what?' another answered.

'I don't know, but . . . she's right. Look at it. It's a sign of . . . something.' It was the older man who was with her.

Gracie remembered being introduced to them on her arrival. He was an American named Greg Musgrave, a glaciologist if she remembered correctly. The woman was his wife.

Musgrave turned to Gracie, waving toward the skycam, jabbing a nervous finger at it. 'Don't send that' – he stammered, struggling with what to call the Draganflyer – '*thing* any farther. Stop it before it gets too close.'

'Why?' Dalton sounded incredulous.

Musgrave raised his voice. 'Pull it back. We don't know what it is.'

Dalton didn't take his eyes off his controls. 'Exactly,' he shot back, 'it can help us figure out what the hell it is.'

Gracie looked out. The skycam was very close to the apparition. She glanced at Finch, then at Dalton, who seemed determined to see it through.

'I'm telling you, pull it back,' Musgrave said, moving toward Dalton now, reaching out to grab the remote control console. Dalton's fingers jerked against the joysticks, making the Draganflyer yaw and pitch wildly, its gyroscopes kicking in to keep it airborne.

'Hey,' Gracie yelled at him, just as Finch and the captain stepped in to restrain Musgrave.

'Grace, what the hell's going on?' Roxberry again, in her ear.

'Hang on, Jack,' she interjected quickly.

'Calm down,' the captain snapped at Musgrave. 'He's gonna pull it back before it reaches it,' then, to Dalton, pointedly, 'aren't you?'

'Absolutely,' Dalton replied flatly. 'You know how much that thing cost me?' He checked out the monitor, as did Gracie. The apparition filled the screen. It was grainy, but there was a subtle, undulating shimmer within the image that really gave the impression that it was bubbling with life. Gracie caught the worry in Dalton's eyes, then looked over at the skycam. The tiny black dot was almost on it.

'Maybe it's close enough,' she told Dalton, under her breath.

Dalton frowned with concentration. 'A little closer.'

'You shouldn't be messing with it before we know what we're dealing with,' Musgrave blurted out sharply.

Dalton ignored him and kept the joystick pressed forward. The skycam glided on, inching its way nearer to the blazing apparition.

'Dalton,' Finch said, low and discreet. It was getting uncomfortably close for him.

'I hear you,' he replied. 'Just a little bit more.'

Gracie's pulse quickened, thumping away in her ears as the skycam sailed ever closer to the apparition. It seemed tantalizingly close now, perhaps fifty feet or less – it was hard to judge the relative distance – when the sign suddenly dimmed right down and disappeared.

The crowd heaved a collective gasp.

'You see that? I told you,' Musgrave rasped.

'You kidding me?' Dalton fired back angrily. 'What, you think I scared it?'

'We don't know. But it was there for a reason, and now it's gone.' The scientist put an arm around his wife, and they both turned and stared out into the distance, as if willing it to reappear, dismay clouding their faces.

'Get real, man,' Dalton shrugged, turning away.

Over the shelf, the Draganflyer continued on its trajectory unbothered. Nothing showed on its monitor as it buzzed through the air that the apparition had occupied. Dalton slid a glance at Gracie. He looked thoroughly spooked. She'd never seen him react that way, not to anything, and they'd been through some pretty gut-wrenching times together.

Gracie was just as shaken. She peered out into the grim sky.

There was no trace of the sign.

It was as if it had never happened.

And then, all of a sudden, Gracie felt the world around her darken, felt a momentous weight above her, and looked up to see the apparition right above her, hovering over the ship itself, a massive ball of shimmering light squatting above them, dwarfing the vessel. She flinched as the crowd gasped and recoiled in horror and Dalton pounced on the main camera to try and get it on film. Gracie just stood there, staring up at it in complete bewilderment, her knees trembling, her feet riveted to the wooden planks of the ship's deck, fear and wonderment battling it out inside her, every hair on her body standing rigid for a brief moment that felt like an eternity –

– and then all of a sudden, the sign just faded out again, vanishing just as startlingly and as inexplicably as it had appeared.

CHAPTER 4

Bir Hooker, Egypt

Yusuf Zacharia puffed ruminatively on his *sheesha* as he watched his opponent pull his hand back from the weathered backgammon board. Nodding wearily to himself, the wiry old taxi driver palmed the dice. Anything less than a double-six meant he would lose the game. He didn't have high hopes for the toss. The dice weren't doing him any favors tonight.

He shook the small ivory cubes vigorously before flinging them across the board, and watched them skitter across its elaborately inlaid surface before they settled into a six and a one. He frowned, turning the fissures that lined his grizzled, leathery face into canyons, and rubbed his mostly bald pate, cursing his luck. To add to his misery, he became aware of a bitter, fruity bite gnawing at the back of his throat. The coals of his waterpipe had cooled down. He'd been so taken by the game and by his miserable run of rolls that he hadn't noticed. Fresh, red-hot replacements would rekindle the soothing, honey-mint taste that helped lull him into a tranquil sleep every night, but he sensed he might have to forgo that little luxury tonight. It was late.

He glanced at his watch. It was time to head home. The other customers of the small café – two young tourists, an American couple, he thought, judging by their familiar guidebooks and newspapers – were also getting up to leave. *Baseeta*, he shrugged to himself. Never mind. There was always tomorrow. He'd be back for a fresh *sheesha* and another game, God willing.

He was pushing himself to his feet when something caught his eye, a fleeting image on the TV set that loomed down from a rickety old shelf behind the counter. It was way past the ever-popular soaps' bedtime. At this hour, here, at the sleepy edge of the Egyptian desert, in the small village of Bir Hooker – haplessly misnamed after a British manager of the Egyptian Salt and Soda Company – and across the entire troubled region, for that matter, TVs would inevitably be tuned to some news program, feeding the endless debates and laments about the sorry state of the Arab world. Mahmood, the café's jovial owner, tended to favor Al Arabiya over Al Jazeera until, aiming to put forward a more tourist-friendly face, he invested in a satellite dish with a pirated decoder box. Ever since, the screen was locked onto an American news network. Mahmood thought the foreign infusion gave his café more class; Yusuf, on the other hand, didn't particularly care for the Americans' never-ending coverage of the recent presidential election there, even though it had been, unusually, keenly watched across the region, a region whose fortunes seemed more and more entwined with the vagaries of that distant country's leadership. But Yusuf's resistance to the channel was counterweighed by an unspoken appreciation for its occasional coverage of pouting Hollywood starlets and scantily clad catwalk models.

Right now, however, his attention was consumed by something entirely different. The screen showed a woman in heavy winter gear reporting from what seemed like one of the poles. In the image behind her, something shone in the sky. Something bizarre and otherworldly, the likes of which he'd never seen before. It was just floating there, blazing over a collapsing cliff of ice, and had – oddly, though it was unmistakable – the distinct, manifest shape of a symbol.

A sign.

The others also took note of the events on the screen and drew in closer to the counter, excitedly urging Mahmood to turn the sound up. The scene it showed was surreal, unimaginable, only that wasn't what disturbed Yusuf most. What really troubled him was that he'd seen that sign before.

His face pinched together with disbelief as he stared at the screen.

It can't be.

He inched forward for a closer look. His mouth dropped by an inch, his skin tingled with trepidation. The camera cut to another angle, and this time, the illuminated symbol took over the whole screen.

It was the same sign.

There was no doubt in his mind.

Unconsciously, his hand rose discreetly to his forehead, and he quietly crossed himself.

His friends noticed his sudden pallor, but he ignored their questions and, without offering an explanation or a farewell, rushed out of the café. He clambered into his trusted old Toyota Previa and churned its engine to life. The people carrier kicked up a small cloud as it fishtailed onto the dusty, unlit road and disappeared into the night, Yusuf riding the pedal hard, rushing back to the monastery as quickly as he could, muttering the same phrase to himself, over and over and over.

It can't be.

CHAPTER 5

Cambridge, Massachusetts

The crowd caught Vince Bellinger's eye as he ambled across the mall. They were massed outside the Best Buy, bubbling noisily with excitement, seemingly about something in the shop's huge window display. Bellinger was more than familiar with the window – it usually housed the latest plasmas and LCDs, including the mammoth sixty-five-incher he'd been fantasizing about for Christmas this year. Covetable, to be sure, but nothing that merited this much attention. Unless it wasn't the screens themselves, but rather what was on them, that had drawn the crowd.

Against the backdrop of piped-in seasonal Muzak and gaudy tinsel decorations, some people were talking animatedly on their cell phones, others waving friends over to join them. Despite being heavily laden with a pile of dry cleaning and his gym bag, Bellinger veered toward the store, wondering what all the fuss was about. Instinctively, he flinched at the possibility of another horror, another 9/11-like catastrophe, images of that terrible day still seared into his mind – although, he quickly thought, today's crowd didn't have that vibe to it. They weren't horrified. They seemed enthralled.

He got as close as he could and peered over the heads and shoulders of the gathered people. As per usual, the screens were all tuned to the same channel, in this case a news network. The image they showed drew his eye immediately, and he didn't quite understand what he was looking at – a spherical light, hovering over what seemed like one of the polar regions, confirmed by the banner underneath. He was watching it with piqued curiosity, in a detached trance, catching snippets of the animated comments bouncing around him, when his cell phone trilled. He groaned and juggled his bag and laundry around to fish it out of his pocket. Groaned doubly when he saw who was calling.

'Dude, where are you? I just tried your landline.' Csaba – pronounced *Tchaba*, nicknamed 'Jabba,' for not-too-subtle reasons – sounded overly excited. Which wasn't unusual. The big guy had a hearty appetite for life – and pretty much everything else.

'I'm at the mall,' Bellinger replied, still angling for a clearer view of the screens.

'Go home and put the news on, quick. You're not gonna believe this.'

Jabba, excited about something on TV. Not exactly breaking news. Although this time – just this once, Bellinger thought – his exuberance seemed justified.

A brilliant chemical engineer of Hungarian extraction who worked with Bellinger at the Rowland Materials Research Laboratory, Csaba Komlosy had a passion for all things televisual. Well-made, high-concept shows were normally his turf, the kind of show where a gutsy and intense government agent repeatedly managed to save the nation from mass destruction or where a gutsy and intense architect repeatedly managed to break out of the most escape-proof prisons. Lately, though, Csaba had veered into seedier territory. He'd embraced the netherworld of unscripted television – reality TV, so-called despite the fact that it had little to do with reality, or with being unscripted, for that matter – and, much to Bellinger's chagrin, he really liked to share the more singularly sublime moments of his viewing.

In this case, though, Bellinger was ready to give him a free pass. Still, he couldn't resist a little dig. 'Since when do you watch the news?'

'Would you stop with the inquisition and put the damn thing on,' Jabba protested.

'I'm looking at it right now. I'm at the mall, outside Best Buy.' Bellinger's voice trailed off as some heads in front of him shifted and the image on the screen snared his attention again. He caught sight of a banner at the bottom of screen, which read, 'Unexplained phenomenon over Antarctica.' There was also a small 'Live' box in the upper right corner. He just stood there, transfixed, his eyes curiously processing what they were seeing. He recognized the reporter. He'd caught some of her specials over the years and remembered her reports from Thailand after the tsunami a few years back, when he'd first noticed her. Shallow as it sounded, the relative hotness of a TV newscaster was directly proportional to how much attention guys paid to the screen – especially if the news in question didn't concern armed conflict, a sports result, or a celebrity meltdown. For most guys, Grace Logan – with the unforgiving green eyes, the tiny, mischievous mole poised just above the edge of her lips, the unsettlingly breathy yet earnest voice, the blond curls that always seemed to have a slightly unkempt tousle to them, and the Vargas Girl body that owed its curves to burgers and milkshakes, not silicone – ticked the hot box with ease.

This time, though, Bellinger's eyes weren't on her.

The camera zoomed in on the phenomenon again, sending an audible shiver through the crowd.

'Dude, it's unreal,' Jabba exclaimed. 'I can't take my eyes off the screen.'

Bellinger couldn't make sense of it. 'Is this a joke?'

'Not according to them.'

'Where is this exactly?'

'West Antarctic ice sheet. They're on some research ship off the coast. At first, I thought it's got to be a stunt for a new movie, maybe Cameron or Emmerich or even Shyamalan, but none of them have a live project that fits.'

Jabba – film geek extraordinaire – would know.

'How long has it been up?' Bellinger asked.

'About ten minutes. It came on out of the blue while la Logan was yapping about the breakup of the ice shelf. First it

33

was like this ball of light, then it morphed to a dark sphere – like that black planet in *The Fifth Element*, remember? Totally creeped me out.'

'Then it turned into this?'

'Yep.' The crunching sound coming through the receiver spurred Bellinger's mind to picture the likely setting for his friend's call: sunken deep in his couch, a bottle of Samuel Adams in one hand – not his first, Bellinger guessed, since they'd both left the lab over an hour ago – and a half-empty pack of sizzlin' picante chips in the other. Which was why he was on speakerphone.

Bellinger's brow wrinkled with concentration as he rubbed his bald pate. He'd never seen anything like it. More people were gathering around now, crowding around him, jostling for position.

Jabba crunched noisily into another chip, then asked, 'So what do you think?'

'I don't know,' he answered, as if in a daze. The crowd oohed as an airborne camera gave a closer look at the unexplained apparition. 'How are they doing this?' he asked, cupping the phone's mike area to cut out the noise around him. As a technology researcher and a scientist, his mind was instinctively skeptical and was immediately trying to figure out ways this could be done.

Jabba was obviously thinking along the same lines. 'Must be some kind of laser effect. Remember those floating beads of light those guys were working on at Keio—'

'Laser-induced plasma emissions?' Bellinger interjected. They'd both seen press coverage of the recent invention at the Japanese university, where focused bursts from a laser projector heated up the air at specific points above the bulky device, causing tiny bursts of plasma emissions that 'drew' small, three-dimensional shapes of white light in midair.

'Yeah, remember? The guy with the weird goggles and the white gloves—'

'No way,' Bellinger countered. 'You'd need a generator the size of an aircraft carrier sitting right under it for something this big. Plus it wouldn't explain the sustained brilliance or the way it's so clearly defined.'

'All right, forget that. What about other kinds of projections? Spectral imagery?'

Bellinger stared closely at the screen. 'You know something I don't? 'Cause except for the droid in – which one's the white one that looks like a fire hydrant?'

'R2-D2.' The roll of the eyes came through in his mocking tone as clearly as if they'd been using high-def webcams.

'Except for R2-D2, I don't think 3-D projectors actually exist.'

Which was true. Something that could achieve a free-floating, uncontained, three-dimensional moving image, like in Princess Leia's seminal 'Help us, Obi-Wan' moment – of any size, let alone something this big – still eluded the best brains in the business.

'Besides, you're forgetting one pesky little detail,' Bellinger added, feeling slightly more uncomfortable now.

'I know, dude. It's daylight.' Jabba sounded spooked at having that realization reaffirmed.

'Not exactly projector-friendly, is it?'

'Nope.'

Bellinger felt uncomfortable having that discussion out there, surrounded by people, his gym bag and laundry inches from getting trampled. But he just couldn't tear himself away.

'Okay, so we can forget about lasers and projectors,' he told Jabba. 'I mean, look at it. It's not contained within any kind of framework, it's not boxed in, there's no dark backdrop behind it, no glass panes around it. It's just there, free-floating. In daylight.'

'Unless there are a couple of monster mirrors on either side of it they're not showing us,' Jabba mused. 'Hey, maybe it's generated from space.'

'Nice idea, but how exactly?'

Jabba bit noisily into another chip. 'I don't know, dude. I mean, this thing doesn't compute, does it?'

'No. Hang on,' Bellinger told him, as he jammed the phone between his ear and his shoulder, grabbed his belongings, and inched back a few steps, out of the ever-growing crowd.

He and Jabba bounced around several other ideas, throwing everything they could think of at it, trying to pin some sensible, plausible explanation on it, but nothing stuck. Bellinger's excitement, though, soon gave way to a sense of unease. Something else was bothering him. An uncomfortable feeling that something buried deep within him was clawing for attention.

Suddenly, the fixed camera got jarred as an altercation took place on the ship's deck. Jabba lapped it up, as did the crowd at the mall, whooping and joking as the people on the ship filming the sighting scuffled, then the aerial camera came back. It closed in on the apparition, which then faded away, only to then suddenly reappear directly over the ship. The crowd around Bellinger shrieked and recoiled in shock as the shaky upward shot from the handheld camera on deck sent a shock wave crackling through them.

'Son of a bitch,' Jabba blurted. 'Is it turning?'

Bellinger focused on the apparition, now aware of a growing lump in his throat. 'It's spherical,' he marveled. 'It's not some kind of projection. It's actually physical, isn't it?'

On the screen, Grace Logan was having trouble keeping calm, clearly rattled by the apparition that was just hovering there, directly over the ship. The crowd in the mall was echoing her reaction, visibly stiffening and going quiet.

Jabba's crunching had also stopped. 'I think you're right. But how . . . ? It's not an object, and yet . . . It's almost like the air itself is burning up, but . . . that's not possible, is it? I mean, you can't light air up, can you?'

Bellinger felt a sudden rush of blood to his temples.

Something clicked. It just rushed in on him, unannounced, out of nowhere. Long-forgotten, dormant neurons buried deep within his brain had somehow managed to reach out and find each other and make a connection.

An unhappy one.

Oh, shit.

He went silent, his mind racing to process that link and take it to its natural conclusion, lost in the dread of the possibility just as the sign faded from view and the sky above the ship went back to normal.

'Dude, you there?'

Bellinger heard his voice go distant, as if he were on the outside watching himself answer. 'Yeah.'

'What? What're you thinking?'

He felt his skin crawl. 'I've got to go. I'll call you when I get home. Let me know if you come up with anything.'

'Dude, hang on, don't just—'

Bellinger hung up.

He stood there, his feet nailed to the cool tiled floor, the commotion around him fading as he turned his thoughts inward. Only minutes earlier, picking up the colorful linen shirts, all folded up and ready for packing, had conjured up a pleasant, warm feeling inside him. With the Christmas holiday days away, the sea, the sun, and the wide blue skies of the Dominican Republic beckoned – his annual pilgrimage, a welcome respite from the claustrophobic, windowless life he led at the research lab. Any feeling of warmth was now gone. A cold, crippling unease had taken its place and, Bellinger knew, wasn't about to let go.

He just stood there for a few long minutes, contemplating the disturbing – and, he hoped, surely unlikely – idea that had clawed its way out from the darkest recesses of his mind.

No way, he thought. *Be serious.*

But he couldn't shake the thought.

He stayed there as the TVs replayed the whole thing, lost

in his thoughts as the crowd dissipated. He finally tore himself away from the screens, gathered his things, and drove home in silence.

No way.

He dumped his bags in his front hallway, decided to try and let it go and move onto other things, and headed for his fridge. He got himself a beer and went back to the hall and rifled through his mail, but it was no use.

He couldn't shake it away.

He switched on his TV. The images it threw back at him were spine-tingling. Snarled traffic in Times Square, where a crowd of people had just frozen in place, mesmerized by the images of the sighting on the Sony JumboTron; people in bars and stadiums, on their feet, their eyes peeled on the screens; and similar chaotic images from around the world. He moved to his desk and fired up his laptop and spent a couple of hours scouring Internet chat rooms while flicking around various news reports, trying to get a clearer picture of what was going on, hoping to come across some ammo to dismiss his theory.

It was insane, outlandish . . . but it fit.

It just fit.

Which brought up an even bigger problem.

What to do about it.

His primal instinct told him to forget about it and leave it alone. Well alone. If what he was imagining was really happening, then he'd be far better off expunging any trace of the thought from his mind and never mentioning it to anyone. Which was the sensible thing to do, the rational thing to do, and Bellinger prided himself, above any other qualities he might have, on his rationality. But there was something else.

A friend had died. Not just a friend.

His best friend.

And that was something that his rationality was finding hard to ignore.

Visions of the tragic accident in the Skeleton Coast sparked in his mind's eye, horrific images his imagination had conjured up long ago, after he'd been told about how Danny Sherwood had died.

He couldn't ignore it.

He had to find out. Make sure. Get the whole picture.

He got himself another beer and sat alone in the dark living room, staring into nothing, his mind alternating between what he'd just seen and what had happened two years ago. A few bottles later, he retrieved his phone and scrolled down his contacts list until he found the entry he was looking for. It was a number he'd been given a couple of years ago, one he hadn't called for almost that long.

He hesitated, then hit the call button.

He heard it ring through three, four times, then a man picked up.

'Who's this?' The man's tone had a detached, no-nonsense ring to it.

The sound of Matt Sherwood's voice brought Bellinger a modicum of solace. A palpable connection, however fleeting, to his long-dead friend.

'It's Vince. Vince Bellinger,' he answered, a slight hesitation in his voice. He paused for a beat, then added, 'Where are you, Matt?'

'At my place. Why?'

'I need to see you, man,' Bellinger told him. 'Like, now.'

CHAPTER 6

Boston, Massachusetts

No one in the crowded arena could tear their eyes away from the huge video scoreboards. Not the fans. Not the players. And certainly not anyone in Larry Rydell's perfectly positioned luxury suite at the Garden.

His guests, the design team working on the groundbreaking electric car he hoped to launch within a couple of years, had been enjoying the treat. They'd spent the whole day in the project's nerve center over in Waltham, bringing him up to speed on the car's status, going over the problems they'd managed to solve and the new ones they'd unearthed. As with everything Rydell did, the project had world-beating ambitions. His friend Elon Musk – another Internet sensation, courtesy of a little online business he'd cofounded by the name of PayPal – had already launched his electric car, the Tesla, but that was a sports car. Rydell was after a different kind of driver: the legions driving around in Camrys, Impalas, and Accords. And so he'd recruited the best and the brightest designers and engineers, given them everything they needed to make it happen, and let them do their thing. It was just one of several pet projects he had running at the same time. He had teams working on more efficient wind farms, solar cells, and better wiring to ferry the resulting power around. Renewable energy and clean power were going to be the next great industrial revolution, and Larry Rydell was nothing if not visionary.

The only resource his projects fought over was his own time. Money certainly wasn't an issue, even with the recent turmoil in the markets. He was well aware of the fact that he had more of it than he'd ever need. Every computer and cell phone user on the planet had contributed his or her share to his fortune, and the stratospheric share price his company had enjoyed had done the rest. And although Rydell enjoyed the good life, he'd found better things to do with his money than build himself five-hundred-foot yachts.

They'd had a long, productive day, overcoming a big hurdle they'd been trying to solve for weeks, and so he'd decided to reward the team by sending them off on their end-of-year break in style. He'd treated them to a great dinner, all the drink they could handle, and the best seats in the house. They'd just watched Paul Pierce slip past Kobe Bryant and slam home a two-handed dunk, and heard the first-period buzzer go, when the suspended cube of screens had flicked over to a live news feed and all noise had drained out of the arena.

As he stood there, mesmerized by the surreal display before him, he felt his BlackBerry vibrate in his pocket. The alert was one of three that never went comatose, even when his privacy settings were on, which was most of the time. One was entrusted to Mona, his PA – or, more accurately, the senior PA among the four who controlled the drawbridge to his office. Another was allocated to his ex-wife, Ashley, although she usually found it easier to call Mona and get him to call her back. The third, the one that was now clamoring for his attention, told him his nineteen-year-old daughter Rebecca was calling.

Something she rarely did when she was on a distant beach, which was currently – and often – the case. The family villa in Mexico, he thought, though he wasn't sure. It could have been the chalet in Vail or the yacht in Antigua. Between her appetite for partying and his scant appetite for anything that didn't concern the projects he lived and breathed, that tidbit of information had some pretty large cracks to slip through.

He pressed the phone to his ear without taking his eyes off the screen.

'Dad, are you watching this?'

'Yeah,' he replied, somewhat dazed. 'We're all standing here at the Garden watching it like zombies.'

'Same here,' his daughter laughed, somewhat nervously. 'We were about to go out when a friend of mine in L.A. called to tell us about it.'

'Where are you anyway?'

'Mexico, Dad,' she half-groaned, with an undisguised you-should-know-this tone.

Just then, the initial shock veered to cheers and claps as the already charged fans let their emotions rip. The noise reverberated through the arena. 'Wow,' Rebecca echoed, 'it sounds wild.'

'It is,' he said with a curious smile. 'How long have they been showing it?'

'I'm not sure, we just switched it on a few minutes ago.' She paused for a moment, then said, 'Dad . . . what do you think it is?'

And, in what was probably a first for a man who was rightly feted around the world as nothing less than a genius, Larry Rydell had no answer for his daughter. At least, not one that he could share with her.

Not now.

Not ever.

CHAPTER 7

Washington, D.C.

A light rain peppered the nation's capital as a black, chauffeur-driven Lexus slipped out of the underground garage and slunk onto Connecticut Avenue and into the sparse late-evening traffic. In the cosseted comfort of its heated backseat, Keenan Drucker stared out in silence, lost in a streaming light show of passing cars, contemplating the events of the momentous day.

The phone calls had begun about an hour ago, and in the days to come, there would be plenty more, of that he was certain.

They were only getting started.

He shut his eyes and leaned back against the richly padded headrest. His mind chewed over his plan, once again dissecting every layer of it, looking for the fatal flaw that he might have somehow missed. As with every previous run-through, he couldn't find anything to worry about. There were a lot of unknowns, of course – there had to be, by definition. But that didn't trouble him. Oversights and miscalculations – now those were different. Those he wouldn't tolerate. A lot of effort had gone into making sure there wouldn't be any. But unknowns were, well, unknowable. A lifetime of making questionable deals in smoke-filled rooms had taught him that unknowns weren't worth worrying about until they materialized. If and when they did, his thoroughness, his focus, and his level of commitment would ensure that, if it pleased the Lord – he smiled inwardly at his little joke – they wouldn't prove too hard to deal with.

His BlackBerry nudged him out of his reverie. The ring tag told him who it was, and a quick glance at the screen before picking up the call confirmed it.

43

The Bullet got straight to the point, as was his norm. They'd already spoken twice that evening.

'I got a call from our friend at Meade.'

'And?'

'He got a hit. A phone call, between two of the peripherals on the watch list.'

Drucker mulled the news for a beat. The Bullet, aka Brad Maddox, had initially suggested using one of his contacts inside the National Security Agency to – quietly – monitor for unexpected trouble. Although Drucker had thought the risk of exposure outweighed the unlikely benefits, it now looked like Maddox had made the right call. Which was why Maddox was in charge of the project's security.

'You've heard the recording?' Drucker asked.

'Yes.'

'Is it anything to worry about?'

'I think it might be. The call itself was too brief to read either way, but its timing raises some concerns.'

Drucker winced. 'Who are the peripherals?'

'One of them's a techie, an engineer here in Boston. Vince Bellinger. He was Danny Sherwood's college roommate. They were tight. Best buddies. The other's Sherwood's brother, Matt.'

A flash of concern flitted across Drucker's eyes. 'And there's no history there?'

'Last communication we have between them goes back almost two years.'

Drucker thought about it for a moment. Two years ago, they had a natural reason to chat. The timing of this new call, though, was indeed troublesome. 'I take it you've got it under control.'

Maddox couldn't have sounded more detached if he'd been sedated. 'Just bringing you up to speed.'

'Good. Let's hope it's a coincidence.'

'Not something I believe in,' Maddox affirmed.

'Me neither, sadly,' Drucker replied. Then, almost as an afterthought, he asked, 'And the girl?'

'Just waiting to be plucked.'

'You're going to need to handle that one with even more discretion,' Drucker cautioned. 'She's key.'

'She won't be a problem,' the Bullet assured him. 'My boys are ready. Just say the word.'

'It's imminent. Keep me posted on the roommate,' Drucker added before hanging up.

He stared at his phone for a moment, then shrugged and tucked it back into his suit's inside breast pocket. He looked out at the streaks of red and white light gliding past his wet window, and played out the next moves in his mind.

It was a good start, no question.

But the hardest part was yet to come.

CHAPTER 8

Amundsen Sea, Antarctica

Gracie watched the screen fade to a fuzzy gray and shook her head. The adrenalin rush was petering out, and she now felt exhausted, battered by a hurricane of exuberance, confusion, and unease. Yet another cup of the ship's surprisingly decent coffee beckoned.

'Let's see it again,' one of the scientists told Dalton.

Dalton glanced over at Gracie, who shrugged, got up, and headed over to the corner bar for her caffeine fix. Her throat felt dry and hoarse, and she'd lost all sense of time. The continuous, seemingly never-ending daylight didn't help.

They'd stayed out on deck, scanning the skies, for about an hour after the apparition had vanished before heading inside for some warmth. Some crew members stayed out on watch, in case it reappeared, while Gracie and the others had crowded into the officers' and scientists' lounge – which sounded a lot more grand than it was – and watched the footage from both of Dalton's cameras on a big plasma screen. Several viewings and countless cups of coffee later, they still weren't anywhere remotely close to explaining what they'd witnessed.

The comfort zone of ascribing it to some spectacular weather phenomenon was quickly dispelled. The obvious candidates – aurora australis southern lights, fogbows, and green flashes – didn't fit the bill. One possibility that did generate a brief debate was something called 'diamond dust.' Gracie had never heard of it. Simmons had explained that it was a phenomenon that involved ice crystals that formed from the condensation of atmospheric water vapor. When these crystals caught the sunlight at a particular angle as they drifted down to earth, they generated a brilliant, sparkling effect, sometimes in the form of a halo. Which might have explained the first part of the apparition, at a stretch, and a pretty big one at that. But it didn't even begin to explain the dazzling symbol that it had turned into.

Looking around the lounge, Gracie could see that the discussion was purely academic. Despite the heated debates and arguments, they were just grasping at straws, skirting the obvious. From the strained faces around her, from the wavering voices and the nervy eyes, it was clear that not one of those assembled really believed that this was a natural weather phenomenon. And this wasn't a simple group of layfolk prone to flights of imagination. They were all highly qualified scientists, experts in their fields, and more than familiar with the unique conditions out there. And they'd all been seriously shaken up by what they'd seen. All of which meant one of two things. If it wasn't natural, it was either man-made – or supernatural.

The first was easier to deal with.

Dalton frowned as he turned away from the footage. 'Well if it isn't a freak of nature, then maybe it's some goofballs messing with us.'

'You think it could be a prank?' Gracie asked.

'Well, yeah. Remember those UFO sightings in New York a few years back?' Dalton continued. 'They had half the city convinced. Turns out it was a bunch of guys flying some ultralights in formation.'

'On the other hand, no one's been able to explain the lights over Phoenix back in 1997,' another scientist, a geophysicist with a thick goatee by the name of Theo Dinnick, countered. The sighting in question, a major event witnessed by hundreds of independent and highly credible people, remained unexplained to this day.

'You're forgetting this was in broad daylight,' Gracie remarked.

Simmons, the paleoclimatologist with the binoculars,

nodded dubiously. 'If it's a prank, I want to meet the guys behind it and find out how the hell they pulled it off, 'cause it sure isn't something I can explain.'

Gracie glanced around the room. Her eyes settled on Musgrave, the glaciologist who'd become testy on deck, and his wife. They were both sitting back, not participating. They were clearly discomfited by the conversation, giving each other the occasional glance. Musgrave seemed really irritated, and finally stood up.

'For God's sake, people. Let's be serious here,' he announced. 'You saw it. We all saw it. You really think something that magnificent, something that . . . *sublime* . . . you really believe it could just be a vulgar prank?'

'What do you think it is?' Simmons asked.

'Isn't it obvious? It's a sign.'

'A sign?'

'A sign,' he repeated. 'From God.'

A leaden silence greeted his words.

'Why God? Why not aliens?' Dalton finally asked.

Musgrave flashed him an icy scowl.

Dalton didn't flinch. 'Seriously. 'Cause that's the first thing that popped into my mind when I saw it.'

'Don't be ridiculous.' Musgrave wasn't making any effort to mask his contempt.

'Why is that ridiculous?' Dalton insisted. 'You're saying it's supernatural, aren't you? You're happy to entertain the notion that it's "God"' – Dalton made some air quotes with his fingers – 'whatever that means, but not that it's extraterrestrial, that it's coming from some intelligent life form from beyond our planet? Why is that any more ridiculous than what you're suggesting?'

'Maybe it's a warning,' Musgrave's wife suggested.

'What?' Simmons sounded incredulous.

'Maybe it's a warning. It appeared here, now, over this ice shelf. During the breakup. It can't be random. There's got to be a reason for it. Maybe it's trying to tell us something.'

'I'll tell you what it's telling me, it's telling me we should get the hell out of here before it shows up again. It's bad news.' Dalton again.

'Goddammit,' Musgrave blurted, 'either take this seriously or—'

'All right, calm down.' Gracie cut off Musgrave before turning to Dalton and flashing him a castigating glance. 'We're all on edge here.'

Dalton nodded and leaned back, taking in a deep breath.

'I've got to say, I agree with him,' Simmons added, gesturing at Dalton. 'I mean, we're all scientists – and even if lasers or holograms or whatever the hell it could have been aren't within our areas of expertise, I'm guessing we're all pretty convinced that what we saw out there is, as far as any of us can tell, *way* beyond any technological capability we know of. Now, the fact that I can't explain it excites me and scares me in equal measure. 'Cause if it's not some kind of laser show, if it didn't come from DARPA or some Japanese lab or from Silicon Valley – *if it didn't originate on this planet* . . . then it's either, as Greg says, God – or, as our friend here was saying, extraterrestrial. And frankly, either one would be just extraordinary, and I don't see that the difference really matters right now.'

'You don't see the difference?' Musgrave was incensed.

'I don't want to get into a big theological debate with you, Greg, but—'

'—but you obviously don't believe in God, even if you're presented with a miracle, so any debate is pointless.'

'No, that's not what I'm saying,' Simmons insisted calmly. 'Look, you're saying this is God, you're saying our maker has, for some reason, chosen this day, this location, this event – and this method – to appear to us, here, today—'

Gracie interrupted, saying, 'Do we know if anything like this has happened elsewhere? Has anyone checked the news?'

Finch said, 'I just got off the phone with the news desk. There are no other reports of any other sightings.'

'Okay, so if He's chosen to show up here and now,' Simmons continued, 'then I've got to think He must have a damn good reason.'

'Half the West Antarctic ice shelf is slipping into the sea. You need more of a reason?' Musgrave's wife said, irritably.

'Why do you think we're here?' Musgrave added. 'Why are we all here?' His eyes darted around the room feverishly before settling on the British scientist. 'Justin,' he asked him, 'why are you here?'

'England's at the same latitude as Alaska,' the man replied. 'The only thing that makes it liveable is the Gulf Stream. Take that away – which is what happens if the ice melts – and that movie, the one with Manhattan swamped with ice and snow? That'll be London. Along with most of Europe, for that matter.'

'Exactly,' Musgrave insisted. 'We're all here because we're worried. All the signs are telling us that we've got one hell of a problem, and maybe this – this *miracle* is telling us we've got to do something about it.'

Gracie and Finch exchanged dubious glances.

'Okay, well,' Simmons conceded, 'all I'm saying is, if that's the reason, if it's a warning, then . . . why couldn't it be coming from a more advanced intelligence?'

'I agree with that young man,' Dinnick said with a slight, disarming grin, pointing at Dalton. 'It's just as ludicrous.'

Musgrave's wife was clearly riled. 'It's pointless to discuss this with either of you. You're not open to the possibility.'

'On the contrary, I'm open to *all* possibilities,' Dinnick countered. 'And if we're talking about some entity making contact with us,' nodding toward Simmons, 'maybe to warn us, which, granted, could justify the here and now of it . . . Well, if you accept the notion of a creator, of creationism, of intelligent design . . . why couldn't that intelligent designer be from a more advanced race?'

Musgrave was incensed. 'God isn't something you find in

a science fiction book,' he retorted. 'You don't even have a basic understanding of what faith means, do you?'

'There's no difference. It's all unknowable as far as our current capabilities are concerned, isn't it?' Dinnick pressed.

'Believe what you will. I'm out of here.' He stormed off.

Musgrave's wife got up. She looked at the faces around her with a mixture of anger, scorn, and pity. 'I think we all know what we saw out there,' she said, before following her husband out.

An uncomfortable silence smothered the room.

'Man. That guy's clearly never heard of Scientology,' Dalton quipped, raising a few nervous chuckles.

'I've got to say,' the British scientist finally offered, 'while I was out there, looking at it . . . there was something rather . . . *divine* about it.'

He looked around for endorsement. A couple of other scientists nodded.

The honesty of his simple words suddenly struck Gracie, their simple, brutal significance sinking in and chilling her more fiercely than any wind she'd felt out on the ice. Listening to the arguments flying around the room, she'd been swept up by the semantics and all but lost track of the fundamental enormity of what they'd all been arguing about. What had happened, what they'd witnessed out there . . . it was beyond explanation. It was beyond reason. It would have been beyond belief if she hadn't seen it with her own eyes.

But she had.

Her mind drifted away with the possibilities. *Could it be?* she wondered. Had they just witnessed a watershed moment in the history of mankind, something for which 'before' and 'after' attributes might be used from here on?

Her innate skepticism, the skepticism of a hardened realist, dragged her back from the swirl of dreamy conjecture with a resounding *No.*

Impossible.

And yet . . . she couldn't ignore the feeling that she'd been in the presence of something transcendent. She'd never felt that way before.

She suppressed a shiver and glanced uncertainly at Finch. 'What did they say?' she asked, away from the others.

Finch said, 'They're getting everyone they can think of to check it out. But they're getting calls from broadcasters all over the world wanting to know what's going on. Ogilvy wants us to send him a high-res clip pronto,' he added pointedly, referring to Hal Ogilvy, the network's global news director and a board member of the parent firm.

'Okay,' she nodded. 'We need to make some calls. You wanna see if we can grab the conference room?'

Finch nodded. 'Yeah. Let's get out of here.'

'Amen to that,' Dalton added.

A barrage of clearly unamused looks greeted his words.

Dalton half-smiled, sheepishly. 'Sorry,' he offered apologetically, and left the room.

They walked down the hall in silence, the sheer magnitude of the discussion sinking in. As they reached the stairwell, Gracie noticed Dalton looking particularly adrift.

'What?' she asked.

He stopped, hesitated, then said, 'What if that Bible-thumping nut back there is right?'

She shook her head. 'There's got to be a better explanation for it.'

'What if there isn't?'

Gracie mulled the question for a moment. 'Well, if that's the case, if it's really God,' she said somberly, 'then for someone who had me totally convinced He didn't exist, He sure picked one hell of a moment to show Himself.'

CHAPTER 9

Wadi Natrun, Egypt

Labored breaths and sluggish footfalls tarnished the stillness of the mountain as the three men trudged up the steep slope. Every step, every scattered rock and rolling pebble echoed, the small sounds amplified by the harsh, lifeless dryness of the hills around them. The moon had been conspicuously absent that night, and despite the fading array of stars overhead, the early dawn light and the chilling solitude weighed heavily on them.

Yusuf had driven straight to the monastery from the café. Like many other devout Coptic Christians, the taxi driver donated as much as he could afford to the monastery, delivering free fruit and vegetables from his brother's stall at the market and helping out with various odd jobs. He'd been doing that for as long as he could remember, and knew the monastery like the back of his hand. Which was why he'd been to the cave, delivering supplies every few weeks to the recluse who was its sole inhabitant, and why he'd seen what was inside it.

Muttering the most profuse of apologies, he'd startled the monk he knew best, a young man with alert gray-green eyes and a gregarious demeanor by the name of Brother Ameen, out of a deep sleep with his startling news. Ameen knew Yusuf well enough to take him at his word and, driven by the old taxi driver's urgent tone, he'd then led him to the cell of the monastery's abbot, Father Kyrillos. The abbot listened, and reluctantly agreed to accompany them back to the café at that ungodly hour.

The monastery's amenities, unsurprisingly, didn't include a media room, and so they'd all watched the footage on the TV at the café. It had thoroughly shocked the monks. And although they were both certain that Yusuf was right, they had to be absolutely sure.

And that couldn't wait.

Yusuf had driven them straight back to the monastery, where they'd counted down the hours anxiously. Then at dawn, he drove them six miles out, to the edge of the desert, where the barren, desolate crags rose out of the sand. From there, the three men had climbed for over an hour, pausing once for a sip of water from a leather gourd that the young monk had brought along.

The trek up wasn't exactly a cakewalk. The steep, uneven slope of the mountain – a barren moonscape of loose, crumbling rocks – was treacherous and hard enough to navigate by daylight, let alone like this, in near-darkness, with nothing more than the anemic beams of cheap flashlights to guide them up the slope that was still bathed in shadow. It also wasn't a path they knew well at all. Visits to the caves were a rare event. Access to the desolate area was, as a matter of principle, fiercely discouraged out of respect for the occasional, driven soul who elected to retreat into its harsh seclusion. They reached the small doorway that led into the cave. A simple wooden door guarded its entrance, held shut by an old, rusted latch. A small timber window, fashioned from a natural opening in the rock, sat beside it. The abbot, a surprisingly fit man with penetrating yet kind eyes, dark, weathered skin, and a salt-and-pepper, square-cut beard that jutted out from the embroidered hood of his black cassock, shone his flashlight briefly into the window and peered in, then retreated a step, hesitating for a moment. He turned to Ameen, unsure of whether or not to proceed. The younger monk shrugged. He wasn't sure either.

The abbot's expression darkened with resigned determination. His hand shaking more from nerves than from the cold, he gave the door a soft, hesitant knock. A moment passed, with no answer. He glanced at his companions again and gave the door another rap. Again, there was no reply.

'Wait here,' he told them. 'Maybe he can't hear us.'

'You're going in?' Ameen asked.

'Yes. Just keep quiet. I don't want to cause him any distress.'

Ameen and Yusuf nodded.

The abbot steeled himself, gently lifted the latch, and pushed the door open.

The interior of the cave was oppressively dark and bone-chillingly cold. It was a natural cavern shaped out of limestone, and the chamber the abbot now stood in – the first of three – was surprisingly large. It was empty, save for a few pieces of simple, handcrafted furnishings: a rudimentary armchair, a low table facing it, and a couple of stools. Beside the window was a writing table and a chair. The abbot aimed his flashlight toward it. The table had a lined notebook on it, a fountain pen lying across its open pages. A small stack of similar notebooks, looking well thumbed, sat on a ledge by the window.

His mind flashed to the notebooks. To the frenzied, dense writing that filled their pages, pages he'd only glimpsed, pages he'd never been offered to read. To how it had all started, several months earlier, unexpectedly.

To how they'd found him.

And to the *miraculous* – the word suddenly took on a wholly different ring – way he'd come to them.

The abbot shook the thoughts away and turned. That could all wait.

He lowered the beam toward the ground and stood motionless for a moment, listening intently. He heard nothing. He took slow, hesitant steps deeper into the cave until he reached a small nook that housed a narrow bed.

It was empty.

The abbot spun around, shining his flashlight across the cave walls, his pulse rocketing ahead.

'Father Jerome?' he called out, his voice tremulous, the words echoing emptily through the chamber.

No answer.

Perplexed, he retreated back into the main chamber, and turned to face the wall.

His hand shook with a slight tremble as he raised the flashlight, lighting up the wall that curved gently into the cavern's dome-like roof. With his heart pounding in his ears, he surveyed its surface, the flashlight's beam lighting it up from the cave's entrance all the way back to its deepest recess.

The markings were just as he remembered them.

One symbol, painstakingly painted onto the smooth rock face using some kind of white paint, repeated over and over and over, covering every available inch inside the cave.

A clearly recognizable symbol.

The same symbol he had just seen on television, in the skies over Antarctica.

Yusuf was right.

And he'd been right to come to them.

Without taking his eyes off the markings, the abbot slowly dropped to his knees and, making no sound, began to pray.

CHAPTER 10

Perched on the crest of the barren mountain, high above the caves, Father Jerome contemplated the majestic landscape spread out before him. The sun was crawling out from behind the mountains, backlighting their undulating crowns and tinting the sky with a soft, golden-pink hue.

The thin, old man with the wire-rimmed glasses, the white, buzz-cut hair, and the dishdasha robe spent most of his mornings and evenings up here. Although the climb up the rocky, crumbling terrain had been harsh on his frail body, he needed the escape from the crushing solitude and the oppressive confines of the cave. And once he was up there, he discovered, the mountain presented him with a reward he hadn't anticipated, a reward far beyond the awe-inspiring magnificence of God's creation.

He still didn't know what had brought him there, what had drawn him to this place. He wasn't the first to come to this valley to serve his faith and to glorify his God. Many before him had done the same, over hundreds of years. Other men like him, men of deep religious faith, who had felt the same divine presence when confronted with the purity and the power of the vast, empty wilderness that stretched up and down the valley. But much as he thought about it, in those endless nights in the cave, he still couldn't explain the calling that had led him to walk away from the orphanage – an orphanage he had only just opened, several hundred miles south, just over the border with Sudan – and wander into the desert, unprepared and alone. Perhaps there was no explanation. Perhaps it was just that, a calling, one from a higher power, one that he couldn't not heed.

And yet, somehow . . . it scared him.

When he thought about it, he knew it shouldn't. It was a

grace from God, a blessing. He had been shown a route, a journey, and even if he didn't understand it or know where it would lead, it was still a great honor for him to be the recipient of that grace. And yet . . .

The nights scared him most. The loneliness in the cave was, at times, crippling. He sometimes arose in a cold sweat, woken up by the howl of the wind, or by the yelps of wild dogs roaming the barren hills. It was in those moments that he was most acutely aware of his extreme isolation. The mountain was a fearsome place. Few could survive it. The early ascetics, the hermit monks who retreated from humanity and lived in the caves long before him, went there to get closer to God, believing that the only path to enlightenment, the only way to get to know God, was through such isolation. Up on the craggy, bare mountain, they could avoid temptation, they could free themselves from all vestiges of earthly desire, and concentrate on the one thing that could bring them closer to God: prayer. But for those who had lived it, the mountain was also a battleground. They were there to pray for us, believing that we were all constantly under assault by demons, no one more so than the hermits themselves, who also believed that the more they prayed, the more they were threatened by the forces of evil they were battling on our behalf.

If he'd been asked about it before coming to this mountain, Father Jerome would have said he disagreed with that rather bleak view of the world. But now, after living in the confines of the cave for months, after going through the hell and torment of solitary reflection, he wasn't so sure anymore.

Still, he had to forge ahead. He had to embrace the challenges before him and not resist them.

It was his calling.

The days were better. When he wasn't up on the mountain, he spent them either in quiet contemplation, in prayer, or writing. And that was something else he didn't understand, something else that troubled him.

The writing.

There seemed to be no end to the words, to the thoughts and ideas and images – *that* image, in particular – that flooded his mind. And when the inspiration came – the divine inspiration, he realized, both exhilarating and scary at the same time – he couldn't write down the words fast enough. And yet, somehow, he wasn't sure where they were coming from. His mind was thinking them, his hand was writing them down, and yet it was as if they were originating elsewhere and flowing through him, as if he were a vessel, a conduit for a higher being or a greater intellect. Which, again, was a grace. For the words were, undeniably, beautiful, even if they didn't necessarily concord with his own personal experience within the Church.

He drank in the view and its sea of haloed crests before closing his eyes and tilting his head slightly upward, clearing his mind and preparing himself for what he knew was coming. And moments later, as it did unfailingly, it began. A torrent of words that flowed into his ears, as clearly as if someone were kneeling right beside him and whispering to him.

He beamed inwardly, locked in concentration, the warmth of the rising sun caressing his face, and drank in the words that were, as with each previous moment of revelation, simply wondrous.

CHAPTER 11

Boston, Massachusetts

Snowflakes dusted the dimly lit sidewalk as Bellinger climbed out of the cab outside the small bar on Emerson, a quiet, narrow street in South Boston.

It was late, and the chill bit into him fiercely. The run-up to Christmas was usually cold, but this was shaping up to be a particularly harsh winter. As he turned to duck into the bar, he slammed into a woman who emerged from the shadows. She pulled back, all flustered, holding up her hands which had come up defensively, and apologized, her clipped words explaining that she was trying to grab the cab before it drove off. She hurriedly sidestepped around him and called out to the driver, and Bellinger managed a fleeting glimpse of her face, soft and attractive, nestling between a bounce of shoulder-length auburn hair and the upturned collar of her coat. It was an awkward moment. Beyond the thin veil of snow and the darkness, he was in a fog of his own, and before he could spew out any clumsy words, she'd hopped into the cab and it was pulling away.

He stood there for a moment, watching it recede and disappear around a corner, then snapped away from the distraction and headed into the bar.

Matt Sherwood had chosen the place. It was a typical, low-key Southie bar. Cheap beer, dim lighting, twenty-five-cent wings, and darts. Some token Christmas decorations scattered around, cheap stuff made in China using paper-thin plastic and colored foil. The place was busy, but not mobbed, which was good. The conversation Bellinger needed to have was one he'd prefer to keep as private as possible.

He paused by the door, taking stock of the place, and realized – oddly – that he was subconsciously scanning for some unseen threat, which surprised him. He wasn't the paranoid type. He chided himself and tried to quash his unease, but as he made his way deeper into the bar, looking for Matt, the paranoid feeling was stubbornly clinging on.

The place had a mismatched cast of topers. Cliques of young, well-dressed professionals were toasting the night away in small, loud circles, in sharp contrast to the lone, sullen mopes who sat perched on their bar stools like narcoleptic vultures, staring into their tumblers through vapid eyes. The music – eighties rock, a bit tinny, coming out of a jukebox in a far corner of the bar – was just the right side of loud, which was good. They'd be able to talk without worrying about being overheard. Which, again, Bellinger realized, wasn't something he normally thought about.

He also didn't normally have sweat droplets popping up on his forehead when he visited bars. Especially not in Boston. In December. With snow falling outside.

He spotted Matt sitting in a corner booth. As he wove his way through the pockets of drinkers to join him, his cell phone rang. He paused long enough to pull it out of his pocket and check it. It was Jabba. He decided to ignore the call, stuffed the phone back into his pocket, and joined Matt.

Even hunched over his drink, Matt Sherwood's hulking stature was hard to miss. The man was six-foot-four, a full head taller than Bellinger. He hadn't changed much in the two years since Bellinger had last seen him. He still had the same brooding presence, the same angular face, the same close-cropped dark hair, the same quietly intense eyes that surveyed and took note without giving much away. If anything, any changes Bellinger thought he detected, minor though they were, were for the better. Which was inevitable, given the circumstances. He'd last seen him around the time of Danny's funeral. Matt and his kid brother had been close, Danny's death sudden and unexpected, the family rocked by an even bigger – and far worse – tragedy to befall its sons this time.

Which made dredging it up all the more difficult.

As Bellinger slipped onto the bench without bothering to take his coat off, Matt acknowledged him with a nod. 'What's going on?'

Bellinger remembered that about him. Laconic, to-the-point. A man who didn't pussyfoot around, which was understandable. Time was something Matt Sherwood appreciated deeply. He'd had enough of it taken away from him already.

Bellinger found a half smile. 'It's good to see you. How are you?'

'Just terrific. I've got orders coming out of my ears, what with all this bonus money floating around.' He cocked his head to one side and gave Bellinger a knowing, sardonic look. 'What's going on, Vince? It's way past both our bedtimes, isn't it? You said we needed to talk.'

'I know, and I'm glad you could make it. It's just that . . .' Bellinger hesitated. It was a tough subject to broach. 'I was thinking about Danny.'

Matt's eyes stayed on Bellinger for a moment, then he looked away, across the bar, before turning back. 'What about Danny?'

'Well, last time I saw you, after the funeral . . . it was all so sudden, and we never really got a chance to talk about it. About what happened to him.'

Matt seemed to study Bellinger. 'He died in a helicopter crash. You know that. Not much more to tell.'

'I know, but . . . what else do you know about it? What did they tell you?'

From Matt's dubious look, it was obvious he could see through Bellinger's tangential, circumspect approach. 'Why are you asking me this, Vince? Why now?'

'Just . . . look, just bear with me a little here. What did they tell you? How did it happen?'

Matt shrugged. 'The chopper came down off the coast of Namibia. Mechanical failure. They said it was probably due to a sandstorm they'd had out there, but they couldn't be sure. The wreck was never recovered.'

'Why not?'

'There was no point. It was a private charter, and what was left of it was scattered all over the ocean floor. Not very deep there, I'm told. But the currents are tough. There's a reason they call the area "the gates of hell."'

Bellinger looked confused. 'What about the bodies?'

Matt winced slightly. The memory was clearly a painful one. 'They were never recovered.'

'Why not?'

His voice rose a notch. 'The area's swarming with sharks, and if they don't get you, the riptides will. It's the goddamn Skeleton Coast. There was nothing to recover.'

'So you—'

'That's right, there was nothing to bury,' Matt flared. He was angry now, his patience depleted. 'The casket was empty, Vince. I know, it was ridiculous, we cremated an empty box and wasted some decent wood, but we had to do it that way. It helped give my dad some closure. Now are you gonna tell me why we're really here?'

Bellinger looked away, studying the faces around the bar. He felt a cold sweat rising through him, and his head throbbed with the strain of his confused, unsettling thoughts. 'Did you watch the news today?'

'No, why?'

Bellinger nodded to himself, wondering how to go on.

'Vince, what's going on?'

Just then, Bellinger's BlackBerry beeped, alerting him to the receipt of a text message. Bellinger kept his hands on the table, ignoring it. He didn't have the patience to deal with Jabba now.

He fixed on Matt and leaned in. 'I think Danny may have been murdered.' He paused, letting the words sink in, then added, 'Or worse.'

Matt's expression curdled, and he looked like he'd been winded. 'Murdered or worse? What could be worse?'

'Maybe he's being held somewhere. Maybe they all are.'

'What?' His face was twisted with utter disbelief. 'What the hell are you talking about?'

Bellinger motioned with his hand to keep it down and leaned in closer. 'Maybe they killed Danny and the others and faked the chopper crash. Then again, maybe they've still got them locked up somewhere, working on it against their will.' His eyes were twitching left and right, scanning the bar. 'I mean, think about it. If you got a bunch of geniuses to design something secret for you, wouldn't you want to keep them around long enough to make sure nothing went wrong when you finally used it?'

His phone beeped again.

'To design what? You're not making sense.'

Bellinger leaned in even closer and his voice dropped down almost to a whisper. 'Something happened today, Matt. In Antarctica. There was this thing, in the sky. It's all over the news. I think Danny had something to do with it.'

'Why would you think that?'

Bellinger was shaking visibly now, the words tumbling out of him nervously. His phone beeped again, but he ignored it. 'Danny was working on something. He was playing around with distributed processing and he showed me some of his stuff and we talked about it and the possibilities were just mind-blowing, you know? I mean, he was brilliant, you know that. But then Reece showed up and whisked him away to work with him on that project of his, the biosensors, and—'

'Reece?'

'Dominic Reece. He taught him. He was his guru at MIT.' Bellinger shook his head, as if trying to block an unwelcome thought. 'He was also in that chopper. With Danny.' He looked at Matt, as if to apologize for bringing it up. After a quiet beat, he added, 'Anyway, it was a great project, the sensors would have saved thousands, tens of thousands of lives, and—'

His phone beeped for the fourth time.

Bellinger lost his train of thought and frowned. He ripped his concentration away from Matt and irritably fished out his phone. He grimaced as he fumbled to get to his inbox, and saw that three messages had come in from the same number.

Not Jabba's. The messages were all from a number he didn't recognize.

He punched up the last of the messages.

The words on the small screen hit him like a sledgehammer.

They simply read, 'If you want to live, shut the fuck up and leave the bar now.'

CHAPTER 12

Boston, Massachusetts

'I think Danny may have been murdered.' The penny-sized mike tucked away under the lapel of Bellinger's coat sucked in the words and rocketed them over to the earpieces of the three operatives who sat in the van that was parked outside the bar on Emerson.

The two other operatives – the ones inside the bar with the barely noticeable, clear earpieces – heard them too.

In the van, the operative leading the surveillance team looked up pointedly at his auburn-haired colleague. She had done well. Her hands had been lightning quick, the move fluidly executed, the tag unnoticed. It had also helped that her beguiling eyes and teasing smile had distracted Bellinger. He hadn't been the first to fall under her spell.

But he now needed to be contained.

The voice of one of the men in the bar shot through their earpieces. 'He's not going for it.'

The lead operative scowled and brought up his wrist mike. 'I'm giving him another prod. Get ready to move in if he still doesn't take the hint.'

The harsh voice came back with, 'Standing by.'

He hit the send button on his cell phone again.

The words on the screen seared Bellinger's eyes. He glanced up, his alarmed gaze raking the bar, a tourniquet of dread choking the life out of his heart. Everyone around him suddenly looked suspicious, threatening, dangerous.

Matt noticed.

'What is it?' he asked.

Bellinger blinked repeatedly. He was having trouble

focusing. For a confused moment, the faces in the bar all seemed to be staring at him with unbridled malevolence.

Matt's voice broke through again. 'Vince. What is it?'

Bellinger turned to him, his words catching in his throat. 'This was a mistake. Forget I said anything.'

'What?'

Bellinger stumbled to his feet. He looked squarely at Matt, his eyes bristling with fear. 'Forget I said anything, all right? I've got to go.'

Matt shot up to his feet from behind the table and reached out, just managing to grab hold of Bellinger's arm. 'Cut the crap, Vince. What's going on?'

Bellinger spun around, yanking his arm free with rabid ferocity before pushing Matt back with both hands. His frenzied reaction surprised Matt, who fell back and landed heavily, jarring his head against the booth's wooden edge and triggering a ripple of commotion that startled the drinkers closest to him and pushed them back a step.

Matt straightened up, his head throbbing from the knock, and staggered to his feet in time to glimpse Bellinger disappearing into the crowd, rushing for the door.

He bolted after him, ducking into his wake, into the clear path that snaked through the drinkers all the way to the bar's entrance.

He burst out onto the pavement and stopped in his tracks at the sight of Bellinger being manhandled by two bulky men and getting dragged into the back of a van.

Matt shouted, 'Hey,' and charged at them, only his feet had barely left the ground when he felt something heavy slam into him from behind, catching him at the base of the neck and across his back, pounding the breath out of him and sending him flying face-first onto the snow-speckled pavement.

He landed badly, his right elbow taking the brunt of his weight and lighting up with pain, and before he could push himself back onto his feet, two sets of strong arms grabbed him, pinned his arms behind his back, and shoved him toward the van before throwing him in through its open doors.

He landed – hard – on the van's ribbed, bare-metal floor, heard the van's doors slam shut somewhere behind him, and felt his weight slide back as the van took off. Jarring images and sensations were coming at him thick and fast and assaulting him from all angles. Still facedown, one eye squashed against the floor, he heard muffled shouts and angled his head up to glimpse Bellinger, the two bulky men over him, and the vague outline of – that couldn't be right – a woman with a shoulder-length bob, seemingly attractive, looking back from the driver's seat, her head silhouetted against the van's windshield, backlit by the streaming lights from beyond. One of the men was sitting on Bellinger's back, pinning him down, one hand covering Bellinger's mouth and blocking his screams of protest. The other was bent down beside them and loomed over Bellinger. He held something that looked like an oversized electric shaver in his hand.

A vaguely familiar high-pitched whine, something powering up, pricked the edge of Matt's hearing, but in his frazzled state, he couldn't quite place it. He turned, trying to shift himself over and onto his back, but one of the men who had grabbed him stomped down heavily on his back and sent him splattering against the van's floor again. A jolt of nausea rushed through Matt as the whine reached a fevered pitch, and his muscles seized up as he realized what it was.

Straining to raise his head an inch, he caught sight of the second man bringing his hand down onto Bellinger and branding him with what Matt now realized was a pocket Taser. Bellinger screamed out in agony as a faint blue light flickered inside the van. A two-second burst was usually enough to bring a fit man down with major muscle spasms, three seconds was enough to turn most men into the sobbing equivalent of a fish flopping around on a dry dock. Bellinger's hit lasted well over five seconds, and Matt knew what the effect on the scientist would be. He'd been at the receiving end of those prods. It wasn't a pleasant sensation, especially not when they were wielded by neolithic prison guards. His skin bristled at the memory, the buzzing noise dredging up the pain of what felt like thousands of needles being shoved simultaneously into every pore of his body.

The van made a left turn, the shift in momentum allowing Matt a brief respite from the weight pinning him down, and he spotted Bellinger's tormentor finally putting down the Taser and bringing out something much smaller, something that glinted at him in the jagged lights cutting in and out of the van, a syringe, which he swiftly plunged into the stricken man's back, just below the neck.

Bellinger's flopping stopped.

'He's done,' the man announced without a hint of exertion or discomfort in his voice, as if what he'd just accomplished was no more than a routine chore.

The bulldozer sitting on Matt asked, 'What about this one?'

The man who'd dealt with Bellinger mulled the question for a moment. 'Same deal,' he decided.

Not the answer Matt was hoping for. Then again, none of the likely answers held much appeal.

One thing he knew: He wasn't about to sit back and let a million volts fry him inside out.

He glimpsed the man moving off Bellinger and making his way over to the back of the van, the pocket Taser in hand, the ominous whine cranking up again.

Just then, the van made another turn, a right one this time.

Time to be a killjoy.

The weight of the bulldozer sitting on top of him shifted slightly from the turn, lightening momentarily. Matt summoned up the furious energy in every corpuscle of his body and suddenly heaved back, as hard as he could. The move caught his captor by surprise, making him lose his balance and sending him flying against the wall of the van. Matt quickly managed to get both hands under him to increase his leverage, then followed through with a full twist, weaving his fingers together and locking them just as he swung around and used his extended arms as a baseball bat.

He caught the bulldozer flat across the nose, a loud, bone-crushing splat erupting in the van. The man's head ricocheted against the van's wall before he curled over, writhing with pain.

Matt didn't pause to watch. There were three other thugs to deal with. The two who'd been busy with Bellinger could wait. The bulldozer's partner, also at the back of the van, was the more immediate threat, and he was already leaping at Matt. Matt steadied himself on his elbow and bent down as he followed through with his roll, the move adding momentum to his leg which lashed out and hammered the incoming attacker across the neck. As the man's head bounced heavily off the van's rear doors, Matt pounced up, grabbed his head with both hands, and pulled it down, connecting it with his knee. Something in the man's face cracked audibly and he went reeling backward, toward the front of the van, falling over the immobile body of Bellinger and interrupting the other two men's advance.

Matt saw them clambering over Bellinger and knew he only had a second or two of clear air. He also knew he wasn't likely to take them out as easily.

There was only one option, really, and he didn't hesitate.

He grabbed the rear door handle, yanked it open, and despite the micro-glimpse of a car trailing not too far back, flung himself out of the moving van.

He didn't have far to free-fall before hitting the asphalt.

It was beyond brutal. His left shoulder and hip took the brunt of it, a lightning bolt of pain shooting through him as he landed. He rolled on himself several times, a cascade of confusing, alternating glimpses of streetlights and tarmac flooding his senses, every inch of his body getting its share of beating. A sudden, ear-piercing shriek hounded him, bearing down on him alarmingly fast, the sound of rubber scraping deliriously across asphalt, the hard-braking car's front bumper only a few feet behind him and gaining fast.

They finally came to a rest together, as if in a synchronized performance, Matt inches away from the car that had fishtailed slightly and was now at a slight angle to the road. Through his dazed whiteout from the pain and the headlights, Matt could feel the heat radiating out from the car's grille, and the air was thick with the smell of burned rubber and brake pads. His shoulder was alight with pain. He steeled himself and straightened up, and glanced down the road. The van was quickly receding, one of the men – it was already too far for anything more specific – looking back before reaching out and slamming the door shut.

Matt pushed himself to his feet. His left leg almost gave way, but he steadied himself against the car's fender. He staggered over to the driver's window. The driver – a man, old, sixties plus – was staring at Matt with a combination of trepidation and disbelief. Matt bent down to look in on him. The old man's window was still closed. Matt gestured for him to open it, but the man just sat there, riven with fear.

Matt rapped his knuckles against the window. 'Open the window, goddammit,' he shouted, gesturing frantically. 'Open it.'

The man hesitated, then shook his head, his brow furrowed with confusion.

Matt jangled the door handle brusquely, but the doors

were locked. He slammed the flat of his hand against the window again, scowling at the old man and yelling, 'Open the goddamn door.'

The man did nervous little mini-shakes with his head again, darted an anxious glance into his rearview mirror, glanced over at Matt again, then turned to face ahead and just hit the gas. Matt reeled back and just watched, dumbstruck, as the car tore off and disappeared into the darkness.

CHAPTER 13

Deir Al-Suryan Monastery, Wadi Natrun, Egypt

A blossoming glint of golden light rose from behind the distant horizon as the three men climbed down the mountain.

They'd waited for close to an hour for Father Jerome to show up, and when he still hadn't appeared, they'd finally given up and made their way back. They didn't speak at all during the hike down or on the drive back. The abbot had simply nodded when asked by the younger monk if he'd been right about what they'd seen, and left it at that.

He needed to think.

Yusuf pulled up outside the monastery and offered to stick around should he be needed. The abbot told him he wasn't, and thanked him, then his expression and his voice darkened.

'Yusuf,' he said gravely, 'I need you to keep what you know about all this to yourself. No one else must be told. For now. Things could get out of hand very quickly if news of this came out. We need to handle this with great care. Do you understand?'

Yusuf nodded somberly, and kissed the abbot's hand. '*Bi amrak, abouna.*' As you wish, Father.

The abbot studied him fervently for a beat, making sure his admonishment sank in, then nodded, giving him permission to leave. He and the monk watched as Yusuf climbed back into the Previa and drove away.

'What are we going to do?' Brother Ameen asked.

The abbot's gaze followed the disappearing minivan. 'First, I need to pray. This is all too . . . unsettling. Will you join me?'

'Of course.'

They entered the monastery through the small gate in the

thick, forty-foot wall that surrounded it. Just inside the enclosure, to their right, the large *qasr* – the keep – a four-storied white cube punctured by tiny, irregular rectangular openings, squatted proudly in the dawn light, its timber drawbridge now permanently lowered and welcoming.

It hadn't always been the case. The sixth-century monastery had been rebuilt several times during its turbulent history.

The valley of Wadi Natrun, which owed its name to the abundant natron in its soil, the sodium carbonate that was a key ingredient in mummification, was the birthplace of Christian monasticism. The tradition had started in the third and fourth centuries, when thousands of followers of Christ had fled there to escape from Roman persecution. Hundreds of years later, still more went there, this time to escape persecution at the hands of the Muslims. The valley held a special resonance for the faithful: It was there that Mary, Joseph, and their infant son had rested while escaping from King Herod's men, before continuing on to Cairo.

At first, the small communities of early Christians had lived in the caves that dotted the low ridges overlooking the desert, surviving off the meager offerings of its scattered oases. Soon, they began to build monasteries where they hoped to worship in relative peace and safety, but the threats never went away, not for centuries. Desert tribes picked up the Romans' baton of aggression and proved even more ruthless. The most vicious of those attacks, at the hands of Berbers in 817, decimated the monastery. When men didn't threaten it, nature itself proved a willing understudy, with only one of the monastery's monks surviving an outbreak of plague in the fourteenth century. And yet, time after time, the persistence and dedication of holy men kept on resurrecting it, and today, the monastery was home to over two hundred monks who followed in the footsteps of the desert fathers of the Old Testament and came here to escape from the distractions of daily life and the temptations of earthly desire to battle their own demons and pray for the salvation of mankind.

The valley had been an oasis of Christianity from the very first days of the movement. The monastic tradition was born there, long before it was eventually adopted by the Christians of Europe. For centuries, profoundly religious men had been drawn to its desolate wilderness. And on the dawn of this portentous day, the abbot thought, it seemed eminently possible that the valley hadn't yet exhausted its relevance to the faithful.

And yet . . . the very thought scared him.

The world was a very different place.

More technologically advanced, undoubtedly. More civilized, perhaps – in certain respects, in certain pockets. But, at its core, it remained as vicious and predatory as it had ever been. Perhaps even more so.

The monk followed the abbot past the keep, through the courtyard that forked off into the Chapel of the Forty-Nine Martyrs – a single, domed chamber that was dedicated to the monks killed during a Berber raid in the year 444 – and into the Church of the Holy Virgin, the monastery's main place of worship. Mercifully, none of the other monks was there yet, but the abbot knew the solitude wouldn't last too long.

He led the monk past the nave and into the *khurus* – the choir. As he passed the grand wooden portal that separated the two areas, his eyes drifted up to a wall painting adorning a half cupola overhead, a thousand-year-old depiction of the Annunciation that he'd seen countless times. In it, four prophets were gathered around the Holy Virgin and the archangel Gabriel. The abbot found his gaze drawn to the first prophet to the right of the Virgin, Ezekiel, and a chill crawled down his neck at the sight. And for the next hour, as he desperately prayed for guidance, he couldn't shake the thought of the prophet's celestial vision from his weary mind: the heavens opening up to a whirlwind of amber fire folding on itself, the wheels of fire in a sky 'the color of a terrible crystal,' all of it heralding the voice of God.

They prayed, side by side, for close to an hour, facing the black, stone altar, prostrating themselves against the cold floor of the chapel in the praying tradition of the early Christians, a posture that was later adopted by Islam.

'Shouldn't we have waited longer for him?' Ameen asked. With the sun comfortably ensconced in the eastern sky, they were now – alone – in the monastery's small, newly restored museum. 'What if something's happened to him?'

The abbot had been concerned about that himself, and not for the first time. Still, he shrugged stoically. 'He's been up there for months. I should think he knows how to handle the mountain by now. He seems to be coping well.'

After a quiet beat, the younger monk cleared his throat and asked, 'What are we going to do, Father?'

'I'm not sure what we should do,' the abbot replied. 'I don't understand what's happening.'

Ameen's eyebrows shot up with incredulity. 'A miracle. That's what's happening.'

The abbot frowned. 'Something we don't understand is happening, yes. But from there to say it's a miracle . . .'

'What other explanation is there?'

The abbot shook his head, lost for words.

'You said it yourself,' the younger monk persisted. 'The sign you described, what you saw on the news.'

A confused tangle of images clouded the abbot's mind. He thought back to that day, in the desert. When their guest had been found, before he took to the caves. The terrible state he was in. His recovery.

The word *miraculous* glided into his thoughts again.

'It doesn't fit any of the prophecies of our holy book,' he finally said.

'Why does it need to?'

The comment took the abbot by surprise. 'Come,

Brother. Surely you don't mean to negate the truth in those writings?'

'We're living a miracle, Father,' Ameen exclaimed, his voice flushed with excitement. 'Not reading about it hundreds of years after the fact, knowing full well it's been translated and embellished and corrupted by countless hands. Living it. Now. In this modern day and age.' He paused, then added, pointedly, 'With all the power of modern communication at our disposal.'

The abbot's face contracted with unease. 'You want people to know about this?'

'They already know about the sign. You saw the woman on the news service. Her images and words will have reached millions.'

'Yes, but . . . until we understand what exactly is happening, we can't allow this to come out.'

Ameen spread out his hands questioningly. 'Isn't it evident, Father?'

The abbot felt cowed by his colleague's fervent gaze, and nodded thoughtfully. He understood the younger man's exuberance, but it needed to be reined in. There was no running away from what was happening, of that he had no doubt. He had to face it. He'd been thrust into this unwittingly, and now he needed to do what needed to be done. But with care, and caution.

'We need to study the scriptures more closely,' he concluded. 'Consult with our superiors.' He paused, weighing the hardest part of the task ahead. 'Most importantly, we need to go back up to the caves and talk to him. Tell him what's happened. Perhaps he will know what to make of it.'

Ameen stepped closer. 'Everything you say is reasonable, but it doesn't detract from the fact that we can't keep this to ourselves,' he pleaded. 'We've received a grace from God. We owe it to Him to share it with the world. People need to know, Father. The world needs to know.'

'Not yet,' the abbot insisted, firmly. 'It's not up to us to decide.'

The younger monk's voice rose with concern. 'Forgive me, Father, but I believe you're making a mistake. Others, many others, will undoubtedly try to claim the sign as their own. And in doing so, they will cheapen and corrupt this most sublime of messages. We live in cynical, amoral times. These charlatans will make it harder for the true voice to be heard. Our message could easily be drowned out by impostors and opportunists, irreversibly so. We can't wait. We have to move quickly before the chaos turns this divine event into a circus.'

The abbot sat down and sighed wearily, massaging his brow with his calloused hands, feeling the room tightening in around him. The young monk's words rang true, but he couldn't bring himself to take that step. The consequences were too frightening to contemplate. He sat there, tongue-tied with uncertainty, staring at the stone floor while the monk hovered nearby, his steps heavy with frustration, waiting. The painting in the chapel crept back into his mind's eye, and he thought again of Ezekiel's vision:

Wheels of fire in a sky the color of a terrible crystal, all of it heralding the voice of God.

After a moment, the abbot looked up, a frown darkening his face. 'It's not up to us,' he repeated. 'We need to consult with the councils and bring the matter to His Holiness. They will decide.'

An hour later, Brother Ameen stood in the shadows and watched from the sanctity of a dark hallway as the library's curator stepped out of his office.

He'd failed to convince the abbot. The old man was visibly overwhelmed by what he'd seen and seemed incapable of grasping the enormity of what was happening. But the younger man wasn't about to let that stop him.

He needed to take matters into his own hands.

He waited patiently, his eyes tracking the priest as he ventured across the courtyard and entered the refectory. Moments later, the young monk sneaked into the priest's office, picked up the telephone, and started dialing.

CHAPTER 14

Less than a mile from the ridge that the two monks and the driver had just climbed down, a boy of fourteen ambled after his small herd with tired feet.

Despite the early wake-ups, the boy did like the mornings best, as did all seven of his father's goats. The sun was still low, the valley cloaked by the long shadows of the hills surrounding them. The cool breeze was a welcome alternative to the sun that would soon be bearing down on them, and the purple hues of the barren landscape were also easier on the eyes and, if he allowed himself to think of them that way, more inspirational.

Humming a tune he'd recently heard on his father's radio, he rounded an outcropping of rocks and stopped in his tracks at the unexpected sight before him. Three men – soldiers, it seemed, from their outfits – were loading equipment into a dust-caked, canvas-topped pickup truck. Equipment like he'd never seen before. Like the sand-beige, drumlike object, perhaps three feet wide but only five or six inches deep, that snared his attention.

Even though the boy had frozen in place and stopped breathing, the men spotted him instantly. His eyes drew a line of hard, unforgiving stares that seared through the black Ray-Bans the men were wearing. He barely had time to register the familiar gear he'd seen on countless news broadcasts of the war in Iraq – the sand-colored camouflage BDUs, the boots, the sunglasses – before one of the men spat out a brief word and the others dropped what they were doing and took quick strides toward him.

The boy started to run, but he didn't make it far. He felt one of the men rush up to him and tackle him from behind, bringing him down into the parched soil headfirst.

With his heart in his throat, he wondered what the hell they wanted from him, why they'd wrestled him to the ground, why he was biting into the sand and grit that also pricked painfully at his eyes. In a mad frenzy of terror, he tried to squirm around and get onto his back, but the man who sat on him was too heavy and had him solidly pinned down.

He heard another man's footsteps crunching their way closer, then glimpsed a pair of military boots from the corner of his eye, looming over him like a demigod.

He didn't hear a word.

He didn't see the nod.

And he didn't feel a thing after the big, practiced hands of the man sitting on top of him quickly and efficiently took up their positions – one around the side of his neck, the other around the other side of his head – and tightened their grip before twisting suddenly and fiercely in opposite directions.

Swift, Silent, Deadly.

It was, without a doubt, a well-earned motto.

CHAPTER 15

Amundsen Sea, Antarctica

'If you figure anything out, call me, okay? Just call me, anytime.' Gracie gave out her satphone number, hung up, and heaved a sigh of frustration.

Another dead end.

She mopped her face with her hands before sweeping them tightly through her hair, massaging some life into her scalp. She'd managed to coax some good video bites from Simmons and some of the other scientists on board, and while Dalton was editing it all into a high-def report to broadband back to the news desk in D.C. – much better than the jumpy, grainy Began live feed they'd used for the first broadcast, more *Armageddon*, less *Cloverfield* this time around – she'd been working the satphone.

Her years on the job had allowed her to build up a beefy Rolodex, and right now, she was mining it for all its worth. She spoke to a contact of hers at NASA, a project director she'd met while covering the space shuttle *Columbia*'s disaster back in 2003. She also called contacts of hers at CalTech and at the Pentagon, as well as the editor of *Science* magazine and the network's science and technology guru.

They were all as baffled as she was.

She'd hardly hung up when the satphone rang.

Another reporter, angling for a comment.

'How are they managing to get hold of this number?' she groaned to Finch.

He pulled a who-knows face and grabbed the phone for yet another polite, but firm, rebuff. For the moment, it was their exclusive – for better or for worse.

It's not that she was camera shy, or that she didn't like being in the public eye. Far from it. Her career as a TV correspondent wasn't an accident: She'd wanted it ever since high school. She'd pursued every opportunity to get those breaks, and once she did, she'd worked damn hard at grabbing her share of airtime and overcoming the endemic misogyny and the subtle bullying in the industry. She thrived on the stories she covered and the experiences she shared with her viewers, she loved stepping in front of that camera and telling the world what she'd found out, and undeniably, the camera loved her back. She had that unquantifiable magnetism that went beyond the purely physical. People just tuned in and enjoyed her company. Focus groups confirmed her broad appeal: Women weren't threatened by her, they took a possessive pride in her expertise, and in an age where public image was everything and every word was carefully weighed for effect, her candor and honesty were a big draw; men, while readily admitting that they fancied the pants off her, more often than not pointed out how they found her brain to be just as much of a turn-on.

And so she'd gone from local reporter at a network affiliate in Wisconsin to weekend anchor at a bigger affiliate in Illinois and eventually to anchor and special correspondent for the network's flagship Special Investigations Unit. In the process, she'd become a face America trusted, whether she was reporting from Kuwait in the run-up to the invasion of Iraq, on board a Greenpeace vessel stalking Japanese whaling ships, or following the unfolding tragedies of the tsunami in Thailand and Hurricane Katrina in New Orleans.

More recently, she'd been unwittingly drawn into the emotionally charged debate on global warming. She'd approached the issue as a skeptic, her instincts compelling her to question – on air – the often lazy assumptions of the ever-more-fashionable, almost religious, environmental movement. She knew how unreliable long-term forecasts were, how history was littered with the failed predictions of the most brilliant minds on everything from population levels to oil prices, and she hadn't minced her words when voicing her skepticism. Up until then, her honesty and integrity had served her well. On this issue, her candor proved to be a problem. The reaction had been nothing less than incendiary. She was lambasted for her doubts from all corners, and her career had hung in the balance.

She decided the subject matter merited her attention, whichever side of the fence she ended up on. She pitched a comprehensive, no-holds-barred, in-depth documentary tackling the issue, and the network's brass signed off on it. And so, with the vast majority of her colleagues mired in the quicksands of the marathon election campaign back home, she focused her energies on examining all the available data on the climate issue and meeting everyone who mattered. She was soon convinced that greenhouse gases had undoubtedly risen in the last few decades, and the earth did appear to be warming, but she still needed to find out if the connection between the two was as direct as it was now being portrayed. And so she'd crisscrossed the globe, from the remote science station of Cherskii in Siberia, where 40,000-year-old permafrost was now thawing and, in the process, releasing huge amounts of greenhouse gases, to Greenland, where massive glaciers were sliding toward the sea at a rate of two yards every hour, taking a forensic look at every new report on the matter during her travels.

Her investigative claws sharpened when she looked into the Global Climate Coalition, the Information Council of the Environment, and the Greening Earth Society – all of them cleverly misnamed, created and funded by the automotive, petroleum, and coal industries with the sole purpose of deceiving the public by spreading disinformation and callously repositioning global warming as *theory* rather than *fact*. It didn't take long for her to become more and more convinced that the planet was indeed in trouble because of us. What was far less clear, however, was what we could

84

realistically – and pragmatically – do about it. That was a far more contentious, and troubling, debate, and one she felt very passionate about.

But she hadn't expected it to lead to this.

She breathed out with exasperation. 'I'm getting nothing here. You having better luck?' she asked Finch as she got out of her chair and walked over to the window to scan the skies.

Finch had been talking to the news desk back in D.C. and trawling through his own contacts list. 'Nope. If it's natural, no one's seen anything like it. And if it's not, they're all telling me the technology to pull off something like this just doesn't exist.'

'We don't know that,' Dalton objected, looking up from his monitor. 'I'm sure there's a lot of stuff out there that we don't know about.'

'Yes, but what we don't know about doesn't really matter in this case, because there's nothing we know about that even comes close.'

'You lost me.'

'Technology breakthroughs – they have to start somewhere,' Finch explained. 'They don't just come out of nowhere. No one suddenly came up with cell phones. It started with Alexander Graham Bell two hundred years ago. There's a progression. Regular phone, cordless home phones, digital phones, and eventually, cell phones . . . Stealth fighters – we didn't know about them, but they're just evolutions of other fighter planes. You see what I mean? Technology evolves. And that thing we saw . . . there doesn't seem to be anything out there that we can point to and say, "Well, if we took that and made it bigger, or more powerful, or used it in such a way, it could explain it." It's in a whole different ballpark. And everyone's trying to figure it out. I mean, look at this.' He pulled up the latest e-mail from D.C. 'It's going ballistic,' he enthused. 'Reuters, AP, CNN. They're all carrying it. Every station from London to Beijing is running it. Same for the big news blogs. Drudge, Huffington. It's been voted up to number one on Digg and we've crossed two hundred thousand hits on YouTube. And the chat rooms are just going nuts over it.'

'What are they saying?'

'From what I can see, people are in one of three camps. Some of them think it's some kind of harmless stunt, a CGI, *War of the Worlds* kind of thing. Others also think it's a con but they see something more sinister in it, and they're throwing out all kinds of crazy ideas about how it could have been pulled off, none of which seem to hold water if you read the mocking replies they're getting from people who seem to know what they're talking about.'

'Is there anyone who doesn't think we're behind it?'

'Yep. The third group: the pro camp. The ones who believe it's the real thing – real as in God, not ET. One of them called us 'the heralds of the Second Coming.''

'Well that makes me feel so much better,' she groaned, her chest tightening with unease. Greed and fear were tugging at her. Part of her was thrilled by the idea of being the face of the hottest story around – she couldn't deny that – but the more reasoned side of her was clamoring for restraint. She knew what she'd seen; she just didn't know what it was. And until she did, she was uncomfortable with how it was all spiraling out of control. If it turned out to be something less momentous than everyone was suggesting, she could already picture Jon Stewart ridiculing her into an early retirement.

Finch spun the laptop back and tapped some more keys. 'And speaking of ET,' he said as he glanced pointedly across at Dalton, 'a guy I know at the Discovery Channel sent me these.' He turned the screen back so it was facing them. 'Some of them are the ones you'd expect, like clouds and Concorde contrails that make people think they're seeing UFOs. I don't know if I should be surprised, but he tells me there are over two hundred reported UFO sightings a month in America. *A month*. But then, there's a whole slew of historic references to unexplained sightings going back thousands of years. We're talking hundreds of references throughout history about bright balls of fire, flying "earthenware vessels," luminous discs. It's not just a modern phenomenon. I mean, check out these historical records: "Japan, 1458: An object as bright as the full moon and followed by curious signs was observed in the sky." Or this one: "London, 1593: A flying dragon surrounded by flames was seen hovering over the city."'

'Opium'll do that to you every time,' Dalton half-joked. 'Seriously. Drugs were legal back then, weren't they?'

'Besides, none of these references are even remotely verifiable,' Gracie added.

'Sure, but the thing is, there are so many of them. Written continents apart, at a time when traveling from one to another was virtually impossible, when most of the world was illiterate. Even the Bible's got them.'

'Big surprise there,' Gracie scoffed. A charged silence hung between them. 'So what are we saying? What do you think we saw?'

Finch pulled off his glasses and used his sleeve to give them a wipe as he thought about it. 'I'd have said mass hallucination if it wasn't for the footage.' He shook his head slowly in disbelief, slipped his glasses back on, and looked up at Gracie. 'I can't explain it.'

'Dalton?' she asked.

His face clouded with uncertainty. He leaned back in his chair and ran his hands tightly through his hair. 'I don't know. There was something . . . ethereal about it, you know? It didn't look flat, like something projected, but then it didn't look like something hard and physical either. It's hard to explain. There was something much more organic, much more visceral about it. Like it was part of the sky, like the sky itself had lit up, you know what I'm saying?'

'I do,' Gracie agreed uncomfortably. The sight of the bright, glowing sign, as vivid as when she first saw it, materialized in her mind's eye. An upwelling of elation, the same one she felt when she first saw it, overcame her again as she remembered how it had formed itself out of nothing. *It was as if the air itself had been summoned by God, lit up from within into that shape*, she found herself thinking. Which didn't sit well with her. She'd stopped believing in God when her mother died, ripped away from her young daughter by an unrelenting tumor in her breast. And now, here it was, this unexplained thing in the sky. As if it were taunting her.

She pushed the thought away. *Get a grip. We're running ahead of ourselves here. There's got to be a logical explanation for it.*

But a nagging question kept coming back.

What if there isn't?

Gracie stared out the window, scanning the sky for another sighting, her jumbled mind desperate for an answer. The satphone rang, and as Finch stretched across the table to answer it, her mind migrated to a UFO hoax from a year earlier. The clip, showing a UFO buzzing a beach in Haiti, had clocked up over five million viewings on YouTube within days of its posting, hogging chat rooms and news aggregator sites across the Web and popping up on every FunWall on Facebook. Millions were taken in by it – until it turned out to be something a French computer animator had put together in a few hours on his MacBook, using commercially available software, reluctantly explaining it away as a 'sociological experiment' for a movie – about a UFO hoax, natch – that he was working on. With the advances in special effects and the proliferation of faked videos of such high quality that they managed to convince even the most staunch of skeptics, a subtle question arose in Gracie's mind: Would people recognize a 'true' event of this kind when – as it seemed – it really happened? She knew what she saw. It was right there in front of her, but everyone else was only seeing it on a screen. And without seeing it with their own eyes, could they ever accept it for what it was, something wondrous and inexplicable and possibly even supernatural or divine – or would it be drowned in a sea of cynicism?

'Gracie,' Finch called out, covering the phone's mouthpiece with his hand.

She turned.

His face had a confused scrunch to it. 'It's for you.'

'Now what?' she grumbled.

'I'm not sure, but . . . it's coming from Egypt. And I think you need to take it.'

CHAPTER 16

There were no cabs around, but it didn't take too long for Matt to get back to his car. The van hadn't traveled that far from the bar before he'd dived out of it. He would've made it back sooner, but he wasn't at his best. He felt groggy and nauseous, his skin had been scraped raw in several places, and every bone in his body felt like it had been hammered by a blacksmith on steroids. And, as if to add insult to injury, it was snowing again.

He was relieved to find his car, a highland-green 1968 Mustang GT 390 'Bullitt' Fastback that was his next restoration project, still where he'd left it, close to the bar on Emerson. It hadn't even occurred to him to check for his keys before he got to it, but, mercifully, they were also still there, safely ensconced in the pocket of his peacoat.

Just a couple of small miracles to cap off a magical night.

Less miraculous, though, was the fact that he'd lost his cell phone. He guessed it had probably flown out of the pocket of his coat during his hard landing on the asphalt, though he didn't dwell on it. He had more pressing concerns.

He leaned against the car and caught his breath, and the brutal images of a helpless Bellinger getting fried and injected roared back into his mind's eye. He had to do something to try and help him, but he couldn't see a move that made sense. He couldn't report it to the cops. The van was long gone, and the inevitable questions he'd be asked, given his record, would only cloud the issue. More to the point, he didn't think the risk of flagging his whereabouts to the goon squad who'd come after Bellinger was outweighed by any positive effect it would have on helping the cops find Bellinger and bringing him back safely.

Which, somehow, he didn't think was going to happen anyway.

The traffic was light and scattered as he drove home, the city now tucked in under a thin blanket of snow. He was on the expressway within minutes, and from there, it was only a short hop down to Quincy and the studio apartment he lived in over his workshop. As he cruised south, his mind ground over what had happened to him, trying to make sense of the rush of events that had come at him from nowhere and figure out what the right move would be.

Bellinger had called. He'd asked for a meeting, one that couldn't wait. He'd then hit him with the news that his brother might have been murdered, or that his death might have been faked and that he might be locked up somewhere. How had he put it, exactly? *Working on it, against their will?*

Danny, alive – but locked up somewhere?

The thought flooded Matt's gut with equal doses of elation – and rage. Matt and Danny had always been close, which never failed to amaze their friends, given how different they were. For a start, they didn't look anything like each other. Matt, three years older, had inherited his dad's olive skin, dark hair, and solid build, whereas Danny – two shades fairer and fifty pounds lighter – took after his mom. The stark difference between them extended to, well, pretty much everything else. Matt had no patience for classes or for schoolwork, whereas Danny had an insatiable appetite for learning. Matt lettered in as many sports as he could cram into his schedule. Danny couldn't sink a basket if he was sitting on the backboard. Off campus, the contrast between the two brothers wasn't any less pronounced. Matt was irreverent, wild, and reckless – in other words, a babe-magnet. Danny was far more introverted and preferred the company of the computer he'd found in a junk shop and rebuilt in his bedroom. Still, despite it all, they had a bond that was unshakable, a deep understanding of each other that survived the nastiest taunts and the most callous temptations that high school could throw at them.

Their friendship had also survived Matt's repeated collisions with the law.

As with a lot of cases like his, things had started small. Matt had built his first car at the age of thirteen, hooking up an old washing-machine engine to a soap-box derby car that became something of a fixture around his neighborhood. The local cops were amazed and even the hardheaded sticklers among them couldn't quite bring themselves to take away his pride and joy – a relationship that would change dramatically over the years. For as he grew older, the disparity between his love of cars, on the one hand, and the bleak part-time work prospects available to him in the Worcester area and his parents' wafer-thin bank account, on the other, became more frustrating. Headstrong and impatient, Matt sought to redress that imbalance his own way.

Those early escapades were classic Matt. He didn't go after any old ride. He would trawl the more affluent neighborhoods of Boston for specific cars on his hit list. He also never crashed or trashed the cars he stole, nor did he ever try to sell them. He would merely abandon them in some parking lot once he'd had the chance to sample them. He managed to test-drive quite a few before he got caught. The judge he came up against on that first conviction wasn't amused or impressed by his antics.

That inaugural stint behind bars proved to have far-reaching consequences. Upon his release from jail, it didn't take long for Matt to realize how his life had changed. Work prospects dried up. Friends shied away from him. People looked at him in a different way. He had changed too. Trouble seemed to come looking for him, as if sensing it had a willing customer. His hardworking, God-fearing parents were overwhelmed and paralyzed by his wild streak. They didn't have the good sense or the strength of character to offer him the guidance he needed. His underpaid and corrupt parole officer was even less of a candle in the dark. And despite Danny's repeated, frustrated arguments about where this was headed, Matt ended up dropping out of high school before graduation, and from there, his life just spiraled out of control. He spent the next few years rotating in and out of jail for theft, criminal damage to property, and battery, among others, his future withering away while Danny's blossomed, first at MIT, then at a highly paid job in a tech company based nearby.

As he motored across the Neponset River, Matt ruefully remembered how he hadn't seen much of Danny before his death. Matt had only been released from jail a few months before Danny had been offered the job with Reece, and he hadn't seen much of him after that. Matt had been busy setting up his business – with the help of a life-altering loan from his kid brother, he thought with a twinge of shame. In a sense, he owed him his life.

It was Danny who'd sat him down and talked some sense into him – finally. Made him realize he couldn't keep doing this. And got him to straighten up.

The way out Danny had suggested was simple. Turn what did the damage in the first place into something positive. Use it to carve out a new life. And Matt listened. He found a small car shop in Quincy that was closing down, and took over the lease. The plan he and Danny came up with was for him to find and fix up classic cars. Matt had a soft spot for American muscle cars from the sixties and seventies, like the Mustang he was now driving, a highly collectible model, a car he and Danny had fantasized about owning ever since they'd watched Steve McQueen catapult one across the streets of San Francisco – a movie they'd only seen about three dozen times. He knew it would be hard to part with it once he was done restoring it, but with a bit of luck, he'd be able to sell it for seventy grand, maybe more, probably to some deskbound executive in need of a weekend toy. In the heady days before the credit crunch, Matt had built up a solid reputation in car enthusiast circles. He'd even sold a couple to guys whose cars he'd stolen years earlier, not that they knew it. Things had been looking up for him, all while Danny had been sucked into the black hole of his new job. A black hole that had ultimately swallowed up his life.

Or had it?

Was it possible that Danny was still alive?

Bellinger had made a convincing argument for it. And he'd been grabbed seconds after making it. That had to mean something.

Whether Danny was still alive or not, the idea that they'd all been lied to, that someone knew the truth and had kept it from them – *the idea that someone, not fate, had taken Danny away from them* – felt like acid in his throat.

He wasn't about to let it slide.

He took the Willard Street exit and turned into Copeland after the roundabout, and his fury swelled even more as he thought back to how the news of Danny's death had devastated their parents. It was bad enough their eldest son was a convicted felon. To lose Danny too – their pride and joy, the redeemer of the family name – was too much to bear. Their mom had died a couple of months later. Despite the complicated medical terminology the doctors insisted on using, Matt knew it was simply a case of a broken heart. He also knew he was partly to blame. He knew the havoc raging in her veins started the day he'd been arrested that first time, if not earlier. His dad hadn't fared much better. Danny's job came with life coverage, and though the insurance payout paid for the nursing home and allowed their dad some minor touches of additional comfort, he'd been left a demolished man. He and Matt had hardly spoken at his mom's funeral, and Matt hadn't been out to see him since that bleak day in

January. Then almost a year to the day later, the local sheriff, a craggy old nemesis, had managed to track Matt down to his garage in Quincy and given him the news of his dad's death. A stroke, he'd said, although Matt had his doubts about that too.

Bellinger's words echoed in his mind. Someone had taken Danny, and it was linked to something that just happened in the skies of Antarctica. It sounded outlandish and surreal. Only it clearly wasn't. The guys he'd just gone up against were very real. Highly professional. Well equipped. Ruthless. And not overly concerned with discretion.

The implications of that last point were particularly worrying.

He coasted east on Copeland, the Mustang's forty-year-old headlights struggling to break through the swarm of cottonlike snowflakes. With no other cars around, the snow had had time to settle, covering the road ahead with a thin, undisturbed white duvet. He passed Buckley and motored on until he reached the 7-Eleven and the turnoff into the alleyway that led to his shop, and just before turning into it, a remote corner of his mind registered a set of tire tracks in the fresh snow.

They belonged to a single car that had veered off Copeland. He couldn't see down the alley. His shop was tucked away about a hundred yards back from the main road, and there were no streetlights that way, but the tire tracks were more than enough to trip his internal alarm, as they could only have been heading to his place. There was nothing else down there.

Problem was, he wasn't expecting anyone.

Which didn't bode well for the rest of his magical night.

CHAPTER 17

Amundsen Sea, Antarctica

'You need to come here. There's something you need to see.'

The caller wasn't a native English speaker, and Gracie couldn't place his accent. And although he spoke slowly and deliberately, his words were laced with an urgency that came through loud and clear, despite the less-than-crystal clarity of the satellite link.

'Slow down a second,' Gracie said. 'Who are you exactly, and how'd you get this number?'

'My name is Ameen. Brother Ameen, if you like.'

'And you're calling from Egypt?'

'Yes. From Deir Al-Suryan – the Monastery of the Syrians, in Wadi Natrun.'

Her internal kook-alert monitor, which had already moved up to yellow before the man had even started talking, got a slight nudge up to blue.

'And how'd you get this number?' she asked again, a slight edge to her voice now.

'I called your Cairo bureau.'

'And they gave it to you?'

Much as her vexation was clear, the man wasn't going out of his way to placate her. Instead, he simply said, 'I told them I was calling on behalf of Father Jerome.'

The name bounced around Gracie's tired mind for a moment, before landing on the obvious association. 'What, *the* Father Jerome?'

'Yes,' he assured her. 'The very same.'

Her monitor took a step back to yellow. 'And you're calling on his behalf from Egypt? Is that where he is?'

It suddenly occurred to her that she hadn't read anything about the world famous humanitarian for quite a while.

Which was unusual, given his highly public, if reluctantly so, profile, and given the huge organization that he'd founded and still ran, as far as she knew.

'Yes, he's here. He's been here for almost a year.'

'Okay, well, now that you've got me on the line,' she said, 'what's this about?'

'You need to come here. To see Father Jerome.'

This surprised her. 'Why?'

'We saw your broadcast. You were the one to see the sign. You brought it to the world.'

'"The sign"?'

Dalton and Finch were eyeing her curiously. She gave them an I'm-not-sure-where-this-is-going shrug.

'For whatever reason,' Brother Ameen said, 'divine or otherwise, you were there. It's your story. And, of course, I'm familiar with your work. People listen to you. Your reputation is solid. Which is why I am telling this to you and you only.'

'You haven't told me anything yet.'

Brother Ameen paused, then said, 'The symbol you witnessed, there, over the ice. It's here too.'

An altogether different alarm blared inside her, one that sent her pulse rocketing. 'What, you've got it there too? In the sky?' Her words also visibly snagged Dalton and Finch's attention.

'No, not in the sky.'

'Where then?'

'You need to come here. To see it for yourself.'

Gracie's kook monitor fluttered upward again. 'I'm going to need a little more than that.'

'It's hard to explain.'

'Why don't you try.'

Brother Ameen seemed to weigh his words for a moment, then said, 'Father Jerome's not exactly here, at the monastery. He was here. He came to us several months ago. He was . . .

troubled. And after a few weeks, he . . . he went up into the mountain. There's a cave, you see. A cave that provides the basics – you know, a shelter with a bed to sleep in, a stove to cook on. Men of God go there when they're looking for solitude, when they don't want to be disturbed. Sometimes, they stay there for days. Sometimes, weeks. Months even.'

'And Father Jerome is there?'

'Yes.'

Gracie didn't quite know what to make of that. 'What does that have to do with me?'

The man hesitated. He seemed uncomfortable with what he was about to tell her. 'He's a changed man, Miss Logan. Something . . . something we don't quite understand has happened to him. And since he's been up in the cave, he's been writing. A lot. He's been filling one journal after another with his thoughts. And on some of their pages, there's a drawing. A recurring drawing, one he's painted all over the walls of the cave.'

Gracie's skin prickled.

'It's the sign, Miss Logan. The sign you saw over the ice.'

Gracie's mind scrambled to process what he'd just told her. An obvious question fought its way out of the confused mire. 'No offense, Brother, but—'

'I know what you're going to say, Miss Logan.' He cut her off. 'And of course, you've every right to be skeptical. I wouldn't expect any less of you, of someone with your intellect. But you need to hear me out. There isn't a television up in the cave. We don't even have one here at the monastery, nor a radio for that matter. Father Jerome hasn't seen your broadcast.'

Gracie's kook-o-meter was having trouble sticking to one direction. 'Well, I'm not sure your word on that's gonna get me hopping on a plane just yet.'

'No, you don't understand,' Brother Ameen added, the restraint in his voice struggling to contain the urgency he clearly felt. 'It's not something he only just started to do.'

An unsettling realization chilled her gut. 'What are you saying? When did he start drawing this sign?'

His answer struck her like a spear.

'Seven months ago. He's been drawing the sign over and over again for seven months.'

CHAPTER 18

Quincy, Massachusetts

Pure instinct took over and Matt turned in early, pulling into the lot of the 7-Eleven just before the alleyway.

Being a twenty-four-hour store, it was open, but there were no other cars outside. He flicked the Mustang's lights off but left the engine gurgling, and just sat there for a moment, bathed by the alternating red-and-green flicker of the store's Christmas lights, taking stock of the situation.

They were here already. Waiting for him. Had to be.

How?

He quickly segued back to Bellinger's abduction. They must have been watching Bellinger. Maybe even listening to his calls. And if they were, they knew about his call to Matt. And if this was about Danny, then they knew all about Matt already.

And Matt had obviously become a problem for them.

Wonderful.

He gave his immediate surroundings a quick scan but didn't notice anything that jarred. They had to be waiting for him near his garage. He put himself in their place and could almost picture the perfect spot where they'd have parked, out of sight, ready to ambush him on his return. *Bastards. How could they react so quickly?* It had only been, what, not even an hour since he'd leapt out of their van?

They weren't short of resources.

Which wasn't helping on the worrisome front.

He switched the engine off, pulled up his coat collar, and climbed out of the car, his eyes stealthily alert for any movement. He took a few quick steps over to the store and huddled under its awning, using the pause to give the area another quick once-over.

Nothing.

Just the single set of tracks headed down the alleyway to the side of the 7-Eleven, disappearing into the darkness, taunting him.

He stepped inside, triggering a two-toned electronic chime that brought him to the attention of Sanjay, the store's congenial owner, who was busy restocking the hot dog grill.

Sanjay smiled, 'Hey, Matt,' then noted the dusting of snow on Matt's head with a bemused expression and said, 'It's really coming down, isn't it?' In mid-sentence, his forehead crinkled with confusion as he registered Matt's battered condition.

Matt just nodded absently, his mind still processing the situation while he made sure there was no one else around. 'Sure is,' he finally replied after the distracted beat, then his face darkened and he said, 'Sanjay, I need to go out the back way.'

Sanjay stared at him for a moment. 'Okay,' he said. 'Whatever you need, Matt.' They'd known each other ever since Matt had taken over the lease on the garage down the road. Matt had been a good customer and a reliable neighbor, and by now, Sanjay knew him well enough to know that Matt wouldn't be asking if it wasn't important.

He led him to the back of the store and unlocked the door.

Matt paused at the doorway. 'Don't lock it just yet, will you? I won't be long.'

Sanjay nodded hesitatingly. 'Okay.' He glanced away, then turned back and added, 'You sure you're okay?'

'Not really,' Matt shrugged, then slipped out the door.

There were no cars around. He stayed low and close to the wall of the back lot and headed away from the main road, making his way past Sanjay's car and the Dumpsters. Any light from the store quickly petered out, and he was soon in total darkness with only a diffused moon glow to guide him. He ducked into a patch of trees and over to a low, single-story brick structure that housed a small law firm. As expected, all of its lights were out, and no cars were around. With his left leg and hip blazing with pain with every step, he scuttled along the back wall of the building quietly until it ran out.

He bent down and chanced a peek around the corner. He'd read it right. A dark Chrysler 300C was parked in one of the law firm's spots, huddled behind the far side of the building, about twenty yards from the entrance to his shop. He could just about make out the silhouettes of two figures inside.

They were waiting for him. Either that, or they were about eight hours early for their appointment with their lawyer, and no one was that enthusiastic about meeting a lawyer.

Matt inched back into cover, his mind racing through his options. His first instinct was to charge in, beat them to a pulp, and pound the truth out of them. A few years back, he might have done just that, despite the odds. But right now, the odds weren't good, and much as he was desperate to take them on, he grudgingly forced himself to accept that it would be the wrong move. He was hurting all over, and his left leg was barely holding him up. He wouldn't stand a chance, and he knew it.

He had a momentary lapse and thought of calling the cops, but again kiboshed that idea. He didn't trust them. Never did and never would. Besides, as far as the cops were concerned, he could always count on losing any his-word-against-theirs contest. And, as he'd realized, the guys in the Chrysler seemed to have a solid setup, which meant they had connections. All he had was a rap sheet that would dry up an inkjet cartridge.

Another idea, a more promising one, elbowed its way into that one's place. He quickly put it through its paces, looking for flaws, and decided it was his best option. His best option out of a total of one, actually. He sneaked a last glance at the

Chrysler, convinced himself that they weren't going anywhere just yet, then made his way back to the 7-Eleven.

He cut through the store, past Sanjay, who gave him a worried, quizzical glance. Without breaking step, Matt flicked him a stay-put, though not hugely reassuring gesture.

'I need some tape,' he told him. 'Something solid and sticky, packing tape, that kind of thing.'

Sanjay thought for a beat, then nodded. 'I'll get you what I have,' he said as Matt disappeared out the front door.

A quick glance around yielded no visible threats. Matt walked to the back of the Mustang and popped the trunk. With practiced fingers, he pulled back the lining along its side wall. He reached in behind it and found the small niche he was looking for. In it was a small black box, not much bigger than a packet of cigarettes. Matt pulled it out and stuffed it in his inside breast pocket. He then pulled out the lug wrench from the spare wheel's tool kit, closed the trunk, and ducked back into the store.

Sanjay was waiting for him. In his hands was a roll of two-inch-thick duct tape. Matt just grabbed it, blurted out a guttural 'Perfect,' and kept going.

He crept back to the corner of the brick building and peered around its corner. The Chrysler was still there, as he'd left it. He checked the perimeter, backed up, and crept into the shrubs and trees behind the parking bay, keeping low. He maneuvered to a spot around fifteen yards behind the Chrysler, making sure he wasn't in the line of sight of their mirrors. From there, he dropped to the ground and crawled the rest of the way.

Matt advanced on elbows that were still suffering from his leap out of the van. He ignored the pain and kept going until he was right behind the Chrysler. He paused to catch his breath and check for a reaction. None came. Satisfied that he hadn't been spotted, he rolled onto his back and pulled himself under the car. He quickly found a strut that would suit his purpose. He reached into his pocket, pulled out the tracker, and taped it to the strut.

He was almost done when he felt a small weight shift in the car, which was followed by the click of an opening door. He turned his head sideways, to the passenger side of the car, and froze as he saw first one foot, then the other, drop to the ground, faintly illuminated by the cabin's inside light. They crunched into the snow, and the light dimmed as the man swung the door back quietly without clicking it shut.

He felt a surge of panic as a sudden realization hit him. Very slowly, he angled his head sideways to look behind the car and saw the trail he'd left behind in the snow. It led right up to the car, a black streak through the pearlescent shimmer of the light snow cover.

His body tensed up as he watched the man take a few steps. He was heading to the back of the car. Matt's eyes stayed on him, fast-forwarding to the moment the man would spot the trail and what the best move would be. With his heart in his throat, he followed the man's feet around past the rear wheel, farther back to the edge of the car – then they stopped. Every nerve ending in Matt's body throbbed with alarm, and his fingers reached under his coat and tightened against the handle of the lug wrench. He was about to swing his legs out in an attempt to kick the man off-balance when he turned so he was now facing the wall. Matt then heard a zipper open, and his body pulled back from Defcon five as he realized the man was just out there to take a leak.

He waited for him to finish, then watched without moving an inch as the man got back into the car. Matt made sure the tracker was solidly attached, then slid back out from under the car and retreated along the same path he'd taken, only pausing briefly to commit the car's license place to memory.

He found Sanjay standing by the cash register, clearly unable to do much, out of worry.

Matt gave him a firm nod of gratitude as he reached over for a pencil and scribbled down the Chrysler's license plate on a flyer. He tucked it into his pocket, then turned to Sanjay. 'Do me a favor. Anyone asks, you haven't seen me, not since lunchtime. Okay?'

Sanjay nodded. 'You gonna tell me what's going on?'

Matt's expression clouded under competing instincts. 'Better you don't get involved. Safer for you that way.'

Sanjay acknowledged his words somberly, then hesitated and said, 'You'll be careful, won't you?' in an uncertain tone, as if unsure about how much he should say or get involved.

Matt half-smiled. 'That's the plan.' Then he thought of something, took a few steps to the fridge, and pulled out a can of Coke. He held it up to Sanjay and said, 'My tab still good?'

Sanjay visibly relaxed a touch. 'Of course.'

And with that, Matt was gone.

CHAPTER 19

Amundsen Sea, Antarctica

'So what's the verdict? Do we believe this guy?'

Gracie leaned her head against the cold glass of the conference room's window. Outside, the light was virtually unchanged, the sky infused with the same grayish pallor, which didn't help her flagging spirit. She needed to rest, to take a step back and give her mind a chance to reboot, if only for an hour or two. It had to be the equivalent of way past midnight, and the continuous daylight of the Antarctic's austral summer had already wreaked havoc on her body clock, but there were still too many questions that needed to be answered.

'Gracie, come on,' Dalton replied. 'He's talking about Father Jerome.'

'So?'

'Are you kidding me? The guy's a living saint. He's not gonna fake something like this. That'd be like – I don't know – like saying the Dalai Lama's a liar.'

Father Jerome wasn't technically a living saint. There was no such thing, since dying was a prerequisite to receiving the honor of sainthood, at least as far as the Vatican was concerned. But he was pretty much a shoo-in for beatification, if not canonization, at some point in the future.

In his case, though, the term *saint* was more than appropriate.

He'd begun his life in 1949 as Alvaro Suarez, the son of a humble farming couple in the foothills of the Cantabrian Mountains in northern Spain. His youth was far from cosseted. His father died when he was five, leaving his mother with the unenviable task of providing for six children in a Spain that was still under Franco's iron fist and recovering from years of war. Raised a Catholic, the young Alvaro – the youngest of his siblings – showed a great resilience and generosity of character, especially during a harsh winter when a viral epidemic almost took away his mother and two of his sisters. He credited his faith with giving him the strength to forge ahead despite overwhelming odds, and with helping his mother and sisters pull through, and their salvation further solidified his bond with the Church. Throughout his youth, he was also particularly drawn to the stories of missionaries, of selfless souls doing the work of God in the less fortunate corners of the planet, and by the time he was in his teens, he knew he would devote his life to the Church. Having narrowly escaped becoming one himself, he chose to concentrate on helping orphans and abandoned children. He left home at seventeen and began his journey, joining a seminary in Andalusia before crossing into Africa, where he soon founded the first of many missions. En route, he took his first vows a few months short of his twenty-second birthday, choosing the name of Jerome after Jerome Emiliani, a sixteenth-century Italian priest and the patron saint of orphans. The modern Jerome's hospices and orphanages were now scattered across the globe. His army of volunteers had turned around the lives of thousands of the world's poorest children. His charitable work, as it turned out, had even outshone that of the historic figure who inspired him.

Forget the technicalities. The man was indeed a living saint, and Dalton's point was hard to ignore. Provided what the monk had told Gracie really did involve Father Jerome.

'Yeah, but that wasn't Father Jerome on the phone, was it? We don't even know if the caller was really calling from Egypt, much less from the monastery,' she argued.

'Well, we do know Father Jerome is really there,' Finch pointed out.

The reports they'd pulled up after the call confirmed that

Father Jerome was indeed in Egypt. He'd fallen ill while working at one of his missions there, close to the border with Sudan, a little over a year ago. After his recovery, he'd pulled back from active duty – he was just shy of sixty now – only going so far as to say he needed to take some time for himself, "to get closer to God," in his own words. He'd subsequently retreated entirely from public view. Crucially, a couple of brief wire reports did have him traveling north and seeking out the seclusion of the monasteries of Wadi Natrun.

'And how could he actually have drawn what we saw? I mean, how would you draw it?' Gracie argued.

'We need to get a copy of that tape,' Dalton suggested.

Before ending his call, Brother Ameen had offered them a tantalizing piece of corroboration. A British film crew, working for the BBC, had visited the monastery several months earlier. They'd spent a few days there, filming part of a multi-episode documentary that compared the dogmatic approach to faith in Western churches with the more mystical approaches found farther east. They'd managed to get a quick peek inside the cave and shot some footage there, before being turned away by Father Jerome. Brother Ameen assured Gracie it included footage of the priest's handiwork across its ceiling and walls.

It was proof that Gracie desperately needed to see. The problem was, getting hold of it would most likely alert the filmmakers to its significance – something they didn't seem to have clicked to, so far – and Gracie could lose the lead on the story. A story that was still virtually exclusively hers.

She let herself sink into the sofa and heaved a sigh of frustration as she pondered Dalton's suggestion. 'No,' she decided, 'not yet. We can't risk it.'

She looked over at Finch, who nodded. After a moment, he said, 'So what do you want to do?'

Gracie felt the air around her resonating with expectation. Warring sensations were tugging her in opposite directions, but, deep down, she knew that she'd already made the decision before she'd put down the phone.

With a conviction that surprised her, she said, 'I have to go there.' Her eyes danced from Finch to Dalton and back, hoping to find some support.

'I want to believe him,' she explained. 'I mean, look, none of this makes sense, right? But what if it's all real? Can you imagine? If what he's saying is true . . . Jesus.' She sprang to her feet, pacing around now, gesturing with her arms, her decision somehow liberating her, unleashing a surge of energy that was intoxicating. 'I don't know how this happened, I don't know what's really going on here, but, like it or not, we're part of it, we're caught up in something . . . exceptional. And the story's not here anymore. It's in Egypt. It's in that monastery. And that's where I need to be.' She fixed on them fervently. 'I mean, what are we gonna do? We can't stay on this ship forever. We sure as hell can't go home, not while this thing isn't resolved.' She paused, studying them, willing a reaction out of them, then she reiterated, 'The story's in Egypt.'

Finch looked thoughtfully at Dalton, turned back to her, and, after an uncertain, so-pregnant-it-must-be-triplets pause, he smiled.

'Let's do it. Even if it means disappointing the kids. Again.' Finch had two under-tens, a son and a daughter. And although he was divorced, he was still friends with his ex-wife and had been planning to spend Christmas Day with them.

Gracie acknowledged Finch's comment with a sheepish, clenched expression. She knew it would be tough on him. She didn't have that problem. She was single and wasn't seeing anyone special. She wasn't a huge fan of the end-of-year holidays anyway. As a kid, she'd hated them, especially after her mom died. The cold weather, the short days, the passing of another year, one less year of life – it all felt morbid and sad to her. She turned to Dalton. He nodded, his expression pensive but supportive. He was in too.

Gracie beamed back. 'Great.'

'I'll go talk to the captain,' Finch said. 'See how quickly he can get us choppered off this ship. You guys start packing.'

A lesser producer would have debated the point to death before covering his ass by getting his news director's approval. Finch was rock solid, and right now, Gracie was hugely grateful to have him in her corner. He looked at her, as if reading the thoughts written across her face, gave her a nod of unflinching support, then left the room.

She crossed over to the window again and looked out. The shelf was still disintegrating, but the sign was long gone. In her mind's eye, she saw it again, and as she relived the shock and awe it had generated in her, in everyone on that ship, a shiver of doubt crept into her.

Her back still to Dalton, she asked, 'What do you think? Are we making the right call here?'

He joined her at the window. She glanced over at him, and thought she'd rarely seen him wearing such a solemn expression.

'We're talking about Father Jerome,' he said, his voice lacking any traces of uncertainty. 'If you're not going to believe him . . . who are you going to believe?'

CHAPTER 20

Boston, Massachusetts

Matt guided the Mustang back onto the expressway and headed north, toward the city. He was cruising on auto-pilot, without any specific destination in mind, just putting some distance between him and the guys in the Chrysler.

He felt shattered. His brain was all tangled up, and he was having trouble making sense of what had happened since Bellinger called him. After the adrenalin rush from tagging the Chrysler, his body was now crumbling from under him. He needed to rest and think things through, but there were no obvious spots where he could crash out and no one to take him in. No spunky-and-resourceful girlfriend, no reluctantly supportive buddy, no irritable-but-still-smitten ex-wife.

He was on his own.

He rode up the expressway for a while, then drifted onto the South Station off-ramp and ended up at a fifties-style diner on the corner of Kneeland, the only place in town that he knew would be open this late.

He looked like a real mess and drew a couple of contemptuous glances as he stepped inside, which wasn't ideal. The last thing he needed right now was to get noticed. He disappeared into the men's room and cleaned himself up as best he could, then grabbed a stool at the far end of the bar. He ordered himself a coffee and decided to add on a cheeseburger, not knowing when he'd have a chance to eat in peace again, and hoping the caffeine-and-protein boost would help carry him through until daybreak.

Although his body still ached from his fall, the food and the coffee helped clear his mind. He asked the waitress for a refill and sifted through his options. He didn't hold out much hope of being able to do anything to help Bellinger. It seemed pretty clear to him that the hit team that came after them were connected to whatever had happened to Danny, and they weren't messing around. He was facing pros with serious resources and no inhibitions, and his options were limited, especially given that he didn't really know much beyond the cryptic words Bellinger had left him with – and the idea that Danny could still be alive. If he was going to get anyone to help him – the press, maybe even the cops, he wasn't sure who at this point – he needed to know more about what was going on. He could think of two threads to tug. One was the tracker. The other was Bellinger. Or, more accurately, whatever it was that Bellinger knew that put him in their crosshairs. His heart sank at the thought of the harmless scientist, his brother's buddy, and the dire situation he must now be in, and he seethed with frustration at not being able to do something about it.

Not yet, anyway.

He needed to check the tracker's position, and he also wanted to see what he could find at Bellinger's place. And for both lines of attack, he needed to go online.

By now, it was well past midnight, and hotel business centers were the only option at this hour. He asked his waitress and got directions to a nearby Best Western, raided an ATM three doors down from the diner, and pulled into the hotel's parking lot fifteen minutes later.

The business center by the soulless lobby was open all night, but it was restricted to hotel guests. Given that his home was off-limits for the time being, the idea of a safe bed and a hot shower had its merits, so he gave the receptionist a fake name, took a single, and paid in cash. He was soon ensconced at a workstation with a high-speed connection pumping information to his screen.

He logged onto the tracker's website and checked its position. Having been a car thief, he appreciated the value of trackers more than anyone, especially when it came to covetable, high-value classics like his Bullitt Mustang. Right now, he was more grateful than ever for having it. The contract he'd taken out had the tracker set up to transmit its location every thirty seconds when the car it was attached to was on the move. It would hibernate and ping its location once every twelve hours if the car was stationary. Assuming the car wasn't spending a lot of time on the road, the tracker's battery would normally last around three weeks between recharges, only Matt was pretty sure it was near the end of that cycle and running low on juice. It probably wouldn't last more than a few days before conking out.

It hadn't moved. Which was both good and bad. If the goons were still there, it meant they weren't on his tail, but then again, it also meant they weren't giving up easily. He moved on and trawled the online white pages for Bellinger's home address, which he found with ease. Clearly, Bellinger wasn't too fussy about his privacy, though it was frightening how much information one could find about anyone online. It was over in Inman Square, a trendy, upmarket enclave in neighboring Cambridge that Matt had visited a few times. Danny had lived there too, right up to his disappearance, Matt thought, preferring the sound of that to the words he would have used before tonight: his death. At this hour, it was only a quick hop there. One that couldn't wait.

Matt jotted down the address and was about to log off when he thought of something else. He Googled 'Antarctica' and 'sky' and 'news' and let the billion-dollar algorithms do their thing. He hadn't taxed them too hard. Almost instantly, they presented him with over a million hits. The first page was dominated by news reports about a huge ice shelf breaking off, and Matt clicked on the first link, the one of the Sky news channel, and read through the report.

It was less than enlightening. He sat back and digested it, perplexed as to how it could possibly be linked to Danny or lead to the vicious reaction that targeted Bellinger. He re-read it and was none the wiser, and was about to get up when a link below the article caught his eye. It mentioned an 'unexplained sighting' on the frozen continent. He clicked on it, and it took him to a related article that had an accompanying, YouTube-like video clip.

This one had more bite.

He felt a tightening at the back of his neck as he read the report and watched the short video of the reporter and the apparition over the ice shelf. He re-read the report and viewed the clip a second time, his face flickering with confusion. He dug deeper and initiated a new search, and got a geyser of hits related to the unexplained sighting, and as he skimmed through them and let the implications they debated sink in, a grim realization dropped further into the roiling pit of his stomach.

This was no small event.

If Danny was somehow involved in it – *against his will,* Bellinger had insinuated, though Matt couldn't even begin to imagine what his involvement could have been – then the stakes were much higher than Matt had imagined.

Minutes later, the Mustang was crossing the Longfellow Bridge and veering onto Broadway, a lone car gliding across the desolate cityscape. There was a stark beauty to the stillness around him, but Matt didn't feel any of it. His mind was swirling with wild theories, and with them came an increasingly uncomfortable feeling, a sense of a sinister malignancy closing in on him.

He tried to stay focused as he made his way to the intersection with Fayette and a three-story Victorian house that matched Bellinger's address. He did a precautionary drive-by, looped back on himself a couple of blocks up the street, and cruised past the house again for another look. It had stopped snowing, and the neighborhood was now huddled under a couple of inches of white frosting. The lights of a lone Christmas tree blinked out of a bay window on the ground floor, but otherwise, the rest of the building was dark, and the street seemed equally comatose. He also noticed that the snow outside the house was undisturbed.

He pulled into a small alley that separated the house from the similar, slightly larger one next door, and switched off the throaty V-8 – not the most discreet of engines. He waited a moment to make doubly sure he was alone, then climbed out of the car. Everything around him was eerily quiet, the air cold and torpid under a moon that shone more brightly now that it wasn't filtered by a veil of snow. He rummaged through his glove box and found what he needed, his trusted Leatherman multi-tool and a small, stiff piece of wire, and pocketed them, then climbed out of the car, pulled up his collar, and walked briskly over to the house's front porch.

The labels on its buzzer showed three occupants, which matched the number of floors – one apartment per floor. Bellinger's name was on top, which Matt took to mean that he had the penthouse. The lock on the communal entrance didn't pose too much of a challenge. It was a five-pin tumbler, a standard household lock that was surprisingly easy to pick, even without his preferred tools for such a job – a pair of paper clips. Getting past the lock on the door to Bellinger's place, up the stairs and on the third floor, was equally effortless. Matt had had way too much practice over the years.

Easing the door closed behind him, he slipped in quietly without turning the lights on, his eyes quickly adjusting to the darkness. He stepped deeper into the apartment, wishing he had a flashlight. The small entrance hall opened up to twin, open-plan living and dining rooms with a two-sided gas fireplace between them, its mantelpiece lined with a dozen or so Christmas cards. Moonlight bathed the wide, bay-windowed space with a delicate, silvery sheen that ushered him farther in. He advanced carefully, all senses on high alert. He spotted an upright halogen lamp with a dimmer switch in a near corner, by a large leather couch and away from the windows, and decided it wouldn't be too visible from the outside on a low setting. He chanced it, barely turning it up. The dimmer buzzed slightly as the lamp suffused the room in a faint, yellowish gleam.

The room was impeccably arranged and ordered. A sleek, glass-and-chrome desk faced a wall on the opposite side of the room, away from the window. Matt angled across to it. It was covered with neat piles of newspapers, books, magazines, printouts, and unopened mail. The clutter of a busy professional with an inquisitive mind. Matt spotted a small box of Bellinger's business cards, picked one up, and pocketed it. He could see that something was prominently missing from the man's desk. A computer. A large flat screen was still there, as was an orphaned docking station for a laptop, and a wireless mouse. The laptop itself was, it seemed, gone.

Had they been here already?

Matt tensed up and gave the room another scan, his ears now listening intently for the slightest disturbance. They wouldn't have had any trouble getting in. They had Bellinger, which meant they had his keys. He thought about it for a beat. If they had been here, they were probably already long gone. It had been maybe three hours since he and their van had parted company.

Still, he had to be sure.

With an even lighter step, he crept across the hallway and checked the rooms at the back of the apartment. He found two bedrooms, one a large master suite overlooking the side street and the back, the other smaller and sparsely furnished, both empty. He checked the bathrooms, also clear. He relaxed a touch and made his way back to the living room, where a blinking light on a coffee table caught his eye. It came from the base unit of a cordless phone that had waiting messages – just one of them, according to its LED display.

He clicked the playback button. An androgynous, digital voice informed Matt that the message came in at 12:47 a.m., which piqued Matt's interest. People didn't normally get calls at that hour.

'Dude, where the hell did you disappear to?' a hyper voice on the machine quizzed. 'What's going on? You're not home, you're not picking up your cell. Come on, pick up the damn phone, will ya? This thing's gathering some serious mass. The blogs are going loco over it, you gotta see this. Anyway, call me back. I'm staying locked on the news in case it decides to make another appearance. Call me, or . . . whatever. I'll see you at the ranch tomorrow.' He sounded deflated before he hung up.

Matt grabbed a pen, picked up the handset, and hit star-69. Another digital voice recited the caller's number to him. It was local. As he wrote it down on the back of Bellinger's business card, a faint noise intruded at the edge of his hearing, a car pulling up outside the building, shortly followed by the dull thuds of car doors closing.

He crossed to the window, but the crackle of brief radio transmissions told him what it was before he peered out and saw the two men walking away from an unmarked sedan and disappearing into the building.

Coming to check out Bellinger's place.

Which meant one of two things.

Either they were more goons, on the same payroll as the guys who'd stuffed him into their van, or they were plainclothes cops and Bellinger's body had already turned up.

Matt could just imagine how that one would play out.

He flinched as the entry phone in Bellinger's apartment buzzed, then sprinted to the front door and cracked it open. He waited, listening intently, his heartbeat thudding in his ears, then it buzzed again, this one longer, more impatient.

The buzzing seemed to confirm the latter scenario. The hit team had Bellinger, meaning they had Bellinger's keys.

They wouldn't need to ring up. Matt felt the blood seep from his face, and a crippling sense of further unreality swept through him as he pictured what might have happened to Bellinger. He waited by the door, his mind racing through possible outcomes, none of which seemed promising.

The entry phone stayed ominously silent.

He decided to take another look, and leaving the door slightly ajar, he scuttled back to the bay window and peeked out.

He could see the two men standing by their car, which he could now tell was a standard issue Crown Vic. One of them was on his cell phone, but Matt couldn't hear what he was saying. Matt relaxed somewhat. They came, they buzzed, no answer, they'd leave. Or so he hoped. Then he saw the other man cock his head toward the entrance, as if reacting to something, before disappearing under the porch again.

Matt's instincts sharpened. He slipped back to the door and, very quietly, picked up the entry phone's handset. He came in mid-conversation.

'—on the second floor,' a woman's voice was explaining. 'Bellinger's got the penthouse directly over me.' She hesitated, then asked, 'Is everything okay?'

The man ignored her question and asked her, 'Does Mr. Bellinger live alone, ma'am?'

Does, Matt thought, for a second. Not *Did*. Present tense. Maybe Bellinger was all right.

The cheery thought was quickly overruled. The guys in the van hadn't looked like they were kidding. Bellinger was dead, he knew it. Why else would these guys be here? Why would they be asking if he lived alone?

The woman's voice had a nervous quaver to it. 'Yes, I think so. I mean, he's single. I don't think he lives with anyone. But I'm surprised he's not picking up. I'm pretty sure he's home.'

Her comment struck Matt like a bucket of ice water.

'What makes you say that?' the man asked, his voice snapping to attention.

'Well, I heard him come back. These are old houses, and even with the refurb, the floorboards have this creak in them that's always there, and I can hear him coming in and out, especially when it's late and it's quiet outside—'

'Ma'am,' the man interrupted abruptly, clearly impatient.

'I think he came in earlier,' she said with more urgency, 'and then he went out again. But then he came back.'

'When did you hear him come in?'

'Not long ago. Ten minutes, maybe? He should be upstairs.'

Matt's nerves went haywire.

He heard the man's tone take on a much harder edge as he ordered the woman, 'I need you to let us in, ma'am, right now,' followed by a shout to his partner and the distinct sound of the entrance door snapping open.

Seconds later, heavy footfalls were charging up the stairs.

CHAPTER 21

Amundsen Sea, Antarctica

Gracie's stomach fluttered as she watched Dalton rise off the deck of the royal research ship. Unlike the *Shackleton,* its stablemate, the *James Clark Ross* wasn't endowed with a helipad. Transfers at sea could only be made by winching passengers to and from a hovering chopper. Which, in sub-zero weather and with a gargantuan wall of ice collapsing a few hundred yards away, wasn't for the fainthearted.

It was now six hours since the sign had first appeared. After their extended, high-definition clip was broadcast and carried by the other channels, the news had simply exploded. It was all over the news updates, splashed across the world's TV screens, and on every Internet news site. Armies of reporters and pundits were talking about it, wondering about it, offering wild theories. People across America and in the rest of the world were being interviewed and asked what they thought the sightings meant. As expected, some of the responses were glib and dismissive, but most people were seriously intrigued. And it was still the middle of the night across North America. Most people there were asleep. The next day, Gracie knew, was when the real frenzy would begin. Her satphone hadn't stopped ringing with requests for interviews and comments, and her inbox was also flooded.

Across every channel, every news network, one expert after another was being wheeled in to try and explain it. Physicists, climatologists, all kinds of scientists, dragged in from every corner of the planet. None of them had a clue. They couldn't offer any remotely convincing insight into how or why it was happening, and while that excited some people, it also scared a lot of them. The religious pundits were faring better. Faith was one explanation that didn't carry the burden of proof. Priests, rabbis, and muftis were voicing their thoughts on the sign with increasing candor. On one clip that Gracie had watched, a Baptist pastor was asked what he thought about it. He replied that people of faith everywhere were watching it very closely, and wondered if there was anything other than the divine to explain it. It was a view that several other interviewees also expressed – and that perspective was gaining ground. Faith, not science, was where the true explanation lay. The thought consumed Gracie as she strained against the downdraft from the Lynx's powerful rotor and shielded her eyes to watch Dalton's slow ascent. A small smile cracked across her face as he waved to her from above, coaxing a wave back. Consummate filmmaker that he was, he held a small camcorder in one hand, capturing every hair-raising moment.

She noticed Finch turn, and followed his gaze to see the ship's captain join them. He looked up, taking stock of the transfers' progress, which had to be swiftly executed, as they were already at the edge of the helicopter's operating range, even with its additional fuel tanks, then turned to Finch and Gracie.

'I got a call from someone at the Pentagon,' he informed them, shouting to be heard against the deafening rotor wash.

Gracie glanced over at Finch, both of them visibly and suddenly on edge.

'They wanted me to make sure no one left the ship before their people got here,' the captain added. 'You in particular,' he specified, pointing his finger at Gracie.

She felt a paralysis of worry. 'What did you tell them?'

The captain grinned. 'I said we were in the middle of nowhere and I didn't think anyone was going anywhere for the time being.'

Gracie breathed out in relief. 'Thanks,' she said and beamed at him.

The captain shrugged it off. 'It wasn't even a request. It was more like an order. And I don't remember signing up for anyone's army.' His words were laced with bemused indignation. 'I'll expect you to kick up a big stink if they ship me off to Guantánamo.'

Gracie smiled. 'You've got it.'

He glanced overhead at the chopper, then leaned in closer. 'We're also getting flooded with requests from journalists and reporters from all over the place. I'm thinking we should seriously bump up our room rate and rake in some cash.'

'What are you telling them?' Finch asked.

He shrugged. 'We've hung up a no vacancy sign for the moment.'

'They'll keep asking,' Gracie told him, 'if they're any good at what they do.'

'I know,' the captain said, 'and it's hard to say no, but this is a research ship. I don't want to turn it into a Carnival cruise. Trouble is, we're the only ones out here. The only other ships within a couple hundred miles are a Japanese whaler and the Greenpeace vessel that's hounding it, and I don't think either of them's in a particularly hospitable mood.' His deep-set, clear eyes twinkled mischievously at Gracie. 'Looks like it's still your exclusive.'

She smiled back, the gratitude evident in her expression. 'What can I say? I must be blessed.'

'I'm kind of surprised you're in such a rush to get off my ship while everyone else seems so desperate to get on,' the captain queried with playful, barely disguised suspicion.

Gracie glanced at Finch; then, without trying too hard to throw their host off the trail, she grinned and told him, 'That's what makes us the best damn investigative reporting team in the business. Always one step ahead of the story.'

As if to rescue her from the uncomfortable moment, the harness appeared again, and a crewmember helped Gracie strap herself into it. Once she was safely locked in, he waved to the winch operator in the chopper, and the slack in the cable began to tighten up.

'Thanks again, for everything,' she yelled to the captain, emphasizing the last word in reference to Finch's request that he keep their departure under wraps. He'd graciously agreed, without asking questions, and she felt a slight pang of guilt at not being able to share the whole story behind their hasty exit with him.

He flicked her a small parting wave. 'It's been our pleasure. Just let us know what you find out there,' he added with a telling wink. 'We'll be watching.'

Before she could react, the cable went taut, yanking her into the ice-speckled air. She breathlessly watched the ship recede beneath her, dreading the marathon journey ahead and the uncertain reward awaiting her at its end.

CHAPTER 22

West Antarctic Ice Sheet

The four ghosts on the ice shelf stayed low and watched as the Royal Navy chopper glided over the ship, just under half a mile west of their position.

They weren't worried about being spotted. Their gear would more than take care of that. They just lay there, hugging the packed snow, invisible in their full 'snow white' camouflage parkas and pants, faces hidden behind white balaclavas, eyes and mouths peeking out from unsettling round openings. Even the soles of their boots, which they scrubbed down every morning before heading into action, were white. Four snowmobiles, also white and without markings, squatted nearby. Hidden under white camouflage netting, they were also virtually undetectable from the sky.

The team leader monitored the chopper through his high-powered binoculars as it lifted the last of the news crew off the ship. A hint of a smile of satisfaction flitted across his chapped lips. Things were going as planned. Which wasn't a given, considering how tight the timing had been and how frantic the deployment of his unit had been.

The operation had gone live four days earlier. They'd left their training camp in North Carolina and flown to Christchurch in New Zealand, where an Air National Guard C-17 Globemaster had been waiting on the tarmac to whisk them down to the National Science Foundation's McMurdo Station, on the ice continent's Ross Island. From there, an LC-130 Hercules aircraft fitted with skis had ferried them to an isolated staging area on the ice shelf itself, fifteen miles south of their current position. Snowmobiles that they'd flown in with them had carried them on the last leg of their thirteen-thousand-mile journey.

The extreme change of climate and the travel through multiple time zones were brutal and would have debilitated most people, but it didn't affect them. They'd trained extensively for this operation and knew what to expect.

To say the job was a high-value, priority-one assignment was underselling it, big-time. He'd never experienced anything quite as intense, nor as uncompromising, as the rigorous interview process and psychological profiling he'd undergone before getting the job. Once that was settled, no expense had been spared in either the training facilities or the gear that was made available to him and his team. The client clearly didn't have budget issues. Then again, a lot of the firm's clients were governments – the U.S. government being its biggest – and they could usually afford what the job requirements would dictate.

In this case, however, it was clear to the team leader that the stakes were higher than on any of his previous assignments. Beirut, Bosnia, Afghanistan, then Iraq – he now saw those frenzied, violent years as mere stepping-stones. They'd led him here, to being selected to lead this unit.

It was, without a doubt, the gig of a lifetime.

And now, after all the preparation and after an interminable wait, it was finally under way. He'd started to think it would never happen. After completing their training, he and the rest of the small team of 'contractors' – the spin-speak name always made him smirk, but he was more than happy to avoid the disdain associated with the more accurate 'mercenary' label – had been put on standby. They'd waited for the go signal for months. The team leader didn't like getting paid to sit still. It wasn't his style. Like the others in his squad, he was ex-Force Recon, the U.S. Marines' equivalent to the Navy's SEALs or the Army's Delta Force. *Swift, Silent, Deadly,* the Force Recon motto, didn't exactly apply to sitting around watching endless hours of TV in isolated, if comfortable barracks. The world out there – misguided, tyrannized, *evil* – was waiting.

Something in his pack warbled. He glanced at his watch. The call was expected.

He checked on the chopper's position again. It was banking away in a wide arc. He pulled out his satellite phone, a tiny Iridium handset. It was no bigger than a regular cell phone, if not for the ten-inch antenna that pivoted out from it and the STU-III voice encryption module clipped onto its base. He pressed the answer key. A sequence of beeps mixed with static told him the call was bouncing its way halfway across the planet. He waited for the red LED to tell him the call was secure, then spoke.

'This is Fox One.'

After the briefest of lags, a computerized male voice responded. 'What's your status?'

It sounded like Stephen Hawking was calling, and he knew his own voice sounded just as robotic at the other end. Although he and the project's overseer had dodged bullets together on more than one continent, the military-level, 256-bit voice encryption made their voices unrecognizable, in case someone was eavesdropping. Which was unlikely enough, but one could never be too careful, which was also why a second safeguard was built into his phone's microchip, enabling a hybrid of hopping and sweeping scrambling. Only another phone fitted with the same chip could decode their transmissions. Any other phone would only pick up a burst of ear-piercing static.

'We're ready to roll,' Fox One replied.

'Any problems I should know about?'

'Negative.'

The synthesized voice came back. 'Good. Pull your men out and initiate the next phase.'

The team leader terminated the call and glanced up at the sky. It was back to its monotone, off-white, bleak self again.

Not a trace, he mused. *Perfect.*

CHAPTER 23

Cambridge, Massachusetts

Matt slipped the phone back into its cradle and eased the door shut before darting through the hallway and into the main bedroom.

He had to get the hell out of there. They were only seconds away.

He ignored the near window in the bedroom and went straight to the back wall where, in the pale moonlight coming in through the window, he'd earlier spotted a half-glazed door that gave on to a ten-foot-square balcony. With his heartbeat throbbing in his ears, he peered out and saw that, as he'd suspected, it led to a fire escape.

He joggled the door handle, but it was locked. He looked left and right for a key, but there was nothing in plain sight. He pulled and yanked at it again, a hopeless, desperate gesture, the door stubbornly refusing to budge, then was glancing back toward the hallway, his brain tripping wildly, like the ever-accelerating countdown of a time bomb, wondering how much time he still had, visualizing the two men bursting into the apartment, when a heavy knock pounded the front door.

'Open up, police.'

He didn't want to get caught in there. He was sure Bellinger was dead, and here he was, in his apartment, an apartment he'd broken into, the apartment of a dead man who was last seen running away from him after they'd had a bust-up in a crowded bar.

A slam-dunk with any jury – if it ever got to that.

Somehow, he didn't think he'd make it that far.

His reflexes took over.

He grabbed a side table by the bed, swung it back, and

hurled it through the window of the balcony door. Glass exploded as the heavy wooden console flew out and thudded heavily onto the decked floor. The posse outside the door must have heard it, as a more pointed shout of 'Open up, police' echoed from the stairwell, a shout with a distinct finality to it. Matt dashed across the room, only he didn't go for the balcony. Instead, he scurried in the opposite direction, away from it, and dived behind the door to the bedroom just as the front door erupted inward.

Two men thundered in, quickly got their bearings, and charged into the master bedroom, rocketing up to the shattered balcony door. Matt squeezed himself tightly against the wall and heard one of them yell, 'He's gone down the fire escape,' adding, 'Check out the rest of the place' while using the muzzle of his handgun to sweep away the shards of glass that stuck up from the window frame, before clambering over and disappearing into the darkness outside. His partner darted past Matt, and just as he felt him go by, Matt slipped out from his hiding place and launched himself after him.

The man was halfway through the dark hallway when Matt tackled him from behind. They tumbled onto the hardwood floor, spilling over each other, something metallic clattering across the floor away from the downed cop. A handgun, by the sound of it. The man wasn't too tall or bulky, but his thin arms had a fierce, coiled energy within them and he fought back like a caged mongoose, twisting around and lashing out with rapid-fire blows to try and get out from under Matt. Matt knew he didn't have time on his side and had to end this fast. He weathered a couple of sacrificial blows to his ribs to set up an opening for a solid hit, then saw one and let loose with an anvil of a punch that caught the downed man just below the left ear and pounded the air out of him. The man curled over, groaning heavily. Matt used the brief respite to roll him back onto his front and felt something under his jacket. He reached under it and found a pair of handcuffs in a belt pouch. He pulled the groggy man a couple of feet to the wall and quickly locked his arms around a radiator pipe. A quick glance around yielded a coat rack overhead that held some jackets, caps, an umbrella, and a scarf that Matt yanked down and stuffed into the man's mouth before roping it around his head a couple of times and tucking it in to secure it in place.

Without even glancing back, he sprang to his feet and flew out of the apartment, hurtling down the stairs three at a time. He plowed to a sudden stop at the main entrance to check out front. There was no sign of the man who'd gone down the fire escape. He took a deep breath to clear his senses, steeled himself for the move, and slipped out into the cold night.

The street was disconcertingly quiet, oblivious to his plight. He scuttled down the steps and crept over to the parked sedan, pulling out his Leatherman and slashing one of the car's front wheels with its blade. He watched for a split second as its air rushed out, then leapt over the small picket fence by the pathway that led up to the house and skirted the front façade, avoiding the sidewalk and scanning ahead and back until he reached the alley.

The Mustang was still there, squatting in the shadows, waiting for him. He slid into it as quietly as he could, and pulled the door half-shut. With his breathing still coming short and fast, he spurred the engine to life without switching on the headlights, and just as it ticked over, the other cop appeared at the mouth of the alley, behind him, backlit by the streetlights. He hollered, 'Stop, police,' reaching for his handgun and holding his other arm up, palm out and flat. He was blocking the way, leaving Matt no way out but to back out and charge him, risking a game of chicken that could end really badly for the one of them who wasn't cocooned inside two tons of steel. It was either that, or –

Matt cursed under his breath, slammed the car into gear,

and floored it. The Mustang's wheels spun slightly in the thin snow cover before biting into the asphalt, and the car leapt forward, howling angrily through the alley, rushing deeper into its dark recess. Matt strained to see where he was headed, what waited for him at the end of the alley, and when it finally came into view, it wasn't good. The alley ended in a mound of bushy terrain that rose into a thicket of trees. A Hummer might have had a chance. The Mustang wasn't built for this. It didn't have a hope in hell of making it through.

He slammed hard on the brake pedal, the Mustang sliding to a halt at the edge of the asphalt, the engine purring in anticipation, waiting to be unleashed again. He glanced in his rearview mirror. He could see the shadowy silhouette of the cop coming at him, weapon raised.

Matt was out of options. He ground down on his teeth and slammed the car into reverse. The car lurched, thundering through the alley – *backward* – its V-8 roaring angrily. Matt hugged the passenger headrest as he steered the car, riding virtually blind. In the best of light conditions, the fastback didn't have the greatest visibility through its rear windshield, and here, in the dark and narrow alleyway, with only the Mustang's feeble reversing light to guide him, all he could do was keep the car in a straight line and hope for the best – hope he could avoid the walls, and hope the cop didn't have a death wish. He stayed as low as he could, tensing up while awaiting the inevitable gunshots, and sure enough, a shot reverberated in the narrow space, followed by several more, one of them drilling through the rear windshield and slamming into the passenger headrest, another pinging off the A-pillar somewhere to his right.

Within a heartbeat, he was almost at the cop's level. Matt twitched the steering wheel to angle the car right up against the wall closest to him, across from where the cop was firing. The Mustang shuddered and squealed furiously as it scraped the side of the house, and with the cop flattening himself against the opposite wall, Matt managed to thread it through without hitting him. More shots followed him as he bounced out of the alley and onto the main road, where he hit the hand brake, spun the car so it was aimed right, and powered away.

He glanced in his mirror and saw the cop emerge into the street and rush to his car, but Matt knew he wouldn't be following him. Still, he wasn't in the clear. An APB concerning his less-than-low-key car would be heating up the airwaves any second now. He had to ditch the car – quickly – and lie low until dawn.

What he'd do the next day, though, was far less certain. He still had the rest of the night to get through first.

CHAPTER 24

Washington, D.C.

Keenan Drucker felt electric. He was well rested, having managed to tear himself away from surfing the news channels and the Internet soon after midnight and get a decent night's sleep. In the morning, over a hearty breakfast of waffles and fruit, he'd gone through the newspapers with quiet satisfaction, something he hadn't felt for years. A feeling he hoped he'd be able to build on as the day wore on.

Presently, sitting in his tenth-floor office on Connecticut Avenue, he pivoted in his plush leather chair, away from his wide desk – nihilistic in its lack of clutter, with nothing on it except for a laptop, a phone, and a framed photograph of his deceased son – and looked out across the city. He loved being in the nation's capital, working there, playing a role in shaping the lives of the citizens of the most powerful country on the planet – and, by extension, the lives of the rest of the world's inhabitants. It was all he'd ever done. He'd begun working his way up the system soon after leaving Johns Hopkins with a master's in political science. He'd spent the next twenty-odd years as a congressional staff member, serving as senior policy advisor and legislative director to a couple of senators. He'd helped them grow in prominence and power while ensuring his own rise in stature, working quietly, behind the scenes, shunning the more visible positions that were constantly on offer – although he'd flirted with taking on that of undersecretary of defense for policy when it had been offered. He preferred the continuity afforded by pulling the strings from behind the curtain, and only left the Hill after an offer that was too good to turn down came in, giving him the opportunity to create and run a well-funded, far-reaching think tank of his own, the Center for American Freedom.

He was made for this life. He was a ruthless and imaginative political strategist, he had a mind like a steel trap, and his appetite for detail, combined with a prodigious memory, made him a master of procedure. And as if that weren't enough, his effectiveness was further enhanced by an easygoing, gregarious charm – one that masked the iron resolve underneath and helped when one was a dedicated polemicist ready to take on the red-button issues that were splitting the country.

The last few years, though, had instilled a new sense of urgency within him. Groups of civilian advisors had firmly gripped the reins of policy – both domestic and foreign – and steered the country to their vision. Their unapologetic, unbridled sense of mission was, to a political animal like Drucker, a thing of beauty; their methods and tactics, breathtaking.

Most impressive, he thought, was their use of 'framing' – the cunning technique of dumbing down complex, controversial issues and policies by using powerful, evocative, emotive catchphrases and images in order to prejudice and undermine any potential challenge to those policies. Framing had been elevated to a fine art in the new century, with deceptive expressions like 'tax relief,' 'war on terror,' and 'appeaser' now firmly embedded in the public psyche, pushing the right emotional buttons and creating a misguided belief that anyone who argued against such measures had to be, by definition, a villain trying to stop the innocent sufferers' champion from giving them their medication, a coward shying away from a full-blown war against an aggressor nation, or – even worse – one too spineless to stand up to Hitler.

Framing worked. No one knew that as well as Keenan Drucker. And he was now ready to do some framing of his own.

He checked his watch. A late-morning meeting had been hastily scheduled with the available senior fellows of the Center to discuss the unexplained apparition over the ice shelf. He'd already spoken to several of them by phone, and they were – understandably – as excited as they were unsettled.

After that, he'd monitor the news channels to check on the project's status. Which seemed well on track, apart from that small complication in Boston. Drucker wasn't worried. He could trust the Bullet to take care of it.

His BlackBerry pinged. The ring tag told him it was the Bullet.

As he reached for his phone, Drucker smiled. *Speak* – in this case, *think* – *of the devil* rarely had a more appropriate or literal embodiment.

With his habitual curt efficiency, Maddox updated Drucker on Vince Bellinger's fate, Matt Sherwood's subsequent escape, and his foray into the now-dead scientist's apartment.

Drucker had absorbed the information with admirable detachment. Maddox didn't like much about Drucker. The man was a politician, after all. A Washington insider. But he liked that about him. Drucker didn't question or second-guess when it came to matters in which he was no expert. He didn't have any ego issues, nor did he assume the annoying air of superiority Maddox had often seen – and enjoyed deflating – in deskbound executives and, even more so, in politicians. Drucker knew to leave the dirty work to those who were comfortable trudging through the muck, something Maddox had never shied away from, and still didn't, even though his 'security and risk management' firm had grown healthily since he first founded it three years ago, not long after he'd been wounded in Iraq.

Maddox was a hands-on kind of guy. He had a tough, single-minded work ethic, an unwavering discipline forged out of a twenty-year career with the Marines and their Force

Recon outfit, where he'd initially earned the sobriquet 'The Bullet' because of his shaved, slightly pointed head. It was a name that took on an even more disturbing connotation after his squad was cut to bits in a savage firefight in the apocalyptic town of Fallujah.

The tragedy that had first brought him and Drucker together and united them.

His unit had been doing good work in the mountains of Afghanistan. Hitting the Taliban and their Al Qaeda buddies hard. Weeding them out of the mountains and caves across the border from Pakistan. Closing in on Bin Laden. Then, frustratingly and inexplicably, they'd been pulled out and reassigned. To Iraq. And nine months into that war, Maddox lost fourteen men and an ear that horrific afternoon. Those who'd survived that attack had left arms, legs, or fingers behind. The word *wounded* rarely conveyed the horror of their injuries – or the permanent, crippling effect on their lives. It was a day Maddox remembered every time he caught a glimpse of his hideous self reflected in a windowpane or a colleague's sunglasses. It was branded on his face, a star-shaped burn that spread out from the small, mangled flap of ear skin that the surgeons had been able to salvage.

He hated looking in the mirror. He relived that day every time he caught a glimpse of himself. Not just that day, but the aftermath. The inquests. The way his superiors had let him down. The way he'd been mistreated and spat out by the system. And if that wasn't bad enough, he then found out he'd been lied to. The whole country had. The war was a sham. A catastrophic sham. And then, to add insult to injury – literally – he watched as the same lying bastards who'd sent him to war, from the lowliest congressman to a war hero who'd come close to becoming president, were voting against funding increases for those who, like him, had come home with debilitating physical and mental injuries. He watched as soldiers were hauled in, tried for every minor trespass of the rules of engagement, and sacrificed for political expediency by men who'd never been within a hundred miles of a firefight. And with each new revelation about the lies and manipulations behind the war – the ones that had cost his buddies their lives, and him his face – he got angrier. More bitter. More vindictive. And out of the anger and the bitterness came a realization that he had to take matters into his own hands if he was going to change anything.

His wounded status made it easier for him to set up shop. Before long, he had dozens of highly trained, properly equipped men on his payroll, working for him in the hellholes of Afghanistan, Iraq, or anywhere else people were paying him to send them. Doing jobs that no one else wanted to touch. Jobs no one wanted to be seen doing. Jobs where they weren't subject to arbitrary rules drawn up by politicians sipping twenty-year-old Cognac. And somehow, with each new job, he found more solace, more satisfaction. It became a revenge fix he couldn't live without. And despite the hundreds of thousands of dollars in government contracts and fees his little operation was pulling in, despite having a small army of trusted, battle-hardened men ready and able to do whatever he asked them to do, he was still out there, on the front line, with them. And when this job came up, he immediately realized it was one he couldn't delegate. To be doing it was satisfying on a whole different level.

If this thing could really achieve what they thought it could, then he sure as hell was going to make sure nothing went wrong.

Still, Drucker didn't sound thrilled by his news.

'I'm not comfortable with Sherwood out there, running around,' Drucker told him. 'You need to put him away before it gets out of hand.'

'Shouldn't take long,' Maddox assured him. 'He's a murder suspect. He doesn't have too many options.'

'Let me know when it's taken care of,' Drucker concluded, before ending the call.

Maddox set his phone down on his desk and stewed on the night's events. Matt Sherwood had proven far more resilient than his brother. They were clearly cut from a different cloth, something Maddox had already known, given Matt's record. All of which necessitated a more concerted approach.

His men were monitoring police communications, but that wasn't enough. Matt Sherwood was taking impulsive, unexpected initiatives like breaking into Bellinger's apartment. Unexpected initiatives that could prove to be a major nuisance.

Maddox cleared his mind and put himself in Matt's shoes, replaying every step the ex-con had taken, trying to get a better feel for the way Matt thought. He extrapolated ahead, looking for the straws Matt would be grasping at, straws he needed to cut down before Matt got to them. He thought back to the reports his men had called in and decided to plow that field.

He turned to his screen and brought up the phone logs of all the peripherals linked to Bellinger and to Matt. His eye settled on the last entry – the phone call from a coworker of Bellinger's by the name of Csaba Komlosy. He clicked on the small icon by the entry and listened to the phone call, a message left on Bellinger's home phone. He listened to it a second time, then went back and listened to the first call between the two scientists. The one that had precipitated the previous evening's confrontations.

The Bullet checked his watch and picked up his phone.

CHAPTER 25

Boston, Massachusetts

Larry Rydell stared blankly at his BlackBerry's screen for a moment before setting it down on his desk. He'd just gotten off the phone with Rebecca. Again. Two calls from his daughter in less than twenty-four hours. Far more than he was used to. They were close, for sure, despite his divorce from her mother almost a decade earlier. But Rebecca was nineteen. She was wild and fabulous and free, in her second year at Brown, and although surprisingly grounded for someone with the world at her feet, regular phone calls to Daddy had – as expected – been increasingly crowded out of the whirlwind of activity that her life had become.

He loved chatting with her. Loved seeing her so excited, so enthralled, so curious about something, even with the undercurrent of fear in her bubbly voice. Loved hearing from her twice a day.

But he hated lying to her.

And he had. Twice now, in less than a day. And, no doubt, he'd have to go on lying to her – if all went well, for the rest of his life.

He felt a small tearing inside at the realization, then the tear widened as the bigger picture of what was going on hit him again.

It's really happening.

It was out there now. There was no turning back.

The thought terrified and elated him in equal measure.

It had all seemed so surreal when he'd first considered the possibility, just four years earlier. And yet it had all come about so fast. The breakup of the ice shelf had been expected. They'd been monitoring it through satellite imagery, but it had come sooner than they projected. And they'd been ready. Ready to capitalize on it.

Ready to change the world.

He thought back to that fateful evening with Reece, three years earlier. A great dinner. A bottle of Brunello di Montalcino. A couple of Cohiba Esplendidos. A long, inspired late-night chat about the possibilities of the manufacturing breakthrough that Reece had achieved. The many and diverse applications it could be used for. The leaps of imagination that great minds sometimes conjured up and actually turned into reality. And then, the mere mention of a word.

Miraculous.

One word. A catalyst that sent Rydell's mind tripping into uncharted territory. Dark, mysterious, wonderful, impossible territory. And here he was, less than four years later, and the impossible had become a reality.

Reece. The brilliant scientist's face drifted into his consciousness. Other faces materialized alongside it – young, talented, dedicated, all of them – and with them, a familiar cold, hard feeling deep inside him. He felt his very soul shrivel at the memory of that last day in Namibia. After the last test. After they'd all shared the elation of watching their hard work bear fruit in such spectacular, bone-chilling fashion. And then it all went wrong. He could still see Maddox, standing there beside him, pulling the trigger. He could hear himself shout, hear the bullet thumping into Reece's back, see his friend's body jerk before toppling into Danny Sherwood's arms.

The sounds and images of that day had been gnawing away at him ever since.

He hated himself for not having been able to stop it. And despite what the others told him, none of the platitudes, none of the clichés about the greater good or about sacrificing the lives of the few for the lives of the many – none of it worked.

He hadn't read them properly. He hadn't realized to what lengths they were prepared to go. And it was too late to do anything about it. They needed each other. If everything he'd worked for was to succeed, he just had to swallow it all and keep going.

Which he did, even though it wasn't easy. He could still feel it, deep inside, eating away at him, piece by piece. He knew it would eventually get him. One way or another, he'd die because of it. He had to. But maybe, before that happened, maybe, if all went well – maybe their deaths would amount to something in the end. Although he knew their ghosts wouldn't let go of him, not even then.

CHAPTER 26

Boston, Massachusetts

Sheltering behind a tall hedge in the brisk, early morning chill, Matt waited and watched, trying to make sure no unpleasant surprises were in store for him at the hotel before breaking cover and making his way in. Tense and alert while avoiding eye contact, he slipped past a few bleary-eyed businessmen who brought a semblance of life to the drab, cookie-cutter lobby, took the elevator to the fifth floor, and reached the refuge of his room.

He was as tired as he was pissed off.

He'd had to dump the Mustang a few blocks from Bellinger's place, and that only fueled his anger. The car represented a personal milestone for him, a notable and particularly satisfying step on his road back from the edge. Danny had not just guided him onto that road, but paid the toll and given him fuel money to boot. And now Matt had been forced to abandon the car on some dark side street, all because of the same bastards who had taken Danny away.

He was seriously pissed off.

After parking the Mustang, he'd scuttled in the shadows for a couple of blocks, then crossed to the north side of Broadway, where he'd hotwired a defenseless, decade-old Ford Taurus. He'd then cut west, heading out of town before looping back on the turnpike, on the lookout for any blue-and-whites. He'd parked in an inconspicuous corner on the backlot of a small shopping center around the corner from the hotel and walked the rest of the way.

He stood by the window of his room, watching the city as it sprang to life. It was another overcast, wintery day, the sun struggling to break through the pasty-gray cloud cover. He lay down on his bed, his muscles and nerves ravaged by tension and fatigue. He hadn't slept, and his body was crying out for a break. He hadn't put it through such a wringer for years. But he knew that would have to wait. He opted instead for a long, hot shower to reinvigorate him and help settle his mind. It bought him a renewed, if rapidly dwindling, lease on life. Twenty minutes later, he was back at a workstation in the austere and windowless business center.

He used the white pages' website to do a reverse listings search on the phone number he got off Bellinger's answering machine. The number yielded the curious name of Csaba Komlosy, with a home address – no surprises there – in the same geek-central catchment area straddling Harvard and MIT that Bellinger – and Danny – lived in. He thought about calling him. According to his message, he and Bellinger had been discussing what was happening in Antarctica just before Bellinger had met Matt, and Matt sensed that this Csaba – he wasn't sure how to pronounce it – could fill in some of the blanks. He decided against making that call. The goon squad seemed to be avid wiretappers. A face-to-face would be better anyway. He jotted down the address, an apartment by the sound of it, clicked on the map link for a more accurate read of its location, then, deciding he couldn't duck it anymore, pulled up the website of the *Boston Globe* and hit the link for the local, breaking news section.

It was the first item.

His face contorted with sadness – and rage.

The report wasn't long. A stabbing. Close to a bar in South Boston, shortly after midnight. They'd identified the body as Bellinger's. There was a brief mention of a brawl in the nearby bar, but nothing more. A murder investigation was under way.

The report didn't mention Matt – yet. But he knew there'd be more to come on that front.

They'd make sure of it.

He exhaled heavily, rubbed some alertness into his face,

and re-read the article. Its dry, clinical words pushed a caustic bile of anger up to his throat, burning him with their finality. His fists hovered over the keyboard, clenched bloodless-white tight, as he summoned up every drop of restraint inside him to keep from bashing it against the desk and ripping the whole workstation to shreds.

It was that simple for these bastards. They could just pluck someone off the street, cut him open, dump him in the snow, and move on to their next assignment without batting an eyelid. A man's life – an innocent, decent man's life, snuffed out in its prime, and all because of what . . . a phone call? An idea?

Matt was boiling.

He took in a deep breath and let it out slowly, willing his fury to subside. A moment later, he raised his concentration back to the screen, keyed in the homepage of his tracker, and logged in.

The Chrysler was no longer outside his place.

A detailed map displayed the car's itinerary in thirty-second increments. Backtracking to the first movement that his GPS tracker had registered, Matt saw that the goons had finally given up their stakeout – or, he thought, merely passed the baton to the next team – almost an hour ago. Which, he noted, was after he'd made it out of Bellinger's place. He wondered if that meant that they were already aware of his little excursion to Cambridge. If they were, it meant they had insights into police activity, either through radio scanners or courtesy of someone inside the department. He made a mental note of it and zoomed in on the Chrysler's current location.

It was parked on a street in Brighton, not far from St. Elizabeth's Medical Center, and hadn't moved for twenty-three minutes. The tracker's website featured a built-in link-up with Google Maps. Matt clicked on the 'street view' option, moved the little orange avatar to the Chrysler's current location, and clicked again. A wide-angle shot popped up, as clear and detailed as if he were standing right in the middle of the street – not in real time, of course, but whenever the Google van with the panoramic camera had done its survey, which couldn't have been that long ago, given that this wasn't exactly Cold War-era technology. It afforded him a detailed view of what the place looked like. He full-screened it, scrolled up the street and back for a virtual drive-by, then rotated the camera to get a good look at the opposite sidewalk.

The narrow, residential street had a string of small, two-story clapboard houses. The fix, accurate to within three yards of the tracker's location if you believed the pitch of the well-oiled salesman he'd bought it from, fell on a tired-looking, seal-gray house with a small balcony over the front porch and a gabled window in its roof.

He needed to take a closer look. A live one.

It didn't take long to get there at this early hour, given that he was heading against the rush hour traffic. The light snow from the previous night was mostly gone, and the old Taurus was, well, functioning. He turned into Beacon and headed west, his mind busy imagining the different ways things could play out once he found them. He tried to rein in his primal instincts. Yes, they were vile, blood-sucking scum, and he knew he'd find it hard to resist beating the crap out of them if he ever got the chance. But there was no need to turn this into a suicide mission. If they were there, he needed to find out more about them – who they were, what they were doing, who had hired them.

What they knew about Danny.

What happened to him.

Once he got all that – well, there was no reason to let them live, really.

The notion just came to him, and it didn't make him flinch. Which surprised him. He'd never killed anyone before. Sure, he'd had his share of fights. Before prison. In prison. He'd taken some serious beatings over the years, but he'd cracked a few skulls too. He hadn't started out that way. He was wild and reckless and played by his own rules, but he wasn't a thug and he never set out to hurt anyone. And although prison had a way of hardening a man, physically as well as mentally, it didn't change what he was about. He was more prone to letting his temper erupt, less shy about using his fists, but he never took pleasure from it. It was always in self-defense, and never went beyond doing no more than was necessary to neutralize any threat facing him.

This felt different. And right now, he wasn't too worried about that. Que sera, sera. He had to find them first.

He turned right on Washington and headed north, his pulse nudging upward with each passing block as he closed in on his target. He hit a red light at the big intersection with Commonwealth, and as he sat there waiting, sitting behind an equally tattered pickup truck in dire need of new piston rings, his gaze was drawn beyond it to the aggressive, toothy grin of a familiar grille – that of a Chrysler 300C. It was waiting at the opposite light, facing him, left indicator on.

He squinted, focusing on it, trying to ascertain whether or not it was 'his' 300C, craning his neck to get a better look past the smoking pickup blocking his view. The opposite light must have changed to green, as the Chrysler cut across the intersection just beyond the truck and motored up Commonwealth, trailing a couple of small imports behind it like a shark with its remoras. As it streaked past, Matt leaned across and got a look at the guy in the front passenger seat, and although his hard features fit the bill, Matt wasn't sure. He'd only seen the goons fleetingly, outside the bar and in the van, and in the shadows outside his place. Sealing it for him, though, was the 300C's license plate. He managed to catch a glimpse of the last two numbers on it, and they matched the number he'd seen on the car that had been parked outside his garage.

It was them.

His pulse rocketed as his eyes followed the rapidly receding car and he wondered what to do, needing to make a split-second decision. He spun the wheel and hit the gas, jinking the car around the pickup truck and ramping its right wheels over the curb, and turned into the avenue, following in the Chrysler's wake.

It was more of an instinctive reaction than a rational move, but as he trailed a few car lengths behind the silky sedan, his decision grew on him. He didn't know what the location was that the tracker had kicked up, whether it was their base or just a random stop they wouldn't be returning to. Besides, there were only two of them in the car, and he didn't mind those odds. Not with the way he was feeling right now.

They drove east on Commonwealth, then turned left on Harvard and took the bridge into Cambridge. As they headed up River, a cold, uncomfortable feeling twitched inside him. They were leading back to the Inman Square area, the one he'd only just escaped from a mere hour or two earlier. His unease flared into full-blown dread when he saw the name of the street the Chrysler turned into and spotted the number of the building where it pulled up.

There was no mistaking it, as it was an address he'd only just looked up.

They were parked right outside Csaba's place.

CHAPTER 27

Cambridge, Massachusetts

Matt coaxed the Taurus past the parked Chrysler, casually turning away as he drove by the brooding sedan, to deny its occupants a glimpse of his face. He kept going and took the first side street he found, and pulled over.

This wasn't good.

He sat in the car, stewing in his thoughts, unsure about what this meant. Was this Csaba character working with them? Had he helped them set up Bellinger, alerted them to what he was up to? Matt didn't know what to think anymore, although somehow, it didn't ring true. The message Csaba had left for Bellinger sounded genuine enough. They were discussing the apparition, and Bellinger – it seemed – had abruptly cut the conversation short.

If Csaba wasn't working with them, then they had to be here for the same reasons they'd gone after Bellinger. Which didn't give Csaba much of a rosy future. Not to mention that the very fact that the goons were after him meant that he knew something, something that could help explain what they were so hell-bent on protecting – and that could shed light on what had happened to Danny.

What *they'd* done to Danny, Matt reminded himself.

He had to do something.

He slipped out of the Taurus and crept over to the corner. He edged out carefully and looked down the street. The Chrysler hadn't moved, the two silhouettes still inside.

They were watching. Waiting.

Stalking Csaba. Matt was now sure of it.

He had to get to him first.

He sized up the block, looking for a way past the goon squad. He couldn't see one. Csaba lived in a modern, six- or seven-story apartment block. The guys in the Chrysler had a controlling view of the street and a clear line of sight to the building's landscaped approach and its entrance lobby, which deep-sixed any notion of going in that way. There was, however, a ramp going down along its side, the kind of ramp that normally led to an underground garage. Problem was, it was also within their sight line.

He pulled back from the corner and sprinted farther up the side street, and found a narrow alley that ran between two houses. He cut into it and advanced cautiously, moving in parallel to the main street, closing in on Csaba's apartment block – only to hit a dead end and a five-foot-tall wooden fence after the second house in. He could see Csaba's building looming ahead, past another couple of houses and fences. He clambered over the fence and kept going. A few minutes later, he reached a side passage that ran alongside the ramp and led back to the street.

Matt peered out. The Chrysler was still there, and he still couldn't make it onto the ramp without them seeing him. From his vantage point, he noticed another problem. The ramp had a keypad-controlled entry. Not only that, it was the kind where the buttons didn't have any numbers printed on them. Instead, the buttons would light up with randomly assigned, non-sequential numbers appearing on them when someone attempted to key a code in, in order to prevent anyone watching from mimicking the sequence and gaining entry.

Just then, Matt heard a mechanical snap, followed by a low, creaking rumble. Although he couldn't see it from where he was, he knew it was the garage door opening. He tensed up and edged back. The nose and roof of a large, black Escalade emerged from the garage. The SUV obliterated a gallon of gas as it charged up the ramp and stopped where it met the street.

Momentarily blocking the Chrysler's view.

Matt seized the opportunity. He charged out and leapt over the low wall that gave onto the ramp. He landed heavily, his bones juddering in protest. It had to be at least a ten-foot drop, more if you counted the height of the wall. He rolled on himself before righting into a low squat. Just then, he heard the Escalade thundering off, turning into the street, and exposing him to the Chrysler. Matt dived through the garage door as it closed, and took cover to one side, hoping he hadn't been spotted.

He peered out, but didn't sense any movement from the car.

He seemed clear.

The apartment numbers were listed next to the floor buttons in the elevator. He rode it to the third floor and made his way to Csaba's door and was about to hit the doorbell when he noticed that the door had a peephole in it. He pulled back, looked up, then took off one of his boots, slipped it on his right hand, and quietly smashed a couple of lightbulbs in the hallway, plunging it into darkness. He slipped his boot back on and rang the bell, which chimed inside. Some footfalls echoed and drew near, then a shadow fell across the bottom of the door.

'Who is it?' It was the same, slightly wired voice from the answering machine.

Keeping a wary eye on the elevator, Matt winged it. 'I'm a friend of Vince. Vince Bellinger.'

Matt heard some shuffling behind the door, as if Csaba were right up against it, trying to get a better look through the eyepiece – not easy given the now-dark hallway.

'A friend of Vince?' Csaba's voice had a stammer in it. 'What's – what do you want?'

Matt tried to sound earnest and unthreatening, but firm. 'We need to talk. Something happened to him.'

A beat, and more shuffling, then, as if with great reticence, Csaba said, 'Vince is dead, man.'

'I know. Would you open the door so we can talk?'

A paralyzing dread seemed to tighten around Csaba's voice box. 'Look, I don't . . . He's dead, he's been murdered, and I don't know what you want, but—'

'Listen to me,' Matt interjected bluntly, 'the same guys who killed him are parked outside your building right now. They heard your phone calls last night, they know what you were talking about, and that's what got him killed. So if you want me to help you not end up like he did, open the goddamn door.'

A charged silence followed for a brief moment, then a decision was evidently reached, as the lock snapped and the door cracked open. A wide, boyish face surrounded by a shock of shaggy hair peered through the slit – then Csaba's eyes suddenly widened in panic at the sight of Matt's face.

'Shit,' Csaba blurted as he tried to push the door shut.

Matt stuck his boot through and shoved the door back and charged in. He shut it behind him as Csaba stumbled back into the room. The big man raised his arms defensively, tripping over himself as he backed away from Matt.

'Don't hurt me, please, don't kill me, I don't know anything, I swear,' he muttered, gesturing frantically.

'What?'

'Don't kill me, man. I don't know anything.'

'Calm down,' Matt shot back. 'I'm not here to kill you.'

Csaba stared at him in muted terror, droplets of sweat popping up all over his face. Matt studied him for a brief moment – then his attention was torn away by an image on the TV behind Csaba.

The big man noticed Matt's sudden distraction and sidestepped hesitantly, giving him a full view of the screen. It was on one of the twenty-four-hour news networks and showed the same glowing sign he'd seen earlier, only this wasn't the same footage. A loud banner on the bottom of the screen proclaimed, 'Second unexplained sighting, now over Greenland.'

Matt inched closer to the screen, his forehead furrowed in confusion. 'This isn't the same one as before, is it?'

It took Csaba a second to realize he was being engaged in conversation. 'No,' he stammered. 'This one's in the Arctic.'

Matt turned to Csaba, feeling lost. It must have come across clearly in his expression, as Csaba was now shaking even more visibly.

'What?' Matt snapped angrily.

'Don't kill me, dude. Seriously.'

Matt was missing something. 'Stop saying that, all right? What is wrong with you?'

Csaba hesitated, then, as if against his will and with a hollow voice, he said, 'I know you killed Vince.'

'What?'

Csaba's hands rocketed up again. 'Your face, dude. It's on the news.'

Alarm flooded through Matt. 'My face?'

Csaba nodded, still riven with fear.

'Show me,' Matt ordered.

CHAPTER 28

Cairo, Egypt

Gracie spotted the man in the black cassock, with the anxious expression, angling for her attention among the throngs of people lining the plate-glass windows of the arrivals hall at Cairo International Airport. She caught Brother Ameen's eye and gave him a hesitant wave, which the monk acknowledged with a discreet, aloof wave of his own before moving sideways through the crowd to meet her.

The journey there had been fretfully long. After the chopper had deposited them at Rothera Station, a DASH-7 had flown them to Mount Pleasant Airport, a military airfield in the Falklands. There, they'd boarded an ageing RAF Tristar that provided commercial service for the long flight to the aptly named Wideawake Airfield on the Ascension Islands and onward to RAF Brize Norton in Oxfordshire. A cab to Heathrow led to the final leg on EgyptAir.

They'd had a brief, tense moment at Ascension, where they'd ducked out of sight and narrowly avoided being spotted by a British film crew headed in the opposite direction. They'd used the journey time to read up about the Coptic religion and, more specifically, the monastery's history. They'd checked their phones for messages at each stop, now that they were back in GSM-land, but hadn't replied to any of the messages that had been left for them. No one back in D.C., apart from Ogilvy, the network's global news director – not even Roxberry, much to Gracie, Dalton, and Finch's bemusement – had been told they'd left the ice continent, or where they were headed. Gracie and Ogilvy knew full well how ravenous their colleagues and competitors could be. The exclusivity of their story had to be ferociously guarded from the rest of the pack.

The new terminal, a gleaming, modern steel-and-glass structure, had surprised Gracie with its efficiency, even more so given that Egypt usually out-*mañana*ed the other countries of the region, no slouches themselves when it came to, well, slouching. The line through passport control had moved swiftly and courteously. The baggage had showed up on the carousel almost at the same time as they did. Even more surprisingly, people seemed to be observing the airport's recently introduced no-smoking policy, no small feat in a country where laws were routinely ignored and where more than half the male population were smokers practically from birth.

More pressingly, Gracie, Dalton, and Finch were already aware of the new apparition over Greenland. Just after the 777 had landed, their BlackBerries had sprung to life almost in unison with urgent messages from the news desk and beyond. The bracing, electrifying news had shaken the tiredness out of their bones and injected them with renewed vigor. And as they sat in the back of Yusuf's Previa, inching their way through the bustling early evening traffic and into the city, they couldn't get their questions in to the overwhelmed Brother Ameen fast enough.

He told them he'd seen it too, on the news, and confirmed that, as far as he could tell, it was identical to the one they'd seen over the ice shelf – and identical to the symbol lining the walls of Father Jerome's cave. The ones he'd started drawing seven months earlier.

Gracie was now certain she'd made the right choice in heeding the monk's call and coming to Egypt. Despite the continent hopping and its associated aches, she couldn't remember the last time she'd felt this energized. The rare, but coveted, sensation – the thrill of the exclusive scoop – was off the charts in this case, given the sheer scale and impact of what was unfolding. Still, there were many questions she needed answered. Starting with the reason for their trip, Father Jerome.

'How and why did he come here in the first place?' she asked the monk.

Brother Ameen hesitated. 'The truth is,' he winced, 'we're not sure.'

Gracie and Finch exchanged a questioning glance. 'He was working in Sudan, wasn't he?' Finch queried.

'Yes. Over the last few years, as I'm sure you know, Father Jerome was very concerned with what was happening in Darfur. Earlier this year, he opened another orphanage there, his fourth, just inside Sudan, near the border with Egypt. And then, well . . . he doesn't quite understand it himself. He left the orphanage one night, by himself, on foot, with no belongings, no food or drink. He just walked out, into the desert.'

'Just like that? He'd just been sick, hadn't he? Weren't they worried he'd be kidnapped or killed? He was very critical of what the warlords were doing out there,' Gracie pointed out. 'He would have been a big prize for them.'

'The fighting, the massacres in Darfur . . . they affected him deeply. It weakened him, and he got very sick. It was a miracle he pulled through.' The monk nodded to himself, his tone heavy with sadness at the thought. 'The night he left, he told a few of his aides there that he needed to go away for a while . . . to "find God." Those were his words. He said he might not return for a while and asked them to make sure their good work continued during his absence. And he just walked away. Five months later, some bedouins found him collapsed, in the desert, a few kilometers south of here. He was in a simple *thawb* – a robe, torn and filthy. The soles of his bare feet were all cut up and calloused; he was delirious, lost, barely alive. He didn't have any water or food with him, and yet . . . it seemed that he'd crossed the desert. On his own. On foot.'

Gracie's eyes flared up with puzzlement. 'But it's, what, five, six hundred miles from here to the border, isn't it?'

'It is,' Brother Ameen confirmed, his voice unnervingly calm.

'But he couldn't have . . . not in these conditions.' Gracie was struggling for words. 'There's nothing but desert out there. The sun alone, his skin . . . Wasn't he badly sunburned? How did he survive?'

The monk turned out his palms quizzically and looked at her with an expression that mirrored her confusion, but said nothing.

Gracie's mind raced ahead, processing his story. It was possible, maybe – but there were too many unknowns to his story. 'What does Father Jerome say happened? He didn't say he walked here all the way from Sudan, did he?'

'He doesn't remember what happened,' the monk explained. He raised a finger, his eyebrows rising as his words took on a more pointed tone. 'But he believes he was meant to come here, to our monastery, to our cave. He believes it was his calling. Part of God's plan.' The monk paused, then a hint of remorse crinkled his face. 'I really shouldn't be speaking on his behalf,' he added. 'You can ask him yourself, when you meet him.'

Gracie snatched a glance at Finch. He tilted his head in a discreet gesture that mirrored her bewilderment.

'What about the documentary?' she asked. 'Tell us about that.'

'What do you want to know?'

'How it came about? Were you there, did you meet these guys?'

Brother Ameen shrugged. 'There's not much to tell. They contacted us. They said they were making a documentary, that they'd heard about Father Jerome's being up in the cave, and could they come over and film him. The abbot wasn't keen, none of us were. It's not in our nature, it's not what we're used to. But they were coming from a very respectable network, and they were very courteous, and they kept on asking and insisting. Eventually, we accepted.'

'Lucky you did,' Finch told him. 'We wouldn't be here otherwise.'

'Oh, I don't know,' Brother Ameen replied, a hint of a smile in his eyes. 'God works in mysterious ways. I imagine he would have found another way to bring you here, don't you?'

CHAPTER 29

Csaba hesitated, then, without turning his back to Matt, he took a few steps back to his desk. It was a mess of piles of magazines and printouts. Coffee cups teetered over them like cardboard watchtowers. Clearly, he and Bellinger were far from twins on more than just the physical front. A large Apple flat screen rose out of the morass and dominated it. It too showed the light over the ice shelf. Flicking his eyes from Matt to a wireless keyboard, Csaba tapped in a few keys and brought up another website. He turned to Matt with an expression that straddled sheepish and terrified.

Matt joined him at the desk. The news report he'd pulled up was a brief crime report. Bellinger's body had been found in an alleyway not far from the bar. The report featured two black-and-white shots from a security camera inside the bar. One was a wide shot, showing Matt and Vince in mid-tussle. The other was a close-up of Matt's face, taken from another frame.

He was pretty recognizable.

Matt's eyes ate up the text voraciously. He didn't see his name anywhere in it, although he knew that wouldn't last. The article mentioned several witnesses, including an 'unnamed woman' who claimed she was outside the bar when she saw Matt chase Bellinger furiously down the street. Which he hadn't done. They'd grabbed them right outside the bar. Matt frowned, his mind flashing back to the woman in the van. He could picture her profile, backlit against the streetlights, the shoulder-length bob framing her face. One and the same, he was certain. He pictured the police showing up at his place, search warrant in hand. He also pictured them finding the murder weapon that bob-girl and her buddies must have planted there.

He noticed Csaba scrutinizing him nervously.

'I know how this looks,' Matt told him, 'but that's not what happened. These guys came after Vince because of this thing in Antarctica.' He pointed angrily at the TV screen. 'He thought my brother might have been murdered because of it. They killed Vince. I didn't. You have to believe me.'

Which, reading Csaba's jittery eyes, seemed like a tall order.

'You and Vince,' Matt asked. 'You were talking about it, weren't you? Before he bailed on you?'

Csaba nodded reluctantly.

It was all Matt had time for right now. 'I need you to tell me what you guys said, but that can wait. They're outside. We need to get out of here.'

'"We"?' Csaba flinched, reaching for his phone. 'Hey, I'm not going anywhere. You can do what you want. I'm calling the cops and—'

'We don't have time for that.' Matt flared up fiercely as he grabbed the phone from him and slammed it back down close to its cradle. 'They're here. Now. Because of your little chat with Vince. Same deal. So if you want to live, you're gonna have to trust me and come with me.' His gaze drilled into him, dead-committed.

Csaba hesitated, his eyes locked onto Matt's, his breathing hard and fast – then he nodded.

'Do you have a car?'

'No.'

'Doesn't matter. Come on.' Matt sprinted toward the door.

'Wait,' Csaba blurted, holding up one hand in a stalling gesture. He grabbed a backpack off the floor and started throwing things in it.

'We need to go,' Matt insisted.

'Just gimme a sec,' Csaba countered as he stuffed his Macbook laptop, charger, and iPhone into the backpack before flicking one last look around the room and joining Matt at the door.

Seeing the phone tripped something in Matt's mind. 'Your cell,' he told Csaba. 'Switch it off.'

'Why?'

'They can track us with it. You must know that.'

Csaba's mouth dropped an inch. Then the words clicked into place. 'Yeah, right,' he said in a daze, and repeated 'You're right' as he fished out the phone and turned it off.

Matt glanced over at the screen for one last look – the blazing sign was still there, taunting him enigmatically – then he dashed out, with Csaba on his heels.

They took the elevator down to the garage. It was home to a dozen or so cars. Matt glanced around, not exactly spoiled for choice. Csaba's neighbors seemed partial to Priuses and Japanese compacts, the Escalade owner notwithstanding. He settled on a marginally beefier Toyota RAV4, a car he was also pretty sure wouldn't resist his charms.

He moved fast. He grabbed a fire extinguisher off the wall and smashed the driver's window with it, then reached in and flung the door open. 'Get in,' he ordered Csaba as he swept the tiny glass flakes off the seat with his hand.

The big man just stood there, slack-jawed. 'That's Mrs. Jooris's car,' he said ruefully. 'She's gonna be seriously pissed, dude. She worships that car.'

'It's just a window. Get in.'

In the time it took Csaba to relent and cram himself into the passenger seat, Matt had popped the hood, yanked out the transponder fuse from the power relay center, and got the engine running. He climbed back in, threw the car in gear, and screeched up to the garage door. An unseen sensor had already instructed it to open. As it rose, the ramp appeared ahead, unobstructed, curving to the left and hugging the building.

'Buckle up,' Matt said.

Csaba gave him a look and glanced down wryly at his bulging midsection. The buckle and its stalk were out of sight, smothered by his doughy thigh. 'You wanna help me with that?'

'Maybe not,' Matt answered with a dry half grin. 'Hang on.'

His fingers tightened against the steering wheel as the garage door rose enough to let them out. Matt nudged the RAV4 up the ramp, slowly at first – there was no point alerting the goons to their presence earlier than necessary. They'd see him soon enough – which happened the instant the small SUV cleared the side of the building.

Matt locked eyes with the two startled men facing him in the Chrysler, committing as much of their features to memory as he could in that nanosecond, his foot poised on the accelerator. He'd already played out his move in his mind's eye. A quick charge across the street diagonally, right at the parked goons, aiming the Toyota's left front bumper at the Chrysler's right front wheel well, hitting it at a slight angle and with enough force to bend its wishbone and disable the car while allowing his own vehicle to keep going, bent but otherwise operational. It was a gamble, and a sacrifice he had to make. He'd lose the benefit of being able to track them, as they'd need to use another car from here on, but he had no choice. The Toyota was no match for the Chrysler. He wouldn't be able to lose them.

He was about to floor the pedal when he sensed something coming from his right. He ripped his gaze off the Chrysler and spotted a car coming down the street toward him. Something clicked into place in his mind. He waited a second or so for the car to get nearer, Csaba watching, not understanding the wait and giving him a low, anxious 'Dude, come on,' the killers in the Chrysler looking at them slightly perplexed now, not sure why they were still there, itching to bolt out of their car after them, probably pulling their weapons out of their holsters and ramming cartridges into their chambers –

– and just as the approaching car was almost at his level,

Matt jammed his foot against the accelerator and charged into the street right in front of it, cutting it off. The car, a lumbering old Caprice from the bygone days of cheap and plentiful fuel and a blissful insouciance about destroying the planet, scraped against the Toyota and bounced off it, its driver – a nervy, ponytailed man wearing thick bone spectacles – swerving into the opposite lane evasively and screeching to a stop almost right alongside the Chrysler. Matt hit the gas and tore down the street, headed in the opposite direction to the one the Chrysler was facing. He watched in the rearview mirror as the Caprice's hapless driver got out of his car and mouthed off at him angrily, and saw the goons climbing out of the Chrysler to get the man to move his car so they could get their car turned around to take up pursuit.

Matt dived into the first turning he saw, pulling a screaming left before charging down one empty street after another, changing directions often as he wove his way out of Cambridge and onto the expressway, all while keeping a wary eye on his mirrors for any sign of the Chrysler.

It was gone.

He relaxed a little and eased off the gas as he pointed the borrowed SUV north, heading out of the city, putting some much-needed miles between him and the streets that seemed determined to ensnare him in their deathly clutches.

He glanced sideways at Csaba. The round man's face was still flushed and glistening with sweat, but his posture relaxed a touch as he gave Matt a pinched acknowledgment. And with a small shake of his head, he said, 'Mrs. Jooris is gonna go mental when she sees this.'

'How you pronounce your name anyway?' Matt asked him.

'"Tchaba." But you can call me "Jabba,"' he replied without a hint of annoyance. 'Everyone does.'

Which surprised Matt. 'Really?'

Jabba nodded. 'Sure.'

'And that doesn't bother you?'

Jabba's expression was one of laid-back, casual bewilderment. 'Should it?'

Matt thought about it, then shrugged. 'Okay then. Let's ditch this car and find us a safe place, somewhere they won't find us. Then I'm gonna need you to tell me exactly what you and Vince were talking about and help me figure out what the hell is going on.'

CHAPTER 30

Before long, the Previa had left the desert behind and was trudging through the snarled traffic leading into Cairo. There was no avoiding cutting across the sprawling city, as the new airport was east of it, with Wadi Natrun to its northwest. By now, it was early evening, and the low sun's fading light punctuated the mist of exhaust fumes and dust that choked the overcrowded, run-down metropolis.

'Does he know what's going on yet?' Gracie asked Brother Ameen. 'Have you told him about the signs?'

'No,' the monk regretted. 'Not yet.' He glanced back at her uneasily, his look signaling that it was something she'd soon be a part of. 'Actually, he doesn't know you're coming. The abbot doesn't know either.'

Gracie was about to ask him to clarify, but he beat her to it. 'The abbot – he doesn't know what to do. He didn't want the outside world to know about it.'

'But you did,' Finch prompted.

The monk nodded. 'Something miraculous is happening. We can't keep it to ourselves. It's not ours to keep.'

Gracie looked over at Finch. They'd been around such situations before: uninvited guests traveling into troubled spots to talk to reluctant interviewees, people whose first instinct was to shut themselves off from outside scrutiny. Sometimes, Gracie and Finch managed to get through; other times, they were locked out. In this case, they had to make it happen. They hadn't flown halfway around the globe to leave empty-handed. Not when the whole world was waiting for an explanation.

The appearance of the tips of the pyramids at Giza told Gracie they were finally leaving the city behind. She'd seen them before, but the sight never failed to inspire awe, even in the most jaded observer. On this occasion, something else stirred inside her, the majestic, stone peaks that jutted out of the sand oddly reminiscent of the nunataks – the rocky crags that rose out of the fields of snow – that she'd looked down on only hours ago from the window of the chopper. The noisy, chaotic mess of Cairo quickly gave way to sleepier, scattered clusters of houses, and as they passed the small town of Bir Hooker, the last town before the desert and the monasteries, they lost the signals in their cell phones. The monk informed them that they'd be limited to the satphone from there on.

Ever since his first call, Gracie hadn't been able to place his accent. 'By the way, where are you from?' she asked him.

'I'm from Croatia,' he explained. 'I come from a small town in the north, not far from the Italian border.'

'Then you must be Roman Catholic.'

'Of course,' the monk confirmed.

'So Ameen isn't your real name?'

'It's not my birth name,' he corrected with a warm smile. 'I was Father Dario before I came here. We all take on Coptic names once we join the monastery. It's the tradition.'

'But the Coptic Church is Orthodox,' she queried. Long before the Protestant Reformation in the 1500s, the Christian world had already been rocked by the great schism in the eleventh century. The long-standing rivalries and theological disputes between Rome and its Eastern counterparts in Alexandria and in Antioch had been festering since the earliest days of Christendom. These petty squabbles finally came to a head in 1054 and split Christendom into two: the Eastern Orthodox Church and the Roman Catholic Church. The Greek word *Orthodox* meant, literally, 'correct belief,' which pretty much summed up the Eastern church's belief that it was the true keeper of the flame, that its adherents followed the authentic and uncorrupted traditions and teachings that had been passed down by Jesus and his apostles.

'Orthodox, yes, but not Eastern Orthodox,' the monk specified. Gracie's confused expression was obviously no surprise, nor was it limited to her. The monk glanced at his three visitors and waved the issue away. 'It's a long story,' he told them. 'The Coptic Church is the oldest of them all, it out-orthodoxes the Eastern Orthodox Church. It was actually founded by the apostle Mark in the middle of the first century, less than ten years after the death of Jesus. But it's all nonsense, really. Ultimately, all Christians are followers of Christ. That's all that matters. And the monasteries here don't make those distinctions either. All Christians are welcome. Father Jerome is Catholic,' he reminded her.

Before long, they rounded the nearby monastery of Saint Bishoi, and Deir Al-Suryan appeared at the end of a dusty, unlit lane. It looked like an ark adrift in a sea of sand – an image its monks had long embraced, believing the monastery to have been modeled on Noah's ark. Detail soon fell into focus as the people carrier drew nearer to it: the two tall bell towers; the cubical, squat, four-story keep – the *qasr* – guarding the entrance gate; the small domes with big crosses on them strewn irregularly around the various chapels and structures inside the walled complex; all of it surrounded by a thirty-foot fortified wall.

They filed out of the minivan, and Brother Ameen led them past the keep and across the inner courtyard, which was presently deserted. The enclosure was deceptively large. It was roughly the width and length of a football field, Gracie noticed, and just as flat. Every exterior surface, wall and dome alike, was covered with a clay-and-limestone adobe of uniform color, a pleasing, sandlike beige, the corners and edges rounded, soft and organic. The walls of the keep were dotted with tiny, irregular openings in place of windows – to keep the heat out – and narrow staircases led in all kinds of directions. With the setting sun's warm, orange gleam adding to the walled sanctuary's otherworldly feel, and its stark contrast to the cold, bleak landscape of the ice continent whose chill still lingered in her bones, Gracie felt as if she hadn't just leapfrogged across whole continents. It felt as if she'd stumbled onto Tatooine.

As they approached the entrance to the library, a monk stepped out and paused at their sight, looking at them first curiously, then with a dour expression on his face. Gracie guessed it was the abbot.

'Please wait here,' Brother Ameen told Gracie and Finch. They stayed behind while he stepped ahead and intercepted the clearly irate abbot. Gracie gave Finch a here-we-go look as they both did their best to observe the heated chat without appearing too interested.

A moment later, Brother Ameen came back with the abbot. He didn't seem thrilled to see them, and wasn't doing much to hide it.

'I'm Bishop Kyrillos, the abbot of this monastery,' he told them dryly. 'I'm afraid Brother Ameen overstepped his bounds by inviting you here.' He didn't offer his hand.

'Father,' Finch said, 'please accept our apologies for arriving here like this. We weren't aware of the, um,' he paused, trying to find the most diplomatic way of saying it, 'internal debate going on here regarding how to deal with it all. We certainly don't mean to inconvenience you or to impose in any way. If you'd like us out of here, just say the word and we'll head back home and no one needs to know about any of this. But I ask you to keep two things in mind. One, no one knows we're here. We only told one person back at our headquarters – our boss – he's the only one who knows where we are. So you mustn't worry about this suddenly becoming a media circus because of us. We won't let it happen.'

He paused again, waiting to see if his words were having any effect. He wasn't sure they were, but thought he detected a softening in the man's frown.

'Two,' he pressed on, 'we're only here to help you and

Father Jerome as you – as we all – try to understand the extraordinary events that we're witnessing. I assume you know that we were there. In Antarctica. We saw it all happening right in front of us. And if we're here, it's first and foremost as expert witnesses. We won't broadcast anything without your permission. What we see and discuss here remains between us until you allow otherwise.'

The abbot studied him, glanced over at Gracie and at Dalton, shot an unhappy frown at Brother Ameen, then turned his attention back to Finch again. After a brief moment, he nodded slowly as he seemed to reach a verdict, then said, 'You want to talk to Father Jerome.'

'Yes,' Finch replied. 'We can tell him what we saw. Show it to him, show him what we filmed. And maybe, he can make sense of it.'

The abbot nodded again. Then he said, 'Very well.' He then raised a stern finger. 'But I have your word you won't let any of this out before talking to me about it.'

'You have my word, Father.' Finch smiled.

The abbot kept his gaze locked on Finch, then said, 'Come.'

He invited them into the most recent addition to the complex, a stuccoed, simple three-story building that dated from the seventies. Finch and Gracie followed while Dalton scooted off down the courtyard. Brother Ameen had told them the monastery didn't have a television, and they were aching to see the footage from the Arctic and the reaction to it.

Gracie and Finch gratefully accepted a drink of water and a small platter of cheese and fresh dates, and they'd barely had time to exchange casual pleasantries when Dalton popped his head through the door.

'We're up.'

They rushed out. Dalton had linked his laptop to the foldable Began satellite dish and was on the network's website. Gracie, Finch, the abbot, and the monk huddled around him while he played the news clip of the sighting over Greenland.

A graphic showed the location of the sighting, by the Carlsbad Fjord on the eastern coast of Greenland, four hundred miles north of the Arctic Circle. The video clip that followed was eerily familiar. The footage was jerkier and grainier than their own. It wasn't filmed by a professional crew. Instead, the sighting had been captured on tape by a team of scientists who were studying the effects of meltwater on the Arctic island nation's glaciers. The apparition had taken them by surprise, with the breathless excitement and hectic activity coming through vividly on the screen. One of them, a white-bearded glaciologist with the National Snow and Ice Data Center in Boulder, Colorado, was then interviewed live, his face heavily pixelated and breaking up from the webcam-linked satellite phone they were evidently using.

'First, Antarctica, and now here,' the offscreen anchorman's voice asked him. 'Why do you think this is happening?'

There was a two-second lag, then the scientist's professorial face reacted to hearing the question. 'Look, I'm . . . I don't know what it is or where it's coming from,' he answered with a gruff voice. 'What I do know is that it can't be a coincidence that this – this *sign* is showing up over what can only be described as disaster areas. I mean, that ice shelf in Antarctica that's crumbling, and this glacier here – they're ground zero. I've been studying these glaciers here for over twenty years.' He turned and waved a gloved hand at the gray-white expanse behind him. 'You'd look out across the land there and it used to be pure white. Nothing but snow and ice, year-round. Now you look at it and it's more blue than white. It's melting so fast that we've now got lakes and rivers all over the place, and that water's working its way down to the bedrock and loosening the bases of the glaciers, which is why they've started to slide out to sea. And if this one goes,' he pointed out gravely, 'we're talking a three-foot rise in global sea levels. Which could then trigger all kinds of nightmare upheavals. So, you ask me what I think is happening? I think it's pretty obvious. Nature's flashing us a red alert here, and I think we need to take that warning seriously, before it's too late.'

Gracie stood there, rooted in silence, as the report cut away to a montage of reactions to the sign's second appearance. The images were breathtaking. A large crowd congregated in Times Square, watching the scenes unfold on the huge screen, the crawler underneath announcing the sighting in bold letters. Similar scenes were captured in London, Moscow, and other major cities. What the first appearance seeded, this second one reaped in spades, in terms of impact. The world was sitting up and taking notice.

Gracie glanced over at Dalton and Finch, and felt a surge of trepidation. Something unprecedented was happening, something big and wonderful and baffling and terrifying all at the same time – and she was right at the heart of it.

The satphone startled her and dragged her attention away from the screen. It was Ogilvy, calling from his cell, as per their agreed communication protocol.

'I just got a call from the Pentagon,' he informed her. 'Two DIA guys just landed in McMurdo and found out you'd skipped town. They're pretty pissed off,' he said with a light chuckle.

Gracie frowned. 'What did you have to tell them?'

'Nothing. It's still a free country. Sort of. But they'll track you to Cairo Airport pretty quickly, if they haven't done it already. From there . . . who knows. You might want to switch off your phones.'

'There's no signal out here anyway,' she told him, 'but we need to keep in touch. We're pretty cut off out here.'

'Check your satphone every hour; I'll text you if anything comes up.' Ogilvy impressed her with his sangfroid.

'We'll do that,' she confirmed. 'And I'll get you the landline of the monastery too, just in case.'

'Good.' Ogilvy's voice took on a more serious tone. 'Did you meet him yet?'

'No, we just got here.'

'Talk to Father Jerome, Gracie. Do it quickly. The whole world's watching. And we've got to keep our lead on this thing. It's ours for the taking.'

Gracie felt a hard lump in her throat. She glanced uneasily at the monks as she stepped away and turned her back to them, lowering her voice. 'We've got to be careful here, Hal. We can't just announce this without taking the necessary precautions.'

'What do you mean?'

'I mean, this is a Muslim country. I'm not sure they'd react kindly to something that smells like a Second Coming, especially not in their own backyard.'

'It's where it happened the first time,' Ogilvy remarked dryly.

'Hal, seriously,' Gracie shot back, 'we need to tread carefully. In case you hadn't noticed, this isn't the most tolerant corner of the planet. I don't want to put Father Jerome in any danger.'

'I don't want to put anyone in danger either,' Ogilvy countered, slightly testily. 'We'll be careful. Just talk to him. We'll take it from there.'

Gracie didn't feel overly relieved. She relented – 'I'll call you after I meet him' – then snapped the phone shut and turned to the abbot. She needed to get something out of the way. 'The documentary footage they filmed in the cave. Can we see it?'

'Of course. It's on the DVD they sent us – I haven't watched it as we don't have a player here.'

'This laptop'll play it,' Dalton told him, tapping his computer.

The abbot nodded and left them.

Dalton glanced worriedly at Gracie and Finch. 'What if the shot we need didn't make the final cut?'

It was a disheartening possibility neither of them wanted to consider right now, as it meant they would then have to contact the filmmakers for the outtakes. The abbot interrupted their concern by reappearing quickly, DVD in hand. Dalton loaded it up and fast-forwarded through it until the screen showed the small film crew climbing up the mountain and approaching what looked like an old door cut into the rock face.

'There,' the abbot exclaimed. 'That's Father Jerome's cave.'

Dalton reverted to play mode, and the screen showed the cameraman's point of view as he entered the cave. Gracie watched, heart in mouth, as it tracked through the dark chamber, an ominous, first-person voice-over describing the cave and its sparse, simple furnishings, giving her a preview of what she would imminently be visiting – then the camera banked around and, in a sweeping pan, covered the curving ceiling of the chamber.

'Right there,' Gracie burst out, jabbing the screen with her finger. 'That's it, isn't it?'

Dalton hit the pause button, backtracked a few frames, and played the clip again in slow motion. They all leaned in for a closer look. It was just a brief shot, no more than a passing glimpse at a curiosity within the cave – but it was all they needed. Dalton froze the image on one of the painted symbols. It was an elegant construction of concentric circles and intersecting lines that radiated outward. Despite its simplicity, it somehow managed to convey what they'd seen over the ice shelf and now, on the video, with surprising ease and clarity.

It was unmistakable.

Gracie turned to the abbot. Her nerves were buzzing with anticipation. 'When can we go there and meet Father Jerome?'

He checked his watch. 'It's getting late. The sun will be gone soon. Tomorrow morning, first thing?'

Gracie winced, her heartbeat having a hard time pulling back from the frenzied quickening brought on by the footage on Dalton's screen. 'Father, please. I don't mean to be a burden in any way, but . . . given what's happening, I don't think we should wait. I really think we ought to talk to him tonight.'

The abbot held her gaze for an uncomfortable beat, then relented. 'Very well. But in that case, we should go now.'

Lying under a sand-colored camouflage net four hundred yards west of the monastery's gate, Fox Two watched through high-powered binoculars as Gracie, Finch, and Dalton, accompanied by the abbot and another monk, climbed into the waiting people carrier.

His Iridium satphone vibrated. He fished it out and checked it. The text message told him Fox One and his team had just landed. On time. As expected.

He locked the phone and tucked it back into his pocket and watched as the Previa drove away in a swirl of dust.

He waited until they were half a mile away before pushing himself to his knees. Crouching low, he carefully folded the netting, stowed it in its pack, then slipped away to rejoin his two men, who waited nearby.

The mountain beckoned.

Again.

CHAPTER 31

Woburn, Massachusetts

The motel was grubby and run-down, but it provided Matt and Jabba with the basics: four walls, a roof, and the anonymity of a check-in alcove manned by a weedy daytime television addict who could barely string together a sentence. And right now, that was what they needed most. Shelter and anonymity.

That, and some answers.

Matt was sitting on the floor, leaning against the bed, his head tilted all the way back, resting against the lumpy mattress. Jabba, on the other hand, couldn't sit still. He was pacing around and making repeated checks out the window.

'Would you stop doing that,' Matt grumbled. 'No one's coming for us here. Not yet, anyway.'

Jabba grudgingly let go of the thin, stained curtain and embarked on another lap up and down the room.

'Just sit the hell down,' Matt snapped.

'I'm sorry, all right?' Jabba fired back. 'I'm just not used to all this. I mean, it's just insane, dude. Why are we even here? Why can't we just go to the cops and tell them what you know?'

'Cause what I know is nothing compared to what the cops think they know, and I don't fancy sweating this one out behind bars. Now do me and this carpet a favor and sit down.'

Jabba stared at him for a beat, then relented. He looked around, frowned at a rickety chair that looked like it would disintegrate if he even thought of sitting in it, and set himself down on the marginally sturdier bed instead. He palmed the remote and changed channels on the small TV that was bolted onto the wall. It matched the room: basic, run-down, but functional. Matt glanced at its screen. The picture was grainy and the set had a meek, tinny sound, but that didn't matter. He could see what he needed to see.

News of the Greenland apparition had whipped up the media into an even bigger frenzy. Coming on the heels of the Antarctic event, it was an irrefutable confirmation that no one could ignore. It was on every channel – endless blathering that ultimately couldn't offer any explanation beyond replaying the same clips over and over and exploring past mystical sightings for any relevance. Clips about previous claims, from Fatima to Medjugorje, were getting airtime, only they paled in comparison. This wasn't a handful of kids claiming to see the Virgin Mary in a field.

The world was, simply, entranced.

Matt tilted his head back again and exhaled wearily. 'Tell me what you and Vince talked about.'

'Tell you what we talked about?' Jabba rambled. 'We talked about everything, dude. Where do you want me to start?'

'Last night,' Matt specified testily. 'What did you guys talk about last night?'

'Last night. Last night, right,' he muttered, pinching the bridge of his nose between two fingers. 'We were watching this thing,' he said, pointing at the screen. 'The first one, anyway. Trying to work out how it could be done.'

Matt sat up. '"Done"? You think it's a fake?'

Jabba gave him a look. 'Dude. Come on. Something like this happens, your first instinct has to be it's a fake. Unless you buy into that whole "the truth is out there" mind-set.'

'Which, I'm guessing, you don't?'

'No, hey, I'm open to it. I'm sure there's some weird stuff they're not telling us about. But there's so much bullshit out there, whether it's from the government or from people who are out to make a fast buck, you've got to look at things with a cynic's eye. And we're scientists, man. Our instinct is to ask questions first.'

Matt nodded, trying to stay focused. 'So you and Vince bounced around some ideas. You come up with anything?'

'No, see, that's the thing.' Jabba leaned forward, and his voice livened up. 'Nothing stuck. Nothing at all. We couldn't even begin to figure it out. If this thing's a fake, then whoever's doing it is using some technology that's straight out of Area 51.'

Matt frowned. He was missing something. 'What is it you guys do, anyway? I mean, if it *was* a fake, what made you think you and Vince could figure it out?'

'We're electrical engineers. We work on . . . I mean, me and Vince, we . . .' He stumbled with visible discomfort. 'We design computer circuits, microchips, that kind of thing.'

Matt glanced at the screen dubiously. 'That doesn't sound particularly relevant to this thing.'

'I'm not talking about Radio Shack walkie-talkies, dude. Or even iPhones. I'm talking sci-fi-level stuff. Like right now, we're building these micro-RFID chips – you remember that scene in *Minority Report*? When Tom Cruise is walking through a mall and all these holographic panels know it's him and start talking to him and showing him these tailor-made ads?'

'Not really.' Matt shrugged. 'I've missed out on a few movies over the years.'

'Too bad, man. Awesome movie. Right up there with *Blade Runner*, the only other Philip K. Dick story Hollywood didn't manage to screw up.' A look from Matt put him back on track. 'Anyway, we can do that now. Not the screen. I'm talking about the recognition part. Tiny chips embedded in the actual fabric of your shirt, that kind of thing.'

'It still doesn't tell me why you think you'd be able to figure this out.'

'What we do . . . it's not just a job,' Jabba explained. 'It's a calling. You live it, breathe it, dream it. It takes over your life. It *is* your life. And part of it is keeping track of everything that's going on, not just the stuff that's directly related to your work. You've got to want to know about what everyone else is doing, whether it's at NASA, in Silicon Valley, or in some lab in Singapore. Because everything's interconnected. One of their breakthroughs could be combined with what you're doing in ways neither one of you intended and could open up a whole new door in your brain. It can give you the one thing you need to make that quantum leap and send your work in a completely new direction.'

'Okay.' Matt didn't sound too convinced. 'So you and Vince kept an eye on what other brainiacs were dreaming up.'

'Pretty much.'

Matt still felt confused. 'Well if the two of you couldn't figure it out, then why was your conversation a threat to anyone? Do you think you might have hit on something without knowing it?'

Jabba did a quick mental rummage of his chat with Bellinger. 'I doubt it. Everything we talked about is public knowledge – at least, among the other "brainiacs" out there. If any of it was relevant in any way – and I don't think it was – someone else would have made the connection too by now.'

'So why come after Vince? And why did it make him think that my brother was somehow involved?'

The word threw Jabba. 'Your brother?'

'Vince thought my brother might have been killed because of it.'

'Why would he think that?'

'I don't know. They were close.'

Jabba's face signaled he was now missing something. 'Who was your brother?'

'Danny. Danny Sherwood.'

A name that clearly struck a chord. A resonant one. 'Danny Sherwood was your brother?'

Matt nodded. 'You knew him?'

'I knew *of* him, sure. Distributed processing, right?

Progamming's holy grail. Your brother's cred was rock solid on that front.' He nodded wistfully. 'Vince loved your brother, man. Said he was the most brilliant programmer he'd ever seen.' He let the words settle as his mind tried to fill in the blanks and see the connections. 'What did Vince tell you, exactly?'

'Not much. He said someone called Reece hired Danny to work with him on something. You heard of him?'

'Dominic Reece. They all went down in that chopper, didn't they? I'm sorry, man.' Jabba's expression tightened. 'Vince told you he thought they'd been murdered? All of them?'

'Maybe. Maybe not.' He didn't want to lose his thread. 'He said they were working on some kind of bio-sensor project. Does that mean anything to you?'

'No. But Vince and Danny were close. Closer than close. He might have told him something in strict confidence. Something he wasn't supposed to spread around. Like maybe the patents hadn't been applied for yet. In our business, one slip of the tongue could lose you a billion-dollar advantage.'

Matt rubbed the exhaustion from his eyes. The sign over Greenland was on the screen again, taunting him. It was hypnotic, and Matt was finding it hard to take his eyes off it. 'You and Vince. That night. He cut the conversation short, didn't he?'

Jabba nodded.

'What was the last thing he said? Do you remember?'

Jabba concentrated. 'He didn't say it. I did. I was just saying that it looked like the air itself was being lit up. Like the air molecules themselves were on fire. Only that's not possible.'

Matt studied the grainy image on the screen. 'What if it is?'

'Setting the air on fire? I don't think so.'

'What about a laser, a projector . . . something that needs the skill set of one hell of a programmer.'

Jabba just shook his head. 'Nothing I know of can do that. And if anyone else knew how it could be done, they'd be on every channel.'

Matt shut his eyes and leaned back, frustrated. He was having a hard time concentrating and getting his head around it all. It didn't help that he was running on empty. He was exhausted, physically as well as mentally. He hadn't slept for well over twenty-four hours, hours that he hadn't exactly coasted through. And it didn't look like whatever it was that had him in its grip was about to let go anytime soon.

'There's a reason they killed Vince. And it has to do with what happened to Danny and the others. Whether this damn sign is real or not, someone's doing something.'

Jabba's face sank. 'And you want to find out who's doing it.'

'Yep.'

Jabba looked at him like a kid studying a three-eyed panda at the zoo. 'Are you nuts? 'Cause that's the wrong play, dude. The right play is we lose ourselves until they're done with whatever it is they're doing. We disappear, maybe drive up to Canada or something, we sit tight and we wait until it's all blown over.'

Matt eyed him like he was now the alien species. 'You think?'

Jabba frowned, a bit discomfited by Matt's sardonic expression. 'You asked me what made me and Vince think we could figure this out. What makes you think you can? I mean, what are you, an ex-cop or something? Ex-FBI? Some kind of ex-SEAL special ops hard-ass maybe?'

Matt shook his head. 'You've got me pegged on the wrong side of that fence.'

'Oh, well that's just wonderful,' Jabba groaned. He shook his head again, then his tone turned serious. 'Dude, seriously. These are bad people. We're talking about guys who kill people by the chopper-load.'

Matt's mind was elsewhere.

Jabba could see it. 'You're not listening to me, are you?'

Matt shook his head.

Jabba's face sank again in exasperation. 'We're screwed, aren't we?'

Matt ignored the question. 'Can you find out who else was on that chopper? What their specialties were? And also . . . who was funding them?'

Jabba sighed. 'Like I have a choice?' He reached into his backpack and pulled out his laptop.

Matt pointed at it. 'Think you can get an Internet connection in this dump?'

'I seriously doubt they have wi-fi here, but . . .' Jabba held up his iPhone and flashed Matt a cheesy, knowing look. Then he remembered and his face clouded. 'Forgot. Can't use this. Dammit.' He rubbed his face with his meaty fingers, thought about it, then looked up. 'Depends on what you need. I can fire it up for forty seconds max. Any longer than that and they'll get a fix on where we are.'

Matt grimaced. 'You get that from watching *24*, or is this for real?'

Jabba held up the phone. 'Dude. First thing I did when I bought this thing? I took it apart to jailbreak it. Just to piss off AT&T.'

'Meaning?'

'Meaning I've set it free. I can hook up its Edge data connection to my laptop.'

'Okay. But just to play it safe, maybe the guy at reception'll let you use his computer.'

Jabba frowned. 'Why? What else do you need?'

'A little update,' Matt said. 'On where our friends with the Chrysler are hanging out.'

CHAPTER 32

Mountains of Wadi Natrun, Egypt

Father Jerome looked very different than Gracie had imagined. That didn't surprise her. In her experience, people often looked different in the flesh than they did in pictures or on film. Occasionally, the change was for the better, though mostly – and more commonly these days, given the amount of Photoshopping that went on – it led to disappointment. In this case, Gracie had expected him to look different, given what he'd been through since the last coverage she'd seen of him. And he was: thinner, more gaunt-faced, seemingly more fragile than she remembered. But even here, in the light of three gas lanterns and a few scattered candles in the oppressively dark cave, his eyes, a piercing green-gray that blazed out of the tanned corona of his face, were more captivating than on film and made up for any frailty his recent ordeal had exacerbated.

'So you don't remember anything at all of your journey?' Gracie asked him. 'You were out there for weeks, weren't you?'

'Three months,' the old man answered, his eyes never leaving hers. Gracie, Finch, and Dalton had been pleasantly surprised by the fact that he hadn't refused to see them. Far from it, he'd been warm and welcoming. He was unperturbed, his voice unwavering and soothing, his words clear and slow. He hadn't lost the trace of Spanish that colored his words. Gracie had immediately warmed to him, no doubt predisposed by her great admiration for the man and the selflessness and humility he inspired.

'And it's just . . . blank,' she added.

'It's not something I've ever experienced. I have vague recollections, fleeting images in my mind . . . Walking, alone. I can see the sandals on my feet, walking in the sand, the endless landscape surrounding me. The blue sky, the burning sun, the hot air . . . I can smell it, I can feel the heat on my face, the hot air in my lungs. But that's all they are. Snippets. Momentary flashes of consciousness in an otherwise blank slate.' He shook his head in despair, slightly, to himself, as if chiding himself for that failing.

Although Dalton and Finch were sitting there with her in the cave, along with the abbot and Brother Ameen, Gracie had decided not to ask for this first interview to be filmed. It hadn't been an easy decision. Although she felt it was best to spend a bit of time with Father Jerome first, to get to know him, to get him comfortable with them, she also wasn't sure how he'd react to seeing the footage of the signs in the sky. And she felt uneasy and disingenuous at the thought of springing the news on him with a camera rolling.

She glanced up at the roof of the cavern. The white swirls, unsettling representations of the sign she'd witnessed over the ice shelf, were all over it.

'Tell me about these,' she asked him, waving her hand across the ceiling.

The priest looked upward thoughtfully, studying the painted symbols above their heads, and thought about her question for a brief moment, before letting his eyes settle on her again. 'Shortly after I arrived here,' he told her, 'a clarity that I'd never experienced came over me. I began to understand things more clearly. It was as if my mind were suddenly liberated of its clutter and freed to see life for what it really was. And these thoughts, these ideas . . . they started coming to me with such clarity, and such power. I just need to close my eyes and they start flowing through me. It's beyond my control. I've been writing them down, there.' He pointed at his desk. A few notebooks sat on its worn surface, some others on the ledge by the window. 'Like a faithful scribe,' he added with a faint smile.

Gracie couldn't take her eyes off him as he spoke. Most unsettling was how steady his voice was, how utterly normal he sounded, how casual his tone was. It was as if he were describing nothing more than the most mundane of experiences. 'And this symbol?' she reminded him, pointing upward again. 'You painted these, didn't you?'

He nodded slowly, his face slightly pinched in confusion. 'It's something I can't quite explain. When the thoughts come to me, when I hear the words in my head just as I hear you, I also see that,' he explained, pointing at the sign. 'It's just there, burning brightly in my consciousness. And after a while, I found myself drawing it, over and over. I'm not sure what it means, but . . . it's there, in my head. I can see it, clearly. And it's . . . it's more than this,' he added almost ruefully as he gestured at the roof of the cavern. 'It's . . . clearer. Richer. More resplendent. More . . . alive.' He glanced away, hesitating to go further. 'It's hard to explain. Forgive me if this sounds too vague, but . . . it's really beyond my understanding. Or control.'

'Could it be something you saw in your dreams?'

Father Jerome shook his head and smiled. 'No. It's there. I just need to close my eyes and I can see it. Anytime.'

Gracie felt a shiver at the base of her neck. 'So you've never actually seen it? I mean, physically?' she specified, weighing her words – then an idea swooped into her mind. 'Could it be something you saw while you were out in the desert? Something you saw but don't remember?'

'Saw? Where?' he asked.

She hesitated, then said, 'In the sky?'

The priest tilted his head slightly, his eyebrows raised, as he mulled her suggestion for a moment. 'I suppose it's possible,' he finally conceded. 'Anything's possible, given how those weeks are nothing but a blur.'

Gracie glanced over at Finch, then at the abbot. With the slightest nods, they seemed to agree with what she was thinking. She turned to Dalton, who had cottoned on and was already keying in the commands on his laptop.

She felt a tightening in her throat as she coaxed the words out. 'I'd like to show you something, Father. It's something we just filmed, something we saw in Antarctica, just before coming here to see you. I'm a bit wary of showing it to you like this, without preparation, but I really think you need to see this. It has to do with this symbol you've been drawing.' She paused, scrutinizing his face for signs of discomfort. She didn't find any. She swallowed hard and asked, 'Would you like to see it?'

The priest looked at her quizzically, but, calm as ever, nodded. 'Please,' he said, spreading his hands invitingly.

Dalton got up and placed the laptop on a low table in front of the priest, and turned it so that they could all watch it. He hit the play button. The video from Antarctica, the edited piece they had sent the network, played. Gracie kept her gaze locked on Father Jerome, studying his face as he absorbed the images unfurling before him. She watched, on edge, expecting to see any one of a number of emotional responses to the clip – surprise, consternation, worry, fear even – and hoping it didn't make the priest distraught. It didn't. But it seemed to confuse him. His posture visibly stiffened as he leaned in for a closer look, his mouth dropped slightly, his forehead furrowed under the strain.

When it was finished, he turned to them, looking bewildered. 'You filmed this?'

Gracie nodded.

The priest was lost for words. His eyes took on a haunted, pained expression. 'What does this mean?'

Gracie didn't have an answer for him. From the silence around her, it didn't seem like anyone else did either. She winced a little as she said, 'There's been another sighting like that. In Greenland this time. Just a few hours ago.'

'Another one?'

'Yes,' Gracie confirmed.

Father Jerome pushed himself to his feet and shuffled over to the window. He stared at his desk, shaking his head in disbelief, then reached down and picked up one of his notebooks. He rifled through its pages until he found what he was looking for, and just stood there, staring at it. 'I don't understand it,' he mumbled. 'It's what I've been seeing. And yet . . .' He turned to face Gracie and the others, the open notebook in his hand. Gracie hesitantly reached out. He placed it in her hand, a faraway, haunted look in his eyes. She looked at the pages before her, then leafed through a few more pages. They were all similar: packed densely with an elegant, handwritten script, and dotted, here and there, with more elaborate renderings of the sign. She looked over at Finch and passed him the notebook, her fingers quivering slightly under the weight of what she'd seen on its pages.

'When I see it,' the old priest continued, 'it . . . it speaks to me. Somehow, it's as if it's putting the words and ideas in my head.' He studied their faces intently, his gaze magnetic, his eyes jumping from one to the other, searching for comfort. 'Don't you hear them too?'

Gracie didn't know what to answer. She felt the others shifting uncomfortably, not knowing what to say either. The abbot got up and crossed over to Father Jerome. He placed a comforting arm around his shoulder. 'Perhaps we should take a small break,' he suggested, nodding at Gracie. 'Let the good father's mind settle down. It's a lot to take in.'

'Of course,' Gracie agreed with a warm, supportive smile. 'We'll wait outside.'

The three of them left Father Jerome with the abbot and the younger monk and stepped out into the small clearing outside the cave's entrance. The last vestiges of day that they'd witnessed on the climb up were now gone. With a total absence of ambient light as far as the eye could see, the ink-black dome above them looked unreal, blazing with a dazzling array of stars, an astounding and humbling display the likes of which Gracie had rarely seen.

No one said anything. They each seemed to be processing what the priest had said, looking for a rational explanation to it all. Gracie glanced absentmindedly at her watch, and saw that it was coming up to the hour. She suddenly remembered what they'd agreed with Ogilvy. 'Where's the satphone?' she asked.

Finch retrieved it from his bag, which he'd left at the door of the cave, inserted the battery back into it, and switched it on. Within seconds, it pinged with several text messages. The one that caught his eye was from Ogilvy. It simply said, in loud, capitalized letters, 'CALL ME AS SOON AS YOU GET THIS.' He handed it to Gracie. 'Something's up.'

The curtness of the message unsettled her as she thumbed the redial key. Ogilvy picked it up inside of one ring, the words somersaulting out of his mouth.

'They just aired the documentary footage from the cave.'

Gracie froze. 'What?'

'They showed it,' Ogilvy reiterated, breathless with urgency. 'It's out. The whole thing's out. Father Jerome, the monastery, the symbol he's painted all over his cave. It's on every TV screen from here to Shanghai as we speak,' he told her, uncharacteristically nerve-racked, clearly struggling to process the implications himself. 'This thing's just blown wide open, Gracie – and you're standing right at ground zero.'

CHAPTER 33

Boston, Massachusetts

Larry Rydell was having a hard time focusing on what his chief advertising strategist and his director of interactive marketing were saying as they stepped out of the elevator. He'd had trouble concentrating on the conversation throughout their lunch at the firm's laid-back canteen – a moniker that seriously understated the fine sushi and Mediterranean cuisine that were on offer. He knew both executives well. They were part of the brains trust that ran the firm – his firm, the one he'd founded twenty-three years earlier, before he'd dropped out of Berkeley. He used to thrive on their informal meetings. They were part of what fueled the company to its global success, and he normally enjoyed them with the enthusiasm of a young entrepreneur hell-bent on conquering the world. Lately, though, he'd been more distant, less focused, and today, he was only there in strictly physical terms. His mind was entirely elsewhere, locked on the events that were taking place continents away.

He gave them a casual half smile and a small wave as they parted, then strode down the wide, glass-covered hallway to his office. As he reached the secretarial pool stationed outside his door, he saw Mona, his trusted senior PA, and his three other assistants clustered around the bank of wall-mounted LCD screens that were constantly tuned to the major international news channels.

The sight surprised him somewhat. They'd already watched the Greenland sighting that morning. Mona turned and spotted him. She waved him over while gesturing at the screen. 'Did you see this?' she asked. 'It's from a documentary they filmed six months ago in an old monastery in Egypt. You've got to see this.'

He felt a pinch of concern as he stepped closer to the screen, then the blood drained from his face as the significance of what it was showing sank in.

He managed to mask his unease and feigned sharing in their excitement for a minute or two before retreating into the sanctuary of his office, where he studied the news reports in private. He was familiar with Father Jerome, of course – who wasn't – but he'd never heard of the monastery. Close-ups of the markings on the cave wall were everywhere he looked, and were definitely renderings of the sign. Which sent Rydell's mind cartwheeling in all kinds of deeply troubling directions.

He flicked around TV channels and websites feverishly, looking for something, anything, to put his mind to rest. Nothing came to his rescue. On the screens, legions of commentators on the news networks were competing to make sense of it.

'Well, if what we're seeing here is true, if this footage was really filmed when they're saying it was,' one notable pundit was saying, 'then clearly, it's an association between this unexplained phenomenon and a highly regarded man of faith, and not just any faith – a Christian man of faith,' he emphasized, 'who somehow foresaw these events we've been witnessing, while staying in one of Christianity's oldest places of worship . . .'

The implications of the footage were obvious and inescapable, and it was already creating a huge stir. Evangelists and born-again Christians, parishioners and preachers alike, had begun staking their claim on the sign and making all kinds of prophetic proclamations. The followers of other faiths – predictably – didn't share in their euphoria and felt excluded and threatened. A few angry denunciations had already been voiced by Muslim scholars. More would inevitably come, and from other religions too, Rydell was certain.

Which wasn't part of the plan.

He pulled back and engaged his mind in a broader, less prejudiced analysis of what this might be. He knew there were a lot of other possible explanations for it. They'd expected people to claim the sign all along. They knew that crazies in every dark corner of the planet would be coming out of their rabbit holes and making all kinds of nonsensical declarations. But this was no nutcase. This was Father Jerome. *The* Father Jerome.

No, he was sure of it. Something was very, very wrong.

He'd misjudged them again.

And that possibility – that certainty – sent a bracing shot of ice rushing through his veins.

He did all he could to keep his anger in check as he picked up the phone and punched the speed-dial key for Drucker.

Seated comfortably in his office on Connecticut Avenue, Keenan Drucker watched his TV monitor with avid interest. He marveled at how quickly the media pounced on any development and whipped it around the planet. The content beast needed to be fed, and ever since the first appearance of the sign, it was positively feasting.

He felt a deeply rooted satisfaction at how things were unfolding, and his gaze ratcheted back from the plasma screen on his wall and dropped down to a framed picture on his desk. Jackson, his son – his dead son – beamed back at him from behind its thin glass plate. Drucker felt the same stab of grief he suffered every time he glanced at the picture. He tried to keep that image of Jackson in his mind – alive, vibrant, handsome, proudly turned out in his crisp officer's dress uniform, the young man's eyes blazing with a sense of pride and purpose – and not let the horrific images from the mortuary seep in and overpower it. But he never could. The images from that visit to the base, when he and his wife were presented with what was left of their son, were permanently chiseled into his hardened soul.

I'll make things right, he thought to Jackson. *I'll make sure it never happens again.*

He tore his eyes off his son's face and looked up at the screen. He surfed away from the mainstream news networks and trawled the Christian channels instead. The sound bites coming through were promising. The footage from the caves was whipping up a storm of excitement, that much was clear. The people in the street were lapping it up. The preachers, however, were being more cautious. He watched as one televangelist after another gave cagey responses about what was going on, clearly unsure about how to handle this unexpected intrusion into their cosseted worlds.

Typical, he thought, knowing they had to be seriously threatened – but also aware that they'd be watching each other, waiting to see who'd be the first to jump into the pool.

'If he's the real deal,' he heard one pundit remark on air, 'these preachers will soon be falling over themselves to embrace him and claim him as their own.'

They'll get there, he mused. *They just need some encouragement.*

Covert encouragement, to be precise.

Which, as it happened, was something Keenan Drucker excelled at.

His BlackBerry pinged. He dragged his concentration away from the monitor and glanced at the phone. It was Rydell.

As expected.

He inhaled a long, calming breath, then picked it up. Rydell's voice was – also, as expected – agitated.

'Keenan, what the hell's going on?'

Time for damage control. Something else he excelled at.

'Not on the phone,' he replied curtly.

'I need to know this isn't what I think it is.'

'We need to talk,' Drucker just repeated, his words slow, emphatic. 'In person.'

A beat later, Rydell came back. 'I'll fly down first thing in the morning. Meet me at Reagan. Eight o'clock.' And he was gone.

Drucker nodded slowly to himself. Anticipating Rydell's reaction, and his call, hadn't exactly taken an act of supernatural-level divination. It was simple cause and effect. But it meant he needed to initiate an effect of his own.

Maddox picked up his call within two rings.

'Where are you?' Drucker asked him. 'Where are we with Sherwood's brother?'

'It's under control,' Maddox said. 'I'm dealing with it myself.'

Drucker frowned. He didn't expect the Bullet to dive in himself unless things were getting out of hand. He decided now was not the time to delve further on that front. He had a more pressing message to convey, in the form of three short words.

'Get the girl' was all he said. Then he hung up.

Almost two thousand miles east, Rebecca Rydell was still in bed and enjoying a late lie-in. By conventional standards, it was past lunchtime, but Costa Careyes was far from conventional. And at the Rydells' sprawling Casa Diva, moreover, as in the other villas and casitas on the sun-kissed Mexican coast for that matter, life was unfettered by such mundane limitations.

She'd been up most of the night, with her friends. They'd watched the latest sighting on the big screen in the open-air living room before adjourning to the beach and wondering about it over ceviche, grilled shrimp, margaritas, and a big bonfire under a pearlescent moon.

Vague recollections of the evening drifted into her mind as she stirred, half-awake, her senses tickled to life by the delicate scents of bougainvillea and *copa de oro* that wafted through the house. She usually liked to sleep with the French doors open, preferring the sound of the ocean's waves and the salty taste of the air to the clinical hum of the air conditioner, but it had been a particularly hot week, hotter than she could ever remember. Still drowsy, she realized something else had nudged her awake. A faint noise outside her bedroom. Footsteps, getting closer.

The door to her room swung open, and Rebecca almost jumped out of her skin at the sight of the two men who hurried in. She knew them, of course. Ben and Jon. The bodyguards her father had insisted should accompany her whenever she left the country. Especially when she was in Mexico. They were normally very discreet and stayed well out of sight, particularly here, in the sleepy, remote playground of Careyes, far removed from kidnap-central Mexico City and the drug warzones farther north. She'd known the two men for over a year now, and she liked and trusted them – which is why she sat up briskly, a sudden ripple of fear rushing through her. For them to be barging into her bedroom like this, without so much as a knock, meant that something very, very bad had happened.

'Get dressed,' Ben told her bluntly. 'We have to get you out of here.'

She pulled the sheet right up against her chest and shrank back against the headboard, her breath coming short and fast. 'What's going on?'

Ben's eyes fell on a light, floral-patterned dress that was strewn across a bench at the foot of her bed. He picked it up and flung it at her.

'We have to get you out here now. Let's go,' he ordered.

Something about the way he said it, something about the way Jon's eyes were dancing back and forth warily, made her uneasy. Her hand fumbled to the night table and she grabbed her cell phone. 'Where's my dad? Is he okay?' she asked as she hit the keypad.

Ben took a couple of quick strides to her bedside and

snatched the phone out of her hand. 'He's fine. You can talk to him later. We have to go now.' He slipped her phone into his pocket and looked at her pointedly.

The finality of his words pummeled her into submission.

She nodded hesitantly and reached for her dress. The two men half-turned to give her some privacy as she pulled it on. She tried to calm herself, to placate the terror that was coursing through her. The two men were professionals. They knew what they were doing. This was what they were trained to do. She shouldn't be asking questions. She knew her dad only hired the best of the best. She was in safe hands. She'd even met her bodyguards' boss, the slightly creepy guy with the granite eyes whose firm handled all aspects of security for her dad's businesses, a man who didn't look like he did anything halfheartedly.

Everything would be fine, she tried to convince herself.

She slipped her sandals on. Seconds later, they were rushing her out of the house and into a waiting car that charged out of the estate and barreled down the bumpy road, heading for Manzanillo.

Everything's going to be fine, she told herself again, although somehow, deep inside, a little voice was telling her she was wrong.

CHAPTER 34

Brighton, Massachusetts

Matt was parked across the street and six car lengths back from the target house. He'd been there for over an hour, sitting low, watching, waiting. Thinking about his options. Not really liking any of them.

He'd ditched the RAV4 and picked up a bathtub-white Camry, pre-'89 and hence pre-car key transponders. Probably the blandest car he'd ever stolen – it even out-blanded the Taurus, which was no mean feat. Regardless, he'd felt a pang of guilt as he'd hot-wired it. Several people were now facing the unpleasant task of dealing with their insurance companies regarding their stolen cars, all because of him. Still, he didn't really have a choice. He figured they'd probably understand if they knew what he'd been going through.

The gray house he was watching was equally unremarkable. Small, run-down, two floors, clapboard siding, gabled roof. Probably leased in the name of a shell company. Rent paid in advance. Practically untraceable, Matt imagined. It squatted there anonymously, its gray boards mirroring the dreary wintery sky overhead, looking as bleak and lifeless as the bare-limbed red oaks that dotted the quiet neighborhood. A small driveway ran alongside it and led to a covered single-car garage out back. The Chrysler was parked outside, as was the van – the one he'd last seen barreling down the snow-lined avenue after he'd jumped out of it.

His nerve endings bristled with impatience and anticipation. The answers he so wanted were probably inside that house, but he couldn't exactly waltz in there and get them. He needed to bide his time. Watch. Study. And come up with a plan. One that had half a chance of working. One that wouldn't end up with him dead.

He'd come up with one earlier, back at the motel, before driving over. A grand plan, one that had him excited – for a short spell, anyway.

He'd call the cops. Do the 'anonymous-tip' thing and tell them Bellinger's real killers were in the house. They'd send a car to check it out. The cops – maybe the ones who showed up at Bellinger's apartment that night – would come up to the door and knock. One of the goons – not bob-girl, presumably, since she was one of the 'witnesses' who'd 'seen' Matt chase down Bellinger – would answer. They'd have a little Q&A. Dance around some questions.

And then Matt would ramp things up a notch.

He'd pick up a couple of empty bottles from a Dumpster on the drive over, along with any old rag he could find. He'd buy a jerrican of fuel and a lighter at a gas station. He'd fill the bottles with fuel. He'd shred the rag into strips and stuff them into the necks of the bottles and use them as wicks. And then he'd firebomb the house.

Maybe from the back. Or from the side. Just sneak up to a spot where he wouldn't be seen and chuck a flaming bottle or two through a window. And watch. It would take them all by surprise. The cops would want to go in to help put out the fire. The goons would probably resist, not wanting them in the house where their gear might be on show. Their behavior would certainly be less than ingenuous, and they would probably behave suspiciously. The cops would get curious, especially given the reason they were there in the first place. They'd probably call for backup. A standoff would ensue. The goons would have a lot of explaining to do. In looking into the unexplained arson attack, the cops would find some forensic evidence in the van, linking it to Bellinger's murder. The goons would get mired in a procedural swamp. They'd be off Matt's back, and, with a bit of luck, Matt would be off the hook for the stabbing.

Maybe.

On the other hand, it could all go wrong and he could get shot by the cops and the case would be closed. And either way, he wouldn't get the thing he most wanted: to find out what they had done to his brother.

So he dropped that plan. Decided to play it more cautiously. Take things one step at a time. Maybe try and get some one-on-one time with one of the goons. In which case a weapon would be good. The van – and the car – could yield one. Something he could use to even out the odds a little. And maybe, with a bit of luck, he could then grab one of the killers and get the answers he wanted.

Maybe.

No one had gone in or out of the house since he'd been there, but the cars and the lights in the front ground-floor room suggested the goons were in. He tried to think back at how many were in the van – four, he thought. Which was bad enough. He didn't know if the two in the Chrysler were part of that crew, or if they were additional, in which case there'd be six of them in there. Which would be even worse.

The house next door looked dark and empty by comparison, with no sign of life apart from a Christmas tree that blinked on and off mind-numbingly in its front window. A five-foot-tall hedge ran between the houses, alongside the target's driveway. Matt thought of waiting till it got dark, to give him more cover, but he didn't feel like loitering around that long and wasn't sure how long they'd be staying in there.

He decided to chance it.

He scuttled alongside the hedge and made his way to the back of the house. He skulked behind the Chrysler and peeked out. He couldn't make out any movement at the back of the house. It was just dark and still. He looked through the 300C's window. Couldn't see anything inside, but the glove box and the trunk were the areas of real interest. The car's doors were locked, which was expected – and unhelpful.

It was a new car, high-specced, with robust locks and both perimetric and volumetric alarms as standard. Which meant that before he could get inside the cabin he'd need to get under the hood without disturbing the car too much. Not the easiest car to break into, certainly not with the basic tools he had at hand.

He crept over to the van. It was slightly older and had a more basic locking mechanism that would surrender more easily. He glanced inside. Again, nothing on view, but once inside, things could prove different.

He knelt by the passenger door and was about to start jimmying the lock when he heard a car slow down by the house and turn into the driveway. He ducked down and slipped quickly around to the front of the van as the other car, a black S-Class Mercedes, pulled up and stopped alongside the house.

Matt crouched low and peered out from under the van. He heard the Merc's door open and watched as a man climbed out of it and walked up to the back door. Matt leaned over and risked a side glance off the van's left fender. The man was close to six feet tall and had a sharp, accurate step. He walked with purpose. He had a shaved head and wore a dark suit that he was subtly packed into, but not with fat. Matt recognized the build from his time in prison. The slightly bow-legged step, the arms cocked out just a touch, limbs whose natural rest positions were impeded by the bulk of muscle. Not huge. Not in-your-face. But there, lurking under the otherwise-slender build, waiting to inflict damage.

As he turned, Matt saw the missing ear and the spiderwebbed burn scar spreading out from it. The unsettling sight took him by surprise. Matt wondered if the man was ex-military. Maybe they all were. And judging by the step, the suit, and the car, this guy didn't seem to be just another one of the drones. He was their boss. As if to confirm it, the rear door of the house creaked open as the man in the suit approached it. One of the goons stepped out and took an instinctive glance around as the hard case in the suit walked right past him without acknowledging him and disappeared into the house. A moment later, the goon followed him in and shut the door behind him.

Matt crouched low, his mind working double-time at interpreting this new variable and adjusting his options accordingly. One move sprang to the forefront of his mind immediately. He embraced it, sneaked over to the 300C, and slid under it.

CHAPTER 35

Mountains of Wadi Natrun, Egypt

'It's not safe,' Gracie told Father Jerome. 'We have to get you out of here.'

She quickly related to the three holy men what Ogilvy had told her. 'Trust me on this,' she concluded, 'I know how it works. The news vans are already on their way and the satellite hookups are already booked. It'll be a zoo out there before sunrise. At least at the monastery, you'll have four walls around you to keep the world at bay until we figure things out.'

What she didn't want to mention was another problem – not the bullying of the press, but an altogether more dangerous one. They were in an overwhelmingly Muslim country, in an overwhelmingly Muslim region. Sure, 10 percent or so of the country was Christian – Coptic, specifically – but that still left more than seventy million other Egyptians out there, and countless others in neighboring Muslim countries, who might take issue with what was unfolding. This was, after all, a region where the moon landings were still believed to be a hoax to promote American superiority, where everything had a 'Christian plot' angle to it, where the Crusades still cast a long and angry shadow.

Father Jerome's face sagged with dismay at the news, but he didn't object. He'd witnessed the savagery that men in the region had a long habit of inflicting on each other for no reason other than what tribe they belonged to or what religion they were born into. The abbot and the young monk didn't argue with Gracie's read of the situation either. What she was suggesting seemed to be the sensible move.

'We should take what we can with us,' she told them,

casting her eyes around the cave's spartan interior before pointing at the journals. 'Everything you wrote, Father. And anything else that's of value to you. I don't know what condition the cave will be in next time you see it.' She looked up at the markings on the ceiling with a sense of foreboding, wondering how long it would be before they'd be defaced, and asked for permission to film their exit, which was given. She got Dalton to shoot a quick take of the cave and of its ceiling while the others helped Father Jerome gather his belongings.

Before long, they were back under the stars and heading down the mountain.

CHAPTER 36

Brighton, Massachusetts

Matt was just sliding out from under the big Mercedes when he heard the back door of the house creak open.

He huddled against the car's front passenger door and froze. He couldn't risk a look, but he didn't need to. The odds were, it was the hard case in the suit, but he knew he was in trouble regardless of who was coming out of the house. The Merc was blocking the Chrysler and the van. Before either of them could be driven out, the Merc would have to be moved first. And the Merc itself was exposed. It had yards of open air in front and behind it, the side and rear of the house to its left and the five-foot hedge that separated the two houses to its right, behind Matt. All of which meant that if anyone was driving anywhere, the Merc was about to move, and Matt was about to find himself out of cover.

He was stuck. He'd known it was a possibility going in, but he'd still gone ahead with it, thinking it worth the risk. Right now, as he listened to the approaching footsteps, he sorely regretted not going with his original firebombing plan. Then again, everything looked better with hindsight, especially when your back was up against a wall – or, in this case, a dense, impenetrable five-foot hedge.

There was more than one set of footsteps, and he figured there were at least two of them approaching. If they were going into the Merc, he'd have someone in his face in a matter of seconds. He crouched down, cheek to the ground, trying to get a handle on how many of them there were and which way they were heading. The backyard sloped upward. He couldn't see anything for a tense moment, then one pair of shoes appeared – black brogues, the hard case's shoes, he thought – closely followed by another. Two of them. Headed for the

Merc. The hard case must have hit his alarm key fob, as the car beeped and the locks popped open with a loud snap.

Matt didn't have a choice.

He coiled up, waiting, his ears straining to pick up the approaching footsteps. He heard a door click open, the driver's door – and then a figure appeared on his side of the car, rounding the front right fender, a guy with high cheekbones and a brush cut that Matt thought he recognized from the car staking out Jabba's place. Matt just sprang up before the guy could react, catching him by surprise and landing a crushing fist on his chin. Brush Cut's face juddered sideways, twisting unnaturally around his neck, a loud, wet wheeze rushing out of his chest and mouth. He was tough and didn't go down. Instead, he tried to turn in and fight back, but Matt was now close enough to inflict more serious damage and hooked him with a ferocious uppercut that lifted Brush Cut momentarily off his feet before sending him staggering backward.

Matt heard movement on the other side of the car and, from the corner of his eye, saw the hard case in the suit stepping back and reaching under his coat. Brush Cut was groggy and having a hard time staying on his feet. Matt grabbed him from behind, curling his left hand around the guy's neck while diving his right hand under the guy's jacket, praying his fingers would find a gun somewhere. On the other side of the Merc, the hard case had his own gun out. He chambered a round and raised the gun at Matt, with Brush Cut between them.

Matt hit pay dirt. Brush Cut had a handgun tucked under his jacket, in a belt holster on his right hip. Matt's fingers found the gun's ribbed grip and yanked it out. He raised it, his right arm extended, level with his hostage's ear, and aimed it straight at the hard case.

'Get back,' Matt shouted, swinging the gun to his hostage's head and back at the hard case.

He sidestepped to his left, putting the car between him and the hard case, who raised his left hand in a calming gesture while keeping his gun aimed at Matt's face.

'Easy, Matt,' he said. 'Just take it easy.'

'Who the fuck are you people?' Matt yelled, still edging sideways, his eyes darting left and right nervously, keeping tabs on the front and rear of the house.

'I'm impressed that you made it here, Matt,' the hard case said, clearly trying to work out how Matt had found them. 'In fact, I'm pretty impressed by everything you've done since this thing started.'

Matt was now at the back corner of the Merc. The hard case wasn't backing away. He was actually tracking Matt, sidestepping smoothly and moving closer to the Merc that was now between them, eyeing the surroundings with radarlike focus. There was something deeply unnerving about him. The missing ear and the scar, the bald head that tapered up in the shape of a bullet – and they only served as a backdrop to the real darkness that emanated from the ceramic-black eyes that looked like they'd been to hell and back without blinking, the dark, eyeliner-like eyelids that rimmed them, and the sharp eyebrows framing the stygian mask that brooded out of the center of his face.

'And what is this thing?' Matt rasped. 'What the fuck's going on? What happened to my brother?'

The hard case shook his face slightly, in a condescending, tut-tutting way. 'You know what, Matt? You're too concerned with the past. You need to think more about your future.'

Matt backed up another step. 'What did you do to my brother?' he yelled again. 'Is he still alive?'

The hard case didn't flinch. He stayed unsettlingly calm, his cold eyes seemingly assessing Matt's position and evaluating possible outcomes. 'You're messing around with something you really don't want to be messing with,' he finally told him. 'My advice to you is to let it go. Find yourself a nice, deep hole, bury your head down, and forget any of this ever happened. Or better still – '

– and he just squeezed the trigger, once, with no discernible emotion, just made a decision and acted on it without a trace of emotion. The round hit the guy Matt was holding up squarely in the chest –

' – let me put you in it.'

Matt felt Brush Cut jerk and felt a sudden burn at his own side, by his left ribs, but he didn't have time to pause and check it out. He had to stay on his feet as everything rushed into a frenzied blur.

Brush Cut's legs gave and he started to fall just as the hard case fired again, then again. One of the shots hit Brush Cut in the shoulder, the bullet exiting close to Matt's crouched head, whizzing past his ear and splattering his face with blood and bone shards. Matt struggled to keep Brush Cut up, using him as a shield while firing back at the hard case, who ducked behind the Merc. He faltered backward, his eyes scanning around, the burning sensation in his left flank getting stronger with each step. The hard case came up for another shot, got Matt's hostage in the thigh. Two more bodies rushed out of the back of the house, guns out. They saw Matt, crouched into firing positions, but they were wide open and Matt got one of them in the shoulder a split second after he realized it was the auburn-haired girl from the van, the night they took him and Vince Bellinger. She tumbled sideways as if her feet had been knocked out from under her. The other shooter dived behind the Merc and joined the hard case. Matt kept moving, still using the bloodied-if-not-dead Brush Cut as a shield, lugging his heavy body back toward the street, step by step, inch by inch, firing away every time he spotted a flash of skin. A couple of shots whizzed by and he retaliated with three more of his own, then his gun's magazine spat out its last round and the slide locked in its open position.

He saw that the hard case and the other shooter cottoned onto it as soon as he did, and they emerged from cover with little concern. He looked around frantically and realized he was now only a couple of yards from the sidewalk. Summoning whatever energy he could muster, he dragged Brush Cut's dead weight back a few steps before letting go of him and bolting into the street.

He didn't look back. He just kept running, the spent gun in hand, hugging the parked cars before sprinting across the street and leaping onto the opposite sidewalk, putting a barrier of cars between him and the shooters' line of fire, hoping one last round wouldn't find him before he got to his Camry, wondering how badly he'd been hit already and whether or not he'd get the chance to find out.

CHAPTER 37

Deir Al-Suryan Monastery, Wadi Natrun, Egypt

As Gracie had predicted, they'd barely managed to beat the news crews to the monastery, and were now safely ensconced behind its walls. A growing number of cars and vans were gathering outside the gates. With the rest of the monks alarmed by the sudden activity – the monastery was home to almost two hundred of them – the abbot set out to calm them while dispatching Brother Ameen to talk to the journalists. The younger monk told those crowding the gates that Father Jerome had no comment as yet, and asked them to respect his privacy. The reporters protested loudly, but to no avail.

The siege had begun.

Gracie's satphone was back up and running. There was no point in staying under the radar any longer. On the contrary. She, Dalton, and Finch were supremely well placed to trump their peers on this story, which was now monopolizing the screens at all the major news channels, commanding continuous coverage and constant live updates. Their exclusive was alive and well, and less than half an hour after getting back, they were sending their first 'live' footage from the roof of the keep that abutted the monastery's entrance gate.

Standing on top of the large, sand-colored cube, Gracie weighed her words carefully as she faced the lens of Dalton's camera.

'He hasn't yet made a statement, Jack. As you can imagine, he's overwhelmed by what's happened in the last couple of days. All I can confirm to you at the moment is that Father Jerome is indeed here with us at the monastery.'

'But you've talked to him, haven't you?' Roxberry asked, through her earpiece.

'Yes, I have,' she affirmed.

'And what did he tell you?'

Roxberry's frustration was coming through loud and clear, and Gracie's cagey replies weren't helping. She'd avoided mentioning to him that they'd shown Father Jerome the footage of the sightings, and hadn't shared what he'd told them in the cave. She and Finch had sifted with great care through what she would or wouldn't say, deciding that it wasn't their place – not yet, anyway – to announce things that the priest had said in confidence and that could be taken wildly out of context and distorted at will, which was inevitable. Hard as it was to keep a huge scoop like that to themselves, they'd agreed that it was more appropriate to give Father Jerome the chance to tell his story himself, if and when he chose to do it. They'd approach him for a live interview as soon as he'd had a chance to rest and let it all sink in.

'He asked us to respect his need for a bit of peace right now, which we fully understand.'

She could almost feel Roxberry's rising blood pressure throbbing through her earpiece.

She and Finch had also debated whether or not to use the material they'd shot inside the cave. Gracie felt they'd been granted a privileged viewing, and she had misgivings about airing the footage, feeling as if she'd be betraying the priest's trust. But, as Finch had pointed out, they couldn't not use it either. It was too good for that, it was part of the story, and besides, the British documentary crew had been allowed to film it for broadcast purposes. It was already airing around the world. He couldn't see the harm in simply confirming it, and Gracie had agreed.

She signed off, expecting an instantaneous and irate callback from the news desk, and stepped over to the edge of the flat roof. The roof had nothing but a low, three-inch lip around it, and Gracie felt a bit uneasy looking at the sharp drop-off. As she gazed beyond it at the flat, barren landscape outside the monastery's walls, she also had a different kind of bad feeling. The trickle of headlights bouncing across the desert was growing ominously as more and more cars converged on the monastery. She knew the region well enough to know how quickly things got out of hand, how suddenly religious passions got inflamed and escalated into bloodshed. She tore her gaze away from the eerie light show and joined Finch and Dalton, who were huddled around the open laptop, watching the Al Jazeera reporter's live broadcast from outside the gates.

'Weird, isn't it?' she observed, overcome by a sudden tiredness and setting herself down cross-legged beside them. 'Sitting here, inside the gates, watching ourselves from the outside in.'

'It's like a bizarro-world version of a hostage situation,' Dalton intoned.

Gracie noticed a shift in the shadows coming out of the roof hatch to her left, and saw Brother Ameen's head pop out. He gave them a subdued nod and climbed up the rickety ladder to join them.

'How's Father Jerome?' Gracie asked.

He shrugged wearily. 'Confused. Scared. Praying for guidance.'

Gracie nodded in empathy, frustrated that she couldn't give him any answers herself. She knew that the pressure he was under was only starting. Watching the streaming news reports on the laptop only confirmed it. The reports coming in from Cairo and Alexandria were troubling. The revelation that Father Jerome had effectively foreseen what was still unexplained was causing a huge stir across the country. The polarization of opinions was already clear, even though the story had barely broken. The clips chosen for broadcast showed the local Christians to be confused, but generally excited, by the news. For them, Father Jerome had long been a beacon of positive transformation, and on the whole, they seemed to be embracing his involvement as something inspirational and wanted to know more. The Muslims who were interviewed, on the other hand, were either dismissive or angry. And, Gracie thought cynically, probably chosen for how inflammatory – hence attention-grabbing – their reactions were. Clerics were denouncing Father Jerome and calling on their followers not to be swayed by what they were already describing as trickery.

She glanced over at the young monk. His face was tight with tension.

'What is it?' she asked him.

He kept his eyes on the screen for a moment, then turned to her.

'I don't understand what this thing is that you all saw. I don't understand Father Jerome's visions either, or how they're both related. But there are some things I do know. Egypt's not a rich country. Half the people around here have little or no education and live on less than two dollars a day. Even doctors in public hospitals don't get paid more than that. But we're also a very religious country,' he continued, his eyes drifting off to the chaotic light show below. 'People take comfort in their religion because they don't see hope in anything else around them. They don't have faith in their politicians. They're tired of traffic and pollution and rising prices and falling wages and corruption. They have no one else to trust but God. It's the same everywhere else in this part of the world. Religious identity matters more to people out here than their common citizenship. And here, in this country – we're on a knife edge as far as sectarian differences are concerned. It's taboo to talk about it, but it's a real problem. There have been a lot of incidents. Our brothers at the Abu Fana Monastery were attacked twice in the last year. The second time, they were beaten and whipped and made to spit on the cross.' He paused then turned, his eyes bouncing between the three of them before settling on Gracie. 'There's a lot of tension and a lot of misunderstanding between the people of this country. And there are millions of them within an hour's drive of here.'

Gracie understood. It wasn't a good mix.

'Bringing Father Jerome down from the cave was a good move,' he added. 'But it might not be enough.'

She'd been thinking the same thing. An alarming vision coalesced inside her: that of two seriously antagonistic groups outside the gates, Coptic Christians on a pilgrimage of sorts to hear what Father Jerome had to say, and Muslims out to repel whatever outrage the *kuffar* – the blasphemers – were perpetrating.

Again, not a good mix. Unless you were cooking up some nitro.

'Where's the army?' she asked. 'Don't they know what's going on here? Shouldn't they be sending people here to protect the monastery? And the cave – it's gonna get trashed if things get out of control.'

'Not the army,' the monk said somberly, 'the internal security forces. They're twice as big as the army, which tells you where the government perceives the real threat. But they don't usually send them out until after a problem catches fire. And when they do show up, things generally get worse. They don't have a problem with using force to bring things back to normal. A lot of force.'

A swell of unease rolled through her. She turned to Finch. 'Can you get hold of someone at the embassy? Maybe they can rustle something up.'

'I can try, but – I think Brother Ameen is right. Might be better to get out of here before it gets out of hand. And that goes for Father Jerome too.'

Dalton indicated the crowd below with a nudge of his head. 'It's not going to be easy.'

Gracie's expression darkened further. 'We have a car and

a driver. And it's still calm out there. We should leave at first light. While it's doable.' She faced Finch again. 'We can take Father Jerome to the embassy. We need to let them know we're coming. We'll figure the rest out from there.'

'What if he doesn't want to leave?' Finch asked.

Gracie turned to Brother Ameen. He gave her an uncertain shrug. 'I'll talk to him, but I don't know what he'll say.'

'I'll go with you. We've got to convince him,' she insisted as she got off the floor. Brother Ameen nodded and crossed over to the open hatch. Gracie turned to Finch. 'First light, okay?' She gave him a determined look before gripping the sides of the hatch and disappearing into the heart of the keep.

CHAPTER 38

Houston, Texas

The Reverend Nelson Darby's cell phone rang just as the tall, elegant man was stepping out of his chauffeur-driven Lincoln Town Car. He was in great spirits, having just witnessed a dress rehearsal of the five-hundred-person choir's Christmas show. The caller ID on his screen prompted him to wave his assistant on, and he stayed back to take the call on the wide stairs that led to the handsome manor that housed the administrative core of his sprawling 'Christian values' empire, an empire whose flagship was the resplendent 17,000-seat glass-and-steel megachurch Darby had built, one of a growing number of full-service Christian cocoons the likes of which hadn't been seen since the thirteenth-century cathedral towns of Europe.

'Reverend,' the caller said. 'How are things?'

'Roy,' Darby answered heartily, as always pleased to hear Roy Buscema's measured voice. A fit man in his early forties, Darby had an angular face, deep-set eyes, and thin lips. With his backswept, perfectly coiffed jet-black mane and Brioni suits, he looked more like a pre-credit crunch investment banker on the make than a preacher. Which wasn't inappropriate, given that both involved managing multimillion-dollar enterprises in a highly competitive marketplace. 'Good to hear from you. How are things with you?'

Buscema, a gregarious journalist for the *Washington Post*, had met the pastor a little over a year earlier, when he'd been commissioned to write a feature profiling him for the newspaper's Sunday magazine. The finely observed and highly complimentary article that he'd written had laid the groundwork for the friendship that followed, a friendship that grew into an unofficial consigliere-godfather relationship with all the hours they spent discussing and strategizing the pastor's endorsements in the marathon presidential primary of the last year. Buscema's take on the events had been impressively astute and always correct, and he'd let the pastor in on more than one scoop that had borne itself out. The pastor was converted. He saw in Buscema a savvy analyst who had the pulse of the people and knew where to go to get his prognoses corroborated, and as such – and given that Darby was one of the Christian Right's political bigwigs – he was an invaluable man to have at hand.

Especially now, with all this going on.

'Crazier than ever,' Buscema replied. 'But hey, I can't complain really. It's what we're here for. Say, you been watching that thing over the ice caps?'

'Who isn't?'

'What do you think?'

'To be honest with you, I'm a bit befuddled by the whole thing, Roy,' the pastor confided with his usual disarming candor. 'What in God's name is going on out there?'

Buscema's tone took on a slightly more serious edge. 'I think we ought to talk about it. I'm gonna be in town tomorrow,' he told the pastor. 'If you have some time, why don't we get together?'

'Sounds good,' Darby replied. 'Come out to the house. I'm curious to hear your take on it.'

I bet you are, Buscema thought as they agreed on a time. He said good-bye and hung up. He then scrolled down his contacts list and made a second, almost identical, call.

A third, similar call followed soon after that.

As did six other carefully coordinated calls, made by two other men of a similar profile to his, to other influential evangelical leaders across the country.

CHAPTER 39

Woburn, Massachusetts

The bullet hadn't done as much damage as Matt had first feared. It had clipped him just below his bottom left rib, punching a small hole through him less than an inch in from his side. Not exactly a graze, but not a major organ-buster either. Still, he had a couple of half-inch holes gouged out of him. Holes that needed to be sealed. Which meant stitches. And given that going to a hospital or to a doctor was out of the question, whatever sewing talents Jabba had would need to be summoned.

Jabba was holding up surprisingly well. He'd managed not to throw up when Matt first staggered back into their room, his clothes soaked with blood. He'd made it to the closest drugstore and picked up the items on a shopping list Matt had hastily dictated to him: iodine to clean the wound; any anesthetic cream he could find, to numb the skin; sewing needles, along with a lighter to sterilize them; some nylon thread; painkillers; bandages.

Most impressively, he'd so far managed to complete three sutures on the entry wound without puking, which he'd come close to doing while attempting the first stitch. Three more would do the trick on that front. Then he had the exit hole to take care of.

They were huddled in the far-from-antiseptic bathroom of the motel room. Matt was in his shorts, on the floor with his back against the tiled wall by the bathtub, grinding down his teeth as Jabba pushed the needle through the caldera of skin that rimmed his raw, open wound. The sensation was far worse than the immediate after-effect of getting shot, when the wound was still warm and the pain receptors hadn't started their furious onslaught up his spine. He felt weak and nauseous and was fighting hard not to pass out. He swam through it by telling himself, over and over, that it would pass. Which it would. He just had to get through this part. He'd had a couple of bad wounds before, and although he'd never been shot, he tried to convince himself that this wasn't any worse than a nasty cut from a blade. Which was something he'd had. Only then, he'd been sewn shut by a real doctor who'd used a proper anesthetic, not an over-the-counter cream more suited to hemorrhoids and leg waxing.

He blinked away tears of pain as the needle came out the other side.

'This look right to you?' Jabba's fingers trembled as he pulled the thread through.

Matt didn't look down. His sweaty face winced under the strain. 'You're the movie buff. You must have seen them do it a few times, right?'

'Yeah, but I usually turn away when they're doing it,' Jabba grimaced as he pulled the two sides of the wound closer to each other and tied a knot in the thread, adding, pointedly, 'which, by the way, they usually do to themselves.'

'Yeah, but then they end up with these Frankenstein-like scars, whereas with Dr. Jabba on the case . . .'

'. . . the Frankenstein look's guaranteed,' Jabba quipped as he cut the end of the thread off. It wasn't a particularly elegant piece of stitching, but at least the wound wasn't bleeding anymore. 'See?'

Matt shrugged. 'Don't sweat it. I hear the ladies just love the hard-ass scars,' he cajoled him. 'When you're done with me, maybe you could take a look at mending that hole in my jacket? It's kind of an old favorite, you know?'

Seven stitches and half an hour later, they were done.

As he cleaned up the bloody mess around them, Jabba filled Matt in on what he'd discovered while he was out, which wasn't much. He'd given the deadbeat receptionist ten bucks to let him use his computer. He'd logged into his

Skype account and made a few calls while burrowing through the Internet, trying to find out more about the team that had died in the helicopter crash.

He'd managed to come up with two other names to add to Danny's and to Reece's – a chemical engineer by the name of Oliver Serres, and a biomolecular engineer named Sunil Kumar.

'Both were at the top of their game and highly regarded,' he told Matt. 'But it's weird, dude. I mean, Kumar's a biologist. So far, we've got him, a chemist, Reece – an electrical engineer and computer scientist – and Danny, a programmer. The last three, I get. But Kumar . . . what's a biomolecular engineer have to do with this?'

The nuance was beyond Matt at the best of times. In his current state, it just streaked past him. 'What do you think?'

'I don't know, man,' Jabba said with visible discomfort. 'These biomolecular guys, they're into rearranging DNA, playing around with the building blocks of life. Pulling apart and rearranging atoms and molecules like they were Lego bricks. And this sign in the sky, the way it looks organic, alive even . . . the gray area between biology and chemistry, between life and non-life, you know? It's giving me a creepy feeling. Like maybe what they're doing has more to do with some kind of designed life-form than a projected image.'

Matt frowned, trying to wrap his head around what Jabba was saying. 'You've spent too much time watching *The X-Files*.'

Jabba shrugged, like it wasn't a bad thing. 'These biotech guys, they're always getting flak for messing around in God's closet. God's closet, man. Who knows what they found in there.'

He let it drift and ran the cold tap. He drank from it, then splattered water across his face before filling up a glass and handing it to Matt. He didn't have much more to tell him. He hadn't been able to find any mention of who was backing Reece's project, let alone what it involved.

Darkness was closing in fast outside their room, which suited Matt just fine. He wasn't going anywhere tonight. He needed to rest. Jabba went back out and picked up some blood-free clothes for Matt and brought back some food and some Coke cans. They wolfed it all down greedily while watching the news. The footage from the cave in Egypt was hogging the airwaves, and the warm pizzas, though welcome, weren't doing much to quell the cold, dismal feeling inside them.

'This is getting bigger,' Jabba noted glumly. 'More elaborate.'

Matt nodded. 'They know what they're doing.'

'That's not what I mean.'

'What then?'

'These people. They've got serious resources at their disposal. Think about what they're doing. First, they rustle up some major brain power, put them to work somewhere for, what, a couple of years? Then they kill them all off.' He noticed a hint of resistance on Matt's face and quickly amended his words. 'Or, whatever, maybe lock them up somewhere and fake their deaths – even more complicated to pull off. But no one seems to know anything about what this scientific dream team was working on, and there's no record of who they were all working for. The one thing that's sure is that there's some serious moolah involved. Danny, Reece, and the others, they wouldn't have gotten involved if they didn't know they had all the backup they needed. And the kind of research they do, it ain't cheap. Plus the rest of it, all this,' he said as he waved at the screen. 'Seriously deep pockets, dude.'

'Okay, so where'd the money come from?'

Jabba thought about it for a second. 'Two possibilities. Reece could've raised the money privately,' he speculated, 'though not from a VC or a public company. There'd be a trace of it, especially after the deaths. No, it would have to be private money. Not easy, given the scale of it. And practically untraceable, given that the entire creative team was supposedly wiped out.'

'What's the other possibility?'

'Reece was doing this for a government agency. A highly classified project. Which sounds about right to me.'

Matt's face darkened with uncertainty. He'd been wondering about the same thing. 'Any particular candidates?'

Jabba shrugged. 'DARPA. In-Q-Tel.'

Matt looked a question at him.

'DARPA. The Defense Advanced Research Projects Agency. It's part of the DoD. They fund a ton of research. Everything from microbots to virtual battlefields. Any technology that can help us win these wars and defeat those who hate our freedom,' he added mockingly.

'And the other one?'

'In-Q-Tel. It's the CIA's venture capital arm. They're early stage investors, which is actually very savvy of them when you think about it. Get in on the ground floor. Find out about any useful technology while it's still being dreamed up. They've got their fingers in a lot of tech companies – and that includes a few of the big, household-name Internet sites you and I use on a daily basis.' He gave him a pointed, big-brother-is-watching-you look.

Matt absorbed what Jabba was trying to say. 'A government op.'

'It's pretty obvious, isn't it? I mean, if what we're saying is true, if they've really faked this thing, they're on their way to convincing everyone out there that God's talking to us. Maybe even through the good Father Jerome. Who else would try to pull off something like this?'

Matt could see the sense in what Jabba was saying, only deep down, something was nagging at him. He winced with doubt. 'You're probably right, but . . . I don't know. Something about the guys in the van. Their place down in Brighton.'

'What?'

'They're a small unit. Working with good resources, but not overwhelming ones. Bunkered down in a small house in a quiet neighborhood. I don't know. If it is a black op, it's not just off the books, it's way off the books.'

'Even worse, then,' Jabba added emphatically. 'Officially, they don't exist. Whoever sent them's got full deniability. They can do anything they want to us and no one will ever know they were there.' He fixed Matt with a sobering stare. 'We need to quit asking questions and disappear, dude. Seriously. I mean, I know he's your brother and all, but . . . we're outgunned.'

Matt processed his warning. He was too tired to think straight, his nerves numb with fatigue and apprehension. But one thought kept coming back to him, a steadying keel that was keeping his head above water in the storm of confusion that swirled around him. He looked at Jabba, and just said, 'What if Danny's still alive?'

Jabba took in a long, sobering breath. 'You really think he might be?'

Matt thought back to the hard case's reaction when he'd asked him that question. The man had an impenetrable poker face, and he hadn't been able to read him. 'I don't know, but . . . what if he is? You want me to just forget about him and run?'

Jabba held his gaze for a moment, a conflicted glimmer in his eyes. It was as if his mind was desperately looking for a way to flush Matt's words back out of his system and was failing miserably to do so. Then he nodded.

'Okay.'

Matt acknowledged his acceptance with a small nod of his own. After a quiet moment, he asked Jabba if he could hustle a few more minutes of online time from the receptionist and check the tracker's website.

Jabba left him alone, then came back a few minutes later

armed with some printed screen shots. He handed them to Matt. The tracker had moved within what Matt estimated had been mere minutes of his escape from the house in Brighton. Which was expected. Neighbors would have reported the shooting. The place would have been swarming with cops pretty quickly.

They'd obviously vacated their safe house in a rush. Hastily. Panicked. Matt's incursion had screwed them up. Which lit a tiny fire of satisfaction deep in his gut.

He checked the tracker's current position. It was stable, at a location in the Seaport district of the city. Which meant the big Mercedes – the hard case's car, the one he'd moved the tracker onto – was there.

Matt glanced over at the handgun on the night table, then let his head loll back against the pillows. His eyelids rolled down and blocked out the world, and the last image that floated into his mind before everything went quiet was the hard case's face.

The man had the answers Matt needed. And hard case or not, one way or another, Matt knew he'd have to wrest them out of him.

CHAPTER 40

Deir Al-Suryan Monastery, Wadi Natrun, Egypt

By dawn, the desert plain outside the monastery was teeming with life. Dozens of cars were scattered far and wide, strewn across the parched wasteland beyond the monastery's walls and all along the narrow road that led up to its entrance gate. People – men, mostly – milled around by their cars or stood in small groups, tense, uncertain, waiting.

It was time to go.

Gracie and Finch sat on either side of Father Jerome in the middle row of the people carrier, with Dalton riding shotgun – his camera locked and loaded – next to Yusuf and Brother Ameen in the back.

The noise coming from outside the walls was disconcertingly subdued for such a large crowd. The general silence only accentuated the tension and the anticipation, like the wait between lightning and thunder. There were some pockets of activity, here and there. Hints of music wafted in from small groupings of worshippers, their heads down in prayer as they chanted traditional Coptic hymns. But there were also many pockets of disturbance, farther back, away from the monastery's walls. Several firebrand clerics were angrily spouting invective, denouncing the priest and the sign to clusters of willing followers. The internal security forces were nowhere to be seen, and while the two opposing groups hadn't collided, it was clear that the plain could erupt into violence at any moment.

Gracie fretted. *It can't last. They're going to be at each other's throats any minute now.* Which was why Father Jerome had agreed – reluctantly – to leave. He was the lightning rod. And if he left, perhaps the storm could be avoided.

She watched as the abbot pushed the people carrier's door shut. He peered in through the dark, tinted glass and gave them a small farewell wave, his face etched with concern. Father Jerome returned the wave with a forlorn look. He seemed even more lost now than he had in the cave.

The abbot waved to two monks manning the gate. They nodded and pulled its huge doors open. As the ancient cedar leaves pivoted inward slowly, creaking on their rusty hinges, a rising cacophony gushed in with them as the crowd outside took note and sprang to life.

Gracie's pulse quickened as she heard the ambient noise rise around her. She shifted uncomfortably in her seat, staring out of her window, the combination of the car's powerful air-conditioning and the musty smell of incense from Father Jerome's cassock making her feel even more heady.

'Time to rhumba,' Dalton said, shifting his camera from the side window and aiming it forward.

Gracie swallowed hard.

The old people carrier lurched forward and charged out of the gate. It advanced quickly along the monastery's wall, and almost immediately, people started swarming across the scrub and converging on it. As the van cleared the perimeter wall and turned down the road that led away from the monastery, the crowd around it swelled. Countless hands reached out, trying to stop their escape. Yusuf had to slow down as the wedge of clear space ahead of him disappeared. With his hand pressed against the horn, he managed to keep going another thirty yards or so at a sputtering crawl before coming to a complete stop, blocked by a wall of people.

Gracie leaned over and looked out past Yusuf and Dalton, who was panning his camera around to capture the pandemonium all around the van. Desperate faces were pressed against the Previa's tinted windows, calling out Father Jerome's name, trying to see if he was inside, pleading for him to talk to them. They rattled the door handles, fighting the locks, their pained, intense features distorted from being squeezed against the van, their sweaty, dusty hands streaking the windows. Father Jerome shrank into his seat as he darted nervous glances left and right at the faces that looked all the more threatening behind the dark glass.

'We've got to go back,' Finch urged Yusuf, 'we've got to get back to the monastery.'

'We can't,' Gracie said as she craned her neck back and saw the mass of bodies pressing against the car from all sides, the loud thumps against the roof and windows echoing like war drums. 'We're boxed in.'

At the edge of the crowd, on a small rise by the crumbling remnants of an old wall, three men in a canvas-topped pickup truck surveyed the unfolding chaos with great interest through military-issue, sand-colored, high-powered binoculars.

As the people carrier disappeared behind the swarm of bodies, Fox Two watched and decided it was time to act.

He signaled his men with a curt hand.

One of his men peeled up a corner of the canvas top, enough to expose the tripod-mounted, drumlike device that lurked underneath. Another man, positioned behind it, looked through its targeting scope and aimed it at the scrum of men crowding the back of the Previa.

He double-checked the settings on the device.

Then he hit the trigger.

The crush of people pressed against the people carrier recoiled back for the briefest of moments, as if struck by an unseen force, their faces contorted in discomfort and pain, their hands rising to block their ears.

The effect only lasted a second, but it was long enough for Finch to catch it – as did Brother Ameen. As the mob jerked back, a crater of clear space opened up behind the Previa.

Brother Ameen caught Finch's eye – both their faces were locked in confusion – then he pointed back frantically and yelled, 'Go back,' to Yusuf.

The driver and Gracie swung their heads back and spotted the opening.

'Back. Go back now,' Brother Ameen shouted again.

Yusuf hesitated.

'Let's go, come on, back up,' Gracie yelled at him, also pointing back fiercely.

The driver nodded reluctantly, slammed the car into reverse, and – with his hand still on the horn – eased the car backward. The men flinched back in surprise, widening the opening behind the Previa.

'Keep going,' Gracie insisted, scanning in all directions. 'Get us back to the gates.'

The Previa gathered momentum, Yusuf taking advantage of the faltering crowd and keeping his foot down. They swerved around the bend at the far corner of the monastery, and the going got easier as they rushed up its long perimeter wall, still in reverse gear and chased by the frenzied horde. Fighting broke out as people lashed out and grabbed at each other, with Father Jerome's followers trying to block the followers of the Islamic firebrands from getting to the van. The Previa kept moving, slipping past the tangle of fists and blood, finally making it to the monastery's gates, which swung open just as it reached them. Yusuf skillfully managed to thread the Previa through the opening before the gates slammed shut and blocked off the crazed posse's advance.

They all tumbled out of the car in a daze, hearts thumping, veins drowning with adrenaline. Dalton was still filming, capturing every moment of their escape.

'Let's go up there,' Gracie yelled to Dalton and Finch, pointing up at the keep that stood next to the gate, jutting in from the perimeter wall. Finch nodded and said, 'Let's get the Began up,' lifting the compact satellite dish out of the Previa. 'The guys on the outside are getting this live.'

Gracie turned to Father Jerome. 'Please go inside, Father. You need to be somewhere safe, away from the gate,' she cautioned. She glanced at the abbot, whose grave face nodded with agreement.

Father Jerome didn't seem convinced.

He didn't acknowledge her words. He seemed distant, his mind preoccupied elsewhere. He was staring beyond her, beyond the gate even, at the people crowding it and shouting out his name, and seemed curiously calm.

'I need to talk to them,' he finally said, his voice settled and certain.

His eyes traveled back to Gracie and to the abbot. Then, without awaiting further words, he stepped away from the car and headed toward the keep.

'Wait, Father,' Gracie called out as she rushed in after him, closely followed by the abbot and Brother Ameen.

'I must talk to them,' Father Jerome insisted, without turning or stopping as he reached the narrow staircase and began marching up its stone steps.

They followed him across the second-floor drawbridge, into the keep and all the way up until they reached the top floor. The rickety wooden ladder still stood there, in a corner of the chapel, poking out through the small hatch. Moments later, they were all standing on the roof.

Gracie, Finch, and Dalton inched forward for a peek at the crowd below.

The scene below was unnerving. Hundreds of people were massed against the gates of the monastery, chanting, shouting, waving their hands and pumping their fists into the air, starved for a response, looking nervously over their shoulders as, behind them, the violence was growing, the pockets of fighting spreading like wildfire, threatening to engulf the entire plain.

Dalton got the live feed hooked up while Finch got through to Atlanta on the satphone. Gracie grabbed her earpiece and mike, mentally running through what she would soon be telling a world audience while watching the old priest as he stood by the hatch, staring ahead at the edge of the roof twenty feet in front of him, the only barrier between him and the clamoring mob below. From where he was standing, he could hear them, but he couldn't see them yet. The abbot and the young monk were talking to him, pleading with him not to expose himself in that way, telling him someone below could easily have a weapon and might take a shot at him. Father Jerome was having none of it. He was calmly shaking his head, a strange mix of resolve and fear radiating from him. His arms were hanging down listlessly, his fingers straight, his sandaled feet idle. He turned his head sideways and met Gracie's gaze, and, with the smallest, most stoic of nods, he started moving forward.

Gracie turned in alarm to Finch and at Dalton. They were huddled by the small, cross-topped dome that occupied a corner of the otherwise flat roof. Dalton had his camera up and was tracking the priest in a low crouch. Finch gave Gracie the sign that they were live. Gracie held up the mike but felt momentarily dumbstruck as she edged forward, tracking the old man, who soon reached the edge of the roof.

He stood there and looked down, and the crowd erupted in a mix of whoops and cheers and angry shouts. The throng pressed forward, calling his name out and waving, the euphoria of the faithful at the front of the mob only riling even more those opposed to Father Jerome's appearance, and the fighting farther back gained in intensity. Shouts of 'Kafir,' Blasphemer, and 'La ilah illa Allah,' There is no God but Allah, resounded angrily across the plain as incensed protesters started throwing rocks up at the keep.

Father Jerome stared down at the raging maelstrom

below, beads of sweat trickling down his face. Slowly, he raised his arms, stretching them high and wide in a welcoming gesture. Again, as his mere appearance had done a short moment earlier, the gesture only seemed to polarize the crowd below even more and fuel the fighting.

'Please,' he yelled out in an Arabic that was heavily accented, 'Please, stop. Please stop and listen to me.' His pleas could hardly be heard over the chaos raging below, and had no effect on the commotion. With rocks still pelting the wall of the keep and flying wildly past him, he remained steadfast and shut his eyes, his face locked in deep concentration, his arms held high –

– and suddenly, the crowd gasped in shock. Gracie saw people pointing upward – not at the priest, but higher up, at the sky above him, and she spun her head up and saw a ball of light, perhaps twenty feet or so in diameter, swirling over the priest. It hovered there for a moment, then started to rise directly above him, and as it did, it suddenly flared up both in size and in brightness and morphed into the sign, the same one she'd seen over the ice shelf. It now blazed overhead, a massive, spherical kaleidoscope of shifting light patterns, its lower edge hovering no more than twenty feet or so directly above Father Jerome.

The throng below just froze, rooted in place, entranced, staring up in openmouthed awe. The stones stopped flying. The brawls ended. The shouting died out. The sign was just there, shimmering brilliantly, rotating very slowly, almost within reach, closer now than it had been over the research ship, its radiant lines and circles mesmerizing.

Dalton was lying on his back at the very edge of the roof, filming the sign and panning back down to get the crowd's reaction. Gracie was still crouching near him, fifteen feet or so away from Father Jerome, who had his head tilted back and was staring up at the blazing apparition above him, dumbfounded. The camera swung back, stopping momentarily to settle on

Gracie. She stared into the dark abyss of the lens, tongue-tied. She wanted to say something, she could feel the whole world watching, hanging on the edge of their seats, willing her to tell them what it felt like to be there, but she couldn't do it. The moment was simply beyond words. She looked up at the blazing sphere of light, then Father Jerome brought his head back down, and as he did, she caught his eye. She could tell that he was shivering, and saw a tear trickle down his cheek. He looked scared and confused, his stricken expression telegraphing an am-I-really-doing-this anguish to her and quietly pleading for some kind of confirmation, as if he didn't believe what was happening. She mustered up a confirming nod and a supportive smile – then his expression shifted, as if something had suddenly startled him from within. He closed his eyes, as if locked in concentration, then, a few seconds later, he turned to face the crowd. He looked down on them for a moment, then he spread his arms expansively and tilted his head upward to face the sign. He shut his eyes again and breathed in deeply, basking in the sign's radiance, drinking in its energy. The masses below were still paralyzed, staring up in shocked silence, their arms stretched upward toward him, reaching out, as if trying to touch the hollow globe of light.

Father Jerome maintained his outstretched stance for the better part of a minute, then he opened his eyes to face the crowd.

'Pray with me,' he bellowed out to them, his voice thick with emotion, his arms raised to the heavens. 'Let us all pray together.'

And they did.

In a stadium wave-like reaction that spread slowly and silently from the front to the back of the crowd, every single person outside the monastery – Christian and Muslim, believer and protester alike – fell to their knees and bent forward, all of them dropping their foreheads to the ground and prostrating themselves in fearful adulation.

CHAPTER 41

Washington, D.C.

'What the hell are you doing? I thought we had an agreement.'

Rydell was seething. He'd been up through the night, monitoring the news. The images from Egypt had exploded across his TV screen a little after midnight, and right now, pacing around the cabin of his private jet by a quiet hangar at Reagan National Airport, his senses still throbbed with the burns of their visual sharpnel.

'We never agreed on it, Larry,' Drucker replied smoothly from his lush, padded seat. 'You just wouldn't have it any other way.'

'So you just went out and did it anyway?'

'We both have a lot invested in this. I wasn't about to jeopardize it all because of your stubbornness.'

'Stubbornness?' Rydell flared up. 'You don't know what you're doing, Keenan. Have you even thought about where this goes from here?'

'It's working, isn't it?'

'It's too early to tell.'

Drucker tilted his head slightly. 'Don't be disingenuous. It demeans you.'

'I don't know if it's working, but—'

'It's working, Larry,' Drucker interrupted emphatically. 'It's working because that's what people are used to. It's what they've been used to for thousands of years.'

'We didn't need it.'

'Of course we did. What did you expect? Did you think people would see the sign and just "get" it?'

'Yes. If we gave them a chance.'

'That's just naïve. What people don't understand they just push away to the far corners of their minds and eventually it fades away and gets forgotten. 'Cause it's safer that way. No, people need someone to tell them what to believe in. It's worked before, many times. And it'll work again.'

'And then what?' Rydell fumed. 'Where do you go from here?'

Drucker smiled. 'We just let him grow his following. Get the message across.'

'That's untenable and you know it,' Rydell flared up. 'You're building up something that's going to be impossible to maintain.'

'Not if you graft it onto an existing structure. One that has staying power. One that can last.'

Rydell shook his head. 'I can't believe you're saying this. You, of all people.'

Drucker chuckled. 'You should be enjoying the irony of it. You should be sitting back and laughing instead of getting all worked up about it.'

'I can't even begin to . . .' Rydell's mind was overwhelmed with indignation. 'You don't get it, do you? You don't see how wrong you are.'

'Come on, Larry. You know how the world works. There are only two surefire ways to get people to do what you want them to do. You either put on an iron glove and make them do it. Or you tell them God wants them to do it. If God wills it,' he scoffed, 'it shall be done. That's when they listen. And given that we don't live under an Uncle Joe or a Chairman Mao – '

'That was the whole point,' Rydell protested. 'God was supposed to be willing it. God. Not his self-appointed, holier-than-thou representatives.'

'That wouldn't work, Larry. It's too vague. Too open to interpretation. You're asking people to decipher the message on their own, and that would be giving them far too much credit. That's never worked. They're not used to figuring things out for themselves. They like to follow, to be led. They need a guide. A messenger. A prophet. Always have. Always will.'

'So you create, what, a Second Coming?'

'Not exactly, but close. And why not? A major chunk of the planet's expecting something like this. All this talk of End of Times and Armageddon. It's a golden opportunity.'

'What about the other religions? 'Cause you do know there are others on the planet, right? How do you think they're going to react to your manufactured messiah?'

'He won't be exclusive. It's been factored in. His message will embrace all.'

'Embrace all and encourage them to follow Jesus?' Rydell said acidly.

'Well,' Drucker mused with a mischievous twist to his mouth, 'That's not the main message he'll be bringing, but I suspect it may well be a secondary effect of his preaching.'

'Great,' Rydell retorted fiercely. 'And in doing that, you'll be propping up this mass delusion we haven't been able to shake for thousands of years. Can you imagine the field day these preachers are gonna have with this? Can you imagine how much power you'd be handing to all those blow-dried, self-serving egomaniacs out there? You'll turn every born-again politician and every televangelist into a saint who can do no wrong. And before you know it, they'll reclassify the pill as a form of abortion and ban it, the *Left Behind* books will become required reading in schools in between mass burnings of Harry Potter, kids will be saying Hail Marys for detention, and we'll have a creationist museum in every town. If that's the trade-off, I think I'd rather stick with global warming.'

'It doesn't have to be that way. See, you're forgetting one thing,' Drucker pointed out as he leaned forward, his face animated with expectation. 'We control the messenger. Think about it, Larry. We've got a chance to create our own prophet. A messiah that we own. Just imagine the possibilities. Think of what we can make people do.'

Drucker studied Rydell through cold, calculating eyes.

'You know we're right,' he continued. 'You know this was the only way to go. These people don't read newspapers. They don't research things on the Internet. They listen to what their preachers tell them – and they believe them. Fanatically. They don't question what the preachers say. They don't bother to fact-check the bullshit they hear in their megachurches. They're happy to swallow it whole, no matter how ridiculous it is, and not even an army of Pulitzer Prize-winning thinkers or Nobel Prize-winning scientists with all the common sense or scientific evidence in the world could convince them otherwise. They'd just dismiss them as agents of the devil. Satan, trying to cloud their minds. We need these windbags. We need them to sell our message. And what better way to get them on board than to give them a new prophet of their own to sell on to their flocks?'

Something in his words jarred within Rydell. 'What about the rest of the world? You're talking as if we're the only problem here.'

'We're the biggest polluters, aren't we? So let's start here. The rest of the world will follow.' He paused, gauging Rydell for a moment, his gaze unwavering. 'Our focus hasn't changed. We're still in this for the same reasons. This is still about survival. It's still about the singular threat facing the planet. It's still about leading people away from the dangerous path they're on.'

'By sending them back to the Dark Ages? By giving those poor deluded sods out there a real reason to believe in their Bronze Age superstitions?'

'See?' Drucker answered him with a smile. 'Now you're getting the irony.' He scrutinized Rydell, then added, 'For better or for worse, the whole movement has become a religious one, Larry. You know that. It's the same old story, the same classic myth that's hardwired into our brains, and in this case it fits like it was tailor-made. It's a story of salvation, after all, isn't it? We're sinners. We're all sinners. We took this perfect Garden of Eden that God bequeathed to us and desecrated it with our orgies of consumption. And now we have to pay. Now we have to make huge sacrifices and flagellate ourselves by driving smaller cars and using less electricity and cutting down on flying and other luxuries we take for granted and choking our economies to death to make things right. We have to defeat the antichrist that is pollution and seek out the salvation of sustainability and save ourselves before Judgment Day rolls over us and wipes us out in an Armageddon of abrupt climate change. That's how it's playing out, Larry. And the reason it's become that is that people like these religious myths. They thrive on them. Sooner or later, they turn everything into a crusade. And this crusade needed a prophet, not just a sign, to get the word across and make it happen.'

Rydell shook his head and looked away for a moment. He was still struggling to fully register that they were actually having this conversation. That, after they'd debated it many months earlier and put the issue to rest – or so he thought – he was actually sitting there facing it in its full, catastrophic glory today. 'The others . . . they're all with you on this?'

'Without hesitation.'

'And where does it end?' Rydell countered. 'Do you really think you can keep Father Jerome in line forever? You really think you can keep this lie alive indefinitely? Sooner or later, someone's gonna figure it out. Something'll screw up, someone'll slip up, and it'll all come out. What happens then?'

Drucker shrugged. 'We're running a very tight ship.'

'Even the best laid plans eventually come unstuck. You know that. I thought that was one of the main reasons you agreed not to go down this route.'

Drucker wasn't budging. 'We'll keep it going as long as we can.'

'And then?'

Drucker thought about it, then waved it off like a minor nuisance. 'Then we'll figure out a graceful exit.'

Rydell nodded stoically, processing it all. He just sat there, hobbled by the shock of it all, his eyes staring into the distance as if he'd just been told he had a week to live. 'No,' he finally told Drucker, his voice thick with dismay. 'This is wrong. This is a huge mistake.'

Drucker's eyes narrowed a touch. 'Take some time to think this through properly, Larry. You'll see that I'm right.'

The words didn't really sink in with Rydell. The image of the priest standing on the roof of the monastery in Egypt, with the sign hovering over him and hundreds of prostrate worshippers before him, shot to the forefront of his mind again. 'Even with the best intentions, even given what we're trying to do . . . I won't be a part of this. I can't help you make this . . . this virus any stronger than it already is.'

'You're gonna have to. We both have too much at stake here,' Drucker reminded him dryly.

'It's wrong,' Rydell flared. 'The plan was to scare them, Keenan. To make them sit up and think about what they're doing. That was it. A few carefully chosen appearances, then it's gone. Keep it unexplained. Keep it mysterious and unsettling and scary. We were in agreement on this, goddammit. We agreed that it would be a good thing if people didn't know where this was coming from, if they ended up thinking it was coming from some alien presence, from some higher intelligence out there. The beauty of this whole plan was that beyond making them sit up and listen, it might also help them pull away from this childish notion they have of this God of theirs, this personal God, this old man in a white beard who listens to every pathetic request they make and who sets down ridiculous rules about what they should eat or drink or wear or who they should bow to, and help them grow into the notion of God being, if anything, something that's unfathomable and unexplainable—'

'—and nudge them to the half-assed mind-set of agnostics,' Drucker commented mockingly.

'Well, yes. It's a step in the right direction, isn't it?'

Drucker was unmoved. He shook his head. 'It's a noble thought, Larry, but . . . this was the only way it was ever going to work. The world's not ready to give up its obsession with religion. Far from it. It's becoming more fundamentalist by the day. And it's not just our enemies. We're doing it too. Look at what's happening in this country. We don't have a single congressman or senator who can admit to being an atheist. Not one. Hell, we had ten presidential candidates on a podium last year, and not one of them dared raise his hand and say he believes in evolution.'

'And you're helping make it even worse.'

'It's a trade-off. It's a message they'll understand.'

Rydell shook his head again. 'No. It's wrong. There was no need to do it this way. You might help get rid of one evil, but you'll be feeding one that's just as vile. One that'll turn our world into a living hell for any rational person.' His face darkened with resolve, and he fixed Drucker with a hard stare. 'We need to figure a way out of this. We need to stop it before it gets too big.'

'You saw what just happened in Egypt. It's too late.'

'We have to stop it, Keenan,' Rydell insisted.

Drucker shrugged. 'We might just have to agree to disagree on that one.'

'I still have a say in this.'

'Within reason. And right now, you're being unreasonable.'

Rydell thought for a moment, then said, provokingly, 'You need me for the smart dust.'

'I do,' Drucker nodded calmly.

'You can't do this without it.'

'I know that.'

Rydell was momentarily thrown by Drucker's lack of even the slightest hint of agitation. 'So?'

'So . . .' Drucker winced, as if pained by something. 'So I had to take out some insurance.'

Rydell studied him, unsure of what he meant – then it fell into place. 'What?' he hissed. 'What have you done? What have you done, you son of a bitch?'

Drucker let him stew on it for a moment or two, then just said, 'Rebecca.'

The word stabbed Rydell like an ice pick. His eyes turned to saucers as he yanked out his phone and stabbed a speed-dial button. After two rings, a voice answered. Not Rebecca's. A man's voice. Rydell instantly recognized it as the voice of Rebecca's bodyguard.

'Ben, where's Becca?'

'She's safe, Mr. Rydell.'

Rydell's heart somersaulted with relief. He shot a victorious glance at Drucker.

The man's face was unnervingly serene.

A bolt of worry ripped through Rydell. 'Put Becca on,' he ordered the bodyguard, hoping for an answer he knew he wasn't going to get.

'I can't do that, Mr. Rydell.'

The words coiled around his gut and twisted it, hard. 'Put her on,' he growled.

The bodyguard's voice didn't waver. 'Only if Mr. Drucker gives the word, sir.'

Rydell threw his phone to the ground and charged at Drucker. 'Where is she?' he yelled.

Drucker sprang out of his seat and deflected Rydell's attack, grabbing his hand and elbow and twisting his arm sideways and back. As he did so, he kicked out Rydell's leg from under him. The billionaire tumbled to the floor heavily, slamming against one of the seats. Drucker eyed him for a beat, then took a couple of steps back.

'She's fine,' he said as he straightened his jacket. His face was slightly flushed, his breathing slightly ragged. He took in a calming breath before adding, 'And she'll stay fine. As long as you don't do anything foolish. Do we understand each other?'

CHAPTER 42

Deir Al-Suryan Monastery, Wadi Natrun, Egypt

Tucked away behind the crumbled wall four hundred yards west of the monastery and veiled by their desert camouflage netting, Fox Two and his two men watched silently through their high-powered binoculars, and waited.

Beside them, nestling under the truck's canvas top, the long-range acoustical device unit sat patiently, ready to wield its unseen power again. It had been painted a matte sand-beige in preparation for their mission, a color that had been matched perfectly to blend in with the terrain outside the monastery and farther up, on top of the mountain, above the cave. They'd left the directional microphone in its casing on this occasion. Today's event had been planned strictly as a one-way conversation, unlike the long hours they'd spent during all those weeks and months, up on the mountain, when Father Jerome had occasionally seen fit to ask a question or two.

Fox Two studied the restless crowd below. So far, he'd been able to push the right buttons and generate the responses he needed without a problem. Father Jerome had reacted as expected to the gentle prodding he'd given him on the rooftop, after the sign had appeared above him – but then, he'd been well primed to react that way. A few whispered words, aimed at the more visibly heated pockets in the mob, were also enough to trigger a cascading reaction, to nudge them into a frenzy at the sight of an escaping car. A high-frequency, ultra-loud pulse using the crowd-control setting was more than enough to hobble their fervor when it was no longer needed and get them to pull away in order to facilitate an escape.

Remarkable, he still thought, even after using the LRAD

device so often that it had become second nature to him. A simple concept, really – projecting noise in a tightly focused audio beam, the same way a film projector's lens magnifies and focuses a shaft of light, so that only the persons – or person, for it was as accurate as a sniper's rifle – in the device's crosshairs could hear it. Even at that distance. And either make it appear as if someone's voice, live or taped, was actually inside the target's head, or – using the less subtle crowd-control mode – send an unbearably loud, caustic sound pulse into the target's ears that, at its highest setting, caused nausea and fainting and crippled the toughest enemy.

Simple, but hugely effective.

His master's voice, Fox Two mused.

The power of suggestion was particularly effective in this case, when the subjects were already burning with the desire to do what was required of them, as in the case of the selected targets in the mob outside the monastery, or, as in the case of Father Jerome, when they'd undergone weeks of forced indoctrination. Electroshocks and sleep deprivation sessions, followed by cocktails of methohexitol to take the edge off. Transcranial mental stimulation. A complete psycho-chemical breakdown. Tripping the switches inside the brain, disarming it entirely before bombarding it psychologically. Implanting visions, thoughts, feelings. Conditioning the brain to accept an alternate reality, like hearing the voice of God or overcoming one's humility in order to embrace the notion of being the Chosen One.

He panned his binoculars across the desert, west of his position. Even though he knew what he was looking for, it still took him the better part of a minute to locate Fox One and his unit. The four men and their gear were also virtually invisible, huddled under camouflage netting in the sand dunes a couple of hundred yards away. Their contribution had been flawless, as expected. Its effect, staggering. He'd seen it before, in a video of a test in the desert. But not like this. Not live. Not in front of an unsuspecting audience.

It had taken his breath away. Even for a battle-hardened cynic like him, it was a heart-stopping moment. A one-two punch that, he knew, would resonate around the world.

Fox Two turned his attention back to the hordes at the monastery's gates. He'd soon be able to leave this dump for good, he thought with a degree of relish. It had been a hellish assignment. Living in hiding, on call at dawn and at dusk, climbing up and down the mountain, lugging the gear, day in and day out. He'd been out here in the desert way too long. He missed the feel of a woman's skin and the smell of a good barbecue, but most of all, he missed living among people.

Soon, he thought.

But before he could do that, he needed to make sure that the mission ended as smoothly as it had begun.

CHAPTER 43

Woburn, Massachusetts

The smell of fresh coffee tripped Matt's mind and coaxed him out of a dreamless sleep. Everything around him looked hazy. He tried to sit up, but did so too quickly and almost blacked out and had to try again, a bit slower this time. His head felt like it was filled with tar as he took in his surroundings and awareness trickled in.

The TV was on, though Matt couldn't really make out what it was showing. He tried blinking the fogginess out of his eyes. Jabba was sitting by the small table next to the window, watching the TV. He turned and grinned at Matt, a smoking cup of coffee in one hand – a venti or a grande or whatever quirkily-original-yet-misguidedly-obnoxious name coffee shops had replaced *large* with these days – and a half-eaten glazed doughnut – or was that 'glazé'? – in the other, with which he pointed at the two other oversized cups and the box of doughnuts on the table.

'Breakfast is served,' he said, in between mouthfuls.

Matt acknowledged the venti-sized scientist with a weary smile before noticing the daylight streaming in.

'How long was I out? What time is it?'

'Almost eleven. Which means you've been out for – ' Jabba did a quick mental calculation – 'sixteen hours or so.'

Which Matt had needed.

Badly.

He also noticed a couple of newspapers on the table. The headlines were in an unusually large font – the type only used when a major event had occurred. An almost quarter-page photograph of the apparition, in color, was also emblazoned across the front pages, next to older, file portraits of Father Jerome.

Matt looked up at Jabba. Jabba nodded, and his expression took a detour into more ominous territory. 'The Eagle has landed,' he said somberly, aiming his half-eaten doughnut at the TV.

Matt watched the footage from Egypt in silent disbelief. Breathless reports coming in from around the world also showed the explosive reaction to what had happened at the monastery.

In St. Peter's Square in Vatican City, tens of thousands of people had assembled, hungrily awaiting the pope's guidance on how to treat the apparition. In the Praça da Sé in São Paulo, hordes of euphoric Brazilians spilled into the square from in and out of the city, invading every available inch of the Sé cathedral, also looking for answers. The reactions reflected the local variations in faith and the different levels of appetite for the supernatural across the planet. The scenes were repeated in frenzied massings outside churches and in city squares in other centers of Christianity, from Mexico to the Philippines, but were different elsewhere. In the Far East, the reaction was generally more muted. Crowds had taken to the streets in China, Thailand, and Japan, but they were mostly orderly and there were only pockets of disturbance. The hotspot of Jerusalem, on the other hand, was very tense, with worrying signs of polarization already apparent among its religious groups. Christians, Muslims, and Jews were taking to the streets, looking for answers, conflicted and unsure about how to treat what many of them saw as a miraculous, supernatural manifestation – but one that didn't match anything prophesized in any of their sacred writings. The same thing was going on in the Islamic world. Confused worshippers had taken over city centers, town squares, and mosques across the Arab world and farther east in Pakistan, Bangladesh, and Indonesia. As always, moderate voices seemed to be either holding back, or crowded out by those of the more radical clerics. Reports were coming in of scattered skirmishes and brawls in several cities, both between followers of different religions as well as infighting among members of the same faith.

Around the world, official reaction was only starting to trickle in, but so far, government and religious leaders had refrained from making public statements about the phenomenon – apart from some fiery rhetoric that a few fundamentalist firebrands weren't shy to express.

Throughout the coverage, Father Jerome's face was everywhere. It was plastered across the front page of every newspaper in the country, if not the world. It beamed down from every channel, the frail priest suddenly thrust into megastardom. Every news outlet was locked in on the story. Anchors and talking heads across the language spectrum were struggling to hold back on the superlatives – and failing. The whole world was firmly gripped by the unexplained event.

As Matt drank and ate and watched the screen, Jabba told him what had happened during the night. The caffeine and sugar worked its magic on him again, slowly injecting a semblance of life back into his veins; the wall-to-wall footage from Egypt and from the rest of the world reached the parts the caffeine had missed. And with each new report, with each new video clip, Matt felt a crippling chill seep through him. The stakes were growing exponentially, along with the realization of the enormity of what he was facing.

When the doughnuts ran out, Jabba turned the volume down and filled Matt in on what he'd been up to. He'd been busy. After Matt had conked out and before the breakfast run, he'd gone back out to the reception alcove, handed the weedy receptionist another ten-dollar bill, and worked late into the night, and again this morning.

He'd gotten an update on the tracker's position, and handed Matt the printouts. They showed that the Merc had left the Seaport district, the last position they had for it, sometime before ten the previous night. It had traveled to the downtown area where the signal had been lost – presumably boxed in by concrete walls deep in the underground parking lot of some building. It had appeared again soon after seven that morning and returned to the same location in the Seaport district, and hadn't moved since.

Jabba had then spent most of his time trying to beef up the thin sketch they had managed to compile on the doomed research team and its covert project. He'd made more calls to contacts in the industry and had given Google and Cuil's search algorithms a real workout, and although he hadn't come up with much, what he didn't find also told him something.

Even though his experience was in non-defense-related research projects, the secrecy surrounding his and his peers' work was often military-like in its intensity. And although defense-related projects were even more cloaked, there was often a whisper, a hint, something that had seeped through the cracks and gave an idea, however vague, of what ballpark the project was in. The critical piece of information to protect was more often than not how a goal was to be achieved; the goal itself was, in most cases, at least obliquely known, especially within the most well-connected techie circles. In this case, however, no one knew anything. The project had been born, and had died, in total and utter secrecy. Which told Jabba that it was unlike anything he'd ever encountered. It also spoke to the resources and determination of those behind it, which made the prospect of going up against them even less appealing – if that was even possible.

He had, however, managed to unearth a real nugget, one he kept for last.

'I tracked down Dominic Reece's wife,' he informed Matt with no small satisfaction beaming across his weary face. 'Maybe she has some idea of what her husband and Danny were doing out there in Namibia.'

'Where is she?' Matt asked.

'Nahant, just up the coast,' Jabba replied, handing him a slip of paper with a phone number on it. 'We can be there in half an hour.'

Matt thought about it for a moment, then nodded. 'Sounds good. But let's see what the tracker's got for us at the Seaport first.'

CHAPTER 44

Deir Al-Suryan Monastery, Wadi Natrun, Egypt

Gracie had been doing almost continuous lives ever since the frenzied moment on the roof of the keep. She'd faced Dalton's lens every half hour or so, feeding the connected world's insatiable hunger for new information, regardless of how much – or how little – new information she actually had. Her throat felt numb, her nerve endings raw, her legs rubbery, but she wouldn't have had it any other way. The whole world was sitting up and listening, hanging on every tidbit of information they could find. Every news broadcast was carrying the story. And she was right there, at the heart of it all, the singular face and voice that everyone on the planet was now hooked on.

And yet she still couldn't believe it was happening, still couldn't fathom the fact that she was there, doing this, living through the epochal events right alongside the man who was quite possibly an envoy from God.

They'd brought Father Jerome down off the roof for safety, given the mob that was massed outside the gates. After the dawn appearance of the sign, the crowd had grown tenfold, and more people were still streaming in from all corners. Father Jerome had been escorted into the bowels of the monastery by the abbot and Brother Ameen. He'd been baffled by the whole experience, and looked visibly drained. He needed time to recover and take stock of what had happened. Dalton, Finch, and Gracie had climbed back up onto the roof on a couple of occasions, and Dalton had crept right up to the edge and filmed the scene outside the monastery's walls. He'd been desperate to use the skycam, but he'd reluctantly agreed with Gracie and Finch that it would be unwise, given the highly volatile nature of the crowd.

So far, ever since the sign had faded fifteen minutes or so after it had first appeared over Father Jerome, things out there were calm, if tense. The violence hadn't flared up again, but the crowd had entrenched itself into separate areas, rival camps that were eyeing each other nervously: Christians who were gathering there to worship and pray, Muslims who were enthralled by the miracle they had witnessed and had joined the others in prayer even though they were unsure about how to interpret the appearance of the sign over a priest's head, and fired-up groups of more fundamentalist Muslims who rejected any suggestion of a new prophet and whose mere appearance was pushing the more open-minded moderates among them to the sidelines.

In between broadcasts, Gracie, Finch, and Dalton were monitoring news reports streaming in from across the globe and getting updates from the network's contacts in Cairo. The first major religious figure to make an official comment on what was happening was the patriarch of Constantinople. Unlike the pope, who was the undisputed leader of Roman Catholics and whose word they considered infallible, the patriarch had little direct executive power in the fragmented world of the Eastern Orthodox Church. It hadn't stopped him from using his resonant historical title to promote his concern for the environment, presenting it as a spiritual responsibility. And in that context, he'd just released a statement that asked the people of the world to pay heed to what they were witnessing and to express his interest in meeting with Father Jerome to better understand what was happening.

Presently, as Gracie looked out over the teeming plain below, she felt increasingly uneasy about their situation. The air was heavy with a charged silence. The threat of a bigger eruption of violence was palpable. She gratefully accepted some fresh lemonade from one of the monks and sat down, cross-legged, on the far end of the roof, her back against a pack of gear. Dalton and Finch, glasses in hand, joined her.

They sat in silence for a moment, allowing their brains to throttle back and their pulses to settle.

'Amazing, isn't it?' Finch just said, looking out over the irregular, domed roofs inside the monastery's walls. 'How everything can change like that, in a heartbeat?'

'Weren't we just freezing our nuts off in the South Pole like yesterday?' Dalton asked in a weary, incredulous tone. 'What just happened?'

'The story of our lives, that's what happened,' Gracie replied.

'That's for sure.' Dalton shook his head, a wry smile curling up one corner of his mouth.

She caught it. 'What?'

'Weird how these things happen, isn't it? I mean, I don't know what you want to call it. Luck. Fate.'

'What do you mean?'

'We could have missed all this so easily. Imagine . . . If you hadn't taken that call from Brother Ameen, back on the ship. Or if he hadn't been able to convince us to come. If the documentary guys hadn't been here before us and shot Father Jerome's wall paintings. We might have passed, right?' His eyes swung from Gracie to Finch and back. 'We wouldn't be here right now, and maybe none of this would have happened.'

Gracie thought about it for a beat, then shrugged. 'Someone else would be here. It'd just be someone else's story.'

'But would it? What if the documentary guys hadn't shot that footage. What if no one had showed up here to talk to him. The mob wouldn't be out there. Father Jerome wouldn't have been up here on the roof. There'd be no sign up there.' He raised his eyebrows in a think-about-it manner. 'Makes you wonder if he's the first, or if there were others before him.'

'Others?' Gracie asked.

'You know, kooks. Nuts with voices in their heads, painting

weird signs all over their walls or filling journals with their ramblings. What if there were others, before him? Others who were also the real deal. But no one knew.' He nodded, to himself, his mind mining that vein further. 'And what about the timing of it?' he added. 'Why now? There were other times when we could have used a sign, a message. Why not just before Hiroshima? Or during the Cuban missile crisis?'

'You always get this lucid with lemonade?' she asked.

'Depends on what the good monks put in it.' He grinned with a raised eyebrow.

Just then, Brother Ameen popped his head through the roof hatch, his expression knotted with concern. 'Come with me, please. You need to hear this.'

'Where?' Gracie asked as she got up.

'Down. To the car. Come now.'

They climbed down and followed him to the Previa, which was still parked by the gates. The abbot arrived as they did. The car's doors were open, and Yusuf and a couple of monks were huddled around it, heads hung in concentration as they listened to an Arabic broadcast coming through on its radio. They looked thoroughly spooked.

Another religious leader was making a pronouncement, only this one wasn't as inspirational as the earlier one. Gracie couldn't understand what was being said, but the tone of the speaker wasn't hard to read. It sounded just like the other furious, inflamed rants she'd heard countless times across the Arab world. And even before Brother Ameen explained it, she understood what was happening.

'It's an imam, in Cairo,' he told them, his voice quaking slightly. 'One of the more hotheaded clerics in the country.'

'He doesn't sound happy,' Dalton remarked.

'He's not,' Brother Ameen replied. 'He's telling his followers not to be deceived by what they see. He's saying Father Jerome is either a *heela* – a trick, a fabrication of the Great Satan America – or he's an envoy of the *shaytan* himself, an agent of the devil. And that either way, they should consider him a false prophet who's been sent to sow fear and confusion among the true believers.' He listened some more, then added, 'He's telling them to do their duty as good Muslims and to remember the preachings of the one true faith.'

'Which is?' Finch asked.

'He's asking for Father Jerome's head,' Brother Ameen replied. 'Literally.'

CHAPTER 45

River Oaks, Houston, Texas

'I've got to tell ya, I'm really confused,' the pastor grumbled as he set down his tumbler of bourbon. 'I mean, what the hell's going on out there? This isn't how it's supposed to happen.'

'How what's supposed to happen?'

'The Second Coming, Roy,' he answered. 'The End of Times. The Rapture.'

They were seated across from each other in the large conservatory, a huge glass house that dwarfed most single-family homes but looked like an outhouse next to the rest of the pastor's massive mansion. An oval-shaped pool lay beyond the chamfered windows, huddled under a glistening tarp cover and waiting for warmer days. The fence around Darby's tennis court winked out from behind a row of poplars that skirted the left edge of the property.

Although they'd met countless times over the last year, Roy Buscema still studied the man before him with the fascination of an anthropologist discovering a new species. The Reverend Nelson Darby was an intriguing specimen. Modern in all things technological and where business practices were concerned, but immovably medieval when it came to anything relating to scripture. Genteel and measured, and yet a fierce right-wing culture warrior and unrepentant agent of intolerance. In all the times they'd met, Darby was never less than a charming, relaxed, and earnest host, nothing like the bombastic, fire-and-brimstone preacher he morphed into on stage. He was also always impeccably groomed, an elegant man who appreciated the finer things in life. Fortunately for Darby, God – according to the inerrant scripture he bequeathed us, in any case – took pleasure in the prosperity of his servants, and the pastor was nothing if not a loyal servant.

His refined style extended to his home. Nestling at the end of a leafy road in River Oaks, it occupied a privileged site, directly overlooking the fairways of the country club. It was a stately, white-columned mansion that dated back to the 1920s – stately, but tasteful and restrained, not a vulgar temple to Prosperity Theology. Darby was particularly proud of his conservatory. He'd had it custom-designed by one of London's leading purveyors of garden houses, who'd then flown over a team of four carpenters to install it. He liked to take meetings there. It was away from the eyes and ears of the small army of staffers who toiled in the sprawling offices on his megachurch's campus. It was a chance to show off and impress his visitors. And, of course, it inspired him. The glass house seemed, to Darby, a prism for the sun's rays, a white hole that sucked in the faintest glimmer of light on even the bleakest of days. It normally helped instill a further sense of wonder in him than he already possessed. It was here that he prepared his most fiery sermons, the ones in which he took on homosexuals, abortion – even in the case of victims of rape and incest – condoms, evolution, stem cell research, and elitist-quasi-Muslim presidential hopefuls, even directing his bombastic, venomous rants at the Girl Scouts, whom he'd branded as agents of feminism, the Dungeons & Dragons game, and, still more bizarrely, SpongeBob SquarePants. It was here that he drafted the sermons he reserved for special occasions, like Christmas, which was now only days away.

Today, though, any inspiration was hobbled by the confused thoughts swarming inside him.

'Maybe this isn't the End of Times,' Buscema suggested.

'It sure as hell isn't,' the pastor agreed huffily. 'Can't be. Not yet. Not when none of the prophecies of the Good Book have happened.' He leaned forward, a studious stare in his eyes, and did the parallel-vertical-karate-chops thing with his hands for emphasis, as he did at his pulpit. 'The Bible tells us the messiah will only return *after* we've had the final battle between God's children and the army of the antichrist out there in Israel. It's only after that happens that we can be saved by the Rapture.' He shook his head. 'This isn't right. Hell, we're still waiting for the Israelis to bomb the crap out of Iran and kick-start the whole thing.'

'God's giving us a message, Nelson,' Buscema put in thoughtfully. 'He's given us a sign – two signs – over the ice caps. And he's sent us a messenger.'

Darby scoffed. 'An Arab. And a Catholic at that, if you can get your head around that one.'

'He's not Arab, Nelson. He's Spanish.'

Darby swatted the correction away. 'Same difference. He's still Catholic.'

'It doesn't matter. What did you think the messiah of the Second Coming was gonna be? Lutheran?'

'I don't know, but . . . Catholic?' Darby groaned.

'That's an irrelevant detail right now. He's Christian. More importantly, he happens to be one of the holiest men on the planet. He's spent the last few months holed up in some cave near a monastery in Egypt. Which is part of the Holy Land. Jesus himself hid in that same valley when he was being hounded by the Romans.'

'What about all that Coptic business?'

'The monastery where he's staying is Coptic, but he's not a Copt. You know much about Copts?'

'Not yet,' Darby answered with a self-effacing smile.

'They're the Christians of Egypt. Maybe ten percent of the population. But they're the ones who've been there longest. They were there long before the Arabs invaded in the seventh century. In fact, they've been there since day one. Uninterrupted. The purest, oldest uncorrupted Christians you'll find, Nelson,' Buscema insisted. He paused to let his words sink in, then continued, 'You do know who started the Coptic Church, right?'

'No,' Darby said.

'Mark. As in Matthew, Mark, Luke, and John. That Mark. He went out there to preach the gospel, about thirty years after Jesus's death. He didn't have too much of a hard time getting the people there to sign up. They already believed in everlasting life, had done so for thousands of years. Difference was, Mark told them it wasn't just for pharaohs. No need to be mummified and put inside a huge pyramid and have priests perform all kinds of weird rituals for it to happen. Everyone was entitled to go to heaven, provided they believed in the One God and asked him to forgive them for their sins. Which, as you can imagine, was music to their ears. And that's where it all started, where Christianity first took shape. The symbolism, the rituals. A lot of it came out of there. Look at the ankh – the ancient Egyptian symbol of eternal life – and the cross. Think about their God, Ra – the God of the sun – and our holy day, Sunday. And that valley where Father Jerome is holed up? It's holier than you think. Those monasteries out there? They're the oldest monasteries in the world. They hold some of the earliest holy books anywhere. Fourth- and fifth-century gospels. Priceless manuscripts. Piles of them. Just lying there. They're still translating them. Who knows what they'll find in them. It's a deeply religious place, Nelson. A deeply religious, *Christian* place. And Father Jerome . . . well, you know all about him. Everything he's done. God's work. How he's helped spread the word. If God was going to choose someone, it seems to me like Father Jerome fits the bill nicely.'

Darby nodded, grudgingly allowing his advisor's sermon to sink in. 'But why now? And why the signs over the poles?'

Buscema's brows rose with uncertainty. 'Maybe he's telling us to watch out. Maybe he'd like us to stick around a bit longer. And who knows?' he smiled. 'You might find people end up preferring that message to the End of Times prophecies you've been telling them about. Regardless of how much they've been looking forward to that.' He smiled inwardly at that last little dig.

Darby's eyes narrowed as it registered. He let it pass. 'It's our destiny, Roy. That's what the Bible says. That's how those of us who've accepted Jesus Christ as our savior are going to be saved. Before Armageddon. Before the earth is reaped. Besides, you don't really believe these greenhouse gases are gonna end up by wiping us all out with their tidal waves or with that new ice age they've been harping on about?'

Buscema gave him a noncommittal shrug. 'I'm not sure it couldn't happen.'

'Hogwash,' Darby shot back. 'War's gonna bring about the End of Times, Roy. Nuclear war between the forces of good and evil. Not global warming.' He sighed and sat back. 'The good Lord created this earth. And if you remember your Genesis, He said, "It is good." Which means, He's happy with how it turned out. It's His divine creation. And He's the Almighty, for crying out loud. You think He'd design it in a way that puny little man could destroy it just by driving some SUVs around and setting the A/C on high? His divine creation? It can't happen. He wouldn't let it happen. Not like that.'

'All I'm saying is,' Buscema countered in his calming manner, 'there's a sign popping up over the planet's climate change tipping points. It's a sign, Nelson. And I just saw the first national polling numbers.'

That fired up a totally different subsection of the pastor's brain, and his face sharpened with keen interest. 'What do they say?'

'People are taking notice. They're listening.'

Darby exhaled with annoyance. 'I bet those "creation care" jugheads are smiling now.'

'"The Earth is the Lord's, and the fullness thereof,"' Buscema quoted playfully.

Darby frowned. 'Thanks for reminding me.'

'It's in the Bible, Nelson. "The Lord God took the man and put him in the Garden of Eden to work it . . . *and to take care of it*,"' he pointed out. 'People are worried about the kind of world their kids are going to grow up in. It's a powerful hook.'

'They're misguided. And dangerous. We've got to be careful, Roy. What are we talking about here? Are we saying the planet's holy? Are we supposed to worship nature? That's a slippery slope. We can't go out there and tell people to love Mother Earth and look after her. Hell, that's what the Indians believed in.'

Buscema smiled. The man understood the subtleties of faith. And he was smart, there was no denying it. A branding whiz, as well as a mesmerizing orator who knew how to entrance his audience. There was a reason thousands of people endured punishing traffic jams every Sunday morning to hear his rousing sermons. Why millions of others tuned in to catch their slick broadcast on national cable and network TV. Why the man's opinions, despite being primitive and bigoted and containing such brain-dead inanities as blaming 9/11 on gays, had helped him build an empire that extended to over fifty different ministries and a global network of over ten thousand churches, a school and a university, a conference center, twenty-three radio stations, and a couple dozen magazines.

'It doesn't have to get to that,' Buscema said. 'Think of it more in terms of man's sinful desires that have led him astray. He needs to see the road to salvation. And it's your job to hold his hand and show him the way.' Buscema studied him, then leaned in for emphasis. 'Unless I've got the wrong end of the stick here, you're pro-life, right?' He teased him by letting the question hang for a beat, always perplexed – and pained – by how pro-lifers applied their zeal to the smallest cluster of cells, no matter how tragically disabled or conceived, but not to any other living species or to the habitat we all shared. 'That's what saving the planet's all about, isn't it? Life?'

Darby breathed out heavily, clearly not liking this, and steepled his hands, buttressing his chin with his thumbs.

'Why aren't any of those bozos in Washington saying anything?'

'They will,' Buscema said, his expression leading Darby to assume he knew more than he was saying.

Darby bought it. 'What have you heard?'

'He's the real deal, Nelson. They know it. They're just mapping out how best to handle it.'

Darby frowned. Small crinkles overpowered the Botox and broke through around his eyes. 'They're worried about the same thing I am.' He waved his arms expansively. 'You build all this, you get to the top of the heap, king of your castle . . . then someone shows up and wants you to call him massa.'

'It's happened, Nelson. We can't change that. And he's out there. I just don't want you to miss the boat, that's all.'

Darby asked, 'What do you think I should do?'

Buscema thought about it for a beat, then said, 'Grab him. While you can.'

'You want me to endorse him?'

Buscema nodded. 'Others are thinking about doing it.'

'Who?'

Buscema held his gaze for a beat, then confided, 'Schaeffer. Scofield. And many others.' He knew mentioning the names of two of Darby's biggest competitors in the soul-saving sweepstakes would generate a reaction. One of them even had the affront to have his megachurch in the same city as Darby.

Judging by Darby's expression, the names hit the sweet spot he was aiming for.

'You sure of that?' the pastor asked.

Buscema nodded enigmatically.

I should know, he thought. *I spoke to them before coming here to see you.*

'The man's a friggin' Catholic, Roy,' Darby grumbled, a flutter of panic in his eyes.

'It doesn't matter,' Buscema answered flatly. 'You've got to endorse him and endorse him big. Big and loud. Look, you're already lagging on this front. The others, your fellow church leaders who signed up for the global warming initiative two years ago . . . they're on board.' Buscema was referring to the eighty-six Christian leaders who, despite strong opposition from many of their evangelical brethren, had signed up for what became known as the 'Evangelical Climate Initiative.' Some of the most prominent church leaders, however, such as the president of the National Association of Evangelicals, had resisted publicly supporting the movement, even if they privately backed it. 'This is your chance to leapfrog over them and take control.'

Darby frowned. 'But what about that sign that keeps popping up? What is it? If it was a cross or something clearly Christian, then fine . . . but it's not.'

'It doesn't matter what it is. What matters is that it's there. It's up there and everyone's looking at it and wanting to be part of it.' Buscema leaned in and fixed Darby with unflinching resolve. 'You're missing the point here, Nelson. Catholic, Protestant, Baptist, Presbyterian, Quaker, or Amish – or even Mormon, Jew, Muslim, Buddhist, or Scientologist for that matter. None of it matters now. You're right that it's not a cross up there. But it's not a Star of David or a crescent or anything linked to any of the other major religions either. It's a game-changer. An entirely new paradigm. It could be the start of something bigger than anything we've seen before, something new, something global. And as we've seen throughout history, when these things happen, they spawn big organizations. Right now, there isn't one. There's nothing. There's just a man and a sign in the sky. But people are coming to him in droves. And you need to decide whether or not you want to be part of it. Right now, you can get a jump on the others by hitching your wagon to him before the rest of them. Things can change . . . in the twinkling of an eye.' He just couldn't resist throwing that one in. 'Because even if it isn't specifically, obviously Christian,' he pressed on, 'if you haven't embraced it while everyone else has, you just might find yourself with a whole bunch of empty pews. And that wouldn't be a good thing, would it?' He winced, trying to stop himself from taking another dig using an End of Times catchphrase, but he couldn't resist, and he kept his voice as even as he could and added, 'You don't want to be left behind, now, do you?'

'Did he buy it?' Drucker asked Buscema.

'Please,' the journalist said mockingly, the sound of rushing air coming through his car phone. 'He's so into it it's almost painful to watch.'

'You gonna see Schaeffer again?'

'He's left me two messages since I last spoke to him,' he confirmed. 'Same with Scofield. I'll let them sweat it out a little bit before calling them back.'

Good man, Drucker thought. It sounded like they'd already reeled in one major marlin. With a bit of luck, they'd be bringing in a record haul.

CHAPTER 46

Boston, Massachusetts

Matt and Jabba were in the bloodstained Camry, parked outside a modern, six-floor office block in the Seaport district.

Matt's face was screened by the shadow of his baseball cap and the upturned collar of his coat. He sat in the passenger seat and eyed the building with quiet fury. It was a bland, architecturally bankrupt tile-and-glass box with a large parking area out front. There was no corporate signage by its front entrance; instead, various tenants probably leased suites there, moving in and out in accordance with the ebb and flow of their earnings. A thin blanket of snow from an early-morning flurry covered the asphalt and trimmed the bare branches of the trees that dotted the lot.

They'd been parked there for half an hour, and had seen only one person walk into the building. There had been no sign of the hard case.

The painkillers had taken the sting out of Matt's wound, but it still hurt every time he moved. He still felt a bit light-headed, which he attributed to the loss of blood. His body was pleading with him to give it time to heal, but the pleas were falling on deaf ears. He could walk, and right now, that would have to do.

'I'm going to have a look,' he told Jabba. He reached for the door handle, grimacing with discomfort as he pulled on it.

Jabba reached out to stop him. 'Not a good idea, dude. You shouldn't even be here. Look at you.'

'Just a look,' Matt repeated; only as he pushed the door open, Jabba put a hand on his shoulder and stayed him.

'I'll go,' Jabba said.

Matt looked at him.

'I'll go,' he protested-insisted, his voice rising a notch, before concern flitted across his eyes. 'If I'm not out in five minutes, call the cops,' he added, slapping his iPhone into Matt's hand. Then he caught himself, and grinned. 'God, I never imagined I'd ever hear myself say that.'

Matt brushed it away, dead serious. 'Just don't get too nosy.'

Jabba looked at him askance. 'Seriously, sometimes, it's like you don't even know me,' he mock-griped, then climbed out of the car.

He scanned left and right as he ambled across the lot, slightly overdoing the casual don't-mind-me attitude, but there was no one around to notice. Matt watched him disappear inside the building's entrance lobby.

Less than a minute later, he emerged.

'Well?' Matt asked.

Jabba gave him a piece-of-cake smile, but his body told a different story. He was breathing fast, and his face was sprinkled with sweat droplets that weren't there before.

'No receptionist. Five names on the roster, one per floor. Third seems unoccupied, or they've been too lazy to put their name up,' he informed Matt in between sharp breaths. 'But I think I know which one we want. Just need to go online somewhere to confirm it.'

Matt thought about it, then said, 'Okay. Do it here.'

Which totally threw Jabba. 'What, you want me to use my phone?'

'Yep,' Matt confirmed, sure of it.

'Dude, they could track our position. My iPhone's got A-GPS, as in "assisted." Makes their job even easier.'

'Fine. Do it. And stay on long enough for them to be able to do it.'

Jabba looked at him like he was nuts. 'You *want* them to know we were here?'

Matt nodded. 'Yep.'

Jabba was now looking at him like he'd sprouted little green antennas from his ears. 'Why?'

'I want to fuck with them a little. Shake them up. Keep them unbalanced.'

'It's my phone, dude,' Jabba specified. 'All they'll know for sure is that I was here.'

'Same difference. They know we're together.'

Jabba looked like he wanted to object more, but he gave up, raised his hands in surrender, and turned on his phone. He checked his watch, then fired up his Macbook and connected it to the phone, using the phone's Internet connection. Matt watched as Jabba's fingers danced across the keyboard and tapped the touchpad a few times. He then swung the laptop so Matt could see the screen.

It was on the home page of a company called Centurion. A slick slideshow showed an oil refinery in a desert location at sundown, then what looked like a gated compound somewhere in the Middle East, then a convoy of cars, again in the same sunny, dusty environment. The last picture showed a steely guy in pristine quasi-military gear, black gloves, and surfer-cool wraparound shades, poised behind a large-caliber machine gun. A slogan flashed up with each image, the last of them announcing the company's motto, 'Securing a Better Future.'

Matt and Jabba read through the 'About Us' paragraph, which described Centurion as a 'security and risk management company with offices in the U.S., Europe, and the Middle East' and a 'security provider to the U.S. government and a registered and active UN contractor.' Jabba clicked on the 'Management' link, and a black-and-white portrait of Maddox leapt out at them. The hard case was the firm's founder and CEO, and the accompanying blurb described his long, stellar career in the Marines and his achievements in the field of 'security consulting.'

'Ouch,' Jabba said, flinching at the unsettling and

unapologetic mug shot of Maddox. He glanced around nervously, clearly uneasy at the thought of taunting this man. He checked his watch again and held up his phone. 'Eighty-five seconds. Can we please switch this off now and get the hell out of here?'

Matt was still absorbing every word of Maddox's bio in silence. After a moment, he said, 'Sure.'

Jabba turned it off as Matt fired up the car and pulled away.

He looked over at Matt. 'So?'

Matt nodded to himself, his eyes a bit distant, his expression dour. 'So now we know who we're dealing with.'

'Dude, the man's got a private army,' Jabba pleaded, his pitch doing its worry rise. 'We've got a white Camry and a handgun with no bullets in it.'

'Then we've got some catching up to do,' Matt replied. 'But let's see what Reece's wife has to say first.'

'You're sure?'

Maddox wasn't shouting. In fact, his voice was unnaturally calm, given the news he'd just been given. But his displeasure was coming through loud and clear to his contact at Fort Meade.

'Absolutely,' came the answer. 'Komlosy's phone signal popped up on the grid for just over a minute before powering down.'

Maddox walked over to his office's window and looked down. Nothing unusual caught his eye. The parking lot and the street beyond were glacially quiet.

Two unexpected appearances from Sherwood in as many days, he fumed. The second one in the immediate vicinity of his office.

The man was good.

A bit too good for Maddox's liking.

'How long ago?' he asked.

'It just went dead.'

Maddox seethed quietly. 'Can't you track him with his phone switched off?'

'Looking at his contract, it seems he's got an iPhone, a 3G one,' the NSA monitoring agent told him. 'If he keeps it on long enough, I can remotely download some burst software onto it that'll let me track it even if it's powered down.'

'I need you to do better than that,' Maddox insisted.

'We're working on some stuff. But for now, it'll get better every time he switches it on. The tracking software will have a head start on him; it'll keep adding data every time he powers up. We won't need as long to get a lock.'

'Okay. Let me know the second it powers up again,' the Bullet ordered. 'And get that download done as soon as you get a chance.' With that, he hung up, stuffed the phone into his pocket, checked his watch, and glared out his window again.

CHAPTER 47

Deir Al-Suryan Monastery, Wadi Natrun, Egypt

'Don't we have anyone who can get here sooner?' Dalton asked. 'Where's the damn sixth fleet when you need it?'

They were standing around uneasily by the base of the keep – Gracie, Finch, Dalton, Brother Ameen, and the abbot. An expectant hum of voices reverberated across the plain, beyond the monastery's thick walls. Closer by, the imam's hateful voice droned on from the people carrier's radio, an angry, never-ending call to arms that was echoed on countless other radios outside the walls. 'Yeah, that'll look real good,' Finch commented wryly. 'American troops flying in to safeguard a Christian holy man in a sea of angry Muslims. That'll clinch the hearts-and-minds battle right there.'

'We need to get Father Jerome out of here,' Gracie said.

'I agree,' Finch said, 'but how?'

'What about bringing a chopper in to whisk him out?' she asked.

'Where's it gonna land?' Finch queried. 'There's nowhere wide enough for it to put down, not inside the monastery's walls.'

Gracie pointed up at the keep. 'What about up there?

Finch shook his head. 'The roof's not strong enough. It's hundreds of years old. There's no way it can hold the weight. And I don't think winching him out is gonna work either. He's too old to take that, and even if he could, someone could take a potshot at him.'

Dalton slid a forlorn nod over at the keep behind them. 'So what do we do? Bunker down?' He pointed up at the keep's second-floor drawbridge, sitting above them. 'This thing still work?' he asked the abbot, only half-joking. The fortified keep, with its food stores, water well, library, and top-floor chapel, had been used as a refuge in times of attack, but that hadn't happened in over a thousand years.

'No, but . . . we should just stay here and wait for the security forces to arrive. They're bound to send them in now. Besides, there aren't just Muslims out there,' the abbot reassured them. 'A lot of them out there, they're our people. Christians. They'll defend Father Jerome if they have to.'

'I'm sure they would, but that's not the point,' Gracie pressed. 'It'd be better to get him out of here before anything like that happens. To make sure it doesn't.'

'There might be another way out,' Brother Ameen offered. All eyes turned swiftly to him. 'How?' Gracie asked.

'The tunnel,' he said, turning to the abbot with a questioning look.

'There's a tunnel? Where to?' Gracie asked.

'It goes from here to the monastery closest to us – the one we drove past on the way in.'

'The Monastery of Saint Bishoi,' the abbot confirmed.

'What, the one across the field?' Gracie was pointing northeast, trying to visualize the second monastery's relative position from when she'd last seen it, from the roof of the *qasr*.

The abbot nodded. 'Yes. The tunnel is older than this monastery. You see, our monastery was built over what was once the monk Bishoi's hermitage, the cave he used to retreat to. Because of the constant threat from invaders, the monks decided to build an escape route from Saint Bishoi's monastery, and they chose his old cave as the exit point. Years later, as the danger receded, a small chapel was built over his cave, and that small chapel eventually grew into this monastery.'

'You think it'll still get us there?' Finch asked.

'The last time anyone went down there was years ago, but it was clear then. I don't see why it should be any different now,' the abbot replied. 'We haven't had any earthquakes or anything like that.'

Gracie glanced doubtfully at Finch. Still, it was all they had.

'If we can make it across, can we get a car to drive us from there? Discreetly?' she asked.

The abbot thought about that for a moment, then looked around at the driver of the Previa and the others, smoking nervously as they listened to the radio. He stepped over to Yusuf and spoke to him in Arabic. Yusuf replied, then the abbot turned back to Gracie. 'Yusuf's brother-in-law also drives a car like his. If he can use your phone to call him, we can get him to meet you at Bishoi.'

'Okay, but then what? Where do we go?' Dalton asked. 'The embassy?'

'It'll be the same thing there,' Ameen put in. 'Maybe even worse. It's safer to fly him out of the country.'

Finch frowned, thinking ahead, stumbling over the logistics. 'Easier said than done. Does Father Jerome even have a passport?'

'We have to sneak him out,' Gracie opined. 'If anyone sees him, it'll get complicated.'

'He can use my passport,' the abbot offered. 'With his robe on and with his hood down, they won't look too closely. And Ameen will be with you to deflect any questions.'

Gracie looked to Finch for approval. He thought about it quickly, then nodded. 'Okay, it's worth a shot. I'll call D.C.,' he told her, 'see how quickly they can get a plane over to us.' He turned to the monks. 'How long do you think this tunnel is? Half a kilometer maybe?'

'I'm not sure,' the abbot said. 'Maybe a bit more.'

Finch frowned. 'We're not going to be able to lug all our gear through.' He turned to Dalton. 'Let's bring it all down. We'll grab as much as we can.'

The speech on the car radio flared up, the speaker's voice rising fiercely. Gracie flashed on iconic, violent images from the region's turbulent recent history, all of

266

them fueled by religious fervor – the storming of the U.S. embassy in Tehran, the stoning and burning of the Danish embassy in Beirut, the beheadings in Iraq and Afghanistan. She didn't want to become one of them, not in that sense, anyway.

'We'd better get moving.' She turned to the monk and the abbot. 'You need to talk to Father Jerome.'

Ameen nodded. 'I'll go now,' he said, before leaving them and disappearing into the doorway, closely tailed by the abbot.

'They're trying to get him out,' Buscema informed Darby.

'Already? Who?'

'I just got a call from my guy at the network,' the journalist told the reverend. 'They've still got that news crew there with him, and they're not waiting for an official reaction. They're handling him themselves.'

'Of course they are,' Darby chortled. 'That inside track's not exactly bad for their ratings, is it? How are they going to do it?'

'I'm not sure. They're scrambling to get a plane out to them as soon as possible.'

'Where are they planning on taking him?' Darby asked.

'I don't know. I don't think they know. They just want him out of there before the whackos rip him to pieces.'

The reverend went silent. After a moment, he exhaled slowly, as if he'd reached a decision, and said, 'Let's bring him here.'

'Here?'

'Hell, yes. This is God's country, isn't it?' he boomed.

'It's not gonna be easy. Everyone else will want him,' Buscema goaded him. 'Did you see the rallies in Rome?'

'The pope hasn't announced his position on this whole thing yet, has he?' An unusual, slight panic crept into his words.

'No. The Vatican's not exactly famous for its quick reactions.'

'So where else is he gonna go? France?' Darby scoffed.

'Spain, maybe. He's from there originally. And the Brits are usually quick to put out the welcome mat for anyone in trouble.'

'No way. We've got to get him over here. Besides, like you said,' he added, 'he's polling through the roof. People here want to hear what he has to say.'

'The government hasn't even made an official statement about him yet.'

'Just as well,' Darby said, gloating. 'Gives me a chance to do it myself and save him from ending up with those heathens back east.'

There it is, Buscema thought. 'You want to handle this yourself?' His voice rose with mock surprise.

'God's sending us a message,' Darby asserted. 'I'm going to make sure everyone hears it, loud and clear.'

Buscema went silent for a moment, then said, 'If the State Department gives the embassy the green light – and they will – it'll be over. If you want to make it happen, you're gonna have to move fast.'

The reverend's tone was as smooth and sharp as a blade. 'Watch me.'

Gracie, Dalton, and Finch had brought the rest of their gear down from the roof of the keep and were now sorting through it in the shade by the entrance to the library. The tunnel would be a long, dark trek through a narrow, dusty passage, and they hadn't thought they'd be able to take everything with them. The camera and live broadcasting gear and as many of Father Jerome's journals that they could carry made the cut. Dalton's skycam rig was almost a casualty of the forced triage before the abbot drafted in a few monks who would accompany them through the passage and help them lug the rest of their gear.

Finch had spoken to Ogilvy, who went to work on rustling up a jet that could fly them out without asking too many questions. They'd still have to get past whatever security checks were in place at the airport, but Finch knew that those controls would be far less stringent for a private plane than they were for commercial flights. Still, they'd have to, pun notwithstanding, wing it at the airport. It didn't give him too much cause for concern, though. They'd gotten out of trickier places before.

As Finch clicked his backpack shut, Dalton's observations from earlier were still bouncing around his mind. Something was nagging at him. As Dalton had noted, everything had hinged on the preexistence of the documentary footage. Without it, he thought, none of this would have happened. They certainly wouldn't have made the trip. Something else was bothering him too. The way the throng surrounding their car had recoiled and given them an opening to back up and return to the safety of the monastery. He couldn't quite put his finger on what it was that bothered him – the moment had been a blur of frenzy. Still, something wasn't right.

He thought again about putting in a call to the documentary's producer to find out more about how it had all happened. He checked his watch and was about to say something when Dalton, looking around impatiently, said, 'Where are these guys? We need to go.'

'I thought Ameen and the abbot went to get him,' Finch answered.

'I'll see if I can find them,' Gracie offered.

She headed down the courtyard, toward the small building that housed the monks' cells. Finch watched her go. He wiped the sweat off his brow and paced around for a beat, and decided to use the dead time to reach out to the documentary's producer. He checked his watch again, made a quick mental calculation of the time difference between Egypt and England, where the producer was based, and found he wouldn't be waking him up at some ungodly hour. He picked up the satphone, then patted his pockets, looking for his cell phone, only it wasn't there.

'You seen my BlackBerry?'

Dalton glanced around. 'No, why?'

He checked his backpack. 'I've been thinking about what you were saying. Thought I'd put a call in to the documentary guys.'

'So use the satphone. Your phone doesn't work here anyway, remember?'

Finch gave him a wiseass grin. 'It's got my contacts list on it, numbnuts.'

Dalton thought about it for a second, then said, 'Last I remember, you had it out when we were up there,' pointing at the *qasr*. 'Before you took that call on the satphone.'

Finch glanced up at the keep that towered over the monastery's walled-in courtyard, and frowned. 'Must have left it up there while we were packing up,' he said. 'Be right back.'

He left Dalton, cut across the courtyard and up to the drawbridge, before disappearing into the keep.

As with each time he entered it, it took a moment for his eyes to adjust from the glare of the Egyptian sun to the dusty darkness of the windowless, low-ceilinged interior of the keep. He made his way down a passage to the narrow stairs and climbed up.

The keep was deserted, as before. Some of its rooms were used for storage, as the darkness and the thick walls kept the temperature relatively cool; others hadn't been used for years, if not centuries. The ceilings were low, the windows were nothing more than thin slits cut into the thick walls – not the most inviting place to work, or sleep, neither of which was what it was designed for. He climbed the staircase up three floors and reached the top, then found the small landing with the wooden ladder that led up to the roof.

The BlackBerry was there, skulking in the dust behind a small stucco smokestack. Finch picked it up. He thought of edging forward for one last look at the teeming plain below, but decided against it. Instead, he found the phone number of the documentary's producer, pulled out the satphone, and called him.

The man, Gareth Willoughby, was a respected, globe-trotting filmmaker with an impressive CV of well-crafted documentaries covering all kinds of topics. Finch only managed to get through to his voicemail, and left him a brief message explaining what was going on and asking him to return the call.

He took one last look across the desert, then headed back down. As his foot settled on the bottom rung of the ladder that came down from the roof, he heard a voice, a low murmur coming from one of the small rooms behind the chapel. A man's voice, no more than a few words, but their rumble carried across the quiet, warrenlike space. Something about it made him listen more closely. He stepped away from the ladder, quietly, and followed the voice around the narrow corridor to a room that faced out, away from the monastery. Finch couldn't make out what he was saying, but it struck him that the man was speaking English.

He reached the doorway and stopped just short of it, hovering, leaning in for a look. The man was inside, alone. It was a monk. Like the others, he wore the traditional black cassock with the distinctively embroidered hood, which was raised over his head. He had his back turned to Finch. Finch stood there, somewhat taken aback, as he realized the man was talking on a cell phone. In English.

'We should be leaving in ten, fifteen minutes,' the man said. 'Shouldn't take more than twenty minutes to get through.' He paused, then said, 'Okay,' and hung up.

Finch stiffened as he recognized the voice, and it must have caused him to pull his foot back an inch, maybe less, nothing significant – except that it was significant enough for the monk to sense his presence and turn.

It was Brother Ameen.

The awkwardness of the moment was stifling. Finch's eyes were drawn to the phone and back – there was something unusual about it, but his frazzled mind didn't latch onto it immediately – and he looked the monk squarely in the eyes before he caught himself and relaxed his face into a casual, sheepish half smile.

'I, um,' he said, wavering, then pointing up at the roof, 'I forgot my phone up there.'

Brother Ameen didn't answer him. He didn't return the casual half smile either. He just stood there, rooted in silence.

Finch sensed the monk's muscles going tight. His eyes drifted down to the phone, then he realized what he'd unconsciously noted. It wasn't just a regular cell phone. They didn't work out there. It was a satphone, with its distinctive, oversized flip-up antenna. Not only that, but it had a small box plugged into its base, which Finch knew to be an encryption module.

CHAPTER 48

Nahant, Massachusetts

'More than anything, Dom lived for his work,' Jenna Reece was telling Matt and Jabba. 'Even when the kids were around, he hardly ever managed to make it up here, and when he did, it didn't make much difference anyway. His mind was always back in his lab.'

They were in the living room-slash-studio of her house in Nahant, a small town that squatted on a tiny crescent-shaped peninsula fifteen miles north of Boston. A couple of miles offshore, it was linked to the mainland by a narrow umbilical cord of sand bank. Reece's house, a fully modernized Dutch colonial, faced the ocean on the town's western coast. It had once been Dominic and Jenna's summer home, she'd told them, but following her husband's death, she'd sold their place in the city and moved full-time out here, where she'd turned the double-height living room into a workshop and lost herself in her sculpture.

'I imagine your brother was probably the same, wasn't he?' she asked. 'They all seemed consumed by their work.' She shrugged wistfully and leaned down to stroke her dog, a ginger-haired retriever that dozed lazily by her feet. A small Christmas tree twinkled in a corner, by the floor-to-ceiling sliding doors that led onto the deck. 'And look what it got them in the end.'

Matt held her gaze and nodded solemnly. 'What do you know about the project they were working on when they died?'

Jenna Reece let out a light chortle. 'Not very much. Dom didn't really go into much detail about his work with me. Not with his ditzy wife,' she laughed easily. 'I haven't really got much of a scientific mind anyway, so it wasn't something I was normally curious about. It was his world. And, well, you must know how obsessive he and the rest of them were when it came to making sure no one knew what they were working on – not until they were good and ready to make their announcements and reap the glory. Which I always thought was a bit too paranoid . . . I mean, it's not exactly the kind of thing I would slip into casual conversations at the coffee shop, is it?' she smiled.

Matt shifted in his seat and leaned forward, steepling his hands under his chin, clearly discomfited by what he needed to ask her. 'Mrs. Reece . . .'

'It's Jenna, Matt,' she softly corrected him.

'Jenna,' he tried again, 'I need to ask you something, but you might find it a bit weird, and . . .' His voice trailed off and he looked at her, hoping for encouragement.

'Matt, you said you needed to talk and you drove all this way to see me, so I figure it has to be important.' She fixed him squarely. 'Ask me what you need to ask.'

'Okay,' he nodded gratefully. 'I just wanted to know . . . Did you actually get to see your husband's body?'

Jenna Reece blinked a couple of times, and her eyes looked away before dropping down to her feet. She reached down and stroked her dog again, somewhat rattled by the memory. Outside, frothy December waves pounded the rocky outcroppings below the timber deck, their metronomic crashes punctuating the uneasy silence. 'No,' she said after a moment. 'I mean, not his whole body. But you know how they died, and . . . the conditions out there . . .'

'I know,' he offered, trying to avoid conjuring up any additional painful imagery. 'But you're sure it was him?'

Her eyes were aimed at Matt, but they were looking through him, far beyond, beyond the room's walls and the town itself. 'All they had for me was his hand,' she said. The words caught in her throat and she shut her eyes for a moment. When she opened them again, they glistened with moisture. 'It was his hand, though. His left hand. His wedding band was still on it. I didn't have any doubts.'

'You're sure of it?' Matt probed again, despite his misgivings.

Jenna Reece nodded. 'He had these really lovely, fine hands. Like a pianist's. I noticed them the first time we met. Of course, it had been . . .' She brushed a painful thought away and straightened up. 'I still knew it was his.' She smiled through it at Matt. 'Why do you ask?'

'Well, there wasn't anything left of my brother, so I was just wondering if . . . I was just hoping maybe someone had made a mistake,' he obfuscated.

'You think your brother might still be alive?'

The way she cut to the heart of his thinking surprised him, and he couldn't help but nod.

She gave him a warming, supportive smile. 'I wish I could tell you something that would help clear it up for you one way or another, but all I can tell you is what I know about my Dom.'

Matt nodded, quietly grateful that he didn't have to explain any further. He thought back to the main reason for their visit. 'Do you know who Dom was working for?'

'He didn't share that with me,' she told him thoughtfully. 'Not that he wasn't very excited about it. He was. But like the rest of them, he was cagey about details. And I'd seen it all before – every discovery of his had the potential to change the way we live. That's how they all thought, it was what they were all chasing after. And I guess some of these things can end up changing our lives, whether it's cell phones or the Internet or electric cars.' She leaned forward, frowning with concentration, trying to see through the cobwebs of her mind. 'But with this project . . . it was different. Like I said, Dom didn't say much about his work at the best of times, but with this one, he was particularly aloof. And I could see that this was different. It was the big one. Much as he tried to hide it, he had this burning enthusiasm about it, this optimism . . . he felt it could really change things, on a more fundamental level. I pressed him on it a couple of times, and he'd just say, "You'll see." And the day he got the green light on the funding – it was usually a big night out for us, a big celebration in some fancy restaurant. This one wasn't like that. He was delighted, don't get me wrong. But it was more than that. It was like the next phase of his life had begun. Like he was on a mission. And he was being more secretive than ever after that. I hardly ever saw him. Until . . .' She looked away, shaking the memory away.

'You didn't know anything about who was backing him? He must have said something about that,' Matt pressed.

Jenna eyed him hesitantly, then said, 'I'm not sure I should be telling you this.'

'Please, Jenna,' Matt said, palms open. 'I really need to know. My brother was part of it.'

Jenna studied him, then heaved out a sigh and nodded. 'Well . . . I always assumed the money was coming from one of the big tech VCs he knew or maybe the government. He only let it slip once, and that was by accident,' she confided.

'What?' Matt asked, gently.

'The money. It was coming from Rydell.'

Matt looked at her, confused. Jabba took up the slack. 'Larry Rydell?'

'Yes,' she confirmed. 'No one was supposed to know. I don't know why, but that's how they wanted it. Rydell has such a big public profile, and I guess he has his share price to worry about. Still, I was surprised – and more than a bit pissed off, to tell you the truth – when he didn't even show up at Dom's funeral. I mean, I can't complain, they took good care of me, I didn't have any trouble with their insurance people or anything, but still . . .'

Jabba looked at Matt pointedly. Matt knew the name – most people did – but didn't quite grasp the significance it seemed to have for Jabba.

'You're sure of this?' Jabba pressed.

'Yes,' Jenna Reece replied.

Jabba looked at Matt with an expression that said they had all they needed to know.

CHAPTER 49

Deir Al-Suryan Monastery, Wadi Natrun, Egypt

'So . . . you've got a satphone?' Finch found himself asking, rhetorically, as if he were in a trance.

Brother Ameen didn't respond in any way.

'I didn't think you had one out here,' Finch added, while trying to drain his tone of any hint of suspicion.

The monk still didn't say anything. He just kept looking blankly at Finch.

'It's funny,' Finch continued, ''cause I just thought the whole point of being here was to isolate yourself from the rest of the world, to allow you to, you know, concentrate on God and . . . and yet you've got a satphone,' he stated again, his attention traveling down to the phone in the monk's hand and back to his eyes.

Finch's forced smile dropped. It rose, fractionally, across Brother Ameen's face.

'I do,' the monk finally said, almost regretfully. 'And it's got an encryption box.'

He held Finch's probing gaze. Finch tried to dismiss the comment with a no-big-deal grimace, but the monk wasn't buying.

'I know you recognized it when you saw it,' the monk added. 'It was obvious from your expression. I expect you've seen them before, given your line of work, the kinds of places you've been.'

'Yeah, but . . .' Finch waved it away, mock-casually. 'I see more and more of them these days. It's safer, isn't it? What with all the scanners and . . .' His voice trailed off as his mind went off on its own, rocketing back over all the events that had led to his being here, in this small, stuffy room; enlightening him with a barrage of revelations that he'd never imagined – and it suddenly hit him that he was in serious danger, an odd, instinctive reaction he didn't quite understand but one that still made him take a hesitant step backward.

The monk mirrored him with a soft step forward.

Finch frowned. 'What are you doing?'

'I'm sorry,' Brother Ameen said as he took another step toward him.

Finch's instincts flared red-hot – and he bolted backward and turned to head back to the stairs, but he'd barely made it past the door's threshold before the monk was right with him, moving lightning fast, slamming him back against the wall while driving a hard knee straight into his groin. Finch pitched forward, exhaling heavily from the kick. His glasses flew off his face as he bent over, and he pivoted around and raised his hands defensively, hoping to stave off another blow. For a split second, he caught sight of the monk's fist. Without the spectacles, it was a bit out of focus, but it looked like the monk had it bunched tight, with its middle knuckle extended, and it recoiled before lunging at his head, fast as a rattlesnake's strike. Its steely tap struck him on the side of his neck, just below his ear, pounding his carotid sinus with the force of a hammer blow. He felt his entire body tense up from the hit, before losing all motor control of his muscles and plummeting to the ground.

It was the oddest feeling – motionless, no control over his muscles, like a big lump of Jell-O dropped on the ground. Through groggy, hazy eyes, he saw the monk hover over him, look away and then back down, think for the briefest of moments, then bend down, grab him by the arm, lift him up, and sling him over his shoulder.

'Where is he?' Gracie asked, scanning the monastery's courtyard.

She was standing with Dalton, ready to go. They'd been

joined by the abbot and Father Jerome, and the other monks who'd be helping them carry their gear across.

Dalton tilted his head up at the top of the keep, cupped his hands around his mouth like a bullhorn, and yelled, 'Finch. We're all set here. Time to move out, pal.'

No answer.

Gracie looked around, then asked Dalton, 'You sure he went up there?'

Dalton nodded. 'It shouldn't be that long. He's just looking for his BlackBerry.'

Gracie glanced around again, impatiently, then frowned at the keep. 'I'm gonna see what's keeping him,' she said, and stepped away.

She'd almost reached the doorway when something inside her made her look up – the barely perceptible noise of a wind rush, a hardly noticeable darkening of the ground to her right – and she turned and looked up just in time to see Finch's body hurtling to the ground and slamming into the hard sand a few feet away from her.

CHAPTER 50

Outskirts of Boston, Massachusetts

'It makes sense,' Jabba concluded, all pumped up, his mouth motoring ahead. 'He's got the money. He's got the technical chops to pull off something like this. And he's a major, major environmentalist.' Jabba shook his head, his face locked in concentration. 'Question is, how's he doing it?'

'Doesn't matter,' Matt replied.

They were back on the mainland, heading down the Salem Turnpike, toward the city. Jabba had told Matt what he knew about Rydell — the way he championed alternative energy projects across the globe, the passion with which he lobbied Washington to take the climate change issue seriously, the support he gave to politicians and to groups who'd been fighting the mostly losing battle against the previous administration's callous disregard for environmental concerns. Every word of it added an additional pixel of clarity to the picture that was forming in Matt's mind: him getting in Rydell's face and hearing what they'd done to Danny straight from the horse's mouth.

'How is it you know so much about Rydell?' Matt asked.

Jabba looked at him askance. 'Dude. Seriously? Where've you been living?'

Matt shrugged. 'So he really thought he could start a new "green" religion? Is that it?'

Jabba cracked a grin. 'We're hardwired to believe from minute one, dude. It's all around us from the day we're born. There's no escaping it. And people will believe all kinds of crap. Look at what a third-rate sci-fi writer was able to pull off, and everyone knew he was only out to get stinking rich. Rydell . . . the man's in a whole different league. He's got state-of-the-art technology and all the money he needs at his disposal. And he's no fool. It's an awesome combination.'

Matt nodded, taking it in. 'And he's set this whole thing up to save the planet?'

'Not the planet. Us. It's like George Carlin said. The planet's gonna be just fine. It's been through far worse than anything we can throw at it. It was here long before us and it'll still be around long after we're gone. It's *we* that need saving.'

Matt shook his head in disbelief, then glanced out the window. The traffic up and down the turnpike was already noticeably heavier, with the Christmas rush home starting to clog the nation's arteries.

'Do you think they knew what they were really working on?' he asked Jabba. 'Danny, the others . . . do you think Reece and Rydell told them?'

'I don't know . . . They had to be aware of the power of what they were putting together.' He glanced sideways at Matt. 'The question isn't just whether or not they were told. It's whether or not they knew about it from day one. Whether or not they were working on it knowing what it was going to be used for.'

Matt shook his head again with denial.

'He was your brother, man,' Jabba added, hesitantly. 'What do you think? Could he have been part of something like this?'

Matt thought about it. 'A hoax like this? Scamming millions of people.' He shook his head again. 'I don't think so.'

'Even if he thought it was for a good cause?'

That one was harder to answer. Danny wasn't any more religious than Matt was, despite their parents' best efforts, so there wouldn't have been any faith issues for him there. And although he was a high-minded, upstanding kind of guy, Matt didn't remember him being particularly concerned with the planet's environmental problems, no more than most well-read, levelheaded people. He certainly wasn't messianic about it. Still, they'd spent a lot of time apart, courtesy of Matt's stints behind bars, and when all was said and done, how well did anyone know anyone else, really?

Jabba was scrutinizing him, unsure about whether or not to say anything more. Matt noticed it.

'What?' he asked.

'I don't know, dude. I mean, I hate to say it, but it doesn't look good. It's been two years. If Danny didn't pull a disappearing act to be part of this, I don't see how they could have kept him locked up and muzzled all this time. He would've found a way to reach out to someone, to sneak a word out, don't you think?'

'Not if they know what they're doing.'

'Two years, man,' Jabba added with a slight wince.

Matt stared ahead, frowning. Suddenly, he was feeling a tightening in his chest. He didn't know what was better – to find out Danny was actually long dead, or that he was part of all this willingly. Part of something that had gotten his own best friend killed and his brother accused of his murder.

'No way,' Matt finally said. 'He'd never want to be part of something like this. Not if he knew what they were really doing.'

'Okay,' Jabba accepted and turned away.

They motored on for a mile or so, then Matt said, 'Get us another lock on Maddox's car, will you?'

'Okay, but we really shouldn't be using this,' Jabba cautioned as he pulled out his iPhone.

'Just don't stay on any longer than you think is safe. You can be in and out in less than your forty seconds, right?'

'Let's make it thirty,' Jabba said and nodded reluctantly. He pulled up the tracker's website. He didn't need to key in the tracker's number – it was now stored on a cookie. He waited a couple of seconds for the ping to echo back, then zoomed in on the map.

'He's stationary. Somewhere by the name of Hanscom Field,' he told Matt. 'Hang on.' He pulled up another website. Punched in his query. Waited a couple of seconds for it to upload. 'It's a small airport between Bedford and Concord. And I'm logging off before they track us.' He killed the phone, checked his watch – twenty-six seconds total – and turned to Matt.

Matt chewed it over quickly. A small airfield. He wondered what Maddox was doing there. He also liked the idea of maybe being able to surprise Maddox and get up close and personal with him outside the man's comfort zone.

He glanced at the clock on the dashboard. It wasn't far, even with the holiday traffic building up. A half hour, forty minutes maybe. 'That's just outside the ninety-five, isn't it?'

Jabba's face sank. 'Yep,' he shrugged.

'Check it again in fifteen minutes or so, will ya? Keep making sure he's still there.'

Jabba nodded grimly and sagged into his seat, sucking in a deep breath and anticipating the worst.

Maddox hung up with his contact at the NSA and scowled. He scanned the skies instinctively for the incoming jet, but his mind was now preoccupied elsewhere.

He'd received three consecutive calls. The first one was innocuous enough: The learning software had delivered on its promise, and the targets were just north of the city, heading into town. The second call told him the targets had changed direction and were now heading west on the Concord Turnpike, which, with hindsight, should have raised an eyebrow, but hadn't. The third call, though, was seriously troubling. The targets had turned north once they'd hit I-95, and were now less than five miles away from the airfield.

Which was, again, seriously troubling. For the simple reason that Maddox didn't believe in blind luck any more than he believed in coincidences. And it was the second time Matt had managed to track him down that day. Which meant he was either psychic, or he had an advantage Maddox wasn't aware of.

Yet.

His mind did a one-eighty and ran a full-spectrum sweep of everything that had happened since he'd first come across Matt Sherwood. He shelved details he thought extraneous and focused on establishing causal links between that first encounter and the present moment and running them against the background skills he knew Matt possessed.

All of which colluded to draw his attention across to his car.

He took a half step closer to it, his eyes scrutinizing it as his operational instincts assessed what the likely culprit could be.

And frowned at the realization.

He wouldn't have time to have the car checked out. Which meant there was a chance he'd have to leave it there for now. Which pissed him off even more. He really liked that car. He checked his watch. The jet's arrival was imminent.

He looked around. The airfield was quiet, as it normally was. Which was good. He decided it was time to put an end to Matt Sherwood's unexpected intrusions – permanently – and waved over two of his men who were waiting nearby.

'I think we're about to have some company,' he told them.

Then he told them what he wanted to do about it.

CHAPTER 51

Deir Al-Suryan Monastery, Wadi Natrun, Egypt

'Finch!'

Gracie's cry shook the walls of the monastery as she dropped to the ground at his side. She was shaking. The blood drained from her face, and her hands shot up to her open mouth. Finch's body just lay there, in front of her, flat against the desert sand. He was on his front, motionless, the puff of dust that he'd kicked up when he'd slammed into the ground drifting back down and settling around him.

Slowly, her hands came down and hovered over him, not daring to touch him. The others, led by Dalton, all rushed to her side.

'Is he . . . ?' Dalton couldn't say it.

There were no visible open wounds, no blood seeping out. It didn't make the sight any less horrific. His head, which must have hit the ground first, was twisted sideways at an impossible angle. He had one arm bent backward, and his eyes were staring lifelessly at the parched soil.

'Oh my God. Finch,' Gracie sobbed as she stared at him, not sure what to do. Her hands finally dropped down onto his body, her fingers pressing softly against his neck, searching for a pulse or for any sign of life she knew she wasn't going to find.

She looked at Dalton through teary eyes and shook her head.

Dalton was shaking. He put his arms around Gracie, his eyes also locked on his fallen friend's body. The monks, waiting hesitantly behind Father Jerome and the abbot, started murmuring some prayers. After a moment, Gracie pulled her hand back, then gently brushed a few errant strands of hair off Finch's forehead and gave his cheek a gentle caress, staring at him, wanting to slide his eyelids shut but not daring to touch them. She sensed movement behind her, turned, and saw Father Jerome advance hesitantly, his gaze locked on Finch. The holy man took a few more steps until he was standing right next to her, then he knelt down beside her, softly, his concentration still focused on Finch's dead body.

A shiver of anticipation rolled through her. *What is he doing?* She watched with rapt attention as he leaned in closer, held out his hands over Finch, and shut his eyes in silent prayer. For a fleeting moment, a wild notion rose within her, an impossible, absurd notion – that she was about to witness something miraculous, that Father Jerome was actually going to intervene with the heavens and bring her friend back from the dead. Her heart leapt into her mouth as she sat there, crippled with fear and hope, and she tried to hold onto that crazy possibility as long as she could, flashing to all the other impossible things she'd witnessed over the last few days and trying to convince herself that anything was now possible, clutching at it with raging desperation even as it slipped away as quickly as it had arisen, driven out by the sight of Finch's mangled, still-dead body and the cold logic that had always guided her. A devastating sense of grief soon came rolling back in and numbed every nerve in her body.

She looked over at Father Jerome, who opened his eyes and made a cross over Finch's head. He turned to face her with a look of profound sadness, and took her hands in his.

'I'm so sorry,' he said simply.

His expression, Gracie saw, was also riven with guilt. She nodded, but said nothing. He rose and shuffled back to join his brethren. The abbot and Brother Ameen were standing a few steps back, and as Father Jerome reached them, the abbot put a consoling hand on his shoulder, and he and the younger monk murmured some words to him. Gracie turned to Dalton, then glanced up at the top of the keep. Its sand-colored edge contrasted sharply against the backdrop of clear blue sky. It looked like a close-up one would find on a hip postcard or coffee table book, disconcertingly perfect with its striking pastel colors – too perfect to have hosted such an ugly death.

'How . . .' she muttered. 'How could he fall like that?'

Dalton shook his head slowly, still in shock. 'I don't know.' His eyes went wide. 'Do you think someone out there took a shot at him? Was he shot?'

Gracie looked at him with sudden horror, then bent back down to Finch's side. Dalton bent down with her. She hesitated; then, with trembling fingers, she straightened Finch's arms and legs and, slowly, turned him over. She scanned his front, but couldn't see any bullet wound.

'It doesn't look like it,' she said. 'I didn't hear a shot, did you?'

'No.' Dalton looked mystified. He turned his gaze back up at the top of the keep. 'The lip of that wall up there, it's so low. Maybe he was leaning over to tell us he found it and just . . .' His voice trailed off.

Gracie scanned the ground around them. The satphone glinted at her from a few feet away, half-buried in the sand. She scanned wider. Spotted it. A small black box, lying by the base of the keep's wall. Finch's BlackBerry. She got up, retrieved the satphone, then padded over to the wall. She picked up the BlackBerry and just stared at it, brushing the sand off it with her fingers, imagining Finch's last moments in her mind's eye as he found it on the roof and crossed over to the edge for – what, one last look? a wave? She wished there was some way to go back and stop him from climbing up there and having his life grind to a halt in one cruel and sudden moment. But there was no going back. She knew that. She'd seen enough deaths in her years and had learned, long ago, to accept their finality.

'What are we going to do?' she asked. Her eyes, still teary, drifted past Dalton, to Father Jerome, the abbot, and Brother Ameen, who were behind him, and the macabre contingent of monks slightly farther back.

'We've got to go,' Dalton told her, his voice hollow.

'What about Finch? We can't leave him here like this.'

'We can't take him with us,' he replied softly. 'We just can't.'

After a brief moment, she nodded, still reluctantly but with a hint of clarity seeping back into her. 'You're right,' she said. She looked over at the abbot. 'Can you . . . ?'

Sparing her the need to say it, the abbot nodded solemnly. 'Of course,' he told her. 'We'll take care of him until we can send him home . . . properly.' He paused, as if to make sure she was all right with that, then glanced over at the Previa and the men huddled around it. She followed his gaze. The faint drone of the radio was still there, threatening like a malevolent siren.

'You should go now,' he added, 'as planned.'

As they gathered their gear, Gracie and Dalton watched as a few monks, aided by the driver, lifted Finch's body onto a makeshift stretcher – an old door that they'd lifted off its hinges – and carried him inside the main chapel. Four other monks picked up the rest of the news crew's gear, and the small troupe followed the abbot out of the sun-soaked courtyard and into the cool darkness of the monastery.

They trudged past the entrance of the Church of the Holy Virgin and the refectory, until they reached an ancient, unlit stairwell.

'You'll need the lamps from here on,' the abbot instructed. The monks lit up a succession of small, camping gas lanterns, casting a cool white pallor across the stone passage. Slowly, they descended a narrow staircase, kicking up a fine mist of pungent dust, and landed in another passage that led them past a couple of olive-oil cellars, where some of the world's earliest dated books – brought to the monastery by monks fleeing religious persecution in Syria and Baghdad in the eighth century – had been discovered in the mid-1800s, and on to the entrance of Saint Bishoi's cave.

The abbot pushed the crumbling timber door open and led them in. The cave was dark and narrow, no bigger than a small bedroom. Gracie held her lantern up for a closer look. The cave's floor was begrimed with dirt, its ceiling vaulted with rough-hewn stone. She saw nothing to support the legend she'd read about during the downtime on their journey over – the legend that Bishoi's devotion to his faith was so powerful that he used to tie his hair to a chain that dangled from the roof of the cave, to make sure he didn't fall asleep for days on end while awaiting the vision of Christ that he was praying for.

'It's this way,' the abbot said.

Gracie swung her lantern in his direction. In a corner of the cave, to the left of the doorway, skulked another rotting timber door, this one even smaller than the one leading into the cave. Two monks helped the abbot pull it open, smothering the tight space with more dust. Gracie edged closer and spotted the entrance to the narrow, low tunnel. It was no more than five feet high and three across, a black hole that sucked in the dim gaslight just as it had barely made it inside.

'God be with you,' the abbot told Father Jerome as, one by one, they dropped their heads and clambered into the tight passage. Gracie was the last one in. She hesitated for a moment, still choking inside at the thought of abandoning Finch, before nodding a parting half smile at the abbot, clenching her jaw with stoic acceptance, and disappearing into the tunnel's oppressive darkness.

CHAPTER 52

Bedford, Massachusetts

Matt slowed the Camry right down as the woods on either side of the two-lane road gave way to a handful of low office buildings that dozed behind snow-dusted lawns.

He slid a sideways glance at Jabba and said, 'Heads up,' before scanning the surroundings.

There were no other cars on the road, and the area seemed very sedate. They cruised past the entrance to a small air force base that was tucked away to their right. A lone, bored guard manned its flimsy red-and-white barrier. The base shared its runway with the adjacent civilian airfield, but little else. From what they could see, it seemed austere and outdated, a stark contrast to the two swanky flight services buildings farther down the road that catered to the well-heeled clientele who favored flying their private jets into Hanscom Field to avoid the air traffic delays and heavy-handed security at Boston's Logan Airport – the twin wonders of twenty-first-century air travel.

The approach road led to the civilian air terminal, which wasn't exactly a hotbed of activity either. There, it doglegged left, then looped back on itself, ringing a disproportionately large, trapezoidal, asphalted central space that served as the visitors' parking lot. Matt counted less than a dozen cars parked there, and none that he recognized.

The hangars and planes were to his right, on the outside of the ring road, across the street from the parking lot. The high-pitched whine of a taxiing jet could be heard behind one of the two main hangars. Given that we lived in a post-9/11 world, the low-level security was surprising. A pretty basic chain-link fence, seven feet high at best, with an extra foot on top canted outward, was all that separated the road from the apron. You could practically reach through the fence and touch the planes that were dotted around the hangar area. As he drove around the return leg of the road, Matt saw two entry points to the airfield. Again, surprisingly basic: chain-link rolling fences, two cars wide, that slid sideways on small metal wheels. No guardhouses. No guards. Just a swipe-card reader and an intercom on a stalk for those who weren't regular visitors.

'Check it again,' Matt told Jabba. 'We need a tighter fix on the bastard.'

'I don't know, dude,' Jabba replied warily. 'We're too close.'

'Just don't break your forty-second rule and we'll be fine, right?'

Jabba studied him with a wry look. 'You think that cocky optimism of yours might have anything to do with your getting that priority pass to prison?'

'Nah. Back then, I was just reckless,' Matt quipped.

'Didn't really need to know that right now,' Jabba groaned as he fired up his laptop and phone. He zoomed right in on the linked Google map, then killed the connection. The tracker was about four hundred yards ahead, at the far edge of the apron, just before the tree line, beyond the second hangar and what looked like a smaller outbuilding.

'What's he doing in there?' Jabba asked.

'Either dropping someone off or, more likely, meeting someone who's flying in.' Matt twisted around, scanning the perimeter. He glimpsed a small private jet crossing from behind one hangar to another. It was rolling toward the tracker's position.

Matt's pulse quickened with a jolt of urgency. His instincts told him he needed to be in there – fast. He frowned at the near gate, giving his options a quick run-through, then saw the other gate, the one farther down and closer to the tracker, open up. He tensed – but it wasn't the Merc, or the 300C, coming out. Just a silver Town and Country minivan, idling as the gate rolled back.

He nudged the throttle, propelling the Camry forward, its narrow tires giving out a tortured squeal. The car accelerated down the ring road, the airfield's perimeter fence to its right. He was eighty yards away when the gate had rolled back far enough for the minivan to nose forward. Sixty yards away when the minivan had cleared the gate, turned right, and was driving off. Forty yards away when the gate had clicked to a stop and started to roll back. Twenty yards away when the gate was halfway shut – and closing. Which, given that it was two cars wide, meant the math wasn't on his side.

Matt didn't lift his foot. Fifteen yards from the gate, he twisted the steering wheel left to send the car swerving wide before flicking it right again while giving the gas pedal a violent kick. The Camry's soft shock absorbers went into cardiac arrest as the rear end swung around and the small car leaned dangerously to the left, the momentum shifting its entire weight onto its two left tires – but Matt got what he wanted. The car had fishtailed into a position perpendicular to the gate and was now rushing toward it. Matt kept his foot down and threaded the Camry in, flying past the gate's fixed post, while scraping the car's right side against the incoming edge.

They were in.

The Bullet watched attentively as the Citation X veered left on the wide apron and pulled up between the outbuilding and the edge of the tree line, by the parked Merc and the 300C.

The X was a fabulous piece of engineering. Its Rolls-Royce turbofan engines took it to within a whisker of Mach 1, which meant it could fly twelve passengers from New York to L.A. in under four hours and in the height of luxury. Little wonder, Maddox mused, that it was the private-jet-du-jour for the lucky Forbes-level big-hitters who weren't even aware there was a credit crunch going on: the biggest Hollywood stars, free-spending Russian tycoons – and evangelist preachers. Humble servants of the Lord like Kenneth and Gloria Copeland, who got their megachurch's army of faithful followers to stump up twenty million dollars for their customized X to help them follow God's personal directive and spread His word more efficiently.

The Bullet had used the spot before: It was tucked away at the far end of the airfield, away from prying eyes. It was well suited for whisking certain camera-shy clients in and out of the city unnoticed – usually, post-operative or post-scandal celebrities, or masters of the universe putting together sensitive transactions.

In this case, things were different.

As the plane's tail-mounted engines whined down, a voice crackled in his earpiece.

'A white Camry just snuck in through the south gate,' the operative said. 'I think it's our boys.'

Maddox casually raised his wrist to his mouth and spoke clearly into his cuff mike. 'Got it. Stay with them. And take them down once the package is in the car.'

He stepped closer to the plane as its door snapped open, his eyes casually sweeping the environment. He didn't see anything suspicious, and turned his attention back to the plane, where Rebecca Rydell and her two bodyguards were now coming down the stairs.

Matt turned left and hugged the back of the first hangar. He reached its corner and stopped, then edged forward slowly, looking out. He whirred his window open, and he could hear the plane in the distance, powering down, but he couldn't see it, so he feathered the throttle again and crossed over to the second hangar. From what he could see on the frozen map on the laptop's screen, there was nothing but open tarmac from there to the tracker's position.

He edged forward. In the distance, about a hundred yards ahead, was the outbuilding, a low, concrete structure with no windows. He could see the tail of the jet sticking out from behind it, as well as the tailgate of a black Dodge Durango. A couple of private jets and a handful of smaller propeller-driven planes sat idly between the hangar and the outbuilding. They provided some kind of cover – which he needed if they were going to get closer without being spotted.

He decided to cut across and get behind the outbuilding. From there, they would be able to see what was going on – and, if feasible, Matt could make his move. He pulled out his handgun. Sat it on his lap. Noticed Jabba looking at him warily.

'You do realize it's empty, right?' Jabba said.

'They don't know that,' Matt replied. 'Besides, I don't plan on needing it.'

Which, judging from Jabba's expression, didn't seem to reassure him much.

'You can get out here and wait for me, if you want,' Matt told him.

Jabba looked left and right at the deserted area behind the hangar, then turned back to Matt. 'I think I'll stick around. It's not exactly Grand Central Terminal out here, you know what I mean?'

Matt nodded, sat the gun in his lap, and eased the car forward.

They shadowed the parked aircraft and pulled in behind the outbuilding. It was a power substation and had a low, metal fence around it. Matt nosed forward, just enough to give them a view of the plane without exposing any more than the side of the car's A-pillar.

Two men were escorting a young, tanned blonde off the plane.

Jabba leaned forward, his jaw dropping with surprise. 'Whoa.'

Matt slid a reproachful glance at him. 'Not now, tiger—'

'No, dude,' Jabba interrupted urgently. 'She's Rydell's daughter.'

Matt studied her with more interest. She stepped off the stairs and glanced around uncertainly as the two men led her over to Maddox, who spoke to her briefly before leading them to the waiting Durango. As he opened the SUV's rear door, he glanced across the tarmac and over in Matt's direction, and their eyes met. Matt flinched slightly, but Maddox didn't. In fact, he didn't seem rattled at all. Which, given that he'd spotted them, could only mean one thing.

The hard steel muzzle that suddenly nudged Matt just above his ear confirmed it.

CHAPTER 53

Half an hour after climbing into the tunnel, Gracie, Dalton, Father Jerome, Brother Ameen, and their four black-robed sherpas all emerged into a musty old cellar at the neighboring monastery. A few anxious monks, led by the local abbot, were there to greet them.

Gracie laid her backpack down, dusted herself off, and stretched her back as the abbot fussed over Father Jerome. He looked haunted. A compact, elderly man by the name of Antonius, the abbot seemed completely awed by the miraculous monk's presence as well as rattled by the turn of events – which was expected. She watched his wrinkled fingers as they trembled while clasping Father Jerome's hand tightly. 'Praise God that you're all right,' he was telling him as he fired off a nervous prattle of words and led them up a stone stairwell and into the monastery's refectory.

They were offered cold water and took a moment to catch their breath before heading out into balmy daylight. The monastery had the same beige, Tatooine-like feel as the one they had just left, and although it was smaller, it was no less venerable. Many Coptic popes had started off as monks there, including the current pope, Shenouda III. It also enjoyed its share of religious myth. The body of Saint Bishoi himself – his name was the Coptic word for 'sublime' – was kept there, sealed inside a wooden container that was wrapped in clear plastic. He was believed to be lying perfectly preserved and uncorrupted by time, even today, a claim that was hard to verify given that the container was locked away in a coffin and the faithful told stories of his reaching out from inside it and shaking their hands, seemingly undeterred by the limitations of physics. The magic wasn't limited to him either. Nearby and similarly sealed were the remains of another monk by the name of Paul, a fellow ascetic who was rumored to have committed suicide – successfully – seven times.

They reached Yusuf's brother-in-law's taxi, a tired white VW Sharan people carrier. It was waiting for them in the shade by a small, multi-domed structure, Pope Shenouda's occasional retreat.

'Are you sure it's safe out there?' Gracie asked the abbot.

'It's relatively quiet here,' Antonius informed her. 'They're not interested in us. So far.' He smiled uncomfortably. 'Come, I'll show you.'

They left the driver and the monks to pile the gear into the car and followed the abbot across the courtyard and up a maze of narrow outdoor stairs that snaked up to the top of the wall.

'Have a look,' the abbot told them, 'but stay low – just in case.'

Gracie and Dalton rose slowly from their crouched positions. The familiar carpet of cars and trucks covered the plain between the two monasteries, but with one crucial difference. All attention seemed focused away from them, toward the monastery they'd just left. Which meant they had a reasonable chance of sneaking out unnoticed.

They climbed back down, thanked the abbot, and got into the car. This time, Dalton and Gracie sat on either side of Father Jerome, while Brother Ameen rode shotgun. Gracie felt a bubble of apprehension as she watched the gate creak open. She steeled herself and straightened up in her seat as the driver gave the throttle a gentle nudge and the Sharan rumbled out into the desert.

There were a few scattered cars and trucks parked on either side of the dusty trail that led away from the monastery. A few men loitered by each cluster of vehicles, talking, smoking, waiting. As their car got closer to the first group,

Gracie turned to Father Jerome and raised his cassock's hood over his head, shielding him from view. Yusuf's brother-in-law kept calm, trying not to draw any attention to them as the Sharan cruised past slowly without eliciting more than a casual glance.

Gracie let out a small breath of relief. There weren't many cars or trucks up ahead. A few more minutes, she guessed, and they'd be free and clear. They were less than a hundred yards out from the monastery's gate when the road doglegged to the left by an old crumbling wall and a clutch of palm trees. A few more cars were parked there, with another bunch of men clustered against the wall, seemingly oblivious to the sun. Gracie felt a flutter in her gut as the driver slowed down to thread through the haphazardly strewn cars, which he managed without fuss – only to find a narrow ditch cutting across them. A lone man was walking toward them, alongside the trail, heading for the trees. Gracie spotted him and tensed up. She tried not to look over at him as the driver slowed right down to a crawl. They were halfway across the ditch when – just as Gracie feared – the passing man drew alongside them, and just as he glanced in, Father Jerome turned and looked sideways, casually, in his direction. It was enough.

The man reacted as if he'd been slapped. His relaxed features took on a sudden alarmed scowl as he put both hands against the car's side window and leaned right in against the glass, trying to see in, side-stepping alongside them.

'He's made us,' Gracie exclaimed. 'Get us out of here – now.'

The driver glanced back, saw the man moving with them, and nudged the gas pedal. The Sharan's engine whined as the rear tires bounced across the ditch and kept going. The man tried to keep up, but couldn't, and quickly fell back into the car's dusty trail. Gracie watched him drift away, but she knew they weren't out of danger yet. Sure enough, she saw the man turn away and start running toward the cluster of men by the trees, waving his hands feverishly, trying to attract their attention. And then, he disappeared. She wasn't sure what had happened, as her view was partially obstructed by the gear in the back of the car and the dust the car was kicking up behind it, but one moment he was there, running and waving and shouting, and then he was gone. She thought she saw him clasp his hands to his head and fall to the ground, almost as if a sudden spasm had crippled him, but she wasn't sure. They weren't about to stop and find out. The driver kept his foot pressed against the pedal, and fifteen minutes later, they were on the highway with a seemingly clear run to the airport.

And then Gracie's satphone rang.

She'd been steeling herself to make that call to Ogilvy, to tell him about Finch, and thought he'd beat her to it. But as she reached for the phone, she didn't recognize the number it was showing. She only recognized the prefix as that of an American cell phone.

'Hello?' she queried curiously.

'Miss Logan?' the voice boomed back. 'We haven't met yet, but my name is Darby. Reverend Nelson Darby. And I think I can help you.'

Fox Two watched the white people carrier streak away down the desert trail, then turned his binoculars back to the stricken man. He was still on the ground, writhing with pain, his hands pressed against his ears. Fox Two relaxed somewhat.

It had been a close call – but they'd been prepared.

He knew the agitator would be down for a while. They'd hit him with a potent blast, just to make sure. Fox Two was surprised the man hadn't lost consciousness, though he knew he still might. Main thing was, he wasn't going anywhere or saying anything. Not for a while, anyway. Which was all the time they needed.

He raised a finger and spun it around, giving his men the signal to move out. Swiftly and silently, they powered down the LRAD and covered it up before pulling away and heading out as innocuously as they'd arrived, shadowing the van from a safe distance and looking forward to finally going home.

CHAPTER 54

Bedford, Massachusetts

The man kept the gun pressed against Matt's temple.

'Easy.' His voice was flat, his arm stable. With his left hand, he reached down to Matt's lap and pulled out his gun, which he stuffed under his belt. Matt cursed inwardly. He'd been so focused on watching the plane and Maddox that he hadn't noticed the man sneaking up on them from the back. Another guy – same general appearance, dark suit, white shirt, no tie, granite-dark shades – appeared a few yards ahead, rounding the other side of the outbuilding, moving toward Jabba's side of the car. He also had a gun out, and it was also leveled at Matt's head. A big gun. A Para-Ordnance P14. It looked heavy. It looked like it could stop a charging rhino in its tracks. Which it could.

Matt's mind rocketed into a manic good news/bad news sift-through. Maddox's drones couldn't really kill them there and then; the airport authorities had to have a record of their being there, there had to be some CCTV cameras scattered around that would have recorded their presence. It was altogether too messy for them, too risky, had to be. Which definitely went under the good news column. But they had plenty of other options. The key was getting him and Jabba off the airport grounds, quietly. They'd either lead them to their cars, or – the cleaner, more obvious option – one of the drones, or both of them more likely, would get into the Camry and lead him and Jabba, at gunpoint, to somewhere nice and quiet where they could pump a few bullets into them and leave their decomposing bodies for some hapless camper to discover. Which definitely went under the bad news column. Matt knew that if he let one or both of the drones into the car, he probably wouldn't be running these good news/bad news exercises ever again. Which in itself wasn't a bad thing, but he did feel like sticking around for other, less life-threatening, pursuits.

It was simple. He couldn't let them into the car.

Which meant he probably had no more than a couple of seconds left to do something about it.

Matt's hands and feet moved like lightning. His left hand shot up and grabbed the man's right wrist – his gun hand – and slammed it forward, crushing it against the inside of the A-pillar. A shot erupted out of it – a deafeningly loud explosion inside the car, a mere eighteen inches from Matt's face. He felt like he'd slammed face-first into a swimming pool. The shot's sound wave hit him like a lead fist that pounded both ears and numbed them into a soundless, disconcerting stillness in the same split second that the .45 ACP round obliterated the rearview mirror and punched through the windshield, a clean, supersonic jab that didn't shatter it but only spiderwebbed it around the bullet's clean, oval-shaped hole of an exit point.

Matt thought he heard Jabba yell out, but he couldn't be sure. He felt like he was still underwater, and besides, he wasn't focusing on him. The other guy was more his concern. So in the same instant that he shoved the first shooter's hand forward and jammed it against the windshield pillar, his right foot stamped on the gas pedal and his right hand twisted the wheel to the right. The car lunged forward and slewed right – straight at the second shooter. The guy to his left jerked backward, but Matt had his elbow locked and managed to keep the guy's gun hand pinned against the pillar long enough for the car to cover the three yards to the second shooter and slam into him before he had the chance to loose a shot, crushing him against the low metal fence that jutted out from the side of the outbuilding. The shooter's midsection was pulverized – his eyes popped wide and he let out a piercing yelp of agony before a gush of blood overwhelmed his vocal cords and came spewing out of his mouth and onto the Camry's virgin-white hood.

Matt still had the first guy to deal with. For a second, the guy's face went rigid with shock at seeing his coworker truncated, then he was all crunched up with renewed determination as he fought Matt's grip and struggled to angle his gun inward. Another round exploded – again mere inches from Matt's face, again deafening, dizzying, like a baseball bat to the ears – and whizzed past Jabba's face before spinning out through his open window. Matt saw the guy reaching down with his free hand – his left hand – moving to pull the gun he'd taken off Matt from under his belt, and Matt spun the wheel to the right – once, twice, full lock, using one arm – then dropped his hand down to the gearshift, slammed it into reverse, and mashed the gas pedal again. The car leapt back, courtesy of the standard tight gearing in reverse, and with the steering locked all the way to the right, the Camry's front swung sideways and outward violently and slammed into the first shooter. He was thrown back and, with his hand still pinned to the pillar, tripped over himself and stumbled to the ground – with the car still arcing backward. The Camry's rear end crunched against the outbuilding's concrete wall just as its left front wheel rode over the fallen shooter's ankles, tearing up bone and cartilage in its wake. The man howled with pain and his fingers let go of the gun, which tumbled into Matt's foot well. Matt threw the car back into drive and howled away in a squeal of rubber.

He threw a glance at the plane – the two bodyguards who were with Rydell's daughter were rushing toward him, guns drawn. He floored the accelerator again and tore back up the apron, found the gate through which he'd sneaked in – it was closed – plowed right through it and tore down Hanscom Drive and into the shelter of its tree line.

'They knew we were coming,' he yelled at Jabba.

'What? How do you know that?'

'They knew. Maddox knew we were coming. They were waiting for us.'

'But . . .' Jabba's mouth was stumbling for words, still in shock from the bullets slicing through the air right in front of him.

'Your phone – they're reading it,' Matt stated flatly.

'No way,' Jabba objected. 'I haven't been keeping it on long enough – '

'I'm telling you they're reading it,' Matt shot back angrily.

'There's no way, man.' He held his iPhone up, examining it curiously. 'No way they can lock onto it that fast, and I haven't had it on long enough for them to download any spyware onto it and—'

Matt just snatched it out of his fingers, and was about to flick it out the window when Jabba grabbed it with both hands.

'No,' he yelled, 'don't.'

Matt looked at him angrily.

Jabba wrenched it out of his fingers and took it back. 'My whole fucking life's in there, man. You can't just throw it away like that. Just give me a second.'

He looked around, checked the car's side pockets, the ashtray, then opened the glove box and rifled through it. He found some paperwork in a plastic sleeve – service documents and a receipt – held together by the very thing he was looking for, a paper clip. He plucked it off, straightened it, and stuck one of its ends into the tiny hole on the top face of the phone. The SIM card tray popped out. He pulled the card out of its slot and showed it to Matt.

'No SIM card. No signal. For all intents and purposes, the phone's dead. Okay?'

Matt frowned at him for a moment, then shrugged and nodded. 'Okay.' He felt his pulse ratchet its way back. He'd just killed two men. Which should have felt bad, but –

strangely – didn't. It was, he told himself, a simple matter of kill or be killed. But he knew he'd have to be more careful if he didn't want to fall on the wrong side of that equation the next time it presented itself.

Jabba sat quietly for a moment, just staring ahead, then asked, 'What are we going to do now?'

'What do you think?' Matt grumbled.

Jabba studied him, then nodded stoically. 'Rydell?'

'Rydell,' Matt simply confirmed.

CHAPTER 55

Wadi Natrun, Egypt

'I understand you're looking to get out of there in a hurry,' Darby said in a casual tone.

Gracie stared ahead quizzically. 'I'm sorry?'

Dalton leaned out and mouthed her a question. She gave him an uncertain glance back.

'You need a ride, Miss Logan,' Darby observed somewhat smugly. 'And I'm calling to offer you one.'

Her mind scrambled to make sense of the call. She recognized the name, of course. She couldn't exactly count herself among the pastor's fans. Far from it, truth be told. But that didn't really matter now, nor did it tell her what she needed to know. 'How did . . . ?' she stammered. 'Who gave you this number?'

'Oh, I have a lot of friends, Miss Logan. Well-connected friends. I'm sure you know that. But that's beside the point, which is that you need to get yourself and my most esteemed brother in Christ out of danger. And I can help you do that. Are you interested?'

She tried to park his offer to one side while she dealt with the competing bits of information that were clamoring for attention and tried to figure out where they stood. Finch had called Ogilvy. The news director was supposed to be arranging a plane, but she hadn't heard back. Hell, she hadn't yet had time to tell him about Finch's death. She didn't even know what Ogilvy had told Finch exactly – whether or not he'd be able to get them a plane and, if so, how soon. She didn't even know where they were headed. The embassy in Cairo? The airport? They didn't have a specific destination – not in Egypt, and not beyond either. The overriding concern had been to put as many miles as possible between them and the mobs outside the monastery. The rest hadn't been mapped out. It was all happening too fast, and besides, that was Finch's domain, and he wasn't there to sort it out.

She needed to know more. 'What do you have in mind?'

The reverend breathed a smile down the phone. 'First things first. Father Jerome is with you, right?'

'Of course,' she answered, knowing that was all he was interested in.

'Can you make it out of the monastery safely?'

Gracie decided to play it out on a need-to-know basis. 'Yes,' she answered flatly. 'We have a way out.'

'Okay, good. What I need you to do is get to the airport in Alexandria.'

'Why Alexandria?' Gracie queried.

Dalton gave her another mystified glance. She flicked him a hold-on gesture.

'It's as close to you as Cairo is, but it's quieter,' Darby told her. 'More manageable. I'll have a plane on the ground in under two hours. How soon can you get there?'

Gracie thought about it. Alexandria made sense. Smaller airport, off the beaten path, far fewer commercial flights, far less chance of being spotted. 'Shouldn't take too long,' she replied. 'We can be there before that.'

'Perfect,' Darby shot back. 'I'll give you my number. Call me when you're on your way.'

'Where are you thinking of flying us to?' she asked, feeling a stab of discomfort at the idea of giving up control and putting herself and Father Jerome in the reverend's hands.

'Where else, Miss Logan?' he boomed. 'The one place we know we can keep the good Father safe.' He paused, then proudly announced, 'Home. You're coming home, Miss Logan. To God's own country. And you can take it from me, the people out here are going to be overjoyed to see you.'

CHAPTER 56

Brookline, Massachusetts

Darkness was moving in impatiently, crowding the low winter sun against the horizon as Matt slowed down and pulled over by the side of the road.

The area was heavily wooded, the traffic sparse. Just ahead, two waist-high stone posts marked the entrance to the municipal service center, which nestled between the forest of Dane Park and the thickets of oak trees that shielded the Putterham Meadows Golf Course. From where he was parked, Matt could make out the low, warehouse-like office-and-garage structure of the Brookline Municipal Service Center, set way back from the road, the drive leading up to it lined with parked cars and lingering thin patches of dirty snow. There wasn't much going on in terms of activity, which suited Matt just fine.

They hadn't driven there directly from Hanscom Field. First priority had been dumping the battered, bloodstained Camry. Which wasn't too much of a problem. They'd ducked into a mall, pulled up to a far corner of its parking lot, and exchanged the car for an equally uninspiring, decade-old, dark polo-green Pontiac Bonneville that didn't look like it had that much longer to live anyway.

Matt had wanted to get a few things first – more bullets for the handgun he'd taken off the shooter at the airfield, most importantly. His options were limited. He couldn't exactly walk into a gun store, not in his current wanted and bruised state. Jabba didn't possess an FOID card, so he couldn't buy them for him either. So they'd rushed down to Quincy, where they'd hooked up with a deeply concerned Sanjay, who'd met them away from the 7-Eleven, at his place. He came through for Matt with two boxes of Pow'RBall rounds, some fresh gauze dressing for his wound, and some cash. Matt had wanted to ask him for another handgun, or maybe his rifle – Sanjay kept a loaded Remington 870 Breecher behind his counter that would have been good to have in hand, given what Matt was planning. But he knew he couldn't ask his friend for it, not in these circumstances.

They'd also used Sanjay's computer to look up Rydell's home address – he lived in a big house in Brookline, where his planning applications to add to the existing house had caused a bit of a stink. Matt also got a refresher course in what Rydell actually looked like. Once that was done, Matt and Jabba had driven across to Brookline and scouted the service center and the area around Rydell's house before staking out the house itself.

They didn't have to wait too long.

Rydell's chauffeur-driven Lexus had pulled into the narrow lane that led to his house and to a couple of other mansions shortly after five o'clock. Matt had thought about making his move there and then, but decided against it. The Bonneville wasn't as meek as the Camry, but it was still weak on muscle, and the bodyguard and the heavyweight riding shotgun looked to be slightly too much to take on, given Matt's condition and who he had riding shotgun next to him.

They'd watched the house for a while, making sure Rydell wasn't going anywhere, then Jabba had stepped out of the car to keep an eye on the house while Matt climbed behind the wheel.

'Remember,' Matt told him, 'if this goes wrong, don't go to the cops. Don't trust anyone. Just do what you thought was the right play right at the beginning, remember?'

'You mean, make like D. B. Cooper?'

'Yep.'

Jabba looked at him and shrugged. 'Just make sure it doesn't go wrong then, all right? I'm already missing my stuff as it is.'

Matt smiled. 'I guess I'll see you in a little while.'

He'd then left him there and looped back to the service center, where he was presently parked.

He double-checked the handgun, then tucked it in under his coat. He emptied one of the boxes of rounds into his pocket, checked the road ahead and the mirror, then got out and walked up the drive to the service center.

He'd taken some more painkillers, which had numbed the wound in his side, and found that he was able to walk halfway decently, in a way that didn't scream out 'walking wounded.' He followed the curving drive, past the parked cars, past the entrance to the reception area and offices, and past the building's 'employees only' door. A couple of guys stepped out, their shift finished, heading home. He met their casual gaze with a small bob of acknowledgment, muttered a laconic 'How's it going?', which only elicited a similarly muttered reply, and didn't break step until he reached the garage area out back.

There were several trucks parked in there, side by side, the wide letters on their grilles announcing they were Macks. Matt looked around. A couple of mechanics were working on a truck that was parked thirty or so yards away. One of them glanced over. Matt gave him a relaxed half wave and a nod, as if his being there was the most natural thing in the world, then walked toward the back wall of the garage with as much of a purposeful step as he could muster, so as not to appear out of place in any way. From the corner of his eye, he saw that the mechanic went back to work. Matt checked the back wall. He noticed a white board with some shift lists marked up on it, then spotted the metal, wall-mounted box where the keys were normally kept. It wasn't locked, which wasn't a surprise – garbage trucks usually ranked pretty low on the 'most stolen vehicles' lists, which probably had a lot to do with the fact that they were garbage trucks.

He quickly matched the number on the tag of one of the

keys with the last three digits of the license plate on one of the trucks, and gingerly picked the keys off their hook. He climbed into the big truck's cabin, gave the surroundings another quick once-over, then stroked the engine to life. The big cab rumbled under him. He pressed down on the heavy clutch, selected first using the thin, long gear shifter, and teased the accelerator. The hydraulic brakes hissed loudly and the truck nudged forward. The same mechanic looked over again, an uncertain expression creasing his face. Matt stopped the truck long enough to give him another friendly nod, then thought better of it and leaned out the window.

'You almost done there? Steve said he was having trouble getting this one into third,' he bluffed matter-of-factly, using a name he'd noticed on the shift list.

The guy looked at him a bit perplexed, but before he could say anything, Matt added, 'Clutch might need some work. I'll be back in ten,' and gave him a short wave before pulling away.

He checked in the side mirror as he turned out of the garage. The man looked his way for a second before shrugging and getting back to what he was doing.

A moment later, Matt was turning onto the main road and guiding the lumbering orange behemoth toward the exclusive enclave that surrounded Sargent Pond.

Feeling numb as he sat in the book-lined study of his mansion, Larry Rydell stared into his tumbler of Scotch and fumed in silence.

Those bastards, he seethed, flinching at the thought of any harm coming to his daughter. *If she so much as gets a scratch*, he flared, a surge of blood flooding his temples . . . but it was pointless. He knew he couldn't do anything about it.

He sagged in his chair and glared at his glass. He'd never felt as helpless in his life.

With his fortune and his power, he could and did take on

the most aggressive hedge fund or shareholder revolt without blinking. He'd had heated debates in Senate chambers that didn't ruffle him in the least. He'd reached a point of his life where he felt he was untouchable. But he was powerless to deal with these . . . thugs. That's what they were, pure and simple. Thugs. Out to pervert his vision, to take his idea and twist it around and use it for . . . what, exactly?

It didn't make sense.

Much as he ground and turned over what Drucker had said, it didn't make sense. They were alike – all of them – when it came to what they believed in. They viewed the world the same way. They saw the risks facing the world – and those facing America – in the same light. They shared the same frustrations with some deeply entrenched aspects of the world's, and the country's, mind-set.

And yet they were doing this? They'd created a fake messiah? An envoy from God? One whose presence would reinforce and vindicate the mass delusion most of the world was suffering from?

It doesn't make sense, he thought again. And yet they were doing it.

He'd seen it.

Drucker had confirmed it.

They were actually doing it.

The backstabbing bastards.

His mind latched onto Rebecca's face, on the last time he'd seen her, shortly before her ill-fated trip to Costa Careyes. He'd wanted to join her there for the holidays – they really hadn't spent much time together, ever, not with everything he wanted to achieve in life, and it was something he now deeply regretted. But he hadn't been able to join her. Not with all this going on. Not with the biggest undertaking of his life in full swing. And, bless her, she hadn't voiced her disappointment. She never did. She'd gotten used to having a mythical dad, in the good and bad sense. Which was something he'd fix, he now thought – if he ever got the chance.

He had to find her.

He had to get her out, put her out of their reach, tuck her away somewhere safe. Nothing else mattered. Even saving the planet now paled into insignificance. He had to get her out of their hands. Then – and only then – he had to try and stop this. He had to find a way to kill it off, to shut it down before it got too big.

But how? He didn't have anyone else to call. He didn't exactly have an 'A-Team' tab in his Rolodex. For years, he'd entrusted all his security requirements – personal and professional – to that rattlesnake Maddox. The security guards 'watching over him' right now, at his house. His driver-slash-bodyguard. The vetting of his pilot, of the staff on his yacht. The corporate security at his companies. E-mail, phones. Everything was covered by one firm. Maddox's. On Drucker's recommendation. 'Keep it all under one roof' had been his advice. 'Use someone you can trust. One of us,' he'd said.

Clearly, Maddox was one of 'us.' Rydell himself, he'd now found out, wasn't.

He felt like a fool.

They had him covered.

He'd been played. From the beginning.

He stared angrily at the heavy tumbler, then flung it at the wall, by the huge, stone fireplace. It exploded and rained shards of glass on the carpet. Just then, he heard a rising whine at the edge of his hearing, the sound of a large engine straining. Curious, he edged over to the window and looked out, down the drive that sloped and curved gently to the mansion's entrance gate.

Matt spotted Jabba as he approached the turnoff into Sargent Lane. Jabba gave him the all-clear, a small thumbs-up, before darting back into the trees. Matt nodded, turned into the lane, and floored the gas pedal.

The Mack's muscular, three-hundred-bull-horsepower engine growled as it raced ahead, straining with each additional mile-per-hour of speed that it managed to add. Before long, the mansion's entrance gate appeared up ahead. Matt stayed in gear, red-lining the engine, not wanting to shift into a higher gear. He wasn't exactly flying, but that didn't matter. Speed wasn't what Matt was after here.

It was bulk.

He reached the gate and wrenched the oversized, horizontal steering wheel left with both arms, fighting the lateral pull from the truck's tires. He didn't lift his foot off the pedal. The truck screeched and leaned a few degrees sideways before its fifteen tons of solid steel plowed into the gate and obliterated it into toothpicks.

The truck charged up the driveway, its heavy footprint scattering gravel and leaving twin ruts in its wake. Matt could see the house through a scattering of stately trees, looming at the top of a manicured, landscaped rise. It was a Georgian revival mansion with separate wings jutting out of the main house and a multi-car garage tucked off to one side. It had a circular gravel drive outside the main entrance. There was no sign of the Lexus or the muscle. Yet.

He aimed the truck right at the entrance and kept his foot down. Just as he reached it, one of the heavies – he thought he recognized him as the guy who'd been riding shotgun in Rydell's Lexus – rushed out of the house. His eyes went wide as he spotted the charging garbage truck, and he was already pulling his gun out from an under-shoulder holster

Matt didn't bother going around the drive. He just beelined for the house's entrance. The truck bounced over the central floral bed and slammed into the bodyguard before he had a chance to fire off a single round. The man splattered against the panoramic windshield, staining it with blood before the truck squashed him against the front door as it bulldozed its way into the house.

Brick, timber, and glass exploded inward as the Mack thundered ahead and came to a rest inside the house's cavernous foyer. Matt kept the engine running as he pulled his gun out and climbed from the cabin just as another heavy appeared from a side room, dumbstruck and gun drawn. Matt had the advantage of surprise and blew him away with two rounds to his chest. Matt stepped away from the truck, sizing up what was left of the house's entrance hall, and yelled, 'Rydell.'

Like a killer-bot on a mission, he advanced through the house, using his handgun like a divining rod, looking for his quarry. He checked the main living room, then a media room next to that, and was on his way into what looked like the kitchen area when a large double-door in a hallway to his right opened up and Rydell's head popped out.

The man looked stunned and confused. Matt recognized him immediately. He looked more gaunt than the photos Jabba had shown Matt on his phone's browser, but it was definitely him.

Matt raised his gun, rushed to him, and grabbed him by his shoulder.

'Let's go.'

He manhandled him back toward the truck, jabbing the gun into his back. Rydell's mouth dropped when he saw the truck squatting in the entrance hall, surrounded by debris, a twelve-foot-square gash eaten out of the house's front façade. As Matt nudged Rydell forward, he heard some approaching footsteps, turned, and saw another guard rushing at them. By now, the adrenalin coursing through him was in control, and Matt was riding its autopilot of heightened awareness. He swung the gun away from Rydell, aimed, and squeezed, dropping the man to the floor.

'Is that all you've got, huh?' he barked furiously at Rydell. 'Is that the best you can do?'

Before the shell-shocked Rydell could answer, Matt grabbed him by the neck, pushed him to the back of the truck, and shoved him against it. Matt glared at him and pointed at its rear-loading bay.

'Get in,' he ordered.

Rydell stared at him, terror-stricken. 'In there?'

'Get in,' Matt roared, raising the gun so it hovered a few inches from the bridge of Rydell's nose.

Rydell studied him for a beat, then climbed in. Matt glared at him crouched there, cowering, and hit the compacting switch. The hydraulic paddle churned to life and inched its way down, swinging over Rydell and herding him into the belly of the truck.

Matt hit the switch again to block the paddle in position, sealing the hold, then made his way back through the debris to the truck's cabin and climbed in. Another man appeared, another drone in a dark suit with a big gun aimed at Matt's face. He fired, the bullets punching through the windshield and hammering the back of the cabin behind Matt's head. Matt ducked, crunched the gear lever into reverse and floored the accelerator. The truck extricated itself from the battered house and emerged onto the gravel drive again. The man followed, still shooting, his bullets digging themselves into the truck's thick carcass. He wasn't doing much damage – the way the truck was built, it was like trying to stop a rhino with a blowpipe. Matt swung the orange beast around and slammed it into first. The truck's smokestack let out an angry bellow of black smoke – its engine probably hadn't ever had such a workout – before hurtling down the drive and out onto the narrow lane again.

He was halfway to the main road when the first of the armed response cars appeared, a yellow SUV with a blaring siren and a rack of spinning lights on its roof. The lane wasn't wide enough for both, and its driver knew it. He didn't stand a chance. He swerved just as the big Mack reached him, but there was nowhere for him to go. The truck plowed into the side of the SUV and flicked it out of its way and into the trees like a hockey puck. The second armed response car didn't fare much better. Matt encountered it just before the intersection of the lane with the main road, clipping its back and sending it pirouetting on its smoking tires before coming to a violent stop in a sewer ditch.

He slowed down at the mouth of the lane, picked Jabba up, and motored on, his neurons teeming with life. He had Rydell, which was good, and Matt was still alive, which was even better.

CHAPTER 57

Washington, D.C.

Too bad, Keenan Drucker thought.

He liked Rydell. The man was a great asset, in any circumstance. And none of this would've happened without him. The term *visionary* was bandied about a lot, but in Rydell's case, he truly was such.

Drucker's mind traveled back to how it had all started.

Davos, Switzerland.

The two-hundred-thousand-dollar-a-table black tie dinner. The Aberdeen Angus beef and pink champagne jelly. Yet another gathering of the planet's rich and famous, the powerful elite who aspired to solve the world's big crises. Insecure egotists and well-meaning philanthropists, getting together not just to assuage their guilt by handing over some money to help a thousand or two poorer souls, but hoping to trigger change that could save the lives of millions.

Rydell and Drucker had sat together, late into the night, going over the growing mountain of data on global warming. Fourteen thousand new cars a day hitting the road in China. The booming industries there and in India building new coal-fired electricity plants every week. The developed world embracing cheap, coal-burning energy more than ever. Congress giving the oil and gas companies back home one tax break after another. The energy companies' disinformation campaigns helping people duck the issue and avoid making hard choices. Every new study confirming that if things looked bad, they were actually far worse.

They were both in agreement: The planet was hurtling toward the point of no return. We were living a defining moment, the defining moment for our continued existence on this planet, and we were ignoring it.

The question was, what to do about it.

Throughout, Drucker couldn't escape the feeling that Rydell was testing him, sounding him out. Seeing how far he'd go.

Drucker smiled inwardly as he remembered how Rydell had finally let it out.

Drucker had said, 'All this,' gesturing at the lavish setting around them, 'it's something, but it won't change much. Governments, big business . . . no one wants to upset the apple cart. Voters and share options, they're the only things that matter. Growth. People don't really want change, especially not if it costs something. The price of oil has quadrupled so far this century, and nothing's changed. No one cares. The "don't worry, be happy, it's all a load of crap" message the fuel lobby keeps pumping out – deep down, that's what everyone wants to hear. It's heaven-sent.'

'Maybe heaven should send them a different message,' Rydell had replied, a knowing – and visionary – blaze in his eye.

The rest had followed on from that.

At first, it had seemed Rydell was talking theory. But the theoretical soon became the possible. The possible became the doable. And when that happened, everything changed.

As far as Drucker was concerned, a whole host of possible uses were on the table. What Rydell and his people had come up with could be used as a weapon that could tackle any number of threats in different, and potentially spectacularly effective, ways. Problem was, Rydell wouldn't be open to that. As far as he was concerned, there was only one major threat facing us.

Drucker disagreed.

There were others. Threats that were far more immediate, far more dangerous. Threats that required more immediate attention. For although Drucker was a concerned citizen of the world, he was, more than anything, a patriot.

The Muslim world was growing bolder and wilder. It needed reining in. Drucker didn't think they'd ever be able to convert that part of the world, to pull its people away from their religion. But there were other ways of using Rydell's technology there. One idea he'd toyed with was using it to foment an all-out war between Sunnis and Shias. China was also a growing concern. Not militarily, but economically. Which was even worse. A spiritual message could have shifted things there. And there were other concerns that troubled Drucker even more. Concerns that were closer to home. Concerns about threats that had cost his only son his life. In any case, using the global warming message as the first hook was the way to go. It was nonthreatening. It was a cause that everyone could embrace, one that transcended race and religion. It would help bring people on board from day one. The secondary message – the one that counted – would sneak in through the back door.

The strategy had to be carefully conceived. He had a head start, given the makeup of the country. Seventy percent of Americans believed in angels, in heaven, in life after death – and in miracles. Even better, fully 92 percent of Americans believed in a personal God, someone who took interest in their individual dramas and whom they could ask for help. The foundation was solidly there. Drucker had also drawn from the work of highly respected psychologists and anthropologists who studied the mental architecture of religious belief. What he was planning had to sit within the parameters such research had laid out. For one, the deception had to be minimally counterintuitive. It needed to be strange enough to capture people's attention and root itself firmly in their memory, but not too strange, so they wouldn't dismiss it. Studies had shown that convincing religious agents had to have just the right level of outlandishness. Also, the manifestation needed to have an emotional resonance in order for belief to set in.

Religions used elaborate rituals to stir up people's emotions: soaring, dark cathedrals filled with candlelight, hymns and chants, bowing in unison. In that context, the environmental movement taking on a quasi-religious aspect was the perfect platform. It wasn't just us coming face-to-face with our mortality – it was the entire planet.

The timing was also helpful. The planet was living through scary times on many fronts. The environment. Economic meltdown. Terrorism and rogue nukes. Avian flu. Nanotechnology. Hadron colliders. Everything seemed to be out of control or have the potential to wipe us out. Our very existence seemed threatened on a daily basis. Which could only feed into the prophecies of some kind of savior, a messiah showing up to sort everything out and bring about a millennial kingdom. And it wasn't just a Christian phenomenon. Every major religion had its own version of how a great teacher would appear and rescue the world from catastrophe. For Drucker, however, only one of them mattered.

Ultimately, though, he kept coming back to one main stumbling block: the notion that at some point, something would go wrong. They wouldn't be able to fool all of the people all of the time. Someone would let something slip. The technology would leak out. Something was bound to screw up. Which was why he'd decided to embrace that fallibility and use it as the starting point of his strategy.

It proved to be an inspirational masterstroke.

Everything was in place. He'd recruited the right partners to help him pull it off. He just needed to wait for the right event, something big, something with enough emotional resonance. He knew that, sooner or later, it would come. The planet was roiling, writhing in anger. More and more natural catastrophes were taking place all around the globe. And the one he got came as if gifted by the gods themselves. The best part of it all was the role the media would play.

They'd buy into the deception without hesitation. It was visceral, it was huge, and – in its crucial launch phase, anyway – it was about saving the planet, an issue that was dear to their hearts.

Too bad, Drucker thought again, his hands steepled in front of his pursed lips. He would have preferred for Rydell to be on board. To be part of it all. He'd tried to convince him about the need to introduce a messenger – a prophet – to the mix. They'd talked about it at length. But Rydell wouldn't listen. Drucker didn't like doing what they had to do to Rebecca either. He'd known her for years, he'd watched her grow into an attractive, free-spirited young woman. But it had to be done. Rydell was too passionate. His commitment and his intensity came with an inflexibility that couldn't be overcome. He'd never be able to accept the trade-off. And, besides, he couldn't be fully included anyway. He was part of the end game. The sacrificial pawn that was crucial to its successful closure.

Drucker's phone trilled. He glanced at its screen. The Bullet's name flashed up. The enabler. The man whose foot soldiers were making it all happen. The charred, deformed marine who was Jackson's commanding officer. The man who'd left half his face in the same Iraqi slaughterhouse that had ripped Drucker's son to shreds.

Drucker picked up the phone.

The news wasn't good.

CHAPTER 58

The hydraulic compactor whined as it swiveled upward. Almost instantly, a sour stench wafted out of the truck's belly, even though the truck wasn't actually carrying any garbage. Matt let the compactor rise two thirds of the way up, then killed its motor. The heavy lid just held there, cantilevered over the yawning, stinking cavity of the truck's hold.

Matt leaned in. 'Get out here,' he ordered.

A short moment later, Rydell stumbled out, shielding his eyes from the day's glare.

The truck was parked in a deserted, narrow alley that ran parallel to and behind a busier, low-rise commercial street, at the back of a closed-down Blockbuster video store. It was six blocks from the municipal service center where Matt had stolen the truck. The green Bonneville was parked nearby. They stood by the mouth of a narrow passageway, out of view, shielded from any potential passing cars by the bulk of the truck.

Rydell stank. His clothes had rips in them, and he was battered and bruised from bouncing around the empty metal box. He was wheezing, his breath coming in brief, ragged bursts. A nasty, bleeding gash had been cut into his left cheek. He was wobbly, totally unbalanced, and had to lean against the truck, breathing in heavily, shutting his eyes, gathering his senses, and probably doing his best not to throw up.

Matt allowed him a few seconds to recover, than raised the big silver handgun the shooter at the airport had lost and held it inches from Rydell's face.

'What did you do to my brother?'

Rydell raised his eyes at him. They were still half-dead, drowning in a morass of pain and confusion. He glanced at Matt, then across to Jabba, who was hovering nervously a few steps back, but Rydell's head was still spinning and he still wasn't totally there. His eyelids slid shut and his head lolled forward again as his hands came up to rub his temples.

'What did you do to my brother?' Matt growled.

Rydell raised a hand in a stiff back-off-and-give-me-a-second gesture. After a moment, he looked up again. This time, his expression was alive enough to telegraph his not having a clue about who Matt and Jabba were or what Matt was asking him.

'Your brother . . . ?' he muttered.

'Danny Sherwood. What happened to him?'

The name resuscitated Rydell. His eyes flickered back to life, like a succession of floodlights getting switched on in a stadium. He winced, visibly struggling with how to answer.

'As far as I know, he's okay,' Rydell said with a hollow voice. 'But it's been a few weeks since I saw him.'

Matt flinched at his words. 'You're saying he's alive?'

Rydell looked up at him and nodded. 'Yes.'

Matt glanced over at Jabba. Jabba put his almost-debilitating unease on hold and gave him a supportive, relieved nod.

'I'm sorry,' Rydell continued. 'We didn't have a choice.'

'Of course you did,' Matt shot back. 'It's called free will.' He was still processing the news. 'So this sign . . . this whole thing. You're doing it?'

Rydell nodded. 'I was.'

'You "were"?'

'The others . . . my partners . . . they're doing it their way now.' Rydell sighed, clearly weighing his words. 'I've been . . . sidelined.'

'What really happened? In Namibia? Was Danny ever really there?'

Rydell nodded again, slowly. 'Yes. That's where we did the final test. But there was no helicopter crash. It was all staged.'

'So Reece, the others . . . they're also still alive?'

'No.' Rydell hesitated. 'Look, I didn't want any of that. It's not how I do things. But there were others there . . . they overreacted.'

'Who?' Matt asked.

'The security guys.'

'Maddox?' Matt half-guessed.

Rydell looked at him quizzically, clearly surprised by Matt's familiarity with the name.

'He got rid of them,' Matt speculated. 'When you didn't need them anymore.'

'It wasn't like that,' Rydell objected. 'None of them knew what we were really planning. Not Reece, not your brother. And then when I finally told Reece, he didn't want to hear of it. I thought I could have convinced him. I just needed a bit of time . . . He would've come on board. And the others would have joined in too. But I never got the chance. Maddox just snapped and . . . it was insane. He just started firing. I couldn't stop him.'

'And Danny?'

'He ran,' Rydell said.

'But he didn't get away.'

Rydell shook his head witheringly.

'And you kept him locked up, all this time.'

Rydell nodded. 'He designed the processing interface. It works perfectly, but it's very sensitive to the smallest variations in air density or temperature or . . .' He caught himself, as if he realized he was rambling on unnecessarily. 'It was safer having him around.'

'So all this time . . . you kept him alive, to use him now.'

Rydell nodded again.

'Why would he keep doing what you asked? He had to know you'd kill him once it was all over.' He studied Rydell, inwardly hoping he wouldn't hear the answer he was dreading. 'He's not doing this of his own free will, is he?'

'No,' Rydell replied. 'We – they – threatened him.'

'With what?'

'Your parents,' Rydell said, then added, 'and you.' He held Matt's gaze, then dropped his eyes to the ground. 'They told him they'd hurt you. Badly. Then they'd get you thrown back into prison, where they'd make sure your life was a living hell.' He went silent for a beat, then added, 'Danny didn't want that.'

Matt felt an upwelling of anger erupt inside him. 'My parents are dead.'

Rydell nodded with remorse. 'Danny doesn't know that.'

Matt turned and stepped away, his face clouding over. He looked away into the distance, hobbled by Rydell's words. His kid brother. Going through hell for two years, living in a cell, cut off from the world, made to wield the fruit of his brilliance for something he didn't believe in . . . going through it all to protect him. To keep Matt safe.

After everything Danny had already done for him.

Matt thought of his parents, how they'd been devastated by the news of Danny's helicopter crash, and a crushing sense of grief overcame him. He glared back at Rydell and felt like ramming his fist down his throat and ripping his heart out.

Jabba watched Matt struggle with the revelation with a pained heart, but didn't interfere. Instead, he took a hesitant step closer to Rydell.

He couldn't help himself. 'How are you doing it?' he asked him, his tone reverent, as if he still couldn't believe he was here, face-to-face with one of his gods, albeit a fallen, battered, and bloodied one.

Rydell tilted his head up to take stock of him, then just shook his head and turned away.

'Answer him,' Matt barked.

Rydell looked at Matt, then back at Jabba. After a brief moment, he just said, 'Smart dust.'

'Smart dust? But that's not ... I mean, I thought ...' Jabba stammered, shaking his head with disbelief, a deluge of questions battering his mind as it stumbled over Rydell's answer. 'How small?'

Rydell paused, reluctant to engage Jabba, then shrugged. 'A third of a cubic millimeter.'

Jabba's mouth dropped an inch. According to everything he'd read or heard about, that just wasn't possible. Not even close. And yet Rydell was telling him it was.

'Smart dust' – minuscule electronic devices designed to record and transmit information about their surroundings while literally floating on air – was still a scientific dream. The concept was first imagined, and the term coined, by electrical engineers and computer scientists working at the University of California's Berkeley campus in the late nineties. The idea was simple: Tiny motes of silicon, packed with sophisticated onboard sensors, computer processors, and wireless communicators, small enough to be virtually invisible and light enough to remain suspended in midair for hours at a time, gathering and transmitting data back in real time – and undetected. The military was immediately interested. The idea of scattering speck-sized sensors over a battlefield to detect and monitor troop movements was hugely appealing. So was sprinkling them in subways to detect chemical or biological threats, or on a crowd of protestors to be able to track their movements remotely. DARPA had kicked in the initial funding, as, although the concept also had a host of potential civilian and medical uses, the more nefarious surveillance possibilities were even more alluring. But funding doesn't always lead to success.

The concept was sound. Breakthroughs in nanotechnology were inching the dream closer to reality. Theoretically, manufacturing the motes was possible. In practice, we weren't there yet. Not overtly, anyway. Making the sensors small enough wasn't the problem. The processors that analyzed the data, the transmitters that communicated it back to base, and the power supply that ran the whole minuscule thing – typically, some kind of minute lithium battery – were. By the time they were added on, they turned the dust-sized particles into hardly stealthy clusters the size of a golf ball.

Clearly, Rydell's team had managed to overcome those hurdles and achieve new levels of miniaturization and power management.

In secret.

Jabba was struggling to order the questions that were coming at him from all corners. 'You were working on it for DARPA, weren't you?'

'Reece was. The applications were endless, but no one could figure out how to actually manufacture them. Until he did. He told me about it before letting them know he could do it. We stayed up late one night, imagining all kinds of things we could use it for.' He paused, reliving that night. 'One of them stood out.'

'So that whole biosensor story?' Jabba asked.

Rydell shook his head. 'Just a smoke screen.'

'But . . . how? Where are they coming from? You dropping them from drones or . . . ?' His voice trailed off, his mind still tripping over the very notion.

'Canisters,' Rydell told him. 'We shoot them up, like fireworks.'

'But there's no noise, no explosion,' Jabba remarked. 'Is there?'

'We're using compressed air launchers. Like they're now using at Disneyland. No noise. No explosion.'

The questions were coming to Jabba fast and furious. 'And the motes . . . How are they lighting up? And how'd you get the power source down to a manageable size? What are you using, solar cells? Or did you go nuclear?' Sensing, sorting, and transmitting data used up a lot of juice. One option scientists were exploring was to sprinkle the motes with a radioactive isotope to give each mote its own long-term energy supply.

Rydell shook his head. 'No. They don't actually need an onboard power source.'

'So what are they running on?'

'That was Reece's brilliant brainchild. They feed off each other. We light them up with an electromagnetic signal from the ground. They convert the transmission into power and spread it across the cloud where it's needed.'

The answer triggered a new barrage of questions in Jabba's mind. 'But how do you get them to light up?'

Rydell shrugged. 'It's a chemical reaction. They're Janus particles. Hybrids. They light up and switch off as needed to take on the shape we want, like skydivers in an aerial display. They burn up after about fifteen minutes, but it's long enough.'

Jabba was visibly struggling to absorb the information and complete the puzzle. His voice rose with incredulity. 'But they're constantly moving around. They've got to be. I mean, even the slightest breeze pushes them around, right? And yet the sign wasn't moving.' He extrapolated his own answer, then his eyes widened. 'They're self-propelled?' He didn't seem to believe his own words.

'No.' Rydell shook his head, then glanced over at Matt, his expression darkening with remorse, his shoulders sagging, before looking away again. 'That's where Danny came in. His distributed processing program . . . more like massively distributed intelligence. He designed it. He came up with this brilliant optical system based on corner-cube reflectors. It lets them communicate with each other very elaborately while using up virtually no energy. It literally brought the motes to life.' He exhaled uncomfortably, then continued,

'We needed the shape – the sign – to stay in one place. But you're right, the motes, they're so small, so light, they're floating around, moving in the air like dandelion seeds. So we needed them to be able to talk to each other. Several hundred times a second. When one mote that's lit up moves away, it turns itself off and the one that drifts closest to where it was lights up instead and takes its place and assumes its position in the display. So the sign appears stationary even though the dust particles are always changing position. Factor in that we wanted the sign to constantly morph in shape to appear like it's alive, and . . . it's a hell of a lot of processing power in a machine the size of a speck of dust.' He lifted his gaze back at Matt, guiltily. 'We couldn't have done it without Danny.'

'Oh, well in that case, I guess you did the right thing by locking him up all this time,' Matt retorted.

'You think this has been easy?' Rydell shot back. 'You think this is something I just got into on a whim? I've put everything on the line for this. And the way things are going, I'll probably end up dead because of it.'

'It's a distinct possibility,' Matt confirmed dryly.

'I had no choice. Something had to be done. This thing's getting out of hand, and no one's paying attention.'

'Global warming?' Jabba asked. 'That's what this is all about, right?'

'What else?' Rydell flared up, pushing himself to his feet. 'You don't get it, do you? People out there – they've got no idea. They don't realize that every time they get into their cars, they're slowly killing the planet. Killing their own grandchildren.' He was gesticulating wildly, all fired up. 'Make no mistake, we're getting close to the point of no return. And when that happens, it'll be too late to do anything about it. The weather will just shift dramatically and that'll be the end of us. And it's happening faster than you think. We owe it to our kids and to their kids to do something about it. Sometime in the next hundred years, people will be living on what will undoubtedly be a very unpleasant planet to live on, and they'll look back and wonder how the hell no one ever did anything about it. Despite all the warnings we had. Well, I'm doing something about it. Anyone who's in a position to do something about it has to. It would be criminal not to.'

'So you decided to go out and kill off a bunch of decent guys to get everyone's attention,' Matt said.

'I told you, that wasn't part of the plan,' Rydell snapped.

'Still, you're going along with it.'

Matt's point must have hit home, as Rydell didn't have a quick answer for him. 'What did you want me to do? Give up on the whole thing and turn Maddox and his people in? Waste everything we worked on for all those years, throw away a plan that could change everything?'

Matt didn't waver. 'But did you ever even consider it?'

Rydell thought about it, and shook his head.

Matt gave him a small, pointed nod with his head. Rydell's face sank and he looked at Matt blankly before turning away.

'What about Father Jerome?' Jabba asked. 'He's not part of this too, is he?'

'I don't know. He wasn't part of the original plan,' Rydell said. 'They came up with that one all on their own. You'll have to ask them about it.'

'He can't be in on it,' Jabba protested. 'Not him.'

'It doesn't matter,' Matt interjected firmly. 'I just want to get Danny back.' He turned to Rydell. 'Where is he?'

'I don't know,' Rydell said. 'I told you, I'm out of the loop.'

Matt raised the big handgun and held it aimed squarely at Rydell's forehead. 'Try again.'

'I'm telling you I don't know, not anymore,' Rydell exclaimed. 'But the next time the sign shows up, you'll probably find him there.'

'What?' Matt rasped, thrown by Rydell's answer.

'That's why we needed him alive,' Rydell pointed out. 'To make the micro-adjustments in real time. On-site.'

'"On-site"?' Jabba asked. 'He has to be there? He can't do it remotely?'

'He could, but data transmission isn't foolproof over such long distances, and even the smallest time lag could mess things up. It's safer having him on location, especially if the sign's gonna do more than just pop up for a few seconds.'

'So he was out there?' Matt asked. 'In Antarctica? And in Egypt?'

'He was in Antarctica,' Rydell confirmed. 'Egypt I don't know about. Again, it wasn't part of the plan. But from what I saw on TV, I'd guess he was there. He has to be within half a mile or so of the sign. That's the transmitter's range.'

An approaching siren wailed nearby. Matt tensed. Through a narrow passage that led to the main drag on the other side of the low, commercial buildings that backed up to the alley, he spotted the flash of a police car blowing past.

It was time to vamoose.

He turned to Jabba. 'We need to move.' He flicked the gun at Rydell, herding him on. 'Let's go.'

'Where?' Rydell asked.

'I don't know yet, but you're coming with us.'

'I can't,' Rydell protested. 'They—'

'You're coming with us.' Matt cut him off. 'They've got Danny. I have you. Sounds like a good trade.'

'They won't trade him for me. They need him. Much more than they need me. If anything, they'd probably be happy to see me dead.'

'Maybe, but if they haven't killed you yet, it means they also need you for something,' Matt observed.

Which, judging by Rydell's expression, struck a nerve. But he seemed to quickly shelve it as he told Matt, 'I can't go with you. They have my daughter.'

Matt scoffed. 'Sure.' Rydell was, clearly, a cunning liar. Which suddenly put everything else he'd told Matt in question.

'I'm telling you they've got my daughter—'

'Bullshit. Let's go,' Matt prodded him, though something about the intensity in his voice, in his eyes – was Matt missing something? His fury at Rydell didn't let it in and plowed ahead. 'Move.'

'Listen to me. They grabbed her. In Mexico. They're hanging onto her as security. To make sure I don't rock the boat. They can't even know I talked to you. They'll kill her.'

Matt wavered, suddenly unsure – and Jabba stepped closer. 'Maybe it's true, dude.' He turned to Rydell. 'She's here.'

Rydell's head jerked forward with attention. 'Here?'

'We saw her,' Jabba informed him. 'A couple of hours ago. Maddox and his goon squad flew her into a small airport near Bedford. We thought they were her bodyguards.'

Rydell's expression clouded.

'They have your daughter, and you only think you've been "sidelined"?' Matt's expression was heavy with contempt. 'I don't know, man. Me, I'd take it as a definite sign that you guys are now enemies.'

Rydell looked at him blankly, Matt's words clearly weighing him down.

Matt shook his head indignantly and just said, 'Let's go.' He motioned to Rydell with his gun.

Rydell's features fogged up as he desperately searched for a glimmer of clarity. He then shook his head and raised his hands in surrender, palms out, and took a step backward. 'I can't.' He took another step back, then another. 'They'll kill her.'

Matt's anger flared. 'You should have thought of that before you started looking the other way while your people got bumped off.'

'How many times do I have to say it?' Rydell blurted. 'I didn't want any of that.' He shook his head stoically. 'Even if

I wanted to help you, I can't. Not as long as they have her. So do what you want, but I'm not going anywhere with you.'

Matt raised his gun at him, but Rydell didn't stop. He kept inching backward, his palms spread, his eyes darting around, taking stock of his surroundings.

'Stop. I mean it,' Matt ordered.

Rydell just shook his head and kept backing up. He was now at the mouth of the small passageway that led to the main drag.

Matt hesitated. Rydell saw it. He gave him a small, knowing, almost apologetic tilt of the head before bolting into the passageway.

'Shit,' Matt muttered as he took off after him. 'Rydell,' he yelled, his voice echoing through the narrow brick canyon as he charged down the grubby passage, Jabba in tow. Within seconds, they burst onto the main road. Matt stumbled to a halt. A few pedestrians stood there, on the wide sidewalk, motionless, eyes locked on Matt, taken aback by his sudden appearance and his gun. Behind them, Rydell was backing away, arms spread out in a calming gesture.

Matt felt too many eyes on him. Rydell was slipping away, and he couldn't do anything about it.

'Let's get the hell out of here,' he told Jabba, before turning and rushing back down the passage toward the Bonneville. He'd lost Rydell, but Danny was alive, and right now, that was all that mattered.

CHAPTER 59

Alexandria, Egypt

The decision to avoid Cairo Airport proved to be an inspired one, although it hadn't started off that way. Gracie had gotten herself into a knot by picturing herself doing what Finch normally took care of – in this case, trying to sneak Father Jerome past an Egyptian passport clerk who would be either maniacally fastidious, sexist, anti-American, or any combination thereof.

The plane was waiting for them when they got there. Darby had come through, as promised. They made their way to the civil aviation office in order to access the tarmac without going through the main terminal, and kept Father Jerome well out of view. They were well aware that the merest glimpse of him could trigger a stampede. He was too recognizable – perhaps the most recognizable face on the planet right now. The clerk manning the small office turned out to be a Copt – a one-in-ten chance in Egypt – and a devout one at that. One look at Brother Ameen's cassock did the trick. Within minutes, their passports had been stamped, the gates had been opened, and they were climbing up the stairs of the hastily chartered jet. The plan was for the driver to wait and make sure the plane took off unhindered before letting the abbot know it was safe to announce that the priest was no longer at the monastery, in the hope of defusing the tense crowd besieging its walls

Gracie started to relax as the Gulfstream 450's wheels lifted off the runway and the sleek fourteen-seater aircraft streaked upward to its cruising altitude, but her relief was short-lived. It only allowed darker thoughts to resurface. Thoughts about Finch. Visions of him, lying there in the sand. Dead.

A veil of grief descended over her. 'I wish we hadn't left him there,' she told Dalton. He was in the seat opposite her, facing back. 'It feels awful. Us being here, while he's . . .' She let the words fade.

'We didn't have a choice,' Dalton comforted her. 'Besides, it's what he would have wanted us to do.'

'And to think, just when he was covering the story of a lifetime.' She shrugged, thinking back. 'After everything he's been through, all the wars and the disasters . . . to die like that.'

Dalton nodded, and they just sat there quietly, crippled by the loss. After a moment, Dalton said, 'We've got to tell the folks back home about Finch.'

Gracie nodded quietly.

'We need to give Ogilvy an update on our ETA,' he added. 'I'll go talk to the pilot. See if he can patch us in to the desk.'

He pushed himself to his feet, but Gracie's hand reached out and arrested his move. 'Not just yet, okay? Let's . . . let's just take a few minutes for ourselves, all right?'

'Sure.' He glanced back at the galley and said, 'I'll see if they have some fresh coffee. You want one?'

'Thanks.' She nodded, then added, 'If they're out, a couple of fingers of Scotch will do just as nicely.'

The false priest who had chosen to be called Brother Ameen watched Dalton rise from his seat opposite Gracie and head his way. He acknowledged the cameraman with a friendly nod as he walked past him to the back of the plane, then turned away and stared out the window.

It was his first kill on this mission, though he'd killed many times before. The war in his homeland had been brutal. It had turned a lot of young Serbian men like him into heartless killers. Once the war was over, some had been able to smother that aspect of their past and morph back into average, amiable folk. Others liked what they'd discovered in themselves. And some of those, like Dario Arapovic, also discovered that the talents that they'd forged in places like Vukovar and during operations like the Otkos 10 offensive were in strong demand. That region of the world was still unstable. It was an ongoing struggle, and any lull was but a temporary pause in the Great Game. A game that people like Maddox were actively participating in, a game where talents like Dario's were coveted – and richly rewarded. And his decision had paid off handsomely, for although Dario had taken great pride in playing a covert role in helping shape his homeland's future, his being picked by Maddox to play this key position in a far more important match was a source of even greater satisfaction.

He would have much preferred not to kill the producer. The risk of detection was high. Equally dangerous was the risk of disrupting a plan that had been working smoothly up until then. The news team had done everything that had been expected of them. They couldn't have done a better job had they been a covert unit themselves. Finch's death had disrupted that. They worked well as a team. They saw things and reacted the way they had been expected to. They were professionals, and professionals who knew what they were doing could be counted on to follow a well-thought-out methodology – and to listen to reason and act accordingly. Finch had been an integral part of that. With him gone, a new door had been opened. One that led down an untried path. Someone else would have to replace him. A new producer. A hardhead who might not be as easy to steer as Finch had been.

Still, he'd had no choice. There was no way out of it. He knew Finch wouldn't have bought into anything he could have come up with to explain his having a satphone, much less one that was encryption-module equipped.

He turned and glanced at Gracie. She was now sitting

alone, her shoulders slightly hunched, looking out her window. He knew she wouldn't bow out because of Finch's death. She was a pro too. And like all pros, she had drive. Ambition. And the cold, rational ability to compartmentalize tragedies like her producer's death and carry on.

Which was good.

She still had a role to play. An important one.

Half an hour after the Gulfstream had taken off from the airport at Alexandria, another aircraft had followed it into the sky and was now shadowing it, a couple of hundred miles back, headed in the same general westerly direction.

The plane, a chartered Boeing 737, was a much larger, and older, aircraft. It had enjoyed stints with various airlines over its twenty-six years of service, though none were as unusual as the one it was undertaking today.

The jet's hold carried a highly covetable selection of state-of-the-art technology. It included a long range acoustic device, canisters of nano-engineered smart dust, and ultra-silent compressed air launchers. Also stowed there was some decidedly less sophisticated, but equally effective, gear: sniper rifles, silencer-equipped handguns, tactical knives, camouflage gear. The jet's cabin held a load that was no less exceptional: seven men whose actions had entranced the world. Six of them were highly trained professionals: a three-man team that had spent over a year in the desert, another that had endured extreme weather all over the globe. The seventh was an outlier. He wasn't highly trained, nor did he share their sense of purpose.

Danny Sherwood was only there out of fear.

He'd been their prisoner for close to two years. Two years of tinkering, of testing and double-testing, of waiting. Two years of worrying, of coming up with devious, complicated plans of escape, of fantasizing about them, of ditching them. And then, finally, it had begun. It was why they'd kept him alive. It was why they needed him. And now it was in play.

He didn't know what their plans were or how it would all end. He'd heard snippets of talk. He thought he knew what they were up to, but he wasn't sure. He'd thought of sabotaging it, of screwing up their plans, of re-jigging the software so that a giant Coca-Cola or Red Sox sign appeared instead of the mystical sign they had designed. But he knew they were keeping a close eye on his work, knew they'd probably figure out what he was up to before he got a chance to use it. He also knew that if he tried it, it would mean a death sentence for him, and, probably, for Matt and for their parents. And so he thought about it, he mulled it over and dreamed of it and enjoyed the brief satisfaction it gave him to imagine it, but he knew he'd never go through with it. He wasn't a fighter. He wasn't a tough guy.

If they'd taken Matt, he knew things would have been different. But Matt wasn't there. He was.

He sometimes wished his survival instincts hadn't kicked in just as the Jeep was launching itself off the canyon's edge. Wished his hand hadn't lunged out and pushed that door open. Wished he hadn't leapt out of the Jeep just as its front wheels ran out of ground. Wished he hadn't ended up clinging to life at the very edge of the abyss, staring up at the circling bird of prey that was about to land and take him away.

But he had. And he was here, now, shackled to his seat, headed for another corner of the planet, wondering when his nightmare would ever end.

CHAPTER 60

Framingham, Massachusetts

The hamburgers were big and juicy and grilled just right, the buns soft but not crumbly, the coleslaw freshly cut and crunchy, the fries thick, crisp on the outside and the right side of mushy on the inside, the Cokes – in glass bottles, not cans – nicely chilled and served in tall, curvy glasses filled with ice cubes that weren't in a rush to melt. It was the perfect meal for Matt and Jabba, given their day – a solid, comfortable meal, a reassuring meal, the kind of meal that dragged one's mind away from troubled times and pulled it back to better days, a meal that drew one into its own comfy world with its hearty offerings and put all thoughts of heavy conversation on indefinite hold.

They sat facing each other in a booth in a small diner in Framingham, about fifteen miles west of Brookline. It was far enough, and busy enough, for them to feel relatively safe. They'd polished off a burger each and hadn't spoken more than ten words throughout. A lot had happened. It had been a charged day, a bad day right on the heels of another bad day. They'd seen a guy get crushed in half, another get his legs mangled up by a Japanese import. Bullets had whizzed by inches from their faces. Matt had shot several guys, possibly – probably – killing one or more of them, which was not something he'd done before. Not even close.

Thinking about it, revisiting those images in his mind's eye, he found it hard to accept it had all really happened. That he'd done all that. He didn't recognize himself. It all felt surreal, like he'd been on the outside, watching it. But it all became real again once he focused on the overwhelmingly good thing that had trumped everything else that had happened: the discovery that his kid brother was still very much alive.

They sat in silence. A small, wall-mounted TV over the cash register was set low. It was on a local channel and had been screening a rerun of an old *Simpsons* episode, one Jabba knew by heart and one Matt couldn't have been less interested in. The end credits eventually gave way to some staggeringly unimaginative ads before segueing into the evening news, starting with the latest update from Egypt. It brought reality roaring back into Matt's face in a flash.

The volume was too low for him to hear what was being said, but even before the waitress turned it up, the visuals themselves were deafening enough. A loud banner on the bottom of the screen informed them that Father Jerome hadn't been seen since the sign had appeared over him earlier that day. Another added that unconfirmed reports had said that he had actually left the monastery for destinations unknown. Reporters and pundits around the world were scrambling to figure out where he was and where he could have gone to. They wondered about whether he might be headed to Jerusalem, or the Vatican, or back home to Spain.

Elsewhere, gargantuan crowds were still massed in St. Peter's Square, in São Paulo, and in many more cities now, holding vigils and praying. The world was holding its breath, waiting for Father Jerome's next appearance. Pockets of violence had cropped up in Pakistan, in Israel, and in Egypt, where men and women of all religions who had taken to the streets to proclaim their faith in Father Jerome had clashed with mobs of unswayed and unwavering believers who were sticking to the rigid tenets of their holy books. Riot police had been deployed, cars and shops had been set alight, and in each case, there had been deaths.

Matt stared at the screen for a moment, then finally said, 'Wherever that priest's going, that's where we'll find Danny.'

'You want to go to Egypt?'

Matt shrugged. 'If he's still there, hell yeah.'

Jabba's shoulders sagged. He took one last bite and pushed his plate off to the side of the table. Wiped his mouth and cast a glance across the diner, then turned his attention back to Matt. Their fates were now intertwined, there was no escaping that. And though he hardly knew the man, he'd seen enough of him to recognize that look – a distant, frowning look that indicated something was bothering him, some kind of itch he needed to scratch. Jabba studied him for a beat, then prompted him by asking, 'What is it, dude?'

Matt nodded his head a fraction, to himself, wheels visibly spinning in his mind. After a moment, he said, 'We need Rydell. They screwed him over. They've got his daughter. Right now, he's real angry. Which makes me think he could help us get Danny back.'

'Not as long as they've got his daughter,' Jabba reminded him.

'Maybe we can change that.'

'Dude, come on,' Jabba protested.

'She's got herself caught up in this thing just like we have,' Matt argued. 'Through no fault of her own. You think this is going to end well for her? You think her dad's gonna kiss and make up with these guys? They're hanging onto her to get him to play nice. Once they're done, they're not going to let them live.'

Jabba gave him a look.

Matt just batted it back. 'You like the idea of Maddox and his storm-troopers keeping her locked up somewhere?'

Jabba smiled despite himself and said, 'Look, just because you throw in a *Star Wars* reference doesn't mean—'

'Seriously,' Matt interrupted. 'We need to do this. Besides, maybe that's where they've been keeping Danny too.'

Jabba tilted his head at him, dubiously. 'You don't really believe that, do you?'

'Not really,' Matt conceded. Then he gave Jabba a slight grin. 'What, you got something better to do?'

343

Jabba shook his head in defeat. 'Even if I did, this is bound to be *so* much more fun.'

Just over three hours later, Maddox took the second call that night from his contact at the NSA.

'I just got another hit,' the man from Fort Meade told the Bullet. 'Very brief. Under twenty seconds.'

'They know we're trying to track them.'

'For sure. They're being very careful. But not careful enough.'

'Location?'

'Same place,' the caller told him. The GPS lock had placed Jabba's iPhone on a busy little commercial strip leading out of Framingham.

'Okay. Keep me posted. In real time. We're in progress.'

Maddox hung up and hit a speed-dial key. The man on the other end picked up the line before it had completed its first ring.

'How far are you?' he asked.

'Should be there in less than ten,' the operative replied.

'Okay,' Maddox said. 'We just got another lock. Same location. They're probably in a hotel or a motel on that block. Let me know what you find.'

CHAPTER 61

Boston, Massachusetts

The presidential suite on the sixth floor of the Four Seasons was as comfortable as it got in the city, or pretty much anywhere else in the world, but as far as Rydell was concerned, he could just as easily have been sitting in a cramped motel room with a coin-operated vibrating bed that didn't work. His mind wasn't registering his surroundings right now. It was elsewhere, stranded on a totally different plane. Grappling with a new reality.

He'd returned to his house after getting away from Matt. It had been swarming with cops and armed response guys – and Maddox. He'd managed Rydell into giving the cops a bullshit story about an attempted kidnapping. Rydell had told them he didn't know who was behind it, saying the men had worn balaclavas. He told them he'd managed to escape from his captors when they'd tried to transfer him from the garbage truck to another car and hadn't operated the compactor properly. He'd left it at that and, wanting to avoid the inevitable paparazzi onslaught, had checked into the Four Seasons. His lawyers could deal with the rest.

Maddox had arranged to have two of his men stationed outside the suite. That angered Rydell, but there was nothing he could do about it. Not as long as they had his daughter. And ever since, he'd been busy reliving his meeting with Drucker, Matt's intrusion, and grinding over what the two men had said.

If they haven't killed you yet, it means they also need you for something, Matt had told him. Which rang true. Worryingly true. But what did they need him for? When Rydell had threatened Drucker and told him they couldn't do it without him, Drucker had agreed. But that wasn't true. Not really.

Rydell had left there believing his own bluff. With a rising dread, he now realized that actually, they could. And were. They had the technology. They knew where the smart dust was being manufactured and stockpiled. They could easily secure the facility. They had Danny.

They didn't need him to make it happen. Not anymore.

And yet they hadn't gotten Maddox to pump a couple of bullets into him.

The realization pulled his doubts regarding what Drucker had in mind back into focus. They'd gone into this together, brothers-in-arms, united for a worthy cause. Was that still the case? It suddenly dawned on him that maybe they weren't after the same thing anymore. Maybe the others were after something else. And in the process, they'd created a messenger that transcended the message. That dwarfed it and buried it in its shadow. The media's shifting focus confirmed his fears.

The story wasn't about God's warning anymore. It was about His messenger.

Drucker wouldn't make such a mistake. Unless he had a different message in mind.

Think of what we can make people do, Drucker had said. The phrase reverberated inside Rydell's head again.

A final thought confirmed his worst fears. Again, it was born out of something Matt had said.

Me, I'd take it as a definite sign that you guys are now enemies. That's what he'd said. And it suddenly dawned on Rydell that Matt was right. There was no way this was ending well. Not for him. Nor for his ill-fated alliance with those bastards. They had Rebecca. There was no point in glossing over it. In pretending that it was a temporary difference of opinion. There was no going back from that. No way to salvage it. It was over.

They were the enemy.

His cell phone rang. It was Drucker. It didn't take long for him to voice the main question.

346

'What did you tell him?'

'All he wanted to know was what happened to his brother,' Rydell said vaguely.

'And?'

'I told him I thought he was still alive. I told him I didn't know where he is. Then I ran.'

Drucker went silent. After a moment, he said, 'Nothing else?'

'Don't worry, he doesn't care what you're up to,' he lied. 'He doesn't know about you, for that matter, although maybe I should have mentioned it.'

'Wouldn't have been ideal for Rebecca,' Drucker reminded him coldly. He paused, clearly putting the news through its paces, then said, 'All right. Stay at the hotel and avoid the press as much as you can. We might have to find you somewhere more discreet to stay until you can move back into the house.'

Rydell hung up and thought about Rebecca again. Matt's words rang through his mind.

He was right. They were enemies now.

And maybe Matt was the only one he could turn to in order to do something about it.

CHAPTER 62

Skies over the eastern Mediterranean

The sea stretched out as far as Gracie could see, a cobalt-blue quilt snugly tucked in around the very edge of the planet. Up ahead and to the left, the sun was teasing the horizon. She leaned forward, right against the glass, and drank in the tranquil view. Although she hopped on planes as often as people took the subway, looking out from an aircraft at high altitude never failed to instill a sense of wonder in her. It was an almost mystical experience – looking out at the planet, the clouds, the sun, the infinite expanse of space beyond what she could see. She never tired of it. She'd normally just sit there and stare out and let her mind wander in all kinds of directions, enjoying that fleeting moment of blissful isolation before getting pulled back into the land of the living by some intrusion.

This time, the intruder was a question, voiced in the dulcet tone of Father Jerome. 'How are you feeling?'

She looked up at him. It felt surreal. To be there, talking to him. After what she'd witnessed. When she wasn't sure what he really was.

She managed a partial smile and a soft shrug. 'Frankly . . . a bit lost. Which is not a feeling I'm used to.'

'You've been lucky,' he commented. He looked uncomfortable, slightly stooped in the cabin despite the fact that its ceiling was an inch or two over six feet high and he wasn't a tall man.

Gracie noticed. She gestured at Dalton's empty seat. 'Please. Won't you join me?'

He nodded, and as he sat down, Dalton came back from the galley.

'I'm sorry, I'm in your seat,' the priest apologized.

'No, that's fine,' Dalton replied breezily as he handed Gracie another coffee. 'I need to talk to the pilot anyway. Find out what the plan is.' He glanced back at Gracie to make sure she was okay with that, then moved forward toward the cockpit.

Gracie watched him go, then turned her attention back to the priest, recovering her train of thought. 'You were saying I'm lucky?'

'I know what it feels like. To feel lost. Ever since I left the Sudan, I've often felt adrift myself. Unsure of where I was, what I was doing. It's been . . . hard,' he said vaguely. 'And now this . . .' He managed a half smile. 'Just to confuse me even more.' He waved his ramblings away and focused on her.

She studied him, then leaned closer. 'Up on that roof,' she asked. 'What did it feel like?' She remembered his mystified look, when the sign was just there, over him, suspended in midair. 'Did you have any control over what was happening?'

He shook his head softly. 'It feels as strange to me as it does to you and to everyone else,' he said. 'There's only one thing that's clear to me.'

'What's that?'

'If I've been fortunate enough to be chosen, then I must overcome my doubts and accept God's grace and His trust. I mustn't shy away from it or deny it. It's happening for a reason. It has to be.' He eyed her reaction, then asked, 'What do *you* think is happening?'

'I don't know. But it's just weird,' she explained, 'to be living it. To be there, watching it happen, to see it going out live, on TV, around the world. To actually have documented proof of this unexplained phenomenon, this miracle I guess, not just some,' she hesitated at which words to use, then went with 'questionable writings from a couple of thousand years ago.'

Father Jerome's brow furrowed with curiosity as he tilted his head slightly to one side. '"Questionable"?'

Gracie glanced away before her eyes came back to Father Jerome. 'I have to be honest with you, Father. I don't believe in God. And I'm not just talking about the Bible or about the church,' she added, somewhat defensively, as if that made it potentially less offensive to him, 'although I never bought into that either.'

He didn't seem offended or perturbed at all. 'Why not?'

'I guess I got that from my parents. They didn't buy into it, so I never had it drummed into me when I was a kid. Which is where it usually comes from, isn't it?'

He nodded.

'The thing is – again, no offense, Father – on the few occasions I did go to church, I never met a preacher I felt I could trust. I never felt they were in it for the right reasons, and none of the ones I met could ever give me an honest, intelligent, or convincing answer to the simplest questions I put to them.'

'Like what?'

'How much time have you got?' she joked. He smiled back, inviting her to continue. 'Anyway, once I was old enough to think for myself, I agreed with my parents and their take on the whole thing. I mean, again, no offense, Father, but historically? It doesn't stand up, does it? Let's be honest here. All those stories, from the Garden of Eden to the Resurrection . . . they're myths. Archetypal, clever, resonant – but still myths. I mean, I tried. I wanted to believe. I wanted that comfort, that crutch. But the more I read, the more I researched it, the more I saw what a primitive masquerade it all was, the more I realized that the faith I saw all around me was really nothing more than a bunch of old tales cobbled together a couple of thousand years ago by some very savvy guys to try and turn a superstitious world into a better place – and one they could control better. We're talking about a seriously primitive bunch of people here. One and a half thousand years later, people were still burning witches. So, to believe in it back then ... that's one thing. But today? With everything we know? When we've mapped the human genome and sent space probes out to the very edge of our solar system?' She sighed, then added, 'And then this happens and suddenly I'm not so sure anymore.' She looked at him with a sheepish, defeated expression.

Father Jerome nodded studiously, allowing her words to sink in more thoroughly. 'Not to believe in one religion or another, that's entirely understandable,' he told her. 'Especially for a well-educated woman like you. Besides, they can't all be right, can they?' He spread his palms out questioningly and smiled, then his expression turned more serious. 'But you're saying something very different. Something much more fundamental. You're saying you don't believe in God.'

Gracie held his gaze, and nodded. 'I don't. I didn't. At least, not until these last few days. Now I don't know what to believe. Or not to believe.'

'But before all this. Why not believe in God, outside religion? The idea of something wondrous and unknowable – and putting aside all the associations the word *God* has in the minds of religious people.'

'Logic. You can boil it all down to the basic "chicken and egg" question. The only reason – the only need – to believe in God is to try and explain where this all came from, right? Where we came from. Where we're headed. But it doesn't work. If there was a creator, a designer who created all this, well then there had to be a creator to create that creator, right? And one to create him. And so on. It doesn't hold water.' She paused, thinking further, about something closer to heart. A deep-seated sadness seemed to emerge from within her. 'And then my mom died. I was thirteen at the time. Breast cancer. She'd been clear for five years, then it just came back and took her away in ten days. It was . . . brutal. And I couldn't see why anyone would create something that nasty or take away someone so wonderful.' Even all these years later, her eyes glistened at the memory.

'I'm sorry.'

'It was a long time ago.' She studied him and hesitated, as if unsure about whether to mention something, then decided she would. 'You know, back at the monastery. When you leaned down beside Finch. For a moment there, I . . .'

'You thought I was going to bring him back?'

She was taken aback by his insight. 'Yes.'

He nodded to himself, as if he had wondered about the same thing. 'I have to say . . . I wasn't sure myself. Of what would happen. Of what I could do.' He looked up at her, his expression foggy.

'But that's what I'm talking about,' she said. 'That's what I can't understand. One minute, something we can't understand – something that could well be what we call God – is sending us some kind of message, showing itself, and it's hopeful and inspiring and wonderful . . . and then, the next minute, a perfectly good man's life is taken away, just like that.' Her whole face was questioning him. 'It's like when my mom died. There wasn't a better, kinder soul on this planet. And I couldn't understand why something like that could be allowed to happen if there was any kind of super-being watching over us. There was no way that could be justified. I talked to a couple of pastors at the time. They just gave me the standard sound bites about her "being with God" and his "testing us" and all kinds of other platitudes that, frankly, sounded like complete nonsense. Their words meant nothing to me.'

Father Jerome nodded thoughtfully. 'The reason your preacher couldn't help you is he's lost. He's still using the same words preachers used to try and comfort people five hundred years ago. But we're a bit more sophisticated than that now.' He paused, as if pained by his own words. 'That's the problem with religion right now. It hasn't evolved. And instead of being open and looking for ways to be relevant in today's world, it's gone all defensive and protective and it's regressed into lowest-common-denominator sound bites – and fundamentalism.'

'But you can't reconcile religion with modern life, with all the knowledge we have, with science,' Gracie said. 'I mean, let me ask you this. Do you believe in evolution? Or do you think men and dinosaurs wandered around the planet together six thousand years ago . . . after it was created in six days?'

Father Jerome smiled. 'I've lived in Africa for many years, Miss Logan—'

'Please, call me Gracie,' she interjected.

He nodded. 'I've been to the digs, I've seen the fossils, I've studied the science. Of course I believe in evolution. You'd have to be a blinkered halfwit not to.' He studied her reaction as she flinched. 'Does that surprise you?'

'You could say that,' she laughed, still stunned.

He shrugged. 'It shouldn't. But then, religion in your country is so focused on fighting science and all these compelling atheist voices that your preachers have lost track of what religion is really about. In our church – the Eastern Church – and in Eastern religions like Buddhism and Hinduism, religion isn't there to offer theories or explanations. We accept that the divine is unknowable. But for you and for a lot of rational people like you, it's become a choice. Fact or faith. Science or religion.' He paused, then added, 'You shouldn't have to choose.'

'But they're not compatible,' Gracie insisted.

'Of course they are. They shouldn't be in competition. The problem is with your preachers – and your scientists. They're stepping on each other's toes. With big, heavy boots.

They don't understand that religion and science are there to serve different purposes. We need science to understand how everything on this planet and beyond works – us, nature, everything we see around us. That's fact, no one with a working brain can question that. But we also need religion. Not for ridiculous counter-theories about things that science can prove. We need it for something else, to fill a different kind of need. The need for meaning. It's a basic need we have, as humans. And it's a need that's beyond the realm of science. Your scientists don't understand that it's a need they can't fulfill no matter how many Hadron colliders and Hubble telescopes they build – and your preachers don't understand that their job is to help you discover a personal, inner sense of meaning and not behave like a bunch of zealots intent on converting the rest of the planet to their rigid, literalist view of how everyone should live their lives. In your country and in the Muslim countries, religion has become a political movement, not a spiritual one. "God is on our side" – that's all I hear coming out of your churches. But that's not what they should be preaching.'

'It didn't exactly work for the Confederacy, did it?' Gracie joked.

'It's very effective at rallying the masses. And at winning elections, of course,' Father Jerome sighed. 'Everyone claims Him at one point or another.'

'The way they're now claiming you,' she pointed out.

'Are they?' he asked, curiously.

'We're in this plane, aren't we?'

Her comment seemed to strike a nerve, and he pondered it for a beat.

'Although,' she mused, 'they might be in for a bit of a surprise. *I'm* surprised. You're much less dogmatic than I imagined. Much more open-minded. Shockingly open-minded, in fact.'

The priest smiled. 'I've seen a lot. I've seen good, kind,

generous people do the most charitable things. And I've seen others do the most horrific things you could imagine. And that's what makes us human. We have minds. We make our own choices and live by them. We shape our own lives with how we behave toward others. And God – whatever the word means – is just that. We feel his presence every time we make a choice. It's something that's inside us. Everything else is just . . . artifice.'

'But you're a priest of the Church. You wear that,' she said, pointing at a cross that hung from a leather strap around his neck. 'How can you say that?'

She thought she detected some nervousness inside him, some uncertainty, as if it was something that had been troubling him too. He looked at her thoughtfully, then asked, 'When the sign appeared . . . did you see a cross up there?'

Gracie wasn't sure what he meant. 'No.'

He smiled, somewhat uncomfortably, and his eyebrows rose as he opened out his palms in a silent gesture that said, 'Exactly.'

CHAPTER 63

Framingham, Massachusetts

At around midnight, the Chrysler 300C swung into the front lot of the Comfort Inn. Two men got out. Dark suits, white shirts, no ties. Lean, hard men, with flat glares and purposeful steps. A third man stayed in the car, behind the wheel. He kept the engine running. They weren't planning on staying long.

The two men entered the austere lobby. It was deserted, which was expected. Framingham wasn't exactly a hotbed of late-night merriment. They strode up to the reception desk. Behind it, a lone man of Latin origin and advancing years was huddled in a corner chair, watching a soccer match on a fuzzy screen. The lead man beckoned him over. His dark suit, surly expression, and sharp tone of voice got the receptionist on his feet in no time. The man reached into the breast pocket of his jacket and pulled out three items, which he spread out on the desk under the receptionist's nose: two photographs – headshots of Matt and Jabba – and a fifty-dollar bill.

The receptionist scanned the items, looked up at the man, looked back down, and nodded. He then reached out and, with a trembling hand, swept back the fifty and pocketed it. Then the man got his answer, but it wasn't the answer he wanted. They had checked in earlier that evening. Taken a room. Occupied it for a couple of hours. Then they'd paid and left. The guy behind the counter had figured something of a carnal nature was going down, and the mental picture it had inspired clearly wasn't one he was comfortable with.

They'd just missed them.

The man from the 300C frowned. He studied the receptionist for a beat, decided there was nothing more to be gained, and walked out. They'd paid, which meant they weren't coming back. Something about it didn't sit well with him. Why take a room for just a couple of hours? He figured something unexpected must have come up. Something that didn't come through on the fat guy's cell phone. Which wasn't good news. It meant they had some other way of communicating with the outside world, one that his own side wasn't aware of.

He led the other man back out, paused by the car, and gave the parking lot an instinctive once-over. Nothing suspicious caught his eye. He pulled out his phone and made the call. Informed his boss what he'd been told. Heard the irritation and anger in his boss's voice. And was ordered to head back to the safe house and wait for further instructions.

The two men climbed back into the 300C. Their driver waited for a passing car, then slid the beefy Chrysler onto the road and drove off, oblivious to the dark polo-green Pontiac Bonneville that pulled out a safe distance back and was now tailing them.

Matt and Jabba kept their eyes peeled on the taillights of the 300C and didn't say much. It was late, the traffic was sparse, the cars few and far between. It all made the risk of them being spotted that much greater. They had to be extra vigilant. No mouthing off or second-guessing their plan. No superfluous chitchat. Just total focus.

They'd baited them by lighting up Jabba's iPhone. The Chrysler's appearance had confirmed Matt's suspicion that Maddox and his goons had been able to track them, despite Jabba's precautions, what with the phone being switched on for such short bursts. Somehow, they had been doing it. Which gave Matt an opening to draw them in. And wait.

The 300C hung a right on Cochituate and curled around to meet the turnpike, which they rode east. There were more cars there, which ramped down the tension of getting spotted, but ramped it up as far as losing the 300C was concerned. Still, Matt had significantly better-than-average driving skills and a keen eye when it came to spotting subtle changes in the attitude of cars, which helped keep them in the game.

They weren't in the least bit sure of what they'd find when the 300C got to wherever it was headed. As Matt had conceded to Jabba, he didn't really think he'd find Danny there, but there was a small chance they'd find Rebecca Rydell. Maddox didn't seem to have an entire brigade of thugs dedicated to this. They were running a lean, mean operation. It wasn't beyond reason to think they weren't running more than one safe house, and that they might be keeping her stashed away at the one. It would be the safest place to keep her, and saved resources. Matt started to reel back to what would have happened had he not moved the tracker over to Maddox's car in the first place, but gave up after finding it was taking away from his concentration. He didn't want to risk losing them. Beyond the possibility of finding Rebecca Rydell, this was also a chance to throw a wrench into Maddox's plans, which, to Matt, sounded pretty satisfying right now

They dumped the turnpike for the 95, which they rode north for a couple of miles before getting off at Weston. Matt pulled back as the traffic got lighter. He stalked the big car and its distinctive, boxy taillights east, all the way to Bacon, where it turned left and headed into Waltham. The going got dicier. There were far fewer cars here, and Matt had to drop way back to avoid being noticed. He also switched from main beams to daytime running lamps at each change of direction to vary the front appearance of the Bonneville in the 300C's mirrors.

The 300C threaded through some residential streets before finally turning into an unlit driveway. Matt already had his lights off and pulled over a couple of houses back. He killed the motor and watched. The three men emerged from the car and headed into the house. The last of them, the driver, beeped the car shut. He hung back and gave the street a cursory sweep before following the two other goons in.

Moments later, the 300C's interior lights automatically faded to black and the car and the house were shrouded in darkness.

The house was a small, two-story structure. Matt knew those houses well – it wasn't far from where he'd grown up, in Worcester, and the internal layouts in that stratum of the housing market were pretty standard. Front or side entrance to a front living room, kitchen at the back, stairs in the middle going up to two or three bedrooms and a bathroom or two upstairs. There was also a basement, and Matt was pretty sure that was where they'd be keeping any prisoners.

There were no lights on in the upper floor, and the front living room was also dark. Traces of light from the back of the ground floor filtered through the bay window of the living room and cast a faint glow on its ceiling.

Matt glanced at Jabba and nodded. There was another car in the driveway. The black Durango they'd seen at the airfield. The one Maddox's goons had stuffed Rebecca Rydell into.

The easy part was over. It was time to crash that party.

Luckily, they hadn't come empty-handed.

The guys from the Chrysler were in the kitchen at the back of the house, talking, having a smoke, sipping cold cans of Coke. Going over the events of the day. Winding down. Not really expecting to be called out again that night.

The loud crash changed things.

It blasted through the house and whipped them to attention. It came from the front, at ground level. From the living room. The distinctive sound of glass, exploding inward: something dense thumping heavily against the wall and landing in a dull thud while a shower of glass cascaded down onto the floor, where it exploded into tiny shards.

The guys moved as one, the lead guy from the hotel barking orders as he rushed to the front of the house, his gun already drawn and out in front. He got one guy to stay behind in the kitchen. Another followed him halfway through the house and stopped at the central staircase, positioning himself at a door that led to the basement. The third was hot on his heels as he burst into the front living room.

It had a wide bay window, and louvered half shutters ran a little over halfway up the glass, to a height of about five feet off the ground. In a defensive reflex, he didn't turn on the lights, relying instead on the dim light that spilled in from the hallway. The room should have been empty, as the rental was unfurnished, and it still was, except for the glass shards that littered the wood floor. They crunched noisily under the man's heels as he advanced into the room, sweeping his gun around. He stopped and looked up at the bay window and saw that its central portion had a huge hole punched out of it, the size of a large pumpkin. He glanced around, trying to make sense of what had happened, and spotted a rock, about the size of a football, at the foot of the back wall. His mind was still processing the idea of someone throwing a big rock through the window when something else came crashing in, something bigger and bulkier that clipped the edge of the broken glass, busted an ever wider gap through what was left of it, and narrowly missed him. It showered him with glass and splashed him with a sour-smelling liquid before it tumbled to the ground and clattered to a rest. He stared at it, dumbfounded for a nanosecond. It was a gas can. Lightweight polyethylene, red, threaded vent. Only its lid wasn't screwed on. In fact, it didn't have a lid. And it had spewed fuel like a

Catherine wheel as it spun through the air on its inward flight, hosing him along the way and now spilling its load all over the floor.

'Fuck,' he rasped as he lunged down and grabbed its handle, turning it upright to stem the flow of gas – only that didn't help, as small geysers of fuel were pouring out of it from all sides, drenching his arms and legs as well as the floor around him. He saw that crude perforations had been cut into it. There was no way to stop the fuel from pouring out. Which wouldn't have been that bad, except that a third projectile came flying into the room. This one was coming right at him, and it was lit.

Matt watched the movement of shadows inside the front room and flicked the lighter on. In his other hand, he held a water bottle that he'd emptied then refilled, half with gasoline, half with motor oil. A wick, in the form of a strip of dust cloth that was soaked with gasoline, was stuffed tightly into its neck, waiting for the flame. Two other identical projectiles were ready and willing by his feet.

The rock had drawn the guys from the Chrysler into the room, in time to receive the gas can he'd cut holes into. He knew he had to move fast and hit them before they understood what was going on. He lit the rag and lobbed the bottle in. The petrol bomb arced through the cool night air and flew into the room through the broken window. A flash of light lit up behind the shutters, followed almost instantly by a bigger fireball as the flames caught the fuel from the gas can. He heard a panicked scream, lit a second bottle, hurled it in through the same opening, grabbed the third bottle, and sprinted around to the back of the house.

The lead guy shrieked as his arms and legs caught fire. He twisted around furiously, trying to bat the flames down with his bare hands, the second guy side-stepping around him in a panic, unsure about what to do to help. The flames were stubborn, more stubborn and stickier than expected – and hotter. The gasoline was easier to smother and kill off. The motor oil was a different story. It stuck like tar and burned stronger and harder. There was no way to get it off his clothes or off the skin on his hands, and it was growing, hungrily consuming everything it touched. Flames had also grabbed hold of the floor and were spreading across the wood.

'Get it off me,' he yelled demonically as he dropped to the ground and rolled on himself, trying to suffocate the flames, unaware of the futility of his moves. Shards of glass were now cutting into his exposed, burning skin, which made the pain intolerable. The second guy took off his jacket and crab-stepped around him, looking for an opening to dive in and wrap it around him. Gray smoke was choking the room, thick with the stink of charred skin and hair and burned motor oil. The third guy, the one who'd been stationed by the stairs, was also in the room, watching his burning partner in horror. He looked around frantically, trying to find something to use to smother the flames, but the room was bare. No carpets, no curtains, no throws over sofas.

'What the fuck's going on?' the fourth guy shouted from the back of the house.

'The kitchen,' the second guy ordered the third guy, 'cover the back.'

But it was too late.

The fourth guy was alone in the kitchen. He had edged right up to the door, by the hall, trying to see what was happening while not wanting to move away from covering the house's back entrance. He could hear the screams and see the flames and the smoke and smell the stink billowing out through the living room's door and getting pushed through the house by the air coming in from the broken window, and it panicked him. It panicked him enough to snag his attention away from the back door and move him away from it enough to make Matt's move feasible.

Matt was hugging the back wall of the house and peering in through the kitchen window. He recognized the man as one of the two guys who'd escorted Rebecca Rydell off the plane, and it gave him a boost of confidence that she might be there. He registered the man's position and decided it would do. He lit the last bottle, took three steps back to give his Molotov cocktail enough momentum to break through the glass, and hurled it with all his strength. The bottle punched its way into the kitchen and exploded against the wall inches away from the guy. He bolted sideways as flames fanned out angrily, looking for food. That split second of diversion was all Matt needed. He kicked the door in right after the throw and caught the guy flat-footed. The guy was still swinging his gun hand around when Matt put him down with two rounds to the chest.

He pushed through the house without hesitating, scanning around for a locked door, sweeping the area with his P14. It felt weird being in there. He wondered if Danny had ever been held captive there. The feeling made him angrier. He stowed it for now and focused on finding Rebecca Rydell. His guess was they'd be keeping her in the basement, and sure enough, the door that led down, by the stairs, was shut. Not only shut, but locked, as someone was desperately hammering against it from the inside and tugging against its handle and yelling. A girl's voice, confirming Matt's thinking.

He didn't veer off to help her. There were at least four of them, and two potentially out of action still left at least two goons to deal with. Matt was easing past the stairs when another guy slipped out of the living room, on his way to help his now-dead colleague in the kitchen. Matt had a flash of recognition from the airfield. He didn't stop to ponder it. He just lunged sideways and down as the guy from the plane loosed off a couple of rounds that crunched into the walls just as Matt let the big handgun rip. A round caught the guy in the thigh and he jerked backward momentarily, then his leg buckled and he collapsed on top of it. The shooter raised his gun, hoping for another shot. The strength had drained out of him and he looked like he was trying to lift a lead brick. Matt was on bent knees, down low against the wall, in a two-handed stance, and squeezed off two more rounds that took the guy out.

Matt stayed there for a beat. He glanced up the stairs, dismissed the idea that anyone would still be up there, and just stayed where he was and waited, arms outstretched, covering the door, watching the smoke and the flames wafting out from the living room, the screaming and the stomping echoing in his ears. He knew the fourth guy had to come back out if he didn't want to get barbecued alive. And there was only one way out of that room.

And then he heard them. The sirens, low and grating squawks, distant but closing in. Just when he needed them. He'd told Jabba to call 911 the instant the first petrol bomb exploded, figuring he'd have enough time to storm through the house before the fire engines got there, and thinking they could come in handy if things hadn't gone according to plan. The sirens grew louder, and he crouched lower, arms tensing up, expecting that the guy inside had heard them and would be needing to make a desperate, Butch-and-Sundance-like breakout. And then he heard something else: glass, shattering furiously, a loud crashing noise, and he understood. The guy had decided to bail through what was left of the bay window.

A stab of panic cut into Matt as he thought about Jabba, out there on his own without a weapon, but they'd parked a couple of houses back and he imagined neighbors were probably stepping out of their houses by now and converging outside the house, alerted by the flames and the gunshots, which would give Jabba some cover.

He waited a beat longer, straining to listen to any telltale noise that contradicted what he thought had happened, then scrambled back to the closed door. Rebecca Rydell – it had to be her – was still banging her fists against the door and shouting.

'Hey! What's going on? Get me out of here!'

Matt tried the handle, but it was locked. 'Step back from the door,' he yelled back. 'I need to shoot the lock off.'

He waited a couple of seconds, then shouted, 'You back?'

She said, 'Yes,' and he fired – once, twice. It more than did the trick. The locks were old and basic, the door frame soft with age. He kicked the door in. Wooden treads led down to a basement where an attractive, tanned girl was cowering against the wall, her face riven with terror.

He extended his arm down toward her, waving her up. 'Come on, we've got to go,' he hollered over the increasing crackle of the flames. She hesitated for a second, then nodded nervously and rose to her feet.

They stormed out of the house, past the startled faces of a few neighbors, past a fire truck that was swinging into the driveway. Matt peered through the darkness, scanning for the Bonneville, and a stab of dread cut into him as he saw that it was no longer there. A scream of horror confirmed his worst fears and he ran faster, his heart fighting its way out of his rib cage, imagining the worst. As he drew nearer, he spotted Jabba's silhouette, flat on his back on the curb outside a nearby house.

He wasn't moving.

A couple of onlookers were huddled beside him, the man checking him out hesitantly, the woman staring down, riveted with fear, her hands cupping her mouth.

'Jabba,' Matt yelled as he slid to the ground beside him.

In the darkness, it was hard to see where the wound was, but a pool of blood was spreading out from under him. He was having a hard time keeping his eyes open, but he caught sight of Matt and tried to say something, but coughed and was having trouble forming the words.

'Did we get her?' he sputtered.

Matt nodded and said, 'She's right here,' turning around to give Jabba a glimpse of Rebecca Rydell, who inched forward, her face flooded with sadness. 'Don't talk,' Matt told him, gripping his hand, tight. 'Just hang on, okay? Hang on. You're going to be fine.' He turned to the couple looming over him. 'Call 911,' he shouted. 'Call them now.'

The woman raced into the house. Matt just stayed there, hanging onto Jabba – hoping to avoid the worst, cursing himself for having dragged him along – for what felt like hours but was actually less than ten minutes until an ambulance finally showed up.

Matt stayed with him as the paramedics fussed over him before bundling him onto their stretcher with breathtaking efficiency.

Matt kept asking, 'Is he going to be okay?' but he couldn't get a straight answer out of them. With a devastating sense of loss choking him, he watched as they wheeled Jabba into the back of the ambulance, shut the doors, and stormed off.

He heard another siren – a police cruiser this time – and glanced at Rebecca Rydell. She was huddled on the lawn, still shivering.

'Come on,' he said as, mouthing a silent prayer for the life of his new friend, he took her hand and led her away from the horror-struck crowd that had gathered around the blazing house.

CHAPTER 64

Houston, Texas

'Where are they now?' Buscema asked the preacher.

Reverend Darby was in his study. It was late, but he didn't mind Buscema's call. He owed him for giving him the heads-up on Father Jerome's predicament. He also didn't mind the ego boost he got from talking about it with virtually the only other person in the country outside his organization who knew what he was doing.

'They should be landing in Shannon, Ireland, about an hour and a half from now,' he told Buscema. 'It shouldn't take more than a couple of hours to refuel the jet.' Darby sounded even more pumped than during his sermons.

'So what time will they get here?'

'I make it around six A.M., Houston time.'

Buscema went silent. Then he said, 'You might want to delay their arrival a bit.'

'Why?'

'Well, I suppose it depends,' Buscema thought out loud. 'You could sneak him in under the radar. Might be safer to play it that way.'

'Or we could turn his arrival into a major event,' Darby said, completing Buscema's train of thought. He pondered it for a moment, then said, 'I was wondering about that. You're right. He deserves to make a big entrance. We shouldn't be sneaking him in like some petty criminal. The man's God's emissary, for crying out loud. We're not like those savages. We're going to welcome him with open arms. Let's show the country and the world where America's moral center really is.'

'I can help leak it,' Buscema told him. 'Just give me as much of a heads-up as you can.'

Darby played it out in his mind's eye. He saw it as something big. Momentous. He flashed to news footage he'd watched a year earlier, of the pope arriving at Andrews Air Force Base. The red carpet, the military dress uniforms. The president and the first lady, greeting him as he stepped off the plane. His mind went back to older footage he'd seen several times. Grainy, black-and-white footage of the Beatles, arriving at Kennedy airport, back in 1964. That was more like it. The frenzied mob, heaving against barricades. The continuous, earsplitting screams. Flashbulbs popping, women wailing. Sheer adulation. That's what this would be like. That's what it should be like. With him at the center of it.

The thought put a smile on his face. It would be a defining moment. For the country and, more significantly, for him.

I'll be upstaging the president, he thought triumphantly. *And that's only the beginning.*

'I'll give you enough time,' Darby said.

'You're going to need some serious crowd control,' Buscema opined.

'Not a problem. The governor is part of my flock.'

'What about beyond that? Any progress on your Christmas offering?'

'The stadium's booked,' the preacher confided. 'It'll be a rush, but we'll make it happen. We're bringing in some performers. Big names. You mark my words, Roy. I'm going to give the people of this country a Christmas they'll never forget.'

Buscema went quiet. The kind of quiet he knew Darby would pick up on.

Sure enough, the pastor said, 'What is it?'

'I'm just a bit concerned about sending out the right message.'

'Meaning?' Darby didn't sound thrilled.

Buscema let out a ragged sigh, as if this were a tough

call. 'I'm hearing grumblings. From other pastors and church leaders.'

'I know,' Darby fumed. 'We've been swamped with calls since the news got out. Every preacher from here to California's been on the line. Even the governor wants in.'

'Wouldn't be a bad idea to share that platform, Reverend. Get the word out more widely. Turn this into a much bigger and broader event. The country could use it right now.'

'I'm the guy flying him in, Roy,' Darby noted calmly. 'I got him out of there.'

'And you'll be the one greeting him when he steps off that plane,' Buscema reassured him. 'You. No one else.'

'The governor's also pushing to be there. I'm finding it hard to keep ducking him.'

'Doesn't matter, Reverend. There won't be any other pastors at the airport. Just you. It'll be your moment. That's the image people will remember when they first see him. But after that, I'd say it's in your interest to show as much generosity as you can handle and invite as many other church leaders to join you on the big day. You've got to think big. You can take the lead on this. America doesn't have a pope. It doesn't have a spiritual leader. But the country needs one. Especially given how tough things are right now. Americans need to be inspired. To feel like they're part of something.' He paused, just enough to let the words settle but not enough to give the preacher an opening to argue back. 'You don't want it to look like just another service at your church. This one's for the whole country. For the whole world. You can't be alone on that stage. But you can do it on your terms. And by extending a welcoming hand, you'll only be elevating your own position as a gracious host . . . and leader.'

Tough part's over, Buscema thought after hanging up with Darby. Now he'd have to wait and see if the self-obsessed blowhard would play nice and share. He needed Darby to play nice. He needed him to share his new toy with the other kids. And that, he knew, was never easy. Not when you were dealing with a spoiled brat, let alone one with a righteousness complex.

He picked up his phone and hit another speed-dial key. The man on the other end had been waiting for the call.

Buscema just said, 'We're on. Leak it,' then hung up.

CHAPTER 65

Shannon, Ireland

The Gulfstream was parked by a service hangar, away from the small airport's terminal. Gracie was pacing around by the plane as she spoke on her cell phone. She was out in the open and wasn't really worried about being spotted. It was night, and there was no one around apart from a few dozy and disinterested maintenance guys who were refueling the jet.

It was much colder there, another shock to her system after the chill of the South Pole and the warm embrace of the Egyptian desert. The cold, though, felt good. Bracing. Numbing. Which was helpful, given that she was on the phone with the abbot and reliving Finch's death in all its grisly detail.

He was on his way back from Cairo. He told her they'd delivered Finch's body to the American embassy there. It hadn't been easy getting there. He told her that fierce clashes had erupted among the hordes outside the monastery once news of Father Jerome's departure had been made public. Jeep-loads of internal security men had stormed across the plain and contained the outburst, and were now clearing away the last troublemakers, but the situation had repeated itself in Cairo and in Alexandria and in other cities across the region.

Gracie saw Dalton coming toward her, waving his BlackBerry, indicating there was a call for her. She was thanking the abbot when he remembered something and said, 'I'm also very sorry about your friend's glasses. One of my brothers broke them by accident. We put the frame in the pocket of his jacket.'

Dalton was right up with her and mouthed 'Ogilvy' to her.

Seemed like it was pretty urgent. Gracie raised a pausing index finger at him, her foggy mind trying to make sense of what the abbot was talking about.

'I'm sorry, Finch's glasses?'

'Yes,' the abbot said. 'One of my brothers stepped on them by accident. He didn't see them.'

'That's all right,' she said, nodding to Dalton like she was done. 'I didn't notice them either,' she added.

'No, you wouldn't have,' he corrected. 'They weren't outside. They were in the keep, and as you know, it's quite dark in there. Anyway, I'm really sorry. I know it's the kind of personal belonging that matters to loved ones at times like these. Would you please apologize to his wife on my behalf?'

'Of course,' Gracie said, still distracted by Dalton. 'Thanks for everything, Father. I'll call you from America.' She clicked off and took the other phone from Dalton.

It was Ogilvy. His news pushed any thought of Finch to the sidelines.

'It's out,' he told her, his tone urgent. 'The word's out that Father Jerome's on his way here.'

'What do you mean? It's been leaked?' Gracie asked. 'How?'

'I don't know. It came up on Drudge half an hour ago and it's everywhere now.'

She scanned around with her eyes, suddenly paranoid. A vision of converging mobs flashed before her, then evaporated. 'Do they know we're here?'

'No, they didn't mention that. All they know is that Father Jerome is out of Egypt and on his way here, to Houston. It doesn't even mention Darby.'

Gracie frowned. This wasn't good. She pictured the media circus and the chaos that would be greeting them.

'We've got to change destinations. Fly in somewhere else. Somewhere quiet.'

'Why?' Ogilvy asked.

''Cause people are going to go nuts when they see him. We'll get mobbed.'

'I called Darby. He told me he's got the cops lined up to help. They're gonna cordon off the tarmac, provide a rolling escort. It'll be fine.'

'You're not serious?'

'Are you kidding me?' Ogilvy asked. 'This is still our story. *Your* story. Every reporter in America would give both arms to be in your shoes. Think about it. Every single TV set in the country is going to be watching you as you walk off that plane right alongside Father Jerome, with Dalton's camera giving us a live inside track. And Darby wants you and Dalton to stick around. He's going to put you up with them. I'm flying out too. So just relax and get some rest and get ready for it. We've got a show to do, and you're about to get the biggest scoop of your life.'

CHAPTER 66

Boston, Massachusetts

'Dad?'

Rydell couldn't believe his ears. His pulse raced ahead with equal doses of fear and hope. He could feel it pounding against his cell phone. 'Where are you? Are you okay?'

'I'm fine,' she said. 'They got me out. I'm fine.'

Rydell's heart cartwheeled. Her voice had a quaver in it, but she didn't sound afraid.

'Hang on,' she said.

He heard some shuffling as the handset evidently changed hands, then he heard the last voice he was expecting.

'Are you alone?'

He recognized Matt's voice. A sudden panic seized him. 'Where are you? What have you done?'

Matt ignored his question. 'She's safe. Can you get out without the escorts?'

'I don't know.' Rydell faltered. 'I . . . I can try.'

'Do it,' Matt ordered. 'Do it right know. And meet us outside the place you took Rebecca for her eighteenth birthday.'

The line went dead.

Rydell didn't know what to think. Was she Matt's hostage now? Was that his plan? He wasn't sure what he preferred – knowing she was in his hands, or in Maddox's.

He wasn't sure either way. What he was sure of was that now that Rebecca was out, Drucker didn't have any hold over him. Unless he tried to grab him and substitute him for Rebecca.

He had to get out.

Now.

He picked up the hotel phone and hit the reception button. Got an answer on the first ring.

'This is Rydell. I need security up here. Right now. As many guys as you can send. My bodyguards are up to something; I need protection right now. From them.' His tone left no room for doubt as to the urgency involved.

The flustered voice on the other end was still fumbling through a reply when Rydell hung up. He darted to the bedroom, found his wallet and his coat, and pulled his shoes on; darted back to the door of his suite and eased against it for a peek through the peephole. He could see the two bodyguards, Maddox's men, standing outside his door. Looking bored, killing time. He waited. About ten seconds later, he heard the whine of the elevator's motor and the clunk of the doors sliding open. Four men rushed out and stormed over to the suite's door. Rydell saw the bodyguards step toward the security guys, arms raised in a halting what's-going-on gesture.

Rydell grabbed his chance. He swung the door open and stormed out, sprinting past the surprised bodyguards and through the wall of security guys, waving a panicked finger back toward his bodyguards and shouting, 'Stop them. They're trying to kidnap me. Help me get out of here.'

The security guys flinched with confusion, as did the bodyguards, who were caught flat-footed by Rydell's rushed exit. Maddox's men stepped forward forcefully, one of them reaching for his holstered handgun, but the security guys weren't cowed. Two of them were beefy bouncer types, and they just stood their ground and closed in on each other, creating a barrier across the corridor. One of them, the biggest one of the lot, held up a stern warning finger and had his handgun out too, a mocking you-really-don't-want-to-do-this grimace across his face. Rydell didn't wait to watch the outcome. He slipped into the elevator, jabbed the down button repeatedly until the doors rumbled shut, and rode down to the lobby, his nerves on fire. The short ride felt like forever. He raced out the second the door opened, flew out of the lobby, and hurtled into a lone, waiting cab. He ordered the guy to just go, and craned his head back as the cab drove off, to make sure they weren't being followed. He made the driver take a few rudderless lefts and rights. When he was satisfied that they were on their own, he told him where to go.

It was a short hop around the Common and past Faneuil Hall to get to the Garden. That late at night, the traffic was light, despite the holiday rush. As the cab turned to pull into the arena's parking lot, Rydell spotted Matt across the street, leaning against a dark sedan. Rydell got the cabbie to drop him off at the gate, waited for him to drive well clear, and crossed the road to join them. He was halfway across when the rear door swung open and his daughter clambered out of the car and ran over to him.

He hugged her tight. He still couldn't quite believe it. He looked over her shoulder. Matt was just standing there, leaning back against the car, his arms crossed, an angry look on his face. Rydell kept a firm grip on Rebecca's hand as he went up to him.

'You did this?' Rydell said. More like a statement than a question.

'My friend's in the hospital,' Matt told him crisply. 'He's been shot. Bad. I need you to make a call and make sure they give him everything he needs.'

Rydell nodded and reached for his phone. 'Of course.'

'He's also going to need protection,' Matt added. 'Is there anyone you can call?'

'I've got the number of the detective who came out to the house,' he said. 'I can call him.'

'Do it,' Matt said.

Rydell kept hold of Rebecca as he made the calls. It didn't take long. His name usually helped speed things up.

They told him Jabba was in surgery, and that the prognosis was uncertain. He hung up and informed Matt.

'He's in good hands,' Rydell told him. 'He'll get the best of care.'

'I damn well hope so.'

Rydell studied him, unsure about where they stood. 'I'm sorry about your friend. I just . . . I can't thank you enough for doing this,' he said, hesitantly.

'I just don't like your friends,' Matt replied tersely. 'They have this habit of locking people up.'

Rebecca turned to meet Rydell's guilty look.

'And . . . ?' Rydell braced himself for more. Were they now both his prisoners?

'And nothing. My friend's been shot and your buddies still have my brother.' Matt stared at him, hard. 'I thought you might want to help me make things right.'

Rydell brought his hand up and massaged his temple. He looked at Matt, then slid his eyes over to Rebecca. She was eyeing him with a mixture of confusion, fear, and accusation.

He didn't know what to do. But he had no one left to protect.

'They're bringing him back,' he finally said.

'Who?' Matt asked.

'The priest. Father Jerome. He's left Egypt. He's on his way here.'

'Where here?'

'They're saying Houston,' Rydell said. 'It's only just hitting the wires. Wherever it is, they're bound to put a sign up over him, and the odds are, that's where you'll find Danny.' He paused, collecting his thoughts. 'You were right,' he finally conceded. 'They're planning something. Something they needed me around for. I don't know what it is, but what I thought the plan was, what they insisted was still their plan . . . it's not it. It's something else. It's all about the priest now.'

'Who would know?' Matt asked him, fixing him squarely.

'The others.'

'I need names.'

Rydell held his gaze, then said, 'You only need one name. Keenan Drucker. It's pretty much his show. He'll know.'

'Where do I find him?'

'D.C. The Center for American Freedom. It's a think tank.' Just then, Rydell's BlackBerry trilled. He fished it out of his pocket, checked its screen. And frowned at Matt.

Matt looked a question at him.

Rydell nodded. It was Drucker.

He hit the answer key.

'What are you doing? Where the hell are you?' Drucker asked sharply.

'Working late, Keenan?' He looked pointedly at Matt, holding up his free hand in a stay-put gesture.

'What are you doing, Larry?'

'Getting my daughter back.' Rydell let that one sink in for a beat. Drucker went mute. Then Rydell added, 'Then I thought I might head down to the *New York Times* and have a little chat with them.'

'Why would you want to do that?'

''Cause I don't know what you're up to, but I'm pretty sure it has nothing to do with what we set out to achieve,' Rydell shot back fiercely.

Drucker let out a rueful hiss. 'Look, I made a mistake, all right? Taking Rebecca was way out of line. I know that. And I'm sorry. But you didn't leave me any choice. And we're in this together. We want the same thing.'

'You're not doing this to save the planet, Keenan. We both know that.'

Drucker's voice remained even. 'We want the same thing, Larry. Believe me.'

'And what is that?'

Drucker went silent for a moment, then said, 'Let's meet somewhere. Anywhere you want. Hear me out. I'll tell you what I'm thinking. After that, you decide if you still want to bring this whole thing down on top of us.'

Rydell swung his gaze around to Matt and Rebecca. Let Drucker sweat it out for a beat. He knew he needed to hear him out. Too much – his whole life, everything he'd achieved, everything he could still achieve – was at stake. 'I'll think about it,' he replied flatly, then hung up.

'What did he want?' Matt asked.

'To talk. To convince me to play ball.'

Matt nodded, then pointed at Rydell's BlackBerry. 'They might have a lock on you.'

Rydell held up the device, a curious expression on his face. 'What, this?'

'They were tracking us. Through my friend's phone. Even though we've been careful. We only had it on for short bursts.'

Rydell didn't seem the least bit concerned. 'We can do it in the time it takes your phone to send out a text message.'

Matt didn't get it.

'It's one of ours,' Rydell assured him. 'A piece of spyware we developed for the NSA. But there's nothing to worry about here. We're fine. My phone's vaccinated against it.'

Matt shrugged, looked away, then swung his gaze back at Rydell. 'What are you gonna do?'

Rydell pondered his question. 'I don't know.' He hadn't had any time to think and strategize. Not that he felt overwhelmed with options. Everything felt like it was crashing down around him. But Rebecca's call had changed all that.

He gazed at his daughter. Her safety was paramount. 'We can't stay here,' he told Matt. 'Not in Boston. Not after your little visit. There's nowhere to lay low, not in this town. Anywhere we go will get flagged to the press – and to Maddox.'

Matt nodded, mulled it over for a moment, then said, 'Don't you want to see it?'

'What?'

'Your handiwork. In all its glory.'

Rydell thought about it for a beat, then said, 'Why the hell not. Let's get out of here.'

CHAPTER 67

Houston, Texas

The crowds were visible from the sky.

Gracie didn't spot them at first. The jet was banking around the small airport, coming in on a low-altitude, looped approach. From a height of around a thousand feet, all she noticed was a solid mass, a dark blot staining the pale wintry scrub that surrounded the acres of gray concrete. The traffic jams gave it away. All the small roads leading to the field were clogged with cars. Vehicles were just strewn all over the place haphazardly, like Lego bricks tossed out of a box. They were all jammed up one against another on the fields on either side of the roads, and weren't going anywhere anytime soon. The traffic was backed up all the way to the Beltway, which was choked for a couple of miles in each direction. People were just abandoning their cars and making their way to the field, following those ahead of them like groupies converging on a big open-field rock concert. They were swarming in from all corners, heading for the northwestern corner of the airport, not far from the northern tip of the runway.

Gracie wasn't familiar with the airfield. Darby had explained to her that the chief of police had requested they avoid Hobby and Bush Intercontinental and use Ellington Field instead. For one thing, it wouldn't disrupt the commercial flights in and out of the city. Ellington was a small, mostly military airfield. A handful of private jet operators had FBOs there, but it wasn't used by any airlines. It didn't even have a terminal. It was no more than a couple of runways and a row of uneven hangars that were home to the Coast Guard, NASA, as well as the Texas Air National Guard, where, famously, George W. Bush had been based during the Vietnam War, ready to thwart any Vietcong attack on Houston. Crowd control would also be easier there. The airfield was used to handling public events, especially since it was home to the annual Wings Over Houston air show.

Still, Gracie was willing to bet they hadn't experienced anything like this.

The jet touched down faultlessly and veered off to the left at the end of the runway. It rolled on for a hundred yards or so before coming to a stop by a large single hangar that had its frontage wide open. A twin-jet helicopter was parked nearby, a couple of men standing beside it. The captain throttled back and killed the Gulfstream's engines, and as they whined down, the noise from outside seeped in, an eerie wave of clapping and cheering that was loud enough to defy the air seals of the cabin and its triple-glazed windows.

Gracie looked at Father Jerome. His face was tight with anxiety and glistened with a sheen of sweat. She reached out and put her hand on his, smiling supportively.

'It's going to be fine,' she said. 'They're here to welcome you.'

He nodded stoically, as if resigned to his new role.

His look brought back the same unease she'd felt on the roof of the keep, and she wondered why she wasn't feeling any relief at being back on safe and solid ground. She glanced over at Dalton. He was already getting his camera ready and turning on the Began to set up a live feed.

'You ready for this?' he asked her.

'No,' she said with an uncertain smile.

Nelson Darby waited by the empty tarmac and drank in the clamor rising up from the mass of onlookers. He was used to big crowds. His megachurch welcomed over ten thousand people every Sunday, and over fifteen thousand on special occasions. This was different. Normally, he was the one providing the fire. He was the catalyst. The crowd would soak up his energy and respond when prompted. He wasn't used to being a passive observer, but the crowd behind the barriers at the edge of the airfield were providing the fireworks themselves. They were clapping and whooping as if they were waiting for Bono to come out for an encore. A large group to the left were singing 'I've Been Redeemed' and swaying back and forth with each line. And Father Jerome hadn't even stepped off the plane yet.

The pastor glanced over to his left, where the governor was standing stiffly by his side. He gave the silver-haired politician as genuine a smile as he could muster and swiveled his gaze over to his right. Roy Buscema met his gaze and nodded solemnly.

Darby leaned closer to him and said, 'Good call, Amigo,' in a low voice.

Buscema just nodded again and kept his eyes fixed on the plane's cabin door as it cracked open.

The crowd roared as the door swung outward. Its retractable stairs slid down and touched the ground, and three of Darby's people rolled a red carpet out to meet it in preparation for Father Jerome's descent.

Without inviting any of his guests to join him, Reverend Darby strode up to the plane, turning briefly to acknowledge the crowd with a regal wave and his signature megawatt smile. The hordes, pressed against the fences that the police had barely managed to put up, roared back their appreciation as the preacher positioned himself at the base of the steps. The governor followed, mimicking Darby's nod to the crowd, but he'd missed the moment and failed to generate the same response.

Inside the plane, Father Jerome straightened his cassock and padded to the front of the cabin. He seemed lost and confused, a stranger in a strange land. He turned to Gracie, the same anxious look darkening his face. Brother Ameen stepped closer to him and took his hand, cupping it with both of his.

'It's going to be fine,' he told the older priest.

Gracie watched, anxious, waiting for him to settle down. Father Jerome sucked in a deep breath, then straightened up, nodding with renewed resolve.

'Is it okay if we start rolling?' she asked, pointing at Dalton and his camera. Brother Ameen studied Father Jerome, then turned to Gracie and gave her a nod. Gracie pressed the earpiece into place, lifted her BlackBerry up to her mouth, and gave Roxberry a low-voiced go signal. They were going out live, as planned – an exclusive for the network.

Father Jerome stooped slightly to pass through the cabin door's low opening and stepped onto the landing at the top of the retractable stairs. Gracie and Dalton were inside the cabin, filming him from behind. The crowd's reaction was thunderous. A tsunami of adulation came barreling over them from all sides. Father Jerome froze and stood there and let it roll over him, his eyes swimming across the sea of faces spread out before him. Gracie craned her neck to get a better look. There were people stretching back as far as she could see. Some carried banners, others had their arms raised. There were cries and wails and tears of joy, a torrent of religious fervor barely held back by the barricades. Television cameras and mobile broadcasting vans were everywhere, their oversized satellite dishes dotted around and giving the airfield the look of a SETI installation. A couple of news choppers circled overhead, their cameras rolling.

Father Jerome raised one hand, then another, an open embrace that spoke of humility, not of showmanship. The crowd went ballistic, clapping and screaming expectantly, their eyes scanning the sky anxiously, wondering if they'd be seeing the miracle for themselves. Father Jerome himself tilted his head up slightly, sliding a glance upward, also wondering if anything was going to appear, but he didn't wait for it. He glanced back at Brother Ameen and at Gracie and climbed down the stairs, straight into Reverend Darby's welcoming embrace.

Gracie and Dalton followed him down and hovered discreetly to one side.

'Are you getting this?' she asked Roxberry. He was back at the studio, anchoring the coverage.

'You bet.' His voice crackled in her earpiece. 'Keep it coming.'

She watched as the reverend kept the priest's hand firmly cocooned inside his own cupped hands and whispered some words into his ear. The priest seemed surprised by what he was saying, then he nodded hesitantly, as if out of courtesy.

Darby turned to the audience, raised his arms, and flapped them down gently in a quieting gesture. The crowd took a moment to settle down, and when they finally quieted, the stillness was eerie. A combination of anticipation and foreboding was palpable. Then one of Darby's assistants handed him a microphone and he raised a hand to the crowd.

'Brothers and sisters in Christ,' he announced in his barrel-organ voice, 'greetings in the name of Jesus Christ, our Lord, to you all, and thanks for coming out here with me to greet our very special visitor, Father Jerome.' He stretched the *o* in Jerome, like a game announcer, and got a wildly raucous reply from the crowd.

'Now as you know, tomorrow is a very special day. Tomorrow is Christmas Day, a special time of celebration for us all, and yet . . . and yet, this year, a time of pause, a time when we must bow our heads humbly and think about these troubled, testing times we're in, think about what we could have done to make things better and what the future holds for us. And up until a few days ago, I was troubled. I was bothered and I was distressed. I was finding it hard to remain hopeful. And like many of you, I've been praying. I've been praying for God to spare our great nation. To spare it from the judgment we certainly deserve for our many trespasses, like the killing of millions upon millions of pre-born children. I've been praying for God to be merciful with the millstone we deserve to have hung around our necks for our sins. For allowing our scientists to experiment with stem cells and colliders. For allowing our living children to be exploited by the deviant anarchists who now control public education and Hollywood. For tolerating those who would like to do away with Christmas altogether. And when a great nation like ours is going through troubled times such as these, when a great nation like ours is on its knees, the only normal and natural and spiritual thing to do is what we, as good Christians, should be doing all the time: calling upon God. Calling upon Him for guidance and for revival.' He paused and let his somber words sink into the crowd, who went silent except for the scattered 'Amen' and 'Bless the Lord,' then he sucked in a deep breath and beamed a kindly smile at the mob.

'Well guess what? I think God heard our prayers,' he bellowed out, to a chorus of 'Hallelujahs' and 'Amens.' 'I know He heard our prayers. And I believe He's sending us a lifeline. A lifeline to help lead a nation and a world that are nearing moral collapse and perhaps even World War III. A lifeline in the form of a pious, deeply spiritual man, a man who has devoted his entire life to the selfless pursuit of helping his fellow man. So I ask you all to please join me in welcoming the good Father Jerome to our great state of Texas,' he boomed, triggering an even more tumultuous uproar.

Father Jerome cast his eye across the crowd, taking it all in silently. He glanced over at Gracie. She was standing next to Dalton, her mike poised in front of her, but she wasn't saying anything. She recognized the same confused, worried look on the priest's face, the one she'd seen on the roof of the *qasr* before the sign had appeared. He seemed clearly uneasy with everything that was happening.

Darby put his arm around the priest and oriented his attention back at the crowd. 'Now I have a special request for Father Jerome, and I hope you'll all join me in this, as it's an invitation from the heart, from the heart of Texas and from the heart of the entire nation.' He turned to Father Jerome, and said, 'I know you're tired, and I know you've been through some heady days, but I'm here to ask you, on behalf of all these people and on behalf of the whole country – will you honor us with a special service tomorrow?'

The crowd whooped its approval in a crescendo of claps and cheers. Darby raised his hand to quiet them, then turned to Father Jerome, moving the mike right up to the priest's mouth and awaiting his answer. Father Jerome looked into his eyes for a beat, then gave him a nod and mouthed, 'Of course.'

'He said yes,' Darby bellowed, and the crowd went nuts again. He raised his hands again to calm them, and said, 'And you're all invited. Every one of you,' pointing at the crowd. 'Spend the day with your loved ones. Enjoy those turkeys and ring out those carols. And at six in the evening, come on down to the stadium at Reliant Park. We've got room for all of you.' He beamed, and the crowd erupted into even louder cheers.

Darby waved to acknowledge his audience and put a guiding arm behind the priest for the best photo op he could have asked for, then herded him away from the crowd toward the hangar to their right.

'We're moving away from the crowd now,' Gracie told Roxberry as she and Dalton followed, continuing their live transmission. 'We seem to be headed for –' she heard the chopper's engines whining up and saw its blades start to spin – 'We're headed for a chopper, Jack. Father Jerome is about to be choppered out of here, which is probably the only way out right now. I guess we're going to lose our connection, but we'll keep rolling the camera and get the pictures over to you as soon as we land.'

They all piled into the helicopter – Darby, two of his assistants, the priest and the monk, Gracie, and Dalton. Less than a minute later, the chopper lifted off the ground, swooped around for a rousing pass over the crowd, and straightened out on a direct trajectory to the city, the two news choppers trailing in its wake.

CHAPTER 68

Houston, Texas

Matt was leaning forward, his eyes fixed on the wall-mounted plasma screen in the FBO's executive lounge at Hobby Airport. Rydell was also there, watching it with him. He had arranged the night flight from Boston, borrowing a jet from one of his dotcom buddies. It had dropped them off in Houston before continuing onward to Los Angeles, whisking Rebecca off to the relative safety of an old friend and a big city. At Hobby, Rydell had arranged for them to have exclusive use of the fixed base operator's facilities, figuring it made sense to hang back at the airport and figure out what their next move would be before going into the city proper and risking exposure. Then they'd sat back and watched.

The live coverage cut away from Grace Logan's feed and segued to the network's fixed camera at the edge of the airport, and the sight of the chopper taking off deflated Matt. He'd been hoping to see the sign show up over the false prophet, and to take its appearance as a sign that Danny was close by. It hadn't happened, but that didn't stop him from scrutinizing every corner of the screen, looking for anything suspicious right until the feed switched over to the aerial view from one of the trailing choppers and cut him dry.

Matt slumped back into the sofa, dropped his head back against it, and shut his eyes. 'Reliant Stadium,' he said. 'That's where the Texans play, isn't it?'

Rydell was already on his BlackBerry. 'Let's see what the weather's like tomorrow.'

'Why?' Matt asked.

'The stadium's got a retractable roof. If it looks like it's not going to rain, they'll have it open – which they'll need to do if they're planning to put a sign up over him.'

Matt kept his head back, staring at the ceiling. He sucked in a deep breath. 'Tomorrow, then,' he said.

They sat in silence for a moment, thinking ahead, trying to let some clarity back into their minds. Matt stared up at the ceiling. He felt a burgeoning optimism. He was getting closer to Danny, and he'd made it alive so far. The continuation of neither of which was a given, not by any measure.

'It's not going to be easy finding Danny,' Rydell added. 'The stadium's huge.'

Matt frowned. He'd been thinking of something else. 'Maybe we won't have to.' He glanced across at Rydell. 'Drucker told you he wanted to talk, right?'

'Last I heard, he was in D.C.,' Rydell told him. Then something occurred to him. 'Unless he's here. For all this.'

'Call him. Tell him you're here if he wants to talk. And tell him to get his ass down here if he isn't here already.'

Rydell weighed it. Seemed to like it, but with a slight reticence. 'He'll suspect something's up.'

Matt shrugged. 'He'll still want to meet with you, and that's something we can control. We'll pick the place. We can be ready for him. Besides, it's not like I'm juggling ten different options here.' He played it out one more time, then nodded, going for it. 'Make the call.'

'You sure?' Rydell asked.

'Get him down here,' Matt confirmed. 'I think we'd both like to hear what the bastard has to say.'

CHAPTER 69

River Oaks, Houston, Texas

The area around Darby's house was entirely sealed off by the police. Running a perimeter four blocks out on three sides, their barricades were blocking all access except for residents. The back of the house looked out over the golf course, and access to the club was also now under strict police control. Officers and dogs patrolled the greens, on the lookout for overzealous believers and angry fanatics. The governor also had the National Guard on standby, should the need for more manpower arise.

The chopper set down in the parking lot of the country club, and its occupants were shuttled across the golf course to their host's mansion under police escort. News vans crowded the edges of the cordon, a long row of white vans and satellite dishes. Throngs of hysterical worshippers were massed against the barricades, clamoring for Father Jerome to come out and talk to them, desperate for a glimpse of the Lord's envoy. A couple of whackos had infiltrated their ranks and were blathering away with incoherent speeches about the imminent end of the world, but more common were the scattered choruses of hymns and carols that could be heard across the neighborhood.

Gracie and Dalton were shown to a room on the ground floor of a guest house that abutted the main building. Brother Ameen was in an adjacent room. Father Jerome was given a cosseted guest suite on the second floor. The plan was for them all to remain at the mansion until the big sermon at the stadium the following evening.

Ogilvy, who was in town, had asked for continual updates live from inside the Darby estate. Gracie and Dalton had given the network's viewers a tour of the compound, but hadn't managed to get a word from Father Jerome, who was resting in his suite and had asked not to be disturbed.

After Gracie signed off, Dalton checked his watch and said, 'I'm off to the airport to get the skycam and the rest of our stuff. I might pick up some fresh clothes if the mall isn't mobbed. You need anything?'

Gracie chortled. 'An alternate reality?'

'I'm not sure Gap sells those, but I'll see what I can do.' He smiled.

He wandered off and left her. She went back to the room, where she collapsed on the bed. It had been a brutal few days, and there was no end in sight. She managed to tune out for all of three minutes before the phone rang.

She fished out her BlackBerry, but it wasn't the one that was ringing. She burrowed deeper into her bag, saw the soft blue glow of another screen, and pulled it out. It was Finch's phone.

She eyed it curiously. The caller's ID was flashing up. It said Gareth Willoughby. It wasn't a name she recognized at first – then it clicked. He was the producer of the BBC documentary.

She took the call.

Willoughby didn't know Finch had died. The news took him by complete surprise. He told Gracie he didn't know Finch and said he was just returning his call.

There was an uncomfortable silence for a moment, then Gracie said, 'I guess you must be glad they finally agreed to let you go up there and talk to Father Jerome, huh?'

Willoughby sounded confused. 'What do you mean?'

'I mean if they hadn't said yes, or if you hadn't kept on insisting . . . who knows what would have happened. I know we probably wouldn't have flown out to Egypt.'

Willoughby wasn't getting it. 'What are you talking about? They came to us.'

His statement pricked Gracie like a dart. She straightened up. 'What?'

'They came to us. I mean, yes, we were there. Making the documentary and all that. But we didn't go looking for him. We had no idea Father Jerome was even there.'

Gracie was having trouble reconciling this with everything she'd assumed. 'So how'd you end up meeting him?'

'Well, it was just one of those serendipitous breaks, I suppose,' Willoughby said. 'We were filming there before heading out to Saint Catherine's in the Sinai. That was our original intention. Not the Syrians' monastery. We were at Bishoi at the time, you know, the other monastery near there?'

'I know the one,' she told him.

'Well, Bishoi's story, the whole thing about him chaining his hair to the ceiling so he wouldn't fall asleep. It's the kind of rather wonderfully creepy detail that adds a bit of spice to this kind of show. And while we were there, we were buying supplies from this small shop and we bumped into this monk from the monastery of the Syrians. We got chatting, and he told us Father Jerome was up there in one of their caves. Acting rather bizarrely. As if he were possessed, only in a good way. Which was really timely for us.'

'Hang on a second,' Gracie blurted, trying to make sense of his words. 'I thought everyone knew Father Jerome was there.'

'No one knew.'

'We looked it up,' Gracie objected. 'It was there.'

'Of course it was – *after* we filmed our program,' Willoughby corrected her. 'That's when it hit the wires. Nobody knew he was in Egypt before we got there and wrapped our piece. He was on his "sabbatical," remember. They wouldn't say where he was. We thought he'd died at one point. And if you think about it, it was all rather fortuitous, in more ways than one.'

'What do you mean?'

'Well, we wouldn't have met that monk in the first place if it hadn't been for our commissioning editor at the BBC. That's what I'm really grateful for.'

'What, that they gave you the green light?'

'No, that they handed us the assignment in the first place,' Willoughby said cheerfully. 'It was their idea. They came up with it.'

Gracie felt a buildup of pressure in her temples. 'Whoa. Back up. You're saying you were sent there? This wasn't your idea?'

'No.'

'So exactly how did this show come about? Give me the whole back story.'

'You know how it is,' the Englishman related. 'We pitch ideas. Programs we'd like to do. We keep pitching until something sticks. We agree on a budget and a timetable, and off we go. This one wasn't like that though. We were bouncing around different ideas. I was more interested in doing a piece on the odd and rather sadistic appeal of End of Times preachings in your country. You know, the lunatics who are rooting for the whole world to blow up. But then the commissioning editor came back and proposed a three-parter that they had American partners lined up for and we ended up doing that instead. Comparing Eastern and Western approaches to spirituality. It was different, but it was still very apropos and they were laying out a decent budget for it.' He paused, taking stock of the conversation, and asked, 'If I may ask, Miss Logan, why all the questions?'

Gracie instinctively put up a defensive wall. Despite the discomfort she felt at what she was hearing, a small voice inside her was telling her to protect what she was uncovering. 'Nothing, really,' she lied. 'I'm just . . . I guess I'm just trying to better understand what got us all out there. Why Finch died.' The second it came out of her mouth, she felt horrible at using his death in that way, and hoped Finch would have forgiven her for it. 'Tell me something,' she asked Willoughby. 'The monk who told you about Father Jerome. Do you remember his name?'

'Yes, of course,' Willoughby said. 'He was a rather interesting chap. Lived through a lot of bad times, you know? He was from Croatia. His name was Ameen. Brother Ameen.'

Gracie felt like she was sinking. She felt like she'd fallen into a great whirlpool of doubt that was sucking her into its dark vortex. A vortex lined with Willoughby's words and with previous sound bites her memory was now dredging up.

She tried to order them up in a nonthreatening way, in a way that defused the most sinister thoughts that were pulling her down, but she couldn't. There was no way to gloss over it.

They'd been lied to.

She focused back on that conversation they'd had in the car after they'd been picked up at Cairo Airport. She closed her eyes and visualized the monk, Brother Ameen, telling them how the filmmakers had badgered them for access to Father Jerome and how the abbot had finally relented.

A clear lie.

The question was, why?

Her darkest instincts were going off in all kinds of directions, and none of them were good. And from that cobweb of conflicting thoughts and suspicions, another worrying sound bite rose up. It freed itself, shot up, and latched onto her consciousness.

She found her phone, pulled up her call log, and rang the number the abbot had called her from. It took a few seconds for the call to bounce its way halfway across the world. Yusuf, the driver, answered on the third ring. It was his cell phone. It was evening there, but not too late. He didn't sound like she'd woken him up.

'Yusuf,' she said, her tone ringing with urgency. 'When the abbot called, when you were driving back from Cairo, he said something. Something about where the glasses of my friend were found. You remember?'

'Yes,' Yusuf said, sounding unsure about what she was getting at.

'He said it was dark inside. That's why whoever it was stepped on them. They didn't see them. They were inside? Inside the keep?'

Yusuf paused for a moment, as if thinking, then said, 'Yes. They were in a passageway on the top floor. Near the roof hatch. They must have fallen from your friend's pocket on his way up to the roof.'

'You're sure of that?'

'Yes, absolutely,' Yusuf confirmed. 'The abbot told me about it.'

Gracie felt a cold stab in the pit of her stomach.

Finch couldn't see without them. And hard as she tried, she couldn't see how he could have climbed up there, much less how he could have found his BlackBerry on that roof, if he hadn't been wearing them.

She hung up and caught herself eyeing the door to her room as if it were a gateway to hell. Something was wrong. Something was very, very wrong. She had to do something. Her first instinct was to speed-dial Ogilvy.

'I need to see you,' she said, her body stiff, her eyes still locked on the door. 'Something's not right.'

CHAPTER 70

Houston, Texas

Matt swept his gaze across the hotel's lobby with caution and walked through its elegant halls slowly. He glanced around casually, checking for security guards, cameras, escape routes, and vantage points. He traversed as far as he could, then doubled back on himself and made his way over to the café that fronted the hotel, the one that overlooked the street. He noted its layout, made a mental list of the ways in and out, took stock of the kind of clientele and their number. Then he went back out to check the service entrance at the back of the hotel.

He was there early. The meeting between Rydell and Drucker wasn't planned for another two hours. Drucker wouldn't even have landed in Houston yet, and besides, the plan was for Rydell to keep from telling him where they'd be meeting until Drucker was actually in the city. Still, Matt felt he needed to check the place out long before any of Drucker's men had a chance to get there. He knew Drucker wouldn't be coming alone. With a bit of luck, Maddox might even be with him. And even though he knew the odds were that he'd be outnumbered, Matt had something going for him that they didn't. He didn't need to be discreet. He wasn't worried about appearances or about causing a panic. He didn't care who saw him whip out a big gun and put it to Drucker's head, right there, in the café. He didn't have anything to lose. The one thing he needed to achieve was to get the muzzle of his gun pressed right against Drucker and walk out of there with him. It didn't matter who saw him do that. It didn't matter how freaked out the hotel's guests got. Only the end result mattered. He would just sit there, bide his time, wait until Rydell got the information he needed out of Drucker, and then he'd move in.

It was easier said than done, and yet, oddly, Matt was actually looking forward to it.

Six blocks west of there, Gracie stood with Ogilvy in Sam Houston Park. Her mind was being pulled in all kinds of directions, none of which were heartening.

They were by the Neuhaus Fountain, an installation that featured three bronze sculptures of coyotes stalking the wild frontier. A few people were ambling by, stopping to experience the peaceful setting before moving on. Gracie wasn't feeling any of that. In fact, she couldn't stand still. She was rippling with nervous energy as she took the network's head of news through what Willoughby and Yusuf had told her.

Ogilvy didn't seem to share her concern. A slick-looking man with an aquiline nose and swept-back hair, he was studying Gracie patiently through rimless spectacles.

'These guys are humble, Gracie,' he remarked with an insouciant shrug. 'So this Brother Ameen character didn't admit he actually pimped Father Jerome out. He was probably hoping to get some screen time himself. Someone in his position would be the last person to admit he found the idea of a little publicity too hard to resist.'

'Come on, Hal. He wasn't the least bit nervous when he was lying about it. He didn't look embarrassed or rattled at all. It wasn't like we caught him out. And what about Finch's glasses?'

'It might explain why he fell. If he couldn't see properly.'

'They should have been down on the ground, somewhere next to him,' she objected. 'Or on the roof, and even that's a stretch. But inside the keep? One floor down from the roof? How'd he even make it up there without them?'

'What if he dropped them and broke them himself. Before he got there?'

'So he just leaves them there? I don't buy that. You step

on glasses, you maybe break one lens. Not both. You can still wear them for some kind of clear vision. You don't just leave them there.'

Ogilvy glanced away and heaved out a ragged sigh. He looked like he was losing patience. 'So what are you saying?'

'I'm saying we've got two lies that need checking out. Something's up, Hal. This is starting to stink.'

'Because of a monk who couldn't admit he got a hard-on when he saw a TV camera and another who's looking for some excuse to explain his clumsiness?'

Gracie was stunned by his dismissal. 'We need to look into this. We need to find a way to talk to the abbot directly, confirm where the glasses were. And get some background on this Brother Ameen. He's from Croatia, right? Where did he come from? How long has he been at that monastery? The guy's been pivotal to getting us to buy into this story and we don't know anything about him.'

Ogilvy paused and looked at her like she was saying she'd been abducted by aliens. 'What are you doing?'

'What?' she protested.

'You've got the inside track on the scoop of the century. This is a huge, huge story. For us and for you. We have unparalleled access. You start poking your nose around and getting Jerome and Ameen all riled up and they could shut us out. Which wouldn't go down well. Not well at all. You can't afford to mess this up right now, Gracie. It's too important. So how about you focus on that instead and put the conspiracy paranoia on hold for a while.'

Gracie looked at him as if he were the one who'd been spouting abductee tales.

'Hal, I'm telling you, something's not right. The whole thing, it's been one "lucky" break after another,' she said, making quotes with her fingers. 'Right from the beginning.' Her mind was running ahead of her now, and she was thinking aloud. 'I mean, think about it. We happen to be there when the shelf breaks off. We happen to be filming nearby. Hell, we wouldn't even have been down there if you hadn't suggested it when we were planning the whole show.'

And then it happened. Her mind plucked out the disparate thoughts that were tumbling around inside her and lined them up so they all fit. Like the sides of a Rubik's Cube falling into place. She saw a connection that was there all along and made a realization that suddenly seemed so obvious to her she couldn't imagine it not to be true.

Almost without thinking, she said, 'Oh my God. You're in on it too.'

And in that briefest of moments between her saying it and his responding, in the nanosecond of his looking at her before he opened his mouth, she saw it. The tell. The tiniest, hardly noticeable hesitation. The one her most basal instincts enabled her to see. The one they wouldn't let her ignore. A visceral pull-focus moment that made her feel like her very soul had been yanked right out of her.

'Gracie, you're being ridiculous,' he said dismissively, his tone even.

She wasn't listening to his words. She was reading through them, reading the creases around his eyes, the dilation of his pupils. And she was now even more irretrievably, horribly sure of it. 'You're in on it too, aren't you?' she insisted. 'Say it, goddammit,' she flared. 'Say it before I shout it out loud to everyone here.'

'Gracie—'

'It's fake, isn't it?' she blurted. 'The whole damn thing. It's a setup.'

Ogilvy took a step forward and raised a calming hand out to her. 'People are starting to stare. Don't make a fool of yourself.'

She shoved his hand away from her and stepped back. Her mind was racing away. 'You played me. You played me all along. This whole assignment. The trip to Antarctica. All that support, all that enthusiasm. It was all bullshit.' She glared at him, questions burning out of her. 'What are you doing? What the hell's going on?' Her mind was racing ahead, drawing on all its processing reserves. 'You're faking this? You're faking a second coming? For what? You're setting up a new messiah? Is that what this is? You want to convert the world?'

Ogilvy's eyes were flicking left and right now. The tell was confirmed beyond a doubt. 'You think I'd want that?' he hissed, trying to remain calm. 'You know me better than that. It's the last thing I'd want.'

'Well, then why?' she insisted. 'Don't tell me this is about saving the planet?'

Something in Ogilvy shifted too. He seemed to give up the pretense and framed her with a fervent glare. 'Maybe. But first and foremost, it's about saving our country,' he stated firmly.

And right then, another realization burst out of the mire, like a diver on his last breath breaking surface and gasping for air. 'Was Finch's death an accident?'

Ogilvy didn't answer fast enough. Something tore inside her.

'Goddammit, Hal,' she shouted, the horror of it making her inch back another step now. 'Tell me Finch's death was an accident. Say it.'

'Of course it was,' he assured her, opening his hands out defensively.

But her gut was telling her otherwise, and his eyes and the lines around them were confirming it. 'I don't believe you.' Her heart thumping wildly, she took another step back, suddenly hyperaware of her immediate surroundings. She didn't see any innocent-looking strollers or joggers. All she could register were two stone-faced guys in short haircuts, dark suits, and no ties, one at each entrance to the fountain area. Their body language wasn't casual.

Her eyes shot back to Ogilvy. He acknowledged the men with a barely perceptible nod. They started toward her with a threatening gait. Closing in. Blocking any escape route.

She looked at Ogilvy in disbelief, still backing away from him. 'Jesus, Hal. What are you doing?'

'Only what's necessary,' he replied, somewhat apologetically.

Gracie couldn't just stand there. She spun on her heels and sprinted off, heading straight for one of the heavies coming at her, screaming her lungs out, calling for help. She tried to fake him out and veered left before swinging right, hoping to slip past him, but his arm whipped out and caught her and pulled her in. The other suit was on them a couple of seconds later. The first guy spun her around and pinned her arms behind her back, immobilizing her. She twisted around, trying to free herself, but couldn't resist his vise-like grip. Instead, she lashed out with her right foot, kicking the suit facing her in the shin, catching it head-on. It must have hurt, as he jerked back and winced hard, but he came back with a backslap across the face that snapped her head sideways and rattled her teeth. She felt groggy and raised her eyes in time to see the suit facing her bring his hand up to her mouth. He pressed something against her nose, a kind of gauze patch. The smell from it was strong and sour. Almost instantly, she felt all the strength in her body seep away. Her eyes jerked sideways and she caught a glimpse of one of the coyotes that suddenly seemed far more threatening than she'd realized, then her head lolled down, her chin thudding against her chest. She saw a few of the flagstones under her feet fall away before everything drifted off into a silent and hollow darkness.

CHAPTER 71

They met in the five-star downtown hotel, as per Rydell's instructions. Located just off the lobby, the Grove Café seemed like a good spot. It was an open, public area with other people around. Rydell felt he'd be safe there.

Drucker was already there when he arrived. He was seated at a low table by a wall of glass that looked out onto the street. It was late afternoon under clear skies, and a few pedestrians were promenading by on the wide pavement outside. Drucker motioned for Rydell to join him.

As Rydell sat, Drucker reached down and pulled out a small box from his briefcase. He placed it squarely on the table, to one side. It was black and heavy and the size of a paperback novel, and had a couple of small LED lights on its side.

'You don't mind, do you?' he asked Rydell, 'just in case you were planning on taping any of this.' He didn't really wait for an answer and discreetly nudged a small button on the box. The LEDs lit up. Rydell shrugged and glanced around to see its effect. A couple of people in the room who'd been talking on their cell phones were now examining them curiously and pressing random buttons to try and get a signal back. Rydell knew they wouldn't be able to. Not until Drucker was done and had switched off his jammer.

Drucker gave Rydell a knowing smile and covered the jammer with his napkin. A waitress came over to ask what they wanted, but Rydell sent her away with a stern shake of his head. They weren't here for an afternoon tea.

'I'm surprised you're down here,' Drucker said. 'Couldn't resist seeing its effect with your own eyes?' He cracked a slight smile, but it didn't hide the fact that he seemed to be fishing for something.

Rydell ignored the question. 'What are you up to, Keenan?' he asked evenly.

Drucker sat back and exhaled slowly. He studied Rydell like a principal wondering what to do about a wayward student. After a moment, he said, 'Do you love this country?'

Rydell didn't get the question's relevance. 'Excuse me?'

'Do you love this country?' Drucker repeated firmly.

'What kind of a question is that?'

Drucker opened his palms. 'Indulge me.'

Rydell frowned. 'Of course, I love my country. What does that have to do with anything?'

Drucker nodded, as if that was the right answer. 'I love it too, Larry. I've devoted my whole life to serving it. And this used to be a great country. A world leader. The Japanese, the Chinese . . . they weren't even a speck in our rearview mirror. We put a man on the moon forty years ago. Fourty years ago. We used to be the standard bearers of modernity. We were the ones showing the rest of the world how it's done, how science and technology and new ideas can help us live better lives. We were the ones exploring new visions of what a twenty-first-century society should look like. And where are we now? What have we become?'

'A lot poorer,' Rydell lamented.

'Poorer, meaner, fatter . . . and dumber. We're moving backward. Everyone else is charging ahead and we're backpedaling to the point where we've become a joke. We've lost our standing in the world. And you know why? Leadership,' he said, jabbing an angry finger at Rydell. 'It's all about leadership. We used to elect presidents who blew us away with their intelligence. With their knowledge of the world and their sharp wit and their dignity. Guys who used to inspire us, guys the rest of the world respected, guys who made us proud. Guys who had vision.'

'We have one of those now,' Rydell interjected.

'And you think we're out of the woods?' Drucker shot

back. 'You think, hey presto, the country's safe now? Think again. We just had eight years of an oil wildcatter I wouldn't even hire to run a car wash, eight years of a guy who thought his instincts were manifestations of God's will, eight years of criminal incompetence and unbridled arrogance that brought our country to its knees, and did we learn anything? Clearly not. Hell, it took the economic meltdown of the century to just barely manage to scrape through this victory. This was no landslide, Larry. Damn near half the country voted for more of the same – or worse. We actually came this close to putting someone who thinks *The Flintstones* is based on fact, someone who only got a passport a year before the election and who wouldn't take an interview for a month while she was whisked away to be quietly educated about what's happening in the real world, someone who actually thinks she's going to see Jesus Christ again on this earth during her lifetime and who thinks our boys in Iraq are out there doing God's work,' he raged, slamming his palm against the table. 'We actually came this close to putting someone as risibly, absurdly unqualified as that within a seventy-two-year-old cancer-weakened heartbeat of the presidency. As ridiculous and insane as that sounds, it actually almost happened, Larry, and it could still happen. That's how blinded we've become when it comes to choosing our leaders. And do you know why it almost happened? You know why they almost got away with it?'

Rydell thought about Father Jerome and started to see what Drucker was getting at. 'Because God is on their side,' he said.

'Because God is on their side,' Drucker repeated solemnly.

'Or so they claim,' Rydell added with a slight, mocking shrug.

'That's all it takes. We'll elect any bumbling fool, any champion of mediocrity to the highest office in the land as long as they have God as their running mate. We'll hand them responsibility for everything – the food we eat, the homes we live in, the air we breathe – we'll give them the power to nuke other countries and destroy the planet, even when they can't pronounce the world "nuclear" properly. And we'll do that proudly and with no hesitation at all just as long as they say the magic words: that they believe. That they have Jesus in their heart. That they seek the guidance of a higher father. That they can look into the heart of a Russian president instead of talking to the experts. We've got presidents making policy decisions based on faith, not reason. And I'm not talking about Iran here. I'm not talking about Saudi Arabia or the Taliban. I'm talking about us. I'm talking about America and this evangelical revival that's sweeping the country. We've got presidents making political decisions based on the Book of Revelations, Larry. The Book of Revelations.'

He settled back to catch his breath and watched Rydell for a reaction before pressing on. 'We were a great country once. A rich country the rest of the world envied. Then they put a guy in there who thought Russia was an evil empire and thought we were living through the prophecies of Armageddon. They got us a guy who found Jesus but can't read a balance sheet, and they're out there running the country down to the ground and waging wars in the name of God and getting our boys blown to bits, and half the country's still marching into church every Sunday and coming out with a big smile and waving the flag of their redeemer nation—'

'I know you're angry about Jackson,' Rydell interrupted, the face of Drucker's deceased son suddenly flashing up in his mind and making him aware of what was really fueling this, 'but—'

'Angry?' Drucker growled. 'Oh, I'm not just angry, Larry. I'm fucking furious. And don't get me wrong. I'm not one to mollycoddle our troops. A soldier's job is to put his life on the line for his country. Jackson knew that when he signed up. But our country was not at risk here. This is a war that never should have happened. Never,' he bellowed. 'And the only reason it did was that we had an incompetent fool with daddy issues and a messiah complex running the show. And that can't be allowed to happen again.'

Rydell leaned in closer. He knew how much Drucker had loved his son, knew of all the grand plans he'd had for him. He had to tread carefully. 'I'm with you on this, Keenan. We're on the same page here. But what you're doing is—'

Drucker headed him off with a quieting hand and nodded like he knew what Rydell was about to say. 'We can't allow this to go on, Larry. They've got it so politicians can't get elected these days if they say they believe in Darwin. They've turned a college degree into a stigma and "elitist" into a dirty word.' His eyes narrowed. 'In the America of the twenty-first century, faith trumps competence. Faith trumps reason. Faith trumps knowledge and research and open debate and careful consideration. Faith trumps everything. And we need to turn that whole mind-set on its head. We need to bring back a respect for fact. For knowledge. For science and education and intelligence and reason. But you can't reason with these people. We both know that. You can't have a political debate with someone who thinks you're an agent of Satan. They won't compromise, because to them, compromising means compromising with the devil, and no God-fearing Christian would want to do that. No, the only way to put an end to this is to make it embarrassing for people and for politicians to flaunt their faith. We've got to take that tool away from the guys who're using it to win elections and advance whatever agendas they have. We need to make it as embarrassing to say you're a creationist as it would be if you said you still support slavery in this day and age. We need to sweep religion into the dustbin of political discourse, just like we did for slavery. And we have to do it now. The country's caught in a voodoo trance, Larry. You've seen the numbers. Sixty percent of the country believes the story of Noah's Ark is literally true. Sixty percent. There are seventy million Evangelicals out there – a quarter of the population, attending a couple of hundred thousand evangelical churches, most of which are run by pastors who belong to conservative political organizations, and these guys are telling them which way to vote. And the people are listening, and they're not voting for the guy whose policies make sense. They're not voting for the guy with the brains or the vision. They're voting for whoever will help them improve their standing when they get to the pearly gates. And it's getting worse. This delusion is spreading. There's a new megachurch opening every other day. Literally every other day.'

Drucker fixed Rydell with blazing intent. 'You think global warming is around the corner? This threat's already here. We may have dodged the bullet with this election, but they're still out there, they'll be back, and they'll fight twice as dirty. They look at it as a war. A war against secularism. A crusade to reclaim the kingdom of God from the nonbelievers and save us all from gay marriage and abortion and stem cell research. And the way things are going, they're going to make it. At some point, these prayer warriors are going to put a televangelist in the oval office. And then we'll have a bunch of whack jobs running Capitol Hill and another bunch of nutcases facing off against them in the Middle East, each of them thinking God wants them to show the other the error of their ways, and guess what? It's going to get ugly. They'll be lobbing nukes at each other before it's over. And I'm not going to let that happen.'

Rydell wasn't following. 'And you're going to do that by giving them a prophet to fire them up even more?'

Drucker just stared at him enigmatically. 'Yes.'

'I don't get it.' Rydell pressed on. 'You're giving them something real, a real miracle man to worship and rally around. A Second Coming to unite them all.'

'Yes,' Drucker repeated, leading him.

Rydell tried to follow his train of thought. 'You're getting all the church leaders to embrace him and hitch their wagons to his train.'

'Yes.' This time, a hint of satisfaction cracked across Drucker's face.

Rydell's brow furrowed. 'And then you'll get him to change his message?'

Drucker shook his head. 'No,' he stated. 'I'll just pull the rug out from under him.'

Rydell stared at him questioningly – then his eyes shot wide. 'You're going to expose him as a fake?'

'Exactly.' Drucker's hard stare burned into him. 'We'll let it run for a while. Weeks. Months. Just let it build. Let every pastor in the country accept him and endorse him as God's messenger. Let them spread the word to their flocks,' he added, spitting out the word mockingly. 'And when it's all sunk in and settled, when it's deeply embedded and they're all on the hook – we'll show him for what he really is. We'll show them what the sign really is.'

'And you'll show them how gullible they are.' Rydell had a faraway look on his face as he imagined the outcome in his mind's eye.

'The preachers will have so much egg on their faces they'll have a hard time stepping behind those pulpits and facing their people. The churchgoers will feel like they've been had – and maybe they'll start questioning the rest of the crap they hear in those halls. It'll open up a whole new discussion, a whole new questioning frame of mind. "If it was so easy to fool us today, with everything we know . . . how easy was it to fool people two thousand years ago? What do we really know about that?" It'll put everything about religion on the table.

And it'll make people think twice about who they're willing to follow blindly.'

Rydell felt heady. He himself had been ready to try and convert the world to his cause, but this . . . this went much further. He let out a weary hiss and shook his head. 'You'll make a lot of them even more fanatical than they already are,' he warned.

'Probably,' Drucker agreed casually.

'And you could also start a civil war,' Rydell added, 'if not a world war.'

Drucker scoffed. 'Oh, I very much doubt that.'

'Are you kidding me?' Rydell flared. 'You're going to have a whole bunch of really angry people out there. And they'll be looking to take it out on someone. Who's going to shoulder the blame? You can't exactly stand up and tell them, 'Hey, we did it for your own good.' The country's already split right down the middle on this. You'll polarize them even more. The blowback will be horrendous. There'll be blood in the streets. And that's before you get the blowback from the rest of the world. You've seen what's starting to happen in Pakistan, in Egypt, in Israel and Indonesia. It's not just Christians who are buying into your little scam. Muslims, Jews, Hindus . . . they're fighting among each other over whether or not he's the real deal. And they're going to be seriously pissed off when they discover it's got Uncle Sam's fingerprints all over it. People don't take kindly to having others mess around with their beliefs, Keenan. They get real angry about that. And it's Americans who are going to pay for it with their blood. You're gonna end up triggering a war you're trying to stop.'

'Well if they're so closed-minded, if they don't see the danger of their ways and insist on marching down that path to destruction, then they're beyond saving.' Drucker seethed. 'We had a war over slavery. Maybe we do need a war over this.' He gave a haughty shrug. 'If it's going to happen sooner or later, might as well just get it over with. And then maybe we can build something more sane from its ashes.'

Rydell felt as if someone had reached in and yanked his lungs out with pliers. 'You're insane,' he told Drucker. 'You've lost all sense of perspective.'

'Not at all.'

'You can't do this, Keenan,' Rydell insisted.

'No. Not without a fall guy,' Drucker conceded.

Rydell stared at him, the words colliding with his tangled thoughts, and instantly got it. 'Me. That's what you need me for.'

Drucker nodded stoically. 'I needed a fall guy. Someone with a completely different motive, one that wasn't in any way related to the politics of this country. Because this can't be seen as a political act, you're absolutely right about that. The only way to do this is to paint it as the desperate act of a visionary genius with no political motive other than trying to save the planet. And who knows? It may well end up giving people more awareness of the global warming problem.'

'But you couldn't care less either way,' Rydell said sardonically.

'Not true, Larry. I care. But I'm not even sure what, if anything, we can realistically do about it. And bringing reason back into politics – that's going to help the polar bears more than pushing Hummer into bankruptcy, don't you think?'

'This isn't about saving the polar bears or the rain forests, Keenan,' Rydell said angrily. 'It's about social justice. For everyone on the planet.'

'Social justice is about freeing people from the clutches of witch doctors and superstition,' Drucker fired back.

Rydell rubbed his brow, letting Drucker's words sink in. The room was suddenly feeling much hotter and tighter. 'How was it all meant to end for me? "Suicide"?'

Drucker nodded. 'Once the hoax is exposed. A tragic end

to a heroic attempt.' He sighed and leaned forward. 'I'm sorry, Larry. But I hope you can see the sense in what I'm trying to do here. The urgency. And that, at some level, you agree that it had to be done.'

Rydell sat back and shrugged. 'I hope you won't be disappointed if I tell you I won't play along.'

Drucker gave him a negative, dismissing wave of his hand. 'Please, Larry. Give me some credit.'

Larry looked at him, waiting for more – and suddenly froze at Drucker's composure.

'You're going to have a stroke,' Drucker told him, casually. 'A bad one. In fact it's going to happen sooner than you think. Maybe right here in this restaurant. In front of all these people. You'll end up in a coma. One we can manage. And during that time, we'll –' he paused, choosing his words – 'massage your personality. You know, like we did with the priest. We'll put the right answers in your mind. Make you more amenable to our plans. And when the time comes, we'll help you take your own life, after leaving behind a detailed, contrite, and moving explanation of why you did what you did.' Drucker studied his face, as if intrigued by Rydell's reaction to his words. 'It's the stuff of legends, Larry. No one will ever forget your name, if that's any consolation.'

Rydell felt a surge of sheer terror – and just then, he noticed something behind Drucker. A man in a dark suit, one of his drones. He swung his head around toward the entrance of the café. Two more men appeared there. His mind tripped over his only option – to make a loud, visible run for it and hope the commotion screwed up their plans – and he was about to push himself out of his chair when he spotted something else. To his side. Out on the street. A white van that had been parked there all along. Its side door, sliding open. Two silhouettes, standing inside, on either side of something big and round and mounted on a stand, something that looked like a projector lamp. His hands slipped off the chair's arms as he tried to push himself to his feet, but he never made it past a couple of inches off the seat cushion. The blast of noise was horrific. It assaulted his senses like a hammer blow that came from inside his skull, overwhelming every nerve ending in his head with an unbearably loud and shrill noise that wouldn't stop. His eyes burst into tears and he yelled out, the force of the caustic sound blasting him out of his chair in front of a stunned roomful of hotel guests. His hands shot up to protect his ears, but it was too late as his legs crumpled under him and he fell to the ground, retching and coughing and sputtering with convulsions.

Drucker's men rushed to his side. They helped him up and instantly bundled him out of the room, avoiding any brusque moves, and displaying the well-trained, expert moves of caring, efficient bodyguards. One of them even called out for a doctor. Within seconds, they'd hustled him out of the café and into a waiting elevator.

Its doors slid shut with a silent hiss, and it glided down to the hotel's underground parking lot.

CHAPTER 72

Matt's pulse thundered ahead as he saw Rydell get blasted out of his seat by an unseen force. There was no noise, no physical disturbance. It was as if he'd been punched backward by a huge invisible fist. Then he was there, bent down on the ground, writhing in agony, the contents of his belly spewing out onto the café's richly textured carpet.

He'd been ready to make his move. Waiting in a corner booth, behind the grand piano by the bar, away from the main seating area, biding his time at a staging point he'd chosen carefully. His fingers were wrapped around the Para-Ordnance's wide grip, ready to yank it out and shove it up against Drucker's ribs. But they'd moved first. Whatever they did to Rydell had sent Matt's plans to the shredder.

He rose and charged toward the café's entrance. He caught sight of Drucker heading out of the room, flanked by two of his men. He was turning right, headed for the hotel's front doors, whereas Rydell had been taken left, to the elevators. Matt hurtled across the café. He skidded to a stop at its entrance. Drucker was leaving the hotel with his escorts. There were a lot of people around him. Hotel guests, bellboys, valets. No way he could get to him. He'd missed his chance. He spun his gaze in the opposite direction. The lights over the elevator Rydell was in scrolled down to indicate he was being taken to the hotel's parking lot.

Matt chose to go after him instead. If Drucker had him again, Matt would be left with no leverage. Leverage he needed if he was going to see his brother again.

He bolted across the lobby, past some shocked guests and through the door to the hotel's internal stairwell. Flew down the stairs, three at a time, gripping the banister at the turns and flinging himself around them like an out-of-control bobsled. Six flights later, he was at the parking level. He burst onto its smoothly painted concrete floor in time to see a dark gray van squealing away and turning onto the exit ramp. His eyes traveled across the garage. He heard a door click open to his left, spun his gaze that way, and rushed toward the noise. A valet was getting out of a car. A big Chrysler Navigator SUV, silver. Matt didn't flinch. He sprinted right up to him, yanked the car keys from his grasp, and shoved him away before climbing in and spurring the big Northstar V8 to life. He slammed the selector into drive and cannoned out of the parking slot and onto the exit ramp.

He emerged into the golden-orange glow of dusk and threw a quick glance in each direction. The city center was an orthogonal grid of alternating one-way avenues, some of them five lanes wide. This one went east-west, and the van was pulling away to the right, heading west. He nudged the gas pedal. The Navigator slid out from under the garage entrance's canopy and accelerated onto the avenue. The van was cruising away, three hundred yards down the road.

Matt threaded the big SUV through a rolling chicane of slower vehicles and caught up with the van in no time. He held back, keeping a car between them. The road was straight and wide, the traffic sparse. The intersections were vast and generous, concrete plains outlined by patterned stone infills that gave them the feel of a Beverly Hills piazza. Two blocks on, a big green sign appeared overhead, announcing the on-ramp to the interstate and, beyond, to the 90. Matt knew he had to do something before they hit the highway. Once they were on it, all kinds of unknowns would come into play. He risked being spotted. He risked losing them. He risked them getting to wherever it was they were going, and having them end up with the home advantage.

He had to make his move.

The road was as wide as a runway and didn't have any

cars parked on either side. The block they were coming up to was lined with a row of thin trees to the left, and some kind of granite colonnade on the right. It wouldn't do. Too brutal. Matt edged the Navigator right and peered ahead. The next block looked more promising. The left side was edged by a bunkerlike parking garage and wouldn't do. The sidewalk on the right, on the other hand, led to a rise of a dozen or so wide, low steps that climbed up to a raised open area outside an imposing stone-clad office building.

Matt settled on it and mashed the pedal.

The V8 growled as the Navigator surged out from behind the buffering sedan and overtook it from the left. Matt went out wide to the left then veered right and aimed the Navigator's nose at the van's left front corner. He didn't lift off. The Navigator homed in on the van like a guided missile. A split second before it slammed into it, Matt jerked the wheel to the left and righted the SUV. It hit the van at a tangent, catching its driver unawares, its momentum flinging the van off its trajectory and sending it shooting off to the right. Matt flung the wheel back to the right, bringing the Navigator right up against the van's left side, hugging it tight and nursing it along its diagonal trajectory, then he swerved right even more to close the deal. The van had nowhere to go, and its driver knew it. He must have stood on the brakes, as the van lurched forward on its front wheels, lighting them up in a cloud of rubber, but he was still going too fast. The van bounced heavily up the stairs before slamming against one of the building's massive square pillars.

Matt ramped the Navigator over the curb and flew out of it just as the van hit the column. He stormed up the steps, the stainless steel handgun out and ready to draw blood, eyes peeled for any movement.

The van had hit hard. Its radiator was smoking and its front end curled around the column. Matt didn't know what state he'd find Rydell in. One thing he knew, though, was that the guys in the front wouldn't be at their healthiest. The van had a steep front rake and little if no hood to protect the engine in case of a frontal collision. Plus, he knew, the guys weren't expecting the hit.

Passers-by and people who worked in the building were edging forward to check out the crash, only to reel away at the sight of Matt and his handgun. He ignored them and rounded the side of the van, knees bent in a wide, low stance, eyeing the van's doors and windows cautiously, looking for any sign of life. The front was badly mashed up, and Matt was pretty sure he wouldn't be getting any grief from there. He side-stepped away to the back of the van, extended an arm across one of its back doors, and rapped on it with his gun. He pulled his hand back quickly, anticipating a few rounds through the bodywork. None came. He reached over and pulled the door open then swung across, looking down the gunsight of the P14.

Rydell was in there, writhing on the floor, shaken up but alive. His hands were held by nylon cuffs. He saw one of the guys he recognized from the hotel, his head bloodied, trying to straighten himself up. The guy glanced up, saw Matt, blinked twice, and fumbled for a gun. Matt squeezed off a round and saw a red splatter burst out from the guy's chest.

'Come on,' he yelled at Rydell, who nodded vaguely like someone who'd been in a solitary confinement sweatbox for a month. As Matt reached in to him, he saw something else. Another body, lying facedown behind Rydell. A woman. Her hands were tied behind her back, same nylon cuffs. Matt climbed in and, carefully, turned her over. She had a fat piece of duct tape covering her mouth. He peeled it off and recognized her instantly. Gracie Logan, the news anchor who'd been covering the sign's appearances. He reached in farther and put his fingers to her neck, looking for a pulse. She was alive.

She stirred at his touch, then flinched, her eyes wide with shock.

'Where are . . . ? Who . . . ?' she mouthed incoherently.

'Give me your hand,' Matt told her as he tucked the P14 under his belt. He helped her up and slung her arm over his shoulders.

'Come on,' he told Rydell. He half-carried Gracie as he cut past a gaggle of dumbstruck onlookers, down the steps to the waiting Navigator. He set her down in the backseat, got in behind the wheel with Rydell beside him, and powered away.

In the rearview mirror, Matt saw Gracie straighten up. She was slowly coming out of it. Her eyes swept across her surroundings before settling on Matt's face.

'You okay?' he asked her.

She stared at him blankly. She looked like she had the mother of all hangovers. Then things must have come flooding back, as her face tightened up with a worried frown.

'Dalton,' Gracie blurted. 'I've got to get Dalton out of there.'

'Who?'

Her hands were rummaging around, looking for something. 'My phone. Where's my phone? I have to call Dalton. It isn't safe.' She turned to Matt. 'I have to warn him.'

Matt looked down the street, saw a bank of phone booths, and pulled over. He helped Gracie out. 'Where are we going? Where shall I tell him to go?' she asked.

'Who are you talking about?'

'Dalton. My cameraman. They'll be going after him too.'

Matt tried to fill in the blanks. 'Where is he?'

'At Darby's mansion,' she said, her expression vague, as if she wasn't exactly sure.

'The preacher?'

'Yes.' She concentrated hard. 'No. Wait. I'm not sure.' She shook her head. 'He went to the airport,' she added after a beat. 'Yeah, I'm pretty sure of that. Either way, he's on his cell.' She picked up the handset. 'What'll I tell him?'

Matt gave it a quick thought. 'Just tell him to get somewhere safe. If he's still out, tell him to stay away from the preacher's place. We'll call him back and tell him where to meet us.'

She started to dial, then paused and studied him curiously, her eyes still foggy, and asked, 'Who the hell are you?'

'Just make the call,' he told her. 'We'll get to that later.'

CHAPTER 73

They were all scattered around the motel room, a motley crew of haggard escapees: Matt, Gracie, Dalton, and Rydell. A week earlier, apart from Gracie and Dalton, none of them had met. They hadn't even come close. They had roamed completely separate spheres, lived disparate lives, had different ambitions and concerns. And then everything had changed, their lives had been upended, and here they were, crammed into the small room, wondering how to stay alive.

Dalton had joined them at the motel, arriving not long after they had. They'd spent the next couple of hours filling each other in on how they'd ended up in that room, each contributing his or her part of the story. The conversation had been urgent and intense as the different pieces had fallen into place, the string of troubling news only brightening up when Rydell had gotten through to the doctor treating Jabba back in Boston. The surgery had been successful. Jabba had lost a lot of blood, but he was stable, and his prognosis was cautiously optimistic.

'What do we do now?' Dalton asked. He still looked spooked, having only just found out that Finch had been murdered, and that the likely suspect was a monk they'd been palling around with.

'I keep thinking of Father Jerome,' Gracie remarked, shaking her head. 'He knew something was wrong. I could see it in his face.' She turned to Rydell. 'You don't know what they've done to him?'

'I don't know the grim details,' Rydell admitted. 'I didn't want to hear about it when they brought it up. They mentioned stuff. About using drugs. Electroshock therapy. Implanting memories and adjusting character. To make him more accepting of his new status, I guess.'

'Nice,' Dalton said with an uneasy wince.

'He said he heard voices. Up on the mountain. He thought God was talking to him,' Gracie mentioned.

Rydell nodded thoughtfully. 'They would have used an LRAD on him. A long range acoustical device,' he speculated. He slid a glance at Matt. 'Same thing they used on me at the hotel. It can also send sound accurately over long distances. Like a sniper rifle, only for noise – or voices,' he explained. 'They were talking to him through it.'

A pensive silence smothered the room.

After a brief moment, Gracie glanced over to Rydell. 'You really thought you could get away with this?' she asked him. Her voice was flat. She was still in shock at Ogilvy's betrayal. At the thought of how she'd been played. At the idea of Finch having been killed because of this.

'I had to do something,' he said with a tired shrug. 'People aren't listening. They're too passive. Too lazy. They don't listen to reason until it's too late. They don't want to listen to politicians. They certainly don't want some tree-hugger in Birkenstocks telling them how to live. They won't take the time to read or to listen to the experts. Look at the financial meltdown. Experts have been warning about it for years. Buffett called derivatives "financial weapons of mass destruction." No one listened. Then it all fell apart overnight.' He looked around the room, as if looking for a hint of understanding, if not empathy. 'I couldn't just sit back. This isn't about your 401(k) losing half its value. It isn't about losing your home. It's about the planet losing its ability to sustain life.'

'It's like Finch said. It's all in the branding,' Dalton remarked, throwing a glance at Gracie. '"Global warming" sounds way too nice and cozy. They should have called it global boiling.'

'It's geocide,' Rydell said before leaning back into the darkness.

A couple of nods sent the tired room back into silence. Gracie finally broke through the weary haze again and asked Rydell, 'If you weren't going to be the fall guy . . . do you agree with what Drucker said? With what they're trying to do?'

Rydell thought about it for a moment and gave a pained shake of his head. 'I agree with what he thinks is wrong with our country. History's shown us, time and again, that mixing religion and politics only brings destruction. And I have no doubt that it's a real danger, maybe more dangerous than anything Homeland Security is worried about. But I don't agree with his solution. And I certainly don't agree with his methods.' He looked around the room. 'No one was supposed to get hurt. Drucker's just out of control. And he's not done. Who knows what message he'll choose to put into Father Jerome's mouth before he's through. He could make him say or do anything he likes. And the whole world's listening.'

'We've got to stop him,' Gracie put in. 'We've got to go live with what we know.'

'No,' Matt said flatly from the corner of the room.

Gracie turned to him. 'What are you talking about? We've got to go public.'

Matt shook his head. 'We can't break the story. Not yet. If we do that now, they'll kill Danny. I need to get him out first, make sure he's safe. After that, you can slap it on the front page of *The New York Times* or wherever you want. It's all yours.'

'You heard what they're planning, Matt,' Gracie argued. 'The show's tomorrow. It's going to be huge – and it'll be watched across the planet. And you've seen what's going on out there. People are buying into it, fighting over it. Every hour we wait, this thing's sinking in deeper. If we wait until after the show to blow the lid off this thing, it might be too late to undo the damage it'll have caused.'

'Once that happens, we'll be kind of doing their work for

them if we expose it, won't we?' Dalton asked. 'I mean, that's their plan, right?'

'We don't have a choice,' Gracie pointed out. 'It's not ideal, but we have to do it and we have to do it now.'

'They can't expose it,' Matt countered. 'Not yet. Not as long as they don't have you,' he said as he chucked a nod at Rydell. 'They don't have their fall guy, right? So who are they going to blame it on? They've got to blame it on someone – someone without a political axe to grind. Plus as long as they don't have you locked up,' he aimed his words at Rydell again, 'they'd be running the risk of you coming out with your side of the story. They'd be screwed. They've got some figuring out to do before they tell the world it's a setup.'

'Which they will, sooner or later, there's no doubt about that,' Gracie interjected. 'No way they'd let this run indefinitely. They'd be handing the Christian Right the keys to the kingdom. And we can't let that happen either.'

Matt paused at the thought. There didn't seem to be a way out, and although all he could think about was getting his brother back safely, he suddenly realized there were bigger considerations he couldn't shy away from.

He chewed over it for a moment, then said, 'We've got a small window before they figure out their fallback position, right?' He glanced over to Rydell. 'They might even be wondering if you'll keep quiet. As a trade-off for getting your green message out there.'

'They'd be wrong,' Rydell confirmed without hesitation.

'Either way, they won't do anything yet. Not until they come up with another endgame that doesn't leave them holding the bag. Which gives me a bit of time to try and get Danny back. Even if it means letting them put Father Jerome up on that stage. You can't ask me to give up on him. Not when I'm so close.'

He looked around the room. The others glanced at each other, weighing his words.

He looked at Gracie. She held his gaze, then nodded warmly.

'The country's already well on its way to buying it,' she finally said. 'Tomorrow night will make it harder to come back from, sure, but . . . we can hold off till then. Besides, it seems to me that none of us would still be around if it wasn't for Matt. We owe him that much.'

She glanced around, judging the others' reactions. Rydell and Dalton each nodded their agreement. Her eyes ended up settling on Matt.

He smiled and gave her a small nod of appreciation.

'Okay, so how do we do it?' Gracie asked him.

'How do we do what?'

'Find your brother.' She caught his confused look and flashed him a slight grin. 'What, did you think we were going to bail on you now?'

Matt glanced around the room again. Saw beaming support from everyone around him. Nodded to himself, accepting it. 'We've got to assume they're going to put a sign up over Father Jerome tomorrow, right?'

Gracie nodded. 'No doubt about that.'

'Then that's how we'll do it.'

They stayed up most of the night, studying maps, plans, and photographs of the stadium pulled from the Internet, examining its layout and the spread of the surrounding area, trying to anticipate where Danny and the launch team were likely to be positioned.

By dawn, they felt they'd reached a consensus on how Drucker's guys might try to stage it. They'd pretty much followed Rydell's lead. Having the guy who'd been in charge of the sign's technology gave them a nice head start, but there were still a lot of unknowns. Then as the first glints of sunlight broke through the darkness, the TV started showing cars and people already setting out on their pilgrimage, and they knew they had to get going too.

They loaded up the little gear they had into the back of the Lincoln. After they were done, Matt saw Gracie standing alone, down the walkway from their room, at the edge of the porch, staring out at the brightening sky. He ambled over and joined her.

'You okay?'

She studied him, then nodded. 'Yeah.' She studied him for another beat, then looked away again. 'It's so weird. To think of how divided the country's become. To think that people need to resort to . . .' She shook her head. 'When did we become so hateful? So intolerant?'

'Probably around the same time some power-crazed douche bags decided it would help them win elections,' he quipped.

She smiled and let out a slight chuckle. 'Now why doesn't Brian Williams ever put it in those terms?'

Her expression darkened as an eclipse crossed over her face.

'What are you thinking about?' Matt asked.

'Father Jerome. He's . . . you couldn't ask for a more decent human being. To think of the hell they must have put him through . . .'

Matt nodded thoughtfully. 'It's not going to be easy for him. When this thing breaks.'

Gracie stared at him, and her face flooded with concern. 'His whole belief system's going to get wiped out.'

'I think it's more than his belief system you need to worry about,' Matt said. 'You're going to need to get him into some kind of protective custody. They'll rip him to shreds.'

Gracie shrank back, winded by the thought. 'We're damned if we do and damned if we don't, aren't we?'

Matt shrugged. 'We don't really have a choice. We have to do this.'

'You're right.' Gracie relented, although it was clear from her haunted look that it wouldn't be that simple.

Matt let a moment pass, then said, 'I want to thank you. For backing me up in there. And for not bailing on me.'

She waved it away. 'After everything you've been through? I owe you my life.'

'Still, I know it wasn't easy,' he insisted. 'Putting the scoop of a lifetime on hold. I mean, there's no doubt you'd be the biggest face on television right now if you walked into any newsroom and just told them what you know.'

'Just how shallow do you think I am?' She smirked.

'Not shallow, just . . . realistically ambitious.'

Gracie smiled and looked wistfully into the distance. 'My Woodward and Bernstein moment,' she chortled, self-mockingly. She laughed inwardly. 'It's like, all your life, you wait for a big moment like this, you hope for it and you work hard to make it happen, you imagine it and picture yourself basking in its glory . . . then when it actually happens . . .'

'When it comes out, it'll change everything for you, you know,' he told her. 'And not necessarily for the better.'

She glanced over at him. 'I know.' Her eyes had lost their disarming sparkle. For something every reporter dreamed about, it was starting to feel more like a nightmare.

He nodded, not really wanting to explore the darker side of what lay ahead. He pushed out a slight, comforting smile. 'Come on. Let's see how the rest of the day turns out first. And take it from there.'

CHAPTER 74

The roads were already jammed by early morning. Miles of cars, streaming in from every direction, choking the Loop and the South Freeway and all the approach roads leading to the stadium at Reliant Park. It was unlike anything the city had seen before. Unlike anything any city had seen before: an antlike procession of packed cars squatting over every square inch of available asphalt for miles around and converging on the biggest sports, entertainment, and convention complex in the country.

It was a clear, perfect day, and by noon, the temperature was in the high seventies and all the parking lots were filled. More than half a dozen of them, scattered around the stadium, the Astrodome, the arena, and the exhibition center. Over twenty-six thousand parking spots, every single one of them taken. The four-wheeled invasion didn't stop there. It spilled over into the vast, empty lot that used to house the Six Flags Astroworld before it was torn down in 2006. Seventy-five acres of flat, bare earth that nestled against the south side of the Loop, soil that was once the proud home of Greezed Lightnin' and the Ultra Twister, now shuddering under the rumble of an unstoppable flood of cars, trucks, and vans.

They came by car, by foot, by any means possible. MetroRail was running extra trains to try and cope with the crush, their cabins struggling to retain the heaving mass of flesh pressed against their walls. Helicopters were ferrying in news crews and reporters, all of whom were busy setting up their satellite dishes and hustling to get the best vantage points to cover the event. Police choppers circled overhead, keeping an eye on the teeming chaos below. The gates of the stadium itself were closed shortly after twelve. Seventy-three thousand people had already filed in by then, after spending hours in long lines, waiting to be frisked for weapons and cleared, the last of them pushing and shoving and fighting their way through in a desperate attempt to make it inside. A few angry, hysterical worshippers wouldn't take no for an answer and were creating scattered spots of trouble. Isolated brawls also broke out in the parking lots as cars jostled for position. Surprisingly, though, most of those who had made the journey were calm and well behaved. The police were doing a commendable job in marshaling the pilgrims around and keeping things civil. Darby's people had also brought in a small army of volunteers to manage the flows on the outside and to help those inside get settled. They were distributing free bottles of water and pamphlets promoting Darby's evangelical empire. The crowds in the parking lots, the ones who didn't make it into the stadium, weren't brooding over missing out. They'd come prepared and were already settling into a festive mood. The lots were brimming with tailgate parties. Turkey, eggnog, and carols were on offer everywhere. Whole families, young and old, people of all shapes and sizes and colors, were joined in one seamless celebration as a rolling wave of Christmas music wafted across the fields of multicolored sheet metal.

They left early, only pulling in briefly at a gas station to pick up some baseball caps and cheap sunglasses to shield their faces, and they still hit the jams. They passed a weathered billboard that said 'Let's meet on Sunday at my house before the game. – God,' and shortly after, the stadium appeared in the distance.

That first glimpse of it, all the way from the freeway, cut through Matt's weariness and gave his spirits a boost. Even at that distance, it was clear that the roof was open. It was the NFL's first retractable-roof stadium, a staggering 500-foot-long and 385-foot-wide sunroof. The big trusses that held it up were far apart, with one side resting over each end zone. Seeing them spread open like that sent a quickening rush through his veins. If they were open, it meant there was a strong chance the sign would be making an appearance. He felt he was getting closer to Danny. He was daring to hope that he might actually see his brother alive again. It felt good to think about that, especially after everything he'd been through over the last few days.

The cars weren't moving. Matt and Gracie left Rydell and Dalton in the big silver SUV and walked the rest of the way. As they approached the center, Matt cast his eyes across the huge complex and tried to fit Rydell's read of the situation onto it: having the launchers outside the stadium and the transmitter inside. The reasons Rydell had drawn that conclusion were simple. It was hardly likely that the compressed air launchers would be placed anywhere near the crowds inside the stadium, or within its walls. In such close proximity, someone was bound to notice the large canisters shooting up into the sky, no matter how silent they were. On the other hand, the laser transmitter that gave life to the motes and controlled the sign's appearance had to be inside the stadium. In imagining how Drucker and his people would stage the event, they were certain that, at some point, the sign would appear within the stadium's envelope. And if that were the case, a beam from anywhere outside the stadium wouldn't be able to reach inside. This wasn't great news. It meant they had to have a look inside – without any weapons, given the security searches at the gates. Of some solace was the fact that it was likely the plotters would want the sign to appear over the stadium as well. That helped narrow down the possibilities. There weren't too many positions inside the stadium from which a transmitter would have a sight line that would allow it to track something as huge as the sign upward through the roof and out into the sky overhead.

The question was, would Danny and his master board be with the transmitter, or the launchers? Or, equally possible, somewhere else altogether?

That third possibility wasn't worth thinking about. As for the first two, they knew it was going to be difficult to cover both angles. They didn't have the manpower, and their limited efforts would be slowed down significantly by the crush of people. As far as the launchers were concerned, the good news was that there weren't that many places they could be. The stadium was surrounded by acres of parking lots on all sides, which were surely too visible to launch from. The bad news was, the few possible spots where they might be were so far apart that covering all of them in the short window of time they had to do it in would be impossible.

That was why they planned to split up. Matt and Gracie would comb the stadium for the transmitter, while Rydell and Dalton would scour the area outside for the launchers.

They braved the onslaught and stood patiently in line and finally made it into the stadium shortly before the gates came down. Nearby, Rydell and Dalton were worming their way to the parking lots and maneuvering the SUV to the east end of the red zone, by Reliant Center. They ended up tucking it into a slot at the far end of the lot, by the fence, somewhere they hoped they'd be less noticed.

Once inside, Matt and Gracie advanced with caution. The noise and the energy inside the stadium overwhelmed them the minute they stepped in. The building itself was staggeringly large, a monumental glass-and-steel coliseum for the twenty-first century. With its roof wide open and the clear sky overhead, it was simply breathtaking. What greeted them within its cavernous embrace was unlike anything Matt or Gracie had experienced. Every single seat was occupied. Tens of thousands of people, talking and laughing and singing and waiting. A hodgepodge cross-section of

Americana, all of them united by a common yearning. Ducktailed older men standing side by side with teenage mallrats. Middle-aged couples, holding hands or carrying young clones on their shoulders. Yuppies in chinos and polo shirts alongside plumbers in stained overalls. Well-coiffed Texas matrons with elegant European scarves next to big-haired strippers in sequined cowboy hats. Whites, blacks, and Latinos of all shapes and sizes, all of them punch-drunk with anticipation, giddy at the idea of being in the presence of a new messiah, cheerful and fired up, hugging and kissing and waving and chatting and singing along to the sounds of Casting Crowns and Bethany Dillon that blared overhead.

Looking down at the stadium floor spread out below them, it was clear to Matt that their initial read of the layout was correct. A large stage had been erected in its center. The area around it was off-limits to the public. A knot of TV news crews, reporters, and photographers were busy setting up around the stage. TV programming across the country, if not the world, was likely to be preempted when Father Jerome got on stage. Matt glanced up at an overhead clock. It was one o'clock. According to Darby's impromptu invitation, the festivities were due to start at five. That gave him and Gracie four hours to do their sweep. It sounded like a lot of time, but it wasn't. The place was enormous. And although the sheer size of the crowd was working in their favor as far as giving them some kind of cover, it wasn't making their task any easier. Getting across the main concourse had taken forever due to the human obstacle course they had to get through. It was like swimming in molasses. The density of the crowd was also masking what lay beyond the bobbing heads and jousting bellies, even for someone of Matt's six-foot-four stature.

Matt's eyes circled around, taking in the tiers of seating that soared about him, looking for a transmitter so small you could hide it in an overhead baggage compartment.

'Where do we start?' Gracie asked.

Matt shrugged. It was a daunting task. He needed to narrow down the search area if they were going to stand a chance. He thought back to the assumptions they'd made. The stadium was a pretty standard shape, a fat rectangle with the long sides arcing outward. It had several levels of seating: five tiers of raked arena seating, intercut by three banks of suites that ran along the sidelines on the second, fourth, and top levels. Matt looked around, trying to picture the invisible cone of the laser signal that would be animating the smart dust. He tried to visualize the sign appearing inside and overhead, and worked back from there to suss out where the best vantage point would be for the transmitter. The banks of suites caught his eye. They provided both the right coverage and privacy. Matt discounted the ones on the highest level. They were tucked away under the sides of the roof. It didn't seem to him that they'd allow enough of an angle to control the sign if the plan was to have it over the stadium. That left the two lower levels of suites to check out, on levels four and two, and the club suites on level three. One bank along each sideline. Six banks of suites in total.

'Up there,' he said, pointing at the upper suites. They'd start up there and work their way down.

Gracie nodded, and followed him out of the seating blocks and back onto the main concourse and the stairwells.

In a far corner of the parking lot, Dalton clicked the Draganflyer's black carbon fiber rotor blades into place and tightened the harness around the airborne camera. He'd recharged its lithium battery overnight, and it was all set to go. He had it laid out on the back deck of the Navigator, away from curious eyes. As he got it ready, he kept looking out, glancing around suspiciously, wary of any danger. He couldn't help it. The idea that Finch had been murdered so ruthlessly and effortlessly was still gnawing at him. Militias and angry mobs in Middle Eastern or African countries he could deal with. Silent, anonymous killers in black robes who snuck up behind you and threw you off roofs – the thought made him shudder.

He checked the remote control unit again. Felt satisfied that he hadn't missed any connections, then set it aside and checked his watch. Less than three hours to go. Even though it would have been really useful to scan the surrounding areas, they'd decided not to use the skycam before the sign came up. It was too risky. They didn't want some overexcited pilgrim or the cops – or Drucker's men for that matter – to blast it out of the sky. Instead, he and Rydell were going to recon the area around the stadium on foot, doing opposite sweeps from the edge of the parking lots, until it got dark.

He looked around. It wouldn't be easy. The lot was heaving with cars and people, huddled against the soaring wall of the stadium. Dalton shrugged, tried to get the image of Finch being shoved off the roof out of his mind, and set out to begin his search.

Keenan Drucker glanced at his watch. Two hours to go. He frowned. Things weren't going well. Not well at all.

Losing Rydell was a huge blow. Drucker hated being in that position. Right now, he couldn't read the man's state of mind. There had been too many upheavals. Rydell had to be unhinged, and unhinged meant unpredictable or, worse, irrational. Would he act impulsively and bring the whole thing down on them all, even if it destroyed him in the process? Or would he retreat and regroup and try to come up with a way out that kept him in the clear?

Drucker wasn't sure. He hoped it would be the latter. That would also give him time to regroup. Time to come up with an alternative. Because right now, he needed one.

He frowned, his eyes burning into the framed portrait of his son that stared back at him from the edge of his desk. He felt like he was failing him. Failing his memory, failing to make up for his pointless death.

I won't fail you this time, he insisted inwardly, his fists clenching tightly, choking the blood out of them and turning them a deathly shade of white.

'We might need to bring our plans forward,' Maddox's voice prompted him from his speakerphone. The soldier sounded bleak, defeated. Not a tone of voice he was used to hearing from him.

'We can't do that,' Drucker grumbled. 'Not with Rydell running around out there. Any sign of his daughter?'

'No,' Maddox said. 'The plane dropped her off in L.A. She's not using her cell or her credit cards. She's out of play for the time being.'

Drucker sighed. 'They'll go for the brother. That's all Sherwood cares about. Are you all set for that?'

Maddox just said, 'We're ready.'

'Then finish it,' Drucker ordered him, and hung up.

CHAPTER 75

Afternoon turned to evening as the sky overhead went from bright blue to a soft pink and the clocks skipped past five o'clock. Matt and Gracie still hadn't found anything. They'd worked their way down from the top of the stadium without success. The show was about to start, and they still had a lot of ground to cover.

Checking out the suites wasn't easy. For this unscheduled event, all the seating in the stadium was free – except for the suites. Matt and Gracie quickly found out that most of those had been allocated to Darby's personal guests, some to the media, and the remainder to the guests of the other preachers that Darby had invited to share the stage with him. Access to the suites sections was restricted and tightly controlled by beefy security guys in black sweatshirts who knew all the scams. Still, Gracie managed to get into both banks of suites on the fourth and club levels by charming some bona fide invitees and tagging along with them, dragging Matt with her. They swept through them, all forty-five suites in each bank, on the lookout for any high-tech gear or for men who didn't look like they were there for a spiritual experience. They didn't find either.

They had just cleared the first bank of suites on the club level when the music faded down and the lights dimmed. Everyone pushed forward for a closer view. Matt and Gracie edged closer. A chorus of voices rose on the overhead speakers and the reverend's hundred-member choir filed onto the stage, taking up their positions solemnly as they sang 'Let There Be Light.' The crowd erupted wildly, clapping and cheering before joining in. The effect was remarkable. Seventy thousand voices, all singing together, soon accompanied by the countless thousands of others outside the stadium's walls, a chorus of worship echoing across the Houston twilight.

Matt frowned. Father Jerome's appearance was drawing near, and they still hadn't found any trace of Danny or of the guys who were holding him. Matt had to make some decisions. He had to go for the likeliest spots and forget about the rest. There wasn't enough time. He scanned the dark stadium, and settled on two target areas beyond the bank of suites they were still checking out: the two banks of suites on level two. Each bank had thirty-nine suites in it, which would take time to vet. They'd have to forgo the main seating tiers and hope for the best.

The singing ended and Darby strolled out onto the stage, basking in the wild applause. Massive overhead video screens beamed a close-up of his face across the stadium.

'Greetings in Christ,' he boomed, drawing the same words back from the excited masses.

Matt and Gracie weren't going to stick around for his speech. They slipped back through the suite and pressed on with their sweep.

They advanced slowly, checking out the rest of the floor. Half an hour later, they'd come up empty-handed. Two other megapastors had come on stage in the meantime, delivering rousing sermons to tumultuous cheers. In between their speeches, the choir sang backup to some of the biggest names in Christian rock. Matt and Gracie descended to the level three concourse and were on their way to level two when Gracie suddenly gasped and spun around and ducked into the cover of Matt's bulk.

'What?' he asked.

She peered out, then slipped out of view behind him again. 'Ogilvy,' she said. 'He's right there.'

Matt's fists clenched. 'Which one?'

'Slick guy, by the concession stand. Graying hair, rimless glasses. He's in a light-colored suit.'

Matt scanned the crowd. The concourse was filled with wall-to-wall people. A couple of heads parted and he caught a glimpse of someone fitting Gracie's description. 'Come on,' he said in a low voice as he took Gracie's hand and cut through the crowd behind Ogilvy. He lost him, then saw him appear again, about fifteen yards ahead, heading for the suites. The fact that Ogilvy was about five-six wasn't helping. Matt tried to press ahead, but the crush of people was like quicksand. He saw a small opening in the crowd and nosed into it, only to slam into a couple of tall rancher types who were cutting across him on their way back from the concession stands. One of them spilled his beer all over his shirt and shoved Matt back angrily.

'Watch your step, doofus,' the man snapped. 'What's your rush?'

Matt's arm tightened and his eyes narrowed and he was about to pounce, but Gracie held him back and subdued him with a forced smile.

'Easy, big guy.' She turned to the angry rancher and cranked her flirt look up to eleven. 'No damage done, boys. What do you say we just forgive and forget and go back to enjoying the sermons. It *is* Christmas, right?'

Matt held back and waited for the other guy to nod. The rancher scowled, thinking about it, then grudgingly gave him a tiny bob of the head. Matt nodded back, took Gracie's hand, and pulled her into the throng of people, but he couldn't see Ogilvy anywhere. He craned his neck and hoisted himself on the tips of his toes and scanned around intently.

There was no sign of him.

Out at the edge of the red lot, Rydell and Dalton watched with awe as the crowd rose into song and settled down again. Some of them had brought small 12-volt-powered TV sets with them, and clusters of people were massed around each set, listening to the sermons and responding with the occasional 'Amen.'

Rydell cast his gaze across the plain of cars, then looked up at the sky. The last glints of daylight had dipped down behind the horizon. 'Let's send it up,' he said. 'We can't wait much longer.'

Dalton brought the Draganflyer out of the Lincoln and set it down on the ground. He checked the light and flicked the HD video camera under its belly to night-vision mode. He then switched the Draganflyer's engines on, glanced around, and guided it up. It rose quickly with the silent whirr of a high-powered household cooling fan and disappeared in the night sky.

Rydell studied the area around them, trying to divine where he would put the launchers. To their right were some low-lying structures, on the other side of Kirby Drive. 'Let's send it out over those buildings over there,' he said, pointing in that direction. Then he seemed to have second thoughts. He shifted his gaze over to the stadium. Something about its north-south axis was tugging at his mind. His eyes narrowed a touch, and he said, 'Actually, send it up there,' pointing behind them, north of the stadium. He checked the image the skycam was sending back onto Dalton's laptop. It had that ghostly, pale-green night-vision look, but the high-definition processor was doing its job and the detail was surprisingly clear. 'And keep your eyes on that screen.'

'Dammit,' Matt hissed. 'We've lost him.'

His eyes scoured the concourse around him. Ogilvy had vanished into the crowd.

'The network,' Gracie blurted. 'Maybe they wrangled a suite here. Maybe that's how they brought the transmitter in.'

'Makes sense. But how do we find out where it is? I didn't see any guest lists. It's all a big mess in here.'

They also had another problem. There were two banks of

suites on level two, but they were at opposite ends of the stadium. One was to the east, facing the Astrodome. The other faced west. Getting across from one to the other meant they'd have to get through another human swamp.

'We won't have time to check both banks,' Gracie said.

Just then, the music changed into a deep, heraldic burst of brass and the lights across the stadium dimmed again. The crowd hushed to a bone-chilling silence. The air was thick with nervous expectation. And Darby reappeared on stage, welcomed by a thunderous uproar. He milked it for almost a minute before raising a calming hand and asking the crowd, 'Are you ready?'

The answer was a thunderous 'Yes.'

'My fellow children of Christ, please give a warm Houston welcome and open your hearts to our special guest, Father Jerome.' Every single person in the stadium was standing up, clapping and cheering rapturously as the slight figure of Father Jerome appeared. He looked unimaginably small on the huge stage, shuffling forward slowly, looking around at the crowd in awe, dwarfed by his own image on the overhead video displays. A blinding fusillade of flashbulbs accompanied him as he padded across to the center of the stage and gave Darby a small, courteous bow. Darby ushered him over to a microphone stand and waved him on before retreating a few steps into the shadows.

Matt and Gracie stood there, rooted to the floor, transfixed by the crowd's reaction. The entire stadium reverberated with an air of majesty. Gracie watched the close-up of Father Jerome's face on the screens. He was looking up, taking in the scene, clearly overwhelmed by the sheer scale of it all. Droplets of sweat were sliding down his forehead. He didn't seem to know what to say. The whole crowd was on its feet and just stood there, silent, hanging on what God's messenger would proclaim. He cleared his throat with a small cough, looking around slightly fearfully – and then his expression changed, as if he'd been mildly startled by something. He cocked his head a little and his eyes blinked, then he swallowed and said, 'Thank you all for being here and for welcoming me here tonight.'

The crowd responded exuberantly with 'Amens' and applause.

As Father Jerome embarked on his sermon down below, an idea burst through the chaos in Matt's mind. 'I need to call Rydell,' he told Gracie. 'Quick.'

Gracie had Dalton's cell phone with her. Rydell still had his. She speed-dialed him and passed the phone to Matt.

Rydell picked up on the first ring.

'Do you have the skycam up?' Matt asked, his tone urgent.

Rydell was eyeing the screen on Dalton's laptop closely. 'It's over the medical center, just north of here,' he informed him. 'Nothing so far.'

'What happens to its video downlink if it crosses into the transmitter's signal?' Matt asked breathlessly.

'It would interrupt it, for sure,' Rydell speculated.

'It wouldn't mess it up so it couldn't fly, would it?'

Rydell thought about it for a beat, then said, 'It might. The laser signal could override the signal from the skycam's remote controller. We could lose control of it while it's in the beam's path. Might fry it altogether.'

Dalton flashed him a concerned look.

Matt's voice shot back. 'We've got to risk it. Send it over to us, inside the stadium. It's the only way we're going to find out where their signal's coming from.'

'Okay,' Rydell said, spinning a finger horizontally in the air to Dalton and gesturing at the stadium. 'Let's just hope it gets there in one piece.' He turned to Dalton, and told him, 'We're going in.'

Dalton used the screen to guide him and fingered the joysticks to turn the black skycam around. Rydell was huddled behind him, his attention riveted to the screen. As Dalton banked the Draganflyer around, he flinched and exclaimed, 'Did you see that?' He jabbed a finger at the screen, but the Draganflyer was zooming back and whatever he was pointing at was gone.

'What?' Dalton asked.

'There was something, back there.' He pointed at the top left-hand corner of the screen. 'On the roof. Can you flip the camera around so it's pointing backward?'

Dalton's face was tight with concentration as his fingers made micro-adjustments to the joysticks. 'Can't do a full one-eighty, it's just a forward sweep. I can spin it around and fly it backward, but it's gonna reach the stadium any second now and I don't want to risk it and fly blind.'

Rydell frowned and nodded. 'Okay, keep going. We'll come back to it.'

'If it's still flying by then,' Dalton worried.

Matt and Gracie scanned the rectangular opening of black sky and waited as Father Jerome finished his sermon.

'Matt, he's doing it,' she told him, pointing at the stage.

Matt looked down, the cell phone still on his ear. 'Come on, guys.'

'It's almost there,' Rydell said, clearly tense.

Down on the stage, Father Jerome tilted his head back and slowly raised his arms outward from his sides until they were slightly above the horizontal, as if he were about to catch a massive beach ball. The crowd shuddered and all eyes turned to the empty air under the stadium's open roof.

'Pray with me,' Father Jerome beseeched his followers. 'Pray with me that God gives us a sign and guides our thoughts and helps us do his will.'

Murmurs rose and lips quivered across the stadium as the crowd started to pray. And then a gasp reverberated throughout the giant hall as a ball of light appeared over Father Jerome. It was small, perhaps eight or ten feet in diameter, a swirling, cloudy sphere of light. An upwelling of flashbulbs lit up the tiers as the apparition just floated there for a few seconds, then started to rise. It reached the halfway point between Father Jerome's head and the stadium's full height and held there for a moment, blazing to a twinkling backdrop of thousands of flashbulbs, then it flared out and expanded into the now-familiar, massive sphere of brilliance.

The crowd was cowed into a nervous silence as the sign rotated before them. Then, like a breaking wave, euphoria rolled across the arena and the crowd erupted into a mighty roar, bigger than anything any touchdown at the stadium had ever generated. Amid wailing 'Amens' and 'Hallelujahs,' the massed faithful waved their arms and hugged their cheeks in adulation and awe. People were crossing themselves. Some people fainted, others wailed hysterically. Most just stared in disbelief while tears of joy ran down their faces.

Matt's skin tingled. It was the first time he'd seen it live, and its power blew him away. He had to keep reminding himself that it wasn't supernatural. That it was Danny's work. That his brother had played a crucial role in making it possible.

He could sense his presence. More than ever, he had to find him.

He looked up and hissed into the cell phone, 'Where is it?'

'It's in,' Rydell announced. 'It just dropped in from the north face of the opening.'

Matt stared up intently, straining to find the tiny black machine – then he spotted it. It was barely visible, its stealthy matte finish blending into the night sky, but it was there. He kept his eyes glued to it and sized up its position relative to the banks of suites. He decided to go for the east bank first.

'Okay, bring it down so it's by the lower end of the sign and take it around the stadium counterclockwise,' he told Rydell. 'And let me know the second you get any interference.'

'Got it,' Rydell acknowledged.

Out in the red lot, Rydell and Dalton watched the laptop's screen breathlessly as the Draganflyer dived into the stadium and circled the sign. All around them, clusters of people were huddled around those who'd brought portable TVs with them, watching the sign in breathless awe.

'Here we go,' Dalton mumbled, nervousness catching in his throat.

Matt struggled to keep the tiny contraption in view as it began its wide circular sweep around the inside of the stadium. The cell phone was glued to his ear and he could feel his pulse thumping against his cheek. Gracie was on alert too, scanning the entrance behind them, still wary of Ogilvy, uncomfortable with his presence there.

Across the stadium, the crowd was still enthralled by the sight before them. The sign was just hovering there, a gargantuan ball of shimmering energy. Matt's gaze kept getting drawn to it. It was incredibly hard to resist staring at it, and as soon as his eyes strayed over to it, he'd pull them away, back to the Draganflyer's last position, trying to stay focused on the tiny black dot.

The skycam had almost reached the southern tip of the east bank of suites when Rydell's voice shot into his ear.

'We've got something. Shit, we're losing it,' he shouted.

Matt's neck flinched forward, as if the extra couple of inches would make a difference. He saw the skycam go into a wobble, then it just arced down violently, as if it had suddenly lost all power or been smacked down by a big invisible swatter, and dropped like a rock.

Matt's heart skipped a beat as he saw it plummet, but his eyes raced back up and lasered in on the suites that faced its last stable position. They were the very last ones, at the southeast corner of the stadium.

'Come on,' he yelled to Gracie, grabbing her hand and bolting back onto the concourse, racing for the escalators.

'Shit,' Dalton yelled as he lost control of the Draganflyer, his heart pounding, his face clenched in panic, his fingers desperately playing the joysticks in search of a reaction.

The image on the laptop's screen fizzled out and was replaced by gray static, its accompanying hiss just making things worse.

'It's gonna fucking kill someone,' he blurted – then the image on the screen suddenly flickered back to life. It was unnerving – a plunging point-of-view from the camera as it dived at a rapidly growing crowd.

'Pull it up,' Rydell yelled.

'I'm trying,' Dalton fired back. The people in the camera's sights grew bigger, their eyes shot wide as they spotted the alien device hurtling toward them and their faces went taut with alarm – and then it came back to life and swooped away just over their heads, avoiding them and pulling up until it just hovered in place by the stadium's roof.

Dalton let out a huge breath of relief and darted a look of sheer delight at Rydell. 'Whose brilliant idea was that?' he asked, his voice shaky.

Rydell gave him a big pat on the shoulder. 'Great job, man. Great job. Now get it out of there and let's check out that building.'

A crescendo of excitement erupted around them. Rydell and Dalton moved back from the SUV's trunk and stared up at the top of the stadium as a wave of gasps rolled across the parking lot.

The sign was now rising slowly into the night sky, a curved sliver of light peeking out above the stadium's roof.

Matt leapt off the escalator onto level two and raced across the landing area that led to the entrance of the suites. Gracie was trailing close behind. The crowds were gone, there was no one around. Everyone was watching the miracle taking place in the arena. The bouncers were also gone, probably watching alongside the guests in one of the suites.

They were coming in from the north side, and the target suite was all the way down the concourse that ran behind the suites, at the south end of the bank. As Matt charged down the curving concourse, two things happened: He thought something must have changed in the arena as a chorus of *oohs* and *aahs* rippled through the suites' doors. And he saw a man walking his way, heading out of the suites area just as Gracie yelled out, 'Matt,' from behind him.

The guy had graying hair, rimless glasses, a light-colored suit, and looked slick. The recognition was mutual as Ogilvy flinched with surprise, but he didn't have time to do much else before Matt just slammed right into him without slowing down, grabbing him by the arms and spinning him and shoving him up hard against the concourse wall. Ogilvy let out a pained gasp as Matt's weight crashed into his back and winded him. Matt felt his wound light up with a spike of pain, but ignored it and belted Ogilvy with a punch to the kidneys. The man buckled forward under the pain. Matt was in overdrive. He didn't let up for a second. He just grabbed

Ogilvy's right arm, yanked it way up high behind him until it almost snapped, then shoved him forward and led him down the concourse at a half jog.

'Which one are they in?' he rasped.

Ogilvy's head was lolling left and right, like a boxer with cut eyes, teetering on his last legs.

'Which one?' Matt asked again, still rushing ahead. He knew the suite he wanted was one of the last ones in the row and didn't really need Ogilvy to answer. He figured the target suite wouldn't be like all the others. They all had their doors wide open, the clusters of people inside them all crowding the front barlike counter. Maddox's boys wouldn't be as welcoming, and their suite would have its door shut. Maybe even someone outside, on guard. Within seconds, they'd rounded the concourse. Sure enough, the last suite had its door closed. Matt pushed Ogilvy up against the door and rapped on it firmly while twisting Ogilvy's arm right up so his shoulder blade was about to pop out.

'Get them to open up, nice and friendly,' Matt hissed into his ear.

'Yeah?' came a low grunt from inside.

Ogilvy swallowed hard, then blurted, 'It's me, Ogilvy,' trying to sound unruffled but not quite pulling it off.

The guy behind the door must have hesitated, as he didn't open immediately, then the door cracked open. Matt lifted Ogilvy off his feet the second he heard the lock jangle, ripping his shoulder tendons in the process, and shoved him against the door like a vertical battering ram. The door slammed backward, hitting the guy standing behind it in the face. The doors to the suites were rock-solid and soundproof. The impact sounded like the guy had been pounded with a baseball bat. It knocked him off his feet and sent his gun flying out of his hand and tumbling heavily to the ground. Matt stormed in, keeping Ogilvy in front of him like a shield. His eyes registered two other guys in there, in addition to the guy on the ground. They were waiting for him and had silenced handguns trained on the door. Matt didn't slow down. He kept charging forward, holding Ogilvy in front of him, flying across the room in five long strides. Ogilvy jerked and flailed as several rounds cut into him, but the shooters didn't have that much time to fire before Matt was right on top of them. He launched Ogilvy at the one dead ahead of him and leapt across at the other shooter, catching his firing arm with his hands and pushing his gun away while landing a heavy elbow across his jaw. He heard it snap as he spun around, still gripping the guy's gun wrist with both hands and tracking it around through ninety degrees until it was facing the other shooter, who was busy pushing Ogilvy's bloodied body off of him. The two silenced handguns pirouetted around in unison to face each other, only the one under Matt's control got there a split second earlier and he squeezed hard against the guy's trigger finger. The handgun belched a round that caught the opposing shooter squarely in the neck. The guy recoiled as a burst of blood geysered between his shoulder blades, just as he let off a round of his own that whizzed by Matt and buried itself somewhere in the wall behind him.

Matt felt the shooter behind him squirm. He slammed his elbow back into him, mashing his throat. He felt the shooter's body go rigid as the man convulsed in a pained gurgle – then Gracie yelled, 'Matt,' again. He spun his gaze back toward the entrance to the suite and to the guy who'd taken the door in the face. Half his face was glowing an angry purply-red. It had to hurt. He was on his knees, straightening up, looking across at Matt. He'd just recovered his gun when Gracie screamed and just hurled herself at him, tackling him from the side. The shooter reacted fast – he just whipped up his arm and deflected her, sending her crashing against the wall behind him, but it bought Matt the precious seconds he needed to play puppet master again and raise the arm of the shooter behind him and fire off a couple of rounds into purple-face.

He took a second to catch his breath and let his heartbeat go back to something that vaguely resembled normal, then wrenched the handgun out of the shooter's hand, kicked him aside, and pushed himself to his feet. Gracie stood up, her face locked in shock, and stepped over to join him.

He cast his eyes around the suite, and a grim realization hit him. There was no transmitter in the room. No control master board. And no Danny either. He thought back to Ogilvy wandering around the stadium, to the shooters' position when he'd come through the door. It had been a trap. They were waiting for him, using Ogilvy to draw him in. The transmitter had to be nearby – the signal had come from that general area – but it didn't matter anymore. He was sure they wouldn't have risked having Danny inside the stadium. He had to be outside somewhere. That is, if he wasn't controlling the transmitter from across the state, or the whole country, for that matter.

Matt's heart sank. He frowned as Gracie took a couple of steps and looked out through the suite's floor-to-ceiling glass pane, into the heart of the arena. He edged over and joined her. The sign had risen through the open roof. Its bottom edge was just beyond the tangent to the roofline, dipping into the cube of empty air over the stadium floor. Father Jerome was still on the stage, his arms outstretched, mumbling a prayer. And every single person in the stadium was still standing.

A warble snapped his attention. It was Dalton's cell phone. Rydell was calling.

He picked it up.

'We think we've got them,' Rydell blurted out breathlessly. 'Get your ass out here. They're here.'

CHAPTER 77

'Where? What's going on?' Matt asked, his voice racing.

'There's a tall building that backs up against the entrance of the red lot on the north side,' Rydell said. 'Might be a hotel, I'm not sure. It's got a pool on one side and a parking lot all around it. There are four guys on the roof. They've got the launchers.'

The words were like an afterburner to his senses. He glanced out the glass wall. The sign was hovering over the stadium now. His mind rocketed back to Rydell telling him it could stay up around fifteen minutes before it burned out. He knew it wasn't long before it would vanish, and once that happened, the crew with the launchers would also be gone. Taking Danny – if he was there – with them.

'Where are you?' Matt asked.

'At the east end of the lot, by the Center.'

Matt was recalling the park's layout from the website they'd studied the night before. 'So if I come out the north gate—'

Rydell jumped in. 'Just head straight up across the lot and you'll hit it, it's about five hundred yards away.'

'I'm on my way. Keep this line open and keep me posted.' He turned to Gracie, his face alight with hope. 'They've got a fix on the launchers. I'm going after them.' He stepped over to the downed shooters, retrieved two of their handguns, and stuffed them under his belt. He pulled his shirt out and let it hang down to cover them. 'Come on. You get back to the car and wait with the guys.'

'You can't go after them alone,' she protested.

'Don't really have a choice,' he told her. 'We've got to go.'

*

Out in the red lot, Rydell and Dalton stood transfixed before the laptop's screen. The Draganflyer was in a holding pattern about two hundred and fifty feet over the target, its night-vision lens on full zoom. They were probably the only people for miles not to be staring at the blazing sign that had now cleared the stadium's roof and was hovering in the night sky above it. It was a mesmerizing, awesome sight, visible for miles around. The thousands of onlookers in the parking lots and on the jammed freeways were just rooted in place, utterly enthralled by the otherworldly apparition.

Rydell checked his watch. He knew what was coming, and sure enough, it happened almost on cue. The sign pulsed slightly, like a beating heart, then just faded out like a snuffed-out candle. The crowd reacted with an audible collective intake of breath and scattered cries of 'Praise the Lord' and 'Amen.'

He glanced at the screen. The guys on the roof were moving fast now, packing their gear. He knew how efficient they'd be. They didn't surprise him. Within a minute, they'd stowed the launch tubes and the rest of their gear and disappeared into the building.

'Come on,' he mumbled, almost to himself, and craned his neck, angling to get a better view of the stadium's north entrance, as if he could spot Matt, but the entrance was too far and his sight line was blocked by all kinds of tall vehicles. He glanced across at the north end of the lot and the big building that loomed over it, behind a row of trees. He shook his head ruefully, and made a quick decision.

'The guns are in the glove box, right?' he asked Dalton.

Before Dalton could answer, he'd already scurried over and pulled out the Para-Ordnance.

'What are you doing?' Dalton felt a stab of fear at the sight of Rydell holding the silver handgun.

Rydell flicked his eyes across at the stadium, then up at the building, then back at Dalton. He handed him his phone.

'I've got to help Matt. Stay with the car.' And before he could object, Rydell was gone.

Matt exploded out of the stadium's north entrance and just plowed on, with Gracie close behind. He reached the lot and stopped, shot a quick glance across the cars to get his bearings, and pointed Gracie in the direction Rydell had said the big SUV was parked.

'They should be around there somewhere, at the back.'

She nodded, and he was gone.

He sprinted through the rows of cars, SUVs, and pickup trucks, cutting around the clusters of revellers, twisting and ducking and weaving like a wide receiver charging the end zone and looking for his own Hail Mary pass. One and a half minutes later, he saw the last row of cars and the low perimeter fence of the lot. He threaded his way through a couple of camper vans and reached the fence, then stopped in his tracks at the sight of Rydell, waiting for him, breathing heavily. He joined him, catching his breath, nodding a question.

'Figured you could use some help,' Rydell said, lifting his jacket to expose the handgun he had tucked under his belt.

Matt tugged his shirttail up to give Rydell a glance of his own arsenal and gave him a slight grin. He held the phone up to his ear.

'Anything?' he asked.

Dalton's voice came back. 'No movement, but the lot on the south side of the building is crawling with people. They've got to have their car on the other – hang on.' He stumbled. 'Okay, we've got one, two, three – four guys, coming out of the east face of the building and heading for what looks like – it's a van, by the trees in the northeast corner of the lot.'

Matt snapped the phone shut and stuffed it in his back pocket. 'You know how to use it?' he asked, pointing at Rydell's silver handgun.

Rydell nodded easily. 'I'll manage.'

Matt flicked him an okay nod and took off for the trees.

They hurdled the low fence bordering the parking lot and cut across the scrub and the thicket of trees that led to the building. A neon sign informed Matt that it was a Holiday Inn. He led Rydell to the right, past the pool area and its terrace café. It was teeming with people, hotel guests who were now discussing the sign's appearance animatedly. They kept going, rounding the hotel and reaching its front parking lot.

Matt hugged the side of the building and looked out. The lot was wide and had poor lighting, and its far reaches were bathed in near-darkness. There was a row of cars, then a lane, then two rows of cars, another lane, and one last row of cars. He could make out the roof of the van all the way down, on the far right. It was parked facing the hotel, with its loading bay backing up against another thicket of trees that separated the hotel from the next property. He looked a question at Rydell. Rydell nodded his confirmation that it was the right van. Matt saw movement around it, figures silhouetted in the night. Saw one of them lifting a big tube and handing it to someone out of sight. He looked to Rydell again for confirmation. Rydell nodded. They were Maddox's men. Loading up.

Matt felt a tightening in his gut. Danny could be right there. Less than fifty yards away.

He pulled out his guns and handed one to Rydell.

'This one will be quieter than that cannon you've got there. Go wide that way,' he whispered, gesturing for Rydell to move in from the left. 'I'll cut across from the right. And stay low.'

Rydell confirmed with a slight nod and slipped away in a low crouch.

Matt crept closer to the van. He hugged the cars, slithering through the narrow gaps between them, his eyes locked on the target. It was a Chevy work van. The big, long-wheelbase model. White and anonymous. He heard one of its doors clang shut and saw one of the men stepping toward the back of the van. The others were out of sight behind it. Matt moved in closer, sucked in a deep breath, and rose just enough to clear the roof of the car in front of him, gripping his handgun in a two-handed stance, ready to pump a couple of silenced bullets into Maddox's men – but there was no one there. They were gone. His nerves bristled as he swept his gun left and right, his eyes and ears at Defcon one – then he heard a rustle off to the right, in the trees beyond the van, and saw a shooter emerge, pulling Rydell along with him, a silenced handgun pressed against the billionnaire's temple.

Matt flinched, unsure about what to do – just as something hard nudged him in the back.

'Drop it,' the voice said. 'Nice and slow.'

Matt's heart cratered. They'd been expected. For a split second, the notion of making a move sparked in his mind, but the guy behind him cut it short with a sudden, hard punch to Matt's ear that sent him down to his knees. He dropped his gun, and his vision went blurry. He stayed down for a moment, waiting for it to settle, and through his bleary veil, he glimpsed the vague outline of someone climbing out of the back of the van. It was Maddox, and – he wasn't alone. He was dragging someone out of the van with him, yanking him by the neck, a handgun pressed against it.

Matt squinted, straining to cut through the fog in his head, but even before it lifted, the recognition was instant.

It was Danny.

He was there. He was actually there.

And very much alive.

Matt's insides cartwheeled. He pushed himself to his feet, and the adrenalin boost coursing through him brought Danny's face racing into focus. He gave Matt a pained smile. Matt nodded back and couldn't suppress a broad smile, even though things weren't looking too promising for them.

Maddox acknowledged Matt's presence with a shrug, but his eyes registered genuine surprise when he saw Rydell.

'Well, what do you know,' he quipped, clearly pleased with the unexpected presence of the tycoon. 'And people say there is no Santa.'

Gracie flared. 'What are they doing?'

The image on the laptop's screen showed the two figures they knew to be Rydell and Matt putting their guns down and stepping back from the van in defeat. Seconds later, two other figures appeared from the van, tightly bunched, one behind the other.

'Is that a gun?' she asked, fear catching in her throat.

'Hang on,' Dalton said. He fingered the joysticks expertly and brought the Draganflyer down slightly closer for a better look.

The top view of Maddox's extended arm grew bigger on the screen. And there was no mistaking the gun that was staring Matt and Rydell in the face.

Danny grunted against Maddox's tight hold. 'I'm sorry, bro,' he told Matt. 'I couldn't warn you.'

'Don't worry about it.' He saw that Danny's hands were tied together with plastic flex cuffs.

Danny glared at Rydell. 'What's he doing here?' he asked Matt.

'His penance,' Matt replied flatly.

Danny shook his head sardonically. His stare burned into Rydell. 'Too little, too late, don't you think? Or do you also have the power to raise the dead?'

Rydell kept quiet.

Maddox swung his right arm straight out, flicking his handgun in a horizontal arc from Matt to Rydell and back.

'Sorry to have to cut this happy reunion short, boys,' he said tersely, 'but we've got to get going. So how about you say good-bye to your pain-in-the-ass brother one last time, Danny-boy.' He settled his gun sight on Matt and gave him a curious, almost respectful nod. 'It's been good knowing you, kid. You did really well.'

'Not well enough,' Matt retorted gruffly.

'No, believe me, you did real well,' he insisted.

Maddox raised the gun a couple of inches for a head shot, no emotion whatsoever registering on his face. Matt's heart stopped at the thought of a bullet shredding into him – then Maddox whipped back as something slammed into him from out of nowhere, something big and black that rocketed out of the night sky with a stealthy whoosh and batted his arm off savagely to one side. His gun went flying off as Maddox howled, the chopper's carbon fiber blades slicing through skin and muscle, and he fell to the ground in a burst of dark blood.

Matt was already moving as the Draganflyer crashed heavily into the van's open door – he rammed his elbow back into the shooter behind him, yelling, 'Go,' to Rydell as he spun around and pushed the man's gun hand away while battering him with a cross that ripped his jaw out of its sockets and sent him tumbling to the ground. Matt went down with him, fighting for the gun, but the man's hand was like a vise around his automatic and he wouldn't let go – they wrestled for it like starved, rabid dogs fighting over a bone, until the gun spat out a shot that caught the shooter in the gut and he flinched back in agony.

Rydell wasn't as quick or as effective – he was grappling with his shooter, his hands clasped around the man's wrist, struggling for the gun. The shooter pulled him in and suckered him into a head butt that caught Rydell flat across the bridge of his nose. Rydell's legs caved in and he ragdolled. Matt rose in time to see the shooter spin around, his gun rising to align itself on Matt –

– then the shooter jerked back to the tune of a couple of silenced coughs. Matt blinked. It took him a second to realize what had happened, then he saw Danny gripping Maddox's gun tightly, a thin tendril of smoke spiraling out of the muzzle of its silencer. Danny stared at the shooter's inert body for a beat, then turned to Matt, his face locked in disbelief at what he'd done –

Danny opened his mouth to say something –

Matt's eyes went wide –

'Watch out,' he blurted, but –

It was too late – Maddox had already sprung to his feet behind Danny. He crashed into him as Matt dived for the gun that had fallen from his shooter. Matt managed to grab it before Maddox made it to the gun Danny had dropped – only Danny was blocking a clear shot. Maddox's eyes met Matt's for a nanosecond before he shoved Danny toward Matt and scurried back away from them, and disappeared behind the van.

'Move,' Matt yelled to Danny, pushing him away, bolting after Maddox – he charged around the van and into the thicket of trees that edged the parking lot, but the darkness had swallowed his quarry up. Matt fired a couple of rounds out of frustration, but he knew he wasn't going to score a hit. Maddox was gone.

The lot went eerily quiet. Matt turned, scanned the area, then stepped around Rydell and his fallen shooter and joined Danny. He embraced him with a big bear hug. Pulled him back and ruffled his hair.

'Merry Christmas,' he told him.

'Best one ever,' Danny replied, his face all lit up with nervous relief. Rydell got up and joined them. Danny faced him for a beat, a hard, angry glare simmering in his eyes. Then he balled his fists and whipped up his still-tied arms in a big, curving swing that caught Rydell on the cheek and knocked him to the ground. Rydell spat out some blood, but stayed down for a moment. Then looked up at Danny, who was just looming over him.

Matt looked on curiously. 'I couldn't have made it here without his help, bro,' Matt told Danny.

Danny eyed Rydell a couple of more seconds, then turned away and shrugged dubiously. 'It's a start,' he grunted.

'Can we get out of here now?' Matt asked, stepping across to help Rydell up.

Rydell looked toward Danny. 'I'm sorry,' he said, his words laced with genuine regret.

'Like I said,' Danny said as he walked away, 'it's a start.'

Less than a minute later, they were in the van, pulling away from the hotel's parking lot and easing past the long rows of parked cars that lined the roads on both sides.

CHAPTER 78

They'd changed motels for safety, moving to a different side of town, just in case – although with Maddox badly hurt and a lot of his men dead, they were starting to feel like maybe the crosshairs had lifted off them a little.

Danny and Matt were in their own world. They had a lot of catching up to do and took turns filling each other in on their tortured journeys.

'I've got to call Mom and Dad, let them know I'm okay,' Danny said enthusiastically, still fired up by his escape.

Matt had skirted around mentioning them, but he couldn't duck it any longer. He held Danny's gaze as he tried to find the words to tell him what had happened, but Danny read his expression before he'd eked out a single word.

'Who? . . . Mom?' he asked.

Matt nodded, but his pained look held more portent than just one parent.

'Not . . . *both*?' Danny mouthed the words in total disbelief.

Matt nodded again.

Danny's face tightened, drowning with confusion. Then it just crumpled with profound grief. Matt had already told him about Bellinger's murder. The triple whammy hit him real hard. He sank to the floor and gripped his head in his hands, feeling as if his veins were flooding with lava.

A more somber mood enshrouded them as Danny told Matt of his despair during those two years. How he'd tried to sneak an e-mail out to him and been caught. How he'd contemplated suicide. How they'd threatened him and drugged him after that.

'You're here now,' Matt finally told him. 'You're out and you're safe.' Matt smiled. 'And that's way more than either of us had a couple of days ago.'

'Tell me more. About Mom and Dad. About how it all happened,' Danny asked him.

In an adjacent room, Rydell stewed alone. He'd found it as uncomfortable to be around Danny as Danny found it to be around him. He also had a lot on his mind.

It was over, that much was clear. Once Gracie returned, the story would blow wide open. And then, whichever way you looked at it, his life was over too. His role in it would be part of the story. A big part of it. There was no way anyone was going to shield him from it. Not Gracie, not Matt or Danny, not Drucker. And even if they'd wanted to, there was no way they'd be able to do it. Not in this blog-rich age. And he wasn't prepared to run either. It wasn't his style. Besides, there was nowhere for him to run to. No, he'd be there to face up to what he'd been a part of.

The hardest part of it all was thinking about what it would do to Rebecca. It would be nothing short of devastating. It would follow her for the rest of her life. His mind kept churning it, desperate to find a way to mitigate that, to keep her out of it, but there was nothing he could think of that could do that.

By the time Gracie and Dalton finally joined them a couple of hours later, the reunion was a bittersweet, subdued celebration. Yes, they were all safe. Yes, Danny was alive – and free. And Gracie and Dalton were about to become superstars. But there was a downside to the forthcoming media feeding frenzy too. A downside well beyond Rydell's very public downfall. One that looked far more daunting the more they talked about it.

In the background, a TV was switched on, replaying the evening's events in an almost continuous loop, with all kinds of talking heads coming in and out to comment on it.

'What's this going to do to all those people who were out

there celebrating tonight?' Gracie asked, pointing at the screen, her voice edgy with concern. 'And not just them, but everyone around the country who was tuning in. Everyone around the planet who's been buying into Drucker's scam, for that matter. What's going to happen to them? How are they going to take it?'

'What's the alternative?' Dalton countered. 'We can't let the lie run. We'd just be digging all those people a deeper hole for Drucker to push them into. The sooner we end this, the better.'

'I know.' Gracie nodded. 'It still feels wrong. It's lose-lose.' She rubbed the bridge of her nose, then spread her fingers out and massaged her forehead. 'I hate this,' she groaned.

'Finch was murdered because of it,' Dalton reminded her.

'Vince too,' Danny added. 'And Reece. And many others.'

Gracie heaved a ponderous sigh. 'They were killed to keep it quiet until Drucker was ready to pull the cover off. And now we're going to do it for him.'

'We have to do this,' Danny chimed in. 'The longer it runs, the more painful it will be when the truth comes out.'

Gracie nodded grudgingly, then said to Rydell, 'I'll need you to go on the record. We'll need the evidence.'

Rydell nodded somberly. 'What choice do I have?'

She shifted her gaze across the room. 'Danny?'

He nodded. 'Hell, yes.'

Gracie acknowledged it, then slumped back in her seat, a frustrated, haunted pallor to her face.

Rydell turned to Danny. 'How were they planning on doing this? Do you know? How were they going to expose him?'

'They made me design a debunking software. They were going to run it over him once they were ready to out him.'

Rydell pressed. 'What does it do?'

'It simulates a breakdown in the technology. Like if you're watching TV and the signal breaks up. It makes it go all

459

jumpy with static, then it just crashes. It's designed to be minimally counterintuitive. What you'd expect to see if the sign was a fake. It'll conjure up a broadcast that's going haywire.' Danny gave him an uncomfortable smile. 'It was either that or a huge Coca-Cola sign.'

'What if we don't do this and it never comes out?' Gracie threw in, thinking aloud. 'I mean, what if there was a way to get Drucker and his guys to keep their mouths shut?'

'The evangelicals would get to keep their new messiah, and Darby and his friends on the far right would get to choose our next few presidents,' Rydell observed gloomily.

'Well by breaking the story and letting people know who was really behind it and what their agenda was, it'll be even worse,' Gracie countered. 'Either way, Darby and all his pals are going to come out of this stronger. Once you and Drucker are exposed, all the heathens and depraved liberals across the country are going to be demonized. We'll be giving the hard-core right their biggest rallying cry since the fall of the evil empire. Branding people as "anti-American" will get a whole new lease on life. They'll run away with the next ten elections and turn the country into a Christian theocracy.'

'Hang on, we're talking about a handful of guys who put this stunt in play, not an entire political party,' Danny protested.

'It doesn't matter,' Gracie argued back. 'What matters is how they'll spin it. How they'll use it to split the country even further. They'll tar everyone with the same brush and make it look like everyone on Drucker's side of the aisle was in cahoots with him. That's what they do. And they're damn good at it too. Just imagine what someone like Karl Rove could do with it.'

'Hey, maybe we could draft him and the other scumbags who sold us the war in Iraq and have them pin this thing on Iran,' Dalton joked.

The others all turned to him with deeply unamused eyes.

'What? I'm kidding,' he protested, his palms turned out.

A dreary silence smothered the room. On the TV, the anchor was back on briefly before the image cut away to footage of violent riots in Islamabad and in Jerusalem. Across the screen, people were clashing furiously as cars blazed behind them. Police officers and soldiers were in the thick of it, trying to stop the carnage.

Gracie sat up. 'Turn it up,' she told Dalton, who was closest to the TV.

'. . . religious leaders have urged their followers to show restraint while the questions surrounding Father Jerome are answered, but the violence here shows no sign of abating,' an off-camera reporter was saying.

An anchor came back on, and a banner at the bottom of the screen said, 'President to make statement on Houston events.'

'Following the unprecedented events in Houston earlier this evening,' he announced, 'a White House spokeswoman indicated that the president would be making a statement tomorrow.'

Gracie and the others didn't need to hear the rest.

Drucker's web was spinning out of control.

'Even the president's getting suckered into this,' Rydell said.

'We can't let that happen,' Gracie insisted. She let out a dejected sigh and sagged back in her seat. 'This is just going to sink us all.' The room went silent. After a moment, Dalton asked, 'So what do we do? 'Cause it seems to me like we need to do this pronto, but we're screwed either way, whether we expose it or not.'

Rydell sat up. 'We can expose it,' he stated. 'We have to. But only if I take the fall for it. Alone.'

That got everyone's attention.

He pressed on. 'It's the only way.' His voice was quivering slightly, a tremble of nerves that was alien to Larry Rydell.

461

'My plan didn't call for a fall guy. It was never intended to empower or undermine any religion. It was just meant to get people to listen. But now . . . after what they've done, the way they've turned it . . . We're all agreed that we can't let this lie go on. But Drucker's right. We need a fall guy with no political motive if we're going to avoid tearing this country apart. And that fall guy's got to be me.' He sighed, then looked around at them with renewed determination. 'There's no other way out of this. If anyone here has a better idea, I'm all ears, but . . . I don't see it happening any other way.'

'Great,' Gracie grumbled. 'So Drucker wins.'

'Don't worry about Drucker,' Rydell assured her quietly. 'I'll make sure he pays.'

Gracie nodded stoically. No one knew where to look. Rydell was right, and they knew it. But the thought of doing what Drucker was going to do anyway, albeit long before he was planning to, was swirling inside them like a tuna melt that was a month past its sell-by date.

Gracie turned to Matt. He hadn't said a word throughout.

'You got somewhere else you got to be, cowboy?' Gracie said, a slightly provoking grin bringing a quantum of light back to her eyes.

'We're forgetting someone in all this,' he said. 'Remember?'

Gracie saw it even before he'd finished saying it. 'Father Jerome.'

'Damn,' Dalton groaned.

'Can you imagine what's going to happen to him if this thing breaks?' Matt asked.

'They'll rip him to shreds,' Rydell said.

'But he wasn't in on it,' Dalton noted. 'You'll make that clear, right?' he asked him.

'It doesn't matter,' Matt frowned.

'They'll protect him,' Dalton argued. 'We can make sure they do. Get him somewhere safe before we go live.'

462

'And after that?' Gracie asked, her voice thick with emotion. 'Where's he going to go? His life will be over, and it'll be our doing.' She glanced at Matt. 'We can't do this,' she argued, resolve hardening her voice. 'Not without letting him know what's about to happen to him. He needs to be part of this decision. We can't just have it all hit him unprepared.' She shifted her focus back to Matt. 'I have to see him. Talk to him – before anything happens.'

'You saw the news. They flew him back to Darby's place,' Rydell reminded her. 'You walk in there, Drucker'll make sure you don't come out.'

'What if you say you want to interview him, one-on-one,' Danny offered.

'Too dangerous,' Rydell grumbled. 'Besides, he's got to be the most heavily protected guy on the planet right now.'

Gracie glanced over at Matt. He seemed to be processing something. 'What?' she asked him.

He turned to Danny. 'How much gear is there in that van?' he asked him, hooking a thumb toward the motel's lot.

'What do you mean?'

'I mean, how much of their gear is in there?'

'The full kit,' Danny said.

'What about the laser transmitter? It was inside the stadium, wasn't it?'

'One was. We had another with us. For when the sign was all the way out over the roof. It took over then.'

Matt nodded. Visibly putting something through its motions in his mind's eye. 'And how much smart dust do you have left in there?' He caught Gracie's expression and noticed her posture straightening up.

'I'm not sure. Why?'

'Because we're going to need it. We can't feed Father Jerome to the wolves.' Matt glanced around the room. 'He was dragged into this, like Danny. And he's a good man,

463

right? As decent as they come, isn't that what you said?' he asked Gracie. 'We can't let Drucker ruin his life. Not until he's had his say on the matter.' He paused to gauge the others' reaction, then turned to Gracie. 'What does Darby's place look like?'

CHAPTER 79

River Oaks, Houston, Texas

The chaotic scene outside the entrance to Darby's gated community was hardly normal, but at least it was quiet. It was almost five o'clock in the morning, and the gathered masses were down for the night. They slept in their cars, in sleeping bags by the side of the road, anywhere they could. Others were still awake, huddled around makeshift campfires, chatting, milling around expectantly. A small, tireless contingent was still crowding the entrance gatehouse, waiting for their messiah to make an appearance. Some wailed in pained desperation while others sang spiritual chants of varying origin. A few diehards goaded the wall of security guards and cops who manned the perimeter barricades. The news crews sheltered quietly by their vans and their satellite dishes, taking turns on watch, afraid to miss out on something. All across the neighborhood, whispered prayers wafted through the evergreen trees that lined the drives, mingling with a thin predawn mist that gave the lushly forested area a portentous, expectant feel.

The sign's appearance changed all that.

It took them all by surprise, lighting up the night sky, blazing out of the stygian darkness, pulsating with mysterious, unexplained life as it hovered in place just above the treetops.

It was right there, up close and huge.

And it was right over Darby's house.

The crowd snapped to attention. The believers, the reporters, the cops, the security guards. Even the dogs went manic. Within seconds, everyone was up, on edge, pointing and shouting excitedly. The worshippers were pressing against the barricades, desperate to get closer to it. The cops were scrambling to contain the sudden swell of people. The news cameras were rolling, the field reporters rubbing the tiredness from their eyes and rambling on into their mikes.

Then it started to move.

Drifting, slowly, silently. Floating sideways, away from Darby's house. Gliding over the trees, heading east, over a neighboring house, toward the country club.

And opening a floodgate of pandemonium.

The crowd broke out and went after it. The sudden shift in their momentum caught the cops by surprise and outflanked them. The barricades toppled over, breached by a wave of hysterical believers who streamed through the trees, chasing the shimmering apparition. Police radios crackled sharply and footfalls crunched heavily as the cops and the security guards raced off to try and control the invading horde.

The cops patrolling the edge of the fairways on the estate's western perimeter saw it too. Their radios squawked to life seconds later. Incoherent bursts of chatter were flying across the airwaves. The six of them, who had been making the rounds in twos, converged by Darby's tennis court to try and make sense of what was going on. They could hear the chaos, an eerie upwelling of noise that subverted the stillness of the night. It was heading away from the house. The rear of the estate, where they were – the part that backed up against the golf course – was calm.

Then one of them saw something. A hint of movement, slipping across the trees at the edge of the fairway. He focused his gaze in that direction and nudged the others to attention. It was hard to see anything in the darkness. The light was coming from behind them, from the porch lights around Darby's garden and pool and, farther away, the sign in the sky. They fanned out a few yards from each other, muscles tensing up slightly, hands resting on their handguns' grips, eyes scanning on high alert. Then another one of them saw something. Looked like two figures, creeping along the far edge of the tennis court, heading toward the house.

'Over there,' he hissed, pulling out his handgun and pointing it through tense fingers – then it hit him. It hit them all. A blast of unbearable static, a hissing shriek from hell. It overwhelmed their senses, an anvil punch to their eardrums that shocked them into unconsciousness. A couple of them wet their pants before they even hit the ground.

Matt glanced into the darkness behind him. He couldn't see them, but he was grateful that Danny, Dalton, and Rydell were there, manning the LRAD, hiding in the trees by the seventh green, covering their back. So far, the diversion was working. But it wouldn't last long. They had to be in and out in fifteen minutes or so.

He waited for a couple of seconds to make sure the guards were staying down, then nodded to Gracie and gave her a let's-go gesture, knowing that she wouldn't hear him through the wax plugs shielding her eardrums.

They struck out over the lawn and crept up to the rear façade of the house. Matt spotted two guards walking past the guesthouse and motioned for Gracie to hold position. They both crouched in silence and waited for them to pass, then slipped across to a set of wide French doors. Matt pulled his earplugs out. Gracie followed suit.

'This it?' he asked her in a whisper.

She nodded her confirmation. 'Stairway's off to the right. His bedroom's upstairs, first door on the left.'

'And the monk's on the ground floor, beyond the stairs?'

Gracie nodded.

He acknowledged it with a tight nod of his own and pulled out his handgun. He'd brought one of the silenced automatics with him, even though he wasn't planning on using it unless things got really desperate. Defending himself against Maddox's goons was one thing. He didn't really have a problem with that. This was different. Gracie had told him that the guys babysitting Father Jerome were cops and private security guards from the estate. They were just doing their job, and he wasn't about to cause them any damage beyond the reparable.

He tried the handle. It was open. He slipped inside. Gracie followed. They waited in a low crouch, by the French doors, listening hard. There was no sound coming from the house. Matt glanced around. They were in the guesthouse's spacious living room. It was lined with bookcases and featured an oversized sofa that faced a big, stone fireplace. It was dark except for a pale glint of light that bounced in from the hallway.

They crossed the room on tenterhooks and slithered up the stairs. Found the first door on the left. Matt tried the handle. It was unlocked. He cracked the door open and slipped through, with Gracie on his heels. Let her in and feathered the door shut behind them. His palm sensed the locking button on its handle, and he pressed it in.

They crossed over to the bed. Father Jerome was fast asleep, breathing in with a slight wheeze. Gracie bent down beside him, glanced hesitantly at Matt, then nudged Father Jerome's shoulder softly. He stirred awake. He turned over, his eyes blinking open. He saw her, inhaled sharply, and pushed himself up.

'What . . . ? Miss Logan . . . ?' He glanced across the room and saw Matt standing by the window, peering out from behind the curtains. 'What's going on?'

She flicked on the small lamp by the bed. 'We have to be quick. You need to come with us. Your life's in danger,' she said, maintaining an even but urgent tone.

'Danger? From what?'

'Please, Father. There's no time. Trust me on this. We have to go now.'

He stared at her, his tired face wrinkled with uncertainty.

Held her gaze for a brief moment, then nodded and got out of bed. He was wearing dark pajamas.

'I have to get dressed,' he told her.

'There's no time. Just put your shoes on,' she insisted.

He nodded, and slipped on his socks and lace-up shoes. Matt came over. He put a friendly hand on the old man's shoulder. 'My name's Matt Sherwood, Father. Everything's going to be fine. Just stay close to Gracie and try not to make any noise, okay?'

The old priest nodded his readiness, the deepening creases in his forehead betraying his unease. Matt glanced at Gracie. They exchanged tight nods, then Matt opened the door and stepped out.

He didn't see it coming. The strike came flying out from the right, his attacker hugging the wall closely. It nailed him just behind his right ear, a downward blow that had a hard leading edge to it, as if the fist had been balled around a hard stump. It lit up the inside of his skull. Matt thudded heavily to the floor as Gracie screamed at the sight of Brother Ameen moving swiftly out of the shadows and landing a heavy kick on Matt's midsection.

Matt grunted heavily as the kick lifted him off the cool tiles of the hallway. He slammed back against the wall, unsure of where the next blow was coming from, his vision blurred. He sucked in a sharp breath and pushed himself onto his hands and knees in time for another kick to explode across his ribs and send him flying back into the wall. Then the monk was right up against him, his thin, taut arms like steel cables around his neck, choking the life out of him. Matt struggled to suck in some air, but the monk's grip wasn't about to cooperate. The energy was seeping out of him fast. He tried hitting back with his elbows, but they only found air, and every thrash was draining the little strength he had left in him. He tried to fight off the encroaching dizziness and drew on his last reserves to try a rear head butt, snapping his neck back as hard as he could. The monk saw it coming and jerked his head sideways to avoid it, then tightened his hold on Matt even more. Matt felt his throat getting crushed, felt all kinds of cartilage in there popping and tearing and twisting, felt his lungs retching for air. He gasped, struggling to breathe now, his eyes feeling like they were about to pop out of their sockets –

Then he heard a loud shriek and a dull, crashing thud and felt the monk's grip slacken. He sucked in a barrel-load of air and sprung backward, shoving Ameen, and turned to see the monk spinning off him before righting himself and shaking his head back to life. Gracie was standing there, her face locked with surprise and fear, the lamp from the old priest's bedside table now upturned and tightly gripped in her hands, its shade all bent out of shape. She was holding it up like a baseball bat, ready for another swing, her body all tight and curled and hunched like a predator's about to pounce. The monk wasn't cowed and he didn't give her another chance. He swung a lightning arm out and whipped the lamp out of her hands, then brought his arm back with its knuckle out again and caught Gracie on the left temple. The blow landed with a sharp crack. It sent her flying back into the room before she hit the ground hard.

Matt shook some clarity back into his own head and leapt at the monk just as he was turning to face him again. Matt was much bigger and bulkier, but Ameen was a tight coil of hard muscle and knew where and how to hit. They wrestled and punched their way across the hallway, then the monk's fist found Matt's bullet wound. A gush of pain erupted across him, causing a momentary blackout that pulled down his defenses and opened him to a frenzy of sharp jabs. Matt recoiled, his body jerking with each blow as if bullets were drilling through him. He was at the edge of the stairs when he heard Gracie scream his name. A flash of lucidity broke through the encroaching darkness, and he saw the monk's fist racing down at his head for a final, crippling blow. He jerked sideways without thinking, tightened every muscle he could still control, and grabbed the monk's arm, twisting it savagely and spinning it around like it was a spoke on a six-foot wheel. The move caught the monk by surprise and bent him forward, lifting him off his feet as his shoulder tore out of its socket. Matt kept a tight grip on the monk's arm and fed his momentum by twisting it even higher in a circular sweep. The monk's head came down and his feet left the ground as he vaulted over the railing backward and flew into the air, before landing in a heavy, sickening crack at the bottom of the stairs.

Matt creaked his body upright, edged over, and looked down. The monk's body just lay there, slack and silent. Matt glanced back at Gracie. She stepped over to him, closely followed by a shell-shocked Father Jerome. She looked down. Frowned. Then nodded.

'Come on,' Matt whispered, his voice hoarse. 'We don't have much time left.'

They slipped down the stairs, past the Croatian's corpse. There was no need to check for a pulse. The man's head was bent at an angle that precluded life. They threaded their way back out of the living room, past the pool and the tennis court, and skirted the edge of the fairways just as the sign faded out and plunged the neighborhood back into darkness.

By the time they got back to the Lincoln, it was loaded up and waiting for them. They all crammed into it and slipped away, a pregnant silence enshrouding the car as they wondered how the city – and the world – would react to their Christmas surprise.

CHAPTER 80

Houston, Texas

Maddox blocked out the pain as he watched the ER team deal with his own Christmas surprise. He'd told the admitting nurse he'd had an accident while fixing up his lawn mower. A valid and well-stocked credit card had taken care of the rest. The surgeons had been working on him for over three hours, cutting and drilling and screwing and sewing away at his mangled arm while a couple of tubes snaked into him and replenished the blood he'd left among the trees by the stadium.

He'd insisted on only having local anesthesia, deciding he'd had enough unexpected surprises for one night and knowing full well that he could have even managed without it. They'd just about succeeded in saving the arm, but he wouldn't have any use of it for a long time, and even then, the doctors had told him that he'd have very limited use of it. The blades had hacked their way through muscle and tendons with abandon. When all was said and done, his arm would be little more than a decorative limb. His right arm. His good arm. In his simmering anger, he'd been tempted to get it over with and have them shear it off at the elbow, but he'd pulled back from the idea, not wanting to make his appearance even more grotesque than it already was. He'd settle for one working arm. He'd just need to train it to compensate.

Even in his weakened, half-drugged state, he registered the commotion in the hospital as news of the sign's appearance over Reverend Darby's house had spread. The news was troubling. He knew that wasn't part of the plan. Which meant someone was going off piste. He wondered if Drucker was behind it, and if so, what he was doing. He realized things were unraveling from all fronts, but he accepted it stoically and knew better than to let his mind fester on what had gone wrong. He knew he needed to focus on the way forward – on completing the task he'd set for himself and, with a bit of luck, on his own freedom and survival. He knew when the time was right to cut one's losses, when it was better to find a new boat than to keep bailing out a sinking ship. And with Rydell, the Sherwood boys, and that reporter running free, that ship wasn't just sinking, it was about to be torpedoed into smithereens.

He knew what he had to do: push forward, press on, and, worst case, live to fight another day. It was what he was trained for. He thought back to Jackson Drucker and the rest of his men, thought of their chewed-up bodies littering that Iraqi ghost town, thought about how he'd failed them all. But he'd lived and he was fighting on, and he had to keep doing that. And that didn't involve him spending any more time in that ER ward than he had to. Which is why, less than an hour after they'd finished patching him up, he was already outside the hospital and making his way to downtown Houston.

CHAPTER 81

They were still debriefing Father Jerome by the time dawn finally made its appearance over the western suburb of Houston, all five of them – Matt, Gracie, Rydell, Danny, and Dalton – helping each other out in the difficult task of telling the frail old man how the last twelve months of his life had been one big lie.

They told him about Rydell's original plan. About the smart dust and the launchers and the planet reaching its tipping point. About Drucker's taking hold of it and perverting it to his agenda. Then they got into the more sensitive topic of what Drucker's people had done to him. The treatments. The drugs. The LRAD talking to him up on the top of the mountain. And with every new revelation, with every additional detail, his bony shoulders sagged further and the creases in his weathered face got deeper.

By the end of it, he looked thoroughly bewildered, but he was holding up better than Gracie had expected. She'd been worried about how he would take it, but he hadn't fallen apart. He'd seen a lot in this life, she reminded herself. Bad things. More than most people could ever imagine. For all his physical frailty, the man seemed to have a remarkable inner strength. And yet . . . surely, it all had to be devastating, she told herself. Then she remembered his comment on the plane, and wondered what his inner voice had been telling him all along.

'The voice on the mountain,' he finally said, looking vaguely into the distance. 'It was amazing. Even though it didn't make sense that it could actually be happening to me, it felt so . . . real. Like it was inside my head. Like it knew what I was thinking.'

474

'That's because they put those thoughts in your head in the first place,' Gracie told him, her tone careful and soft.

Father Jerome nodded, a sanguine acceptance darkening his face. He sighed heavily, and after a moment, he lifted his gaze toward Rydell. 'And you're going to say it was all your idea?'

Rydell nodded.

Father Jerome's brow furrowed with a dubious shrug.

Gracie caught it. Her eyes darted across to Matt, who seemed to catch it too, then she swung back to the priest. 'What is it?'

The priest didn't answer. He seemed to be in his own world, processing everything he'd been told, weighed down by it all.

'I'm tired,' he finally said in a hollow voice. 'I need to rest.'

Gracie and Dalton retreated to their room, Rydell to his. In the fourth room, Danny and Matt stretched out on their beds, staring at the ceiling, sharing a moment of peaceful reflection. They'd caught the early morning news on the in-room TV. The top story was, as expected, the sign's appearance over Darby's mansion and the subsequent frenzy, but there was no mention of Father Jerome going missing. So far, they were keeping it quiet.

After a while, Danny asked, 'What are you thinking about?'

'Same thing you're thinking about,' Matt said.

'Drucker?'

Matt replied by way of a slight grunt.

'It just really gets my goat, you know?' Danny said. 'The idea that he might weasel out of this without damage.'

'Look, the guy's a dirt bag, no argument. But there's not much we can do, short of putting a bullet through his skull.'

Danny didn't answer.

After a beat, Matt asked, quite matter-of-factly, 'You want to go put a bullet through his skull?'

Danny tilted his head to one side, gave Matt a maybe look, then stared at the ceiling again. 'Not really my style.'

'Didn't think so.'

'But if Rydell doesn't take care of him in a big way, I might want to reconsider.'

'We could grab him and lock him up in my cellar for a couple of years as payback,' Matt remarked flatly. 'Just feed him dog food and toilet water.'

Danny pursed his lips and nodded, mock-mulling it over. 'Nice to know we've got options,' he said with a smile.

Matt tilted his head over to him. 'It's good to have you back, man.'

Danny nodded warmly, then turned to stare at the ceiling. 'It's good to be back.'

In his room, Rydell wasn't staring at any ceiling. He was pacing around, racking his brain, trying to think of another way out. He needed to call Rebecca. He needed to hear her voice. He checked the clock on his cell phone. It was still too early on the West Coast. Especially for Rebecca. That thought brought an inkling of a smile to his face. It also released a tear that trickled down his cheek.

He wiped it off with his sleeve and sat down on the edge of the bed. What an end, he thought. Everything he'd achieved. A true master of the universe, self-made, from nothing. And it was all about to be flushed down the toilet.

He had to talk to Rebecca. He tapped an *R* into his contacts list, pulled up her number. Poised his finger on the call button. But couldn't do it. Not because of the time difference. Because he didn't know what to tell her.

He set the phone back down next to him, felt his eyes filming over, and watched his hands shiver.

*

It was almost noon when Matt stepped out of his room to hit the vending machine again. Gracie was out there too, leaning against the grille of the Navigator, a cold can of Coke in her hand. He downed some coins and pulled out a can of his own. Snapped the lid open, took a long sip, and joined her.

'Can't sleep?' he asked.

'Nope.' She smiled. 'My body clock's so out of whack I don't even know what day it is.'

'It's the day after Christmas,' Matt said with a knowing smile.

'Really?' She grinned and looked around. 'Not exactly a white one this year, huh?'

Matt nodded. Took another sip. Said, 'You should get some rest. You're about to have the most intense few months of your life. Of anyone's life.'

'What, even worse than the last few days?' she quipped.

'Oh yeah.' He shrugged. 'That was a cakewalk.'

'Some cakewalk,' she said, dreamily. She caught his glance, then looked away, staring through the scenery around them, her mind wandering off.

'What?' he prodded.

She shrugged. After a quiet moment, she said, 'It seems like such a waste, don't you think?'

'What?'

'All those people, at the stadium. Around the world. Hanging on his every word. Singing. Praying. Did you ever hear anything like that in your life?'

He didn't reply.

'They were loving it. They loved believing in him. They were lifted by it. I know, it's primitive and it's cultish and it's even a bit creepy, but somehow, some part of me thought it was beautiful. For a moment there, they were all happy. They'd forgotten about their problems and their jobs and their mortgages and everything that was wrong in their lives. They were happy and they were hopeful. He gave them all hope.'

'False hope,' Matt corrected.

'What's wrong with that?' she asked, as much to herself as to him. 'Hope isn't real by definition, is it? It's just a state of mind, right?' She shrugged, falling back to earth. 'If it wasn't for all those self-serving leeches using him . . . twisting everything for their own purposes. Using something as beautiful and as inspirational as that to fill their own pockets and grab more power . . .' She looked at him forlornly. 'Such a waste, you know?'

'Same-old same-old.' He shrugged. 'It's the way of the world.'

She nodded ruefully. Stood there quietly for a moment, then asked, 'So what are you going to do? You're part of this story too, you know. People are going to want to hear your side of it.'

He cocked his head at her with a pleased look on his face and said, 'Good.'

'Why?'

'I thought I might get me a ghostwriter,' he mused. 'Knock out a book about it. Something punchy. Like something that guy who wrote *The Perfect Storm* would write. Maybe flog the movie rights to some studio for a cool mil.' He flashed her a grin.

'Yeah, well, get in line, bub,' she countered.

He let out a slight chuckle. Turned to look at her. It suddenly occurred to him that she was a great-looking girl. Great-looking and, with all the rest of it, everything any man could ask for. And much as he wanted to put the whole nightmare of the last week behind him, the thought of it keeping them involved in each other's lives for a while longer had taken over as the preferred option.

But they had to get through the tough part first.

'When are you going to hit the button?' he asked her.

Her face tightened at the uncomfortable thought. 'I don't know. How about we let everyone out there enjoy a few more hours of peace. Christmas was only yesterday . . .'

'Tomorrow?' he asked.

'Tomorrow,' she nodded.

They dunked their empty cans in the trash and trudged back to their rooms. They were outside Father Jerome's door when it cracked open. The old priest was standing there, holding it open, a knot of concentration etched across his forehead.

'I'm sorry, did we wake you?' Gracie said.

'No,' he said. He didn't look like he'd slept at all, and seemed deeply consumed by his thoughts. He studied them for a beat, then said, 'Can you get everyone together? I've been thinking about everything that's happened, and . . . We need to talk.'

CHAPTER 82

The sky was still as balmy and clear as it had been on the big day itself. A relative calm had reasserted itself over the city, even though the air was still heavy with expectation. There hadn't been any fresh news about Father Jerome in over twenty-four hours, and the city was trying to carry on with life while awaiting the next moment of revelation.

The first people to see the ball of light pulsating over the reflecting pool were the families and couples and joggers who were out enjoying a day in the park. It was small and spherical, maybe twenty feet across, and was hovering innocuously around a couple of hundred feet up over the south end of the long, rectangular ceremonial pool, by the Pioneer Memorial obelisk, at the northern tip of Hermann Park. Curious onlookers gravitated toward it, scanning the grounds around them with wary eyes. They soon spotted the man underneath it, the one in the black cassock and the richly embroidered hood. The light was hovering over him as he walked slowly away from the obelisk.

The onlookers converged on him, calling others over, pointing him out. The park was hugely popular and was surrounded by some of Houston's most beloved attractions: the zoo, the Garden Center, the Museum of Natural Science with its cylindrical butterfly greenhouse, and the iconic Miller Outdoor Theater. Given the weather and the holiday, there were a lot of people out there, and it didn't take long for most of them to swarm in on the frail old man who was walking innocently along the edge of the tranquil body of water. They spoke to him, greeted him, and threw hesitant questions at him, but he didn't answer or meet their eyes. He just nodded enigmatically and kept ambling quietly, seemingly lost in his thoughts. They kept a respectful distance, staying back a few yards from him. Those who breeched that private zone were told off by others and made to pull back. Throughout, Father Jerome kept moving, slowly, until he made his way up the ceremonial steps to the platform that looked down over the pond.

He stopped there and turned, looking out onto the wide open area before him, framed against the statue of Sam Houston and its monumental arch. The park police were quick to get involved; they reeled in as much backup as they could muster and soon set up a protective cordon around the platform. The news vans rushed over too. Before long, hundreds of people were spread across the grounds of the park, their eyes locked on the tiny figure with the sphere of shimmering light floating above him who just stood there and looked down on them in silence.

Once everything was in place – the crowd, the coverage, the protection – he took a step forward and raised his hands to a wide, welcoming stance. A ripple of sh-sh-sh's rolled over the crowd, and the entire park was shrouded in silence. Even the birds and the branches of the trees seemed to fall into line as any trace of noise seeped away from the ceremonial plaza and was replaced by an ominous stillness.

Father Jerome's eyes traveled slowly across the field of onlookers and back. He then tilted his head up to look at the sphere of light floating over him, nodded thoughtfully, clenched his fists with resolve, and addressed the crowd.

'Friends,' he began, 'something wonderful has been happening these past few days. Something amazing, something breathtaking and strange and surprising and . . . something I don't quite understand,' he confessed. A murmur of surprise coursed through the crowd. 'Because the honest truth is . . . I don't know what's happening. I don't know what this is,' he said, pointing upward at the hovering ball of light. 'I don't know why it's here. I don't know why it chose me. What I do know, though, is that its meaning hasn't been properly understood. Not by others. Certainly not by me. Not until last night. And now I think I do understand. I understand what it's trying to tell us. And I'm here to share that with you.'

Keenan Drucker stood in his hotel room, openmouthed, staring at the TV screen, wondering what the hell was going on.

He'd been on edge since he'd gotten news of Father Jerome's disappearance from Reverend Darby's mansion, and he'd been worriedly anticipating a quick press blowout from Rydell and his new friends. The fact that it hadn't happened threw him. He'd wondered why they hadn't gone public, what Rydell was up to. And the sight on the screen before him, of Father Jerome walking through a park with a growing horde of followers congregating around him, wasn't making things any clearer.

He heard his suite's doorbell ring, and crossed to see who was there, his mind still in thrall to the events taking place less than a mile away. He checked the peephole and stiffened at the sight that greeted him, then he composed himself and unlocked the door.

'Jesus,' he said when he saw Maddox's heavily bandaged arm and his sweaty face. 'You didn't tell me it was that bad.'

Maddox pushed into the suite, ignoring the comment. 'There's a lot of commotion in the lobby. Have you seen what's happening?' He'd barely said it when he saw the live coverage on the TV. He stepped closer to the screen, then turned to Drucker with a suspicious frown. 'What are you doing?'

'It's not me,' Drucker protested. 'I don't know what's going on.'

Maddox studied him dubiously. 'It's not you?'

'I'm telling you this has nothing to do with me,' Drucker

insisted. 'It's got to be Rydell. He's running things now. They got the priest out last night.'

'The sign,' Maddox realized, filling in the gaps mentally. 'I thought it was something you'd planned. Then I tried Dario's phone and got some cop, and that didn't add up.'

'Dario's dead,' Drucker confirmed.

Maddox nodded. Things were unraveling even worse than he'd thought. He turned to the screen, his mind processing what he was seeing. 'So what's he up to? What are they doing?'

'I don't know. Maybe Rydell's got the others convinced the global warming message is too important to kill.'

'But he knows you can blow it all up for him,' Maddox remarked.

'He can also take me down with him,' Drucker reminded Maddox, then added, 'and you too, in case you forgot. He was the fall guy, remember? Without him, we're out of options.' Then his face relaxed with a comforting realization. 'They're not going to expose him. They can't. Not yet. Not before they figure out who they're going to pin it on.' His face lit up. 'Which gives us time. Time to figure out how to expose him without fingering ourselves as his puppet masters. Time to come up with another way out.'

Maddox studied him for a beat, then came to a quick conclusion. If he was going to disappear – if he was going to live to fight another day – he had to make sure he didn't leave anyone behind who could ruin things for him. Like a career politician who wouldn't think twice about selling him out to save his own skin.

But what he was seeing brought back to life a far more attractive option. One he thought had been wiped off his playbook.

He pulled out an automatic before Drucker had time to blink and shoved it right up against the man's forehead. 'I already have. Sit down.'

He herded Drucker backward and into an armchair facing the TV, then in one swift movement, he bent down, grabbed Drucker's shaking hand with his gun hand, and arced it up so the silencer's muzzle was jammed against Drucker's mouth.

Drucker stared at him, terrified and confused.

'Thing is, right from the get-go, I never thought exposing Jerome was a good idea,' Maddox told him. 'He's much more useful this way. The truth is, we're not out of options here, Keenan. You are.' And he pulled the trigger.

The bullet ripped out the back of Drucker's head and sent a gray and burgundy mess splattering across the wall behind him. Maddox placed the gun in Drucker's limp hand, pressed Drucker's fingers tightly against the grip and the trigger, then let it drop as it would have had Drucker been alone.

Swift, Silent, Deadly. It was one hell of a good motto.

He pulled out his cell phone and hit the well-worn speed-dial number. 'I think we're back in business. How's our boy?' he asked.

'He's still put, at home,' his NSA contact told him. 'Watching the live coverage from the park.'

'Good. Let me know if he moves. I need him to be home.' He glared at the screen, then slipped out the room, already calculating the quickest route to Hermann Park.

CHAPTER 83

Father Jerome stared at the crowd and hesitated, and felt a shiver spread across his lips and a tremble in his fingers. His forehead went sweaty as other thoughts started rising out of the caverns of his mind, fighting for attention. His eyes strayed, darting left and right nervously, clouded with uncertainty. Then a familiar voice echoed in his ears.

'You're doing great,' Gracie told him. 'Just keep going. Remember everything we talked about. Think about what you really want to tell these people. Block everything else out and open up your heart to them, Father. We're right behind you.'

A ghost of a smile broke across his face, and he cast his gaze over the crowd, a renewed resolve blossoming within him. He bobbed his head in a slight gesture of confirmation, and pressed on.

Crouched in the back of the van, Gracie put her binoculars down and turned to address Matt across the big drum of the LRAD.

'This thing's just incredible.' She grinned, patting it. 'I want one.'

'Why not. It *is* Christmastime, right?' Matt said with an easy smirk. Then his expression tightened and he said, 'Let them know I'm going in. And keep your eyes on Father Jerome in case he wobbles again.' He popped the door open.

'Good luck.' She smiled.

He smiled back and said, 'I'll see you in a little while.' He pushed his cell phone's earpiece into place and glanced across at Dalton, who was behind the wheel. They exchanged a tight nod, then Matt slipped out of the van and headed for the plaza.

Across the field from the plaza, tucked away behind the Miller Outdoor Theatre, Danny watched the proceedings through another set of binoculars while Rydell liaised with Gracie on the phone. The Navigator was parked nearby, tucked away in the service lot behind the theater, its rear door open. The launch tubes were huddled beside them, now freshly stacked with the last of the smart dust canisters.

'Matt's on his way,' Rydell told Danny.

Danny nodded. 'Launchers ready?'

'They're all set,' Rydell told him. 'You sure you had enough time to write the new programs?'

'They'll be fine,' Danny said flatly.

Their eyes met. An unspoken anger still festered behind Danny's gaze. Rydell winced and said, 'I'll make it up to you. I promise.'

Danny shrugged, and said, 'Let's make sure we pull this off first,' then turned his attention back to Father Jerome. 'Ready?'

Rydell nodded. 'Ready.'

'Let 'em rip.'

'We're living in a fractured world,' Father Jerome announced. 'Others have come before me. Blessed with revelations, with inspirations. With wise and noble thoughts that they tried to share with those around them. To help humanity. To give us food for thought. But all it's done is turn man against man. Their wise and noble words and their selfless deeds have been misinterpreted, twisted, abused . . . hijacked by others for their own glorification. Institutions have been built in their names . . . great big temples of intolerance, each one of them claiming to be the true faith and pitting man against man. Turning their words into instruments of control. Instruments of hate. Instruments of war.'

He paused, breathing in short, ragged bursts now, sensing the unease spreading among the crowd. He frowned and redoubled his concentration, pushing the conflicting thoughts back, and said, 'We have to try and fix that.'

Just then, the sphere of light spread out, growing outward until it dwarfed the piazza below it. The audience gasped, staring in wonderment as the sign pulsed and rippled with life before morphing into the sequence of geometric patterns it had previously displayed – only this time, it ended up settling on a different image. A cross. A large, blazing cross, burning in the sky over Hermann Park.

A loud cheer and shouts of 'Praise the Lord' and 'Amen' burst through the throng of onlookers as the cross just held there – but their joy was cut short when the sign started morphing again. The crowd gasped once more as the sign seemed to ripple and stretch outward and around before settling into another sign. Not a cross, this time. A star. The Star of David. The crowd flinched with surprise, roiled by the change, confused and scared and caught off-balance – but the sign wasn't done yet. It held that shape, then changed again. It didn't stop. It kept going, shape-shifting into a rotating sequence of symbols associated with other religions – Islam, Hinduism, Buddhism, Bahaism – and kept going, reaching back into history, assuming representations of all kinds of religious movements stretching back through the spider cults of Peru to the sun gods of ancient Egypt and Mesopotamia and all the way back to the very dawn of civilization.

The changes sped up, the symbol spinning from one shape to the other, faster and faster, a haphazard and dizzying light show. It sped up until the symbols became almost indistinguishable, the intensity almost blinding – and then, all of a sudden, it just vanished. Just died out. In the blink of an eye, and without any sound or warning, it was just gone.

The crowd went silent, as if they were all robots and someone had hit a mute button. The stunned onlookers just stared around at each other, mystified, not knowing what to think – then the sign burst out in its former glory, assuming its familiar pattern, the shape that was first seen over the ice shelf, and just held it and shimmered above the priest's head.

'Interesting light show you're putting on,' the voice rasped from behind them.

Danny and Rydell turned and froze at the sight of Maddox approaching them from behind. He had a long, black case slung over his shoulder and held a gun in his left hand, his uninjured hand. A curious mix of anger and confusion lined his weary face.

He stepped closer until he was about ten feet away from them and stopped. He guided his gaze above their heads, at the massive sign lighting up the sky a couple of hundred yards farther away, by the monumental arch.

It hadn't been that hard for him to find them. Not for someone who knew what to look for. A vantage point, within a certain range, somewhere where they could work and watch and not be seen. There hadn't been that many options. The third spot on his sweep turned out to be the right one.

'I'm feeling all warm and cuddly inside,' he chortled, gesturing for them to raise their hands. 'Love and peace and goodwill to all men. Is that what you're selling them?'

'It's working,' Rydell told him, glancing across at Danny as he set down his cell phone without killing the line. He raised his hands slightly. 'They're listening.'

'And you think that's going to make a difference?' His voice rose with his anger. 'You think our enemies are going to buy into that horse shit too? Wake the fuck up, Larry. They may be listening, but it's not going to change anything.'

'It could. Look, I don't know what you and Keenan have in mind, but I don't want them to stop believing in God,' Rydell said, raising his voice and volleying the anger back at Maddox. 'I'd just like them to use their own minds a bit more. Just listen to Father Jerome. Listen to what he's saying.'

'It's an admirable thought,' Maddox said mockingly. 'We are the world, we are the children, right? It's great. Everything he's saying out there, it's just great – but you know what it's going to do?' He set his pack down on the ground, reached into it, and pulled out a sniper rifle. 'It's going to get him killed.'

Gracie stiffened the second the words echoed through the headset of her cell phone.

Maddox was alive – and there. And by the sounds of it, he'd taken them by surprise.

An icy panic stabbed the back of her neck. She turned to Dalton in alarm and said, 'I need to call Matt. We've got trouble.'

CHAPTER 84

The crowd was thoroughly rattled and exploded with awe at the appearance of the familiar sign before Father Jerome raised his hands to calm them and his voice burst out, cutting through the confusion.

'Many of us have preached the same message, the only message that counts,' he bellowed as they quieted to listen to his words. 'A message of humility. And charity. And kindness and compassion. That's all that matters. And yet it hasn't worked. All these religions we've built have been around for hundreds, for thousands of years. And yet the world is angrier and more divided than ever. And we need to do something about that.'

'Matt.' Gracie's voice burst through his earpiece. 'It's Maddox. He's got Danny and Rydell.'

Matt's feet froze for a beat – he missed one step, maybe two – then he was suddenly weaving through the crowd, hurtling toward the Miller Outdoor Theater, a tangle of horrific images tumbling through his mind.

Maddox swung the rifle at Rydell and Danny. 'As soon as he's done talking, he's going to get his head blown off. We'll make it look like some towelhead nutjob took him out, we've got a bunch of them on watch. 'Cause that's how all good prophets end up, isn't it? They have to die for their cause.'

Rydell started to say something, but Maddox cut him off sharply.

He mocked him loudly. 'Come on. You can't do these things half-assed. You've got to go all the way. You've got to close the deal. If you really want people to believe his words, if you really want his words to be seared into the minds of all those millions of people out there, he needs to die. He has to. To become a martyr. 'Cause martyrs . . . they're so much harder to ignore, aren't they?'

Danny studied him for a beat, then said, 'And after he's dead . . .'

Maddox nodded casually. 'Yep. With you both out of the picture, it'll clean things up, nice and tidy. They won't find you. They will find the Iranian whacko who shot Jerome, though. A card-carrying fanatic with a great CV, someone we've been watching for quite a while. He'll have his head blown off, of course. Self-inflicted. One for the team.'

'You weren't planning to expose Father Jerome?' Rydell asked.

Maddox shook his head. 'Nope.'

'But Keenan . . .' Rydell got it. 'He didn't know.'

Maddox flashed him an icy smile. 'Of course not.'

'So the Iranians, the Muslim world,' Danny said. 'They'll get the blame?'

'Of course,' Maddox smiled. 'Beautiful, isn't it? The prophet who wanted to set us free, shot by an agent of intolerance.'

'You'll start a war,' Danny blurted. 'The people who've bought into Father Jerome – they're going to be mad as hell.'

'I'm counting on it,' Maddox replied coolly.

Rydell took a step forward. 'Think about what you're doing here, Brad – '

'I've thought about it, Larry,' Maddox hissed, anger flaring across his face. 'I've done nothing but think about it while I've watched us pussyfoot around and let these savages slaughter us. "Rules of engagement,"' he spat out indignantly. 'Geneva Conventions. Senate hearings the minute you try and bitch-slap the truth out of some kamikaze who doesn't think his life's worth anything anyway. We're just too weak. We don't have the balls to get things done. We're playing by the rules against an enemy who knows wars don't have rules. They're laughing at us out there; we're getting our asses handed to us and you know why? Because they get it. They know how to get things done. They know that if someone slaps you, you don't turn the other cheek. You rip their fucking arm off. And the only way we're going to win this thing is to get people really angry, so angry that they'll be baying for blood.'

'You'll be dragging millions of innocent people into a war just to punish a few extremists—'

'It's not just a few extremists, Larry. It's all of them. It's the whole fucking region. You weren't out there. You haven't lived among them. You haven't seen the hatred in their eyes. Your "we are all one" bullshit won't work. We can't live together. It's just not going to happen. There's a fundamental difference between us and them on every level. They know it. We know it. We're just too gutless to face up to it. And they're coming after us. They're not going to give up. Make no mistake, they're our enemies, plain and simple. They want to destroy us. They want to conquer us, and it's not a land grab. It's a holy war. And to win a holy war, you need a crusade. We have to go after them with everything we've got, no holds barred. Once and for all. We need to wipe them off the face of the earth. And the death of your fake prophet will make it happen. It'll be one hell of a call to arms, one that'll be heard around the world.' He leveled the gun at them. 'So you just keep that sign up there and settle back until he's done. Then we'll finish this.'

Father Jerome fixed his eyes fervently on the massed onlookers and jabbed a stern finger in their direction.

'We all pray to the same God,' he told them. 'That's all that matters. Everything else – all these institutions we've built in His name, all the rituals and public expressions of faith – we created those. We did. Humans, people like you and me. And maybe we were wrong in creating them and giving them the power they have over us. Because God doesn't care about what you eat or what you drink. He doesn't care about how often you pray to him or what words you use or where you go to do that. He doesn't care who you vote for. He only cares about how you behave toward one another. That's all that matters. He gave you all great minds, minds that have allowed you to achieve great advances. You sent a man to the moon from this very city. That's how clever you are. You can create life in test tubes. You can wipe out the planet with the weapons you keep creating. You hold life and death in your hands, and you are all gods. And like it or not, you control your lives with everything you do, with every action you take. What you do. What you buy. Who you vote for. And you have infinite powers stored inside you. You have minds that allow you to achieve the impossible. Minds that allow you to reason. To talk to one another and debate things openly. And those same minds should be enough to tell you how you should treat one another. Every single one of you knows that. You can see that for yourselves. You know that hurting and killing one another is wrong. You know that sitting idly while others die of starvation is wrong. You know that dumping lethal chemicals in rivers is wrong. Every day, each and every one of you is faced with a choice, and it's how you choose to behave that matters. It's that simple.'

'Almost done.' Maddox seethed as he watched Father Jerome from their vantage point.

Rydell watched him inch toward the Navigator and prop the rifle on the SUV's side mirror. He turned to Danny.

'Run the debunking software.'

'What?' Danny asked.

'Run the damn software,' Rydell yelled. 'Better to expose him than get him killed and start a war.'

'Don't,' Maddox growled, spinning the rifle at them –

'Wait,' Danny blurted, raising his hands. 'Just calm the hell down, all right? I'm not doing anything.'

'Danny, listen to me,' Rydell urged him. 'He can't kill us both. He needs the sign to stay up. Run the goddamn software.'

'Don't even try it, Danny boy,' Maddox warned. 'It doesn't matter to me if the sign dies out right now. It's done all I needed it to do.'

Rydell turned to Maddox in exasperation. 'Listen to me,' he pleaded. 'This is good. This can change things. It can make things better for everyone. It'll achieve what you're trying to do without—'

'Enough,' Maddox yelled, his voice ripping up the air like a mortar shell. 'You know what, Larry? You're no longer needed here.' He raised the gun, three inches maybe, and squeezed the trigger –

– just as Matt tackled him from the side. The bullet flew wide, missing Rydell and ricocheting against the side of the theater as Maddox and Matt fell against the hard ground. Maddox spun around and lashed out with a fierce kick that caught Matt across the chest and winded him.

Matt recoiled in pain as Danny and Rydell rushed Maddox. The soldier scrambled to push himself off the ground, but he forgot his right arm was mangled as if a dingo had been at it and instinctively used it to right himself, causing a torrent of agony to flood through him. He fell back again and glared at Matt as his left hand dived under his jacket. Matt saw the grip of an automatic sticking out from behind Maddox's belt, saw the rifle he'd dropped lying a few feet away, and dived for it.

Maddox's hand had less distance to travel and came up first – but he didn't count on Danny, who was already there and threw his weight against him and shoved him to one side, hard. Maddox flew sideways and landed on his right arm again, and his scream sliced through the empty lot before Matt shut him up permanently with three high-powered rounds to the chest.

*

'You don't need anyone to tell you what to believe or who to worship,' Father Jerome was telling the crowd. 'You don't need to follow any set of rituals. You don't need to worry about an angry God not allowing you into heaven. You don't need to march into these great temples of intolerance and be told what is God's inerrant and infallible word, because the simple truth is that nobody really knows that. I don't. All I know is that you're not slaves and you're not part of any grand master plan. If there is a God, and I believe there is one, then you are all God's children. Each and every one of you. You create your own destiny. And you need to accept that responsibility and put aside your egocentricity and stop looking for excuses in tired old myths. You make your own fate every single day. You need to look after each other. You need to look after the land that feeds you and gives you the air you breathe. You need to assume your duty toward all of God's creation. And you need to accept the credit for the good and take the blame for the bad.'

He looked across the stunned crowd and smiled. 'Enjoy your lives. Look after your loved ones. Help those less fortunate. Make the world a better place for all. And allow me one last humble request. Please don't allow my words to you here today to be used and abused in the same way.' He cast his gaze across the onlookers again, shut his eyes, and raised his hands. The sign held there for a moment longer – then it dropped down, slowly, until it engulfed the entire platform around Father Jerome in its dazzling light, obscuring him and his protective ring of cops and park patrolmen from view. The massed audience flinched backward, gasping in horror – then the sign split up and divided itself into smaller balls of light that shot outward, over the crowd, spreading themselves evenly all over them. A horizontal field of hundreds of smaller signs, each no more than three feet across, now hovered over the sea of onlookers, almost within reach of their outstretched hands.

It took a couple of seconds for the first gasp and the first shout to draw the crowd's attention back to the platform at the top of the steps.

The cops and the park patrolmen were looking around in puzzlement. The whole crowd looked on, also bewildered.

Father Jerome was gone.

CHAPTER 85

River Oaks, Houston, Texas

Across town, at his mansion in River Oaks, Reverend Nelson Darby glared at his massive TV. His land line was ringing.

Again.

As was his cell phone.

The preachers he'd invited onto the stage with him were clearly watching the live telecast too. And they weren't thrilled either.

He sucked in a deep, angry breath.

Grabbed the big phone unit from the limed oak coffee table in his study.

Ripped its power cord out of the wall.

And hurled it straight through his TV screen.

They all watched the endless replays of the coverage in the executive lounge of the FBO at Hobby Airport with relief. They'd pulled it off, and so far, there was no sign of any vicious reaction, not from anywhere around the world. They all knew they'd opened a huge Pandora's box, opened up a debate that would surely rage on for months and years ahead. But it was an opportunity none of them could resist.

Rydell had booked the FBO for their exclusive use. The plane bringing Rebecca from L.A. was due any minute. It would then take them all to their various destinations: D.C. for Gracie and Dalton; Boston for Rydell, Matt, and Danny. Father Jerome would be Rydell's guest until they figured out how to reintroduce him into public life – if at all.

In the well-stocked lounge, Gracie studied Father Jerome as he watched himself on the TV screen.

'No regrets?' she asked him.

He looked at her with warm, smiling eyes. 'None whatsoever.

We need this. We need a new level of consciousness to deal with the challenges we're now facing. And who knows? Maybe it'll work.'

'You have more faith in human nature than I do, Father,' Rydell commented.

'Do I? You created this.' He pointed a bony finger at Rydell. 'You created something wonderful. And you did it with the best intentions. It was a shame to let it all go to waste, when it could be used to do so much good. And you had to think it would work, or you wouldn't have tried it in the first place. Which tells me you also had some level of faith in mankind heeding its call and doing the right thing, no?'

Rydell smiled, and nodded. 'Maybe, Father. And maybe they'll surprise me and listen and take in one tenth of what you said.' He paused, then told him, 'I owe you my life, Father. Anything you want, just name it.'

'I can think of a few places that could use hospitals and orphanages,' Father Jerome said casually.

'Just write me up a list,' Rydell told him. 'It'll be my pleasure.'

Gracie gave Father Jerome a soft pat on the shoulder. She looked over at Dalton, who was listening intently as Danny told him all about the technology behind the sign. She wondered if Dalton would bail on her and join Danny and Rydell in geekland, then spotted Matt over by the coffee machine, walked over and joined him.

'So I guess your Hollywood blockbuster's not gonna happen, huh?'

Matt crinkled his face in mock pain. 'Nah. Just as well, really. I wouldn't know how to deal with all those groupies.' He paused, then added, 'Your Woodward and Bernstein moment's also gone up in smoke.'

'Thanks for reminding me,' she groaned.

Something in her eyes told him it wasn't that much of a lighthearted retort. 'You okay?' he asked her.

'I don't know. It just feels weird. Pulling off a big scam like this. It feels a bit, I don't know, condescending. Like we know better.' She chortled. 'I feel like Jack Nicholson on that stand, remember? Barking out, "You can't handle the truth."'

'You're way hotter,' he ventured.

It was just the disarming comment she needed. 'I sure as hell hope so,' she shot back, then beamed a melting smile at him. 'But thanks for noticing. Now would you please do me a favor and find something else for us to talk about?'

He studied her smile, basked in it for a moment, then said, 'You like classic cars?'

AUTHOR'S NOTE

Faith by itself has never caused evil. What causes evil is what *people* have faith in, how they *interpret* it and—most of all—a *weakness* within them that, all too often, makes their faith (against its very definition) waver unless it is shared by everyone around them.

Consider Christianity's beginnings: Few came to the manger, fewer still claimed to have witnessed the Resurrection; the faith spread nevertheless. How, a few centuries later, its sublime and bighearted message would be ignored and countless people would be terrorized in its name, is baffling. What's happening in America today, the growing number of hate-filled, amped-up fanatics who claim they have a God-given right to define their nation and impose their fundamentalist vision on all of its citizens and, ultimately, on the rest of the planet, is no less baffling—or dangerous, all the more so when combined with their collective death wish regarding the supposedly approaching End of Days. The inquisitors only had torture chambers and burning stakes. Today's leaders have rather more potent weaponry at their disposal.

Religion is universal, and its central role in the lives of many as well as its wondrous effects hardly need advertising. It is part of what makes us human. But the *combination* of religion with that human weakness—with the illnesses of insecurity, intolerance, ignorance, hatred of life, and megalomania—is frightening, and nowhere is that evidenced more than when religion seeps into politics. If history has taught us anything, it's that mixing the two is a very bad idea. It's something the Founding Fathers understood very well. Somehow, too many of us don't seem to be sharing their concerns.

Consider our recent past:

'I turn back to your prophets in the Old Testament and the signs foretelling Armageddon, and I find myself wondering if we are the generation that is going to see that come about. I don't know if you have noted any of those prophecies lately, but, believe me, they describe the times we are going through.'

– President Ronald Reagan, speaking in 1983

'If people aren't involved in helping godly men in getting elected, then we're going to have a nation of secular laws. That's not what our founding fathers intended and that certainly isn't what God intended ... We need to take back this country ... And if we don't get involved as Christians, then how could we possibly take it back? If you are not electing Christians, tried and true, under public scrutiny and pressure, if you're not electing Christians then in essence you are going to legislate sin.' And: *'Florida is key with regard to a shift in this nation, and no doubt these elections in Florida are key as well. That is why there is such spiritual warfare ... Father, once again, once again, we'll rejoice with Your son and bring this nation into alignment with Your government, with Your Kingdom's principles and authority.'*

– Katherine Harris, secretary of state of Florida, on why she chose not to allow a recount of the Florida vote, despite the numerous charges of election fraud and irregularity, and with Al Gore trailing George W. Bush by only several hundred votes in the contest for Florida's electoral votes, thereby handing Bush the 2000 election

'I recall the election in 2004. Hollywood was against us. The media were against us. The universities were against us. And despite them all the church of Jesus Christ put George W. Bush back in the White House. We're on the winning side. We are going to win because we have the truth. We have the inerrant word of God.'

– Jerry Falwell

'Gog and Magog are at work in the Middle East ... The biblical prophecies are being fulfilled ... This confrontation is willed by God, who wants to use this conflict to erase his people's enemies before a New Age begins.'

– President George W. Bush, in a phone call to French President Jacques Chirac in early 2003 to convince him that Iraq had to be invaded to thwart Gog and Magog, the Bible's satanic agents of the Apocalypse

---

"Put on the full armor of God, so that when the day of evil comes, you may be able to stand your ground.'

'It is God's will that by doing good you should silence the ignorant talk of foolish men.'

– Biblical quotes on the March 31, 2003 and April 7, 2003 covers of the Worldwide Intelligence Update, the daily briefing document sent to President George W. Bush by the Pentagon under Donald Rumsfeld. Such quotes were featured routinely on the covers of the documents during the early years of the Iraq war

'Yes, I think I will see Jesus come back to earth in my lifetime.'

– Republican vice presidential nominee Sarah Palin, when asked if she believed in the Rapturist theology of End of Days

Compare that to where we were more than two hundred years ago:

'Merely the ravings of a maniac, no more worthy, nor capable of explanation than the incoherences of our own nightly dreams.'
  – Thomas Jefferson, the third president of the United States, writing about the Book of Revelation

'The purpose of separation of church and state is to keep forever from these shores the ceaseless strife that has soaked the soil of Europe with blood for centuries'; also, 'I have no doubt that every new example will succeed, as every past one has done, in showing that religion and Government will both exist in greater purity, the less they are mixed together'; and: 'If Tyranny and Oppression come to this land, it will be in the guise of fighting a foreign enemy.'
  – James Madison, the fourth president of the United States

Would Jefferson or Madison stand a chance of getting the nomination, let alone winning the election, in the America of the twenty-first century? I wouldn't bet on it.

ACKNOWLEDGMENTS

Writing is essentially a solitary effort, and in an effort not to end up typing 'All work and no play makes Raymond a dull boy' over and over and looking for the nearest axe, I take every opportunity to pick the brains of my friends and other hapless victims whenever I can muster up a reasonable excuse to call on them. Fortunately, they happen to be a very clever and clear-thinking bunch of people who always manage to find the time to humor me, and for that I'm very grateful to them all. In no particular order, and surely forgetting one or two, my stellar posse on this book included Richard Burston, Bashar Chalabi, Carlos Heneine, Joe and Amanda McManus, Nic Ransome (sorry I couldn't work in the line 'He's not the Messiah, he's just a very naughty boy!'), Michael Natan, Alex Finkelstein, Wilf Dinnick, Bruce Crowther, Gavin Hewitt, Jill McGivering, Richard Khuri, Tony Mitchell, and my parents.

Hearty thanks go to my editors Ben Sevier and Jon Wood for their advice and their patience. Your insights were, once again, invaluable to me. Big thanks too to Brian Tart, Claire Zion, Rick Willett, and everyone at Dutton and at NAL, Susan Lamb and everyone at Orion, and Renaud Bombard and Anne Michel and everyone at Presses de la Cité, for all their hard work and their enthusiasm, and for making it possible for me to hassle all the above mentioned people for so-called research on a continual basis.

A very special and long overdue kudos goes to Ray Lundgren and Richard Hasselberger, who as art directors at Dutton were responsible for the iconic covers, starting with *Templar,* that have made such a powerful impact. Ray, that cross with the Manhattan skyline was pure genius. The success of my books owes a lot to the brilliance of your cover designs. Many, many thanks to you both.

Thanks, too, to Lesley Kelley and to Mona Mourad for generously donating to charities and bidding to have characters named on their behalf.

And finally, a big nod of gratitude to my fabulous consiglieres at the William Morris Agency – Eugenie Furniss, Jay Mandel, Tracy Fisher, and Raffaella De Angelis.